THE LETTERS OF
DANIEL DEFOE

DANIEL DEFOE
from the frontispiece to *Jure Divino*, 1706

THE LETTERS OF
DANIEL DEFOE

EDITED BY

GEORGE HARRIS HEALEY

OXFORD
AT THE CLARENDON PRESS
1955

Oxford University Press, Amen House, London E.C. 4

GLASGOW NEW YORK TORONTO MELBOURNE WELLINGTON
BOMBAY CALCUTTA MADRAS KARACHI CAPE TOWN IBADAN

Geoffrey Cumberlege, Publisher to the University

———

PRINTED IN GREAT BRITAIN

PREFACE

BIOGRAPHERS and historians have long turned to the letters of Defoe for authentic information about a fascinating and complicated personality, and have long called for a published collection in which, for the first time, all of his extant letters might be made accessible. This volume is intended to meet their need. In it are drawn together all that I have been able to discover of the surviving letters, reports, and memoranda that came from his pen, or that were addressed to him by others. The correspondence amounts to 251 letters, of which 16 are written to Defoe and 235 are written by him. In the course of more than two centuries, nearly all of these letters have, at some time or another, appeared in print, some prominently, some obscurely, some given in full, some not, some transcribed accurately, some very inaccurately indeed. The largest accumulation of printed letters appeared a half century ago in vols. iv and v of the Historical Manuscripts Commission's *Report on the Manuscripts of His Grace the Duke of Portland*; these texts, in spite of their announced and obvious limitations, have been well known and often used. The other printed letters, however, have been widely scattered, and some of them deeply hidden; Defoe's fine letter to William Penn, for instance, was printed in 1902 but will be new nevertheless to most readers. Unpublished letters by Defoe or his correspondents are rare. Still, a few have been turned up. Six letters are here printed for the first time, two of them to Defoe (Nos. 26 and 161), the other four by him (Nos. 41, 43, 46, and 162). Almost none of the letters previously published has received full editorial treatment. None of them has been annotated sufficiently, and few of them have been annotated at all. Explanatory notes and comments are here appended to each. Many of Defoe's letters were not dated by him, and though dates have since been assigned to most of these, I have felt obliged in fifteen instances to reject such dates in favour of more reasonable ones. To seven of his letters, dates are here assigned for the first time. At the end of each letter will be found a formulary which gives whenever possible the name of the owner and the whereabouts of the original, the publication in which the letter appeared for the first time, the address as given in the manuscript or otherwise recorded, and the endorsement.

Throughout the course of his long life, Defoe's correspondence must have been enormous. He had a quick pen, an abundance of opinions, a widely dispersed multitude of acquaintances, and a relish for communicating his thoughts. If on the one hand we lament that so much of his personal writings has been lost, on the other we are grateful, and a little surprised, that so much has survived. The level of society to which he belonged, and within which presumably he carried on most of his correspondence, was not the class most likely to preserve files of personal papers. For instance, one searches in vain for a single letter written to his parents, or to Mary Defoe, patient helpmeet of a half-century of small triumphs and great calamities, or, with one exception, to any of his children, the delight and despair of his old age. Still, of his ordinary, everyday letters, not everything is lost. We have at least a sampling, various and probably representative, addressed to small tradesmen, business associates, publishers, political workers, fellow Dissenters, and other acquaintances.

But Defoe directed a voluminous and unusual correspondence to one man who did save most of his letters, his benefactor Robert Harley, Speaker of the House of Commons and Secretary of State, later Earl of Oxford and Lord Treasurer. The cautious Harley was a collector, and it is to his instinct for keeping things that we owe the happy preservation of most of the letters in this book. One may wince at his occasional practice of tearing off the now-prized signature of his secret agent, but he did not destroy the letter itself, and for that the student of Defoe must always be the debtor of Harley. In addition to this trove, the property of the Duke of Portland and now deposited by him in the British Museum, there survive a score of other letters written to persons of high station, most of them statesmen, who, like Harley, had facilities for preserving their correspondence and reasons for doing so.

Chronologically, the letters run from 1703, when Defoe was about 42 years old, to 1730, a few months before his death. The intervening years are covered sometimes fully, sometimes sparsely, sometimes not at all. There are no letters for 1709, for 1715–16, for 1719, or for 1721–7. But if some periods are poor, others are rich. The year 1705 is represented by 20 letters, in the majority of which Defoe exhibits in unique detail the political complexion of the West in that turbulent election year. Exactly a hundred letters of Defoe and his correspondents illumine the great period from 1710 to 1714, and the last years of the Queen. The richest coverage of all, however, falls to the years 1706–7; for that period, 78 letters, 74 of them by Defoe, have been preserved. It is a fortunate preservation, for most of Defoe's letters for those years were written during his long sojourn in Scotland as reporter and what today would be called 'promoter' of the most remarkable event of that time, the legislative Union of England and Scotland. No one tries to tell that story without turning to Defoe's letters from Scotland. Nowhere else is recorded so vividly and excitingly the spectacle of two ancient nations, separated by centuries of distrust, contempt, and warfare, struggling over Union. Whether Defoe's letters stem from this period or from another, whether they recount great national events or small personal ones, whether they were set down in the comfort of a home or the misery of a jail, all of them tell us something, and some of them tell us a great deal, about the life and strange, surprising adventures of the man who wrote them.

All the original manuscripts that can now be found have been made available for this edition, and I have been allowed to examine and transcribe all of them. Of Defoe's 235 known letters, I have been able to trace the holographs of 218, or 93 per cent. When the manuscript could not be traced, I have presented here the text of the earliest published version, unless a later one was both more complete and no less authoritative. In general, I have preserved Defoe's spelling, but I have expanded a number of his contracted forms. Defoe often employs the symbol ⫪þ to stand for the combinations pre-, per-, and par-. I have not retained that symbol: 'ⴶþsume' becomes 'presume', 'ⴶþform' becomes 'perform', 'ⴶþliament' becomes 'parliament', and so on. When the letter c is to receive the soft pronunciation, Defoe writes c̄. I have omitted the mark: 'sinc̄e' becomes 'since'. He employs the same device when the c is to be pronounced as sh. I have changed that c̄ to whatever the more familiar spelling calls for: 'acc̄on' becomes 'action', 'pretenc̄on' becomes 'pretension', and 'pačenče', in which both usages appear, becomes 'patience'. When Defoe indicates a double letter by placing a line above a single one, I give the double letter: 'cōmon' becomes 'common'. The contracted forms of a number of words have been expanded; the most frequent examples follow: 's^r' has been changed to 'sir', 'y^e' to 'the', 'y^t' to 'that', 'y^m' to 'them', 'w^{ch}' to 'which', 'o^r' to 'our', 'yor' to 'your', 'yo^{rs}' to 'yours', 'wth' to 'with', 'acco^t' to 'account', 'accqua^t' to 'accquaint', 'allow^a' to 'allowance', 'comp^a' to 'company', 'comm^a' to 'commander', 'complim^t' to 'compliment', 'Lond^o' to 'London', 'merch^a' to 'merchant', 'ordin^a' to 'ordinary', and 'rec^t' to 'receipt'. Throughout, superscribed letters have been lowered to the line. Where such lowering might result in confusion, I have abandoned the contraction and given the whole word: 'fa^{ll}' becomes 'faithfull', and 'Coll^{ll}' becomes 'Collonell'. Defoe's punctuation is sometimes confusing and often lacking. Whenever his pointing leads to distraction rather than clarity, I have abandoned it, and in order to provide a readable text I have been obliged to do so often. Most of the holographs are now easily accessible to any of Defoe's countrymen who may wish to observe his orthographical peculiarities, and Americans will find photographs of virtually all the manuscripts in the Cornell University Library.

G. H. H.

CORNELL UNIVERSITY

ACKNOWLEDGEMENTS

For permission to transcribe and publish original letters and other manuscripts I am grateful to His Grace, the Duke of Portland; Mrs. Margaret De Foe Latham, Woodhall Spa, Lincs.; the British Museum; the Public Record Office, London; Dr. Henry Clinton Hutchins, New Haven, Conn.; Mr. M. F. Bond, Clerk of the Records, House of Lords; the Rosenbach Company, New York and Philadelphia; the Historical Society of Pennsylvania, Philadelphia; the Victoria and Albert Museum; the Pierpont Morgan Library, New York; the Bodleian Library; Lieut.-Col. F. E. D. Fremantle, Essendon, Herts.; the Yale University Library; the Library of the Society of Friends, London; the Henry W. and Albert A. Berg Collection of the New York Public Library.

For permission to publish letters that have already appeared in print, I am obliged to the Controller of Her Majesty's Stationery Office, London; Longmans, Green & Co., London; Methuen & Co., London; C. J. Farncombe & Sons, Ltd., Croydon, Surrey; Professor G. M. Trevelyan, Cambridge University; Mr. Philip A. Wright, Olney, Bucks.

For help in searching for Defoe's letters and for generous assistance of many other kinds, I wish to thank Professor William M. Sale, Cornell University; Professor R. C. Bald, the University of Chicago; Professor James Sutherland, University College, London; Professor Charles W. Jones, Cornell University; Mr. Francis Needham, Reading, Berks.; Dr. Herbert Davis, Oxford University; Dr. David Daiches, Cambridge University; Professor Arthur Secord, the University of Illinois; Mr. M. Radford, Sotheby's, London; Miss Hannah Buchan, the University of Glasgow; Mr. James McGloin, Glasgow; Mr. Anthony Geiss, Queen Mary College, London; Professor Juliet Reeve, Friends University, Wichita, Kans.; Sir Harold Williams, 43, Albert Court, Kensington; Mr. John Fleming, New York; Mr. Roger Thomas, Dr. Williams's Library, London; Mr. P. J. Dobell, Tunbridge Wells, Kent; Mr. James Ross, City Librarian, Bristol; the editors of the *English Historical Review*; the Reverend G. J. Grieve, Secretary of the Presbyterian Fund, London; Dr. Felix Reichmann, Cornell University Library; Miss Mildred E. Jenkinson, Bideford, Devon; Mr. M. A. Vardill, Brentford, Middx.; Miss Dorothy Greene, Rotherham, Yorks.; Mrs. Dorothea Hill, Crowthorne, Berks.; Mr. John L. Hobbs, Borough Librarian, Shrewsbury; Messrs. Maggs

Acknowledgements

Brothers, London; Mr. John Robertson, Librarian, Stirling, Scotland; Mr. J. A. C. West, Librarian, Weymouth, Dorset; Mr. Donald De Foe Baker, London.

For the award of the Martin Sampson Fellowship, for a grant which enabled me to carry my investigations to England and Scotland, and for many other favours, I am grateful to Cornell University.

I wish to record particularly my obligation to the kindness and erudition of Professor John Robert Moore of Indiana University, who for many years has cheerfully made available to me his unmatched knowledge of Defoe.

CONTENTS

REGISTER OF LETTERS

xix

ABBREVIATIONS USED IN THE NOTES

*Here and throughout, place of publication
is London unless otherwise noted*

Aitken ed.   *Romances and Narratives of Daniel Defoe*, ed. George A. Aitken, 1895, 16 vols.

C.B.E.L.   *Cambridge Bibliography of English Literature*, 1941, 4 vols.

Defoe Papers.   A volume of manuscripts, owned by the Duke of Portland, entitled 'Harley Letters and Papers, De Foe, 1703–1714'. The volume is foliated in two sequences, ff. 1–267 followed by ff. 1–147. In citations from this volume the two sequences are distinguished by a '1' or a '2' preceding the folio number.

Dottin, *Defoe*.   Paul Dottin, *Daniel De Foe et ses romans*, Paris, 1924.

Fasti Ecclesiæ Scoticanæ.   Hew Scott, *Fasti Ecclesiæ Scoticanæ*, Edinburgh, 1915–28, 7 vols.

Harley Papers.   The 51 volumes of manuscripts, owned by the Duke of Portland, so entitled.

History of the Union.   Defoe, *The History of the Union*, 1786.

H.M.C. Bath.   *Calendar of the Manuscripts of the Marquis of Bath*, 1904–8, 3 vols.

H.M.C. Mar and Kellie.   *Report on the Manuscripts of the Earl of Mar and Kellie*, 1904.

H.M.C. Portland.   *Report on the Manuscripts of His Grace the Duke of Portland*, v.d., 10 vols.

J.H.C.   *Journals of the House of Commons.*

J.H.L.   *Journals of the House of Lords.*

Journal to Stella.   Jonathan Swift, *Journal to Stella*, ed. Harold Williams, Oxford, 1948, 2 vols.

Later Stuart Tracts.   *An English Garner: Later Stuart Tracts*, introduction by George A. Aitken, Westminster, 1903.

Lee, *Life*.   William Lee, *Daniel Defoe: His Life and Recently Discovered Writings*, 1869, 3 vols.

Lockhart Papers.   George Lockhart, *The Lockhart Papers, Containing Memoirs and Commentaries upon the Affairs of Scotland from 1702 to 1715*, 1817, 2 vols.

Luttrell, *Brief Relation*.   Narcissus Luttrell, *A Brief Historical Relation of State Affairs*, Oxford, 1857, 6 vols.

Mackinnon, *Union of England and Scotland*.   James Mackinnon, *The Union of England and Scotland*, 1896.

Abbreviations Used in the Notes

Mathieson, *Scotland and the Union.*   William Law Mathieson, *Scotland and the Union,* Glasgow, 1905.

Parliamentary History.   *Parliamentary History of England,* vol. vi, 1810.

Shakespeare Head ed.   *Novels and Selected Writings of Daniel Defoe,* Oxford, 1927, 14 vols.

Somers Tracts.   *A Collection of Scarce and Valuable Tracts on the Most Interesting and Entertaining Subjects,* 2nd ed., 1809–15, 13 vols.

Sutherland, *Defoe.*   James Sutherland, *Defoe,* 2nd ed., 1950.

Tour thro' Britain.   Defoe, *A Tour thro' the Whole Island of Great Britain,* introduction by G. D. H. Cole, 1927, 2 vols.

True Collection.   Defoe, *A True Collection of the Writings of the Author of the True Born English-man,* 1703.

Wentworth Papers.   *The Wentworth Papers, 1705–1739,* ed. J. J. Cartwright, 1883.

Wilson, *Life.*   Walter Wilson, *Memoirs of the Life and Times of Daniel De Foe,* 1830, 3 vols.

Wodrow, *Analecta.*   Robert Wodrow, *Analecta: or, Materials for a History of Remarkable Providences,* Maitland Club, 1842–3, 4 vols.

Works, 1705.   Defoe, *A True Collection of the Writings of the Author of the True Born English-man,* 1705, cited as vol. i; and *A Second Volume of the Writings of the Author of the True-Born Englishman,* 1705, cited as vol. ii.

Wright, *Life* (1894).   Thomas Wright, *The Life of Daniel Defoe,* 1894.

Wright, *Life* (1931).   Thomas Wright, *The Life of Daniel Defoe,* revised ed., 1931.

1. *To* DANIEL FINCH, EARL OF NOTTINGHAM.[1]

9 *January 1702/3*

My Lord

I am Exceding Senceible That I have Given her Majtie and The Governent Offence, and Severall Poor and Some Innocent People being in Trouble on my Account, Moves me to Address your Lordship in This Manner, for which Rudeness I humbly Ask your Pardon.[2]

I had Long Since Surrendred to her Majties Clemency, had Not the Menaces of your Lordships Officers, Posest me with Such Ideas of her Majties and your Lordships Resentments, as Were Too Terrible, and Such as Respected former Things,[3] which I have had No Concern in, Tho' I have had the Missfortune to pass for Guilty by Common Fame.

To Flee from her Majties justice, Seems my Lord to be a kind of Raiseing Warr Against her, and is Very Irkesome to me. I Beseech your Lordship to Assist me in Laying Down These Arms, Or at Least in Makeing Such a Truce, as may Thro' her Majties Condesension Obtain her Pardon.

My Lord a Body Unfitt to bear the hardships of a Prison, and a Mind Impatient of Confinement, have been the Onely Reasons of withdrawing My Self: And My Lord The Cries of a Numer-

---

[1] Daniel Finch (1647–1730), second Earl of Nottingham, high Tory, conscientious but reactionary minister, was Secretary of State for the Southern Department. On 3 Jan. he had issued orders 'to make Strict and diligent Search for Daniel Fooe and him having found you are to apprehend and Seize together with his Papers for high Crimes and misdemeanours and to bring him before me to be examined concerning Such matters as shall be objected against him touching the premises and be further dealt with according to Law' (P.R.O., S.P. 44/352/103). Defoe never forgave Nottingham for the ill treatment that followed, assailed him often in the *Review* and elsewhere, and attacked him violently in *The Dyet of Poland*, 1705.

[2] Defoe was a fugitive from the wrath of the embarrassed Tory Government. His ironical *Shortest Way with the Dissenters*, published during the previous month, had first deceived and then infuriated the high Tories, subject of its satire, who controlled both the Ministry and the House of Commons. Nottingham had penetrated his anonymity, ordered his arrest, and offered a reward for his apprehension (*London Gazette*, 11 Jan.).

[3] Among them, perhaps, writing his defiant *Memorial to the K[night]s, C[ommon]s, and B[urgesse]s in P[arliamen]t Assembled. Addressed to R[ober]t H[arle]y, Esq., S[peake]r of the H[ous]e of C[ommon]s* ('Legion's Memorial'), 1701, which Defoe may have delivered in person to the House of Commons, and which, in his own words, 'struck such a terror into the Party in the House, that, from that time, there was not a word ever spoken in the House, of proceeding against the Kentish Petitioners' (*History of the Kentish Petition*, 1701, in *Later Stuart Tracts*, p. 169). Defoe denied authorship of 'Legion's Memorial' but it was, and is, commonly believed to be his.

ous Ruin'd Family,[1] The Prospect of a Long Banishment from my Native Country, and the hopes of her Majties Mercy, Moves me to Thro' my Self at her Majties Feet, and To Intreat your Lordships Intercession.

I Beseech your Lordship to Assure her Majtie, That I am Perfectly Free From any Seditious Designs,[2] and However I have Unadvisedly offended, I am, and Ever was Entirely Devoted to her Intrest and Service.

With the Lowest Submission I Intreat her Majties Pardon For This Mistake, For which I am Ready To Make any Publick Acknowledgement, and Further humbly Beseech your Lordships Pardon and Patience in Makeing a Proposall on my Own Behalf, For Tho' it Must be Unusuall Condesension, in her Majtie to Capitulate with an Offending Subject, yet Offences Differ in Their Nature, and her Majties Mercy is Unbounded.

I Was Inform'd My Lord, that when my Distress'd Wife, made Application to your Lordship, you were pleas'd to Direct, I Should Surrender, and Answer to Such questions as Should be asked me;[3] My Lord would your Lordship Condescend to Permitt any Questions you Think Fitt, be Writt Down, and Sent to, or left at my house, I will as Soon as I Can Recieve them, give your Lordship as Plain, Full, Direct, and honest Answers, as If I were in Imediate Apprehensions of Death from your Resentments; and Perhaps my Lord my Answers may be So Satisfactory, as may Encline you to Think you have been Mis Inform'd Concerning me.

But My Lord if after This I Should Still have the Misfortune to Remain Under her Majties Displeasure, I am Then her Most Humble Petitioner, that She will please to Remitt the Rigor of Prosecution, and That Pleading Guilty I may Reciev a Sentence from her Perticular justice, a Little More Tollerable to me as a Gentleman, Than Prisons, Pillorys, and Such like, which are Worse to me Than Death.[4]

---

[1] His father, wife, and six children.

[2] Defoe may have felt, and been, within his rights in opposing the Tory Government's attitude toward Dissenters, but the Government threatened him just the same by charging that his pamphlet was 'seditious'.

[3] When Nottingham finally did examine Defoe, he learned nothing; but he had apparently hoped to sift Defoe concerning not only his present pamphlet but also his past associations with the late King William and the Whigs. See Sutherland, *Defoe*, p. 93.

[4] On the advice of his counsel, William Colepeper (one of the five Kentish Petitioners), Defoe did plead guilty, but his punishment of pillory, indeterminate jail sentence, and heavy fine was hardly lightened thereby. See J. R. Moore, *Defoe in the Pillory and Other Studies*, Bloomington, Indiana, 1939, pp. 3–38.

I Beg Leave To Observe to your Lordship, that Felons, and Thieves, whose Punishmt is Death are Frequently Spar'd upon Entring into her Majties Service. If her Majtie Will be pleased to Order me, to Serve her a year, or More at my Own Charges, I Will Surrendr my Self a Voluntier at the head of her Armyes, in the Netherlands,[1] To any Collonell of horse, her Majtie Shall Direct, and without Doubt my Lord I shall Dye There Much More To her Service than in a Prison; and If by my Behaviour I Can Expiate This Offence, and Obtain her Majties Pardon, I shall Think it much More honourable to me Than if I had it by Petition.

And Least I Should Seem to Prescribe to her Majties Mercy, My Lord, If her Majtie abateing Prisons, and Corporall Punishments, shall Please To Pass any Sentence upon me, That I am Capable To Put in Excecution, I Resolve Chearfully To Submitt To it, and Thro' my Self upon her Native Clemency.

But if her Majtie Shall Extend her Grace to a Totall Remission of This Offence,[2] and if I may Presume to Say shall Further be pleas'd to Accept my Service, I Will Raise her Majtie a Troop of horse, at my Own Charges, and at the head of Them Ile Serve her as Long as I Live.

At Least my Lord This may Assure you, I am Ready with my hand, my Pen, or my head, to Show her Majtie The Gratitude of a Pardoned Subject: and To Give her Majtie all The Satisfaction I am Capable of, being Extreamly Griev'd That I have Offended her. Humbly Entreating your Lordships Favor and Intercession which Possibly your Lordship will not Repent, when you shall find you have Gran[ted][3] it, To a Zealous, Thankfull, and Faithfull Subject, and To

> May it Please your Lordship,
> Your Most Obedient, Distressed
> Humble Petitioner and Servt
> DE FOE

Janua 9th 1702

MS.: P.R.O., Museum Ped. No. 100. *Pub.*: G. A. Aitken, 'Defoe in

[1] In the Netherlands, Marlborough's British and Dutch troops were in winter quarters preparing to open the second campaign of the War of the Spanish Succession.

[2] Defoe was released from Newgate in late Oct. or early Nov. 1703. The Queen ordered the Lord Treasurer to pay his fine and costs and to relieve his family. His official pardon, however, seems to have been delayed until July 1704. See W. P. Trent, 'New Light on Defoe's Life', *The Nation* (New York), lxxxvii (1908), 260; Defoe, *Appeal to Honour and Justice*, in *Later Stuart Tracts*, p. 77; and Godolphin to Harley, 31 July 1704, *H.M.C. Bath*, i. 61.   [3] MS. torn.

Trouble', *The Athenaeum*, 22 Dec. 1894, p. 862. *Address*: 'To the Right
Honoble Heneage [in error for Daniel] Earl of Nottingham, Her Majties
Principall Secretary of State'. *Endorsed*: 'De Foe, Jan 9 1702.'

2. *To* WILLIAM PATERSON.[1] *April 1703*

Sir

I can Not Omitt That in the Little Information I have from
my Very Few Friends, I Meet with from Every hand The
Notices of your Concern for my Present Suffering, And as I am
Assur'd my Gratitude for the Kindness of my friends will be the
Last Vertue That will forsake me, So my Sence of your Regard
for me, on whom I have Laid No Obligation, Lays a Debt On
Me I Can No Otherwise Pay Than by my Thankfull Acknow-
ledgements.

Tis Vain for me To Complain of the Misfortune of my Present
Condition, Since you Can Render me No Services for which you
Shall not Recieve Reproaches from all Partyes. Nay Even the
Dissenters Like Casha to Cæsar Lift up the first Dagger at me:
I Confess it makes me Reflect on the wholl body of the Dissenters
with Something of Contempt More Than Usuall, and gives me
the More Regrett That I Suffer for Such a People.[2]

Shall I Own to you That the Greatest Concern I have Upon
me is That the Govornment, whom I Profess I Did not foresee
would be Displeas'd, Should Resent This Matter. I had it not
in my Thoughts That the Ministers of State would Construe
That as Pointing at Them, Which I Levell'd Onely at Dr
Sachavrell,[3] Dr Stubbs,[4] and Such People, my More Direct

---

[1] William Paterson (1658–1719) helped found the Bank of England, conceived
the idea of the Darien Settlement, and strongly supported the Union with Scotland.
Like Defoe, he was a London merchant, a writer on economic themes, a man of
affairs, and an enthusiastic 'projector' of schemes. Both he and Defoe had enjoyed
the confidence of King William. For a sketch of Paterson, see J. H. Burton, *History
of Scotland*, 1897–1901, viii. 13–20.

[2] The Dissenters had been as outraged at the extravagance of *The Shortest Way*
as the high-flyers had been at its impudence.

[3] Henry Sacheverell (1674–1724), Fellow of Magdalen, Oxford, was already
known as a High-Church enthusiast and an enemy of occasional conformity. His
Oxford sermon of the previous year, published as *A Discourse Showing the Dependence
of Government upon Religion*, had alarmed the Dissenters by its talk of hanging out the
bloody flag of defiance against them. He came into more general public notice
seven years later, on being impeached for his famous sermon on the perils of false
brethren, an attack on the Whigs, moderate Tories, and Dissenters. See A. T.
Scudi, *The Sacheverell Affair*, New York, 1939. Defoe denounced Sacheverell for
many years. For an early public attack, see the *Review* for 16 Dec. 1704; for a later
private one, see Defoe's letter to Stanhope, No. 132.

[4] Philip Stubbs (1665–1738), high Tory, Fellow of Wadham, and first chaplain
of Greenwich Hospital, was at this time rector of St. Alphage, London Wall. Defoe

4

Antagonists; Thus Like Old Tyrrell[1] who shot at a Stag and Killd the King, I Engag'd a Party and Embroild my Self with the Govornmt. Sir, My Sence of This has Led me to the Lowest Submissions I was Capable of in a Letter I wrott to my Lord Nottingham[2] and Some Other Applications Made Since, Nor is there any Thing So Mean (which I Can Honestly Stoop to Do) That I Would not Submitt to To Obtain her Majties Favour.

I Accquainted my Ld Nottingham That whereas Persons Condemn'd for Capitall offences were Frequently Spar'd upon Their Entring Into her Majties Service, If her Majtie would Grant me the Like Favor I would Surrendr my Self at the head of her Armyes To any Coll. of Horse her Majtie Should Appoint, and Serve her a year, Two, or More at my Own Charge, Not Doubting I Should Dye There more to her Majties Service Than in a Prison, And that if by my behavior I Could Expiate This Folly, I Should Esteem it More honour to me Than If I Obtain'd her Majties Pardon by Petition; I Omitted Nothing to Express the Unfeigned Sence I had upon my Mind of haveing offended her Majtie, and I Repeat This to you that you May kno' and be assur'd and May if you Please So farr Answer for me, that I Really am a hearty Penitent on That Account and That I am Not asham'd, to be asham'd of it.

I Can Not but with Regrett Look back on the Former Discourses we have had Concerning Things Done before Now, and you Must Remember how Willingly I allwayes Offred you To make my Acknowledgements To a Certain Gentleman,[3] who I allwayes Honour For his Character Among Wise Men, More Than the Greatness of his share in the Royall Favour; If I have

named Stubbs as one of those who 'branded the Dissenter with Rebellion and Faction, not only in their Nature, but in their very Principles; they have laid it down in their Writings and Sermons, and Multitudes of their ignorant Hearers believe it, that *the very Doctrine of the Dissenters is made up of Principles in their own Nature tending to Confusion and Rebellion* . . . and that 'tis the Religion of a Dissenter to disturb Government, kill Kings, and oppose Laws' (*New Test of the Church of England's Loyalty*, in *Works*, 1705, i. 404).

[1] Walter Tirel was supposed to have discharged the arrow that killed William Rufus in the New Forest, Aug. 1100.

[2] The preceding letter.

[3] Robert Harley, Speaker of the House of Commons. Paterson did not send the letter to Harley until 28 May (see endorsement), four days after Defoe's arrest (*Daily Courant*, 24 May 1703). Harley was at least in some measure responsible for Defoe's present plight. In an undated note (perhaps of late December) to Nottingham, Godolphin had written: 'I had last night some talk with the speaker, & he has had a mind to speak to you abt a book lately Come out, Call'd, *a short way with the Dissenters*. He seem'd to think it absolutely necessary to the Service of the Governmt that your Lp. shd endeavour to discover who was the Author of it' (Brit. Mus., Add. MSS. 29,589 f. 400).

Rendred the hopes you gave me of his Favour Desperate by This Disaster, Tis a Missfortune as Great as all the Rest. If Not, Beseech him To Suspend his Resentments Till my Future behavior may Convince him That (of all the Gentlemen known to me Onely by Character) he is the Last I would Disoblige and the First I would Humble my Self To Because of The just Respect I have Entertaind of his Wisdome and Honesty.

As to my Present Circumstances I Can Onely Say as of him that Repents without hope I Find Them Desperate and That Neither Sence of the Offence Nor Future Amendment will attone. So I am Fled, and Tho' I Do allready Find Tis No Very Difficult Thing for me to Get my Bread, yet as I Exprest to My Lord N: Methinks fleeing from her Majties Justice is a Sort of Raiseing Warr against her, and I would Fain Lay Down These Arms. Nor had Death been the Punishment Should I ha[ve been][1] So Long before I had Come in and Thrown my Self upon her Majties Clemency, but Jayls, Pillorys and Such like with which I have been So Much Threatn'd have Convinc't me I want Passive Courage, and I Shall Never for the Future Think my Self Injur'd if I am Call'd a Coward.

I hope by my Missfortunes I Shall Not Loose the Influence of your Friendship, and if you Find it Necessary To Make any Postulata of Future Loyalty and my Obedient Submission to or Service for the Govornment, If you Believ me Master of any Faith, or That I have any Principles of Honour or honesty Left, you May Depend upon my Punctuall Performance.

If you Should Find Room for my Name in your Conversation with the Gentleman I Mention'd, I Suppose I Need Not Name him, If you Find him Enclin'd to have Compassion for One who Offended him Onely because he Did Not kno' him, Venture in My Name in the Humblest Terms to Ask his Pardon, and whether Ever I am Restor'd to my Native Country Or Not,[2] I shall Never Name him but with Some Epethite Suited to Express his Merit; Let him kno' That I Sollicit you with More Earnestness To Convince him of my Sence of his Resentment, and My Earnest Desire to be set Right in his Thoughts, Than I Do for the Obtaining a Recall from This Banishment Forasmuch as I Vallue the Esteem of One Wise man above abundance of Blessings.

---

[1] MS. torn; words supplied.
[2] Defoe's hiding-place remains unknown. When captured, he was at the house of a French weaver in Spitlefields.

Accept my Repeated Thanks for the Friendship you show in Concerning your Self for me, my Vows for your Welfare and Prosperity, and Continue your Goodness and kindness To

Your Exil'd Friend
D F

Aprill. [   ]th. 1703[1]

MS.: Duke of Portland, Defoe Papers, 1 ff. 1–2. *Pub.*: *H.M.C. Portland*, iv. 61–62. *Address*: 'For Mr William Paterson in London, in Covert.' *Endorsed* (by Robert Harley): 'Received from Mr Wm Paterson, Fryday May 28: 1703: at one a clock.'

3. [To WILLIAM PENN].[2] 12 July 1703

Sir   July 12th, 1703

Tho' a Long Apology Suites Neither your Own Temper, Nor my Condition, yet I Can Not but Let you Kno' with all The Thankfullness I am Capable The Sence I have of your Extraordinary Kindness:—Concerning your Self For me So Much a

---

[1] Blank in MS.

[2] William Penn (1644–1718), founder of Pennsylvania, had long before been victim himself of three imprisonments for non-conformity, and though at this time beset by troubles of his own, was attempting to save Defoe, who was now in Newgate, from the humiliation of the pillory. Penn was popular with the Queen, and though he failed to obtain a mitigation of Defoe's sentence, he did manage to gain a brief deferment. On 17 July, two days before Defoe was to have begun his sentence, Godolphin wrote to Nottingham: 'After I had the honor to see your Lp yesterday, Mr William Penn came to mee to tell mee he had acquainted my Lord privy seal [Buckingham] that *de Foe* was ready to make oath to your Lp of all that he knew, & to give an Account of all his Accomplices in whatsoever he has been Concerned, for the information of the Queen, & the Lords of the Councill, provided by so doing, he may bee excused from the punishment of the pillory, & not produced as an Evidence against any person whatsoever, & upon my acquainting the Queen with this just now at noon, her Maty was pleased to tell mee she had received the same Account yesterday from my Lord pr-seal, & seem'd to think, this if there were no other occasion, would make it reasonable for the Cabinett Councill to meet here [at Windsor] tomorrow, & has Commanded mee to tell you soe, because, she says, you seem'd to think yesterday, that it might bee an unnecessary trouble' (Brit. Mus., Add. MSS. 29,589 ff. 28–29). On 18 July Penn wrote to an unidentified 'Noble Friend' as follows: 'For the Queens service I beg this mans disgrace may be deferr'd if not pardon'd. I inclose a lettr to Lord Treasr who desireing to be by at his examination with Ld Notingham, before he sufferd the Sentence, which cannot be if he suffer to morrow' (P.R.O., S.P. 34/3/3). On the same day, Nottingham ordered the sentence to be deferred (P.R.O., S.P. 44/104/316). Defoe was examined at Windsor on 21 July. On the following day, Godolphin reported to Nottingham: 'As to *de Foe*, the Queen seems to think, as she did upon your Lps first acquainting her with what he said, that his Confession amounts to nothing, however she is willing to Leave it to the Lords of the Committee to Lett the sentence bee executed tomorrow [Friday], or not till after Sunday, as they think proper' (Brit. Mus., Add. MSS. 29,589 f. 46). Defoe stood in the pillory on the last three days of July (*London Gazette*, 2 Aug. 1703).

Stranger to you, Nor Can I Doubt whether To One who Appeares So Much my Friend as to attempt being my Saviour From This Distress, I should Scruple to use the uttmost Freedome with Relation to the Present Case.

Sir The Proposall you are pleas'd to hint By your Son[1] from My Ld Nottingham, of Discovering Partyes is the same which his Lordship has often Put upon me before.

Sir In Some Letters[2] which I have Sent his Lordship I have Answer'd him with the Same Assurance I did to the Privy Council, Vizt That in the Manner which they Proposed it I really had No Person to Discover: That if my Life were Concern'd in it I would Not Save it at the Price of Impeaching Innocent Men, No More would I Accuse my Friends for the Freedome of Private Conversation.

It has been my Character Sir among those who Kno' me, That I Scorn to Lye, and by Gods Grace Ile preserve it while I live. I Take the Freedome to give you the Trouble of repeating it, Onely To affirm to you with the More Confidence the Protestation I make. I Sollemnly Affirm that Other than what Passes in Conversation, and Perhaps There is ill blood among people of my Opinion More than Enough, but other Than that I have no Accomplices, No Sett of Men, (as my Lord Call'd Them) with whom I used to Concert Matters, of this Nature, To whom I us'd to show, or Reciev hints from them in Ordr to These Matters, and Therefore to Put it upon Condition of Such a Nature is to Offer me Nothing Attall.[3]

But Sir My Case is this. I came in upon the Honour of the Govornment, being Under Baile that (at least Some of them) Consented to Let me go away, and presst me to it. I agreed to give the Court No Trouble but to plead Guilty to the Indictment, Even to all the Adverbs, the Seditiously's, The Malitiously's, and a Long Rapsody of the Lawyers et Ceteras; and all this upon promises of being us'd Tenderly. I am Ready To do the Church of England any justice by Vindicateing her in the Same Publick Manner They Suppose her affronted I mean in Print.

This is what I Thot Fitt to give you the Trouble of, For

---

[1] William Penn the younger.
[2] They do not survive.
[3] Yet four days later Penn was assuring Godolphin that Defoe was ready 'to give an Account of all his Accomplices' if by so doing he could escape the pillory (p. 7, n. 2,). 'No doubt he was firm and weak by turns in those trying weeks of July' (Sutherland, *Defoe*, p. 93).

which I ask your Pardon, and Entreat the Continuance of those Kind Offices you have So Generously undertaken for

An Unknown Captive, Your Disstress'd Servt

DANIEL DE FOE

MS.: untraced; the text is taken from the MS. copy, once owned by Mr. Philip Justice of Philadelphia, now in the Library of the Society of Friends, London. *Pub.*: Norman Penney in *The Friend* (Philadelphia), lxxvi (1902), 1–2. *Address*: 'For William Penn Esqr., Humbly Presd.'

4. *To* JAMES STANCLIFFE.[1] [*c. 9*] *November 1703*

Mr Stancliffe

One Trouble allwayes brings on Another, and as you have Embarkt for me in the First part of this Matter, you must not Refuse to be the Messenger of my Acknowledgements.

I Can hardly Promise my Self that what I have wrott will Express my Sence of the Obligation I have upon me to Mr Harley, and I Wish you would make it up, by Saying Every thing you Can Immagin a Man Overcome with Kindness Ought to Say.

I am at Some Loss about the papers I told you I had prepar'd to publish on my Enlargement. I would do nothing of that Nature that should be offensive to my benefactors, but I am perswaded None of that party of Men which are Touch't by me have any hand in an Action So Generous as this, and am of Opinion what was in my thoughts that way would Rather please than Dissoblige those that Can Entertain any thoughts of kindness or Compassion for my Case. Yet I shall Continue to stop the press in this Case till I hear your Opinion, tho' the Substance was never So Necessary to my Own Vindication.[2]

I am your Oblig'd Friend & Servt

D F

No [   ][3] 1703

MS.: Duke of Portland, Defoe Papers, I f. 3. *Pub.*: *H.M.C. Portland*, iv. 76. *Address*: 'To Mr James Stancliffe, in Ironmonger Lane, London.'

[1] James Stancliffe had been a business associate of Defoe's early in the last reign, had lent him money to further an unfortunate venture in breeding civet cats, and was soon to become a referee in Defoe's present bankruptcy. Flight and imprisonment having ruined his tile business, Defoe's creditors agreed to a composition. Defoe delivered up all his assets to Stancliffe, who was then to pay to the creditors the amounts that they had agreed to accept in discharge of Defoe's indebtedness to them. See J. R. Sutherland, 'A Note on the Last Years of Defoe', *Modern Language Review*, xxix (1934), 137–40; and T. F. M. Newton, 'The Civet Cats of Newington Green', *Review of English Studies*, xiii (1937), 10–19.

[2] If the stop was for a short time only, Defoe may be referring to his *Challenge of Peace*, which appeared on 23 Nov. (Dottin, *Defoe*, p. 807).

[3] MS. torn. Since this letter was apparently a cover for the following one, dated 9 Nov., it was probably written on or about the same date.

5. *To* ROBERT HARLEY.[1] *9 November 1703*

Sir

As there is Something Surprizeing in your Bounty To a Morti-fyed Stranger,[2] So I am more than usually at a Loss in what Manner to Express my Sence of it. But Sir at the Same time that you Stoop to do good you Subject your Self to a Necessity of bearing The Impertinence of a Thankfull Temper.[3]

Of all the Examples in Sacred Story None moves my Indigna-tion like That of the Ten Lepers who were healed by Our Saviour. I Sir Like that One Gratefull wretch am Come back to Pay the Tribute of thankfullness which this So Unexpected Goodness Commands from me.

And Sir Tho' I think my Self bound to Own you as the Principall Agent of this Miracle, yet haveing Some Encourage-ment from you to Expect More Perticularly to *kno' my Bene-factors*; I can Not but wish for that Discovery that my Acknow-ledgements may in Some Measure be Proportion'd To the Quallity of the Persons, and the Vallue of the Favour.

It Remains for me to Conclude my Present Application with This Humble Petition that if Possible I may By Some Meanes or Other know what I am capable of Doeing, that my Bene-factors whoever they are May Not be Asham'd of their Bounty

---

[1] Robert Harley (1661–1724), moderate Tory, was at this time Speaker of the House of Commons, and in spite of personal characteristics not usually considered promising, was looked upon as a coming man. In his private life he was easy-going, soft-tempered, and fond of good wine, old books, and learned company. In public affairs he was enigmatic, muddling, and dilatory, but was also tolerant, calm under attack, and moderate in an age not really much given to the moderation it affected. He and Defoe, dissimilar though they were in station and character, had some qualities in common. They were of about the same age. Both were of Puritan heritage, though Harley now attended church rather than meeting-house. Both rather enjoyed secrecy and mystification. But it was their common belief in moderate principles, both religious and political, that enabled the two to work together so long in common cause. Harley privately recognized Defoe's ability, but never acknowledged it publicly. He never adequately rewarded Defoe for his years of diligent service, never found him the permanent post so often requested, and some-times left him in serious straits for want of money to pay expenses incurred in government service. Yet Defoe never forgot his indebtedness to the man who got him out of Newgate. He admitted his obligation in correspondence and in print, and seems to have maintained toward his 'Benefactor' a warm and lasting affection. See Defoe, *Minutes of the Negotiations of Monsr. Mesnager*, 1717, pp. 48–53; Thomas Bateman, 'The Relations of Defoe and Harley', *English Historical Review*, xv (1900), 238–50; and E. S. Roscoe, *Robert Harley, Earl of Oxford*, 1902, pp. 47–74.

[2] This letter is evidence against the notion—held occasionally in our day as well as in Defoe's—that Harley and Defoe had been acquainted before 1703 and that Defoe had been writing at Harley's instigation and indirectly in his support.

[3] Harley had obtained Defoe's release from Newgate.

as Missapplyed. Not Sir That I Expect to be able to Meritt So Much goodness, But as A Gratefull Temper is Allwayes Uneasy to be Loaded with Benefitts, So The *Vertue* which I Call Gratitude, has Allwayes So Much Pride in it, as Makes it Push at a Retribution, Tho' tis Unable to Effect it.

Whoever Sir Are the Principalls in this Favour, I Can Not but Profess my Self a Debtor wholly to your Self, who Till I May be Otherwise Instructed Appeares the Originall *as to Me*. And in the kindness the Manner is So Oblidgeing, and all the Articles of it So Generous, that as a Man Astonish't at the Perticulars, I am Perfectly Unable to Express My Sence of it, Onely in the humblest Manner I Can, Most Earnestly Pray That I May have Some Opportunity Put into my hands by Providence to Make More Explicit Acknowledgements; And that as I have Recd Such an Obligation as few Ever Reciev'd, I Might be Able to Make Some Such Sort of Return as No Man Ever Made.

And as I am Sure I write this from an honest heart, Readyer by Farr to Perform than to Promise; So I Take The Freedome to Repeat the Assurance of A Man Ready to Dedicate my Life and all Possible Powers to The Intrest of So Generous and So Bountifull Benefactors, Being Equally Overcome with The Nature as well as the Vallue of The Favour I have Reciev'd. Asking your Pardon for The Freedome of This Address and For Subscribeing My Self

     Your Most Obedient Infinitely Oblidged Humble Servant
                         Daniel De Foe

Novembr 9° 1703

MS.: Duke of Portland, Defoe Papers, 1 ff. 4–5. *Pub.*: *H.M.C. Portland*, iv. 75–76. *Address*: 'To The Honoble Robert Harley Esqr., Speaker To the House of Commons, Humbly Present.'

6. *To* [?   ].[1] *18 April 1704*

Sir

I Was Very Sorry To heare you were So Suddainly Goeing away, and Came a great way to have Wisht you a good Journey.

This I thot my Self Oblig'd to in Return for those Many and Kind Visits you bestow'd on me in a house of Bondage and affliction.

As This was all my Reason for offring you the Interruption of a shake by the hand, So I supply your Absence by putting it

[1] The addressee remains unidentified. He may have been William Penn, but the possibilities cannot be narrowed down to him.

into Writeing, Onely Assureing you I shall be Glad To hear by a Line, whether you Get Safe Down, and if it be worth your while to Correspond you may be Sure Twill be welcome To

Your Oblig'd Frd & Servt
D FOE

Aprll 18. 1704

MS.: Historical Society of Pennsylvania, Philadelphia. *Pub.*: *A Catalogue of the Collection of Autographs Formed by Ferdinand Julius Dreer*, Philadelphia, 1890, i. 157. *Address*: none.

7. [*To* ROBERT HARLEY]. *12 May 1704*

Sir

Tis a Perticular Missfortune to me That I had Not the honour of Seeing you Last Night,[1] and Tis the More So, in that I Recd No Orders when to give My Farther Attendance.

And yet Sir I had waited with all the Patience became Me in This Perticular, Till your Affaires had permitted or your Pleasure Approv'd of giveing Me Audience; had not my Uneasyness at This Time Prevail'd On Good Manners from the Following Occasion.

I kno' the Duty Lay on me To Conceal the Favour I Recd in your Admitting a Man Lately Made Despicable to So Near and So Advantageous a Conversation, and Therefore have Carefully Conceal'd from all the world what Otherwise I should have Vallued my Self upon on all Occasions, That I had the Honor So Much as to be known to you.

But Sir It is Impossible for me to Describe the Confusion I was in, when I was Publickly Told On Wednsday Last, when, where, and How often I had the Honour of your Conversation, and Imagining Their Intelligence was *Ab Inferis*, Expected to hear Every Mom[ent][2] the perticulars of Our Discourse.

I am Confident you will Pardon the Importunity of This Letter, when you Reflect how Earnest I was Not Onely to Accquaint you with This, but Also to Let you kno' the Accident which brought it to Pass; and the Method by which any ill Consequence from it may be Prevented.

I am your Most Humble Petitioner, That you will Please to abate me all Those Extasies and Extravagancyes a Necessary Acknowledgement of your Generous Concern for me would Lead me to. I Can No More Express my Self, Than I Can for-

[1] For the explanation, see the following letter.
[2] MS. torn.

gett the Obligation. And I Choose to be Perfectly Silent, from the Impossibillity of Putting my Sence of it into words, and the hopes I have That the Same Providence which I humbly Recognize as the first Mover of your Thoughts in My favour, will yet Put an Occasion into my hands, by Faithfull, and usefull Application, to Satisfye you, That I am the Gratefullest wretch Allive.

[Half a page, including the signature, torn out.]¹

Fryday May 12° 1704

Sir

If you please to Let a Note be left (or any Other way) with the Maid Servt at Mr Auditors Chambers² I shall Call there for your Orders, Or Directed [to me]³ at Jones's Coffee house in Finch Lane Near the [Exchange].

MS.: Duke of Portland, Defoe Papers, 1 ff. 6–7. *Pub.*: *H.M.C. Portland*, iv. 83. *Address*: torn out.

8. *To* ROBERT HARLEY. [*16 May 1704*]

Sir

It is Very Unhappy That I, who have So Seldome the Advantage as well as honour of your Notice, should Meet Such United Interruptions in the least Occasion of its Return.

I Recd Sir Last Fryday a Letter Appointing me to wait on you on Thursday⁴ Evening at 6 a Clock. I was at the Coffee house after Four that Evening⁵ and No Letter was Come, and by the Exactest Notice I Can have, the Messenger did Not Leave it Till after the Time I was to ha' been at the Place.

As Soon as I Recd it, I Took Care by a Letter⁶ left at your house, to Signify the Dissappointment; and to Entreat your farther Ordrs, but To my Surprize They Tell me the Person who left the Letter Call'd again, to kno' if it had been Delivred.⁷ This Causes me to Suppose Sir my Letter has Not Reach'd your hands, Tho' left with your Porter Last Fryday Night.

¹ Doubtless to conceal the identity of Harley's clandestine correspondent and visitor. Hereafter, until the autumn of 1706 when he was in the North, Defoe signs his letters to Harley with a symbol, or, on one occasion, with the initials of his pseudonym, 'Alexander Goldsmith'.
² Edward Harley, brother of Robert, was an Auditor of the Imprest.
³ Blot on the MS. affects two lines.
⁴ That is, the day before the letter arrived.
⁵ Thursday.
⁶ The preceding one.
⁷ That is, Harley's messenger called at Jones's Coffee House to ask if Defoe had yet received Harley's letter.

I Impatiently Wait to Reciev your Ordrs, and to Inform you of The Dissapointment, Wishing if Possible the Time May Come, that you May find this Neglected fellow Servicable, or at least Make him So.

Your Most Obedt and Humble &c
[symbol]

Tuesday Noon

MS.: Duke of Portland, Defoe Papers, 1 f. 8. *Pub.*: *H.M.C. Portland*, iv. 83. *Address*: 'To the Right Honble Robert Harley Esqr., One of her Majties Principll Secretarys of State, Present.' *Endorsed*: 'Upon being disappointed in receiving a Letter from the Secretary.'

9. *To* ROBERT HARLEY. [*May–June 1704?*]

Sir

The Hurry of your Affaires[1] is my Mortification as it Deprives me of the Opportunity of waiting On you, and I take this way to supply it because In Our short Interviews I Omitt too Much what I would Say.

Before I go on to what I would Now write I desire to Premise to you Sir That your Proposall of my Goeing to H——[2] is Really and Sincerly Very Acceptable to me, And perticularly as you were pleasd to Tell me I might do you Some Service there, the present Useless posture I am in being my perticular affliction.

I Entreat you to believ me without Compliment That besides my being by Inclination and principle heartily in the Intrest of the Governmt, So I am perticularly in A great Varyety of Obligations and More Than Commonly by my Own Affections link't to your personall Intrest, and shall be Glad to Distinguish my Self in any Thing and at Any hazard for your Service.

I Confess my Own Pressures[3] which are Sometimes Too heavy and Apt to Sink the hopes I Conciev'd from your Goodness Force me to Importune you, but I Can not but believ you Resolve to help me without my so Frequent sollicitations. I

---

[1] A Cabinet crisis had forced the Queen to choose whether she would be served by high or by moderate Tories. Nottingham, unenthusiastic about the war and inimical to Marlborough and Godolphin, was among the high Tories dismissed. Hedges, the other Secretary, was moved into Nottingham's vacated position, and Speaker Harley, on 18 May, stepped into Hedges's place as Secretary of State for the Northern Department.
[2] Perhaps Hanover. Defoe did not, however, make the journey.
[3] i.e. straits or difficulties.

Therefore Ask pardon for my Impatience and Go On to Tell you That the Voyage you propose is Very Acceptable to me, and My Very Choice Unless I may Render you More Service Elce where which you will Determine for me.

But Sir This Need Not hindr, but if you please To Move my Ld Treasurer[1] in my behalf One Thing may be Done for me which I humbly represent to your Thoughts.

Either That One Branch of the Auditors office (for I am Assur'd it is Divided)[2] May be bestow'd on me which I Can Ordr to be Done privately and put in a person to supply for me till my Returne, Or That his Ldship will appoint me a Convenient Private Allowance for subsistence On which I might Comfortably Depend and Continue to be servicable in a private Capascity whether abroad or at home.

I Sollicit the first Sir On 2 accounts first because Matters of Accounts are my perticular Element,[3] what I have Allways been Master of, and secondly Because Twill be a Certainty in which I may bring my Sons up Under me to be in Time Servicable to Their Fathers Benefactor.

I perswade my Self Sir a word from you To my Ld Treasurer would Do this for me and I Humbly tho' Earnestly press you to Consider it for me.

I beg Leav to Tell you That I will Ordr my Affaires So in This Office that no One shall kno' me to be in it till Something may happen to make it Reasonable to Appear in it.

If This Can Not be Then I Refer the Last to your Goodness that if possible I may be Delivered from the Unsufferable Disorders of my affaires,[4] and That my Goeing Abroad may be as speedy as you please. Pardon my Urgency in this Matter and admitt me I Entreat to as speedy an Audience as possible that I may at last Enter into your Intrests and Service and show you whether I am quallifyed to Merit your favour or no.

I am, Sir, your Depending but Oblig'd Obedt Servt
[symbol]

Thursday morning

MS.: Duke of Portland, Defoe Papers, 1 ff. 12–13. *Pub.*: *H.M.C. Portland*, iv. 89. *Address*: 'To the Right Honble Robert Harley Esqr., Principall Secretary of State, Prest.'

[1] Godolphin.
[2] There were two principal Auditors of the Imprest, and two Deputies.
[3] Defoe had once been an accountant to the Commissioners of the glass duty (*Appeal to Honour and Justice*, in *Later Stuart Tracts*, p. 72).   [4] See No. 10.

10. *To* Robert Harley. [*May–June 1704?*][1]

Sir

As I Took the freedome to Say to you So I Can Not but Repeat to your honor I am at a Loss how to behave my Self undr the Goodness and Bounty of the Queen. Her Majtie Buyes my Small Services So Much too Dear and leaves me So Much in the Dark as to my Own Merit That I am Strangely at a stand what to Say.

I have Enclos'd My humble Acknowlegemt to Her Majtie and Perticularly to my Ld Treasurer but when I am writeing to you Sir Pardon me to alter my Stile. I am Impatient to kno' what in my Small Service pleases and Engages. Pardon me Sir Tis a Necessary Enquiry for a Man in the Dark that I may Direct my Conduct and Push That Little Little Merit to a proper Extent.

Give me leav Sir as at first to Say I Can Not but Think Tho' her Majtie is Good, and My Ld Treasurer kind, yet my wheel within all These Wheels must be your Self, and There I Fix my Thankfullness as I have of a Long Time my hope—as God has Thus Mov'd you to Reliev a Distrest family, Tis my Sincere Petition to him, that he would Once Put it into my hand to Render you Some Such Signall Service, as might at least Express my Sence of it, and Encourage all Men of Power to Oblige and Espouse Gratefull and Sincere Minds.

Your farther Enquiry Into the Missfortunes and afflicting Circumstances That attend and Suppress me fills me with Some Surprise. What Providence has Reserv'd for me he Only knows, but Sure The Gulph is too Large for me to Get ashore again.

I have Stated the black Case. Tis a Mellancholly prospect Sir and My feares Suggest That Not less Than a Thousand Pounds will Entirely Free me.

Tis True and I am Satisfy'd 500*l* or 6 at Most Joyn'd to This I Now Reciev will Open the Door to Liberty and bind all The hands of Creditors That I may have Leisure to Raise The Rest [in][2] perhaps a year or Two, but the Summe is Too Large for me to Expect.[3]

Indeed This Debt is Rais'd by Doublings of Intrest on bonds, The Length of Time haveing Encreased the Burthen. I was Rise-

---

[1] The preceding letter requests aid; this one acknowledges receipt of it. Hence I have reversed the order in which the two were placed by the editor of *H.M.C. Portland*, iv.

[2] Omitted in MS.

[3] See J. R. Sutherland, 'Some Early Troubles of Daniel Defoe', *Review of English Studies*, ix (1933), 275–90.

ing Fairly to Clear it all when the Publick Disaster you kno' of began, but Sir That Entirely blasted all my affaires, and I Can Easily Convince you was above 2500*l* Loss to me all at Once.[1]

I forbear to Say all the Moveing Things to you I Could on This head. All my prospects were built on a Manufacture I had Erected in Essex; all The late kings Bounty to me was Expended There. I Employ'd a hundred Poor Familys at work and it began to Pay me Very well. I Generally Made Six hundred pound profit per Annum.

I began to live, Took a Good House,[2] bought me Coach and horses a Second Time. I paid Large Debts Gradually, small Ones wholly, and Many a Creditor after composition whom I found poor and Decay'd I Sent for and Paid the Remaindr to tho' Actually Discharged.[3]

But I was Ruin'd *The shortest way* and Now Sir had Not your Favour and her Majties Bounty Assisted it must ha' been One of the worst Sorts of Ruine. I do Not mean as to Bread; I firmly and I Thank God Comfortably Depend on the Divine Goodness That I shall Never want That, But a Large and Promiseing family, a Vertuous and Excellent Mother to Seaven[4] Beautifull and hopefull Children, a woman whose fortunes I have Ruin'd, with whom I have had 3700*l*, and yet who in the worst of my afflictions when my Ld N. first Insulted her[5] Then Tempted her, scorn'd So much as to Move me to Complye with him, and Rather Encourag'd me to Oppose him.

Seaven Children Sir whose Education Calls on me to furnish Their heads if I Can not Their Purses, and which Debt if not paid Now Can Never be Compounded hereafter is to me a Moveing Article and helps Very often to make me Sad.

But Sir I am I Thank God Furnisht with Patience. I Never Despaird and In the Worst Condition allways believ'd I should be Carryed Thro' it, but which way, has been and yet Remaines a Mystery of Providence Unexpounded.

---

[1] His flight and imprisonment of the previous year had caused the ruin of his pantile business at Tilbury in Essex (Lee, *Life*, i. 31–32).

[2] At Hackney.

[3] Cf. Defoe's *Dialogue between a Dissenter and the Observator*, reprinted in *A Collection of the Writings of the Author of the True-born Englishman*, 1703, pp. 223–4. The *Dialogue* was repudiated by Defoe, but see J. R. Moore, 'Defoe's First Collected Works', *Defoe in the Pillory and Other Studies*, Bloomington, Indiana, 1939, pp. 54–58.

[4] This is the earliest notice of a seventh child, perhaps Martha, who died in 1707 (Lee, *Life*, i. 59).

[5] Nottingham's insulting Mary Defoe has been doubted (G. M. Trevelyan, *Blenheim*, 1930, p. 336 n.).

I beg heartly your Pardon for This Tedious Epistles. The Miserable are allways full of Their Own Cases and Think Nothing Impertinent. I write This for tis too Moveing for me to Speak it. I shall attend the Ordrs and houres you Appointed To morro' Even and am

Sir, your Most obedt Servt
[symbol]

I Presume to send the Enclos'd¹ Open for your Approbation. You will please to put a seal to it—

MS.: Duke of Portland, Defoe Papers, 1 ff. 10–11. *Pub.*: *H.M.C. Portland*, iv. 87–89. *Address*: 'To The Right Honble Robert Harley Esqr., Her Majties Principall Secreta of State, Prest.'

11. To ROBERT HARLEY. [June 1704?]²

Sir

I can Not but Retain a Very Deep Sence of the Candor and Goodness with which you Recd me Last Night. The Perticulars Sir Admitt of No Epithets to Illustrate them. It Remaines to me Onely To Tender you all the Acknowlegemt of a Gratefull Temper Highly Oblig'd.

Persuant, Sir to the Plainess I have your Leave to Use, The Enclosed Papers are written for your Perusall— They are Observations from the Discourse of the Town on the Affair of the Fleet. Tis an Unhappy Subject, and I assure you There is Much less than is Discours'd on that head— I have Onely One Thing to Premise, and which I Entreat you to believ of Me, That I have No Manner of Personall Design as to Sir Geo: R——.³ I Neither kno' him, Nor am Concern'd with him, or with any that Does kno' him, Directly Or Indirectly. I have Not the least Dissrespect for him, or any Personall Prejudice, on Any Account

¹ His acknowledgements to the Queen and Godolphin.
² Both the letter and its enclosure are undated. The enclosure clearly belongs to the summer of 1704, and the editor of *H.M.C. Portland*, viii, suggests July of that year. I have assigned it (and hence also the covering letter) to June, because on the 24th of that month Defoe published a *Review* containing in substance the same indictment of Rooke that appears in the enclosure. Defoe would have reason for sounding Harley before printing so grave a criticism of the Admiral, but none for writing his thoughts to Harley after they had already been made public. Wright, who had not seen the enclosure, assigned the letter to May 1705 on account of its reference to *The Dyet of Poland*, which was published in that month (*Life* [1931], p. 120). But this letter was written before the *Dyet* was published or even finished, for Defoe here asks permission to 'Perfect it and Turn it abroad into the World.'
³ Admiral Sir George Rooke (1650–1709) was Commander of the Grand Fleet.

whatsoever—[1] I hope you will please to give Full Credit to me in This. Otherwise It would be Very Rude and Presumeing to offer you the Paper.

I am Prepareing with Joy to Execute your Commands For Thursday Next and Furnishing my Self with Horses &ca and Entreat the Liberty Since the Time is short and I Can Not Expect to See you often, of Troubling you the More with my Visits of This sort, and Fill you with my short Requests.

First Sir That you will Please to Order the Letter of Leave for Mr Christopher Hurt[2] to be Absent on his Private Affaires For 2 Months or More.

That you will Please to Think of Some Instructions for my speciall Conduct and whether it may Not be Proper for me to have something About me like a Certificate, Pass, or what you Think fitt to Prevent being Question'd, Searcht, or Detain'd, by an Accident, which often happens on the Road. The Nature and Manner of Such a Thing I Remit to your Judgement— It will be Very Necessary that I should be provided Against the Impertinence of a Country Justice.

The Poem Sir of the Diet of P——d[3] I Omitted to Mention to you last Night but Certainly Twill be Very Necessary to Carry in the Country with me, and As I am Sure of its being Very Usefull, I Can not but Importune you to Let me Perfect it and Turn it abroad into the World. I Expect strange Effects from it as to the house.[4]

The Other Papers which I Purpos'd to Finish I Referr[5] with your Licence to send you per Post—Perticularly some Notes Relateing to the Parliamt and a scheme of an Office For Secret Intelligence at home and Abroad.[6]

This last as I kno' you are Not Ignorant of the Vallue, the Magnitude, and necessity of the Design, with the Want of such

---

[1] Defoe's disclaimer is not wholly acceptable. His friend Colepeper, one of the Kentish Petitioners and counsel for Defoe during the 1703 trial, had been challenged to a duel and then threatened and assaulted by three of Rooke's friends for criticizing the Admiral. The affair had ultimately got into court, where at least one of Rooke's henchmen was found guilty and fined. Defoe had given a brief account of the proceedings, so discreditable to Rooke, in the *Review* of 20 May 1704. See p. 61.
[2] Wilson (*Life*, ii. 358), Lee (*Life*, i. 112), and Wright (*Life* [1931], p. 120) assumed that 'Christopher Hurt' was a name Defoe himself was adopting for the occasion; but Hurt was another person, a customs employee and fellow Dissenter, who accompanied Defoe on the journey through the Eastern counties.
[3] Defoe's *Dyet of Poland*, published May 1705 according to Lee (*Life*, i. xxxii), but see also T. F. M. Newton, 'William Pittis and Queen Anne Journalism', *Modern Philology*, xxxiii (1935), 176.　　　　[4] i.e. as to Parliament.
[5] i.e. defer.　　　　[6] For the intelligence scheme, see No. 14.

a Thing in This Nation, So I shall Take [time][1] while I am abroad to Finish a Perfect scheme, and Such a One as I [hope] you will Approve, and Put in Practice, that if Possible the Affaires [of] all Europe may Lye Constantly before you in a True light and you may [know] what is a doeing all Over Europe, Even before *tis a doeing*, and In This weighty Perticular Go beyond all that Ever Were in That Place before you.

I Confess Sir I had the Enclosed Papers in My Pockett when I was with you But was Unwilling to Rob my Self of So Much of your Obligeing Conversation as to Produce them. I Comitt them to your Serious Thoughts as a Subject, *Pardon me if I Think Amiss*, Not atall Triviall, and at Present Much Wisht for in the Nation.

When I Sir Take the Freedome To Lay any of these Things before you, Tis for you to Judge from as you Think Fit. I hope you will not find Me Assumeing Either a Positiv Determination, or So Much as Arguing Absolutely. I may Mistake, the wholl Town may Mistake, Tho' in This Case I Doubt They do Not. However, I am forward to Lay Such things before you because I Can Not but Think Tis Necessary you should kno' in This as well as any Thing Elce what the People Say—

I am, Sir, your Most Obedt &ca
[symbol]

[Enclosure]

Of The Fleet and Sir Geo: Rook

It will Easily be Allow'd the Fleet May be Made more Usefull Than it is. If The Enemy did Not kno' by happy Experience that Our Navall Force does Them no harm, They Would Allwayes be Oblig'd to keep More Forces on Their Coasts and Consequently want Them Elce where.

Tis Plaine They have a Most Despicable Opinion of Our Navall Expeditions and have Too Much Reason for it.

Our Fleet with about 5000 Men on board Might keep them in Continuall allarm. They Must have 20 Battallions at Least to Guard the Coasts of Provence and as Many Those of Languedoc.

We Talk of Relieving the Camisars.[2] Nothing Can Do it So

---

[1] This and the following bracketed words are hard to make out on account of the manner in which the MS. is bound.

[2] In France, 4,000 Huguenots were waging bloody civil war against Louis XIV and were hence quasi-allies of the Confederacy. Villars, having left the Danube

Effectually as to have Our Fleet Hovering on that Coast Sometimes Landing a Few Men here Sometimes There. The Mareschall De Villars Must Draw Down to Monpellier and the Sea Coast and by Consequence give the Camisars Room to spread Themselves and Act at Large.

But Our Fleet does Nothing of all this. Tis Commanded by a Person The People hates, and all Miscarriages will lye at his Door, whether the Fault be his or No.

No Reflection Can Lye Against the Person Employ'd, but Tacitly Affects the Govornment Employing, and Nothing Reflects on the Govornmt but it Touches the Ministry.

Portugall is an Instance of This. All Our Complaints of Conduct are stopt at Once, by her Majties Displaceing the Generall. People Say her Majtie has found herself ill serv'd, has Altred her Measures, and Chang'd the Generall.[1]

But when the People Ask One Another of the fleet, the Common Answer is, how should We Expect better with such an Admirall, A Man that Never Once fought Since he was an Admirall, That Allwayes Embrac'd the Party That Oppos'd the Govornmt, and has Constantly Favourd, Preferrd, and kept Company with the high furious Jacobite Party, and has Fill'd the Fleet with Them.[2]

How should we have Good Capts while Such a Man Promotes Them, and This is a Reason why We have No Officers in the Navy Fitt to Preferr—

The French Presume Upon This Misconduct of Ours. Tis Not to be Suppos'd the french Admirall Durst ha' Ventur'd into the Mediteranean with 29 Sail when Our fleet was there before him with a Force Very Superior.

It must be a Scandall on Our Admirall or On the Nation.

Either on the Admirall that They knew he Durst not Fight Them, which Affects his Courage, or That They Understand One Another, which is Worse and Affects his Fidellity.[3]

command, was at present combating the insurrection. Schemes for the relief of the Camisards were popular but impracticable, as Defoe himself had admitted (*Review*, 22 and 25 Apr. 1704).

[1] The incompetent Duke of Schomberg, commanding British troops in Portugal, had just been relieved in favour of the Earl of Galway.

[2] After his victories at Gibraltar and Malaga later in the summer, Rooke was set up by the Tories as their party hero, in answer to the Whigs' similar exaltation of Marlborough, victor of Blenheim. See p. 60, and G. M. Trevelyan, *Blenheim*, 1930, pp. 420–1.

[3] In May the French admiral, Toulouse, with the Brest squadron, had set out to round the Straits and join the Toulon squadron, which was expected to come down and meet him. Rooke's mission was to prevent this formidable junction. He

Or it is a Scandal on the Wholl English Nation, as if 29 French Men of War Could be a Match for 45 English.

The Manner of the Conduct afterwards is Perfectly Scandalous. Our Fleet Saw the Enemy at the Distance of Three Leagues Sayes the Relation.

Why Did We Not Fight them, Say Our Old Tarpaulins—and all the Exchange after them, why did we not Chace them? *Why, We did Chace them but found they Gain'd Upon us.*[1]

What, do They Out Sail us Allwayes? There Never was a fleet but That some ships Saild better Than Others—

What! did the Worst of Their Sailers Outgoe the best of Ours? Then Our Navigation, or building, or Sailes are Defective, and should be Enquir'd into; and the Charge of a Fleet Sav'd, Till they Are fitt to Match the Enemye, at Sailing as Well as fighting.

But They Tow'd Away with all Their Boates. So Might we ha' Done too, and Ought to ha' Continued the Chace Till We had Seen them in Port, ha' Waited On them to their Own doors, and ha' Insulted Them there.

But at last what Can be said how They Got by us, how They Gott beyond Our Fleet. Why did Not Sir G R, when tis Plain he knew the French were in The Mediterranean, why did he Not Post himself at the Isle of Heires[2] and keep his Guard Upon the Very Road of Thoulon, where they Must ha' Come of Course and where it had been Impossible to have Entred without Fighting him?

To Say They Might ha' fallen Upon him There and the ships from Thoulon ha' Joyn'd in the Fray, is Imposeing Upon us, for We all kno', They Durst Not stirr Till the Very Action, Ours Lyeing before Their Port, and There Must be so Many Concurring Accidents of Wind and Tide, all which must hitt the Very Minute of Action, that the hazard of it is not Worth Nameing.

These Sir are some of the Town Discourses and There are Scandalous Letters in Town from the Fleet it Self on This head.

The Action at Barcelona is Counted as Monstrous as all the

---

sighted Toulouse off Minorca and offered to engage; but the French declined, sailed around Rooke's force, and escaped his pursuit to come safely into Toulon (Julian Corbett, *England in the Mediterranean*, 1904, ii. 252–3; and *Review*, 24 June 1704).

[1] The French squadron, fresh from its own harbours, was in better sailing condition than the English. Rooke's ships had been fitted out at Lisbon, which lacked proper facilities, and the squadron lost way on account of foul bottoms (*Manuscripts of the House of Lords, 1704–1706*, 1912, p. 152; and Corbett, op. cit. ii. 252).

[2] Hyères, off the south-east coast of France, not far from Toulon.

Rest. To Land a Force Inferiour to the Enemy and Indeed Disproportion'd to the Attempt had some Most Scandalous Circumstances in it.[1]

'Twas hardly Rationall To Expect the People of Barcelona had they Ever so much Inclination to the thing should Appear when They saw the Force landed was Not Sufficient to Protect Them. Had There been Landed 3 to 4000 Men And the Fleet in Good Earnest Applyed themselves to Their Assistance, There's No Room to Doubt the Town had been taken.

The Country Thinking Their Friends Were Come and Not knowing Their Force was So Small began to show Themselves, and as Severall Hundreds Did Come in, Many More were in the Road and the Wholl Province was at the very Point of Revolting, when the Fleet being bound on another Expedition Resolvs to be gone, and all The Well Meaning Inhabitants are left to the Fury of an Enrag'd Enemy to be Drag'd to Execution and Destruction by the hand of the hangman, just as the French did at Messina.

The Complaints of all Sorts of People on This head are Very Severe and The More so because not to be Answerd.

If it be Answerd the king of Portugall Deciev'd Them,[2] Tis Reply'd Then the attempt should Not ha' been Made, And the Poor People Not Expos'd.

If Sir G. R Alleages his Orders for the Relief of Niza or Vill. Franc,[3] Then he should ha' Saild Thither First and ha' Made This Attempt at his Return when he had Leisure to ha' Carryed it on. There Seems No question but if he had Stay'd, The Catalans Were so Dispos'd to Joyn They would soon ha' been strong Enough to ha' Forc'd the Town.

These are the Present Grounds of Complaint as to the Fleet which as to the Matter of them are Very Considerable as to Fact.

[1] Previous to his chase of the Brest squadron, Rooke had landed Prince George of Hesse with 1,200 English and 400 Dutch troops at Barcelona in the hope that the disaffected Catalans, thus encouraged, would rise and declare for 'King Charles III'. But the landing force was too small, the plan did not succeed, and after two weeks the allied forces re-embarked. Rooke was blamed unjustly for the fiasco (Corbett, op. cit. ii. 248–50).

[2] Pedro II had been expected to advance against Spain in the west, a move that would have brightened the prospects of a revolt in Catalonia; but Pedro dawdled the summer away and the diversion did not come off (H. V. Livermore, *History of Portugal*, 1947, pp. 333–4).

[3] Nice and Villa Franca, two strategic Savoyard ports, had been threatened by the French, and Rooke was to proceed to their relief if the operation developed. The French abandoned their plan (Corbett, op. cit. ii. 240–50).

As to the Defence the Admirall Can Make &ca.

This with Submission I do not See Materiall. It Remains to Consider whether in such Cases it has Not been Generally Thought Needful by all the Politick Princes and states in the World, to Recall any Generall or Admirall who Comes Under The Unhappyness of any of These Circumstances

1 Either to ha' Comitted any Capitall Mistake, Tho' Not by Design, want of Courage, or Negligence.

2: That has the Misfortune to Fall Under the Generall Censure and Hatred of the People, whether Deserv'd or No.

3 Or That Generally speaking is Allwayes Unfortunate.

In all these Cases The Generall may be Really Clear, but yet all Ages are Full of Instances of Such being laid by, as at least Improper Persons if Not Otherwise Culpable.

The Grecians, the Romans, and the Carthaginians Allwayes Laid by Unfortunate Generlls as Persons the Gods were Angry with and would Not Prosper. The Turks do the Same to This day, of whom tis well Observ'd that they Are Never Betraid.

Our Easy Way of Accquitting Men in Councils of War and by Examination of Partys perhaps Concern'd in A Mistake gives Room for Men to Abuse their Trust, in Confidence of Comeing off Upon the Artifice of Future Mannagement.

Tho' to Miscarry Ought not in justice to be Criminall, yet in Pollicy it should allwayes Entitle a Man to be Useless. Otherwise a Generall shall be Indiffrent as to Success, his Own Fortunes being Not Concern'd.

Besides, who knows whether Sir G. R. has Miscarry'd for want of Discretion, or for Want of Honesty, or for Want of Judgement, Courage, or any Thing Elce, and if This be Doubtfull how Can Such a Man be Trusted with the English Navy before the Case is Decided? If a Miscarriage has happend There Ought at least be a Suspension of Command Till the Man Charg'd is Justifyed, For tis an Unaccountable Risque and Such an Error in Polliticks as No Minister of state would be Seen in to Committ The Charge of the English Fleet, the Safety and Honour of the Nation, to a Traytor. If Such a Thing should Chance to be Made Out, what Can be Said To Excuse So Much Credulity? For to be Suspected is Certainly Reason Enough Not to be Employ'd.

The Queen Can Not do an Action More Agreeable or Obligeing to the Generallity of the Nation than to Remove This

24

Gentleman and Committ the Navy to Another.[1] If he be after wards Accquitted, her Majtie may Restore him with Honor to himself and Satisfaction to the World, but to Employ him while all the World Suspects him is Takeing all the blame of a Miscarriage On the Queen and Ministry if he be prov'd Guilty:

To Remove a Man from his Power Cleares the Way to Proof of Fact, which his station screens him from, and which Discourages Complaints from Attempting.

Tis Enough to A Govornment That the People in Generall Decrye The Man, for Tho' Common Fame is often a Lyer, yet Universall Clamour Allwayes Demands a suitable Regard, Or is Apt to Affect the Govornmt as Wanting in a Due Care of Things and Careless of the Publick Dissatisfaction.

Tis true To have Enemyes is No Crime, but to have Wise Men Ones Enemy and Men of Moderation and Temper be Uneasy is a Sufficient Ground to Suspend a Man From a Charge of Such Consequence Till it appeares whether there is a Crime. He Ought to be Try'd Indeed before he is Condemn'd,[2] but shall Such a Man Command Till he is Try'd?

If he Appeares Guilty then the Navy, the Honour, the Safety of England, is Put in the hands of a Criminall. If he be Dissmisst and yet Innocent, the Injury is but to One Man. But if he be Continued and be Guilty, the Injury is to the Wholl Nation and the hazard is too great to be Ventur'd:

The Nations Safety, the Publick Reputation, and the Creditt of the Ministry, Calls for a Suspension at least of this Obnoxious Suspected Man.

MS.: the letter, Brit. Mus., Birch's MSS. 4291 ff. 219–20; the enclosure, Duke of Portland, Harley Papers, 37 ff. 279–84. The enclosure, though unsigned, is in the handwriting of Defoe. Its relationship to the letter has not hitherto been noted. *Pub.*: the letter, Wilson, *Life*, ii. 358–60; the enclosure *H.M.C. Portland*, viii. 135–9. *Address*: 'To the Right Honble Robert Harley Esqr., One of Her Majestyes Principall Secretarys of State, Present.'

12. *To* ROBERT HARLEY. *7 July 1704*

Sir

I can Easily Suppose your being Full of good News[3] This

[1] Rooke was removed from command in the following January and was succeeded by Sir Cloudesley Shovel, a Whig.

[2] During the following winter, a select committee of the House of Lords investigated Rooke's conduct in the Mediterranean but submitted no report to the House (*Manuscripts of the House of Lords, 1704–1706*, 1912, pp. viii–xiii).

[3] Word of Marlborough's victory of 21 June at Schellenberg had reached London.

week has Left you Little Leisure, and Undr That head am a Little in Pain for the Dyet—¹ I Confess my Self also Something Impatient to have it from your Self, that I had Explain'd the Review to your Satisfaction and That in Reading it you have been Pleas'd to Note the Caution I Mention'd That it was to be wrott Not as if the Objectors Were of Such quallity as to whom The Stile Shou'd be Unsuitable.²

But Sir I Must Own Neither of These Mov'd me To give you This Trouble. I Can Not Put it from my Thoughts That Success of Affaires as it is the Prosperity of a Nation, So Tis the Felicity of a Ministry. Methinks This Victory Abroad Might have its Advantages at home.³

Tho' I Think it my Duty to give This hint I shall presume No farther without your Comand, which I shall be as Glad to Reciev as faithfull to Obey.

A New king They Say is Chosen in Poland.⁴

I am, your Most Obedient Faithfull Servt

[symbol]

July. 7. 1704

MS.: Duke of Portland, Defoe Papers, 1 f. 14. *Pub.*: *H.M.C. Portland*, iv. 98. *Address*: 'To the Right Honble Robert Harley Esqr., One of her Majties Principall Secrs of State.' *Endorsed*: 'About the Review, 7 July 1704.'

¹ His *Dyet of Poland*, for which he was seeking Harley's approval. See p. 19.
² Since its inception, the *Review* had been describing and explaining the great strength of the national enemy, France. Defoe's motive, to awaken the country to concern, unity, and effort, was patriotic to be sure; but his unembarrassed praise of French power, resources, and shrewdness had sounded strange in war-time, and readers were continually questioning and objecting. On 4 July, annoyed but patient, Defoe interrupted his programme to explain both it and himself once and for all in a *Review* given almost entirely to apologia. But the objectors only objected all over again, this time to that very explanation by which Defoe had hoped to allay them. He was now thought too condescending, too patronizing, and his explanation, they charged, 'was with too much Contempt of the objectors, as if no body might mis-understand him, but what deserv'd the name of Fools' (*Review*, 11 July 1704). Defoe answered this second grievance by declaring that he did not disdain the objectors, nor think them fools, but that he had not 'receiv'd any Remarks from Persons of Character, who therefore might demand a more particular distinction of Stile; and for this Reason, I chose not to alter my way of Expression, but talked à la Vulgaire' (*Review*, 11 July 1704).
³ The high Tories, many of whom wanted a merely defensive war, had been infuriated at Marlborough's stealing the British Army and marching it to the Danube. Now, through his unexpected victory there, the Ministry found a rare opportunity to confound their critics and enemies.
⁴ Stanislaus Leszczynski, placed upon the throne by the conquering Charles XII of Sweden to supplant Augustus II.

13. [*To* ROBERT HARLEY]. [*July–August 1704?*][1]

Sir

I am Convinc't you are Throng'd with Bussiness of So Much more Weight Than the Perticular before me, that I Ought Not to Expect you Can think this way; but Sir tis the Debt I Owe to your Orders as well as my Willingness to Embark in your Service which Obliges me to Accquaint you, That Persuant to your Directions of Getting Ready For this Very Day, I ha' been Prepareing and Fitting Out in Ordr to have been on horse-back this Morning.

I Confess it Afflicts me to See the Day Appear and My Self Unfurnisht with The Main Thing, the Very Substance of all the Rest, *your Instructions*. Methinks I Look Like the Muscovite Ambassador at Constantinople, who Appear'd as Envoy and had Every Thing Ready, but his Orders. Indeed Sir I Can not jest with my Self heartily on this head, because I Reckon it my Great Missfortune. And tho' I shall Never Attempt to Dictate to you, yet from the Leave you have given me to Use More Freedom than Otherwise I should, I Crave a Liberty with all Possible Respect both to your Judgement, and to your Design, Humbly to Represent, That if This Journey be for your Service, As I hope it is or I Should be Very Sorry to be Employ'd, it Can Not be for the Advantage of that Service to have me Straightn'd in Time, and the Latter Part of the Season Come on before I Shall have Room to Answer Either your Charge or Expectation— I would Not be An Unprofitable Servant, the Unfortunate as I have Noted Elce where[2] Are Criminalls in Politicks, and Ought to be Laid by; if Sir I have the Season for Acting I Dare Answer for it *I Won't Miscarry*, but Sir The *Night Comes*, Winter will be upon me *in which* of This Affair I may Say *No Man can Work*.[3]

I Acknowledge when you first did me the honour to Converse with me and began the Discourse of These things in Perticular, That Very Part So hit what I have had On my Thoughts Some yeares that I adjourn'd all my hopes, and all the Thoughts I had, Some of which were of Much Greater Appearance,

---

[1] The proposal with which Defoe concludes this letter appears in the *Review* for 29 July 1704.

[2] See p. 24.

[3] Defoe's reference to riding horseback and his anxiety about bad weather seem to indicate that Harley's earlier plan to send him to Hanover (p. 14)—if Hanover it was—had already been abandoned and that Defoe's journey through the eastern counties was now in prospect.

believing this a Thing So Absolutely Usefull, So Exceedingly Profitable in its Event, and So Suitable to my Genius, that tho' I had Some Things of a More Capitall Nature before Me, I Clos'd with this as *the Thing* which I Thought the Ministry most wanted and My Self most Capable of.

I had before Now Tendred you a Scheme of Generall Intelligence[1] but I Thought this would Much better go before it.

I had a Designe to propose your Settling a Private Office for the Conducting Matters of This Nature, So Directed as Neither in Generall to be Suspected of what it should act, and yet be as Publickly known as any Other; That in This office Openly and without the help of Mr *St Johns Back staires*[2] a Correspondence may be Effectually Settled with Every Part of England, and all the World beside, and yet the Very Clarks Employ'd Not kno' what Thay are a doeing.

But all this I thought would be Better Subsequent to This Journey and I firmly believ This Journey may be the foundation of Such an Intelligence as Never was in England. If I did Not Think So I would be your humble Petitioner Not to Let me go and Earnestly Remonstrate Against it.

Sir I Can Not Close This Long Letter without Observing something from your Last Discourse with me.

You Were Pleas'd to Note that the Queen held the hands of the Dutch and the Dane from Falling on the Swede, and the Reason was just, because in Case of a Rupture the Daneish, the Prussian, and The Lunenburgh Troops must be Recall'd &ca.[3]

Sir I Entreat you to Consider whether a Squadron of English and Dutch Men of War May Not Effectually bring the Swede to Reason without Concerning the Dane or the Prussian in the

---

[1] For such a scheme see the following letter.
[2] Henry St. John (1678–1751), later Viscount Bolingbroke, had become Secretary at War in May.
[3] The Dutch were incensed at Charles XII for dictating conduct to the free city of Danzig, where Dutch commercial interests were numerous and important. The Danes were smarting under a humiliating defeat after a brief war against Charles and were being encouraged by the Russians to renew hostilities. Both Dutch and Danes were at this time neutral in Charles's war against Poland, Saxony, and Russia, and it was to the interest of the Grand Alliance to keep them so. The Dutch had as much as they could do in their struggle against France, and the Danes, not in anyone's war at the moment, supplied Marlborough with splendid troops. If, 'in Case of a Rupture', Charles of Sweden should turn from Poland and Livonia to wage war farther west, he would flutter the dovecots of northern Europe and thousands of mercenaries would be called out of Marlborough's command and returned to their own duchies and cities to defend their own people. See R. N. Bain, *Charles XII and the Collapse of the Swedish Empire*, 1895, pp. 56–65, 82–125, and 130.

Matter, and if he will break with the Rest he will be ill handled at last, but I am perswaded Our Fleet may (if well Directed) Do all the Work and the Empire would soon have another Face.

I Need Not Tell you the Advantages of a Saxon Army On the Danube and a Gratefull king in your Intrest who will Certainly Acknowlege his being Sav'd by Our hands.[1]

I have Said too Much. I ask Pardon for the Freedome I use and Am &ca
[symbol]

Thursday Morning

MS.: Duke of Portland, Defoe Papers, 1 ff. 16–17. *Pub.*: *H.M.C. Portland*, v. 106–7. *Address*: none. *Endorsed*: 'A Scheme of General Intelligence &c.'

14. [*To* ROBERT HARLEY]. [*July–August 1704?*][2]

I allow That in Our Constitution we Admit of No Supreme Ministry,[3] That the Nation is Perticularly Jealous of Favourites. These Are the Two Chief Obstructions in the Way of a Refin'd[4] and Riseing States Man and These Are the Two Reasons why we have had No Capitall Men in the Civill Administration, No *Richlieus, Mazarines,* or *Colberts*[5] in the State.

But I must Go Back for A Reason for These Two Principles, and Must Say

1 : It wou'd be best to have a Supreme Ministry.

2 : The Nation May Easily be Reconcil'd to it.

[1] Charles XII had clearly won his war against Poland but would not stop fighting the Saxons and Poles so long as his personal enemy Augustus, the deposed king, remained unpunished. Defoe's notion is that if the English and Dutch by a display of sea power could awe Charles into peace and hence relieve a grateful Augustus, then the latter's troops would be available to support Marlborough on the Danube. Cf. *Review*, 29 July 1704.

[2] The manuscript of this memorandum is undated. G. F. Warner, who first published it, suggested that since it mentions the 'new post' to which Harley succeeded on 18 May 1704, it was perhaps written in May or June of that year. I place it a little later than that because, like No. 13, it contains Defoe's proposal of sending a naval squadron to the Baltic, a proposal which appears in the *Review* for 29 July. The memorandum probably came later than No. 13, because the latter mentions as yet unwritten the 'scheme of intelligence' which appears here. On the other hand, the memorandum must have been written before 10 Aug., the date upon which the news of the victory at Blenheim reached London, because after that date Defoe would hardly be worrying about 'bringing Down Such a Force on the French as Should in all Probability Turn the Scale of the Warr On the Danube' (p. 38). The scale had turned at Blenheim.

[3] That is, no Prime Minister.   [4] i.e. subtle.

[5] Armand Jean du Plessis (1585–1642), Duc de Richelieu, Jules Mazarin (1602–61), and Jean Baptiste Colbert (1619–83), French ministers of the preceding century.

Twill be Needless to prove the Advantage of a Chief Ministry. Our Confusions in Council, Our Errors in Excecuting and Unwaryness in Directing from the Multitude and bad Conduct of Ministers make it Too plain.

To Prove the Nation May be Easily Reconcil'd to it, Twill be Needfull to Go back for the Reasons why Former Favourites have So ill Pleas'd the Nation, and how Others have Discharg'd Themselves with Honour.

The Spencers, the Gavestones,[1] of Former Reigns Are too Remote; the Prime Ministers of Modern Times have been Principally the Earle of Leicester, the [Dukes][2] of Somersett, Buckingham, &ca.[3]

These all Incur'd the Displeasure of the people by One Crime, Persueing Their Private Intrest, Enriching and Aggrandizeing themselves and Familyes, and Raiseing Vast Estates Out of the Spoils of the Publick, and by Their Princes favour heaping up Honors and Titles to Themselves from Mean Originalls.

I Need Not Search hystory for the Perticulars, the Fact is too plain.

The Consequences of this Spirit of Covetousness were allwayes Extortions, Oppressions, Bribes, Sale of Publick Employments, Intrenchments on the Publick Moneys, Exorbitant Grants of Roya[ll][4] Bounty and the like.

If any Man will sho' me the Man That Serv'd the State Abstracted from his Own Intrest, Ile show Them the Man who was as Much the Peoples favourite as the kings.

Tho: Lord Cromwell[5] was Such a One and Tho' he Fell, as who in the Reign of That Fickle Unconstant king Could stand, he Fell a Sacrifize to the Protestant Party, Universally belov'd, and Lamented of the People.

Sir Francis Wallsingham,[6] Tho' Not a Prime Minister, yet if we Read his Story The ablest statesman and the Longest Employ'd, The Most Employ'd in Difficult Cases and the Greatest Master of Intelligence of the Age.

---

[1] Hugh Despenser (1262–1326), Earl of Winchester, and Piers Gaveston (d. 1312), Earl of Cornwall, favourites of Edward II.

[2] Left blank in MS.

[3] Robert Dudley (1532?–88), Earl of Leicester, favourite of Queen Elizabeth; Edward Seymour (1506?–52), Duke of Somerset, the Protector after the death of Henry VIII; and George Villiers (1592–1628), Duke of Buckingham, favourite of James I.   [4] MS. torn.

[5] Thomas Cromwell (1485?–1540), Earl of Essex, holder of many great offices under Henry VIII.

[6] Walsingham (1530?–90) was Secretary of State under Elizabeth.

Both These Dyed Poor. They spent Their wholl Time in the Service of Their Country, and No Man would ha' Repin'd at Their Enjoying their Princes favour Longer.

This Premis'd, I Bring home the Matter To the Case in hand. How shall you Make your Self Prime Minister of State, Un-envy'd and Unmolested, be Neither Address'd Against by Parliament, Intreagu'd Against by Partyes, or Murmur'd at by the Mob—?

With Submission Tis Very feasible with an Accurate Conduct. They Say Those Designs Require Most Policy which have Least of honesty; This Design must be honest because it must be honest To Serve Our Country.

If it be Objected, But I wou'd Not be Prime Minister, I Returne, Then you Can Not be Secretary of State. The Secretaryes Office Well Discharg'd Makes a Man Prime Minister of Course; and you Must be prime Minister with Applause, or you will be Secretary with Disgrace.

Popular Fame Never Thinks a Man too high, Popular Hate Never Thinks him to Lowe.

A Generous, free, Noble, Uncontracted Conduct, as Effectually Secures the affections of the People, as a Narrow, Covetous, Craveing Spirit Effectually Engages Their Mortall Aversion.

Tis Certainly a Noble Design to be Popular, from a Principle of Reall Meritt. I Observ when all Our people Clamourd at Dutchmen, And Even the king Cou'd Not please Them, because he was a forreigner, No Man Ever had a Bad word for Monsr Overkirk.[1]

Nothing wins This Nation like Generous, free, Open handed Courtesye.

The king of Sweden[2] in his German Warrs, Allwayes Employ'd Trusty Persons in the Towns and Cittyes he Reduc'd, to Inform Themselves of any known Case where one was Oppress'd, or any Family That had the Generall Pitty; and Unlook'd for, Unask'd, he would Send for, Right, and Reliev Them.

Sir, That Noble Soul is a Rare Pattern; he gaind[3] his Very Enemyes by Surprizeing Acts of Bounty.

In your New Post,[4] Joyn'd with the Influence you have on the

---

[1] Overkirk, the ablest of the Dutch generals, was now one of Marlborough's most dependable supporters and later distinguished himself at Ramillies.

[2] Gustavus Adolphus. Defoe celebrated him in the *Review* of 15 July 1704 and, many years later, in his *Memoirs of a Cavalier*.   [3] i.e. gained over.

[4] Harley had become Secretary on 18 May.

Royall hand, you will have Infinite Opportunitys to fix an Invulnerable Reputation. May Not These heads be Proper.

1 : To keep a Sett of Faithfull Emissarys Selected by your Own Judgement. Let Them be your Constant Intelligencers of Private affaires in the Court.

2 Sett your friends by, *if They Are Such They'l Wait*, but Surprize your Enemyes if you have any with Voluntary kindness.[1]

3 Communicate your Favours with Unbyast hand, That all Partyes may Court you.

4 You have Estate Enough, and Honor Enough. Let the World kno' you Covett Nothing; all Men Then will Covet you.

Let No Man Under you, Make a Profitt of your Favours. One Gehezai[2] in your Attendants Will undo the Merit of all your Actions. He will Gett the Money, and you the Curse of the Person that Payes it.

Tis Absolutely Necessary to be Popular. The Peoples Darling May be a Few Mens Envy, but The peoples hate is a Statesmans Ruin.

This Opinion of the People is Easily gain'd at first, and if Lost at first Never Reestablish'd.

Tis Gaind by Little Acts of Courtisy. One Generous Man Oblig'd, One Opprest Man Reliev'd, does a Man of Trust More honour, than Twenty ill Tongues Can blott Out.

In Ordr To This, your Trusty Servants will Enquire you Out Occasions Enough, A Generall forwarding, and Dispatch of Petitions, and a Thousand Things which a Man in Such a Post, with Such a Soul, Never wants Opportunity for.

In the Old Prince of Oranges Army,[3] a Captn That had Long Serv'd in the Warrs, Talking to a Friend, was heard to Say, he would give 10000 Guilders for Such a Regiment, the Coll. being Newly Dead. Why do you Not Put in For it, Sayes his Friend. Because, Saies he, the Prince has No kindness for me and I kno' he will Denye me. The Prince knowing him to be a Man of Meritt Sends the person who Told him the Story with Orders to Take his bond for the 10000 Guilders Upon Condition that he procur'd him the Regiment, which he did Accordingly. The Next Day the Prince Sends for him, Gives him the Regiment, and as he was goeing Out, here, Sayes the Prince, and here's

---

[1] Defoe had given similar advice to King William. See p. 68.
[2] See 2 Kings, v. 20–27.
[3] Identified as 'Maurice' by Defoe's note on the MS. Maurice, Prince of Orange (d. 1625), was Stadtholder of the Dutch Republic.

Something for your Equipage, and Threw him his Bond. The Man was So Surpriz'd with the Generosity of it he Turn'd from a Prejudic'd person To the Greatest admirer the Prince had.

Sir, This Proposall of a Generous Bounty and Courtisye, is Not Directed because you want it, but because you have it. To Suppose you want it wou'd first be an Insolence Unpardonable, as it would propose your Feigning it, and So Make a Vertue of Hypocrisy; But as I have More Than Ordinary Proof of your being Master *of the Quallity*, I Take the Freedome To hint the Uncommon Advantage it Gives you, to Make your Self Truly Great, and have all Men Pleas'd with it.

Envy allwayes Goes with her Mouth Open,[1] and you are Not to Expect That an advanc't Post will shut it, but There is a Secret in Mannagement That Checks it Effectually, (Viz:) a Generall, Unaffected Goodness of Temper. Julius Cæsar was Remarkable for it, and Conquer'd More Enemyes in the Forum Than in the Field.

A Man Can Never be Great That is Not Popular, Especially in England. Tis Absolutely Necessary in the Very Nature of Our Constitution, where the People have So Great a Share in the Govornment.

Besides, the People here, in Recovering their Just Rights, have Usurpt Some, That are Not Their Due, Vizt Censuring Their Superiours,[2] But the Govornmt is bound to Submit to the Grievance because tis Incurable.

Tis True A Wise Man Will slight Popular Reproach, but No Wise Man slights the Generall Approbation, because Nothing but Vertue Can Obtain it.

Tis Therefore Absolutely Necessary for a States man to be Popular.

A States Man Once in the Peoples favor has a Thousand Opportunityes to do with Freedome, what in a Contrary Circumstance he would Not Dare to Attempt; For as the People often Condemne hastily, They Approve with More blindness Than They Censure, and yet Generally Speaking the Common People have been Allwayes in the Right.

A Statesman Envy'd[3] Dares Not Attempt a Thing, which he knows is for the Publick Service Least the Miscarriage falls Upon himself.

---

[1] '*Envy always goes with Her Mouth open, and Truth can seldom shut it*' (*Review*, 4 July 1704).
[2] Cf. *Review*, 16 Sept. 1707.　　　　　　　　　　　[3] i.e. disliked.

Cardinall Richlieu Supply'd the Want of the Peoples favour by Meer force, and So Ruin'd those that Oppos'd him, as in the Case of the Duke D Momorency,[1] and a Multitude of Others. Tho this would be Impracticable here, it showes the Absolute Necessity of the Thing, *or of an Equivalent*; And yet we find this Cardinall strove hard for the Publick Voice, and Us'd a Thousand Artifices to Obtain it, Among which This was One, That he Never Appear'd to his Own Resentments, and tho' a Multitude of Persons of all Ranks, were Sacrifiz'd to his Politick Intrest, yet he Never would be seen in a Matter of Punishment; if a Pardon was to be Granted, he Took Care the Debt should be to the Cardinall, but if Justice was to be Done, That was In the king.[2]

A Popular States Man Shou'd have the Obtaining all the Favours, and Let Others have the Mannagement of Offences, and the Distribution of Justice.

In your Perticular Case Sir, you have but One Publick Missfortune Vizt That your Friends for want of Judgement are Affraid of you, Not Affraid you'l Hurt them but your Self. Twou'd be Necessary to Confirm them in the belief of all they hope to find.

A Perticular Step will Absolutely Effect it—of which by it Self.[3]

A Scheme of what I Mean by Popularity in your Own Perticular, and how to be both Obtaind and Improv'd for the Publick Service, Shall be Drawn if you Please to admitt it.

Also A Method to Make the Office of Secretary of State an Inner Cabinett, and Excecute Necessary Parts of Private affaires without the Intervention of the Privy Council and yet have Their Concurrence as farr as the Law Requires.

When a Prince is to Act any Thing Doubtfull or any Thing likely to be Disputed Either at Law, Or in Parliament, the Council is a Necessary Screen to the Secretaryes of State.

But in Matters of War, Treatys, Embassys, Private Instructions, Expeditions, how Many Such has the Delay, the Hesitations, the Ignorance, or Something worse of Privy Councelors Overthrown.

---

[1] Defoe had been reading a life of Richelieu (*Review*, 1 July) and alludes to him again and again in the *Reviews* of late May and June. Henry II, Duke of Montmorency (1595–1632), revolted against Richelieu, but was defeated and beheaded.

[2] Cf. *Memoirs of a Cavalier*, Shakespeare Head ed., pp. 14–15.

[3] In the margin, this and the two statements that follow it are each marked with a 'hand' and are numbered 1, 2, and 3. In the concluding pages of this memorandum, Defoe returns to these topics (and to a fourth farther on which is similarly marked) and develops each of them, referring to them by number.

Matters Maturely Advis'd, Deliberately Concerted, and Absolutely Resolv'd, Require but Two Quallifications to Legitimate Their Excecution.

1. That They Are Legall.
2. Really for the Publick Good.

Such Need No Council Table to Screen Them, Fear No Parliamentary Enquiry, and yet the Authors are Not Answerable for the Success.

Cabinet Councils in England are Modern, and Excentrick, and I Question whether an Action which is Not Justifyable Unless Transacted In Council, is Justify'd by being So in the Cabinet. But Cabinets of Ten or fourteen are Monsters and Useless.

If her Majtie Leaves the Course of Things to follow the Nature and Custome of English Kings, her Privy Council shou'd Take Cognizance of all Needfull Affaires, But her Treasurer and Secretary of State should be all her Cabinet[1] Unless she had a Well quallifyed Chancelour to Add to Them.

Six Sorts of Great Officers are the Moveing Springs of the State and I Can Not but Own without Flattery England was Never Capable of being better Supply'd, I Do Not Say is fully Supplyed.

a Lord Chancelour	a Secretary of State
a High Admirall	an Arch-bishop who Perhaps might
a Generallissimo	Expect to be Put first but
a Lord Treasurer	Not by Me[2]

Of These The First Should be a good Lawyer, The Second a good Sailor, the Third a good Soldier, The Last a good Divine, But the Treasurer and the Secretary Ought to be Good States Men. The Weight of all the Publick Affaires Lyes on Their shoulders.

One for Mannageing the Revenues, Provideing Needfull

---

[1] Godolphin, Harley, and Marlborough had already formed such an inner Cabinet, and Harley had served therein even before he was Secretary. The office of Lord Chancellor was unfilled at this time. See G. M. Trevelyan, *Blenheim*, 1930, p. 289.

[2] Compare Defoe's ideal Cabinet with that proposed by Sunderland in the year before Anne's accession: Archbishop, Lord Keeper (or Lord Chancellor), Lord President, Lord Privy Seal, Lord Steward, Lord Chamberlain, First Commissioner of the Treasury (or Lord Treasurer), two Secretaries of State, Lord Lieutenant of Ireland, and, if the King wished more, the head of the Admiralty and the Master of the Ordnance. See G. M. Trevelyan, op. cit., p. 288 n.

Funds, Maintaining Publick Credit, and Regulateing Abuses and Exactions &ca.

The Other For Forreign Intelligence, Correspondence with the Courts Abroad, Mannageing, Settling, and Obtaining Confederates, Observing and Suiting affaires with the Circumstances and Intrest of Princes.

Intelligence is the Soul of all Publick bussiness.

I have heard That Our Secretaryes Office is Allow'd 12000*l* per Annum for This Weighty Article,[1] And I am Credibly Inform'd the king of France has paid 11 Millions in One year for the Same Article and Tis Allow'd he Never Spares his Money on That head, and Thereby Out does all the World in the knowledge of his Neighbours.[2]

How Much of the 12000*l* Allow'd for Intelligence, is Expended in Our Secretarys office, I Will not guess at, But This I Presume, That Such a Summe being So Vastly Disproportion'd to the Necessary Expence, the Work is Not Done, and Consequently the Money that is Given for it is Lost.

Our States Men have been So farr from Accquainting Themselves with Other Countryes, that They are Strangers to Their Own, A Certain Token That they ha' Sought Their Private Advantage, Not the Publick Service. The Secretaryes Office should be an Abrigemt of all Europe.

Her Majties Secretary of State Ought to have Tables of all the Following Perticulars To Referr to, Stated So Regularly, That They Might ha' Recourse to any Perticular Imediately.

They Ought to have

    1st A Perfect List of all the Gentry and Familys of Rank in England, Their Residence, Characters, and Intrest in the Respective Countyes.

    2 Of all the Clergy of England, their Benefices, Their Character, and Moralls, and the like of the Dissenters.

    3 Of all the Leading Men in the Cittyes and Burroughs, with the Partyes they Espouse.[3]

They Ought to have a Table of Partyes, and Proper Callculations of their Strength in Every Respective Part, which is to be

---

[1] Doubtless an exaggeration. By 1707 each Secretary of State was receiving £3,000 annually for secret service (M. A. Thomson, *Secretaries of State, 1681–1782*, Oxford, 1932, p. 150).

[2] Cf. *Review*, 24 June 1704 and 13 Nov. 1707.

[3] Defoe himself later undertook to provide this sort of information. For one of his reports, see No. 44.

36

had by haveing the Coppyes of the Polls Sent up on all Elections, and All the Circumstances of Such Elections Hystorically
Collected by faithfull hands, and Transmitted to the Office.

They should kno' the Names of all the Men of Great Personall
Estates, that they May kno' how and where to Direct any Occasionall Trust. They should have the speciall Characters of all
the Justices of the Peace, and Men of Note in Every County, to
have Recourse to on all Occasions.

Two Trusty Agents would Easily Direct all This So, if Their
hands are Not too Much Tyed up as to Money, and yet the
Persons Entrusted Not kno' who they Serv Nor for what
End.

The Secretary of State Should have a Table of all the Ministers of State, Lists of the households, The Privy Councils, and
Favourites of Every Court in Europe, and Their Characters.

With Exact Lists of Their Forces, Names of The Officers,
State of Their Revenue, Methods of Govornment, &ca So just
and Authentick and Regularly amended as Alterations happen
That by This he may Duly Estimate Their Strength, judge of
Their Intrests and Proceedings, And Treat with Them Accord-
ingly.

He should keep a Correspondence of Friendship in all Courts
with Ministers of like Quallity, as far as may be honourably
Obtain'd, and without Prejudice Carry'd on.

Mr Milton kept a Constant Epistolary Conversation, with
Severall forreign Ministers of State, and Men of Learning, Abstracted from Affaires of State, but So Woven with Politicall
Observations that he found it as Usefull as any Part of his forreign Correspondence.

A hundred Thousand Pounds Per Annum Spent Now for 3
year in forreign Intelligence, Might be the best Money Ever
This Nation Laid Out, and I am Persuaded I Could Name
Two Articles where if Some Money had been well Apply'd,
Neither the Insurrection in Hungary Nor the Warr in Poland[1]
should ha' been So Fatall to the Confederacy as Now They
are.

If it may be of Service I Shall give a Scheme for the Speedy
Settleing those Two Uneasy Articles, and Consequently bringing

---

[1] The Hungarian rebels were ravaging England's ally Austria and had in part
necessitated Marlborough's march to the Danube. Sweden's invasion of Poland
had robbed the Grand Alliance of a potential ally, Augustus II, King of Poland
and Elector of Saxony, whose troops otherwise might have been free to fight the
French and Bavarians. See the *Review*, 25 July and 2 Sept. 1704.

Down Such a Force on the French as Should in all Probability Turn the Scale of the Warr On the Danube and the Po.[1]

A Settl'd Intelligence in Scotland, a Thing Strangely Neglected There, is without Doubt the Principall Occasion of The present Missunderstandings between the Two kingdomes.[2] In the Last Reign it Caus'd the king to have Many ill things Put upon him, and worse are Very likely to follow.

I beg Leave to give a Longer Scheme of Thoughts on That head, than is Proper here, and a Method how the Scotts may be brought to Reason.

There is a Large Article of Spyes abroad Among the Enemyes. This I Suppose to be Settld, tho' by Our Defect of Intelligence, Methinks it should Not; But It Reminds me of a Book in Eight Volumes Published in London about 7 or 8 yeares Ago Call'd Letters writ by a Turkish Spye—[3] The books I Take as They Are, a Meer Romance, but the Morrall is Good, A Settl'd Person of Sence and Penetration, of Dexterity and Courage, To Reside Constantly in Paris, Tho' As tis a Dangerous Post he had a Larger Allowance Than Ordinary, Might by One happy Turn Earn all the money and the Charge be well bestow'd.

There are 3 Towns in France where I would have the like, and They might all Correspond, One at *Thoulon*, One at *Brest*, One at *Dunkirk*.[4] They three might Trade together as Merchants, And the Fourth also with Them.

As Intelligence Abroad is So Considerable, it follows in Proportion That The Most Usefull Thing at home is Secrecy.

For as Intelligence is the Most usefull to us, So keeping Our Enemyes from Intelligence Among us, is As Valluable a head.

I have been in the Secretarys Office of a Post Night when Had I been a French Spye I Could ha' Put in my Pockett my

---

[1] This statement is marked in the margin with a 'hand' and is numbered 4. See p. 34, n. 3. Defoe returns to the subject in the concluding pages of this memorandum under the caption 'No. 4'.

[2] This was a period of grave tension between the two countries on account of the Scottish Act of Security, under the provisions of which upon the death of Anne the Crowns of England and Scotland would almost certainly be separated. For a summary of the state of this contention at about the time Defoe was writing this memorandum, see G. M. Trevelyan, *Ramillies and the Union with Scotland*, 1932, pp. 242–3.

[3] *Letters Writ by a Turkish Spy, Who Lived Five and Forty Years at Paris; Giving an Account of the Most Remarkable Transactions of Europe from 1637 to 1682*, 7 vols., 1687; vol. viii, 1694, is attributed to Giovanni Paolo Marana, a Genoese. In 1718 Defoe entitled one of his own works *A Continuation of Letters Written by a Turkish Spy at Paris*.

[4] All three were important naval bases.

Lord N——ms[1] Letters Directed to sir Geo: Rook and to the Duke of Marlebro' Laid Carelessly on a Table for the Doorkeepers to Carry to the Post Office.[2]

How Many Miscarriages have happen'd in England for want of Silence and Secresy!

Cardinall Richlieu, was the Greatest Master of This Vertue That Ever I Read of, in the World, and if hystory has Not wrong'd him, has Sacrifyz'd Many a faithfull Agent, after he had Done his Duty, that he might be sure he should Not be betraid.

He kept Three Offices for the Dispatch of his Affaires, and One was so Private, That None was admitted but in the Darke, and Up a pair of back Remote Stairs, which Office being at the Apartments of his Niece Made Room for a Censure past upon her Character, which the Cardinall Chose to Suffer, that he might have the Liberty To Transact Affaires there of Much More Moment.

This is a Principall Reason why I object Against bringing All Things before the Council[3] for I Will Not Affirm that the Minutes of Our Privy Council have Not been Read in the Secreatryes Office at Versailles. Tis Plain the French Out do us at These Two Things, Secrecy and Intelligence, and That we may Match them in These Points is the Design of the Proposall.

Further Schemes as to Trade, funds for Taxes, &ca Relateing to the Ld Treasurers place in the Publick Administration I Omitt, haveing Taken up too Much Room with This—

No. 1[4]

What I Mean by a Step to Confirm your Friends in the Belief of what They hope for From you Can Not be Explain'd without Filling your Eares with Some of those ill Natur'd Things They Take the Freedome to Say, Vizt

That you are a Man wholly Resolv'd to Make your fortunes and to bring it to Pass will Sacrifize your Judgement as well as your Friends to your Intrest.

---

[1] Nottingham's.

[2] Harley would have done well to take heed. In Jan. 1708 one of his clerks, William Greg, was convicted of treasonably communicating to France information he had picked up in the Secretary's office (G. M. Trevelyan, *Ramillies and the Union with Scotland*, 1932, pp. 329–33).

[3] As a matter of fact not everything was brought before the Council or even the Cabinet. Marlborough's spectacular plan to march into Germany was probably known ahead of time in England only to the Queen and Godolphin (G. M. Trevelyan, *Blenheim*, 1930, pp. 334–5).

[4] See p. 34, n. 3.

That you gave Proofs of this in Embraceing the Party of
Those People who Pleas'd themselves, and Strove to be Popular
at the Expence of king William.

That you forsook the king who Treated you kindly, and That
his Majtie Spoke of it in Very Moveing Terms as what he was
Concern'd for.[1]

That Now you have forsaken the Dissenters, and Fallen in
with Their Enemyes and Promoted the First Occasionall bill.

Cum Multis Allijs &ca.

Sir, It is Not That I Suppose the Dissenters Ought to be
Deciev'd Or That you will Deciev Them that I Repeat it Again
they are to be Pleas'd with words.

But Sir as Good words are usefull in Their Place So when
Not Spoken with Design are Honoble in Themselves. There is
No Imediate Action by which you Can Demonstrate you will
Serve Them.

Onely Let Some Proper Persons Carefully Inform Them That
on all Occasions They may Depend On your Good Offices with
the Queen, and Give Them Some Notices by Such hands as
may be Trusted That you are Their Friend.

Perticularly it May be Very Easy to Posess the Dissenters
That They Owe the Change of her Majties Sentiments with
Relation to the Occasionall bill to your Mannagement And
Councils.

And That her Majties Changeing Sides was together with
the Measures you Prescrib'd the Onely Reason of the Majority
Obtain'd in the house of Lords against the Said bill.[2]

To Effect This a short Paper shall be handed about, Among
the Dissenters Onely, giveing Them a Pretended View of the
Measures taken by Some Persons, *Nameing None*, to Convince
the Queen of the Unreasonableness of This bill.

It Can Not fail to Open their Eyes that you are their Friend
and yet if your Affaires Should Require you to Dissown Such
a Paper it shall Easily be True that you had No knowledge of it,
for you May Really kno' Nothing of it—

If My Service in Another Case is Accepted I shall Take

---

[1] Harley had begun his public life as a Whig, but had gradually taken up with
the Tories. He had opposed King William on the questions of the standing army
and the Irish forfeitures. For an account of Harley's political development, see
Keith Feiling, *History of the Tory Party*, Oxford, 1924, pp. 330–59.

[2] But the House of Lords had rejected the Bill during the session of 1702–3 even
though at that time Anne had openly favoured the measure. There is hence no
reason to accept Defoe's suggestion that their second rejection of it, in the session
of 1703–4, was due to Anne's change of heart.

Care to Make Such a Paper be Read in all parts of the kingdome.[1]

I Allow the Perticular Steps Mention'd in Such a Paper May Not be Fact, yet if it be Really Fact That you have Appear'd Against the bill, That you have Influenc'd and Advis'd her Majtie in Favour of the Tolleration &ca, The Generall is Truth and Therefore the Design Just.

This is Part of the Perticular Step Markt No. 1.

No. 2 Of Popularity

That which I Call Popularity, May a Little Differ From the Thing which Goes by That Name in the Generall Opinion, and Therefore Tis Needfull to Distinguish the Term.

Popularity in Generall, is the Generall Esteem of the People.

But The Popularity I Mean Must have an Adjunct, Vizt, A Generall Esteem Founded upon Good Actions, Truly Meriting The Love of the People.

Tis True the People are Not So Apt to Love, as to hate, and Therefore when the Former is Fixt on a Person, it Ought to Implye Some Merit.

But This is Not Universally True for the People Sometimes Love by Antithesis, and Sho' a Generall Affection to One Person, to sho' Their Disesteem of his Enemy, and This May be Visible in the Case of the Duke of Munmouth, who Really had Not a Great Deal of Personall Merit.

We Say happyness Consists in being Content; but I Must Denye it, Unless the Contentment be fixt on a Centre of Vertue, for a Vicious Man may So be More happy Than a Vertuous, and A Mad Man Than both; So here, A Man May be Popular without Merit, But That Popularity will Neither be usefull, nor Serviceable.

For Tho' by Wicked Acts Men Gain Applause,
The Reputation's Rotten like The Cause.[2]

A Wise Man is willing to be Popular, and a Wise States man will be So, but it is Such a Popular Esteem as Rises from Acts of Vertue, Bounty, and Noble Principles.

Tis my Opinion Sir as to your Self, and I speak it with the Same Plaineness as I do Things Less Smooth, That I Ought to

[1] Harley apparently declined the offer; no such paper can be identified.
[2] From Defoe's *Character of the Late Dr. Samuel Annesley*, reprinted in *True Collection*, p. 114.

use More Arguments with you to Perswade you to Desire This Popular Esteem, Than to Deserv it.

And Therefore Sir I Leave the Phylosophy of the Argument to your Own Speculation, and Go on to the Present Case.

The Popularity I Mean Now, is—A Politicall Conduct of your Self, between the *Scylla* and the *Charibdis* of Partyes; So as to Obtain from Them all a generall Esteem.

Tho' this Part of Conduct is Call'd Dissimulation, I am Content it shall be Call'd what They will, But as a Lye Does Not Consist in the Indirect Position of words, but in the Design by False Speaking, to Deciev and Injure my Neighbour, So Dissembling does Not Consist in Puting a Different Face Upon Our Actions, but in the further Applying That Concealment to the Prejudice of the Person; for Example, I Come into a persons Chamber, who on a Surprize is Apt to Fall into Dangerous Convulsions. I Come in Smileing, and Pleasant, and ask the person to Rise and Go abroad, or any Other Such question, and Press him to it Till I Prevail, whereas the Truth is I have Discovred the house to be On Fire, and I Act thus for fear of frighting him. Will any Man Tax me with Hypocrisye and Dissimulation?

In your Perticular Post Sir you may So Govorn, as That Every Party Shall believ you Their Own:

I Think I may Answer for One Side; and Shall Think Very Meanly of my Own Designs, if I Do Not bring the Dissenters to believ it firmly, if you please to give me Leave to Act as Effectually as I may Convince you will be Needfull.

The Dissenters Sir May be brot

1. To believ better of Past Actions, of which I Mean in the scheme No. 1.
2. They Shall allwayes believ you Their Friend with the Queen.
3. Take you for Their Advocate and Applye to you on all Occasions.
4. Freely Accquaint you of all Circumstances Relateing to what They Desire, or Fear.
5. If Ever you Find Occasion, you may be the head of The wholl Party, and Consequently Influence them as you Please.
6. You will have the Opportunity upon all Occasions both to Represent Them Right to the Queen, and the Queen Right to Them, the Want of which has been Injurious to both.

7. You Will Caution Them against Indiscretions, and any Thing that may be to Their Dissadvantage.
8. You May at Second hand Accquaint Them of the Designs of a Party Against them; and have the honour of Saveing them from the Mischief Intended.

The Influence your Office, as well as Personall Merit Gives you on the Queen, will give you Opportunityes Either to bring off Many of the Hott Men on the Other Side, or So to Discourage Them that They may Cease to Disturb—and as to the Moderatest of Them you will often by Serving them Oblige Them to Acknowledge you.

Of the Moderate Men you are Secure, and They Can Not but both Aprove your Conduct as They See it Moves towards the Reall happyness of us all.

This is the Dissimulation I Recomend, which is Not Unlike what the Apostle Sayes of himself; becoming all Things to all Men, that he might Gain Some. This Hypocrise is a Vertue, and by This Conduct you Shall Make your Self Popular, you shall be Faithfull and Usefull to the Soveraign and belov'd by The People.

No. 3 Of Makeing the Secretarys of State an Inner Cabinett to the Queen

If the Secretarys of State have a Right Understanding and Act Entirely in Concert it will forward it Exceedingly.

The Secretarys Should have a Sett of Able heads, Under a Secret Management, with whom to Make Generall Callculations, and from whom to Recieve Such Needfull Informations, as by Other Agents Under Them may be Obtain'd, in all Necessary or Difficult Cases, & yet These Secret heads Need Not Correspond.

From This fund of Advice all Things Needfull to be Concerted for the Occasions of State, May be Form'd into schemes, and Come Out Perfect. The Proposalls Made by The Secretarys Shall No More be Embrios, and be brought before the Council to be Argued, and Amended, but shall be born at Once, and Come before them wholl and Compleat, and the Council have Little to do but to Approve a thing as it is Proposed.

If all the Proposalls Relateing to Publick Matters were Thus Digested, her Majtie would find There was a Secret Sufficiency Some where in her Secretarys Office, that in Time would bring both her Self and Council To Depend upon the Secretarys of State, for all the Modells of Action, as well as the Mannagement, and Thus Sir I have brought Out what I Affirm'd at First, That the Secretary of State Must of Course be Prime Minister.[1]

An Essay or Two of This Nature shall be Made when you Please.

I Acknowlege the Conjunction of the Lord Treasurer, for the Time being, would Make a Compleat Conduct, because Tis Impossible but his Lordship must be furnisht, with Such helps as may finish Things with Less Difficulty.

In This Concert All the Great Actions of State, all Orders Given to Admiralls, and Generalls, all Forreign Treatyes, and Forreign Intelligence, would Reciev Their Last Turns, be Digested, and Finisht, and the Queen See her Self Mistress of the Most Capitall Part of her affaires, before They Come before The Council.

All Funds for Taxes, Wayes and Meanes, Projects of Trade, &ca shall be here form'd into heads, and Either be Fitted For Excecution, or Laid Aside as Impracticable, and My Lord Treasurer be Eased of the Intollerable Impertinence of Fund Makers and Projectors.

Secret Matters Relateing to Partyes, to Private Persons, home Mannagemt &ca will here be Settl'd, Determin'd, and prepar'd for Excecution.

Here all the Bussiness of the Crown, the Affaires of Law Onely Excepted, will Center and the Secretarys Office be Thus the Onely Cabinett—

This would Make Our Actions Uniform, Our Councils Secret, Our Orders Regular and Practicable and The Excecution Punctuall.

This would bring the Secretarys Office and Above all the Secretary into Such Reputation that Orders Issued would have more Regard Since Resentments of Miss Conduct would Lye in the Breast of the Secretary and be Very Certain and Severe—

Here would be a Prime Ministry without a Grievance, The People Pleas'd, the Govornmt Serv'd, Envy Asham'd, Intreagues Fruitless, Enterprizes Successfull, and all Our Measures be both better Directed and Better Excecuted.

---

[1] Lord Treasurer Godolphin was at this time the leading minister, but his leadership depended upon the influence of his personality rather than the authority of his office. Later, some Secretaries of State did become Prime Ministers. See M. A. Thomson, *Secretaries of State, 1681–1782*, Oxford, 1932, pp. 12–18.

Att home Partyes would be Suppresst, Furious Tempers on all Sides Check't and Discountenanc't, Peace Promoted and Union Obtain'd.

All the Leading Men of all Sides, would be Influenc'd here by a Rare and Secret Mannagement. They Should Never Stir or Speak as a Party but it Should be known.

Not a Mayor or an Alderman in Any Corporation, Not a shereif of a County, Not A Member of Parliamt, Or Convocation Could be Elected, But the Govornmt Should kno' who to Oppose, and how to Do it if They Saw Fitt.

This would be The wheel of All Publick bussiness, and all the Other branches Must of Course Depend on the Mannagement of This Office.

No. 4 Some Considerations with Relation To
the Affaires of Hungaria and Poland[1]

First I Lay it Down as a Principle—That the Present Insurrection of the Hungarians be Their Pretensions Never So Just, or Their Provocations Great, The Invasion of Poland by The Suede and Dethroneing The king, However Unjustly he may have Acted, Are Fatall Embarrasmts to the Present Confederacy, and in Effect Great helps to the French in Their Over Runing the Empire, and in Their Attempt on The Libertyes of Europe.

This being Allow'd, the Wholl Confederacy Are bound in the Consequence to Support the Emperor Against the Hungarians and the king of Poland Against the Swedes.

If it be Objected why Not as well the Swede Against the Pole and the Hungarians Against the Emperor Since Otherwise you fight Against the Protestant Religion, I Return *This is Not a War of Religion*.[2] The Present Question is Not Protestant or Papist But Liberty Or Universall Monarchy, and if it were a War of Religion Tis Not Protestant or Papist in Hungary and Poland but in England, Holand, and the Empire.

Now if the Hungarian or Swedish Protestants will have So Little Regard to the Intrest of the Protestant Religion in Generall as to Make Their Private share in it Clash with the Generall We Must do by Them, as We Do by Our Neighbours

---

[1] Defoe's strictures on the wars between Hungary and the Empire and between Poland and Sweden were reiterated in the *Review* throughout the entire second half of 1704. For the Swedish affair see especially the issues from 15 July to 29 Aug.; for the Hungarian rebellion see those from 2 Sept. to 5 Dec.

[2] Cf. *Review*, 29 July 1704.

when the Street is on fire, blow up Their houses to Save the Wholl Town.

Twould be preposterous Temporising if we should Suffer Our Selves to be Over Run for fear of Their being Ruin'd. These Unfortunate Christians of Hungaria have had the Missfortune Once before to attempt Their Liberty in a juncture and in A Manner as Improper as This, and That was when the Turks Came Down, Or Rather when They brought The Turks Down to the Siege of Vienna. Now Tho' Some People here were So Weak to wish the Turks shou'd Take the Citty because Thereby The Protestants would be Establish'd, yet No Man That Could See an hour before him Could Say but it were Better for all the Rest of Europe That the Protestants of Hungaria were Entyrely Rooted Out and Destroyd, Than That the Turks Should Take the Citty of Vienna.[1]

And Therefore we find the Protestant Princes of Germany were the first and Forwardest to March to the Relief of it, and the Hungarian Protestants Could Expect No less.

On This Accont *Delenda est.* The work Must be Done. Protestant or Papist the Troubles in Hungary Must if Possible be Appeas'd One way Or Other and the Onely Remaining Question is how it must or may Rather be brought to Pass.

I Grant, That as in the Simily before, Endeavours Are Allwayes Made Use of to Quench the fire before the blowing up of any houses. So here Negotiations Should first be Attempted and Accomodations Propos'd.

The Hungarians without Doubt are an Opprest People, and On the Other hand the Emperor is in Danger and the Juncture favourable. The English and Dutch Forming a Project of Peace and Pacification and Entring into a Close Imediate Treaty On both hands, There is Great Reason to believ both Sides might be brought to See Their Intrest.

First the Reall Grievances of the Hungarians to be Considred, Drawn by way of Abstract from Prince Rakocsi's[2] Declaration,

---

[1] What was perhaps Defoe's earliest political writing—now lost—was given to this same subject (*Appeal to Honour and Justice*, in *Later Stuart Tracts*, p. 104).

[2] Francis Rakoczy (1676–1735) was leader of the insurrection that had started out as a peasants' revolt against religious intolerance in 1703. By now the insurgents had achieved very considerable success, and at one time had advanced almost to the gates of Vienna itself. A two-front war was more than Austria could successfully wage, and a settlement with the Hungarians would have enabled her to turn her waning energies entirely against the French, now advancing towards her frontiers. Rakoczy was demanding the restoration of constitutional rights to Hungary and of his own title as Prince of Transylvania, concessions that the

And if any Mittigation of Demands were Tho't Reasonable, Room left to Adjust Them by a Treaty.

Here it May be Considred Some are Capitall articles which Must be Granted on both sides.

As Restoreing The Prince, Restoreing The free Excercise of Religion, Retrenching the Usurpations of the Romish Clergy, Calling the Assembly of the Estates & Leaving Them at Full and Entire Liberty to Act, withdrawing forreign Forces, and the like.

On the Behalf of the Emperor Some Capitall Articles Must be Insisted on, Such as Laying Down Arms, Restoreing Towns, Delivering Magazins, Renewing Alleigance, and Aiding him Against the French and The like. As to Matters of Taxes, Trade, Imposts, Freedome of Passages, Bounds of Estates, and all Things Relateing to Property and Civill Justice, These may be and Must be Settled Among Themselves by Treaty or in an Assembly of Estates.

But for the Other, an Imediate Envoy to be Sent to the Emperor or Instructions to The Resident There as Follows

In the Name of the wholl Confederacy to Represent to the Emperor the Necessity of Complying with the Hungarians, and to Let Him kno' That On These Terms Peace is both honoble and Reasonable and That if his Imperiall Majtie will Not yield to Such a Proposall, Allowing Such Alterations, or Additions, as are Reasonable, They shall Think themselves Dissengag'd From any Extraordinary Care of the Empire, Any Farther Than by Treatyes They are bound, And that They will Imediately Supplye the Hungarians with 1000000*l* Sterling to Enable Them to Settle Themselves Independent of the Empire, and Establish Prince Rakocsi king of Hungary and Transilvania, and Maintain him in The Posession of the Same.

At the Same Time a Faithfull Agent to be sent to Prince Rakocsi, to Represent to him: That as Now he has a Favourable Opportunity to Restore Religion, and Liberty, in Hungary, and Reestablish himself and his Family, So he Ought to Let his Demands be Govorn'd by The True and just Reasons of his Takeing Up Arms, and Not Build Upon the Prosperity of his Affaires, Designes which may Embark Other Nations in A Necessary Quarrell Against him; That They will Concern Themselves to Mediate with the Emperor Such a Peace as may

Emperor, at this gloomy moment, might have been induced to make. See Henry Marczali, *Hungary in the Eighteenth Century*, Cambridge, 1910, pp. lix–lxi.

Secure Hungary Against Future Opressions, but That if he Pushes on his Designes beyond the just Demands of Reason, They shall be Oblig'd to Concern Themselves against him.

That as They are Ready on the Project of Peace Tendred them, to Oblige the Emperor to Complye with it, So if Not Accepted They have Resolv'd to Assist the Emperor with 25000 Men to be Rais'd and Maintain'd at Their Own Charge, i.e. the Confederates, In Order to Reduce Them by Force.

These Proposalls Warmly Made, Positively Insisted on, and Resolutely Carry'd on, together with a Dextrous Management, would in all Probabillity Soon bring the Matter to A finall Conclusion.

It is Not Sufficient to Say This is Talking big to No Purpose, and is like Thunder at a Distance, which Scares No body because They are Out of the Danger, for where will the Confederates find 25000 Men &ca for the Service.

To This I Answer we Can find the Money, and There's No Fear of the Men if the Money be Ready. The Emperor if he wanted Money No More Than he wants Men would Beat the French Out of the Empire in One Campaigne.

On the Other hand The Protestants in Hungary want No Men, They want Onely Arms, Amunition, and Officers. The last may be Supply'd Them Very well, and Money will Supply the First with Very Little Difficulty.

The advantage of This Peace No body will Dispute.

As to Poland

The Swede is Now Agressor, and as he was Really Injur'd by The Pole in an Unjust Invasion of the Swedish Livonia, yet he Ought to be Prevail'd with Not to Carry his Private Resentments On, to Affect The Present Confederacy of which the king of Poland is a Member.

When the Swede was Embarrast with the Dane, the Muscovite, and the Pole, The English and Dutch Interpos'd, and gave the king of Danemark the Mortification of Seeing the Conquest of Holstien, which was allmost Compleat, Turn'd upon him, and a Powerfull Army allmost at the Gates of Copenhagen.[1]

[1] Patkul's coalition of Denmark, Poland, and Russia had opened the Great Northern War against Sweden five years before. Fearing the possible defeat of the youthful Charles XII and a subsequent unbalance among the Baltic countries, England and Holland had supported Sweden to the extent of sending naval forces to join those of Charles. The three fleets overwhelmed the Danish Navy and allowed Charles to invade Denmark and threaten Copenhagen. The frightened

They have the Same Right and as much Reason to Restrain
the Swede from kindling a War in the Bowells of the Empire,
which will Certainly be the Effect of his Dethroneing the King
of Poland, and Marching a Swedish Army into the Dukedome
of Saxony, which Appeares Now to be the Design.[1]

How shall This be Done?

Embassyes and Memorialls have been Try'd Allready, and
we Do Not Pretend Our Envoys In That Case have been Very
well Treated, haveing been Made to follow the Swedish Camp
and been Deny'd Audience.[2]

One Positive Memoriall Delivred him, with Subjoyn'd Pre-
liminarys of a Treaty between the Poles and Their king, and
Between himself and the king of Poland, Upon Conditions both
honourable and Advantageous for himself—with a Resolution
of the English, The States Generall, and the king of Danemark,
to Declare Warr Against him In Case he Refuses to Treat, would
Effectually End that Warr in Two Months Time.

First, I Grant the Conditions Ought to be Very Good, and
Very Mortifying to the king of Poland, because The Swede was
Injur'd in the Invasion of his Subjects.

Second, But There is a Great Difference between Demanding
Satisfaction of a Prince, and Setting his Own Subjects To De-
throne him. There is Something More Dishonoble in That,
Than in the Injury he Recd.

But Suppose he shall Reject the Proposall.

Act like The French, Make the Offer with Sword Drawn,
Send a Strong Squadron into the Baltick,[3] Not After the Ambassador, but with him.

If the Swede Refuses, Assist the Muscovite, Let him Take
Narva, which he would Soon do if the Swedes are kept from
Relieving it.—

This fleet will Effectually Cut off his Comunication with his
Own Dominions, Expose all Liefland[4] to the Muscovites, Deliver
Dantzick from the Insults of the Swedes, and Force him to
Complye Or be Ruin'd.

Danes, by quickly retroceding their conquests in Sweden's protectorate, Holstein,
had assuaged Charles and made peace. See R. N. Bain, *Charles XII and the Collapse
of the Swedish Empire*, 1895, pp. 56–65.
   [1] Charles's enemy Augustus was both King of Poland and Elector of Saxony.
   [2] Charles XII disliked diplomatists and though friendly with England's Minister,
John Robinson, would not discuss state business with him (R. N. Bain, op. cit.,
pp. 115–16).
   [3] Cf. No. 13, and *Review*, 29 July 1704.
   [4] Livonia.

But if it be Objected he will Joyn with France
If he does he is Undone. France Can No way Reliev him but by Sea, and the Confederates will Command the Sound & the Passages of the Belt.

Here a Project for Obligeing the Swede by an Invasion of Schonen[1] will be to the Purpose.

MS.: Brit. Mus., Lansdowne MSS. 98 ff. 223–45; unsigned, but in the handwriting of Defoe. *Pub.*: G. F. Warner, 'An Unpublished Political Paper by Daniel Defoe', *English Historical Review*, xxii (1907), 132–43. *Address*: none.

15. [*To* ROBERT HARLEY]. [*August–September 1704?*]

The First Principle of Govornment is Allow'd to be The Publick Safety, The Capitall Branches Whereof are

> Union at home
> Power Abroad

I Humbly Conciev the Most Difficult Point at Present is Union Among Our Selves, and as This Nation is Unhappily Divided into Partyes and Factions, It Seems a Much Nicer thing to Form a Union Since Some Articles Seem Absolutely Irreconcileable.

Tis Plain Those Gentlemen who Propose This Union by Establishing One Party and Suppressing Another, Are In the Dark as to This Matter, and Offer That which has been often Essay'd, and has as often Miscarryed.

The Papist, The Church of England, and The Dissenter, have all had Their Turns in the Publick Administration; and when Ever Any One of Them Endeavourd their Own Settlemt by The Ruine of The Partys Dissenting, the Consequence was Supplanting themselves.

The Papists in the Reign of Queen Mary Drove The affair of Persecution to that highth that They Thought to Extirpate the Beginings of the Reformation, but as the Nobillity had Entertaind a Suspicion of the Resolution taken to Restore the Abbey Lands, Tis plain from the Memoirs of those Times, the people of England had borne it but a Little While Longer Tho' Queen Mary had liv'd.

The forwardness shown in the Generall Establishment of the Protestant Religion at The begining of Queen Elizabeth Con-

---

[1] Modern Skåne, southernmost province of Sweden.

firms This, For Popery Sunk So Absolutely in the Wholl kingdome That it hardly Struggl'd at its Parting.

The Church of England had almost Enjoy'd the Settlement
of 100 yeares when in the Civill Warrs it Sunk Under the hands
of Those Dissenters it had attempted to Suppress.

These proceeding Upon the Same Unchristian principle,
Vizt Ambition, and Persccution, Driveing Things to Extreme-
tyes, Overthrew Themselves and Open'd the Door To the
Returne of The Party They Oppresst.

This has allwayes been the Fruit of Immoderate Principles.

I Might Carry On The Paralell to the Reign of King James
when Popery Seem'd to Make A New Effort but Overshooting
the Mark Fell in the Attempt.

To Bring This Home

Her Majsty Came to the Crown on the Foot of a Legall
Settlement. All the Fatall Encroachment of Partyes which had
Embroil'd us for Some Ages, had Suffred an Operation, and
Submitted to Legall Right, Law, and Constitution; Persecution
was Checkt by Authourity, and Liberty of Conscience Declar'd
a Native Right, the Gust of Unlimited Power was Damn'd by
Parliament, and all the Depredations on the peoples property
Made Void, and Declar'd illegall.

Her Majtie had the Fairest Opportunity in the World to
have United us all upon her Accession to the Crown, had Not
Some Unhappy Councils Directed That Early Mistake when in
her first Speech She Told the Nation her Resolution of Bestowing her Favours Upon the Most Zealous Church Men, in Perticular.[1]

I am Very Sure her Majtie Neither foresaw the Effect of her
words, Nor Imagind that those she Designd her Favours for,
would So ill Improve her Goodness. But these Gentlemen haveing No Power To Restrain Their Warmth, Immediately Gave
a Loose to The Imoderate heat of Their Temper, and boldly
Construed the Queens Perticular Favour to them as a Commission Given them to Insult the Dissenters. Tis hardly Credible
with what Insolence we were Treated in all Socyety, That Now

---

[1] On 25 May 1702, in dismissing the Parliament that was sitting at the time of
her accession, Anne had said: 'My own principles must always keep me entirely
firm to the interests and religion of the Church of England, and will incline me to
countenance those who have the truest zeal to support it' (*Parliamentary History*,
vi. 25). The high Tories had promptly seized upon this declaration as a royal
endorsement of their position and had used it effectively against the Whigs and
Dissenters in the election of that summer. See Keith Feiling, *History of the Tory
Party*, Oxford, 1924, pp. 362–5.

we had a Church of England Queen And The Dissenters Must all Come Down, Our Ministers were Insulted in the Street, Down with the Whigs, was a Street Phrase, and Ballads were Sung of it at Our Doors.

From Hence It proceeded to Libells, and Lampoons, and From Thence to the Pulpitt and the Press; Till Mr Sachavrell, in a Sermon Preach't at Oxford,[1] and Licensed by the University, Told his Hearers that whoever was a True Son of the Church or Wisht well to it, Was Oblig'd to hang Out the Bloody Flag of Defiance Against the Dissenters.

If This Treatment fill'd the Dissenters with Terrible Apprehensions of what They had to Expect; Her Majtie Can Not blame Them without forgetting The use These Gentlemen Made of her first Speech, and Resenting it Accordingly.

From This Came the Book Call'd *The Shortest Way*, with all the et Ceteras of it to the Unhappy Author, Unhappy Onely in Saying too Much Truth.

All her Majtie has been Able to Say Since, has Not been Able, Either to Check the Fury of a Party, who had posest Themselves with the hopes of Ruining The Dissenters, Nor Could it lessen the Feares the Dissenters Too Justly Entertain'd of The Reall Design they Thot was laid for Their Destruction.

If I am Ask'd how This wrong Step is to be Retriev'd and Peace of Partyes to be Procur'd, I Must Answer in Generall:

By Removeing The Dissenters Jealousyes,[2] and Checking the Destructive Fury of the present hott party.

The Dissenters Jealousyes May Effectually be Remov'd, The wholl Party Entirely Engag'd, and Brott to an Absolute Dependence Upon her Majtie, and a Conjunction with her Intrest, and yet No Concessions Made to Them which May give Reason of Distast to the Church.

Of This, if I am Ordred to give a scheme, possibly it would Appear both Reasonable and Feasible. But I wou'd be Very Loth it should be Seen but where it May be usefull.

Those Gentlemen who Are for Engrossing all the Places of Profitt and Trust in The Kingdome in The hands of Church Men, should by my Consent be Gratifyed, tho' without the Necessity of a Law: The Dissenters shou'd Content Themselves with Their Liberty of Conscience, and I am Perswaded wou'd

---

[1] Published as *Political Union, a Discourse Shewing the Dependence of Government on Religion in England*, Oxford, 1702.

[2] i.e. suspicions.

be So Content, and being Secur'd in Their Property and Religion, and Out of the Feares and Taunts of Their Enemyes They wou'd of Course Correspond together, and in Time Unite.

A Bill for Occasionall Conformity would be Needless, and I am Perswaded The Gentlemen who were forwardest for it Now would ha' Thought it less Significant Than They Seem'd to do if They had Design'd to follow it with Some Other Steps More Effectuall and More Perticularly Mortifying.

There Are Differences in This Unhappy Nation which Respect the State wholly and Not Religion, There Are High Church and Low Church as well as Conformist and Dissenter.

Tis my Opinion the Moderate Men of both Partyes are the Substantiall part of the Nation. They are its Refuge when the Men of Heat Carry Things too farr.

These Are the Men in whom alone the Govornment Can be Safely Lodg'd and when it is So No Men That are Lovers of Their Country Can be Uneasy.

I Can Never Believ We are Safe in Any hands but These. The Lords May be Hott on One hand, and the Commons On Another. So far as Either Run On to Extreams, So farr they Are to blame, Injure The Peoples Peace, Foment Partyes, and Hazard Our Safety.

These Breaches May Perfectly be heal'd by The Queen. Two words at the Opening the Next session[1] shall Finish it all without a Dissolution.

Dissolving Parliaments Allwayes Lessens the Crown, and Never lessens Grievances. Time was we Could Not have Grievances Redresst and Parliament Could Not be Suffr'd to look into Them. Tis hard Now We have a Prince That would Make us all Easy We Can Not Correspond in Our Demands and Let her kno' wherein Our happyness Consists.

All This May be Cur'd by Wise Conduct, Wary Councils, Moderate Measures and Moderate Men.

Methods of Mannagement of the Dissenters

I allow Previous to the proposall That 'Tis Not Necessary in the present Conjuncture to Restore The Dissenters to Offices and Preferments.

This would Make the Govornmt Seem Byast in Their Favour.

---

[1] In the following October, Anne opened the session with a plea that 'we should be entirely united at home' and that 'there will be no contention among you but who shall most promote the public welfare' (*Parliamentary History*, vi. 356).

The high Church Men would Reflect on her Majtie as Not True to her Own Principles or her Promise.

I Might Possibly Grant The Temper of the Dissenters Not So Well Quallify'd for the Prosperity of Their Princes favour as Other Men, and Grant They are Better kept at a Due Distance Provided Not Made Uneasy.

But This would be Certainly the Effect of bringing them into Action, That it would add Nothing to Our Union; it would Onely Make One Party Easy and An Other Discontented and we should be Still Divided.

I Premise Also by the Way That I am Perswaded Freedom and favour to The Dissenters is The Directest Method to Lessen Their Numbers and bring Them at last into the Church. I Verily Believ the 18 yeares Liberty They have Enjoy'd[1] has weakn'd Their Intrest. A Tenderness and Moderation to Them will Still Lessen Them and I Could Say Much on This head.

The Dissenters Are Divided and Impolitick. They Are Not form'd into a body. They hold No Correspondence among themselves. Could they ha' been brought to do So, Their Numbers would ha' Made Them Formidable. But as they are Onely Numbers Irregularly Mixt They are Uncapable of Acting in Any Capascity.

They are Consequently Passiv in all Matters of Govornment. The Most That Ever They do is to Address by Their Ministers.

The Proceedings to Restrain Either Their Liberty as Dissenters or Their Other Privileges Must Necessarily Make Them Uneasy and Fill Them with Feares. And as Words have given Them So Much Uneasiness, Words May Restore it and Cure all the Breach without Changing the Mannagement Other Than what is in Prospect.

The Uneasyness of the Dissenters Consists in Their Feares That the Queen is in the hands of That Party of Men who would Ruin Them.

Her Majtie is Easily Able to Clear This by shifting but a Few Obnoxious hands, and Putting her Self upon the Fidelity and Prudence of Such a Ministry as Neither Side Can Object Against without Manifestly Discovering that Tis the Places, Not the Men, They are Concern'd About.

One Speech from Her Majtie Either in Council or at the Next session of Parliament would Effectually Stop the Mouth

---

[1] Reckoning since James II's first Declaration of Indulgence, 1687. See Sutherland, *Defoe*, p. 277.

of Rallery and Strife and Make us all Easy but Such Unreasonable people on both Sides as might Easily be Silenc't if Once publickly Discourag'd, or if Not Silenc't Would be Expos'd and Contemn'd.

Some Small Mannagement Among the Dissenters by Fathfull Agents Might be Very Usefull to Settle The Generall Temper of The Party and Methods shall be propos'd at Demand.

What hands to be laid by, What perticular Expressions in Such a Speech, what Methods to Satisfye the high Church Malecontents, I Dare Not Presume to Make an Essay at, Tho' Possibly On a Liberty Granted I Could Say what I hope would Appear Reasonable.

These Generalls Extended to Perticulars, I am Perswaded The Dissenters May be brought to be So Perfectly Easy, That if it Were in Their Power Or Choice to Alter the Face of The Govornment They would Not Attempt it. This way They Shall Convince the World that the Liberty of Their Consciences and assurance of its Continuance is a Full Satisfaction to Them without Civill Preferments and Advantages, and That They Desire No More Than the Tolleration They Enjoy.

With This Management it shall Never Disturb Them if They Are No way Concernd in the Govornment, while They See at the Same Time, it is in the hands of Such as Sincerely Design Their Protection, and Not Their Destruction.

And he That will Not be Content in Such a Case will be Dissown'd as a Hypocrite, and Pass for a Politick, Not a Religious Dissenter.

Those Gentlemen of the Church who were Not Content with This Mannagement would Discover plainly That Twas Not the Churches Safety but the Dissenters Ruine They Aim'd at in all Their Unnecessary Clamours, and Her Majtie would Easily Disscern the Men.

The Gentlemen of the highest Temper in These Matters Generally Conform to the Face of the Court. Such as Continued Averse to peace Might be Either Taken off by Methods Or Discourag'd, and Tho' ill Nature would Not be Supprest at Once, Twould lessen and Dye away by Time

Should her Majtie Declare That as she had Often given her word to Maintain the Tolleration, So She should Never Consent to any Act that Seem'd to Restrain The present Liberty of the Dissenters.

That she So Desired the Generall Peace of her People That

any person That Either by Writeing, Preaching, Or Printing promoted the Fatall Strife of Partyes should Meet with No Encouragement from her.

That she would Perticulary Recomend it To the Clergy to Preach up Moderation, Charity and Peace with people of Different Opinions, and To strive by Their pious lives and painfull Preaching to prove whether[1] were The Best Christians.

Nor Could her Majtie Need to Say Much of her Zeal or Care for the Church; No body Doubts her Steadyness. But Such a Declaration would Imediately Stop the Clamours of the Pulpitt against the Dissenters and Care might be Taken to prevent the Dissenters Takeing any Unjust advantage of the Churches Silence.

These with a Little Application and Private but Very Nice Conduct Might give the last Step to a Generall Union of Affection in the Nation; and as to a Union in principle, As it Can Not be Expected, So blessed be God it is Not So Necessary as that we Can Not be happy without it.

MS.: Brit. Mus., Harl. MSS. 6274 ff. 227–34; unsigned, but in the handwriting of Defoe. *Pub.*: Sutherland, *Defoe*, pp. 277–82. *Address*: none.

16. *To* SAMUEL ELISHA.[2] *31 August 1704*

Sir

I had your obligeing Letter, for which, tho' its now very Late, I presume to give you my Sincere Thanks.

I had Given Mr. Rogers[3] over, and knew not how matters were with him; supposing he was marry'd and had forgot his friends, or something else was befallen him.

This made me give you the Trouble of a Parcell yesterday, by the Carryer, in which are 50 books, which you will find are a few Thoughts on the late Victory:[4] if you please to Let him have them, or any Friends that Desire them. If they are too many, he may returne what he mislikes.

I can not Enlarge, but you'l see, by the Enclos'd, what wonderfull Things God is Doeing in the World; of which I could

[1] 'Whether' in the old sense of 'which of the two'.

[2] Of Samuel Elisha (1670–1745) little is known. He was the son of a Shrewsbury maltster, practised law at Shrewsbury, was admitted a Burgess of the town in 1707, and became Mayor in 1725 (*Shrewsbury Burgess Roll*, ed. H. E. Forrest, Shrewsbury, 1924, p. 95). For another letter to Elisha, see No. 20.

[3] Mentioned also in No. 20. Perhaps Gabriel Rogers, Shrewsbury bookseller.

[4] Defoe's *Hymn to Victory*, celebrating the military and naval triumphs of that summer, had just appeared (advertisement in the *Review*, 29 Aug. 1704).

not forbear putting you to the Charge, that you might let our friends have the first of it. 'Tis midnight. I hope you will Excuse the hast.

I am, Sir, Your sincere Friend [and]¹ Servt,
DE FOE

Ultimo Augo 1704

MS.: untraced. *Pub.*: John Forster, *Oliver Cromwell, Daniel De Foe, Sir Richard Steele, Charles Churchill, Samuel Foote: Biographical Essays*, 3rd ed., 1860, pp. iv–v. *Address*: 'To Mr. Samll Elisha in Shrewsbury.'

17. [*To* ROBERT HARLEY]. [*September 1704?*]

State of Partys in England

County of Hertford

This County is under Severall Characters.

That part of it adjoyning to Bedfordshire and Buckinghamshire is whiggish and Full of Dissenters.

That Part adjoining to Huntingdon, Cambridg and Essex, Entirely Church and all of the High Sort.

The Gentlemen of the Royston Club² Settle all the affaires of the Country and carry all before them, Tho' they behave with Something More Modesty or at least Carry it Closer, than in former Dayes.

This is a Monthly Meeting of the Gentlemen of all the Neighborhood the First Thursday in Every Month. They used to Drink Excessively, and do a Thousand Extravagant Things, but they behave much Better now.³

They have Built a large, Handsome, Square Room, well wainscotted, and Painted. Tis Hung with the Pictures of King Charles the 1st, the 2d, King James, and King William, at their Full Length, well painted in Good Frames, 10 or 12 Foot High.

They Have a Monteth of Silver of about 4 Gallons which cost them 50*l*. They raise Some Fines and Forfeitures, which Formerly were improved to the Encrease of Drunkeness, but now they do Some Charity's, and are much reformed.

Here Justice [   ]⁴ and the then Club resolved

¹ Forster's brackets.
² A political and convivial society that had set up rooms in the Red Lion at Royston. See the *Gentleman's Magazine*, l (1780), 474, and liii (1783), 813–15.
³ Defoe had deplored the drinking habits of the Club in his *Reformation of Manners*, 1702 (*Works*, 1705, i. 88).
⁴ Blank in MS. The offending Justice was Sir Ralph Radcliffe. See R. L. Hine, *Mirror for the Society of Friends*, 1930, pp. 34–35.

the Pulling down the Quakers meeting at Hartford in 1683 for which the Proprietor afterwards Sued him and recovered Sufficient Damage to rebuild the house.

Mr Freeman[1] is Master of all this part of the County as to Parties.

Of the Royston Club[2]

MS.: Duke of Portland, Defoe Papers, 1 f. 26; unsigned, but in the handwriting, somewhat disguised, of Defoe. *Pub.*: *H.M.C. Portland*, iv. 153–4. *Address*: none.

18. [*To* ROBERT HARLEY]. *28 September 1704*

Sir

I did my Self the honor to write To you from Cambridge on Saturday the 16th Insta[3] and was in hopes to have Recd your Ordrs as hinted There by Fryday— How I have Spent the Time the Last week—how I Recd an Odd Alarm from London Occasion'd by Mr Stephens the Messenger of the Press, who Really Treats me ill,[4] how This Occasion'd me Makeing a Trip to Town, how staying but Two dayes There I happend of a smart Rencounter with Mr *Toke* of East Greensted,[5] These are things I Purpos'd Not to ha' Troubl'd you with, Till I had the honour to finish the Affair I am Upon.

As my Last Signify'd my Desire to Come to This Place, and That Not Recieving your Countermand I Should persue that Design, I have Accordingly Spent a Few Dayes here. Sir R Davers[6] who Rules This Town Carrys Matters Very high. Sir

    [1] Ralph Freeman was M.P. for Hertfordshire and belonged to the Royston Club.

    [2] With this caption the page ends; the succeeding matter, if there was any, has not been found.   [3] Letter missing.

    [4] Robert Stephens, known as 'Robin Hog' among those authors, printers, and booksellers who were victims of his High-Church zeal, had reported that he was ordered to arrest Defoe; and Luttrell had recorded under date of 26 Sept. that 'Daniel de Foe is ordered to be taken into custody for reflecting on admiral Rooke' (*Brief Relation*, v. 469). Defoe had criticized the Admiral in the *Review* for 22 Aug. Moreover, a reward was offered for the discovery of the author of *Legion's Humble Address to the Lords*, and Defoe was suspected, probably justly, with having had a hand in that attack on the Tory House of Commons (*Review*, 3 June 1704; J. W. to Harley, *H.M.C. Portland*, iv. 93; and Hedges to Harley, ibid. iv. 138). Vulnerable though he was, Defoe returned to London, accosted the Messenger of the Press, and forced him to admit that he had no warrant for Defoe's arrest. For Defoe's account of the episode, see the *Reviews* for 7 and 10 Oct., 4 and 7 Nov. 1704, and 16 Nov. 1706. For notice of Stephens and his activities, see Dunton, *Life and Errors*, i. 253–4, and Laurence Hanson, *Government and the Press*, 1936, pp. 36–39.

    [5] John Toke, M.P. for Grinstead. Dottin interprets this 'smart Rencounter' as a duel (*Defoe*, p. 141).

    [6] Sir Robert Davers, M.P. for Bury St. Edmunds.

. . . Felton[1] the Other Member we heare to Day is Dead or Dying, and I Doubt They will make but an ill Choice. If it be possible to bring that Gentleman off, it would do Great Service, his Intrest in This County being Very strong; but of This I Crave leave to be Perticular hereafter.

I Can Not but beg leave to Lay before you That I am Surpriz'd to find my Name in the Written News Letters of this day as Taken into Custody, and Comitted by her Majties Order for Ill Treating Sir Geo: Rook &ca. I hope if there be any Suggestion Against me, on That or any Case, you will please to Reserve me to Answer to your Self; It Can Not be, that I Can be Guilty of any Thing to Displease you, Nor of any Thing Willingly to give you Cause of Dislike. If Sir Geo: is Scandaliz'd at me for any thing, at the Same Time professing I have Not Design'd him any Affront, I beseech you Sir to Take me into your protection, upon that head, and am Ready To Make Such Acknowledgemt as you shall Think Reasonable.[2]

I have been Exceedingly Concern'd at This Case, and was Comeing Up Post to Thro' my Self at your feet and Put my Self into your hands, but being Very Unwilling to leave what I am Upon, Till it is Finisht, I have Venturd to Stay, Depending on your Goodness to me in This Case.

I Write This from *Bury* where I hope I have Not been Useless. Norwch I have Perfectly Dissected,[3] and Was Directing my Course To *Lyn*, but This Unhappy News paper I Confess Discompos'd me, and I spend the Time in Visiting The Sea Coast Towns here, till I may have a line from you at This Town, where your farther Orders will both Comfort and Direct me. If I do Not Reciev Some Signification from your Self by Certificate, or other wise, I shall hardly kno' how to govorn my Self, For my Stirring about may be Dangerous, and I am in Danger of being Taken up as a Person fled from the Queens justice, and in Such a Case may have my Papers Taken from me, and at Least Seen, which would be as bad. For This Reason I am Very shye of my Self, Till I have the honor of your Protection, which I Entreat by First Post.

I am Inform'd here this News Paper is Written by one Mr

---

[1] Sir Thomas Felton. He survived to become a Tacker next session.
[2] Perhaps on Harley's advice, Defoe mollified Rooke in the *Review* for 7 Oct.
[3] He did not go there himself; perhaps he sent Hurt, his companion. A short time later, Fransham was writing to Defoe: 'I heard you were within a few miles of Norwich and had it not been for the impertinence of a News-Writer had made us a visit' (p. 64).

Fox who they Say belongs to the Secretarys Office.[1] If any Thing Could have been in it, I flatter my Self I should have it from your Self, from whom (if I were Guilty of high Treason) a Letter or a Verball Comand should Cause me To Come and Put my Self into your Power.

I Can Not Conciev what I Can have offended in, and shall Desire but This favour, That Sir Geo: Rook may be Referr'd to the Law; if I have Offended him I am Willing to be left to the Law, and Ask him no favour, but if the Govornmt will Espouse the Quarrell of a Single person against another, any Man May be Crusht.

I have Not Taken the freedome my Inclination guided me to, and which I Really Thot the Case of Sir G R Requir'd; because I Saw you Dislik'd another man[2] upon that head, and as I hope I Act from Different Principles with Those people, So Sir I allwayes Remembr'd my Obligation to you, and believ and hope to Satisfye you, I shall Never do any Thing to Make you Think I forgett it.

Tis Something hard that while I am Spreading Principles of Temper, Moderation, and Peace Thro' Countrys where I go, and Perswadeing all People That the Govornment is Resolv'd to proceed by those Rules, I should be Chosen Out to be made the Object of a Private, high flying Revenge, under Colour of the Govornments Resentments, for be it Sir that you find Sir G. R faithfull, and that This fight or Victory at Sea be the first Proof of it

I Can at This Distance Accquaint you, That the Improvemt Made of This Victory Abroad by The Mad Men of his Party at home, is Such, that *speaking of The Peace at home*, which is the Design I am Upon, and which I Suppose her Majtie, your Self, and all Good Men Embark't in, perhaps we may See good Cause to wish that Victory had been a Defeat— And tho' I were to Suppose Sir Geo: himself under the Mannagemt of your hand, yet Sir I am free to Tell you, that the high Church Party look on him as Their Own. The Victory At sea they look upon as Their Victory Over the Moderate Party, and his health is Now Drunk by Those here, who wont Drink the Queens Nor yours. I am Oblidg'd with Patience to hear you Damn'd, and

---

[1] Joseph Fox (1686?–1746) was a news-letter writer and bookseller at Seven Stairs, Westminster Hall. He is not known to have had any connexion with either Secretary's office.

[2] Perhaps John Tutchin, who had criticized the conduct of the war (*D.N.B.*).

he Prais'd, he Exalted and her Majtie Slighted, and the Sea Victory Set up against the Land Victory, Sir Geo: Exalted above the D of Marl . . . . , and what Can the Reason of this be, but that they Concieve some hopes from This, that their high Church Party will Revive Under his Patronage.

Now Sir I leave This to your judgemt whether be Sir G R Concernd or No, whether this Unreasonable Acclamation be not made from Other Principles than joy at a Victory. If he is to be the Patron of that Party, whether he Sees it or Not, if he is to be a head for Them to Vallue themselves Upon, whether Purposely or Not, he is a fatall Instrumt to Ruine the Peace we speak of.

Indeed Sir Tis my Regard to your Orders, and that Onely, Restrains me On that head, for the Case Requires to be Spoken to, and if the Govornmt Espouse the Case against me in This, the broil will be Remov'd from high Church and Low Church To Rookites and . . . .[1]

The Consequences This has allready in the Country, and the Check it has put to the Advances Peace has Made, are Visible, and I Shall Give you Perticulars as Soon as I Come up, And Conclude with This presumtion—Sir at least Sir G. R must be won Over to Dissown the proceedings of This Party, and to Check those which affront the Govornment on his behalf, or the Civill feuds of Partyes will Encrease, Rather than Diminish, my Comission will be in Vain, and you will find the Temper of the Gentlemen who are to Come up the 24th of Next Month,[2] less Govornable than you Expect.

I am Running Out Sir into the Usuall Freedom, with which I hope you will not be offended. I Can not but Think it my Duty To Let you See there, what you would be Displeas'd to See if you were here.

Sir I have Another Grievance to Lay before you, with an Earnestness Perticular to my Usuall Sollicitations. Mr Chris: Hurt of the Custome house, The Same whose Name you have in your Pocket book, has been with me all This Journey, and a Very Usefull person I have found him in the work I am Upon,— He is Under Concern at my staying Longer than I Expected, and haveing Ask't No Leav at the Custome house where he is Not a Little Mark't Out as a Dissenter, Expects to be ill Treated for This absence. The Least Notice from you Sir will Remove the Possibillity of it, and Tho' I Conceal the bottome of the

---

[1] Thus in MS.   [2] The session of Parliament was about to open.

bussiness, yet he Serves it faithfully, and I kno' Not how to want him.

I Therefore Entreat you will please to get a Note of Leav from My Ld Treasurer Directed to the Comissrs of the Customes for *Christopher Hurt, Key*[1] *Man*, to be Absent on his Private Occasions.

I would ha' hinted that the Magazin Runs Lowe, and is Recruited by Private Stock, which is but Indifferent. I acknowledge myself Not a Good Husband, But as my ill husbandry is Onely where I find it Absolutely Needfull, I Venture Not to be spareing, and hope you will find Cause to Approve it, and Trust my Choice of Instruments and Methods.

I Again Entreat your Care of my Assistant. It would heartily Concerne me, and I believ yourself, if he should be Divested of his Livelyhood for the absence here, while the bottom of it is your and the Nations Service.

I Cease to Importune you farther and waiting to hear farther from your Self Ask your Pardon for The length of This, and am
Your Most faithfull, Oblig'd, and Obedt Servt
[symbol]

The Extraordinary goodness of the Season (here haveing been No Rain these 3 Weeks) makes me Offer it if for the Service to Stay Out as long as you please.

Bury Sept 28. 1704

If I should be straightn'd and you please to Ordr me To Draw for a Supply and on whom, I hope the Success of the affair will answer it beyond your Expectation.

Please To Direct to Alexandr Goldsmith[2] at Mr John Morleys[3] in Bury.

MS.: Duke of Portland, Defoe Papers, 1 ff. 20–21. *Pub.*: *H.M.C. Portland*, iv. 136–8. *Address*: none.

19. [*To* GABRIEL ROGERS?]. [*October 1704?*]
Sir
I am much concern'd That the books are not come to hand. I was out of Town when they were sent but They were Delivr'd

---

[1] i.e. Quay.
[2] One of the names assumed by Defoe during his service under Harley.
[3] Morley, unidentified, is mentioned again later (p. 118).

at the Falcon¹ without Aldersgate. I hope you have them before this comes to hand else please to Give me Notice that I may Enquire for you.

I as much long to see you, where you tell me of Friends I have no merit to purchase nor reason to Expect, but fear the season is too farr spent to expect it. Pray give my service to all that think me worth their concern and let them kno' if I live till Spring I purpose to give them Trouble enough. My due respects and Service to Mr. Owen and Mr. Elisha.² Jure Divino goes on.³ Pray forget it not.

I am, Your hearty Faithfull Servt
D E F O E

One of my letters about the Battail⁴ are here enclosed.

MS.: untraced. *Pub.*: Sotheby's Sale Catalogue for 15 Dec. 1931, No. 351a. *Address*: none.

20. [*To* SAMUEL ELISHA].⁵ *11 October 1704*

Sir

I have your kind Letter and had Answerd it sooner but I have been Out of Town for above 3 weeks.

What Treatmt I have had since I have been Abroad you will See in the Review where I have been Oblig'd to Vindicate my Self by an Advertisement, and had Not the Malice of people Reported me fled from justice, which made me think it Necessary to Come up and sho' myself, I dont kno' but I might ha given you a short Visit.⁶

I am Glad to hear you had the Hymns⁷ and Thank your Acceptance of the single One but I must own myself Sorry Mr Rogers⁸ is leaving you.

I Thank you for your kind proposall, but tho' I have a Family

---

¹ The Castle and Falcon, Aldersgate Street, from which wagons departed for points to the north-west (*Blundell's Diary and Letter Book, 1702–1728*, ed. Margaret Blundell, Liverpool, 1952, p. 182).

² Since Defoe admired James Owen, dissenting minister at Shrewsbury (*Present State of the Parties*, 1712, p. 308), and was a friend of Samuel Elisha of the same city (Nos. 16 and 20), I suggest that this letter was intended for a Shrewsbury correspondent.

³ In Shrewsbury, subscriptions to *Jure Divino* were taken by 'Mr Rogers' (p. 64) who may therefore have been the person to whom this letter was addressed.

⁴ Missing and unidentified.

⁵ See p. 56, n. 2.

⁶ See No. 18, and the *Review*, 7 and 10 Oct. 1704.

⁷ Defoe's *Hymn to Victory*. Cf. p. 56.

⁸ Perhaps Gabriel Rogers, Shrewsbury bookseller.

Large Enough, would not have my useless Accquaintance Burthensome to my Friends, Especially you of whom I have been Capable to meritt Very Little.

I Rejoyce that I shall see you in Town and wish you a good journey up— I beg the favour of you to Remind Mr Rogers of Jure Divino¹ which Now Draws near putting forward.

I am, Sir, Your Oblig'd Humble Servt

D F

Octobr. 11. 1704

MS.: Pierpont Morgan Library, New York City. *Pub.*: John Forster, *Oliver Cromwell, Daniel De Foe, Sir Richard Steele, Charles Churchill, Samuel Foote: Biographical Essays*, 3rd ed., 1860, pp. v–vi. *Address*: none.

21. JOHN FRANSHAM² *to* DEFOE. [*October 1704?*]

Sir

I have sent you a List of the Subscribers to your Book³ which I have procur'd in our Town pursuant to the request you made me. I could have wish'd it longer and can assure you there was nothing wanting on my part to have made it so but when I consider First how few there are amongst Tradesmen of which our City chiefly consists that set any great value upon Books, secondly of such as do how many have resolv'd never to subscribe for a Book again having been bit in former Subscriptions, Thirdly that the greatest part of this City would have subscribed for the contrary subject, and lastly of them that like the undertaking how many of them that like their Money much better; I say when I consider these several Classes I flatter myself that you'll think I have done tollerably well.

I heard you were within a few miles of Norwich and had it not been for the impertinence of a News-Writer had made us a visit.⁴ I wish you had put your designe in execution upon a

---

¹ The *Review* for 26 Sept. 1704 announced that subscriptions for *Jure Divino*, by the author of the *True-born Englishman*, would be accepted not only in London but 'at most of the Principal Towns in *England*'. The book was delayed, and Defoe did not publish it until 1706.

² John Fransham (d. 1753) was a linen-draper of Norwich. He was the reputed author of two religious tracts and other miscellaneous writings, and later became rent-agent to Horace Walpole, brother of Sir Robert. The surviving correspondence between Fransham and Defoe, published by Francis Norgate in *Notes and Queries*, 5s., iii (1875), 261–3 and 282–4, consists of eleven letters. Norgate made no attempt to assign dates to letters lacking them, and as a result, his sequence, though numbered, is not chronologically correct. For the other letters, see Nos. 23, 24, 28, 29, 31, 32, 45, 49, 83, and 122.

³ *Jure Divino*.   ⁴ See p. 59.

double account, one the pleasure of your conversation, the other the increasing the List for an Authors presence you know do much. If you had been here as this day you might have read in Dyers Letter the following paragraph, 'The Weaver in Spittle-fields that was taken up for dispersing a poem call'd the Address is admitted to Bail by my Ld C. Just. Holt, but his Tenant Mr De Foe is absconded so that a Messenger can't get to speak with him notwithstanding he falsly asserts the contrary in his Review.'[1] Tis possible (seeing it seems that you have not his Letter in London)[2] that this may prove a piece of News to you which is all that you can be at present furnisht with by

Sir, your humble Servt
JNO. FRANSHAM

MS.: untraced. *Pub.*: Francis Norgate, 'Correspondence between De Foe and John Fransham, of Norwich', *Notes and Queries*, 5 S, iii (1875), 261. *Address*: none recorded.

22. [*To* ROBERT HARLEY]. *2 November 1704*

Sir

I am Very Shye of Burthening you with Triffles while the Nations Burthens Load you, but *Pardon me* That I am Extremely Sollicitous on your Account: If it be So that My Low station Renders my Concern Very Useless to you, yet I shall Not less show My Sincere Endeavour, and at worst Incur your Censure as Impertinent, Not as Unfaithfull.

The Freedome you Allwayes gave me, and which I Think it was Never More my Duty to Take, Oblidges me to Talk to you, in Terms Too Course for the Distance between your Character, your Person, your Merit, *and Me*. I Beseech you Place my want of Decency, to the Account of my Passion if Possible to Render you Service.

I wish for an Occasion to Show you by any thing besides This Cheap Empty way of word Service, what I would Do, Suffer, or Risque for your advantage, That the Sincerity with which my Soul is Swell'd For your Service Might by Some Demonstra-

---

[1] In September, Secretary Hedges had ordered the arrest of Nathaniel Sammon, a weaver of Old Street, Cripplegate, for dispersing copies of *Legion's Humble Address to the Lords* (P.R.O., S.P. 34/5/35, and Hedges to Harley, *H.M.C. Portland*, iv. 138). Defoe denied that he had written the *Address* and maintained that, far from fleeing, he was ready to expose himself to public view 'at Two Pence a time' (*Review*, 3 June 1704). According to Hedges, Sammon was a 'tool' of Defoe's. In 1703 Nottingham's men had discovered Defoe hiding in the house of an unnamed Spitalfields weaver —perhaps Sammon.

[2] Dyer's *News-letter* was not circulated in London (*Review*, 23 Aug. 1705).

tion Challenge your belief; and I Might If Possible Discharge My Self of the weighty Debt of Gratitude, and Please my Self with haveing Done Something worthy of you Obligeing, and of me Oblig'd, beyond The Common Rate of Service and Obligation.

Among the Croud of Things which Press my Thoughts, and the Various wayes my Impotence of Thought Offers both to Discharge my Exceeding Obligation, and if possible be Usefull to So bountifull a benefactor, admit Sir as the best I Can offer a Genuine Candid Observation On the Publick Affaires as Undr your Conduct—and yet who Am I that I Should Pretend to Advise you, Quallifyed to Advise a Nation.

It Wounds me to the Soul to hear the Very whigs Themselves, and who for Saying So I Fancy in the Confederacy which you hinted you had Some Notice of, Tell Me and Speak it Openly *you are Lost,* That your Intrest in the house wont keep you in the Chair, That the Party Suppressing you There will Consequently Ruin your Intrest in The [Queen's favour, and give a new turn to your management at Court.][1]

I Confess it Fills me with Indignation, to hear This Spoken with an Air of Satisfaction by a Party who Ought to kno', if Blindness From Heaven had Not Seiz'd Their Understandings, That in your Fall, *Pardon my Calling it So,* from the Mannagemt, The Ruin of Their Intrest is as Effectually Contain'd as tis Possible for Consequences to be in Their Originall Causes.[2]

But the Children of Light were allwayes Darker in Temporalls, than the Rest of their Neighbours, and we are willing to be Fools to please Our Fancys, tho' to the Destruction of Our Judgements; but above all They are the Most Implacable in Censure,—and They Can Not believ Mr H. . . . honest, and True to the Moderate Intrest, because They Once Thought him Otherwise; But the Principall Reason I Find, because They Saw themselves in The Case of the Disciples, who were Dissapointed when they Found Our Lord Did Not Restore the

---

[1] This passage is obscured by the manner in which the MS. is now bound; the reading is taken from *H.M.C. Portland,* iv.

[2] The opposition Whigs, in some quarters at least, were entertaining the notion of combining with the opposition Tories against the moderate 'Triumvirate', Godolphin, Harley, and Marlborough, who had no majority of their own in either House. Defoe's anxiety for Harley and the Ministry was well founded. But the threatened coalition of the two oppositions did not come off; Whig party-discipline was strong enough to prevent it. When the session opened, Harley, though a Secretary of State, was allowed to continue as Speaker of the Commons. See G. M. Trevelyan, *Ramillies and the Union with Scotland,* 1932, pp. 4 and 6.

Temporall Kingdome to Israell, or like the Mother of Zebedees
Children who look't to have Them all to be Lord Chancellors,
and Lord Treasurers, and One to Sitt on the Right hand and
the Other on the left, and were Angry Our Lord Did Not Grant
it, Tho' he Declar'd *it was None of his to give.*

I Rejoyce Sir That I have had the honour of Doeing your
Character Justice, and have Some Converts to boast of, but as
my Little Merit Shall be the Last Thing Ile Plead, So Sir I Onely
hint it Now to Let you kno' The blemish, as they would have it
Call'd, on you as a Person Not in the Right Intrest, has had a
Vast Extent, and Requires Some Conduct to Rase Out. Pardon
me Sir, had your Enemys Nothing to boast of but the Voice of
Our Foolish Friends, I Grant this Not worth your Notice, but as
it is Apt to fall in with Other Capitall Mischiefs, It Merits your
Consideration, and some Methods to Suppress it.

If you'l allow the Vanity of the Expression, *If I were a Publick
Minister* I would if Possible kno' what Every body Said of me,
and I have formerly Instanc'd Cardll Richlieu to you on that
head. Please Sir to give me leav, tho' the words shock my Soul
as I write them and I believe them to be Impotent Forgerys,
yet to Repeat Them that you may Make use of them as you See
Cause.

'Mr Harley is *Out*, he has *Lost* his Intrest, the house will
Certainly *lay him by*, and if There be Nothing Elce in it, 'tis a
Tryall of the Strength of the house, and a Proof he *has lost
Ground*; besides, both Sides are against him, he has Trim'd So
Long On both Sides, and Cares't both Partys, Till both begin
to See themselves ill Treated, and Now, as he Loves Neither
Side, Neither Side will Stand by him. All the Whigs of King
Williams Reign Expected to ha' Come In Play Again, and
had Fair words Given Them, but They See it was but wording
them into a Fools Paradise, and Now The Two Ends will be
Reconcil'd to Overturn his Middle Way:

'If he is Out of the Chair They will Soon Work him Out of
the Seales, and the Lord Godolphin Out of The Treasury.'

They Call The Duke of Marlebro', My Ld Treasurer and
your Self *the Triumvirate* who Mannage the State, and That if
This knot be broke in the House First, They will prevail with
the Queen to Continue the Duke of M abroad, all This winter,[1]
Under Pretence of Goeing to Concert Measures with the Princes

[1] Marlborough would ordinarily be in England during the winter, since field
operations were customarily suspended during the bad weather .

of the Empire, and So they will Easyly Put by all This scheme of Mannagement.

This Ridiculous Stuff had Never Reach't your Eares if I had Not Observ'd Some Coherence between it and what you were pleas'd to Mention to me as Design'd, and by which it Seems Either to be publickly Concerted or at least Concluded and Talkt on as a Thing finished.

As Our Friends[1] were allwayes Fools, it Amazes me to hear Them Promise Themselves a Generall Ease On a Capitulation with the high Church, Liberty, Occasionall Licence, and God knows what.

I shall give you No Comments On This Ungratefull Text, I leave it To your Sedate Thought. I Struggle with my Uttmost to Expose the Folly of it, and with Encourageing Success. Nor is it the Danger to you from These people I hear Discourse that would ha' Mov'd me thus far to assume a Post that So ill becomes me. But as These Little Capilary Veins of Mallice, Reciev the Little Venome They Contain from Some Fountain of Larger Dimension, so I Recomend That Fountain to your Discovery and Prevention.

I Remember Sir when haveing had the honor to Serve the *Late King William* in a kind like this, and which his Majtie had the Goodness to Accept, and Over Vallue by Far, Expressing Some Concern at the Clamour and Power of The Party, at his Express Command I had the heart or Face or what Elce you will Please to Call it, to give my Opinion in Terms like These:

'Your Majtie Must Face About, Oblige your Friends to be Content to be Laid by, and Put In your Enemyes, Put them into Those Posts in which They may Seem to be Employ'd, and Thereby Take off the Edge and Divide The Party.'[2]

Twould be an Unsufferable Vanity to Offer you the Detail of That Affair, but Sir the End of Thus Arrogantly Quoteing My Self is as Follows.

Sir, The Whigs are weak; they may be Mannag'd, and Allways have been So. What Ever you do, if Possible Divide Them, and they are Easy To be Divided. Caress The Fools of Them Most, There are Enough Among Them. Buy Them with here and There a Place; it may be well bestow'd.

If you have him Not allready, as all I Can Talk with That are

---

[1] The Dissenters.
[2] Defoe had given Harley this counsel before (p. 32).

Friends *Wish* you had, My Ld Somers,[1] who all allow to be a great Man, Must if Gaind From Them, weaken and Distract the Party.

Such a Man Can Not be bought too Dear, and if Gaind Entirely would Secure your Intrest.

Tis Pitty Two Such Men should Not Understand One Another (if it be So). *United*, what may you Not do! *Divided*, what Mischiefs Must Ensue to both, and the Nation in Generall!

Sir, I Humbly Entreat your Accepting These hints. Tis my Fear of a Conjunction of Extreams, which are Doubled from The Connexion of what I hear Abroad and what you observ'd. They Talk of This Conjunction as of a Thing done, and you would wonder at the Follys and hopes Some Weak People Discover at This Novelty.

I have had Some Thoughts, Tho' it be but a Project, That the bringing an Occasionall Bill upon The Anvill in Such a juncture would be of the last Service in This Case. Twould break the Confederacy,[2] Twould blacken, and Expose The Party, yours Are Sure of giveing it a Toss at last, and There are a Croud of Present Advantages to be Made of it.

To bring it in by Trusty hands,[3] and blast it at last, would Confound the Thing it Self, Ruine all the Confederacy, Brand the Party with the Scandall of Opposeing the Queen, and breaking their Promise in The Address;[4] Twould Sink Their Character, and They would go home with Such a Fame, as would Cause Fewer of The Same Men to Come back Again Next session than may otherwise be Expected.[5]

These Two Things have Layn So Strongly on my Thoughts, allways Employ'd and Sollicitous to Serve your Intrest, That I Could Not Satisfye my Self without giveing you the Trouble of Peruseing Them, and Pardon me Sir if I Say, I Think I write

---

[1] John Somers (1651–1716), Baron Somers, member of the Whig Junto and former Lord Chancellor, was at this time in retirement. The Queen did not like Somers, and he did not enter the Cabinet until 1708.

[2] That is, the threatened alliance of Whigs and Tories. The Whigs, part of whose political strength lay in the support they received from the Dissenters, would not now have been willing to alienate the latter by endorsing the Tories' favourite Bill, coalition or no coalition. Seven years later, however, the Whigs did join the Tories in passing an act prohibiting occasional conformity.

[3] The Bill was brought in during this session, but by high Tories rather than by any 'Trusty hands' selected by the Ministry. See Keith Feiling, *History of the Tory Party*, Oxford, 1924, p. 376.

[4] In their Address of 30 Oct., the Commons had assured the Queen that they would avoid division and contention (*Parliamentary History*, vi. 357).

[5] A general election was to take place in the following summer.

of Them with More Earnestness and Concern, Than I Should If I were Petitioning you for a Repriev from the Gallows.

I Beseech you Sir, Place it all To the Account of my Zeal to Serve you, and to Prevent if Possible a Publick Disaster to the Nation, which I Think must be the Consequence of a blow to your Present Greatness and Conduct, to whom we all Owe Much of, if not all the Present Prosperity of England.

I have Some Subsequent Thoughts On This Subject, which if This Pleases you you May Command at a Word, as you all-ways May

Sir, Your Most Obedient Servt
[symbol]

Nov. 2. 1704

MS.: Duke of Portland, Defoe Papers, 1 ff. 22–24. *Pub.*: *H.M.C. Portland*, iv. 146–9. *Address*: none.

23. JOHN FRANSHAM *to* DEFOE. *10 November 1704*

Sir

It was with no small Sattisfaction that I read your Justification in your Review[1] which I doubt not on the other hand prov'd as great a Mortification to Dyer. I read it to several Gentlemen (before I receiv'd your Letter) in the chief Coffee-house here where we have it as oft as it comes out and is approv'd of as the politest paper we have to entertain us with. I had some difficulty to prevail with the Master of the house[2] to take it in but now he finds I advis'd him well there being no paper more desir'd. If there be any that you have a mind to convey to Norwich if it be left at my Bro: Franshams and you let me know I'll take care to have it down.

Dyer lets us know yesterday that the Observator was found Guilty[3] and hopes that he will be exemplarily punish'd but were there such scales as could weigh Incendiaries exactly into which put a Tutchin in one scale and a Dyer in the other and I doubt not 'twould appear that the lowest scale contain'd the lightest man.

I have nothing of news to impart but only that 2 or 3 nights since one of our worthy Justices being at the Coffee-house above nam'd was inform'd by some of the company that there was a

---

[1] See the *Review*, 4 and 7 Nov. 1704.
[2] Identified as 'Mr. Brady' in Norgate's note.
[3] On 4 Nov. John Tutchin had been found guilty of reflecting upon the Ministry in his *Observator* (Luttrell, *Brief Relation*, v. 484).

very topping address in the Gazet from Marlborough.¹ Ay quoth the Justice has the Duke sent an address? Pray Mr M . . . I see you have got the Gazet in your hand be so kind as to read me the Dukes address. The Gentleman pursuant to his request read (without the Title, to humour the mistake) the address from Malbrough, which done his worship said twas a fine address truly, and so (to the great sattisfaction of the company) went away with the opinion that it was sent by the Duke notwithstanding the many high encomiums given his Grace therein. I write you this story not as a subject for your Society² to discant upon but only to afford you some diversion in your privet conversation, and whenever your multiplicity of business will permit you to make returns of like nature they will be gladly receiv'd by

Sir yours &c.
J. F.

Norwch Nov. 10, 1704

MS.: untraced. *Pub.*: Francis Norgate, 'Correspondence between De Foe and John Fransham, of Norwich', *Notes and Queries*, 5 S, iii (1875), 261. *Address*: none recorded.

24. *To* JOHN FRANSHAM. [*2 December 1704*]³

Mr. Fransham,

I can now tell you that the dead doing Tool of Occasional Conformity having been brought into the House on Thursday was sevennight last⁴ rec'd on Tuesday a fatal blow in the House of Commons by being offer'd to be consolidated or tack'd as they call it to the Land Tax Bill, which notwithstanding a very great struggle was carried in the negative by 117 voices.⁵ It has

---

¹ That is, from the town of Marlborough, Wilts. See the *London Gazette*, 30 Oct. 1704.
² That is, the 'Scandalous Club', to whose supposed proceedings a part of each *Review* was at present being given. Defoe embellished Fransham's story with details and political implications, and published it in the *Review* for 2 Dec. 1704.
³ Although Wright (*Life* [1931], p. 111) assigns this letter to 'about 18 November', the allusion in the last paragraph to 'the Review of today' clearly establishes the date as 2 Dec.   ⁴ i.e. a week ago.
⁵ In two previous sessions the Occasional Conformity Bill had passed the Commons only to be rejected by the Lords. This time the Tory managers proposed to tack it to the Land Tax Bill in the belief that the Lords, rather than throw out the war taxes, would pass the two together. But the Tackers were defeated in their own Commons, which rejected their plan 251 votes to 134. See G. M. Trevelyan, *Ramillies and the Union with Scotland*, 1932, pp. 14–15.

been to-day before the House as a Bill,[1] and they have made some amendments to it, but we are in hopes that it has had a Death's wound in the last Stroke. Last week I rallied some Forces against it and brought out some thoughts on that subject in print.[2] I have sent about 25 of them to you and should be glad to hear how our Friends approve it. I have not done this that I would impose any thing of mine on you, but as my purpose of writing is to furnish our Friends with arguments to defend the cause against a clamorous noisy Enemy, so it must be necessary that they should see them as much as possible, and for this purpose we are establishing a method to send them in small parcels amongst Friends all over England.[3] And yet I am so far from making a profit of it that if any are so poor as not to afford it or too narrow spirited to spare 6*d*. I am very free to give them to such rather than they should not be improv'd by any thing I am able to do, and you have my free consent to give them to any body you think fit. I wish I could afford to print twenty thousand of these and give them all over the nation.

If you approve the method and think it worth while you shall have a parcel like this or a few over or under always sent you when I do any thing I think worth your while.

I have now in hand a small piece[4] against Sir Humphrey Mackworth's Bill for employing the poor, which unless you contradict I'll send you some of, because it concerns you all as Manufacturers and employers and it is fit when you are to be ruin'd you should know it.

In the Review of today you will find the story of the Justice of peace who thought the Malbrough address was by the Duke. I wish you would send me his name and the story at large. I hope 'tis told to your Sattisfaction. Pray let me know if you receiv'd the Books.

I am, Sir, your sincere Friend
DE FOE

MS.: untraced. *Pub.*: Francis Norgate, 'Correspondence between De Foe and John Fransham, of Norwich', *Notes and Queries*, 5 S, iii (1875), 261–2. *Address*: none recorded.

[1] Although the motion to tack had failed, the Occasional Conformity Bill was immediately reintroduced in the Commons. It passed that House but was defeated, as usual, in the Lords (G. M. Trevelyan, op. cit., p. 16).

[2] *Queries upon the Bill against Occasional Conformity*.

[3] See No. 46 for an example of such distribution.

[4] *Giving Alms No Charity*, an attack on Mackworth's plan to set up parochial factories, supported out of public funds, for the employment of the poor. Defoe believed the idea economically unsound.

25. [*To* THE SELECT COMMITTEE OF THE HOUSE OF LORDS] [*c. 30 January 1704/5*]

Of The Seamen[1]

Humbly Craveing your Lordships Pardon if I mistake, I Presume your Lordships Commands are Included in The Following Question, Vizt

How May the Fleet be Mann'd, without the Delays, Expence, Violences, and Other Intollerable Inconveniences of Impressing Seamen?

It is my Humble Opinion, That Searching for the Causes of This Evill will Imediately Direct to the Cure.

The True, and Originall Causes of the Scarcity of, or rather the Difficulty in Procureing, Seamen, Are These Two.

[1] The Navy had not at this point distinguished itself in the war, either in combating the enemy's fleets or in protecting English merchant shipping. One reason for this indifferent showing was the scarcity of seamen to man the warships, a difficulty that was now grave but by no means new. Defoe had examined that problem back in King William's time, and had published his solution, substantially the same as that given here, in his *Essay upon Projects*, 1697 (pp. 312–34). In the *Review* for 13 Jan. 1704–5 he repeated his basic argument, that the way to man the fleet was not through impressment, which was both evil and inefficient, but rather by cutting the 'extravagant wages' whereby the merchant shippers were at present enticing seamen who might otherwise be willing to serve in the Navy. He could, he said, easily prescribe a method whereby the wage differential would be adjusted, impressment of seamen abandoned, the fleet fully manned, waste of time and money prevented, and, incidentally, the price of coal reduced in London. And in the following issue (16 Jan.) he offered to make available his scheme and to accept exile if it did not work.

These confident statements soon came to the attention of an interested body, the Select Committee of the House of Lords which was just then investigating the deficiencies of the Navy. On 25 Jan. the Committee summoned 'Daniel Du Foy' and directed that he submit his proposal in writing on 30 Jan. On 10 Feb. the Duke of Bolton read Defoe's communication before the Committee, after which Defoe was summoned, asked to write out the details of his scheme in a supplementary report, and informed that the whole matter would be laid before Prince George, Lord High Admiral. On 3 Mar. Bolton, 'acquainting the Committee that Mr De Foe desired in reguard the Session was like to be short that he might have time till the next meeting of the Parlt to prepare the schemes lately proposed by him, It is Ordered that Mr D'Foe doe agst the next Session prepare the Schemes he proposed for the more effectual manning the Fleet' (Minutes of Committees, 24 Oct. 1704 to 5 Apr. 1710, House of Lords, MS. 2058).

Here the matter seems to have dropped. Twenty-three years later, in a pamphlet renewing the proposal, Defoe wrote that at one time it 'went so far as to be thought worth considering of by his Royal Highness Prince *George*, then High-Admiral, and to be laid before a Committee of Parliament', but that 'it was at last declined only upon some Scruples about Liberty and Compulsion, which some nice People, who have got over all these Difficulties in other Cases not less dangerous, pretended to raise. Upon this Foot, I say, it was laid aside, (not rejected) and had the Prince lived a little longer would, I believe, have been brought to be practicable' (*Some Considerations on the Reasonableness and Necessity of Encreasing and Encouraging the Seamen*, 1728, pp. 35 and 38).

73

1. The Exorbitant, Unreasonable, and in All Respects Disproportion'd wages given to Sailors, in the Service of The Merchant.
2. Want of Some Due Measures to Procure Able bodyed Land men, on any Emergency of State, to Embrace Willingly the Service, and Thereby Encrease the Number of Seamen in Time of war.

The first of these I Humbly Think to be the True, and Perhaps the Onely Reason, why Our Seamen Skulk, and hide Themselves from the Publick Service; Since it can not be Expected The Sailors Should Covet to Serv the Queen at 23*s* Per Month, when at The Same time, they can have 55*s* Per Month in The Service of The Merchant.

This Premis'd I humbly Propose

That an Act to Limit the Wages of Seamen in The Service of the Merchant May be Past, wherein a Fixt Rate of Wages Per Month, where the Custome of Trade is to Sail Per the Month, and Per the Voiage where they Sail by the Voiage, and Per Share, where the Sailors are paid by the Share, may be Appointed, Proportion'd to, and Limited by the Rates Now paid by her Majtie in the Navy, Or as Near Thereto as to your Lordships Shall Seem Convenient, with Stated Penaltyes both to Masters, Owners or Seamen, who Shall give or Take beyond it.

If your Lordships Command me to Lay before you, any Reasonings on the Perticulars; or Schemes for the Performing this; your Orders Shall be Readily Obey'd; The Proposer Not Presumeing to offer Those things without your Lordships speciall Directions.

For the Supplying with Land men on any Emergency of The State, The Proposer Humbly represents:

That the Act of Parliament Empowring the Civil Magistrate to List or Enter men into the Service, has this Defect in it.

That Many Thousands of Able body'd men, Proper Subjects for That act and Perhaps Enclin'd Enough to the Service, are hindred from Entring or at Least are not oblig'd to Enter as the Law Directs, The Church wardens, Overseers &c. Screening them from the Law, to prevent Their wives and Children becoming Chargeable to The Parish.

To Rectifye This the Proposer humbly Offers,

That a Clause be brought in, Empowring The Proper officers of Every Parish in Case any Man Shall Voluntarily Enter him-

74

self into The Service, who has a family in The said Parish, to Take Such care of, and make Such allowance to Their Said Familyes, as shall be Thought fitt by your Lordships Dureing Such time as the Said Person Continues in her Majties Service, the Same to be Repaid Out of the Treasury of the Navy, or allow'd on Their Taxes, and Discounted Out of the Pay of the Person So Serving.

And The Said Paymt or Such other Pension or Allowance as Shall be Thought fitt, and for as Long Time to be Continued to the Said Family in Case The Man should Lose his life, in The Said Service.[1]

This tis Presum'd will not Onely Encourage Great Numbers to List, but will Remove the Obstruction, which Now prevents the Parish Officers Marking Out those That are Proper, and Some Methods for the Makeing this yet more Effectual shall be Laid before your Lordships if your Commands Require Them.

By This Method the Proposer Humbly Supposes, at least Ten Thousand able body'd Land men may be Rais'd, on Any Emergency for the Publick Occasion without Force, Charge, or Oppression.[2]

Another Method Every way as Certain and in all its Parts Superiour to any yet Practis'd Either here Or Abroad is as Follows

By an Act to Cause all the Seamen in England at Once to be Entred into the Publick Service, and Imediate Pay.

Under This Regulation The proposer Offers to Satisfye your Lordships,

1. The Navy Shall at any Time be Compleatly Mann'd at a months Notice, all the Seamen in the Nation being at Command, and Easy to be Found.
2. The Merchant Never be Delay'd.
3. Trade Never Opprest.
4. Exorbitant wages Effectually Supprest.
5. Seamen Entring into Forreign Service Prevented.
6. The Merchants be gainers.

---

[1] Defoe was half a century ahead of his time. Pensions for the dependents of deceased seamen were not provided until 1747, and allowances for the families of men absent on sea-duty were not possible until 1758. See W. L. Clowes, *The Royal Navy*, 1897–1903, iii. 18.

[2] The foregoing portion of this communication covers three pages, and is separated from what follows by three blank pages. These six pages have been folded together and bear their own endorsement: 'Mr De Foe's Proposals, Read 10⁰ February 1704.'

7. The Seamen be Pleas'd and Thankfull.

8. A Large Summe of Money Rais'd annually for The service of the Govornment.

The Clauses of This Regulation are too Many to Trouble your Lordships with here.

An Abstract of Them the Proposer humbly Presents, and shall at any Time be Ready on your Lordships Commands to Enter on the Perticulars.

1 That In Proper Offices in Every Port, and Subjected to the Same Powers now Employ'd, all the Seamen or Seafareing Men in the Nation be Imediately Listed or Entred into the Queens Pay, in Classes, and Degrees, according to the usage of the Navy.

2 That They shall all Reciev half Pay when Out of Employmt: 23*s* Per Month in her Majties Service, 26*s* Per Month in the Merchants Service, 36*s* Per Voiage to Newcastle, and Proportion'd Rates for other Voiages, and [ ]*s*[1] Per Month half Pay, or other Rates as to your Ldships shall Seem fitt.

3 That the Same Provision be made For Seamen Maim'd in the Service of the Merchant as in her Majties Service.

That No Man Presume to hire, Employ, or Carry to Sea, any man as a Sailor, but what he shall Reciev from the Proper officers Appointed.

That the Mercht, Masters, &ca shall Reciev any Number of Men they want at 8 Dayes Demand, with Liberty of Choice, and Refuseing; showing Reasons for it; without Delay, Fee, Payment, or any Manner of Consideration.

That the Merchant Shall Pay The Govornmt Not the Seamen, and the Seamen be paid by the Govornmt.

In Time of war the Mercht To Pay the Govornmt 30*s* Per Month for able Seamen, and No More, the Overplus of 4*s* Per Month to be Reserv'd to make good the half Pay.

A Table of Regulations, Differences, Avarages, stoppage of Pay, Methods of Discharge, Rules of Subordination, allowance to seamen Abroad, orders for Dissmiss of Men at Delivring Ports, Tradeing Voiages, Rules for the seamen, in Case of the Loss of ships abroad, and all the Proper Niceties of Trade, in Such Cases: The Proposer shall be Ready to Offer to your Lordships when Ever your Commands shall Require it.

The Summs the Govornment Shall Save are So Great, and will be So Easily Paid, and So willingly by The Mercht, that

[1] Left blank in MS.

No Proposall on Our Marine affaires can Equall: the Perticulars whereof I am Ready to Offer, when Ever your Lordships Think Fitt.

By This Proposall the Tax to be Levy'd, will be Easy, because all that Pay it will be gainers, and all the advantages Proposed will be Gain'd Out of the Present Exorbitant wages of Seamen, which is Now the Great and most Destructive burthen of Trade, and which Costs This Nation at This Time above a Million Per Annum.

Of The Coal Trade

The Extravagant Price of Coals is Not Occasion'd as Some Imagin from Engrossments of Merchants, Pressing Their Men, or Private Combination among the Owners, but from the Excessive Rate of Wages given The Seamen.

This Indeed has its foundation in the Length of the Voiage, and That in the Danger of the Passage, which Obliges the Colliers to wait for Convoys, Stay to go in fleets, Companies, and the like.

This I Humbly Propose may be Cur'd by a Generall Assureance on the wholl Colliery, and The scheme of Which when Ever your Lordships please to Command it, shall Make it Appear, That for The small Premio of One Per Cent, The wholl Colliery May be Assur'd, Either by The Queen or by Private hands, The assurers to find the Necessary Convoys, and So Guard the Passage, That the Coliers may Run Single, as in Times of Peace, and Coles be Near as Cheap in The Pool as in Time of Peace, and the assured to be paid all losses, by an Imediate Method without Delays or Deduction.

All which is humbly Submitted to your Lordships
May it Please your Lordships
By your Most Obedt Servt
D E   F O E

MS.: House of Lords, 2058 (ak). *Pub.*: *Manuscripts of the House of Lords, 1704–1706*, 1912, pp. 223–6. *Address*: none. *Endorsed*: 'Mr De Foes Proposals, Read 10° February 1704' and '10 Febry 1704, Mr De Foes Proposal.'

26. [JOHN RELFE][1] *to* DEFOE. *3 March 1704/5*

Sir

His Grace the D[uke] of Bolt[on] haveing this Day acquainted the Lds Committees appointed to consider the state of the Nation in relation to Naval Affairs that you desired, in reguard the session is like to be short, that you might be allowed time till the next meeting of the Parlt, to prepare the Schemes lately proposed by you to their Ldpps, for the more effectual maning Her Matyes Navy, their Ldpps ordered you should be allowed the time desired, and His Grace the D of B commanded me to acquaint you therwith.

I am, Sir, Your

3 March 1704[2]

MS.: draft, House of Lords, 2058 (al). Hitherto unpublished, but noted in *Manuscripts of the House of Lords, 1704–1706*, 1912, p. 226. *Address*: 'for Mr De Foe.'

27. *To* JOHN RELFE. *9 March 1704/5*

Mr John Relf

According to your Request by The Messengr who brought an Ordr of the house of Lords for me to Mr Nutts,[3] I send you This to Signifye I have Recd The Said Ordr Importing That Their Ldships are pleasd to Ordr me to Prepare the schemes I have proposd to The Lords Committees for the more Effectuall Manning her Majties Navy, Against Next session of Parliament, which I shall Carefully Obey.

Your Humble Servt
DANIEL DE FOE

March. 9. 1704

MS.: House of Lords, 2058 (am). *Pub.*: *Manuscripts of the House of Lords, 1704–1706*, 1912, p. 226. *Address*: 'To Mr John Relfe, Present, March 9. 11 a Clock, At the House of Peers.'

[1] Relfe, to whom Defoe addressed the answer to this letter, was usher to the House of Lords (Luttrell, *Brief Relation*, v. 108).
[2] The draft is so dated, but the minutes to which the draft is pinned say: 'Memo that on the 7th March the D of Bolton commanded me to acquaint Mr De Foe by letter and not by order that his desire was granted, which I accordingly did by Mr Davis senior' (Minutes of Committees, 24 Oct. 1704 to 5 Apr. 1710, House of Lords, MS. 2058). Perhaps the draft was prepared on the 3rd and the letter not ordered to be sent until the 7th. Defoe replied on the 9th.
[3] John Nutt was one of Defoe's publishers.

28. JOHN FRANSHAM[1] *to* DEFOE. *29 March 1705*

Mr De Foe,

The cause of my present writing is this, a Gentleman of our Town and a great admirer of your Writings obtein'd of me sometime since a promise of sending you a Letter by him at his next going to London, for which place he sets out this day and carry's with him accordingly such a Letter which he is pleas'd to call his credentials which he'll deliver into your hands if you'll be pleas'd to direct a penny post Letter to him at the 4 Swans in Bishopgate Street where he lodges or at the Gàrter Coffee house behind the Exchange where he is 2 or 3 times a day, and in it let him know where he shall meet you any day near Change, or if it suits not your convenience there any where else you shall name.

And now to make his company the more acceptable to you (which his own merit would sufficiently do by a little acquaintance) I shall give you a brief character of him, with a short history of what has been and is still transacting in our Town relating to him.

His name is Thomas Dunch, a Wine Merchant, a person of clear Ideas, a member of the Church of England, and in fine so staunch a Whigg as to be accounted the Head of that Interest here by the Tory's who for that reason only have acted in that unaccountable manner as follows.

He was upon the 14th Instant by the Freemen of the Ward put up one of the Candidates for Alderman, the other was one of our present Sherifs. The first had the Majority of 21 Votes, yet was a Scrutiny demanded & granted which being gone through Mr Dunches Majority was thereby increas'd notwithstanding which the Jack-Daw-Gentlemen of the Court were so affraid of admitting him that they refus'd to swear him on his demand to be sworn, and to justify their arbitrariness pretended to bring presidents (even less to the purpose than the Commons were relating to the Ailesbury men)[2] to shew that if the Court did not approve of the Freemens choise they could order them to proceed to a new Election. When these presidents and power came to be examined into they appear'd to be founded on some

---

[1] See p. 64, n. 2.
[2] The celebrated Aylesbury election dispute was the biggest news of the day, and had at this time risen to such a pitch that the two Houses of Parliament were close to 'open and violent conflict'. See G. M. Trevelyan, *Ramillies and the Union with Scotland*, 1932, pp. 24–25.

obsolete charters but totally destroy'd by our last which it
seems expressly says That upon the death of an Alderman the
Freemen of the Ward to which he belong'd shall by the Mayor
be requir'd to proceed to a new Election and the person elected
by the Majority shall be sworn Alderman for Life. Yet these
Gentlemen particularly the Mayor and the other Sherif (who
is said to have the whole management of him) have thought fit
to enter Mr Dunch (thus duly elected) in their Book as a person
Contentious, Seditious and pernicious and therefore not fit to
be admitted amongst such Men of Peace and Moderation, so
that he is now gone up an elected but unsworn Alderman.
What he has farther to do he knows best.[1]

I thought it proper to give you this brief account of this
Gentlemans affair not knowing but it might prove a subject
in your conversation and for that reason you'll pardon the
prolixity of

Sir yours &c.,
J. F.

Norwch March 29th 1705

P.S.—If I have misstated the case in any particular (as I do
not know I have) upon reading it to Mr. Dunch if there be
occasion he will set it right.

MS.: untraced. *Pub.*: Francis Norgate, 'Correspondence between De Foe
and John Fransham, of Norwich', *Notes and Queries*, 5 S, iii (1875), 262–3.
Address: none recorded.

29. JOHN FRANSHAM *to* DEFOE. [*c. 29 March 1705*]

Mr De Foe,

The Gentleman[2] who delivers you this Letter would have it
of me under the notion of a credential, but you that read Mankind so much will by a little conversation quickly perceive that
he's a person that wants no recommendation. His Merit is
not like that of the Occasionall Conformity Bill, it wants no
crutches,[3] his Character I have allready acquainted you with
and therefore need nothing farther than to wish you an agree-

---

[1] Defoe reported the case in detail a year later (*Review*, 11 Apr. 1706). See also
P.R.O., S.P. 34/6/49 *et seq.*
[2] Thomas Dunch (see the preceding letter).
[3] An allusion to 'the Tack' of the previous Nov. See p. 71, n. 4.

able conversation which knowing both the Gentlemen so well
is not the least doubted by

Sir yours &c.,

J. F.

MS.: untraced. *Pub.*: Francis Norgate, 'Correspondence between De Foe
and John Fransham, of Norwich', *Notes and Queries*, 5 S, iii (1875), 263.
Address: none recorded.

30. *To* CHARLES MONTAGU, BARON HALIFAX.[1]
5 April 1705

My Lord
 I Most humbly Thank your Lordship for Expressions of your
favour and Goodness which I had as Little Reason to Expect
from your Ldship as I have Capascity to Merit.
 My Ld Treasurr has frequently Express't himself with Concern on my behalf, and Mr Secretary Harley The like, But I
my Ld Am like the Cripple at the Pool, when the Moment
happen'd No Man was at hand to put the Wretch into the
water, and My Talent of Sollicitation is absolutely a Cripple,
and Unquallifyed to help it Self:
 I wish your Lordship Could Understand by my Imperfect
Expressions the Sence I have of your Unexpected Goodness,
in Mentioning me to My Ld Treasurer.[2] I Could be Very well
pleas'd to wait, Till your Merit and the Nations want of you,
Shall place your Lordship in that Part of the Publick affaires,
where I might Owe any benefitt I shall Reciev from it, to your
Goodness; and Might be able to act something for your Service,
as well as that of the Publick.
 My Ld The Proposall your Lordship was pleas'd to make by
my Brother[3] the bearer, is Exceeding Pleasant to me to Perform, as well as usefull to be done, agreeable to Every Thing the
Masterly Genius of your Lordship has Produc'd in This Age;
But my Missfortune is, the bearer, whose head is not That way,
has given me So Imperfect an Account, That Makes me your

---

[1] Charles Montagu (1661–1715), Baron Halifax, later Earl of Halifax, was one
of the ablest Lords of the Whig Junto and had enjoyed a brilliant public career
during the late reign, but now, like the rest of the Junto, was in comparative eclipse.
He had recently been impeached, though unsuccessfully, by the Tory Commons,
and had been dropped from the Privy Council. But his voice was still powerful in
the Lords, and the moderate Ministry was slowly beginning to move towards an
understanding with his Party.
[2] The nature of Halifax's good offices is not known.
[3] Robert Davis, Defoe's brother-in-law.

Lordships most humble Petitioner for Some hints to Ground my Observations Upon.[1]

I was wholly Ignorant of the Design of that act, Not knowing it had Such a Noble Originall.

Pardon my Importunate Application to your Ldship, for Some hints of the Substance, and Design of that act, and if your Ldship Please the Names Again of Some books which my Dull Messengr forgott, and which your Lordship was Pleas'd to Say had spoke to This head.

I The Rather Press your Ldship on This head, because The Very Next Article which of Course I Proposed to Enter upon in *the Review* being that of Paper Credit, I shall at Once do my Self the honour to Obey your Lordships Dictate, and Observe the stated Order of The Discourse I am Upon.[2]

I Shall not Presume to offer it against your Lordships Opinion, and would be farthest of all from Exposeing your Lordship to any Tongues, but if Ever your Lordship shall Think this Despicable Thing, who scorn'd to Come Out of Newgate at the Price of betraying a Dead Master,[3] or Discovring those Things which No body would ha' been the worse For, fitt to be Trusted in your Presence, Tho' Never so Much Incognito, He will Certainly, Exclusive of what he may Comunicate to your Lordship for the Publick Service, Recieve from you Such Instructions as are Suitable to your known Genius, and The Benefitt of This Nation.

I have herewith Sent your Lordship Another book.[4] I kno' your Lordship has but a Few Minutes to spare, but I am your Ldship humble Petitioner, to bestow an hour on its Contents, because it is likely to Make Some Noise in the World, and perhaps to Come before your Lordship in Parliamt.

I Forbear to Divert your More Serious Thoughts with perti-

---

[1] Although Defoe's circumspection conceals the nature of Halifax's proposal, it appears from what follows farther on that Defoe was being asked to support the 'Act for giving like remedy upon promissory notes as is now used upon bills of exchange' (*J.H.L.* xvii. 645, 660, 664, and 717).

[2] Two weeks later he announced that in due course the *Review* would examine the subject of credit and that 'the late Act of Parliament for the Currency and Regulation of Promissory Notes [would] be Examined; [and] the Extensive Benefit of it Explain'd' (*Review*, 19 Apr. 1705). But he did not get round to the subject until the following January, and by then could say only that the Act, though it 'came from a Noble Hand', had proved ineffective (*Review*, 12 Jan. 1705/6).

[3] King William, under whom both Defoe and Halifax had known happier days, and the secrets of whose Whig Government Defoe had refused to reveal to Nottingham. See Sutherland, *Defoe*, pp. 49 and 93.

[4] Probably *The Consolidator*, which Defoe advertised as 'Just Published' in the *Review* for 26 Mar.

culars. I humbly Thank your Ldship for the freedome of Access you were Pleasd to give my Messenger; and am Extreamly ambitious of Listing my Self Under your Lordship, in That Cause, in which your Lordship was Allwayes Embarkt, Vizt of Truth and Liberty.

> I am, May it Please your Ldship
> Your Ldships Most Humble and Obedt Sert
> D Foe

Aprll 5. 1705

MS.: Brit. Mus., Add. MSS. 7121 ff. 23–24. *Pub.*: Sir Henry Ellis, *Original Letters of Eminent Literary Men of the Sixteenth, Seventeenth, and Eighteenth Centuries*, 1843, pp. 321–2. *Address*: 'To The Right Honble The Ld Hallifax, Humbly Present.' *Endorsed*: 'De Foe, April 5 1705.'

31. JOHN FRANSHAM *to* DEFOE. [*c. 5 April 1705*][1]

Mr De Foe,

Your Consolidator[2] (which I could have wish'd much longer) I have just now got through, which contains (according to the opinion of a high *Solunarian*[3] Gentleman I had some discourse with about it) too much Wit for Mr De Foe to be the author of it; he will have it wrote by a Genius superior to any *Crolians*,[4] which shews that let a man be never so great a Bigot to his party let him but have a Tast of starling sence and ingenuity such a one must be forc'd to confess that it abounds with masterly strokes of both. I thought to have proceeded no farther in relation to this Book, but can't forbear telling you one Instance more of the approbation it met with here. Another Gentleman of my acquaintance said he was so well pleas'd with reading it that he would have gone through had it contein'd as much as Fox's 3 Volumes.[5]

I receiv'd as mention'd in yours 6 of them, 12 of Gill's case and 24 of the Supplements.[6]

---

[1] This letter is undated, but the *Review* 'of this day' mentioned towards the end can be identified as that for 3 Apr. and Fransham could have been reading his copy in Norwich on about the 5th.

[2] *The Consolidator, or Memoirs of Sundry Transactions from the World in the Moon* had been published on 26 Mar. (*Review*, 27 Mar. 1705.)

[3] In *The Consolidator*, the Solunarians represented men of the Church of England.

[4] The allegorical name for the Dissenters in *The Consolidator*.

[5] John Foxe, *Acts and Monuments*.

[6] That is, 6 copies of *The Consolidator*, 12 copies of *The Experiment: or, the Shortest Way with the Dissenters Exemplified. Being the case of Mr. Abraham Gill, a Dissenting Minister in the Isle of Ely* ('just published' according to the *Review* of 7 Apr.), and 24 copies of the Dec. *Supplement* to the *Review*, which had appeared belatedly on 10 Mar. 1704–5 (see the *Review* of that date).

Gill's case you perceive by my last[1] I had read before yours arriv'd and had given such a representation thereof to some topping Dissenters that they were very glad to hear I had some coming to dispose of amongst them.

The Bearer of this was very desirous of having charge of it; all that I can say to recommend him to you is that I believe he is a very honest man, and one that has as great a value for the memory of King William as any man in the kingdom, and that he is one of the Subscribers for *Jure Divino* and the Review. That of this day concerning persons born deaf I cannot subscribe to.[2] I wish you had the convincing of me by word of mouth, till which time I shall not think of entring the argument.

You have follow'd the Heels of Truth so close in your Consolidator that the danger of a kick[3] gave some pain to

Sir yours &c.

J. F.

MS.: untraced. *Pub.*: Francis Norgate, 'Correspondence between De Foe and John Fransham, of Norwich', *Notes and Queries*, 5 S, iii (1875), 282. *Address*: none recorded.

32. *To* JOHN FRANSHAM. [*c. 1 May 1705*][4]

Sir,

I have your obligeing Letter. You can give me no greater pleasure than to hear that any thing I can do or have done in this world is usefull and helps to forward that good which every honest man ought to wish and which I believe I was brought into the world and am suffer'd to live in it only to perform.

This is the Token for good to me that the work I am upon is of him whose immediate hand by wonderful steps have led me through Wildernesses of Troubles and Mountains of popular Fury to see this day in which I may in some way or other honour him whose cause I espouse, and who is the support of that Truth and peace of which I am the mean and unworthy advocate.

---

[1] The letter here referred to is missing.

[2] See the issue for 3 Apr. 1705.

[3] Fransham is echoing Defoe's 'If I can therefore follow Truth close at the Heels, without a kick in the Face, 'twill be well; if I can't, I see no Remedy, I must venture' (*Review*, 29 June 1704).

[4] This undated letter appears to answer Fransham's of *c*. 5 Apr. and to refer to the *Review* for 1 May.

I am still farther delighted in observing by what secret steps in his providence he has furnish'd me with or directed me to such sincere propagators of this blessed work as you are whose hearts he have touch'd with a sence of the obligation we have all upon us to assist in the establishment of his Interest in the world.

This is the glory of his infinite Wisdom that brings to pass the great ends appointed by his foreknowledge by the agency of us his most despicable Instruments and the interposition of the minutest Circumstances.

To him be all the praise both of his own work and our little, little, very little share in it, and let the success of his service encourage all the Lovers of Truth to stand up for the Lord against the Mighty, who knows but now is the day of our deliverance.

As to the contents of your Letter, I am glad you receiv'd the several parcels, but I hear not whether 100 Reviews sent you every time since according to your order came to hand.

I thank your care about the Jure Divino money, and by the Review of to day you will see in what forwardness it is.[1]

There is a paper come out weekly call'd Truth & Honesty, in which if you think fit the story of your Mayor may be inserted, and I can manage it there.[2]

I am your Sincere Friend
D. F.

I hope to day's Review will please you.[3]

MS.: untraced. *Pub.*: Francis Norgate, 'Correspondence between De Foe and John Fransham, of Norwich', *Notes and Queries*, 5 S, iii (1875), 262. *Address*: none recorded.

33. *To* CHARLES MONTAGU, BARON HALIFAX.
[*Early summer, 1705?*][4]

Pardon Me my Lord

If to a Man that has Seen Nothing for Some yeares, but The Rough face of Things, The Exceeding goodness of your Lordsps

[1] The *Review* for 1 May announced that *Jure Divino* was 'now in the Press, and shall go on to be Printed with all Expedition'. It did not appear, however, until July 1706.

[2] The story appears under the heading 'Resolutions upon the present Posture of Affairs by TRUTH and HONESTY', in the *London Post* for 14 May 1705.

[3] The issue for 1 May denounces the Tackers.

[4] Although this undated letter has hitherto been considered of later date than No. 38, also to Halifax, to which it is related, I have here placed it earlier. Comparison with No. 38 will show that the present letter, so profuse in its expressions of gratitude for the mysterious 'bounty', must have preceded the other, which, while mentioning the gift, is hardly likely to have been Defoe's first acknowledgement of it.

discourse Softn'd me Even to a Weakness, I Could Not Conceal.

'Tis a Novelty my Lord, I have Not been Us'd to, to Reciev Obligations from Persons of your Lordships Character and Merit, Nor indeed from any Part of the World, And the Return is a Task too hard for me to Undertake.

I am (My Lord) a Plain and Unpolish'd Man, and Perfectly Unquallify'd to Make formall Acknowledgements, and a Temper Sour'd by a Series of Afflictions, Rendres me Still the More Awkward in the Recd Method of Common Gratitude, I Mean the Ceremony of Thanks.

But My Ld if to be Encourag'd in giveing my Self up to That Service your Lordship is pleas'd So Much to Overvallue, if Goeing On with the More Cheerfullness in being usefull to and promoteing the Generall Peace and Intrest of this Nation; If to the Last Vigorously Opposeing a Stupid, Distracted Party, that are for Ruining themselves Rather than not Destroy Their Neighbours, If This be to Merit So Much Regard, your Lordship binds me in The Most Durable, and to me the Most pleasant Engagement in the World, because 'tis a Service that with my Gratitude to your Lordship, keeps an Exact Unison with my Reason, my Principle, My Inclination, and The Duty Every Man Owes to his Country, and his Posterity.

Thus My Lord Heavenly Bounty Engages Mankind, while The Commands are So far from being Grievous, that at the Same time we Obey we promote Our Own Felicity, and Joyn The Reward to the Duty.

As to the Exceeding Bounty I have now Recd, and which your Lordship Obliges me to Reserv my Acknowlegemts of For a yet Unknown Benefactor, Pardon me My Ld to believ your Lordships favour to me has at Least So much share in the Conduct of it, if Not in the Substance, that I am Perswaded I can Not be More Oblidged to the Donor, than to your Lordships Singular goodness; which tho' I Can not Deserve, yet I shall Always Sencibly Reflect on, & Improve. And I should be Doubly blest, if Providence would put it into my hands, to Render your Lordship Some Service, Suited to the Sence I have of your Lordships Extraordinary Favour.

And yet I am your Lordships Most Humble Petitioner, That if Possible I may kno' the Originalls of This Munificence. Sure That hand That Can Suppose me to Merit So Much Regard, Must believ me Fitt to be Trusted with The knowledge of my benefactor, and Uncapable of Discovering any Part of it, That should be Conceal'd; But I Submitt This to your Lordship and the Persons Concernd.

I Frankly Acknowlege to your Lordship, and to the Unknown Rewarders of my Mean Performances, That I do Not See the Merit They are Thus Pleasd to Value.[1] The most I wish and which I hope I Can Answer for is, That I shall Allwayes Preserv the Homely, Despicable Title of *an Honest Man.* If This will Recomend me, your Lordship shall Never be Asham'd of giveing me that Title, Nor my Enemys be able by Fear Or Reward to Make me Other wise.

In all Other things I justly Apprehend your Lordships Dissappointment and That your Ldship will find little Elce in Me worth your Notice.

> I am, May it Please your Lordship
> Your Ldships Highly Oblig'd
> Most Humble and Most Obedt Servt
> DANIEL DE FOE

MS.: Brit. Mus., Add. MSS. 7121 ff. 27–28. *Pub.*: Sir Henry Ellis, *Original Letters of Eminent Literary Men of the Sixteenth, Seventeenth, and Eighteenth Centuries,* 1843, pp. 323–4. *Address*: 'To The Right Honble Charles Ld Hallifax, Humbly Present.' *Endorsed*: 'From Mr De Foe.'

34. [*To* ROBERT HARLEY]. [*June 1705?*]

Memorandums

To be Furnish't with Some thing New to Informe the people I Converse with, at Least when any Thing Extraordinary happens which may be had More Authentick than Ordinary.

To have a Certificate as from the Office, that being Travailling on my Lawfull Occasions I may not be stopt by any Malitious persons on the Road—or which may be worse—Search't.

To Settle a Method how To write &ca.

Charges to be Directed as shall Reciev Ordr—

To get Leave for the Same Person who went with me before[2] to be Absent at the Custome house—

To be goeing as Soon as Possible. The Assizes will Elce Not Overtake me Onely but be before me.

---

[1] Even though Defoe professes ignorance of why Whig money should be falling into his purse, he hardly could have been unaware that his long and vigorous campaign against the tacking, high-flying Tories was of extraordinary value to their political opponents in an election year.   [2] Christopher Hurt. See p. 61.

If May Suit with Convenience—be gone Fryday Next.
Some speciall Instructions—

MS.: Duke of Portland, Defoe Papers, 1 f. 28; unsigned, but in the hand-writing of Defoe. *Pub.*: *H.M.C. Portland*, iv. 200. *Address*: none.

35. *To* ROBERT HARLEY. *9 July 1705*

Sir

When with your Usuall Goodness you were pleasd the Last
Time I was with you, to Ordr me to Put Down in writeing any
Thing I had to propose on My Private Account, it Put me On
Considering whether The Same Secret hand that first Put it
into your Thoughts to do me Good, Might Not Perhaps yet
Farther Move you on My behalf.

Sir I am Not Insensible of the Tenderness you Treat me with,
and tho' I am Not Ever Crowding you with my Empty Acknowlegemts as Things I kno' you are Above the Ceremoney of, yet
you have bound a Gratefull Fellow So Close to you that Nothing
Can be too great for me to attempt for your Service. I Onely
want the Occasion which Must Come from your Self.

When I Come to Talk of my Self Sir, The story is Mellancholly Enough and yet I am Loth to give you The Trouble of
it.

What I write of Peace it Seems Raises war to me, and Those
people[1] who were Easy before grow Troublesome Now, tho'
they Must Needs kno' me less able Than before The Last
Trouble to Discharge Them, and as Those who Offer this are
Most of Them of the Contrary Party, I See The Design is if
possible to put a stop to my writeing.

But why do I Trouble you with This? To Ask you Any Thing
that Can Reliev This Capitall Defect, is what I have Not Merit
to pretend to. But I Remember when you were pleas'd, The
last Bill I Recd from you for which I Ought to Repeat my
Thanks, to Say Something of bringing it to a Certainty—Pardon
me for Restraining My Requests, tho' you Give me too Much
Freedome. I kno' Not whether what I have from you be from
the Publick Or your Own Private. Tho' the bounty to me is
Equally yours, yet This Difference it will have; That tho' I hate
to be craveing, yet as I hinted Once, I was Fitter for a Pension
than an Office, by which I Meant Respecting the Service I may
do Among the Party. So Sir Might the Service I may do Merit a

[1] His creditors. See the *Reviews* for 7 and 17 July 1705.

Private Allowance, by which The Necessary Craveings of a Large Family of 7 Children might be answer'd, What Elce I Can Raise in the World would Soon Set me at Ease as to Creditors, whereas the Eager prosecution of Enemyes will at Last Disable me Either to Support the first or Discharge the Last.

I kno' Not how to build this proposall but on This Foundation, That I hope 'tis in your Power to Make me Deserve it.

I hope you have More Confidence in Me Than to Think what you Supply me with for the Expence of the Service I go On, shall be in The Least Missapplyed, and Tho' I can Not Perswade my Self that Good husbandry should Straighten the Work, and was Something too Expensive in the Last,[1] yet Really Sir the many Perticulars Obtaind and the short Time perform'd in, Oblig'd me to Expence and I Thought it well bestow'd. Nor Unless you prescribe me shall I spare where the Service I am Upon Requires, Since I am Satisfyed This Thing will be of Various Uses to the Publick.

All This is to Signifye to you, Sir, that the Money you are pleas'd to Furnish, for This affair, which I hope is Out of the Publick stock, as the Use is for The Publick, Relates to its Proper Expence; Subsistence or Allowance being hitherto Unconcern'd in it.

Nor should I Take This Freedome but Wait your Leisure, to Reward me as your Own Judgement shall perswade you I Merit, haveing allwayes Reason to Acknowlege you forward to Assist me, But— Sir, The Man is Demolish'd, and the Wound is too Deep [for][2] Common Industry to heal; and he That made you The First Physician, has Entail'd The Rent Charge on you, and Makes My Ld Rochesters Verses, on Women, True of me.

> That Authors Beggar like, will haunt the Door,
> Where They Recd a Charity before.[3]

Make me Merit Sir all you Do for me. If I Can do Nothing, why Assist me attall? If any Thing, Then the Publick Bounty will not be Lost. Tis The hopes of the Party to See me flye, and I believ They would bribe me to be gone. If my stay is a harm to Them,

[1] His journey to the eastern counties in the previous autumn.
[2] MS. torn.
[3]   But Women, Beggars like, still haunt the Door,
          Where they've receiv'd a Charity before.
('A Very Heroical Epistle, in Answer to *Ephilia*', *Poetical Works of John Wilmot Lord Rochester*, ed. Quilter Johns, 1933, p. 196.)

tis a use to the Contrary. My petition to you Sir is, to make me Servicable, and The Queens Bounty will follow, for No Man Servs her Majtie for Nothing.

I have Answerd This high Church Legion.[1] I have Dedicated it to my Ld Treasurer. From your hand Sir, My Ld Can Not but accept it, and I hope to my Advantage; if not, I am Sure tis for the publick good, and if I Loose by it Ile publish it,[2] and flatter my Self you will Not be Asham'd of the performance.

I Forbear to Trouble you any More with my Cases. I Lay This at your Feet, and Throwing my Self wholly on your Goodness, humbly ask your Pardon for the Freedome and am

[symbol]

July 9. 1705

The Messengr Stevens[3] has brought or will bring some people up for the Dyer. I pray that a seeming[4] Reprimand, &c. may Suffice, Elce the Charge will lye——&ca.[5]

MS.: Duke of Portland, Defoe Papers, 1 ff. 32–33. *Pub.*: *H.M.C. Portland*, iv. 203–5. *Address*: 'To The Right Honble Robert Harley Esqr.'

36. *To* ROBERT HARLEY. [*10 July 1705*]

Sir

I wrott the Enclosed[6] last Night, Tho' had I Seen you I believ my heart had Faild me in Delivring it, for I Could Never yet speak for my Self.

I Wait with Impatience your Last Orders and shall attend at 4 This afternoon According to your Direction.

[1] Defoe's name for the notorious *Memorial of the Church of England*, and also the title under which he published his answer to it. The *Memorial*, perhaps by Dr. James Drake, was a complaint against the persecuted state of the Church of England and the favour shown to the Dissenters, and reflected the ever-growing wrath of the High Church against the Ministry. It sharply criticized Godolphin, to whom Defoe dedicated his reply. In addition to publishing *The High Church Legion*, Defoe denounced the *Memorial* in the *Review* for 12 July and thereafter in every issue from 19 July to 21 Aug. See Wilson, *Life*, ii. 369–80.

[2] It was published on 17 July (*Review* of that date).

[3] See p. 58, n. 4. [4] i.e. suitable.

[5] In a *News-letter*, Dyer had reported that the *Neptune*, an East-India ship, had run aground and been lost with £46,000 in bullion aboard. But he had added that the bullion had been derived from '*Good Crown Pieces melted down, which are National Losses, and to be Deplored*' (quoted from the *Review* for 23 Aug. 1705). The charge that one of the East India companies was illegally melting down English coinage raised a furore, and Defoe, who was on bad terms with Dyer anyhow (No. 21), attacked him in the *Review* for 23 Aug. Defoe here reminds Harley that unless Dyer is punished, the story may be accepted by the public as true.

[6] The preceding letter.

I Long to Accquaint you That I am Told Dr Atterbury[1] is Author of The Memoriall and That Geo: Sawbridge and Abell Roper[2] are the Publishers but your Messenger Stevens[3] (too Much a friend to That Party) Took Such Care of the Orders given him to Discover the Printers, that Some houres before his Search, a Person was Sent Privately to all the Booksellers and Gather'd Them in Again.

Mr Pooley[4] in Some Company yesterday gave a great Encomium of the book Very Publickly.

I have Sent you herewith the Rough of the Answer.[5] I hope Twill please you and any hint you please to give shall be added. If you please to give me Leave I would address it to My Ld Treasurer or to your Self; it should be in the press to Day if possible.

I beg the Favor of your Perusall of it— The printing shall Not stop my Journey an hour— I am

Sir Your Honrs Most Obedt Servt
[symbol]

Tuesday Morning

MS.: Duke of Portland, Defoe Papers, 1 ff. 34–35. *Pub.*: *H.M.C. Portland*, iv. 205. *Address*: 'To the Right Honoble Robert Harley Esqr., One of her Majties Principll Secreta of State, Present.' *Endorsed*: 'About the Memorial & Answer and about Subsisting the Author of the Answer, 9 July 1705.'

37. *To* ROBERT HARLEY. [*16 July 1705?*][6]

Sir

I am Sincerely Thankfull to your Sollicitous Thots for me, tho' I Avoid Extasies on That Subject.

I have the Pass Sir and Doubt Not its being Effectuall, and Assure you of my Makeing No use of it, but at the Last Extremity.[7]

[1] Francis Atterbury (1662–1732), at this time Dean of Carlisle, later Bishop of Rochester.

[2] George Sawbridge, publisher of Defoe's *The Storm*, 1704, and frequent advertiser in the *Review*, was ultimately fined £200 for publishing the *Memorial*. Abel Roper (1665–1726) was publisher of the Tory *Post Boy*.

[3] Robert Stephens, Messenger of the Press. See p. 58, n. 4.

[4] Henry Pooley (or Poley), Tory M.P. for Westlow, who was himself suspected of having had a hand in the *Memorial* (*Remarks and Collections of Thomas Hearne*, Oxford, 1885–1921, i. 203).

[5] *The High Church Legion*, published 17 July.

[6] In *H.M.C. Portland*, iv, this letter is tentatively assigned to 2 July. But in view of its mention of *The High Church Legion* (first advertised on 17 July) and of Defoe's departure 'This Minute' (on 16 July according to No. 44), it may better be assigned to 16 July, which fell on 'Monday'.

[7] He found use for his pass. See p. 99.

I give you Joy Sir of the Good News[1] which I Recd with One hand the Same Moment I Recd yours with the other, and which I Take as a good Omen, and both Contribute to Send me Out Chearfull and Easy.

I Send you herewith Six of the High C Legeon. The bearer, who is My Brother in Law,[2] and who May be Depended on, and is The Same Person Carrye'd the Coventry Affair,[3] yet knows Nothing of The principall affair—

He is Charg'd with the Like Number for My Ld Treasurer, But if you Demand Them will Deliver Them, Since if you would please to Concern your Self So far as to Let my Ld Treasurer kno' They Come by your hand, It would be a Double Favour.

I Perswade my Self Now Sir you are Convinc't Lesly[4] has Not been the Author of the Memorial. I am fully posess't with a Belief that Not him, No Nor Dr D . . . ke,[5] But the Latter as a Tool, an Amanuensis, to his Grace.[6] Lætantur Lares &ca. There are [h]is[7] Marks, his strokes. There is his spirit, his Gall and in short his Picture.

I am Concern'd to See your Orders betraid and Buffoon'd. That Wretch Stephens[8] Makes the Govornmt perfectly Impotent in These Matters and The Booksellers and he Together make sport at your Orders.

Indeed Sir I write This without private Design or ill will to the Man. His being a Rogue was Usefull to me, and I brib'd him allways to my Advantage, But in This Case They act undr his patronage.

An Instance of This you will have Tomorro', when The Memoriall is to be publish't Answer'd Paragraph by Paragraph.[9]

---

[1] Marlborough's success in forcing the so-called Lines of Brabant at Elixem. See G. M. Trevelyan, *Ramillies and the Union with Scotland*, 1932, pp. 53–54.

[2] Robert Davis.

[3] The meaning is not clear, but Davis may have delivered to Harley a report by Defoe on the Coventry riots of the preceding April and May. See the *Reviews* for 10 May 1705 and 17 Aug. 1706.

[4] Charles Leslie, author of the Tory journal, *The Rehearsal*.

[5] James Drake (1667–1707), Tory political writer.

[6] John Sheffield (1647–1721), Duke of Buckingham, recently dismissed from the office of Lord Privy Seal, and bitterly attacked by Defoe in his *Dyet of Poland*, pp. 48–49. See the following letter.

[7] Letter omitted in MS.   [8] See p. 58, n. 4.

[9] He probably refers to *An Answer, Paragraph by Paragraph, to the Memorial of the Church of England*, thought to be by William Pittis. A pamphlet entitled *The Memorial of the Church of England, Humbly Offer'd to the Consideration of All True Lovers of Our Church and Constitution, Considered Paragraph by Paragraph* had already appeared, and Defoe (to whom it has sometimes been attributed) had attacked it in the *Review* for 12 July.

As This is Done Purely to Sell the book,[1] which The Town is Eager for, and which I Think the Govornmt is highly Concernd to prevent, So The Answers are Allways Triffles, and the Design, which is Dispersing the Originall, is fully Answer'd.[2]

If you Send for That Fellow[3] and Severely Reprimand him, Charge him in it, you May Effectually Damn This project in its Embrio, for he knows the hand it Comes by and may Go and Seize it in the press, and will be Frighted by your Threats, For Villains are Allways Cowards.

The License you Give me to use This Freedome, Joyn'd to My Concern For the Case, is my Excuse for This and I hope shall be Accepted So.

This Minute I go Away and shall do my Self the honour to write at Large on all Occasions. Interim I am

&ca

[symbol]

Monday Morning

MS.: Duke of Portland, Defoe Papers, 1 ff. 30–31. *Pub.*: *H.M.C. Portland*, iv. 200–1. *Address*: 'To The Right Honble Robert Harley Esqr., Principal Secretary of State &ca.'

38. *To* Charles Montagu, Baron Halifax.
16 July 1705

July. 16. 1705

My Lord

I had Gone on farther to Replye to This Most Insolent Memoriall, But that the Subject of the Review being before This book came Out, Entred Upon the Same Article, Vizt The Danger of the Church,[4] I Shall handle it apart.

I Think it my Duty to Lay it before your Ldship as it is, and have Sent Six of Them,[5] Not That I Think it worth your Ldships Recommending, but That, if your Ldship Please to Concern your Self for me So far, your Own hand May Make This Empty Returne to The (to me Unknown) Benefactors of whose Goodness to me your Lordship was Pleas'd to be a Medium, and which I have No Other way to Acknowlege.[6]

If I knew how to Ask my Ld Treasurer Pardon, Either for the Weakness of my Defence in his Case, or the Rudeness of a Dedication without a Name, I Should be Glad to do it, But I

[1] Publication of the original had been stopped.
[2] Cf. *Review*, 11 Aug. 1705.   [3] Stephens, the Messenger.
[4] See the *Reviews* from 14 July to 21 Aug.
[5] Copies of his anonymous *High Church Legion*, just published.   [6] See No. 33.

am too Obscure and Remote to do it Personally, and the Same Reason That Obliges me Not to Sign the Dedication Obliges me Not to do it Publickly.[1]

The Writeing This book I hear is Charg'd upon Dr. Drake. I Can Not forbear Assureing your Ldship, That however he Might be The Drudge or Rather Amanuensis in the work—his Master The Duke of Bucks is as plainly Pictur'd to me with his Pen in his hand Correcting, Dictating, and Instructing, as if I had been of the Club with Them.[2]

I Ask your Ldships Pardon for This freedome and Am

Your Ldships Most Humble and Obedt Servt
DE FOE

MS.: Brit. Mus., Add. MSS. 7121 ff. 25–26. *Pub.*: Lee, *Life*, i. 115. *Address*: 'To The Right Honble Charles Ld Hallifax, Humbly Prest.' *Endorsed*: '16 July, 1705, From De Foe.'

39. *To* ROBERT HARLEY. *30 July 1705*

Sir

I do my Self the honor to Accquaint you That I Reacht This Town yesterday tho' Extreamly Fatigued with the Violent heat, but This Country has been Cool'd with plentifull Rains and is Now Very Refreshing.

I have Nothing to Complain of in the Success of my Design Except in Dorsetshire where the Exceeding Harmony between the Dissenters and the Low Church, The Disposition of the former to peace one with Another and of the Latter to Moderation, Makes my Remarks Something Useless.

The Onely 2 warm People, Coll Strangeways and Sir N Napier,[3] have acted with More Caution and less Success than Ever and had Lt Gen. Earle and T Freak[4] put in for the County they had Carryed it beyond all possibillity of Miscarriage.

The Dissenters are Indeed too Easy and Do not struggle, have-

---

[1] *The High Church Legion* is dedicated to Godolphin and defends him against the attacks of *The Memorial of the Church of England*.

[2] Cf. the preceding letter.

[3] Thomas Strangeways and Sir Nathaniel Napier, Members respectively for Dorset and Dorchester in the previous Parliament. Strangeways was re-elected, but Napier's seat was taken by Awnsham Churchill.

[4] Both Thomas Erle and Thomas Freke had been returned for Dorset constituencies, Erle for Wareham and Freke for Lyme Regis. Defoe wishes that one or the other had stood rather for the County; the election of either to that seat would have ousted the troublesome Strangeways. Cf. p. 109.

ing Met with No ill Treatment to Move them, and Perticularly
the Inferiour Clergy are the Most Temperate here of any place
I kno', A Certain proof that the Different Temper of Other
Counties is Owing (at Least much of it) to Their Inflameing
the Gentry.

At Salisbury 'tis quite Another Thing. The Bishops Candidate
for the Town, Mr Harris, Lost it[1] and the Bishops friends were
Very ill Treated by The Clergy.[2] At the County Election the
Bishops Gentlemn, the Dukes of Somersett and Bolton,[3] Recd
Strange Insults and his Grace of Somersett was Insulted in the
streets of Salisbury by The Mob.

Here also Things are in Terrible Disordr. The Election of
Honyton is an Abridgemt of Coventry,[4] and F Gwin[5] has Perticularly Distinguisht himself.

In Excester the Conquest the Bishop made Over his Clergy[6]
and the Further Improvement his Ldship makes of his Victory
Renders him Formidable and Exceedingly Chagrins the Party;
But his Ldships (as they say) still Declaring himself for the
Occa: bill Comforts Them. *Fisher*[7] The former Representative
of the Clergy was Expell'd by The Bishop last week for want
of Institution and Induction and had a Severe Admonition
given him to be Residt at a Small Cure he has in the Country
on pain of Suspension. Severall others of the high C Clergy
feel the Effect of his Ldships Displeasure and are Under like
prosecution.

[1] Bishop Burnet, at the wish of the Queen, had supported Harris in the hope of
defeating Charles Fox, M.P. for Salisbury (T. E. S. Clark and H. C. Foxcroft, *Life
of Gilbert Burnet*, Cambridge, 1907, p. 417).

[2] Earlier in the summer, Lord Poulett had written to Harley that Burnet's clergy
'preach nothing but the Church being in greatest danger, and the Bishop himself is
often named in their pulpits as an enemy of the Church' (*H.M.C. Portland*, iv. 177).

[3] Charles Seymour (1662–1748), 'the proud Duke', was a moderate Whig and
Chancellor of Cambridge University. Charles Paulet (1661–1722), second Duke
of Bolton, was Custos Rotulorum and Lord Lieutenant of Dorset. He had been
chairman of the Select Committee of the House of Lords which had consulted
Defoe on naval affairs a few months before. See No. 25.

[4] The election at Coventry had been attended with so much violence and corruption that the Commons later refused to seat the Members chosen (*Review*,
17 Aug. 1706, and T. W. Whitley, *Parliamentary Representation of the City of Coventry*,
Coventry, 1894, pp. 133–5).

[5] Francis Gwyn (1648?–1734), Tory politician, denounced by Defoe in *The
Dyet of Poland*, pp. 49–50.

[6] Sir Jonathan Trelawny (1650–1721), at this time Bishop of Exeter, had
recently deserted the Tories to join the Whigs and Ministerialists and had induced
many of his clergy to make a like change (G. M. Trevelyan, *Ramillies and the Union
with Scotland*, 1932, p. 29).

[7] Probably Peter Fisher (d. 1739), Prebendary of Exeter (*Fasti Ecclesiæ Anglicanæ*,
i. 428).

All agree here had My Ld Treasurer Given his Letter to the Bishop to ha' Set up his son,[1] Sir Ed: Seymour[2] had lost it here. If That had happen'd The Party had Recd Such a blow They would Never ha' Recovred.

I Go this day to Excester Again to finish my Informations at That Place and Thence to Plymouth, shall Come Round by the North Coast of This County and be at Tiverton in about 10 dayes where the honor of a Letter from you would be a Satisfaction and Encouragemt, Directed to Alexa G . . . th,[3] in a Cover to the Revrd Mr Josiah Eveleigh, at Mr Francis Bere,[4] Merchant in Tiverton.

I Met an Express and Two Lisbone Mails on the Road fryday Last. Some Little Perticular of That affair Other than the Prints Informe would furnish me with means to Let them kno' I shall be Usefull, for all Our Party here are Politicians, Especially the Parsons (God bless us), who Once a week Settle the Consciences, Twice a week the state; and It Could not but afford me some speculation, to See, at This place, where the Dissenting parson is my Friend, the Post Comeing in on Sunday morning, The people Devoutly Resort to the News house as they Call it first, and then to Church.

I am Allmost asham'd to Tell you how Expensive I am, and yet Not Extravagant, but I am Resolv'd not to Baulk the Design, leaving all things of that Sort to your kindness, and to judge by The Effect, wherefore haveing a Little Supply of my Own at Plymo, I forbear to press you on That head, if you please to Convey to Kingsland[5] what you Think Convenient for the Support of This affair against I may Reach Bristoll. I shall then be Oblig'd to Draw—and My wife who is my faithfull Steward will Not Diminish it One Penny.

[1] Francis Godolphin had stood for Cambridge University but had been defeated.
[2] Sir Edward Seymour (1633–1708), uncompromising high Tory and a former Speaker of the Commons, had so powerfully influenced elections in Devon and Cornwall that those counties were sometimes spoken of as 'Seymour's Western Empire'. He appears as 'Old Seymsky' in Defoe's *Dyet of Poland*, pp. 19–23.
[3] 'Alexander Goldsmith' was one of Defoe's pseudonyms.
[4] Both Josiah Eveleigh (d. 1736), dissenting minister at Bowden Hill, Crediton, and Francis Bere (or Bear) of the neighbouring Tiverton, were agents of Defoe. See p. 116. Eveleigh perhaps served the Dissenters at Tiverton as well as at Crediton.
[5] This passage strengthens the suggestion of A. W. Secord ('Defoe in Stoke Newington', *PMLA*, lxvi [1951], 212) that at this period Defoe resided at Kingsland, in the Parish of Hackney. Defoe was living at Kingsland in 1693 (J. R. Sutherland, 'Some Early Troubles of Daniel Defoe', *Review of English Studies*, ix [1933], 286), wrote a letter from there in Jan. 1707–8 (No. 123), and did not move to Stoke Newington until 1708 or 1709 (Secord, op. cit., pp. 212–15).

I have Nothing More worth your Notice Save That I am, as Allways, Oblig'd.

> May it Please Your Honr
> Your Most Humble and Most Obedient Servt
> > [symbol]

Crediton July 30. 1705.

MS.: Duke of Portland, Defoe Papers, 1 ff. 36–37. *Pub.*: *H.M.C. Portland*, iv. 213–14. *Address*: 'To the Right Honble Robert Harley Esqr., One of her Majties Principall Secretarys of State, Present.'

40. *To* ROBERT HARLEY. *14 August 1705*

Sir

I Recd but This Day the honor of yours at Tiverton. Your Concerne for me Sir fills me with Gratefull Thoughts how to Render my Self a yet more Suitable Subject for So Much Goodness, and Encourages me to bear up undr the Desperat Resolutions Taken to Ruine me.[1]

Providence and Some Dexterity of Conduct (pardon my Vanity) has hitherto Rendred all the Measures of the Party Impotent and Unsuccessfull and yet I have not Omitted One part of my work Nor Bauk'd One Town I purposed to Call at, Barnstaple Excepted.

I Can not however but Divert you with the short history of this Matter. The Misscarriage at Weymo happened by Such a Cassualty as no Man Could forsee; my Letters, Directed for the Friend Now with me Call'd Capt Turner,[2] to be left at Weymo, were Taken up, by One Capt Turner, Commander of a Guernsey privateer[3] Then in that Port. The Ignorant Tarr when he found Things written Darke and Unintelligible shows them to all the Town. At Our Comeing however he Restores the Letters, Drank a pint of wine with us and Calls for One himself, which it seems afterward he went away, and Never paid for. The

---

[1] See the *Reviews* for 7 and 17 July.
[2] 'Captain Turner' cannot be identified with assurance. Defoe had a friend of that name and title who took subscriptions for *Jure Divino* 'in the Auction Room near the House of Commons-Door (*Review*, 26 Sept. 1704). Before setting out, Defoe had asked Harley to allow Christopher Hurt to accompany him (p. 87), but Hurt, who may of course be 'Captain Turner', is named in none of the letters written during this journey. Defoe later wrote that his companions at this time were 'one Friend, and his Friend's Servant' (*Review*, 25 Aug. 1705). Robert Davis, Defoe's brother-in-law, was his attendant on part of the circuit, but not until the two met at Bath (p. 103).
[3] Capt. James Turner of the privateer *Diligence* (Weymouth Corporation Minute Book, 1699–1724).

people of the house Demanding Money for it next Day Put him
in a frett, and that Vented it Self in his Railing at this Letter all
about Town Till the Mayor[1] sent for him. The Imperfect account he gave fills the Mayors as foolish head with Jealousyes,[2]
and the Assises being at Dorchester, away he Runs to the
Judges and Getts a summons for Mr Fenner[3] the Dissenting
Minister and Two or 3 More who I had Visited, and Carryes
them to Dorchester where the Judge Whose Name I think is
Price[4] Examin'd them and Dissmiss't them.

But This blunder has had a worse Effect Since— When I
Came to Excester and haveing Appeard publickly among my
Friends and being after at Crediton a Day or Two, the party
Thot I was Gone, One of the Aldermen blustred that he was
Sorry he Did not Take me up and list me for a soldier, Coll
Brittons[5] Regimt being There.

At my Returne I appear'd publickly, walk'd severall Times
on the Walks of the Church Call'd the Parade of the Party, went
to the Church, the Bowling Green, the Coffee house &ca with
some of the Principle of the Citizens, and Mr Alderman & his
brethren took no Notice of it.

I went from Thence to Totness, Dartmo, & Plymouth, and
the Day before I went, the Judges Came to Town. The party
then Took heart and as I Understand applyed to Mr Justice
Price, who in his Charge to the Grand Jury Tells them There
are Severall Seditious persons Come Down into the Country
spreading Libells &ca and Embroiling the people, and advises
the Justices to Apprehend them.

The first Effect of This was that at Crediton a Country
Justice[6] Grants the Enclosed warrant[7] Against me and searches

---

[1] Capt. William Harding.   [2] i.e. suspicions.
[3] John Fenner, Independent minister.
[4] Justice Robert Price (1655–1733), a Tory.   [5] Col. William Britton's.
[6] Hugh Stafford. See No. 41.
[7] The warrant, copied in a hand that is neither Defoe's nor Stafford's, follows:
   To all Constbles and Tythingmen and other her majesties officers within the
County of Devon and allso to Charles Sugg.
   Whereas I have recieved Information against Daniel de Foe for spreading and
publishing divers seditious and scandalous Libels and false news to the great
disturbance of the Peace of this Kingdom and that He is a Person of ill Fame and
Behaviour, and is now lurking within some or one of your Parishes, Tythings, or
Precincts—These are in her Majties name to will and require you and every of
you on Sight hereof to make diligent privy Search within your said Parishes,
Tythings, and Precincts, in all suspitious Houses and Places within the same, and
to be assistant to the sd Charles Sugg in searching for and apprehending the sd.
Daniel de Foe, and when found and apprehended forthwith to bring him before
me to be examin'd concerning the Premises, and to be dealt with as the Law

the Town with Constables, and perticularly the Dissenting Ministers house. But I was Then at Liskard in Cornwall.

The first Account of This I mett with at Bideford where Some Gentlemen on Comeing into the Town from the Assizes Told the people the Judge had Nam'd me to the Grand Jury and Given Directions to Apprehend me wherever I might be found.

By This Report I had been Insulted in Bideford the Next Morning; But the Mayor being Out of Town, the Next principle Magistrate, whom they Call a Justice as haveing been Mayor The year before, was my perticular Friend,[1] And here was the first and Onely Time I show'd your Pass, Takeing the hint from your Letter of useing it with Caution.

This So Encourag'd the Magistrate and all my Friends That I might have assur'd my self here of Protection, and the Measures of the Other party in the Town Seem'd Entirely broke. But I was privately Informd that they had sent away a messenger Express to have me stop't at Barnstaple as I Came along.

Had not the Danger of my Own private affaires and the warrant from London[2] being Rouz'd by this Noise layn a Little Upon my Thoughts, I had more publickly Ventur'd the Worst Effects of Their Mallice, but not knowing what of that Sort might be in it, I Avoided Barnstaple, and haveing a perticular friend a S. T. P.[3] Dissenter who I Carryed with me all this Circuit from Exon, I have Visited Every Town So securely by being lodg'd among friends that I am Now under the Nose of the Justices Concern'd in the Enclos'd warrant and yet Out of their Danger.[4]

To morrow I leav this Town and County and, Presumeing your Directions for my Returne proceed from your Apprehensions of my personall hazards and are the Effect of your Concern for me which I Can Never Enough Acknowlege, and Not from an alteration in your Opinion or Design of haveing this work Done, I proceed with Resolution thro' More Difficultyes than these to persue all the Ordrs I shall at any time Reciev from you.

directs. Hereof you and every of you may not fail at your utmost Perils. Given under my Hand and Seal the 9th day of August in the 4th year of the Reign of our soverain Lady Ann over England &c. Anno Dom. 1705.

HUGH STAFFORD

Across the bottom, Defoe has written: 'Pray Sir Do not loose this paper.'

[1] John Darracott.
[2] Three actions had been entered against him by creditors (*Review*, 17 July).
[3] Professor of Sacred Theology. At Exeter there was a Dissenting Academy.
[4] A fuller version of these adventures appears in the *Review* for 25 Aug.

The success I have had in this part I perswade my self will fully Satisfye you as it has Encouraged me to Say That Seymskyes Westerne Empire[1] may with Much Ease be Overthrown and his successor[2] Defeated, and had I Come here Sooner by half a year it had felt a great blow Ere Now.

As to Apprehensions of my Friend who is with me betrayeing me, I assure you of the Contrary, Nor are you Sir betraid to him, Nor does he suspect I Correspond with you or have the honour to Converse with you. I am not Serving a Master I have so little Vallue for. You may Sir Depend upon me That Neither by Fraud or Folly the Confidence you are pleasd to place in me shall Ever be Dissappointed.

I wrott you Sir from Exon[3] which I hope is Come Safe. In that I Took the Freedome to Mention a supplye. Indeed I have been more Expensive here than I Expected, but it has been purely to perfect the work, and I Think I may say I have a perfect skeleton of this part of England and a Settled Correspondence in Every Town and Corner of it.

I go Directly to the Bath where my Companion leaves me and Mr Davis my Brother in Law who has the honor to wait on you Comes to me with another Friend who will Travail into the North with me.

By my Brother any thing you please to Convey to my Wife will Come Safe, But Rather by Bill than in specie, and Seal'd because Sir I have Learnt in all these things to make Agents without Accquainting them with Perticulars.

I Humbly Entreat your Letter, which Mr Davis will bring me to the Bath and So No Danger of a Misscarriage, and Till Then forbear Troubling you any Farther.

But am, Your Faithfull Obedient Servt
[symbol]

A Terrible storme On Fryday night Last has done Incredible Damage in the Country besides what has been at Plymouth.[4]

Tiverton Augt. 14. 1705

MS.: Duke of Portland, Defoe Papers, i ff. 39–40. *Pub.*: *H.M.C. Portland*, iv. 221–3. *Address* (on a separate sheet and in another hand): 'To the Right Honoble Robert Harley Esqre, Principal Secretary of State, Present.'

[1] See p. 96, n. 2.
[2] Francis Gwyn was prepared to take over full control of Tory politics in the western counties as soon as the aged Seymour relinquished the share of it he now held. See Defoe's *Dyet of Poland*, pp. 49–50.
[3] He probably refers to No. 39, written from Crediton, which he had visited on a side trip from Exeter.   [4] See *Tour thro' Britain*, i. 229–30.

41. To HUGH STAFFORD.[1] *14 August 1705*

Sir

I am not att all Surprized att the malice of my enemies in their vain attempts to insult me, But I am concerned to hear a man of your Charac[ter,][2] honour, and Office, Should Soe freely grant your warrant for apprehending a man Travailing about his Lawfull Occasions, and not in the least misbehaving himselfe to any man.

I doe my Selfe the Honour to acquaint you that foreseeing the possibillity of Such dealings I have with me a Certification from her matyes Secretary of State of my haveing acquainted the Goverment of my Occasions to travaile and of my giveing security for my Fidelity to her matye, requireing you as well as all other magistrates to offer me noe disturbance or molestation in my Journey,[3] and being att Biddeford when I had the notice

---

[1] The Devonshire Justice of the Peace who had issued the warrant for Defoe's arrest. Defoe did not soon forget Stafford's officiousness and later ridiculed him from time to time in the *Review*. See especially the issue for 25 Aug. 1705.

[2] MS. torn.

[3] Stafford assumed that Sir Charles Hedges was the Secretary here referred to, and hence sent to him a copy of Defoe's letter and the following explanation (P.R.O., S.P. 34/6/88):

Pynes Aug: 27th 1705

Sir

I haveing the honour of being one of her Majtyes Justices of the peace for this County of Devon, and hearing from very Cridible hands, that Severall letters of dangerous Consequence to the Queen, and Goverment, were directed to Mr De' Foe att Weymouth, (which Came to his hands) and that he had been att Lyme, Honyton and Exeter, and being in my neighbourhood, in his way for Crediton, thought it my duty (the Assizes being att hand) to acquaint Mr Baron Price, one of the Judges of Assize att Exeter therewith, who advised me to Issue out my warrant to apprehend him, hopeing to have found some of his dangerous Letters about him; which accordingly I did, but missing my aime in not takeing my Sparke, (tho' I did it with all possible diligence and secrecy,) had only in returne, an impudent reflecting letter Sent me, wherein he pretends he has Authority, and license, for his Sd Travailing from your Honour, as you will finde when you please to peruse the inclosed, which is a true Coppy of a letter I received from him, upon which I did not think fitt to proceed therein, till I had your further Commands which Shall alwayse be punctually obay'd by, Sir, Your honours most obedient humble Servt

HUGH STAFFORD

Since writeing of this I have further information from very good hands that he deals very freely in his common conversation with the young parliamt men, in basely reflecting on them lately in my neighbourhood, by Saying, as for them, they generally lay drinking att Some Tavern or other near the house, and leave the concerns of the Nation to halfe a Score Old Stagers to mannage; till any business of moment, and then they are Sent for, who as soon as they come into the house imeadiatly whisper to one, and soe to another, to know how Sir Edward, Sir Humphry, or Sir John, how they voted, and haveing learnt that, without ever hearing the meritts of the cause, or indeed any thing of the matter Says he, immeadiatly cry out they give their vote the same way lett it be right or

of your unjustice-like as well as ungentleman-like warrant, I went Imeadiately to the principall magistrate of the Town to Show my Selfe and the Authority aforesd to any man that had reason to question it.

By this Sir I publickly Confute, that Scandalous Falsity affirmed in your warrant of my Lurking in the Countrey, and I am Sorry my Occasions will not permitt me to tell you soe to your face.

As to my dispersing Libells Sir, and disturbing the peace, I am extreamly desirous of knowing what Information of that Sort can be brought you Since my respect for your Character forbids me to beleeve you would grant your warrant for me unless it was Informed upon Oath, and if it was Sworne I shall Certainely pursue the perjured Villaine as farre as the law directs, assureing you it is false in fact and malicious in Suggestion.

I wish all men would pursue the peace and publick Tranquillity and as earnestly perswade to it [as][1] I doe, and I Claim this Justice of you that what is Charged on me to the contrary may be fairly prov'd or the forgers of it detected.

I am now att Tiverton, and goe from hence to Wells where I doubt not to convince that Honble person[2] who tis Suggested pointed att me in publicke that he as well as you have been imposed upon. If you have assurance enough of your Information and thinke fitt to Send after me, you Shall finde I doe not Lurk about, but dare Show my face to you or any man.

If Sir you please to doe me the honour of your reply to this and the Justice of acquainting me who are the Informers, I shall receive it, if directed to me att the Essex Coffee house[3] att the Temple, London.

Your humble Servt
DANLL DE FOE

MS.: untraced; the text is taken from a copy made by the addressee, P.R.O., S.P. 34/6/106. Hitherto unpublished. *Address*: none.

wrong Soe long as Sir Edward and they vote Soe, and many more Such Scandelous reflections as these are, which makes me very much doubt he comes into our country with noe good designe, for he keeps Company with none but presbytarian and Independent preachers, for he has made it his business to visitt them almost in every town and parish throughout our County, and I hear throughout all the Countys through which he has past.

[1] Omitted in MS.

[2] Unidentified.

[3] Where Defoe must have had a henchman, for subscriptions to *Jure Divino* were received there. See advertisement in the *Review* for 28 Nov. 1704.

42. *To* ROBERT HARLEY. *10 September 1705*

Sir

My absence from the Bath, where I had Appointed my Brother to Meet me and where having waited Two dayes I Could not Satisfye my Self to spend my Time, Occasion'd me to Miss him Longer then I Intended and Consequently to Deferr my Giveing you an Account That by him I Recd as well the Supply as the Repeated Expressions of your Concern for my Safety, for both of which Sir I Owe More Acknowlegements than I Can Express this Way.

I spent about 8 dayes, the Intervall I Mention above, in Goeing back into Somersetshire and that Great Vale of Trade Extending from Warminster on the south bordr of Wilts to Cirencester in Gloucester shire, which lyeing so Out of the Road I Could no Otherwise take Either Goeing or Comeing without Omitting places of Equall Moment.

Here I shall give you an Account & I hope to satisfaction of strange and Unaccountable people as well as practises in the late Elections, with a survey something perticular of the Towns of Warminster, Westbury, Bradford, Trubridge, Chipenham, Caln, Divizes, Malmsbury, Bedwin, Lutgersall, Marleboro', Cirencester, &ca.

Here I am to Note to you Sir that *Watt White*[1] Member for Chipenham is Dead, and that all the Gentry of the high party who here act like Devills more than Men, *pardon the Expression,* are Embark't to get in if possible that scandall of the County Coll Chivers,[2] and the Design is not so Much to have the Man in the house as to shelter him from the prosecution of my Ld Bishop of Salisbury who prosecutes him for most Impudent language, of all which I have the perticulars.[3]

Sir there Can not be a greater peice of Service to the publick nor Can any Thing Tend more to Carrying future Elections in this County, which Now Run higher and worse than in most places in England, than to prevent this project, and One step above would do it Effectually Viz: putting Chivers Out of the Commission of peace to which he is Really a horrible scandall— for by being in that power he Influences the Town, Sitts Dilligently at Every petty sessions, and Aws the people. He was at this work when I was at Chipenham— This may be done

---

[1] Walter White had died in July.   [2] Henry Chivers.
[3] See John Oldmixon, *History of England,* 1735, p. 368.

Obliquely; No Man Need kno' who hurt them. His Character will most Clearly Justifye it and No man Can Object. If he is Out of the peace he Certainly looses the Election.

My Ld Mordaunt[1] stands against Mr Chivers but his Intrest is but weak yet.

Bristoll, Gloucester, and Bath[2] are Entirely Reform'd Cittyes and the Moderate Intrest prevails amain.

Divizes and the wholl County of Wilts are Corrupted and abused by the *Iron-Chest*, a Modern proverb now known in this Country as Universally as the Alphabet. The Meaning is the Reciever Genll of the County is Sir Fra: Childs Bro:[3] whose Influence so Rules by Lending Money that who ever is Needy is sure to be bought off.

The Remove of that One Article would make 20 Members more, of which I Reserve till I have the honour to see you.

I am Now Moveing North, shall be at Shrewsbury to morrow and at Manchester Thursday from whence Ile do my self the honour to write again, and where I may Reciev any Ordrs from you if you please to Direct to Robt Davis, to be left at the post house at Manchester Till Call'd for, for I shall Go to Leverpool & Come back thither.

I am I bless God Got Clear of all the Enemies I apprehended and am Every where Recd with Unusuall Respect.

It a little supriz'd me At Gloucester when Mr Forbes[4] the Dissenting Minister bid me at parting Give his humble service to you for he knew I had the honour [to][5] be known to you. I Can no way Divine his Intelligence unless Mr Auditor[6] might mention it to him.

I am, Sir, Your Most Obedient [   ][7]
A G[8]

Kiderminster, Sept. 10. 1705

MS.: Duke of Portland, Defoe Papers, I ff. 41–42. *Pub.*: *H.M.C. Portland*, iv. 244–5. *Address* (in Defoe's hand, though disguised): 'For The Right Honoble Robert Harley Esqr., Principall Secretary of State.'

[1] Son of the Earl of Peterborough. In the subsequent election he defeated Chivers (Luttrell, *Brief Relation*, v. 618).
[2] Defoe added 'Tewksbury', then crossed it out.
[3] Sir Francis Child, banker and former Mayor of London, was M.P. for Devizes. His brother John was removed from the Wiltshire receivership in the following spring (Luttrell, *Brief Relation*, vi. 31).
[4] James Forbes (1629?–1712).   [5] MS. has 'the'.
[6] Edward Harley, brother to Robert, was one of the Auditors of the Imprest.
[7] MS. torn.
[8] For 'Alexander Goldsmith', one of Defoe's pseudonyms.

43. *To* EDWARD OWEN.[1] *26 and 27 October 1705*

Mr Owen

I Can Not but with Some Satisfaction look back on the Conversation you had with the Gentlemen at the Bull.[2]

Mithinks I See all our English Gentlemen would Come to Their Reason if They would but Allow themselves to Argue Against us without Prejudice. I Can Not but Own The Sence and Parts of both the Gentlemen with you and I Vallue Them as Such, and It Appear'd Perticularly in Two Things which as they Frankly Ownd So all the Gentlemen of That Party would Own them also if they were Masters of the like Understanding.

1. The Dr Allow'd That On Extraordinary Occasion The Collective or Representative body of This Nation May Limitt, alter, or Interupt the Succession of the Crown and that the Said body of the people are the Judges of That Occasion—and indeed they must all allow it or Deny the Queens Claim to The Crown.

2 The Dr Allowed it was Scandalous to the Church of England that the Non Jurants should joyn and pretend to Defend the Church of England which at the same Time They Denye to be a True Church and Declare to be scismaticall.

I know but One Thing more I Could wish of those Gentlemen to bring us all to be Of One mind, and That is That These Gentlemen would practise What they Also Allow'd to be Reasonable, that they might live like Christians, Neighbours, and Gentlemen with their Brethren who Differ in some Cases and not Two Partyes being Eternally Cutting One Anothers Throates on Chimeras of a Presbyterian Govornmt which I Dare

---

[1] Edward Owen was formerly Mayor and at this time an Alderman of Coventry, and had long supported the Whig cause in the turbulent political contests of that city. In 1702, when he was Under-Sheriff, the House of Commons had demanded his apprehension for 'having been guilty of divers illegal and partial proceedings in the late election for the City of Coventry'. He had then absconded, and the Queen had offered a reward of £50 for his capture. The consequence, if any there was, is not known. See T. W. Whitley, *Parliamentary Representation of the City of Coventry*, Coventry, 1894, pp. 122–35. In May 1705, in spite of the Queen's concern for the peace of the city, the election in Coventry resulted in three days of riot, during which a mob took possession of the town hall and 'many voters were beaten, knocked down, dragged along the ground by the hair and inhumanly abused'. Owen joined the Mayor and five other Aldermen in a report to Harley which placed blame for the riots upon the Tory candidates (*H.M.C. Portland*, iv. 187–8). Defoe reported two Coventry riots in the *Reviews* for 10 May 1705 and 17 Aug. 1706. His information probably came, at least in part, from Owen, who was one of his agents (No. 46).

[2] A Tory rendezvous (T. W. Whitley, op. cit., pp. 141–2).

Undertake to Convince Men of their sence and Candor No Dissenter in his witts Can Desire, and he that Does Must act against the Intrests of the Dissenters in Generall and be Fitter to Go to Bedlam than to be a Magistrate.

I have thot Some times those Gentlemen may Expect I shall Reflect Publickly on their Discourse when they may learn who I am. Their Opinion of me I kno' Not, but pray Assure them I kno better Than to Invade Conversation or to make use of any words a Gentleman may Unwarily let fall when in Company they kno' not. And as I kno' Nothing said for which they Can be justly Reproach't, the Concessions above being I hope Their Naturall Sentiments, I wish all those we Call high Church men would act the Gentleman Equally with these to whom Pray give my humble service.

Your Humble Servt

D FOE

Daventry Octo. 26. smith speaker[1]

Pray also Mr Owen Remind those Gentlemen that as to the Character They were pleas'd to give of me that night by Report Vizt that I Owe 3000*l* and have Taken advantage of all the acts of parliamt against my Creditors, it shows them too Credulous and too forward to Report things they can not be sure of, for that

1. Tis false in Fact. I Never took advantage or indeed made Use of any act of parliamt against any Creditor tho' to make use of Law must be lawfull.[2]

2: If I do Owe 3000*l*, I presume a great many men that hold up high Now, if they were to fall into the hands I have been in, would hardly Come Out less in Debt, Since I Can make it appear I lost above 3000*l* in the broil they and all the World kno' of.[3]

3. It is not actually a Crime to Owe 3000*l*, but to Owe it and being Able to Discharge, Omitt or Refuse it.

---

[1] The new House of Commons met on 25 Oct. and the two parties immediately tested their strength in the election of a Speaker. The Tory candidate was William Bromley, Member for Oxford University and leader of the Tackers. The Whigs put forward John Smith, Member for Andover and later Chancellor of the Exchequer. In a heated contest, the Whigs won; Smith received 248 votes, Bromley 205. The result was gratifying of course to Defoe, who disliked Bromley and ridiculed him under the name of 'Bromsky' in *The Dyet of Poland*, 1705, pp. 39–41.

[2] In the following August he was compelled to seek relief from his creditors by taking advantage of the Bankruptcy Law then newly enacted (No. 50).

[3] His arrest and imprisonment in 1703 for writing *The Shortest Way with the Dissenters*. See Lee, *Life*, i. 31–32.

So that if Debt be the Objection and the Occasion So plain,
I think they do me some wrong there and question not but upon
Reflection they are Men of So much Sence they will own it.

Your Humble servt

D F

What Cowards are these Coventry Whigs that now Barcelona is taken,[1] Mr Smith Chosen, and all the Torys Dead
hearted, yet they Dare not so Much as make a bonefire—or
Ring the Bells.

Nay there's that Ned Owen is such a Cowardly Ro . . . that
he Dares not go to Greens Coffee house and Read a balad there.

Fye Ned, Coventry Men Cowards! Fye! Fye!

If you are So Dastardly now, what wou'd ha' become of you
if B B B Bromley had been Chosen.

Courage! men of blew,[2] the job is Done. Rouze up Jere
Withers,[3] the Gold is all your Own.

What a Toad is this de foe. He is old Dog[4] at a guess. He Said
we should have a majority of 60—and behold 52,[5] which put
against 63, which they had of us last parliamt, makes near the
120 I Computed.

And about 25 more Recovred by Controverted Elections[6]
secures the Nation, bewildres the Jacks,[7] Disheartens the high
Church, and I hope makes an End of all these brangles.

Amen

Daventry Saturday morning[8]

Mr Cater[9] & Mr Owen

I Can not write here. You See how all things go. That affair

---

[1] The Earl of Peterborough had entered Barcelona on 3 Oct.

[2] In the preceding reign the rival factions in Coventry had adopted party colours.
The Whigs wore orange, in honour of King William; the Tories were 'true blue'
(T. W. Whitley, *Parliamentary Representation of the City of Coventry*, Coventry, 1894,
p. 118). Defoe elsewhere alludes to the high-flying party at Coventry as a '*true blue
Specimen* of a *Coventry* Dye' (*Review*, 17 Aug. 1706).

[3] Jeremy Withers was a Whig attorney of Coventry (Whitley, op. cit., p. 125).

[4] i.e. expert.

[5] The Whig majority in the election of the Speaker was actually 43 (G. M.
Trevelyan, *Ramillies and the Union with Scotland*, 1932, p. 86).

[6] 'Most of the controversial elections were carried in favour of the whigs: in
some few they failed, more by reason of private animosities than by the strength
of the other side' (*Bishop Burnet's History of His Own Time*, Oxford, 1823, v. 224).

[7] Jacobites.   [8] 27 Oct.

[9] Probably Joseph Cater, who was later designated to receive mail for Defoe at
Coventry (p. 128).

Requires Now your Uttmost speed— Ile be in London God willing on Fryday.[1] Thanks and Service to all friends.

Yours

D F

MS.: Dr. Henry C. Hutchins, New Haven, Conn. Hitherto unpublished. *Address*: 'To Mr Edward Owen in Coventry.' *Endorsed*: 'Obr 1705, Dan: Defoe's Politicks.' In a corner of the fourth page, which otherwise contains only the address and endorsement, Defoe has drawn a line through his note: 'Mr steph Wright, Daventry.'

44. *To* ROBERT HARLEY. [*c. 6 November 1705*]

An Abstract of My Journey
with Casuall Observations on Publick Affaires

I Sett Out from London July 16° haveing Concluded to Make No Observations within 20 Miles of London. I proceed to the Severall stages.

July

16 Brentford. Lodg'd at Justice Meriwethers—he was a justice but Turn'd Out of Commission in the Genll Displaceing Moderate men.[2] Note. Justice Lamb of Acton who was a Goldsmith in Lombard street is now the high flyeing & Ruleing Justice of That Side of Midsx, the same who swore to the flash of his pistoll in the Case of Ni: Charleton.[3]

Reading. They are all well there and there is No Doubt of a Good Member in the Room of Mr Vachell.[4] I have the Exact list of the Magistracy of all the Chief Towns in Berks.

17 Newbury. A large Tradeing Town but Choose no Members, but they Influence the Elections at Ludgersall and Great Bedwin, and a Very Good story about the Bruces[5] who now petition is to be told here.

[1] That is, on 2 Nov. He does not appear to have reached London, however, until the 6th (p. 113).

[2] Lord Keeper Sir Nathan Wright had dismissed large numbers of Justices of the Peace in order to replace them with Tory Party men. Defoe's host must have been Justice Richard Merrewether (mentioned in the 'Braintford Journall', a MS. preserved in the Public Library at Brentford).

[3] See Luttrell, *Brief Relation*, iii. 18 and 87.

[4] Tanfield Vachell, elected for Reading, had died in October (Luttrell, *Brief Relation*, v. 604).

[5] Charles, Lord Bruce, and James Bruce, the defeated Tory candidates for Great Bedwin. See *J.H.C.* xv. 8.

18 Salisbury. Here I have the wholl account of the County Elections and the parsons Rustling my Ld of Salisbury[1] and Mr Westfield his steward, and the Mob Insulting the Duke of Somersett and stopping his Coach in the street.[2]

19, 20 at Blandford. No Corporation, the County too much Govorn'd and this Town Entirely by Seymour Portman and Coll Strangeways.[3] Had Majr Genll Earle[4] plyed his Intrest well they all Say the Other had lost it.

21. at Dorchester. A good for nothing Town. One Member is Churchill[5] the bookseller, the other [   ][6] Chose by the Intrest of Coll Strangewayes. People here Very Moderate.[7]

22 Weymouth. Here the Disorders of my letters hindred me stayeing to do what I purposed.[8]

23 Lyme. A Town Entirely United and all the Church men Very Moderate and well affected.

24 Honiton. A Terrible Mob Election here, but Sir Jno Elvill[9] of Excester is so Cow'd by Sir Wm Drake[10] and Fra: Gwin[11] that he Dares not petition.

25 Excester. Here I have the List of all the partyes Exactly and a Modell how Sir Ed Seymour[12] may be Thrown out against Another Election without any Difficulty at all. Here I learnt the history of the Family of Coll Rolles[13] and how the young Gentleman[14] Kt of the shire for Devon will be brought off from high Church.

Augt

1 I left Excester and Went to Totness, Sir E. S.[15] Town as we Call it, tho' he has not One foot of Land nor a house in the Town.

---

[1] Bishop Gilbert Burnet.   [2] Cf. p. 95.
[3] Seymour Portman, born Henry Seymour, was a brother of the high Tory magnate Sir Edward Seymour, but took the name of Portman upon succeeding to the estate of Sir William Portman, another Tory politician of the western counties. Col. Thomas Strangeways was M.P. for Dorset.
[4] Lieut.-Gen. Thomas Erle was perennial M.P. for Wareham. See p. 94, n. 4.
[5] Awnsham Churchill.
[6] Nathaniel Napier. Left blank in MS.
[7] Cf. *Tour thro' Britain*, i. 210.   [8] See No. 40.
[9] Misspelled. Sir John Elwill was one of the displaced Justices. See Richard Duke to Harley, *H.M.C. Portland*, iv. 122.
[10] M.P. for Honiton.
[11] Tory politician of the western counties. Cf. p. 95, n. 5, and p. 100, n. 2.
[12] See p. 96, n. 2.
[13] Samuel Rolles (or Rolle or Rolls), M.P. for Kellington.
[14] Robert Rolles.   [15] Sir Edward Seymour's

2 Dartmouth. A Bubbled Town Engrosst by the Herns[1] but the story of a ship Call'd the Constant Tacker is a Mistake.

3 To Plympton. A Little Town all Low Church and Very well United but a poor place. Ld Chief *Baron* Treebys[2] Town.

4 To Plymo. I have the skeleton of this Town.

5 To Saltash.

6, 7 To Liskard and Bodmin.

8 To Launceton. There is nothing to be done in these Towns. They are wholly Guided by the Gentlemen, and the Townsmen kno' Little but act just as they are bid. My Ld Granville Govorns severall of them, my Ld Treasurer More.[3] I Thot it was Throwing away Time to stop among them.

9 & 10. Bidiford.

11. Barstaple.

12, 13 Tiverton. Here the Alarm of the Devonshire Justice Hurryed me too fast[4] but I have Establish't Correspondence at all these Towns.

14. Taunton.[5] Have an Exact account here.

15. Bridgewater. And here also.

16. To Bristoll.

19. Bath. A Contest here between the People and the Magistracy will Come before the house.[6]

20. To Chippenham. Here Watt White[7] being Dead That scandall to all Good Manners Coll Chivers puts up. He is the profoundest Rake and Bully in the County and is put up here by the Gentry on purpose to skreen him from the Bishop of Salisbury who sues him for Most Impudt Scandalous lyes Raised of him. Of This I have the perticulars as also of his Scandalous history and Tis the humble Request of all the County on that Side at least that he may be Out of the Commission of the peace for he is a scandall to the Country.[8]

---

1 Frederick and Nathaniel Herne, Members for Clifton.

2 The late Sir George Treby (1644?–1700), formerly M.P. for Plympton and Chief Justice of the Common Pleas. Above '*Baron*', Defoe inserted 'Justice'.

3 John, Lord Granville (1665–1707), Tory politician, had been Lord Lieutenant of Cornwall until the previous spring, when Godolphin, slowly moving away from his old Tory colleagues, assumed the post himself.   4 See No. 40.

5 But according to Nos. 40 and 41, Defoe was at Tiverton on this date.

6 See *J.H.C.* xv. 12.

7 Walter White, the newly elected M.P. for Chippenham.

⁸ f. p. 103.

22 To Divizes. Here is the Same petition against the Iron Chest, the story of which is worth Relateing.[1]

23 To Bradford, Trubridge, and Westbury. The skeletons of all these Towns are Compleat with all the Vale here for 50 miles.

24 To Devizes again and from thence to Visit young Ducket Chosen for Caln, the same Sir Cha Hedges petitions agt: of him the story how the Atheist Club at Oxford Us'd him, his Character.[2]

25 To the Bath.

26 Back to Bristoll. The history of the Revolution of this Citty is large and Edifyeing and I have an Exact scale of the people, their Trade, and Magistracy. Stay'd here 4 dayes.

30, 31 To the Bath again, Chipenham and Caln, thence to Malmsbury, Tutbury,[3] and Cirencester. Here I had the story of the Election which it seems Mr Cox[4] has Given Over, or Elce the briberys on both sides would ha' Made Strange work.

Septembr

1. To Gloucester. A perfect Change here, the hystory of which I had from Mr. Wade, Bro: to Major Wade[5] of Bristoll, and from Mr Forbs.[6] This City and Bristoll are perfectly Reformd and New Modelled.

2. Teuxbury. A Quiet Tradeing Drunken Town, a whig bayly and all well.

3 Pershore and Evisham. Great Contest at the last for Sir Richard Cox[7] and a Great Deal of Fowl play.

4 Worcester. Here I forbore to Examine as to the Magistracy, you haveing full knowlege of persons and things.

[1] See p. 104.

[2] George Duckett (1684–1732) later turned author, criticized Pope's translation of *The Iliad*, and, like his visitor, was enrolled in *The Dunciad*. Hedges was Secretary of State and former M.P. for Calne. The affair of Duckett and the Atheist Club appears in the *Review* for 9 Oct. 1705, and in Defoe's 'Vision of the Angelic World' in *Serious Reflections during the Life and Surprising Adventures of Robinson Crusoe*, ed. G. A. Aitken, pp. 296–314.

[3] Corrected in another hand to 'Tedbury' (i.e. Tetbury, Glouc.).

[4] Charles Cox. See *J.H.C.* xv. 12, 15, and 26.

[5] Nathaniel Wade, pardoned by King James for commanding a regiment in Monmouth's rebellion, was now a city official in Bristol. Of his brother nothing seems to be known.

[6] James Forbes, the venerable dissenting minister.

[7] Sir Richard Cocks had not been returned.

5 To Leominster. I went on a perticular Obligation to Visit a Quacker, One Bowen that I had been Engag'd to by his brother here, but as being Mr Harleys Town I did nothing here.[1]

7 Beawdly. Of this Town I have a long and Usefull hystory and of the Election there.

8 Bridgnorth. Of this Town I have a full account and of the Throwing Out Sir Sir Ed Acton.[2]

10 Shrewsbury.[3] Of this Town I have an Exact list.

11 Wrexam.

12 Chester. And of this also.

13 Leverpool. And here also.

16 Warrington.⎫

17 Manchester.⎪ No Magistrates in any of these Towns. Choose

20. Boulton. ⎬ no Members nor have any officer but a Con-

21. Rochdale. ⎪ stable.

22. Hallifax ⎭

23, 26 Leeds, Wakefield, and Sheffield. No members Chosen here neither. Here I have made usefull Remarks on Trade and Observe that Frequent Elections haveing no Influence here to Divide the people, They live here in Much more peace with one another than in other parts.

29. Darby. The partyes were Exceeding Inveterate here but begin to Unite Very well.

October

2 Nottingham. This is a Violently Divided Town. I have the Exact schedule of their Leaders.

6 Leicester. A monstruous story here about the Elections and the Contending partyes here Dayly together by the Eares.

8 Lutterworth. Here Justice Bradgate Rod a horseback into the Meeting house and Told the parson as he was preaching he Lyed.[4] A high flyeing Town but no Corporation.

9. Coventry. Of this Town you will see the history at large in print.[5]

---

[1] Edward Harley (1664–1735), brother to the Secretary, was Recorder and M.P. for Leominster. Bowen is unidentified.

[2] Sir Edward Acton had been M.P. for Bridgnorth.

[3] But according to No. 42, Defoe was in Kidderminster on this date.

[4] Cf. *Review*, 10 Nov. 1705.

[5] Defoe had written one *Review* (10 May 1705) on the Coventry election riots, and in another (5 June 1705) had indicated his intention of drawing up an 'exact account' of the affair. Although that proposal is repeated here, again in the Preface

15. Daventry. Famous for an Infamous parson who among
other things swore himself a Freeholder whereas he is not
the Incumbent but Curate Onely.
16 Northampton. Of this town I have a Draft.
18 Wellingboro'.
19 Huntington.
21 Cambridge. Done before,[1] but the story of the Colleges
Disscomoning Mr Love the late Mayor[2] and his Indiscretions are very Remarkable.
25 Bury. Here the Case of my Ld Harvey and Sir Dudly
Cullumb[3] and the measures taken on both sides for the
Approaching Election are Observable.
28 Cambridge again, to Move some Friends that Came thither
from London on private bussiness of my Own.

Nov.

1 To Sudbury, and have the perticulars of their Mannagemt
of the last Election.
3 To Colechester.
5 To Chelmsford.
6 To London.

In all Parts the Greatest hindrance to the forming the
People into Moderation and Union Among Themselves, Next
to the Clergy, are the Justices.
Wherever There happens to be Moderate Justices The people
live Easy and The Parsons have the less Influence, but the Con-
duct of the Justices in Most parts is Intollerably scandalous,
Especially in Wilts, in Lancashire, in Nottingham, Leicester,
Warrwick, Northampton, Suffolk, Essex, and Midsx.[4]

MS.: Duke of Portland, Defoe Papers, 1 ff. 44–49; unsigned, but in the
handwriting of Defoe. *Pub.*: *H.M.C. Portland*, iv. 269–72. *Address*: 'To The
Right Honoble Robert Harley Esqr., One of Her Majties Principall
Secretaryes of State, Present.' *Endorsed*: 'Abstract of a jorney from July 16:
to Nov: 6: 1705.'

to volume ii of the *Review* (issued 29 Dec. 1705), and yet again in the *Review* for
11 Apr. 1706, Defoe is not known to have published any such work.
[1] During the previous autumn (p. 58).
[2] In university parlance, to 'discommon' a tradesman was to deprive him of the
privilege of trading with undergraduates. For what may well be the story of Mr.
Love, see *Tour thro' Britain*, i. 89.
[3] John Hervey (1665–1751), Baron Hervey of Ickworth, later became Earl of
Bristol. Sir Dudley Cullum (1657–1720) had been M.P. for Suffolk in the previous
Parliament.
[4] For Defoe's general observations on the state of the nation as observed by him
on this circuit, see the *Reviews* for 9 and 11 Oct. 1705.

45. JOHN FRANSHAM *to* DEFOE. [*c. March–April 1706*]

Mr De Foe,

In one of your Letters[1] you were pleas'd to promise me a correspondence tho' accounts were now ceas'd between us, but I am affraid you have forgot it or the hurry of affairs have not given you permission, however I hope now you have labour'd so heartily and gain'd your point for the publick good in the act of Bankruptcy[2] you are a little more at leisure and will acquit yourself of the promise above, and not to make it only a complemental correspondence I will give you a subject relating to the said act. Know then that I have all along during this Bill's being the subject of all conversation been a vigorous defender of the reasonableness and justice of it, endeavouring to make the equity of it appear as clear to others as it did to me and in these little Rencounters I have sometimes occasion to defend my Friend the author of the Review and particularly last night upon my reading the Abstract of the Act and approving it I met with opponents who had receiv'd some prejudice agt you (who they suppos'd was the contriver of it) by some of your creditors in these parts vizt Mr Emperor and Mr Gibbs[3] both whom indeed I have heard reflect upon you, but it was no great Surprise to me as well knowing that there are great numbers of persons in the World that fix the same epithet upon those that can't as on those that will not pay their Debts. However I say these Gentlemen with whom I was last night in discourse having heard the above nam'd persons storys were credulous enough to believe that in your case practice and principle did not exactly correspond. Amongst other things in your defence I read them your Review which contein'd advice to the Bankrupts after the Act pass'd.[4] Can it possibly be suppos'd said I that the author of this paper can have justly any thing dishonest fixt upon him— does not he here allow the Title of an Honest Man to be the most glorious that can be given and consequently the contrary to be the worst, and yet knows it belongs to himself. Can he thus in the Face of the World triumph in his Honesty which is an appeal to all that know him, and yet be conscious that he may easily be

---

[1] Missing.

[2] Defoe strongly supported the Bill, aired the question in all the *Reviews* from 9 Feb. to 26 Mar., and published in April a tract entitled, *Remarks on the Bill to Prevent Frauds Committed by Bankrupts*.

[3] Neither is identified.

[4] See the issue for 26 Mar.

prov'd the contrary—have he not in his reply to Ld Haversham[1] declar'd to all the World that he has uncompounded reduc'd his Debts from £17000 to under £5000, is not that an evident proof of his honesty? Yes reply'd the Gentleman, supposing the Fact, but where's the proof of that? His creditors in these parts are altogether unacquainted with it. No doubt, said I, Mr De Foe has proper reasons for their coming amongst the number of the last to be paid, but I have heard tho' I can't assert it from my own knowledge that one of his creditors in Yarmouth have been fully sattisfy'd his Debt which was considerable. If you could give me any proof of that, reply'd the gentleman, I shall never doubt of his being just, for I readily agree his writings are very much so.

If you think fit to enable me to give him a positive answer I shall receive it with a great deal of Sattisfaction[2] because I shall be thereby likewise better able to vindicate a person whose defence is at all times undertaken with pleasure by

Sir yours &c,

J. F.

MS.: untraced. *Pub.*: Francis Norgate, 'Correspondence between De Foe and John Fransham, of Norwich', *Notes and Queries*, 5 S, iii (1875), 282–3. *Address*: none recorded.

46. [*To* ROBERT HARLEY]. [*April 1706?*]

Remarks &c. Sent into the Country[3]

100 to Plymo & Biddiford   Mr Barron, Minr[4]

[1] *Reply to a Pamphlet Entituled, the L[ord] H[aversham]'s Vindication of His Speech*, published 28 Feb. according to the *Review* of that date.

[2] For Defoe's reply, see No. 49.

[3] This report of the distribution of a publication identified only as 'Remarks &c.' is undated. But in the whole period during which Defoe was associated with Harley, only two of his pamphlets begin with the word 'Remarks', and both of these were published in the spring of 1706. Of these two, the one here referred to is probably *Remarks on the Letter to the Author of the State-Memorial*, a defence of Marlborough and Harley which the Government would have wished to be widely distributed, and which bears at the beginning of the text the caption 'Remarks &c.'. The date given on the title-page is 1706. The exact date of publication has never been established, but the piece probably was comparatively fresh when it drew forth a comment upon it in the *Rehearsal* for 10 Apr. The other tract, a less likely possibility, is Defoe's *Remarks on the Bill to Prevent Frauds Committed by Bankrupts*, a commentary on the Bankruptcy Act of Mar. 1706, which was published on 18 Apr. (Dottin, *Defoe*, p. 811).

In the report, persons whose names are followed by no note remain unidentified.

[4] Peter Baron, or Barron, dissenting minister at Plymouth, was ordained in 1704 and died in 1759 (MS. 36.28, and Wilson MS. D*, p. 179, both in Dr. Williams's Library, London).

100	to Excester	Mr. Eveleigh, Do.[1]
25	to Tiverton	Mr Bear, Mercht[2]
25	to Taunton	Mr James, Mr[3]
12	to Bridgewater	Mr Codrington
100	Bristoll	Benja Cool, Quaker[4]
25	Do.	Mr Wraxall, Mercha
25	Lime & Bridport	Mr Gay, Mr[5]
12	Weymo	Mr Fenner, Mr[6]
12	Dorchester	Mr Nowell, Mr[7]
25	Salisbury	Mr sloan, Mr[8]
25	Divizes	Tho: Webb, Clothr
12	Newbury	Ja Pearce, Mr[9]
25	Reading	Timo Westley[10]
25	Cirencester &c.	Mr Dixe
12	Bath	Dr Parker[11]
12	Caln & Chipenham	by Mr Dukett[12]
25	Gloucester	by Mr Dixe
12	Hereford	Mr Bolow
12	Worcester	Mr Fitzer, Clothr
12	Leominster	Mr stansbury
12	Bewdly	Mr Oasland, Mr[13]

[1] Josiah Eveleigh, dissenting minister at Bowden Hill, Crediton, 1702–36 (G. E. Evans, *Vestiges of Protestant Dissent*, Liverpool, 1897, p. 60). See also No. 39, p. 96.

[2] Francis Bear, or Bere. See p. 96.

[3] Stephen James, tutor at Taunton Academy for Dissenters from 1706 until his death in 1725 (Alexander Gordon, *Freedom after Ejection*, Manchester, 1917, pp. 291–2).

[4] Benjamin Cool, or Coole, a well-to-do merchant of Bristol, one of the founders of the Bristol Brass Co. and of the Bristol Friends' Workhouse (Isabel Grubb, *Quakerism and Industry before 1800*, 1930, pp. 50–53).

[5] Mathew Gay, dissenting minister at Lyme Regis (MS. entitled 'Records of Nonconformity No. 4', p. 32, in Dr. Williams's Library).

[6] John Fenner, dissenting minister at Weymouth from about 1691 to 1712 (Gordon, op. cit., p. 262). See also No. 40, p. 98.

[7] Baruch Nowell, dissenting minister at Pease Lane, Dorchester, from 1689 to 1739 (Evans, op. cit., p. 74).

[8] Sloan is recorded as being dissenting minister at Salisbury, but his first name is not given (MS. 35.4 in Dr. Williams's Library).

[9] James Peirce (1674?–1726) was dissenting minister at Toomer's Court, Newbury, from 1706 to 1713. He was later charged with Arianism and became a principal in the Salters' Hall controversy (*D.N.B.*).

[10] Timothy Westley, or Wesley, brother of Samuel Wesley (Defoe's fellow student at Morton's Academy) and uncle of John Wesley, founder of Methodism (A. G. Mathews, *Calamy Revised*, Oxford, 1934, p. 521).

[11] Henry Parker (1655–1736) attended Oxford, received the B.A. in 1675 and the M.A. in 1678, and was incorporated at Cambridge in 1705. He practised medicine at Bath (John and J. A. Venn, *Alumni Cantabrigienses*, iii. 306).

[12] George Duckett. See p. 111, n. 2.

[13] Edward Oasland, or Osland, attended Sheriffhales Academy for Dissenters

25	Evisham & Parshore	Mr Gibbons
50	shrewsbury	Mr Elisha[1]
50	Chester	Mr Hinks
50	Leverpool	Mr Done[2]
50	Whitehaven & preston	Mr Gale
12	Warrington	Mr Owen, Mr[3]
25	Manchester	Mr Cuningham, Mr[4]
25	Bolton	Mr Crompton, Mr[5]
25	Hallifax	Mr priestly, Mr[6]
25	Leeds & Wakefield	Mr Ibbetson[7]
100	Newcastle	Mr Button[8]
50	York and Hull	by Mr Ibbetson
25	Gainsboro'	Mr Coates, Mercha[9]
25	sheffield	Mr symmonds
25	Nottingham	Dr Woodhouse[10]
12	Leicester	Mr sympson
12	Mount sorrell	Mr Matthews, Mr[11]
12	Wigston	Mr Chambers, Mr[12]

(as did Harley) and was dissenting minister at High Street, Bewdley, from 1704 to 1750 (Evans, op. cit., p. 15, and Gordon, op. cit., p. 322).

[1] Samuel Elisha, attorney and later Mayor of Shrewsbury. See Nos. 16 and 20.

[2] Done, whose first name remains unknown, was active in municipal affairs and had invited Defoe to his house when the latter visited Liverpool in the previous September (*Norris Papers*, ed. Thomas Heywood, Manchester: Chetham Society, 1846, pp. 144–5).

[3] Charles Owen, dissenting minister at Cairo Street Chapel, Warrington, was also tutor at Warrington Academy for Dissenters (H. McLachlan, *English Education under the Test Acts*, Manchester, 1931, p. 15).

[4] James Coningham, M.A., was dissenting minister at Cross Street, Manchester, from 1700 to 1712 (Evans, op. cit., p. 165).

[5] Unidentified. John Crompton had been a dissenting preacher at Bolton, but had died in Aug. 1703, before Defoe became acquainted with Harley (p. 10) and hence before this report was written. Crompton left a son, also John, but there is no evidence that the son was a minister (Mathews, op. cit., p. 145). Joseph Crompton, baptized at Bolton, served as a dissenting minister from about 1701 to 1719, but not at Bolton (Francis Nicholson and Ernest Axon, *The Older Nonconformity in Kendal*, Kendal, 1915, pp. 602–3).

[6] Nathaniel Priestley was dissenting minister at Northgate End Chapel, Halifax, from 1696 to 1728 (Gordon, op. cit., p. 335).

[7] Unidentified. The Ibbetsons were one of the leading nonconformist families of Leeds.   [8] Joseph Button, bookseller. See No. 152.

[9] Unidentified. Perhaps related to the 'Matthew Coats the elder, mercer', who before his death in 1701 provided a chapel for the Gainsborough dissenters (Gordon, op. cit., p. 239).

[10] John Woodhouse, M.D. His late father, the Rev. John Woodhouse, had succeeded Dr. Samuel Annesley at Little St. Helen's, London, where the Defoe family for many years worshipped (Gordon, op. cit., p. 389).

[11] Michael Mathews (Gordon, op. cit., p. 310).

[12] Probably Abraham Chambers (Presbyterian Board Minutes, ii. 187 and 223, in Dr. Williams's Library).

12	Lutterworth	Mr Dowley, Mr[1]
25	Coventry	Mr Owen[2]
25	Daventry & Northampton	Mr smith
50	Cambridge	Mr Jardin
25	Wisbich	Mr Kinderly
25	Bury	Mr Morley[3]
1405		

Ditto

12	To stamford	Mr
12	Beccles	Mr Nokes, Mr[4]
100	Norwich	Mr Fransham[5]
12	Leostoff	Capt Pacy
12	Ipswich	Mr Whitaker
25	sudbury	Capt Fenn
50	Colechester	Mr Wheely
25	Canterbury	Mr Fenner
50	Cranbrook	Mr Jellard
25	Maidstone	Mr Tongue
50	Portsmo	Mr Johnson
25	Braintry &c	Mr Ruggles
25	Hartford &c	Mr smart[6]
25	Aylesbury	Mr Mead
50	to Dublin	Mr Rogers
12	to shirborn	Mr Dix
..	Oxford	Mr Woodcock[7]
510		
50	laid Down in Coffee houses	
100	Given about by hand	

MS.: Duke of Portland, Defoe Papers, 1 ff. 49–50. Hitherto unpublished.
Address: none.

[1] Peter Dowley, or Dowely, or Dewly, dissenting minister at Lutterworth from 1696 to 1715 or later (Gordon, op. cit., p. 255).
[2] Probably Edward Owen. See p. 105, n. 1.
[3] Unidentified but mentioned earlier, p. 62.
[4] William Nokes was pastor of an Independent congregation at Beccles from 1703 to 1709. He later conformed (Walter Wilson, *History and Antiquities of Dissenting Churches*, 1808–14, ii. 536).
[5] John Fransham, linen-draper. See p. 64, n. 2.
[6] A family of prominent Dissenters in Hertfordshire was so named.
[7] Perhaps Josiah Woodcock, dissenting minister at Oxford (Wilson, op. cit. iv. 393).

47. [*To* ROBERT HARLEY]. *6 May 1706*

Sir

As the last Time I had the favor of Audience with you, you Were pleasd to Tell me you Desir'd to speak with me on Account of The Review &c. I have Often Endeavour'd to have the like honor and began to hope Some thing might Offer in which I might be usefull to you.

But I am Not Onely Unhappy in frequent Dissappointmts, but my Unhappy Circumstances Makeing those Dissappointmts more Severe to me than I believ you Would have them be, forces me to give you This too Tedious Narrative, Humbly to state to you My present Case and Earnest Request, and Entreat your pardon for the Importunate plainess, a Liberty you were pleas'd Frankly to give me and which I have been too Apt to Accept of.

My Case Really Sir admitts no Ceremony, being Come to that Crisis, that without Some powerfull aid, or Some Miracle which I Ought Not to Expect, I Shall Soon be Rendred Entirely Useless both to the publick and My Self.[1]

But why do I look to you, or Move you in This Matter? is a question Offers Some shock in My Writeing this.

Pardon my Positive way of speaking. I don't Say I Merit, at least any Thing but Pitty—But Sir you have had the Goodness to put me in hopes that something was Reserv'd in My favour. If I have Mistaken you, I am Wrong Indeed, and would be Glad to be Sett Right, that I might not Expect and make you Uneasy with my Importunityes.

This Reserv Sir you were pleasd to Say with your Usuall Tenderness for me, you would have be Usefull to me, and therefore kept till I was free. But Sir The prospect of that Freedome looks Every Day More Dull upon me, and I foresee I shall Never Master it, Unless I can Take off Some of the most Furious people who Resolutely Oppose me, and which is worse I find it Will be if Contested a Very Doubtfull point whether I am within the Meaning of This Act[2] or no, and am Therefore advis'd Not to attempt it.

Now Sir as the Risq of Disputeing is too Great, Since I must

---

[1] Three weeks later, in writing to Fransham of his pecuniary difficulties, he was saying that he might have to 'quit the kingdom unless reliev'd' (p. 123).

[2] Although the new law was entitled *An Act for Preventing Frauds Committed by Bankrupts*, it was designed to protect not only creditors but bankrupts too. See the *Review* for 23 Mar. 1705–6.

Surrender my Self first into the hands of the Unmercifull, and that to take them off by Treaty is Absolutely Necessary, No Man that is my Friend Advises me to attempt it by Law,[1] Since when they in perticular are Taken off, I shall be as Effectually Free as by the act, all the Rest being Undr Obligation to a Composition which they have Recd part of and Can not go from.[2]

Thus Sir my Freedome Depends Upon a private Treaty, which Treaty without assistance I Can Not Carry on, and Mean Time have been So Close persued Since I saw you, that I am but by Miracle yet Out of their hands, and am Oblig'd to quitt all Conversation, and Make a Retreat altogether Disconsolate, and Such as Renders me Useless and Uncapable.

This Urges me Sir to Say if There is Such a Thing, if her Majties Bounty has any Thing In Reserv for me, I Entreat of you One of The Two following perticulars, And tis fitt I should leave it to you to Choose.

1st Sir That I may be assisted as far as 2 or 300*l* will do it, to Free my Self from the Imediate fury of 5 or 6 Unreasonable Creditors, after which I shall by my Own strength work Thro' the Rest in Time.

2dly Or Sir That According to your kind promise which I Can not but Claim, you will please to send me Somewhere Abroad, Out of The Reach of Their hands, and That her Majties Bounty may be someway Applyed to the support of my Family.

I Really kno' not Sir whether This thing I Call her Majties Bounty be what I Ought to speak of in this Manner or No. I pretend to no Meritt, I have done but my Duty—But Indeed I have been Unjustly Ruin'd and that in her Majties Name, and I am Now Implacably persued purely on Account of my Endeavours for her Majties Service:[3] if these are Merits, I have some Claim, And I flatter my Self your Intercession Sir will Improve it: I Cease to go On with This Sad story, and Tho' my Case Renders me Now Next to Desperate, yet I Can not Enlarge upon my Complaint.

I am not weary attending at your Door, nor do I Repine at stayeing your Leisure—But Sir the Risque I Run So Much as to

---

[1] Nevertheless he did seek relief under the Act (*Review*, 20 Aug. 1706) and apparently received it (p. 124).

[2] After each of his failures, Defoe had negotiated compositions with at least some of his creditors, whereby they accepted a proportion of his assets in discharge of their claims (Sutherland, *Defoe*, pp. 44 and 272).

[3] See the *Review* for 11 Oct. 1705.

pass and Repass is of the last Consequence to me, and Tho' I Resolv if possible not to be Taken by Them, yet Theres no Defending against a surprize.

The loss I sustain also in the want of Conversing with you, appeares to me Destructive of all the Designs layd by me for your service. The Correspondence I had Settled by your Ordr in most parts of England and from which on all Occasions I Could have Rendred you Service, Dyes and Declines for want of That Assistance which you were pleasd to Allow was necessary to me, Vizt of a Servant to assist, and of frequent Communication of things to keep Intelligence alive.

The Very Charge is too great for my Reduc't Condition, and the Number of Letters too many for the few Undisturb'd houres which I have left me.

Thus I am Rendred Useless to you, in that which I hoped Once to have brought to a perfection beyond Even your Own Expectation, and in which I have been at no Inconsiderable Charge Over and Above what you have been pleasd to allot for that work.

I hope you will think all this proceeds from a mind Griev'd that I Can not be made that usefull Instrumt to the publick I would be, and what Ever may look self Intrested, you will pardon, for tho' Tis True I Importune you in the first, I above all Covet to show you That I would not be thought to Enjoy your favour, not to your advantage:

I have Severall things to Move you in that I Can not Comprise here. Mr Ducket[1] has been in Town. That Affair being Delay'd, not Onely sinks my Intrest and Correspondence in that County, but puffs up the high Intrest in the Country to a Vast Disadvantage, and I have much to say on that head worth Notice.

I would be your Humble Petitioner for a private Appartmt in Whitehall, where I am Told It is in your power to admitt me, and haveing an Opportunity now to Clear my Self of the Queens Bench by an Accidt which I want to Inform you of, I might by the shelter of Such a Retreat prevent any New attempts upon me there.

I have also Something to Inform you of, of a Design forming Agat your Self, which I should be Glad to be Instrumentall to Dissappoint, but all these things Reciev their Interruption, as I a Continued Mortification in the Want of that Access to your Self which formerly I Enjoyd.

---

[1] See p. 111, n. 2. Duckett's 'affair' is unexplained.

I am Impatient to Mention also the subject of the Three last Reviews[1] which if you have not seen is my loss, Since without doubt I might be Enabled by you to have Carryed on that subject Exceedingly to the Govornments advantage.

I humbly Referr all these things to your Consideration and wait to Dispose my Self by your Direction.

I am, Sir, Your Most Obedt Servt
[symbol]

May. 6. 1706

MS.: Duke of Portland, Defoe Papers, 1 ff. 52–53. *Pub.*: *H.M.C. Portland*, iv. 300–2. *Address*: none.

48. *To* ROBERT HARLEY. *21 May 1706*

Sir

I am Loth to break in upon your Joy, and No Man More Sincerely Congratulates it Than I,[2] Tho' my Clouds Darken my Own Expression of it, and Makes me Reflect That 'tis hard all the Queens friends Rejoyce but I.

My Mellancholly Story however is Not the Design of This. I Can not Expect but you are in Hurrys too Great to Think of my Triffling affair, but I Could not but Send you the Enclos'd.[3] Perhaps you may Make Use of Them to my advantage; if not Tis Fitt I should Recommend Them to you Sir to use at your Pleasure.

It is allways a Cordiall to me to See you but Now when So Much more Suppress't than Ever it would be Peculiarly So.

Will a short Essay on These mighty Affaires be Accepted from me in This juncture? is a question which if answerd by you Sir would help Inspire the performance.

Your Most Obedt St
[symbol]

May. 21. 1706

MS.: Duke of Portland, Defoe Papers, 1 ff. 54–55. *Pub.*: *H.M.C. Portland*, iv. 305. *Address*: 'To the Right Honble Robert Harley Esqr., Principll Secretary of State.'

[1] In the *Reviews* for 2, 4, and 7 May, Defoe had defended the Ministry against criticism prompted by the conduct of the war in Spain.

[2] The news of Marlborough's victory at Ramillies had just reached London. Defoe celebrated the triumph in a poem, to which he gave most of the *Review* of this day.

[3] Missing, but perhaps his verses on the victory.

49. *To* JOHN FRANSHAM. *24 May 1706*

Sir,

I have several times been going to reply to your long Letter[1] but have been interrupted by continual hurry of business and have so little time to correspond with my Friends that I every day loose them who cannot bear with it.

I am sorry to see you assaulted about my Integrity, and wonder you should expect any man can be persuaded to believe a man honest whom they loose by.

I appeal to all the World, and in it to my worst Enemy's for these articles of my Honesty, and let any man in Trade shew better if they can.

1st If my Disaster was not from plain known inevitable causes which humane wisdom could not foresee nor humane power prevent.[2]

2dly If I did not first leave off early according to my advice now to others,[3] nay while my Estate was sufficient to pay all men their full demand.

3dly If I did not immediately offer a full surrender of all I had in the World in Sattisfaction to my Creditors.

4thly If after they had driven me to all extremities till all was consumed and I had not 5*s* in the World but by Providence and my own Industry in the World I began to rise again I did not pay every one according to my utmost ability.

5thly If notwithstanding this it has not cost me £5000 since I have been in these Troubles to maintain my Liberty to work for them and to defend myself against such as would have all their Debt before others and indeed before I could get it.

As to people paid at Yarmouth I can not but admire you should suffer yourself to be prevail'd upon to bring that as a proof of my honesty which is a snare laid for me that finding some people paid more than others they may have room to complain and pretend to take out a Commission of Bankrupt to recover it again.[4]

The thing is true in Fact, and as true that these people to whom I have been so particular are now the only people who pursue me so close that I must at last I doubt quit the kingdom

---

[1] No. 45.
[2] The exact cause of Defoe's bankruptcy in 1692 has never come to light. See Sutherland, *Defoe*, pp. 42–47.
[3] See the *Review* for 19 Feb. 1705–6.
[4] A Yarmouth creditor was still pursuing him seven years later (p. 401).

unless reliev'd by this late Act of Parliament[1] in which I am not yet sure that I shall find neither.

I have not time to enlarge on this melancholy story, which is perhaps the severest ever you heard. I desire to submit, but methinks people that call themselves protestants should be content to take all a man have and not pursue him to death.

I am now to acquaint you and all my Friends that Jure Divino at last is finished and waits only your order how many and whether bound or in sheets it shall be sent.[2]

There is also a picture of your humble Servant[3] prepar'd at the request of some of my Friends who are pleas'd to value it more than it deserves, but as it will cost a shilling I shall leave it free for those that please to take it or leave it.

I am Your humble Servt
D. F.

May 24, 1706.

MS.: untraced. *Pub.*: Francis Norgate, 'Correspondence between De Foe and John Fransham, of Norwich', *Notes and Queries*, 5 S, iii (1875), 283. *Address*: none recorded.

50. *To* ROBERT HARLEY. [*21 August 1706*]

Sir

Tho' I had Not the honor to Wait on you last Night your Letter forbiding, I Can Not but give you the Trouble of Letting you kno', God almighty has heard the Cries of a Disstresst Family and has given me at last a Compleat Victory Over the most Furious, Subtill and Malitious Opposition That has been Seen in all The Instances of the Bankrupts act.[4]

I Earnestly Wish and Long to give you the perticulars in which Something Very Unusuall will Divert you.

[1] See the *Review* for 23 Mar. 1705–6.
[2] But two months passed before the volume finally appeared (*Review*, 18 July 1706).
[3] The so-called *Jure Divino* portrait. See frontispiece.
[4] 'The Commissioners in a renewed Commission of Bankrupt against Daniel Foe, late of London, Merchant, give Notice, That he hath surrendred himself to the said Commissioners, and been thrice examined; and that he will attend again on Thursday the 22d Instant, at 4 in the Afternoon, at the Chamber of Mr. Robert Davis, in Essex-Court in the Middle Temple, in order to finish his Examination; when and where his Creditors may attend, to shew Cause why a Certificate should not be signed pursuant to the late Act of Parliament' (*London Gazette*, 8 Aug. 1706). This letter indicates that his final examination was held a day earlier than the date announced for it. For his own account of the 'Malitious Opposition', see the *Review* for 20 Aug. 1706 (not to be confused with the issue of Thursday, 22 Aug., incorrectly dated 20 Aug.).

Sir I Can Not but Comunicate to you One Thing Nor Can I stay till the Time I am to wait on you for it.

There is a Letter or Manuscript, for tis as big as a book, brought I Suppose by a Messenger Express from Scotland, to be printed here. Tis Unhappily Written and full of Mischief against the Union, but perticularly address't to the Dissenters and Insinuateing that their Destruction is Intended and will be Compass't in it. It Seems to Imply that the presbys in Scotland Are alarm'd at it, that the Ministers and assistants keep Dayes of Prayer and fasting against it, that they foresee it will be fatall to their Establishmt and would Invite the Dissenters into the same Notions.

It is Something perticularly wonderfull that has brought this to me but I Suppose I shall be Applyed to to get it printed. I Encourage Them to it as far as I Can without appearing too forward. If I Can lay my hands Upon the Manuscript, you will be Sure to see it,[1] and if I Can not prevent its publication then I shall but Ill Recomend my Capascity to you as fitt to be Employd abroad.

I shall more Largely Explain this when I have the honour to see you On Saturday Night.

I am Exceedingly Fateagu'd with this afternoons Struggle.
Your Most Obedt &c
[symbol]

Wednsday Night[2]

MS.: Duke of Portland, Defoe Papers, 1 ff. 56–57. *Pub.*: *H.M.C. Portland*, iv. 323. *Address*: 'To The Right Honble Robert Harley Esqr., Principall Secreta of State.' *Endorsed*: 'Mr Goldsmith, Ḥ Aug: 22–23: 1706.'

51. [*To* ROBERT HARLEY]. *13 September 1706*

Sir

I Was Comeing to Wait Upon you and Take your Last Instructions, when I Met with your Ordr to Dispatch[3] without any farther Conferences; Tis the More Afflicting to me because you are pleas'd to Signifye That Something Unhappy Relateing to your Self Sir is the Occasion, in which I Condole tho' I kno' Not Directly the Occasion—But on My Own Account Sir This is a

---

[1] Harley received the manuscript (Duke of Portland, Harley Papers, 39 ff. 10–27) and endorsed it 'γολδσμιθ Aug: 29: 1706.'
[2] This letter is misdated 23 Aug. in *H.M.C. Portland*, iv. It was received on 22–23 Aug. according to the endorsement; the previous Wednesday was the 21st.
[3] For Scotland, to further the interests of the Treaty of Union.

Perticular Disaster because I had a great many Enquiries to make Sir in Ordr to my Conduct in The Affair I go Upon.

Not but That as Abraham went Chearfully Out Not knowing whither he went, Depending on him that Sent him, So Sir I Willingly go On, Entirely Depending that I shall have Such Instructions as shall Not Dissable me from Effectually Answering your Expectation.

I Onely Entreat your leav to Remind you, that as you have accquainted Her Majtie & My Ld Treasr with my goeing, The Success of my Journey is the More my Concerne, least want of Information Rendring me Useless, The want of Capascity or Dilligence, be judg'd the Reason of my Miscarriage.

Under These Anxious Thoughts I beg you to Considr Sir That I am without the heads of the Treaty,[1] without the Characters of the Gentlemen who were here, and without the knowlege of what has been Transacted In the Councils here, in Ordr to Dictate to me what I am to Observ.[2] Hence I shall Seem Ignorant, of the Sence of England, and of what is Expected here, or Intended from Hence, and Thus I shall be so far from knowing the people I go to That I shall appear Not to kno' those I Come from.

However, That if my Notions are wrong, I may be Set Right by your Instructions, I beg leav, tho' it be beginning at the wrong End, to Set Down how I Understand my present bussiness—as foll.

1 To Inform My Self of the Measures Takeing Or Partys forming Against the Union and Applye my Self to prevent them.

2 In Conversation and by all Reasonable Methods to Dispose peoples minds to the Union.

3 By writing or Discourse, to Answer any Objections, Libells or Reflections on the Union, the English or the Court, Relateing to the Union.

4 To Remove the Jealousies and Uneasyness of people about Secret Designs here against the Kirk &c.

Sir I beg the Ordrs you please to give me may Mention if I

---

[1] The Treaty consisted of 25 Articles. See G. S. Pryde, *The Treaty of Union of Scotland and England, 1707,* 1950, pp. 83–102.

[2] Early in the year, the Queen had appointed a Commission of 62 members to draw up proposals for a Union. The 31 Scottish Commissioners had come to London to negotiate with their English colleagues, and by 22 July the two groups had agreed upon a tentative Treaty of Union, the 25 Articles of which were to be placed before the two Parliaments for ratification. Since by far the greater opposition was thought likely to come from Scotland, it was arranged to lay the Treaty before the Edinburgh Parliament first.

am Right in my thoughts of these Things—and that you will give me as much light as possible in your farther pleasure Concerning my Conduct.

I Can Not Quit This without Mentioning the Matter of Expence. I Confess Sir when you Told me it is Out of your private, and that the govornmt should be at no Charge, it straightn'd my Thoughts and I am the More Limited in My Designs— Indeed Sir Ile put you to No Expence for Extravagancies, but in the Affair, if I am a good husband I shall ill Serv you.

If it be proper to print any thing there—Some Charge will attend it, and for Intelligence of things I would not be spareing.

I Entreat you to give me the proper limits of Expence, that I may not make you Uneasy on that score; for Tho' I hope I Need Not Assure you That what I shall Take shall not be Missapplyd, and That I shall bring nothing back, leaving any Consideration for me or Mine to your Usuall Goodness; yet I beg you will please to hint to me for my Governmt what you think fit on the head of Charges.

I have Recd Sir your bill of £25—and with the Uttmost Expedition have Equipt my Self as the Summe and the Time will permitt.

I Mention the first not Sir by way of Complaint, of any thing but my Own Missfortune—who haveing as I accquainted you before Parted with So much as horse, Sadele, bridle, pistols and Every thing,[1] I am Forc't to buy all New— Yet Refurnisht Sir with Two horses and all Necessarys, I Assure you I have No fear of highway men. *Cantabit Vacuus*—is my Motto,[2] and if I Reach N Castle I shall be in Condition Very Fitt to wait upon Mr Bell—[3]

As to Family, 7 Children—&c. Hei Mihi—

No Man Sir That Ever Serv'd you shall Trouble you less than I with Complaints of This Nature—But if I have been honest I Must be Naked, & am less Asham'd to Tell you So Than I should be to Tell you I am foresworn and have Made Reserves.

I Need Say No More. Sir you were pleasd Once to Make me hope Her Majtie would have Some Concern for me when free— I have Now Naked Liberty—and Can Not but Recomend the

---

[1] As a result of his bankruptcy in the previous month.
[2] *Cantabit vacuus coram latrone viator* (Juvenal, x. 22).
[3] John Bell, Postmaster at Newcastle upon Tyne, was the intermediary through whom Harley communicated with his agents in the North.

Circumstance to That Bounty which I Trust you will Move on my Account.

Thus Sir you have a Widdo' and Seaven Children On your hands, but A word I presume from you will Ease you of the burthen.

I Ask your Pardon for This Representation to which My Present Circumstance Compells. I shall be No More Importunate in That affair.

I have been Considering About Treating of Union in the Review and Unless your Judgemt and Ordrs Differ believ as I shall Mannage it, it Must be Usefull, but beg hints from you if you find it Otherwise.[1]

I Entreat Letters from you Directed to Alexa Goldsmith[2] to be left at Mr Joseph Caters[3] in Coventry where I shall be God Willing On Thursday or Fryday at Farthest.

If any thing supplimentall offers the Next post, For Ditto to be left at Mr John Drury,[4] Bookseller in Nottingham, and the Next at Mr John Coninghams[5] at Manchester.

Your Most Obedt &c

[symbol]

Pray Sir please to give me the positiv day the Parliament are to sit Down.[6]

sept 13 1706, just takeing horse.

MS.: Duke of Portland, Defoe Papers, 1 ff. 58–59. *Pub.*: *H.M.C. Portland*, iv. 326–8. *Address*: none.

52. *To* ROBERT HARLEY. *22 September 1706*

Sir

The short Jornall of my Travail hither is Not worth your Note Onely to Tell you I was lockt up by a Rain of 48 Houres without Ceasing and that we have not had One Dry Day Since I Set Out. This tho' I stayd but One Day at sturbrige fair made me March Very slow, The Country here being Very Deep and wett. I hope to Make More hast when I get Over the Trent, the Ground being hardr.

---

[1] Defoe's long run of *Reviews* on the Treaty of Union began on 26 Sept.

[2] 'Alexander Goldsmith' was one of Defoe's pseudonyms.

[3] Unidentified, but perhaps the Cater mentioned on p. 107.

[4] Unidentified.

[5] Unidentified, but perhaps associated with—or even confused with—James Coningham, the dissenting minister at Manchester, who was one of Defoe's agents (p. 117). As it happened, Defoe did not get to Manchester (p. 129).

[6] The Scottish Estates were to convene on 3 Oct.

I am Dissapointed in Not Meeting your Instructions at Coventry as by my last In Obedience to your Ordr I Directed. If It Meets me not at Nottingham I shall hope for it at New Castle to be left at the post House or with Mr Bell.[1]

I have put off my Design of Goeing to Manchester because I doubt it being late and yet kno' not the Day the houses will meet at Edb, and the badness of the Waye makes it long Enough getting thither.

Sir I Entreat the favour that I may not fail of your letters at New Castle without which I shall be Extreamly at a loss how to proceed. Till Then I go On Chearfully

As Your Depending Obedt Servt

[symbol]

Leicester Sept. 22. 1706

Sir

I think it my Duty to accquaint you that there is a book published in Town whose Title I do not Remember—Nor Unless I Could see the Courant Can not Describe it Other than that tis Sd Wrott by One that Calls himself a High Church man, in which besides a great Deal of Virulence and High Church poison, I am told the wholl Memoriall is Couch't and as it were Reprinted.[2]

Tis boasted of in this Country as a Defiance to the Court and Indeed the Impudence of the party is Intollerable in these parts and such as I never met with the like in England. They Say here that tis wrott by the Coventry parson Kinderly,[3] Others that Mr Bromley[4] & a Club are the Authors, Others that the Memoriall authors have done it, and perticularly I am told it was printed by — Taylor in Pauls C yard. I mean the young man,

[1] He eventually received instructions (No. 55), but his first mention of them in these letters is on 24 Oct. (p. 132).

[2] *The History of the Church, in Respect Both to its Ancient and Present Condition: To Which Is Added, a Continuation of the Same, with the Opinions of Several Bishops and Learned Divines concerning the Doctrine and Discipline of the Church of England. By One Call'd an High Churchman* (*Daily Courant*, 31 Aug. 1706).

[3] Misspelled. Jonathan Kimberley was at this time Vicar of Trinity Church, Coventry, and Canon of Lichfield. He later became chaplain to Speaker William Bromley and Canon of Westminster. In 1713 Kimberley was appointed Dean of Lichfield, an office for which Swift was a disappointed candidate. Defoe maintained that Kimberley was one of the originators of the movement against occasional conformity (*Review*, 14 July 1705).

[4] William Bromley (1664–1732) was M.P. for Oxford University and one of the champions of the Occasional Conformity Bill. It was Bromley who proposed the motion to tack that Bill to the Land Tax. In 1710 he became Speaker, and in 1713 Secretary of State.

Not old Taylor who I suppose has More Witt—[1] This I thought my Duty to Accquaint you Sir and ask your pardon if it be officious.

Idem &c.

MS.: Duke of Portland, Defoe Papers, i ff. 60–61. *Pub.*: *H.M.C. Portland*, iv. 331–2. *Address*: 'To the Right Honble Robert Harley Esqr., Her Majties Principal Secret of State, Present.' *Endorsed*: 'Mr De Foe.'

53. *To* ROBERT HARLEY. *30 September 1706*

Sir

I have Every Thing here According to my Expectation and yours Sir as to Mr Bell; and am Unhappy Onely in wanting your Letter, Instructions, &c.

Your Letter to Mr Bell put me to Some Difficulty, Mentioning to him That you should Draw a bill on him, whereas I had No bill, but your Letter without your Name and with Some Other Circumstances in it which were Inconvenient to show him; But Mr Bell was pleasd to believ me, and has Supplyd me 25*l* and Given me his Letter of Credit to Edenbg for a Supply in Case of Farther Occasion, in which I shall be as spareing as may Consist with the Duty I Owe to your Service, and the More So because you have not been pleased to limit me in Perticulars.[2]

I have had a Severe Journey hither but it begins to Mend Now and The Two last have been the Onely Dayes without Rain since I left London which has made me longer Getting hither than I Expected.

I shall lose no Time. I came hither last night and shall go away to Morrow morning for Edenbg. If you will please to

---

[1] John Taylor and his son William were partners at 'The Ship', one of the largest establishments of the period. It was William Taylor who thirteen years later published *Robinson Crusoe*.

[2] Next day John Bell wrote to Harley: 'Yester Night Came to towne Mr Alex Goldsmith in his Jurney to Scotland & Sent for me & Enquird if I had an Ordr to pay him Som money. I told him I had a letter from a gentleman that Mention'd him & would Supply him with what he had Occation for. He told me about 25 guineas would Serve him at present & Desird a letter of Cridit to My friend at Edenbrough for what he Shall want there. I Shall give him a letter to the Generall post Master at Edenb to furnish him with what he has Occation for, with Som Restrictions. I Dranke a botle with the gentleman & perceive he is Not Nice in telling his Name, & will Owne it at Edenb. He Sa's he is So publiccly Knowne that it would Not be prudence to goe under an Other Name. I have red part of a booke under his Name; it May be his Owne but be pleased to let that pass. What I write is wholly to your Selfe. He is to Dine with Me to day & then Shall be further Acquainted with him' (Duke of Portland, Harley Papers, xxiii f. 323; pub. in *H.M.C. Portland*, iv. 333–4).

favor me with yours Directed to Mr Bell Till I can write from Edenbg he will forward it to me.

Methinks I look Very Simply when to my Self I Reflect How I am your Messengr without an Errand, your Ambassador without Instructions, your Servant without Ordrs. I beseech your Honr to let me Not be to seek for any thing which may furnish me to Answer your Expectations to do her Majsty & the Nation the Service which you Design, and for Justifyeing your choice in the honour you do me in Singling me Out for this work.

I Need say no More. Sir you kno' without a strict Correspondence it will be Impossible for me to Act by your Measures or to kno' what course to steer.

I Entreat your pardon for my Importunity on This head and Am

Sir Your Obedt Servt
[symbol]

New Castle Sept. 30. 1706

MS.: Duke of Portland, Defoe Papers, 1 ff. 62–63. *Pub.*: *H.M.C. Portland*, iv. 333–4. *Address*: 'To The Right Honble Robert Harley Esqr., One of her Majties Principal Secretas of State, Present.'

54. *To* ROBERT HARLEY. *2 October 1706*

Sir

My Last of the 30th past From hence Inform'd your Honor of my Arrival here.[1] I had parted from Hence This Morning but have had the Missfortune of One of my Horses failing, Worn Out with the fategue of the Journey.

Mr Bell has however Cur'd This breach by Furnishing me with a horse which tho' it has Encreasd the Expence of The Journey 12*l* yet The Necessity I presume will Excuse me to you and the Horse shall be at your Honrs Service at Demand.

This as Now Ordred will Retard me not above half This Day and I shall God willing Reach to Morpeth to night.[2]

I am, Sir, Your Most Obedt Servt
[symbol]

Octo. 2. 1706

MS.: Duke of Portland, Defoe Papers, 1 ff. 66–67. *Pub.*: *H.M.C. Portland*, iv. 336. *Address*: 'To the Right Honble Robert Harley Esqr., One of Her Majties Principll Secrs of State, Present, London.'

[1] Newcastle upon Tyne.
[2] Two days later Bell wrote to Harley: 'I have had the Favor of Mr A: G[oldsmith]'s Conversation for 2 or 3 dayes & find him to be a Very Engenious Man & fit for that busness I guess he is goeing about. I wish him good Success. He had

55. [ROBERT HARLEY *to* DEFOE?]. [*October 1706?*][1]

Instructions

1. You are to use the utmost caution that it may not be supposed you are employed by any person in England: but that you came there upon your own business, & out of love to the Country.

2. You are to write constantly the true State how you find things, at least once a week, & you need not subscribe any name, but direct for me under Cover to Mrs Collins[2] at the Posthouse, Middle Temple Gate, London. For variety you may direct under Cover to Michael Read[3] in York Buildings.

3. You may confidently assure those you converse with, that the Queen & all those who have Credit with her, are sincere & hearty for the Union.

4. You must shew them, this is such an opportunity that being once lost or neglected is not again to be recovered. England never was before in so good a disposition to make such large Concessions, or so heartily to unite with Scotland, & should their kindness now be slighted—[4]

MS.: Duke of Portland, Defoe Papers, 1 f. 64. *Pub.*: *H.M.C. Portland*, iv. 334. *Address*: none.

56. *To* ROBERT HARLEY. *24 October 1706*

Sir

According to your Commands in the Onely paper of your Ordrs Vizt of writeing Constantly To you, I Continue to give you The Generll state of Things here.[5]

Occation for More Money than I Mentiond to your Honor in My Last. Haveing Occation to buy a horse at this place, he had of me forty pounds, 17:6d, & I have given him a letter of Cr to the post Master Generall for twenty pounds More, & if his Stay be long there, he is to write to me to give him fresh Cr, which I Shall Doe if your Honor Approve of itt. Inclosed I Send your Honor his letter he left with me. He went for Scotland on Wednesday Last [2 Oct.]' (Duke of Portland, Harley Papers, xxiii f. 327; pub. in *H.M.C. Portland*, iv. 336).

    [1] On 30 Sept. Defoe was still begging for instructions (p. 130); on 24 Oct. he acknowledges having received them.

    [2] Unidentified.

    [3] Harley's porter and, according to Swift, 'an old Scotch fanatick, and the damn'dest liar in his office alive' (*Journal to Stella*, i. 335).

    [4] The MS., apparently a draft, is written in a professional hand. The single page is unaddressed and undated, and breaks off in the middle of a line.

    [5] Defoe probably reached Edinburgh about 6 Oct., and was certainly there by the 13th (Mar to Sir David Nairne, *H.M.C. Mar and Kellie*, p. 292), but his earlier letters from Edinburgh have not come to light.

I am Sorry to Tell you here is a Most Confused scene of affaires, and The Ministry have a Very Difficult Course to steer. You allow me Freedome of speaking Allegories in such a Case; it Seems to me The Prebyterians are hard at work to Restore Episcopacy and The Rabble to bring to pass the Union.

We have had Two Mobbs Since my last and Expect a Third and of these the Following is a short account.

The first was in the Assembly Or Commission of Assembly where Very strange things were Talk'd of and in a strange Manner and I Confess Such as has put me Much Out of Love with Ecclesiastic Parliamts.[1] The Power, Anglice Tyranny, of the Church was here Describd to the life and Jure Divino Insisted upon I[n][2] prejudice to Civill Authourity—but this was by some Tumultuous spirits who are Over ruld by men of More Moderation, and as an Assembly they act with more wisdom and Honesty than they do in Their private Capascities in which I Confess they Contribute too Much to the Generall Aversion which here is to the Union, at the Same Time they Acknowlege they are Unsafe and Uneasy in Their present Establishment— I work Incessantly with them. They go from me seemingly Satisfyed and pretend to be Informd but are the Same Men when they Come Among Their parties— I hope what I say to you Sir shall Not prejudice them; in Generall They are the Wisest weak men, The Falsest honest men, and the steadyest Unsettled people Ever I met with. They Mean well but are blinded in their politicks and Obstinate in Opinion.

But we had the last Two Nights a worse Mob than this and that was in the street, and Certainly a scots Rabble is the worst of its kind.

The first night[3] they Onely Threatned hard and follow'd their Patron D. Hamilton's[4] Chair with Huzzas from the Parliament house quite Thro' the City— They Came up again Hallowing in the Dark, Threw some stones at the Guard, broke a few windows and the like, and so it Ended.

I was warn'd that night that I should Take Care of my Self

---

[1] The Commission of Assembly, the deputation of the General Assembly of the Church of Scotland, was then in session and on the 22nd had heatedly debated the question whether a proposed public fast should be appointed on their own authority or referred to Parliament (Mathieson, *Scotland and the Union*, p. 182).

[2] Letter omitted in MS.   [3] Tuesday, 22 Oct.

[4] James Douglas (1658–1712), fourth Duke of Hamilton, was head of the nationalist, anti-English, 'Country' Party in Scotland, and a leading opponent of the Union. His personal prestige was very great, but his policies were equivocal, his motives enigmatic, and his leadership unstable.

and not Appear in the street which Indeed for the last five dayes I have done Very Little haveing been Confin'd by a Violent Cold. However, I went up the street in a Friends Coach in the Evening[1] and some of the Mob Not then Gott together were heard to say when I went into a house, There was One of the English Dogs &c.

I Casually stayd at the house I went then to Till Dark and Thinking to Return to my Lodging, found the wholl City in a Most Dreadfull Uproar and the high street Full of the Rabble.

Duke Hamilton Came from the House in his Chair as Usuall and Instead of Goeing Down the City to his Lodgings Went up the High street *as was said* to Visit the D of Athol.[2]

This whether Design'd by the D. as Most think or No, but if not was Exactly Calculated to begin the Tumult—For the Mob in a Vast Crow'd attending him thither waited at the Door— and as those people did not Come there to be Idle, The Duke Could have Done Nothing more Directly to point Out their bussiness, The Late Ld Provost Sir Pat. Johnston[3] liveing just upon the spot.

The Mob had Threatned him before and I had been Told he had Such Notice of it That he Remov'd himself; Others Say he was in his Lodgings with 11 or 12 Gentlemen besides Servants Resolved to Defend himself; but be That as it will

The Mob Came up staires to his Door and fell to work with sledges to break it Open, but it seems Could not. His Lady in the Fright with Two Candles in her hand that she might be known, Opens the Windows and Cries Out for God Sake to Call the Guard.

An Honest Townsman, an Apothecary, that Saw the Distress the Family was In went Down to the Guard which is kept in the Middle of the street, and Found the Officers Very Indifferent in the Matter, whether as to the Cause or is Rather Judg'd Thro' Reall fear of the Rabble, but Applying himself to One Capt Richardson, a brave Resolute Officer, he told him he Could Not go from the Guard without the Ld Provosts Ordr but if he would Obtain that ordr he would go up— In short the

---

[1] The following evening, 23 Oct. (*History of the Union*, p. 237).

[2] John Murray (1659–1724), first Duke of Atholl, in spite of Jacobite leanings had been loyal to both William and Anne, but the consequences of Fraser's 'Scotch Plot' had driven him into full opposition against both the London and the Edinburgh Ministries. Like Hamilton, Atholl opposed the Union, but their mutual jealousy prevented them from concerting their opposition.

[3] Johnstone had been one of the Union Commissioners and at this time represented Edinburgh in the Scottish Parliament.

Ordr was Obtain'd and the Capt went with a Party of the Guard and made his way Thro' the Rable to Sir Pat. Jonston's stair Case— The Generallity of them fled, some were knock't Down and the stair Case Clear'd, and Three or four Taken in the Very assaulting the Door.

Yet they fled Not far but Hallowing and Throwing stones and sticks at the souldiers Severall of Them are Very Much bruised and the brave Capt I am Told keeps his bed.

However, he brought Down his prisoners and the Toll booth being at hand Hurryed them in and made his Retreat to the Guard.

In This posture Things stood about 8 to 9 a Clock and the street seeming passable I Sallyed Out and Got to my Lodging.

I had not been Long There but I heard a Great Noise and looking Out Saw a Terrible Multitude Come up the High street with A Drum at the head of Them shouting and swearing and Cryeing Out all scotland would stand together, No Union, No Union, English Dogs, and the like.

I Can Not Say to you I had No Apprehensions, Nor was Monsr *De Witt*[1] quite Out of my Thoughts, and perticularly when a part of This Mob fell upon a Gentleman who had Discretion little Enough to say something that Displeased them just Undr my Window.

He Defended himself bravely and Call'd Out lustily also for help to the Guard, who being within Hearing and Ready Drawn up in Close Ordr in the street, advanc't, Rescued the Gentleman, and took the person he was Grappld with prisoner.

The City was by this time in a Terrible fright. The Guards were Insulted and stoned as they stood, the Mob put out all the lights, no body could stir in the streets, and not a light be seen in a windo' for fear of stones.

There was a Design to have shut the Gate at *the Nether Bow* as they Call it, which is a Gate in the Middle of the Great street as Temple barr may be, and the Design was to hinder the Guard in the City and the Guard in *the Cannongate* as they Call it from assisting one Another and Cut off their Communication.

But My Ld Commissionr[2] prevented that by sending a Detach-

---

[1] Jan De Witt (1625–72), Dutch statesman and Grand Pensionary, was literally torn to pieces by an angry mob.

[2] James Douglas (1662–1711), second Duke of Queensberry, supporter of the Union, had emerged from the temporary eclipse he suffered as a consequence of the 'Scotch Plot', and now headed the Scottish Ministry as High Commissioner. Defoe dedicated his *Caledonia* (1706) to Queensberry, and his *History of the Union*

ment of his Guards up the Cannon Gate street as from white hall to Temple bar who seiz'd upon the Nether Bow and took post there with Every Souldier a link in his hand beside his Arms.

Dureing this Hurry,[1] whether they Omitted shutting the North port as they Call it which goes to Leith or that it was not yet Ten a Clock I kno' not, But a Second Rabble of 500, Some say a Thousand, stout fellows Came up from Leith and Disporting themselves in the street Continued the Hurry in a Terrible Manner.

About 11. a Clock My Ld Commissioner sent for the Ld Provost[2] and Desir'd him to let him Send a body of the Guards into the City—which they say is what Never was admitted before and some say the Ld Provost Hesitated at it for a long time.

I Can not send you the perticulars of That part—but about Midnight A body of the Guards besides those posted at the Cannon Gate Entred the City, Drums beating, March't up the High street to the Parliament Close, and His Grace the Duke of Argyle[3] Mounted at the head of the Horse Guards to have seconded them.

After the foot Came my Ld Provost, the Bayliffs and Magistrates with Their officers and links, and These Clearing the streets the Mob was Disspersst. They have 6 I think or there about in Prison and The Council is Now sitting—to Take Some farther Ordr for preserving the Peace.

Two Regiments of Foot are sent for to quarter in the City and I hope, as before, this Mob will like Our Tackers be a Meer plott to Hasten what They Design'd to prevent.

What Further happens in This Matter I shall as it Occurs not fail to Accquaint your Honr With and am

Your Most Obedt Servt
[symbol] D F

Edinb. Octob. 24. 1706

MS.: Duke of Portland, Defoe Papers, 1 ff. 68–71. *Pub.*: *H.M.C. Portland*, iv. 339–41. *Address*: 'To The Right Honble Robert Harley Esqr., Principall Secreta of State, Present, to be forwarded to him.' *Endorsed*: 'Mr De Foe,' and 'Edenburg Octr 24 1706, R̶ Nov: 3:, Riot.'

(1709) to Queensberry and Queen Anne. The Duke befriended Defoe and entertained him at Drumlanrig (*Tour thro' Britain*, ii. 729–30).
  [1] i.e. tumult.   [2] Sir Samuel McClellan.
  [3] John Campbell (1680–1743), second Duke of Argyll, in spite of his youth was already a distinguished soldier and had preceded Queensberry as High Commissioner. Argyll, Queensberry, and Seafield comprised the triumvirate of peers who eventually brought the Treaty of Union successfully through the Scottish Parliament.

57. *To* ROBERT HARLEY. *29 October 1706*

Sir

In my Last you had an Account of Two Mobs, in perticular Church and street, but as you were put in Expectation of a Third Mob There, I purposely Refer'd it to This post to let you know That this perticular Sort is Expected within the house it Self.

There is an Entire Harmony in This Country Consisting in Universall Discords. The Church men in perticular are goeing Mad. The parsons are out of their wits and those who at first were brought Over, and pardon me were Some of them My Converts, their Country brethren being now Come in are all Gone back and to be brought Over by no perswasion.

The Mob you have heard of are affrighted with the loss of the scots Crown—and the parsons Malitiously Humour it, and a Country parson who preach't yesterday at the high Kirk before the Commissionr took this Text, *Behold I Come quickly. Hold fast that which thou hast; let no man take thy Crown.*[1] He pretended not to mean an Earthly Crown but made his Wholl sermon a bald allegory against the Union. I Confess I had patience to hear him but to an Exceeding Mortification.

The house is Now goeing on. They have Confirmd the act of the Council for suppressing the Rabble and bringing in souldiers[2] and thereby Suppresst a New Clamour which was Raising Against the bringing in souldiers into the City at which it was begun to say this was not a free parliamt, but that is Over.

Now tis said this was a Mob Raisd by my Ld Commissioner[3] and that his Grace did it on purpose to have an Opportunity to suppress them.

The Third Mob is Expected in the house where tis said when the party see the Articles put to the Vote, if they Can not Carry their part, they will Protest, take Instruments as they call it here,[4] and leav the house, and then they pretend to say the Nation will take Arms and the high lands are to be brought in— and Indeed if this should Run so far I fear the Church will Joyn the Worst of their Enemies against the Union.

They are now a goeing to fast all Over the kingdome and

---

[1] The Scottish Parliament later amended the 24th Article of the Treaty to provide that the royal crown, sceptre, and sword of state should be retained in Scotland (*History of the Union*, p. 474).

[2] The text of the Act appears in *History of the Union*, pp. 610–12.

[3] The Duke of Queensberry.

[4] That is, make a formal attestation of their action.

therein to give the ministers Occasion to pray and preach against it, and soon as that is done Tumultuous addresses are prepareing in severall parts of the Country.

And thus you see Sir what a nation you have to do with here— I am as Diligent, with Caution not to be suspected, as possible. I have not the success I hop't for but I Continue to push on and think I do no harm.

I have printed One Essay which I Transmitted the last post. I have the second in the press, which if it does Equall Service with the first I shall not So much Grutch the Expence.[1]

I wrot you last post how I hear I am Treated in England as to my Ld C. J. Holt.[2] I beseech you Sir to Concern your Self in the Case that I may not be Ruind while I am at this Distance, my secret Enemies being Very Vigilant and Furious. I am told they will bring the publisher to a Tryall while I am absent and he Can not procure me, for which I shall be Eternally Reproacht.

Sir you may Depend upon it I shall be persued to the Uttmost if your power be not my screen. I Earnestly therefore Entreat you will not forget me in this Condition.

I am, Sir, Your Most Obed Faithfull Servt
D F

Edinb. Octo. 29. 1706

MS.: Duke of Portland, Defoe Papers, 1 ff. 72–73. *Pub.*: *H.M.C. Portland*, iv. 342–3. *Address*: 'To The Right Honble Robert Harley Esqr., Principall Secreta of State, Present.' *Endorsed*: 'Edenburg Oct: 29 1706, R̸ Nov: 11:'

58. WILLIAM MELMOTH[3] *to* DEFOE. [*November 1706?*][4]

Sir,

    The regard you have shewn to the request I lately made you

[1] The two essays here referred to may well be (1) *An Essay at Removing National Prejudices against a Union with England*, Part III, and (2) *A Fourth Essay at Removing National Prejudices; with Some Reply to Mr. H[o]dges and Some Other Authors*. Both were published at Edinburgh at about this period.

[2] But this subject is not mentioned in No. 56, which Defoe here calls 'my Last' (p. 137). In the *Review* for 1 Oct. 1706 Defoe had reflected on the opposition to the Union offered by 'a certain grave, great and learned Man'. He was understood to be referring to Lord Chief Justice Holt, and proceedings were opened against him (*Remarks and Collections of Thomas Hearne*, Oxford, 1885–1921, i. 297). Defoe protested in print that he had not meant Holt (*Review*, 16 and 21 Nov.), and there the matter seems to have dropped.

[3] William Melmoth (1666–1743), lawyer and religious writer, in 1705 had begun an anonymous correspondence with Archbishop Tenison in which he urged the closing of the theatres as the only remedy for the depravity of the stage (*D.N.B.*).

[4] No date is recorded for this letter, but Defoe was criticizing the stage in the *Reviews* for 26, 29, and 31 Oct. 1706, and his attack may have elicited these

to persue your designe of exposeing the stage,[1] obliges me to repeat my thanks to you; which I assure you I do with great sincerity, being alwaies pleased, I must own, whenever I see the playhouses attacked; for I am persuaded they have greatly contributed to corrupting the present age. I have taken the freedome to send you Mr. Bedford's new book,[2] by which you will see my charge was not ill groundcd, when I told you how little respect had been shewn to her Majesties order.[3] I am the more induced to trouble you with this book, as thinking it might be of some use to you in the designe in which you are engaged. I have likewise sent you the opinion of Archbp. Tillotson touching players, which has been lately printed,[4] and dispersed in great numbers, and which, if it were still made more public, (as it might be, if printed in one of your *Reviews*)[5] would prove, I hope, of some use. *His* opinion, perhaps, may be of weight with those who are proof against other arguments, at least one would think it should make them consider a little what they are doing, when they give countenance to a set of men who seem to bid defiance to all that is serious. . . .[6]

MS.: untraced. *Pub.*: William Melmoth, Jr., *Memoirs of a Late Eminent Advocate*, 1776, pp. 54–55. *Address*: none recorded.

59. *To* ROBERT HARLEY. *2 November 1706*

Sir

I have not faild Since I Came hither to give you a Constant and Faithfull Account of Every thing which Occurs on this stage of Confusion.

I am Every day a Member of the Generall assembly[7] and I Confess I make a very odd figure here, for all Day the Commission Sitts, and night and Morning I have a Revrend Committee with me to Answer their Cases of Conscience.

acknowledgements. See E. G. Fletcher, 'Defoe and the Theatre', *Philological Quarterly*, xiii (1934), 382–9.
    [1] This 'request' may possibly be the letter written on 14 Aug. and published without signature in the *Review* for 26 Oct. 1706. It resembles this one in some phrases, and applauds Defoe's earlier attacks on the playhouses in the *Reviews* for 20 June, 8 and 10 Aug. 1706.
    [2] Arthur Bedford (1668–1745), a Bristol clergyman, was author of *The Evil and Danger of Stage-Plays*, Bristol, 1706.
    [3] On 17 Jan. 1704 the Queen issued a proclamation against impropriety in theatrical performances (John Ashton, *Social Life in the Reign of Queen Anne*, 1882, ii. 10–11).   [4] Unidentified.   [5] Defoe did not accept this invitation.
    [6] The remainder was not published.
    [7] The Commission of Assembly. The General Assembly itself was not in session.

Pardon my Vanity Sir. I take upon me more Mod[esty when][1] I Argue with the Right Revrend fathers of this Church, and if I pass for much more of an Oracle among them than I Merit, Tis Owing to that Secret Mannagement for which I suppose my Mission hither is Designd.

And yet Sir, Pardon me I do not boast my Success; they are a hardened, refractory and Terrible people; They have now kept a Fast,[2] Thursday was the Day in this City, and tho' the Ministers spoke with more Modesty than I Expected, yet in the Country they Enflame the people strangely:

And yet not a man of them Can say they would Venture to stand alone, or Dare think of falling Out with England.

This Day Came in severall addresses from E. Louthan, Perth-shire, and they say Three more, but I do not find they were sign'd by many hands.[3]

But the worst Apprehension I have is from an Association forming in the North and West to which they say there will be 50 thousand hands. It is in the form of an Oath that they will stand by One Another in Defence of the present Establishment in Church and state— I am promised the Coppy of it which I shall not fail to Transmitt and as it proceeds you shall hear.

I this day fortifyed a Minister who Enclind to sign and promote it, but will now Oppose it, and I purpose to go to St Andrews and Glasgow the next week, on the same Errand [havin]g[4] some hopes to prevent its progress in *Fife* and all [that] side and perhaps as far as Perth.

There has been no Mob here Since the proclamation[5] but at *Sterlin, Glasgow* and some Other places they seem forward & have been Turbulent Twice.

At Blantire, a Town in Duke Hamiltons Estate, I hear to day when the minister Dissmisst the people he Desird the Men to stay. When the women were Gone he presented an address to the parliamt for them to sign, and publickly Exhorted them to it. They all signd it Except about 9 or 10 of the most Judicious who Refused. Thus you see who are the fire-brands.

One Balanton an Incendiary Minister has handed about the

[1] MS. torn.
[2] See *History of the Union*, pp. 233–6.
[3] Midlothian, Linlithgow, Perth, Stirling, Dumbarton, and Forfar had submitted addresses against the Union by 4 Nov. (J. H. Burton, *History of Scotland*, 1897–1901, viii. 148).
[4] Tear in MS. affects the two bracketed words.
[5] The Act drawn up by the Privy Council as a result of the October tumults (*History of the Union*, pp. 610–12).

Enclosed paper of Queries[1] which I send for your perusall because they are the heads of Mr Hodges's book[2] which I presume you have heard of if not seen.

I think to answer these Queries to morrow— I am writeing a Poem in praise of scotland.[3] You will say that is an odd subject, to bear a Panegyrick, but my End will be answerd. I make them believ I am Come away from England, and resolv if the Union goes on to settle in scotland,[4] and all Conduces to perswade them I am a friend to their Country:

I Confess Sir doeing all this without any Instructions or the least hint of your Approbation. I am perfectly at a loss what to say— I stay here for your Orders. I spend your Money (and that not a Little) for I have had £45 besid a horse. I beseech you Sir let me not Run On to any length beyond your Satisfaction. I am Remanded with a word, and being wholly yours, would fain act not for your Service Onely, but by your Direction, and to your Content.

If you please yet to favour me with a line Enclosed to Mr Bell he will forward it to me.

I am, Your Most Obedt Servt
D F

Edinburgh. Novembr 2. 1706

MS.: Berg Collection, New York Public Library. *Pub.*: H.M.C., *Ninth Report*, Pt. 2, 1884, p. 469. *Address*: 'To The Right Honble Robert Harley Esqr., Principall Secretary of state, Prest.' *Endorsed*: 'Edenbg Nov: 2: 1706, R̸ at London Nov: 9: 1706, De Foe.'

[1] *Some Queries, Proposed to Consideration, Relative to the Union Now Intended*, written by John Bannatyne, minister of Lanark (*Fasti Ecclesiæ Scoticanæ*, iii. 307–8). The pamphlet no longer accompanies the letter, but see *Catalogue of the Collection of Autograph Letters and Historical Documents Formed between 1865 and 1882 by Alfred Morrison*, 1885, ii. 13 n.

[2] James Hodges was the author of *The Rights and Interests of the Two British Monarchies*, in which he listed 32 conflicting interests of England and Scotland, and maintained that to unite with so sinful a nation as England would bring God's judgement upon the Scots. Hodges's book was widely distributed in Scotland. Defoe answered the argument and rebuked the author in his *Fourth Essay at Removing National Prejudices; with Some Reply to Mr. H[o]dges and Some Other Authors Who Have Printed Their Objections against an Union with England*, Edinburgh, 1706; and in several issues of the *Review*. See, for instance, those for 9, 12, and 14 Nov., and 12, 14, 19, 21, and 24 Dec. 1706.

[3] *Caledonia, &c. A Poem in Honour of Scotland and the Scots Nation*, Edinburgh, 1706; London, 1707.

[4] A few days later Defoe announced publicly that he was 'not only at present out of the Town, but out of the Kingdom, pursuing my private, lawful and known Design of settling my Family abroad, and letting the World know, I do not live by Scribbling, as is suggested' (*Review*, 16 Nov. 1706).

60. *To* ROBERT HARLEY. *5 November 1706*

Sir

Since my Last the Face of affaires I hope are a little Mended and after a Very Long and Warm Debate on Fryday[1] whether they should proceed on the Union or Go first on the security of the Church, it was past proceed.

On Saturday they sat till near 8. at night and the speeches on both sides were long and Warm.

D Hamilton Rav'd, Fletcher of Saltoun,[2] and the Earle of Belhaven,[3] Made long speeches, the Latter of which Will be printed— The Clamour without was so great That a Rabble was feared tho' the Guards are Numerous and were Drawn Out in Readyness.

Addresses are Delivred in from Severall places and More prepareing but tis observ'd the addresses Discover a Fraud which shows the party here at their shifts.

The addresses are found in the Cant of the Old Times Deploreing the Misery of scotland for want of a Further Reformation and the security of the Church and the Lords Covenanted people, but when the Names Come to be Examin'd they Are all sign'd by known Jacobites and Episcopall men.[4]

[1] i.e. 1 Nov.

[2] Andrew Fletcher of Saltoun (1655–1716), M.P. for Haddingtonshire, believed that Scotland's troubles were caused by the English Government, and could be mitigated only by limiting the prerogative of the Crown and increasing the autonomy of the Scottish Parliament. He was of course bitterly opposed to an incorporating Union. See W. C. Mackenzie, *Andrew Fletcher of Saltoun*, Edinburgh, 1936, pp. 248–76.

[3] John Hamilton (1656–1708), Lord Belhaven, opposed the Union, and on this occasion delivered the celebrated speech of which the best-known lines are: 'I think I see our ancient mother Caledonia, like Caesar, sitting in the midst of our senate, ruefully looking round about her, covering herself with her royal garment, and breathing out her last with an *Et tu, mi fili*.' The Earl of Marchmont's mocking reply is equally celebrated: 'Behold he dreamed, but lo! when he awoke, he found it was a dream.' See P. Hume Brown, *The Legislative Union of England and Scotland*, Oxford, 1914, p. 117. Defoe bantered Belhaven in *The Vision*, Edinburgh, 1706, but later became Belhaven's friend and acknowledged the friendship publicly (*Review*, 10 July 1708).

[4] Defoe examined the addresses against the Union in the *Review* for 26 Nov. In questioning their validity he aroused the wrath of the Jacobite George Lockhart, who wrote of him: 'I know very well that the Author of the History of Europe, for the year 1706, and that vile Monster and Wretch *Daniel De Foe*, and other mercenary Fools and Trumpeters of Rebellion, have often asserted, that these Addresses and other Instances of the Nation's Aversion to the Union, proceeded from the false Glosses and underhand Dealings of those that opposed it in Parliament, whereby the meaner Sort were impos'd upon and deluded into those Jealousies and Measures' (*Memoirs Concerning the Affairs of Scotland*, 1714, p. 229).

There has been a farther Expectation of a Mob and some practises have been used to Infect the souldiers, but the E of Leven[1] Call'd the Guards together to day and made a speech to them. They had been posesst with a Notion that they should be sent to the West Indees as soon as the Union was Over.

My Ld Leven I hope has Reestablisht them, and the proceeding since is more favourable.

Last night the Grand question was put whether the first Article—Or in short the Union it self should be approved or Not—and Carryed in the Affirmativ which being On King Williams Birthday is to me Very Remarkable and Encouraging.

I had to day the Honour to be sent for by the Lds Comittee for Examining the Equivalents and to assure them in the Calculateing the Draw back on the salt, the proportion of the Excise and some addenda About Trade.[2]

They profess themselves Oblig'd to me more than I Merit and at their next Committee I am Desir'd to Dine with them. I am lookt on as an English man that Designs to settle here and I think am perfectly Unsuspected and hope on that foot I do some service— Onely I spend you a great Deal of Money at which I am Concern'd but see no Remedy if I will go thro' with the work.

I have Now Great hopes of it tho' to day the assembly men make a great stir; in short the Kirk are *au Wood*,[3] pardon the scotticisme.

Your Most Obedt Servt
D F

Edinb. Nov. 5. 1706

MS.: Duke of Portland, Defoe Papers, 1 ff. 74–75. *Pub.*: *H.M.C. Portland*, iv. 345–6. *Address*: 'To The Right Honble Robert Harley Esqr., Principall Secreta of State, Present.' *Endorsed*: 'Edenburg Nov: 5: 1706, R̸ Nov: 11:'

[1] David Melville (1660–1728), third Earl of Leven, was Commander-in-Chief of the Scottish Forces and Governor of Edinburgh Castle.

[2] To bring Scotland's system of taxation, customs, excise, and the like into accord with that contemplated for her under the Union Treaty required an intricate machinery of fiscal adjustments, under which Scotland was to be recompensed for such immediate financial disadvantages as her acceptance of the Union would impose. The 'equivalents' were moneys to be paid to Scotland outright; the 'drawbacks' were refunds, under certain conditions, of customs duties that Scotland as a party to the Union would have to pay. The Committee which sought Defoe's counsel consisted of Montrose, Argyll, Tweeddale, Sir Alexander Campbell of Cessnock, George Baillie of Jerviswood, John Hadden of Gleneagles, Robert Inglis, Lieut.-Col. John Erskine, and Hugh Montgomery (*H.M.C. Portland*, viii. 251).

[3] i.e. 'a' wud' (all mad).

61. *To* ROBERT HARLEY. *9 November 1706*

Sir

In my last[1] I hinted to you what the Church was doeing as to Their Address or protest against the Church of England Constitution.

I herewith Send you the thing it Self[2]—and as to the Generall Opinion it gains here I must Own it does some harm—but Not what it Was Expected, for while it was in Debate, like the English Fleet while it lay at Torbay it kept all France in suspence,[3] so the Country Expected the Kirk would have protested as the Burghs have done[4] Against the Union in Generall as Destructiv to the Civill Intrest and the Intrest of the Church in Generall, but Instead of That it Containes Six heads as you will see, all which suppose the Union as Reall and Certain.

I had this Day the Honor to be in the Committee of parliamt Appointed to Examine the Drawbacks and Equivalents and they have Desir'd me to assist them. Their Debates will End in makeing Explications on the heads of Excise and Drawbacks and I believe I shall have the honour to form them. I shall in my next I hope be Able to give you a scheme of their Demands, and as I believ I shall have the Honour to Draw them for them, I Would be Glad that after I send you a Draft of the subject I might be Instructed what will Or will Not be Conceded in England, since it is so Ordred that I am in their Cabinet by some Mannagemt and Can Influence them more than I Expected.

Now to Lead them to anything which England will Not Complye with, or to put them off anything which Makes a Difficulty here and may be Complyed with, is Equally acting against the Union.

Their Ldships have Resolved to Committ the Drawing up the Explanations to me, and if Directed I might do more service to both Kingdomes than I Could have Expected. If therefore my service here be of any Moment I shall beg to be Instructed or If I take wrong Aims to be Excused.

---

[1] Missing.

[2] Missing, but the text of the Address and Defoe's comment upon it appear in the *Review* for 30 Nov. 1706.

[3] In the previous summer. See *Bishop Burnet's History of His Own Time*, Oxford, 1823, v. 265–6.

[4] See the *Review* for 26 Nov. 1706, and Mathieson, *Scotland and the Union*, p. 132.

Next post I shall Transmitt a Draft of the things in Debate.
I am, Your Most Obedt Servt

D F

Nov. 9. 1706

All the Gentlemen Lay Elders protested in the assembly against the address.

MS.: Duke of Portland, Defoe Papers, 1 ff. 76–77. *Pub.*: *H.M.C. Portland*, iv. 346–7. *Address*: 'To The Right Honble Robert Harley Esqr., Her Majties Principall Secreta of State, Present.' *Endorsed*: 'Edenburg Nov: 9: 1706, R̤ Nov: [date blotted].'

62. *To* ROBERT HARLEY. [*13?*] *November 1706*

Sir

In my Last I Accquainted you with the present posture of the Affair before the Committee of Parliamt. The Difficulties before Them are The Draw backs and The Equivalents, The Taxes and The Trade.

The First head is—Vizt, speaking as themselves

We have Some Difficulties, how Can we Remedy Them. We Can Not add any Article or Take off any. That will Require a New Treaty, and Consequently a New delay and the Lord ha' Mercy On us if we have another Session here. Will England admitt of Explanations?

My Answer (Pardon me Uninstructed in the Case) without Doubt England will admitt the Parliamt of Scotland to Declare Their Construction of any Article of the Treaty provided it be agreeable to the True Intent and Meaning of The Treaty and to Reason and justice.

Upon This foot Sir you will have an Explanation Offred on the following heads, and were I better Informd from England I Could perhaps lessen, Encourage, or Disscourage Those Explanations.

1. That Their Twopenny Ale which is sold but for 2.4*d* per Gallon More Than our small beer, should pay as small beer Onely, Or (as I offer) be advanced to a Middle Rate of Excise between strong and small in Proportion to its advance of Price, which seems just.[1]

2. That Their Own acts of Parliamt Obligeing Them to Cure fish with forreign Salt and those Acts being by the Union to be Continued, They are to Understand English Salt as forreign

[1] See *History of the Union*, pp. 378–82.

Salt in the Sence of those Acts, It being So Now. Or Elce After the Union they shall be prohibited useing The Rock Salt of England which will be to the Loss of England as well as a hardship on scotland.[1]

3 That Whereas They are Obliged to Salt all flesh for Exportation or for Victualling their ships, with forreign Salt, They may Use Their Own or English Salt, Paying the Duty for it. Elce They are Not on Equallity with England who Salt Most of Ther ships beef with English Salt.

4 That the Tax Upon Coals payable by The Chalder in England be Explain'd On the Weight of scots Coal in proportion, They Not Selling by Measure, (5) and the Bounty on Corn be Explain'd to Include a Grain Calld Bear which is much the same as Barly but Differs a little.

These are what are at present before Them and as the Rest offer (for There will be More) I shall Accquaint your Honor. Mean Time It would be Very Servicable if I might kno' whether These Explanations are Agreeable to England or No, Since it will be in My power to shorten them Very much, tho' if allow'd it will give some Ease here to a Nation that Really are in a Terrible Ferment, and it is Unaccountable how it Encreases.

At Dumfreis They have burnt the Articles in the Market place.[2] At Glasgow They were about it but the Magistrates prevaild with them to forbear On promise to sign an adress against it.

It would amaze you if I should give you The Trouble of Repeating The Ridiculous Notions people here have Entertaind Against Their Own happyness. The Libells, The Absurdities and The Insults on That head are Intollerable.

The High Commissioner has had Letters Sent to Threaten him with Pistoll, Dagger and Variety of Assassination,[3] and the Unusuall Numbers of Highlanders Makes Some people Very Uneasy here, There being More of Them here Now than has been known— Indeed they are Formidable Fellows and I Onely Wish her Majtie had 25000 of Them in spain, a Nation Equally proud and Barbarous like Themselves.

They are all Gentlemen, will Take affront from No Man, and

---

[1] See *History of the Union*, p. 419.
[2] This letter was received in London on 21 Nov. and appears to have been written on the 13th. Yet, *An Account of the Burning of the Articles of Union at Dumfries*, a contemporary broadside, places the date of the Dumfries incident as 20 Nov., and Defoe, who followed that source, does likewise in his *History of the Union*, p. 250.
[3] See *History of the Union*, pp. 365-7.

Insolent to the last Degree. But Certainly the Absurdity is Ridiculous to see a Man in his Mountain habit with a Broad sword, Targett, Pistol or perhaps Two at his Girdle, a Dagger and staff, walking Down the street as Upright and Haughty as if he were a lord—and withall Driving a Cow. Bless us—are These the Gentlemen! Said I—

Sir As to the Union Tho' I hope well and The Govornmt sticks Close to it, yet I Must Own tis yet a Dark prospect. The Difficultyes are Many and the people Obstinately Averse, and if any Insurrection happen, which I Must acknowlege is Not Unlikely—I Crave leav to say—The few Troops They have here are Not to be Depended Upon— I have this Confesst by Men of the best Judgement— The officers are good but Even the Officers Own They Dare Not Answer for Their Men, and Some of the Wisest and Most Discerning Men here Wish Two or Three Regiments of Horse or Dragoons Were Sent but Near the borders as Silently as might be. All the Force This Governmt has to make a stand is Not 2000 Effective Men and of Them I Question whether 1500 Could be Drawn together.

I have More Objections of Trade to make but They are Not Ripe. I Wish I Might kno' what steps to Take in This affair.

Mr Bell has Sent me a farther Supply.[1]

I am, Sir, Your Most Obedt Servt

[symbol]

Edinb. November [13?][2] 1706

Sir, I am wrott to—to offer my Service to My Ld Hallifax to Accquaint him with Matters here. My Respect and Indeed Obligation to My Ld Makes it Very Agreeable to me, and I have This post wrott to his Ldship.[3] But as I am yours Sir in Duty Abstracted from and Exclusive of all the World, I Thought my Self Oblig'd to Accquaint you of it and on your Orders shall at any Time Desist.

MS.: Duke of Portland, Defoe Papers, 1 ff. 78–79. *Pub.*: *H.M.C. Portland,* iv. 348–50. *Address*: 'To The Right Honble Robert Harley Esqr., Her Majties Principall Secreta of State, Present, in Cover.' *Endorsed*: 'Edenburg Nov: 13: 1706, ℞ Nov: 21.'

[1] According to John Bell's account, Defoe received £52. 10s. 6d. in November (p. 170, n. 2).
[2] The date is somewhat smudged, but it looks like '13' and Harley so read it.
[3] This correspondence has not come to light. For Defoe's 'obligation' to Halifax see No. 33.

63. *To* ROBERT HARLEY. *14 November 1706*

Sir

I Sent you a Post or Two Since My Ld Bellhavens speech which I presume has Diverted you. I Enclose you a short Comment Upon it[1] which has made Some sport here and perhaps Done More Service than a More Solid Discourse.

Since my last the Parliamt Voted the act for the security of the Church and Refused the Articles the Church Recommended,[2] at which the Church are Very angry and the Rabble at Glasgow has been Very Tumultuous upon that [head].[3]

The Church has to day Voted an Adress[4] to Cure the suggestion [too][5] justly Cast on them against the succession Viz: that the Growth of popery may be prevented, the Open profession of it suppresst—That the succession being Undeclard Gives the Greatest hopes to the party of the prince of Wales &c.

This is a Healer but Does not fully Recompense the folly of their last.

To Day the house has Debated whether they shall go upon the second article with a proviso or begin at the 4th Article, and have Agreed to go upon the second,[6] but the Majority is not above 25 whereas they Carryed it against the Church affair[7] by a Majority of 70; and a good joke at the End of it, that all the protestors and adherers, which were 25—were of such as were the known Enemies of the Church.

---

[1] Missing, but perhaps a draft of his bantering poem later published as *The Vision*. See p. 142, n. 2, and p. 162, n. 1.

[2] The Union Commissioners had been forbidden to deal with the worship, discipline, or government of the Church of Scotland, and hence as the Treaty left their hands it made no provision for the security of the Church. The Commission of the General Assembly had requested Parliament to take legislative action that would fill this gap, and an Act based upon their petition was introduced. The Commission then decided to request that yet further and more specific safeguards be added to the Act. Parliament declined to go all the way with this second petition, but did incorporate some of the requested provisions into its Act, which was passed and subsequently embodied in the Treaty. Defoe is not quite accurate, therefore, in saying that Parliament 'Refused the Articles the Church Recommended'. See the *Review* for 30 Nov. 1706, and Mackinnon, *Union of England and Scotland*, pp. 298–304. This Act of Security (for the Church) should not, of course, be confused with the Act of Security (for the Kingdom) passed in 1703, which threatened separation of the Crowns of Scotland and England.

[3] MS. reads 'had'.

[4] Yet another communication, the third, from the Commission of Assembly to Parliament. It is published, with Defoe's comment, in the *Review* for 5 Dec. 1706.

[5] MS. reads 'to'.

[6] The second Article provided for accepting the Hanoverian Succession.

[7] That is, the second petition of the Commission of Assembly. See n. 2 above.

Twas Very odd and Diverting to find these Gentlemen Vote that the Act was not a Security sufficient for the Church, and Especially Sir Alexa Bruce Now E of Kincarn[1] formerly Expelld the house for sayeing the prebyterian Church was Inconsistent with Monarchy.

I Ask your Pardon for my Brevity and am

Sir, Your Honrs Most Obedt Servt

D F

The floods here are so great I question Even the post being able to Travail.[2]

Edinb. Nov. 14. 1706

MS.: Duke of Portland, Defoe Papers, 1 ff. 80–81. *Pub.*: *H.M.C. Portland*, iv. 350. *Address*: 'To The Right Honble Robert Harley Esqr., Principall Secreta of State, Present.' *Endorsed*: 'Mr. De Foe,' and 'Edenburg Nov: 14, R̃ Nov: 20.'

64. *To* ROBERT HARLEY. *16 November 1706*

Sir

Since My Last the Parliamt have Voted The Second Article of The Treaty[3] Vizt yester-Night after long struggle and Severall attempts to put it off, as First—a Motion to Make a Recess To Accquaint her Majtie what a ferment the Nation was in and how the Matter was Vigorously Opposed by The wholl Country, and to lay it before her Majtie in An Humble Address.

This was put to the Question and past in the Negativ or Rather According to the Method here Delay or proceed, and Carryed proceed—

Then the Main Question was Put, Approv the second Article or Not Aprove, and Carry'd Approv by a Majority of 58.

Thus in Parliamt Sir Things go Right Enough, but Really Every Where Elce the Nation is in strange Confusion, and The Threatnings of the Church Party are Very high and playn.

The Rabble at Glasgow has Driven the Provost[4] Out of the

---

[1] The Earl of Kincardine. See P. Hume Brown, *The Legislative Union of England and Scotland*, Oxford, 1914, pp. 38–39.

[2] Of the many circumstances that combined to make possible the Union, not the least was 'the excessive Rains and unusual wet Weather, which prevented the People, that thought and contriv'd the Mischief of Rabbles and Arms, putting any thing in Practice' (*Review*, 1 May 1707).

[3] By which Scotland accepted the Hanoverian Succession.

[4] John Aird the younger.

Town and he is fled hither; the Reason was he would Not Address. They have sent up Their Address, and a great Many whose hands Are to it have Sent Up Letters to the Ld Chancelor[1] That They were forc'd to sign it Against Their Minds.

Yet The Address was Recd and Read, The Provost flyeing for his life. They have broken up his house and Plundred or Defac't his goods.[2] The Lenity of the Governmt is Taken as Fear and the Kirk is stark Mad that They have as They Say No Security and that their Articles are Rejected.[3]

The Cameronian Adress, tho' of No great Moment, I send[4] because you should See some of the spirit; for tho' Hepburn[5] that Sends it is a Mad Man (that is, Mad in Zeal) and has been Deposed and Disowned by The Kirk, yet They Talk his Very Language Now Every Day in Their Common Discourse, and I Dined to Day with a Minister who Told me were the Weather permitting They would have been at Edinburgh before Now with 15000 men. They Excercise Their Men and Appear with Arms and Drums in Glasgow, and Indeed these Things Tend to a strange Conclusion.

The Next Sitting of Parliamt will Enter On the Main question, I Mean the 3d Article,[6] and If it pass we shall see whether they Dare make any Disturbance or no.

I Wish her Majtie would be pleased to have Some forces On the bordr for if There is the least Violence here all will be in Blood. An Appearance of some Regiments on the Border would at least Encourage the Troops here, who are not otherwise to be Depended on.[7] You will Excuse my presumtion in Offring any thing that looks like Direction. No Doubt her Majtie Will let Nothing be wanting here to Succor That Intrest which Appears So hearty and which if They are Not supported will if

---

[1] The Earl of Seafield.

[2] For a full account of the Glasgow Address and the attendant disturbances, see *History of the Union*, pp. 266–80, and Mackinnon, *Union of England and Scotland*, pp. 310–13.

[3] See p. 148, n. 2.

[4] Missing. To the Cameronians the Union was yet another violation of the Covenant.

[5] John Hepburn (d. 1723), stormy Cameronian clergyman, was often in trouble with the Kirk, which sometimes suspended him, and with the State, which sometimes imprisoned him. His real position in the disturbances of this time is far from clear. He publicly opposed the Union, as all the Cameronians did, but 'appears to have systematically betrayed their proceedings to the Government, while counselling and encouraging them' (J. H. Burton, *History of Scotland*, 1897–1901, viii. 162).

[6] Providing for a single Parliament of Great Britain.

[7] English troops were later sent to the Border and to northern Ireland (P. Hume Brown, *The Legislative Union of England and Scotland*, Oxford, 1914, p. 120).

an Accidt happens be Sacrifiz'd to all Manner of the Most Barbarous Insults.

Your Most Obedt Servt

D F

Nov. 16. 1706

MS.: Duke of Portland, Defoe Papers, 1 ff. 82–83. *Pub.*: *H.M.C. Portland*, iv. 351–2. *Address*: 'To The Right Honble Robert Harley Esqr., Principall Secretary of State, Present.' *Endorsed*: 'Edenburg Nov: 16, 1706, R̸ Nov: 22:'

65. *To* ROBERT HARLEY. *19 November 1706*

Sir

I have the Satisfaction to write your Honr that the Parliamt has Now Voted the Third Article[1] by a Majority of 30.

I am not Willing to fill you with the Apprehensions of people here, Nor am I Very Flegmatick on That head my Self, and Therefore when I shall Tell you that the Commissionr[2] has been Threatned with Daggers, pistols &c. and Now That the last Two Sittings being within Dark he was Insulted by the Rable in the street at his Return, Great stones Thrown at his Coach, and One of the Guards wounded—I yet shall add that [I][3] am Of Opinion his Grace will go Thoro' with the Matter.

I Confess I Thought it an Ill Concerted Measure that last night the Commissioner Drove thro' the Town so hastily, The foot Guards Runing and the Horse Galloping, at which the Mob Hallood and the Enemy Insults To, thus, The Commisr was Run away &c. Indeed it betray'd too Much Concern but That is not my bussiness.

The Church has not yet Done, and Tho' In the Review I am Defending her proceedings,[4] which you will Easily perciev Sir I do Not that I like them, but to Checq the Ill use will be made of it in England, yet I doubt she will go On till no honest man Can Defend her.

Addresses are Now Comeing In from the Respectiv presbyteries in Ordr to Justifye the Comissions first address, and as by the Enclosed[5] which is the First of them you will see the Nature of them, so I doubt Others will be Worse yet.

All the west is full of Tumult. Glasgow is mad. I was goeing

[1] Establishing a single Parliament of Great Britain.
[2] The Duke of Queensberry.　　　　　　　　　　[3] Omitted in MS.
[4] See for instances the issues for 31 Oct., and 2, 5, 7, 9, 12, 14, and 16 Nov. 1706.
[5] Missing, but probably that from the Presbytery of Lanark.

to see what I Could do there but met severall of the honest people flying and all advised me not to Venture, so I have much against my Will playd the Coward and made my Retreat, but I think to go the Next week Incognito if it be practicable, onely to Observ and be Able to giv you Exact perticulars.

The Commissionr is Come Down from the house to day by Daylight, where they have Debated but not yet Voted the Fourth Article.[1] They Came Down without any Disturbance as I yet hear of.

The Ministers are quieter here now than before but in the Enclosed petition or address you have Two in perticular who were here in the Commission and have been in the Country to procure it Viz: Jo Bannatyne[2] and Linning,[3] Two Firebrands and who Merit to be Markt as Incendiaryes of whose actions I Doubt I shall have Occasion to give you farther Accounts, and I Wish they dont bring them selves to want her Majtes Mercy.

I Do myself the Honour to Congratulate your Saf arrivall from the Country[4] and Especially if the Waters have been Equally Violent as here where it Exceeds all that has been known in this Age—

　　　　　　I am, Sir, (Tho' Impatient to hear from you)

　　　　　　　　　　　Your Obedt Servt

　　　　　　　　　　　　　D F

Edinb. Nov. 19. 1706

MS.: Duke of Portland, Defoe Papers, 1 ff. 84–85. *Pub.*: *H.M.C. Portland*, iv. 352–3. *Address*: 'To The Right Honble Robert Harley Esqr., Her Majesties Principall Secreta of State, Present.' *Endorsed*: 'Edenburg Nov: 19: 1706, ℞ Nov: 25:'

66. [*To* ROBERT HARLEY]. [*22*][5] *November 1706*

Sir

In my Last I gave you the address of the Pressbytery of . . .[6] and it was feared that all the presbyterys would do the like,

---

[1] Providing for equality of trading privileges.

[2] See p. 141, n. 1.

[3] Thomas Linning (or Lining, or Linen), minister at Lesmahagow (*Fasti Ecclesiæ Scoticanæ*, iii. 314).

[4] Of which Defoe had learned not from Harley but from John Bell. See *H.M.C. Portland*, iv. 353.

[5] Defoe blotted the date on this letter. Harley read the blot as 23 Nov. (see endorsement) but that date fell on a Saturday and Defoe says that the fifth Article is to be taken up 'to morrow'. The House did not sit on Sundays. Since in fact the fifth Article was considered on the 23rd, I have assigned this letter to the day previous. See *History of the Union*, p. 369.

[6] Probably Lanark.

Nor do I question but Endeavours have been and Are still Used to procure them, tho' I hear of no more yet Come in.

The Eyes of the people begin a little to Open and I had the honour to hear an Assembly man tell me yesterday he was afraid Some were gone too far and that they were to be onely the Cats foot, and he would have no more to do in it. I do not Claim the honour of Converting him tho' he Compliments me on that head.

But my last Essay[1] which I Transmitted to your honor by post has had some Effect, for Hodges's book[2] which Indeed has done more Mischief than a thousand men is so much Exposed Now that it is grown into Contempt and a Gentleman did me the honour to Tell me to day that it has stopt Three addresses which were Comeing Out of the North, and that a Gentleman Reading it among about 20 that had Resolvd to address, they all layd it aside.

I am not pleading my Merit Sir but to let you see how Easily this people have been Imposed upon that a Little plain arguing would bring them to Reason again.

I hope things begin to look a little better here. They have Given some Vent in the partyes to the first fury and Now the three first Articles are Over they seem to be Calmer.

At Glasgow we hear of no more Tumults tho' here was a flying Report of 15000 men Got together.

Coll Areskin[3] is highly blamd, Even by his Own friends, for his Imprudence; who being Provost of sterling Drew Out the Militia to sign an adress, and with his sword Drawn in One hand, and his pen in the Other, signd it, and made the Rest do so also; with some Very Indecent Expressions, which in any Governmt but One so Mild and forbearing as this Would have been Otherwise Resented; but he is a Malecontent and Declining in his fortunes, tho' otherwise a Very honest Man.

However, these things do them no service, Nor has it been any help to them—that Fletcher of Saltoun made a speech to Tell the parliamt the Trade to England was No advantage to them: or to see 20[4] Members Vote against a Communication of

---

[1] Perhaps his *Fourth Essay at Removing National Prejudices*. See *H.M.C. Mar and Kellie*, p. 322.

[2] *The Rights and Interests of the Two British Monarchies*. See p. 141, n. 2.

[3] Col. John Erskine of Carnock, M.P. for the Burgh of Stirling, not to be confused with Col. John Erskine, Governor-Depute of Stirling Castle, who favoured the Union. See *Tour thro' Britain*, ii. 756–7.

[4] Actually 17 (A. V. Dicey and R. S. Rait, *Thoughts on the Union between England and Scotland*, 1920, p. 374).

Trade with England in which Even Duke Hamilton himself abandon'd them, and a Very pretty proposall was Offred as follows, which None of them Could answer.

Why Gentlemen are you against the Clause? If the Communication of Trade be no advantage, is it Not a passive Article? Can't we let it alone, and make no use of it? The English by this Article dont bind us to Trade, they Onely lay Open their Trade to us, to Enter into or let it alone. Why should we Refuse the liberty?

They go to morrow on the 5th Article.[1] They have been Debateing it last sitting, and here is a mighty popular Objection against on Account of their shipping.

The Enclosed[2] will Explain it more perticularly, which I Wrot at the Desire of the E's of Abercorn, sutherland,[3] and some Members of the Commons, to prepare them against to morrows Debate.

And thus I believ I must do, on Every article as they Come to be Debated. The Objections in some Cases are so Dull and so gross, and yet so puslie[4] on One side, and the honest Gentlemen So Ill informed of things here on the Other, that Really I blush for them sometimes, and am asham'd to Instruct men, who I thought I had not been Able to Informe of any thing.

They have Reprinted the book of Rates[5] here, tho' it is not yet published—but I foresee they will want an Exposition upon it, for many that have seen it are Not One Jott the Wiser, and honestly protest not to Understand it.

They go on Calmly now—but some foresee that there will be the Greatest struggle about the Generall, when after the perticulars are Run Thoro', they shall be in Danger at last in passing the Generall questions. On this some of the Lds that are Sincere friends to it, and Undr some Concern on that perticular Account, sent to me yesterday, to Desire I would write One Essay more On the Generalls of the Union, the Common Intrests of Trade, Governmt and Religion[6]— This as within my sphere and the substance of my silent Commission hither, (pardon me that

[1] Which provided that vessels belonging to Scotsmen be deemed 'ships of the build of Great Britain'.   [2] Missing.
[3] James Hamilton (1656–1734), sixth Earl of Abercorn, and John Gordon (1660?–1733), fifteenth or sixteenth Earl of Sutherland.
[4] Meaning perhaps 'petty'. See *O.E.D.*, 'pusill'.
[5] For customs duties.
[6] Defoe's *Fifth Essay at Removing National Prejudices, with a Reply to Some Authors Who Have Printed Their Objections against an Union with England* appeared in the following January (Dottin, *Defoe*, p. 812).

freedom) I have accepted with some seeming Reluctance, as haveing Raised me Enemies here allready &c.

If this be finished time Enough, I hope it may be of service, and I shall not be spareing to Disperse them tho' I Venture putting you to some Charge Sir, and Indeed I am a Chargeable Messengr to you, but if I had been to spend my Own Money, I protest I Could not have forborn these things, and for the sake of publick service I should have Ruin'd my Self.

If I am too forward, I beseech you Sir Restrain me by your Ordrs, for I have no Other Uneasiness— I seek the service by the Directest methods, I am master of— If I Err, the missfortune will be mine, but Indeed Indeed Sir Want of Instructions, is a Mellancholly Reflection, and makes me Frequently think my self an Unworthy Instrument.

However, to my Power I Resolve to be Diligt and Faithfull as becomes

Your Obt Servt
[symbol]

Edinb. Nov. 2[?]. 1706

I Can Not but hint Sir my Own Missfortunes to your Remembrance and by you to her Majties goodness as you were pleased to give me Room to Expect.[1]

MS.: Duke of Portland, Defoe Papers, i ff. 88–89. *Pub.*: *H.M.C. Portland*, iv. 356–7. *Address*: none. *Endorsed*: 'Edenburg Nov: 23: 1706, R̸ Nov: 29:'

67. [*To* ROBERT HARLEY]. [*22 November 1706*][2]

Sir

Since the Other part I have attended the Committee; The first false step I Discovred was that the Vote yesterday Upon the fourth Article[3] was Design'd as an alteration of the Articles.

I Took the Freedom to say if they broke in Upon the Articles to alter the Terms of them, they Unravelld the Treaty and would Come to the Necessity of a New Commission—But that I Conciev'd all their Amendments or Regulations Might be brought into an act Explanatory of the Articles and founded Upon them,

---

[1] His wife had written to him at about this time that she had been without money for ten days (p. 159).

[2] The editor of *H.M.C. Portland*, iv, suggested 21 Nov. as the date of this letter. But since in the first paragraph Defoe mentions 'the Vote yesterday Upon the fourth Article', and since that Article was voted on 21 Nov., I assign the letter to the 22nd. See *History of the Union*, p. 367. Furthermore, this correction gives meaning to the phrase 'the Other part' (first paragraph), which can now be understood as referring to the other letter written earlier on the same day, No. 66.

[3] Which provided for equality of trading privileges.

and while these Explanations Consisted with Equallity, proportion and Reasonable Constructions they might Expect the
parliamt of England would hear Reason, whereas if they went
on to Direct Alterations they would fall into Inextricable
Difficulties and indeed Dissolve the Treaty or at least Endanger
it— This They all adher'd to and Resolve to Call the Vote of
yesterday an Explanation in the Minutes if they Can, tho' perhaps that may be too late.[1]

Then they Desir'd my Opinion of their Demand of a Draw
back on Peas, Oats and Oat Meal which the Northern Members
press for and the people are Very Clamarous About.

I put them off from a Bounty on Oates or Peas by assureing
them England Will allwayes buy them and there Could be
No Pretence for a Drawback or bounty for Exporting that Was
allwayes wanted at home. The justice of this prevaild with the
Committee and so they Have agreed to wave that.

But On Oats Ground or Oat Meal they are positive and
Really the Reason of it Convinces me—They Drive a great
Trade to Norway for Deals and Timber and they puchase them
and sometimes bring Silver to boot with their Oat Meal.[2]

On the Other hand from Ireland They do the like, and
Undersell Scotland, and This Bounty will Enable the scots to
Send larger quantities—and I Can not but Add (to you Sir)
This May Help England who Now Trades to Norway wholly
for Ready Money and perhaps in Time May Come to save a
Great Deal of it by supplyeing them with Oatmeal—

So their Explanation On this Article is to have 2*s*:6 Draw
back on Oatmeal Onely per Quarter.

Then we had a long Debate what Price the Oat meal must
bear when the Bounty should be Due, and the price of Oat meal
being an Uncertain thing Especially in England and hard to
Determine, I Offred an Expedient Vizt that the price should
be stated in the wholl Corn. I proposed 12*s* per Quarter, My Ld
presidt[3] Demanded it at 20, Mr Paterson[4] Offred it at 13*s* 4*d*,
and there it passed, and so the Amendment will be thus

---

[1] In spite of Defoe's warnings, several of the Articles were altered, but the
changes were not so numerous as to jeopardize ratification at Westminster. See
Mathieson, *Scotland and the Union*, pp. 135–7.

[2] The drawback on oatmeal eventually was allowed (Mathieson, op. cit.,
p. 136).

[3] James Graham (d. 1742), fourth Marquis of Montrose, later first Duke of
Montrose, was President of the Council and a member of the Committee for
equivalents.

[4] William Paterson, promoter of the Bank of England and of the Darien scheme,

That a Bounty of 2*d* 6*d* per Quarter on Oatmeal shall be Allowed when the price of Oates in the Port where the Sd Oatmeal shall be Exported does not Exceed 13*s* 4*d* per Quarter.

This I presume will be the Work of the next meeting of the parliament and if they get it pass'd as proposed and the Amendments Offred by way of Explanations, I hope all will be agreeable to England and to the Common Intrest.[1]

The Committe then proceeded to the Matter of the Excise and Very great Difficultys Appear'd there.

They all Insisted that by True proportion and the Rules of Equallity their two penny Ale here Ought to pay but as small beer—But the people are Uneasy and affraid to be left to the Mercy of the Excise Office to Construe the Law Upon them.

And Indeed the Clamour of the people would be Intollerable should the strong beer Duty be Demanded on their Ale, which tho' Called Ale is little better than small beer and really sells Under 10*s* per barrel.[2]

However, to Come to a Certainty they are Content that the Excise Come up to a proportion and this they Calculate at 2*s* per Barrell and so the people pay 9*s* per barrell Onely to be sure, and to bring this to be offred in the Terms of an Explanation Their Ldships put it Upon me to Draw it up for them against the next meeting of Parliament, which Will I Suppose be Wednesday— The Rough of the Said Draught I herewith Enclose[3] Your Honor and wish I had Time to have your Opinion of it— I have done it with as Much Indifference and Impartiallity to both Sides as I Can, and as I See no shadow of any Other Medium I believ it will be Approv'd here, and I hope in England too.

The Draw back on Salt will be the Next Difficulty, and There is a strong Demand for a Draw back on Their Pork Exported for Sale— I Mentioned it and Mr P . . . . n[4] Thought I had started it for them, and hinted as Much after we Came Out, which Onely Serv'd to Convince me he Converst with but few, Since The Merchants Concernd are Many, and Make a great Crye about it, and I Think it Every Mans bussiness that wishes well to This work to Allay The spirits of this Agitated

was financial consultant to the managers of the Treaty of Union. See Mackinnon, *Union of England and Scotland*, pp. 259–60. For a letter from Defoe to Paterson, see No. 2.   [1] See *History of the Union*, pp. 373–4.

[2] See *History of the Union*, pp. 378–82.

[3] Missing, but see *History of the Union*, p. 378.

[4] William Paterson.

people at the Expence of Every Thing that Can be Easily parted with.

Tis true Draw Backs and Bountys will Put back the Equivalent,[1] but They are but Few and the Consequence of Denying them Very Great. When pd They are pd by Themselves and I Dare say the Reasons will sway England to do any Reasonable Thing to make This people Easy.

I Wish my Ld Treasurer Inform'd That a Report was spread here, when My Ld Anandale proposed the succession with Limitations instead of the Union,[2] That There was a Letter in Town From his Ldship to Direct the accepting it—and That his Ldship Wonderd They Did Not Close with it at the First offer—

D F

MS.: Duke of Portland, Defoe Papers, 1 ff. 86–87. *Pub.*: *H.M.C. Portland*, iv. 354–6. *Address*: none.

68. [*To* ROBERT HARLEY]. *26 November 1706*

Sir

I Can Not Express to your Honr what a Cordial the favour of your Letter[3] was to me After Such a strange and Surpriseing Silence. I Thank God my Faith in your Regard to me was too firmly Fix't to suffer me to Neglect my Duty, but I Own I have been Undr Perplexitys and Discouragemts Inumerable. I shall Trouble you no More with them.

My Success here I am In hopes will Answer your Expectations, tho' the Difficultyes have been Infinite. If No Kirk Devills More Than we yet Meet with appear, I hope all will be well and I begin to See thoro' it.

If I Understand the Cautions you are pleasd to give me in your Letter, they Respect England as much as scotland, And Indeed I am afraid of Erring Most that way, and am Therefore Very Wary.

Tho I will Not Answer for Success yet I Trust in Mannagemt you shall not be Uneasy at your Trusting me here. I have Compass't my First and Main step happily Enough, in That I am Perfectly Unsuspectd as Corresponding with anybody in England.[4] I Converse with Presbyterian, Episcopall-Dissenter, papist and Non Juror, and I hope with Equall Circumspection.

---

[1] That is, will require a recalculation of it.
[2] See *History of the Union*, pp. 345–53.   [3] Missing.
[4] 'He was therefor a Spy amongst us, but not known to be such, otherways the Mob of Edin. had pulled him to pieces' (*Memoirs of the Life of Sir John Clerk of Penicuik*, Edinburgh, 1892, p. 64).

I flatter my Self you will have no Complaints of my Conduct. I have faithfull Emissaries in Every Company And I Talk to Everybody in Their Own way. To the Merchants I am about to Settle here in Trade, Building ships &c. With the Lawyers I Want to purchase a House and Land to bring my family & live Upon it (God knows where the Money is to pay for it). To day I am Goeing into Partnership with a Membr of parliamt in a Glass house, to morrow with Another in a Salt work. With the Glasgow Mutineers I am to be a fish Merchant, with the Aberdeen Men a woollen and with the Perth and western men a Linen Manufacturer, and still at the End of all Discourse the Union is the Essentiall and I am all to Every one that I may Gain some.

Again I am in the Morning at the Committee, in the Afternoon in the assembly. I am privy to all their folly, I wish I Could not Call it knavery, and am Entirely Confided in.

Youl Pardon me this Excursion on my Self And bear with This allay to it, that I Really have spent a great Deal of your Money and am like to do More—yet perhaps not So Much as by Mr Bells Account, Since he sent me in his last more and sooner than I Expected, of which however I am not the Worse husband and have about £20 yet in hand tho' the press Dreins me and I am something behind to it.

I Assure you Sir and Entreat you to believ me I am not in anything Extravagant in this sharping Dear place. But where the Design I am in presses me, Then Indeed I am not spareing— My Own Affaires I have Recommended to you but too often, and had not mentioned them Now tho' severely presst there, Onely to assure you I Can not Relieve them from Hence Tho' My Wife wrott me last week she had been 10 dayes without Money— I submitt it all to that providence which when he sees Good will smile, & Till then I must wait—

I shall strictly observ your Directions and act with the Uttmost Caution in Every Thing.

The Regulation of the Clause about forreign ships has pass'd agat the scheme I Offred,[1] but I shall Take the first Occasion with my Ld President[2] to see them to Rights in Method.

While I wrott the Above I am Sent for by My Ld Cessnock[3]

---

[1] See *History of the Union*, pp. 369–72.   [2] The Marquis of Montrose.
[3] Alexander Campbell, born Hume (1675–1740), was a son of the Earl of Marchmont and had been elevated to the Scottish Bench as Lord Cessnock. He was at this time M.P. for Berwickshire and a member of the Committee for equivalents. See *H.M.C. Portland*, viii. 251.

to the Committe where I Understand Mr Paterson is to be also. Tho' I Never saw him there yet the Result I shall add to this, that Gentleman is full of Calculates, figures and Unperforming Numbers, but I see nothing he has done here nor does any body Elce speak of him but in Terms I Care not to Repeat.

I am, Sir, Your Most Obedt Servt

D F

Edinb. Nov. 26. 1706

MS.: Duke of Portland, Defoe Papers, 1 ff. 90–91. *Pub.*: *H.M.C. Portland*, iv. 358–9. *Address*: none. *Endorsed*: 'Edenburg Nov: 26: 1706, R̸ Dec: 2:'

69. [*To* ROBERT HARLEY]. *28 November 1706*

Nov. 28. 1706

Sir

I have the honor of your Second Letter[1] with the Enclosed paper of Observations which I have Transcrib'd and here Returnd According to your Directions, and shall not Fail to Observe The Cautions you were pleasd to give me.

The Gentlemen kept me So late the last post night that I Closed your Letter in Some Confusion, the post being just goeing Elce I had sent this paper back that night.

I Observ by These papers it is Expected the parliamt here should pass the Articles Entire— I fear they will Never be Able to do that, but as I wrott you in my last they will Onely make their Demands and Explanations in an act of parliamt which they will Annex to the Union.

It is my Dayly bussiness to Convince them and Remove New started Difficulties in this Case, and If it had not been my Good fortune to be there that Night, they had blindly Gone into Direct Modelling the Articles.[2]

The parliamt has been Two dayes Upon the Sixth Article[3] and have at last Referr'd it back to the Committee where I shall have some more Opportunity to Debate it with them.

I gave you an Account what I had Done in the severall Cases of the Oatmeal,[4] which I hope the parliamt will Confirme, but

[1] Missing.

[2] The Scottish Parliament did in fact change some of the Articles, but all of the alterations proved acceptable to the English Parliament. See Mathieson, *Scotland and the Union*, pp. 135–7.

[3] Which provided for uniformity with England in matters of allowances, encouragements, prohibitions, restrictions, and regulations of trade.

[4] See p. 156.

they have Altred the Rate of Oates from 13*s* 4*d* to 15*s* per Quarter as the standard of Price.

I have also proposed a Medium by which I put them off from layeing any Duty or prohibition on Oates from Ireland, Not that it signifyed Much but that I Avoid Loading the Case with Amendments— I had a Great Tug about this Triffle for they would have 16*s* per Quarter on their Groats or Oatmeal and 8*s* per Quarter on the Oates, which must then have been Altred in England.

Looking in the book of Rates it Appeares that in England there is 5*s* per Quarter on Oates now as Imported from Ireland— This I showd them was sufficient still and might stand for the wholl Island, Onely with this Addition—that Every Quarter of Groats or Oatmeal shall be Deemd as three quarter of Oates within the said act.[1]

This I believe will pass; the house to day has been warm Upon the Drawbacks on Oats and Peas, but the Gentlemen of the Comitte stood their Ground On my Notion of their being allwayes a Market in England.

I Omitted Encloseing the Draught of my proposall for the Excise for they kept me so long I had not a Minute for the post. I Ask your pardon for the Ommission and have sent it herewith.[2]

This Terrible people the Church men have not yet done. They have now in Debate a protestation Against the Act of security as Insufficient.[3] *God almighty Open their Eyes.*

Also here is a protestation to day from the West, where they burnt the Articles. I shall get a Coppy of it to send next post.[4]

I am Sorry Sir to see in the paper you Enclosed me that all the Amendments seem to be Desir'd here to be Referrd to the parliamt of Brittain.

I Dare say the Gentlemen here would Come in to it but should they Attempt it the wholl Treaty will be lost. The Very word Parliamt of Brittain is Grown Terrible here, and the people are so foolishly possest with their haveing No justice there that tis to Say Nothing to attempt it.

On the Other hand the Entring into these few Amendmts or Explanations mightily quiets and Eases the minds of the people Especially of the Wiser Sort.

---

[1] See *History of the Union*, p. 373.
[2] Missing.
[3] See Mathieson, *Scotland and the Union*, p. 185.
[4] The protest of the Dumfries men who had publicly burned the Articles of Union. The protest is reprinted in *History of the Union*, pp. 614–15.

I Take this Liberty Sir On Two Accounts.

First Sir that I may have your Ordrs that if I must not go on to Lessen their Demands or put them off from some by Granting Others and the like, but Insist plainly that They must pass the articles and referr the Rest &c., I may know how to Obey you punctually—but then I beseech you to bear with me In saying all the Intrest here would Never Carry the Union without blood.

Secondly I offer this, That if you Encline as I hope you will in England to Grant the heads, I Daresay they shall be Triffles and I hope to put them off from a great Deal that they now Insist upon.

> I am, Sir, Your Most Obedt Servt
> [symbol] G——

I Could not Refrain sending you a peice of my Ld Beilhavens Poetry in Answer to the Ballad.[1]

I Daresay you will believ it a meer Originall and I believ he may Challenge all the World to match it or to Answer it.

You will also see by it I have mannagd so in the Ballad that he does not suspect it but believs it my Ld Haddington.[2]

The Dr he means is your Next Neighbour—Dr W—d.[3] This morning I put abroad privately the Enclosed lines upon it also.[4] The ballad is printed.[5]

MS.: Duke of Portland, Defoe Papers, 1 ff. 92–93. *Pub.*: *H.M.C. Portland*, iv. 360–1. *Address*: none. *Endorsed*: 'Edenburg Nov: 28 1706, R̷ Dec: 4:'

[1] The 'Ballad' is doubtless Defoe's *The Vision*, in which Belhaven's speech is ridiculed. See p. 142, n. 3. Belhaven's poem was probably the one entitled *A Scots Answer to a British Vision*.

[2] Thomas Hamilton (1680–1735), sixth Earl of Haddington, a member of the Squadrone, which was now supporting the Union.

[3] Defoe refers to the following stanza:

> By this World may see
>   Whence the maggot does bite,
> Since a rake and a cullie,
> A doctor and a bullie,
> Much touch a Court's fee,
>   And do their worst to Unite.

Professor James Sutherland kindly points out to me that the doctor was probably Dr. James Wellwood who, like Harley, lived in York Buildings. See *D.N.B.*

[4] Missing, but probably his *Reply to the Scot's Answer to the British Vision*.

[5] It must have been circulating in manuscript. A few days later Mar wrote to Sir David Nairne: 'I have sent you a song about Balhaven, but it's not in print, which is a pittie' (*H.M.C. Mar and Kellie*, p. 351).

70. *To* ROBERT HARLEY. *30 November 1706*

Sir

The Parliamt has Sat Three times since I wrott to you— They have passt the 7th Article,[1] not in the Exact Terms, but on the foot of the paper I sent in my last.

I am Sorry to say it but tis Really True the Union may be Carryed on and I hope perfected on Reasonable Explanations, Never with leaving it to the parliamt of Brittain. Tis my sphere to lessen them as much as possible and in this I think I do my Country good service and this Country no Injury.

I am Sorry to Tell you the war here is begun. The Glasgo men, 100 Onely Very well Arm'd, are Marcht and 200 are to follow. The Sterling men, Hamilton Men and Galloway men are to meet them.[2]

Expresses Comeing in to day of this, the Privy Council who had yesterday Ordred a proclamation against them have Dispatcht a body of Dragoons to meet them and I must Own the well affected people here attend the Issue with Great Uneasiness.

I had heard of the west Countrymens Resolutions and purposed to have Gone among them myself, but the Committee Calling Every Day for me I thought myself able to do more service here—and Mr Pierce[3] whom you kno' of Offering him-

---

[1] Which provided that Scotland levy the same excises that England did; it was passed on 28 Nov.

[2] The Glasgow men numbered actually only about 45. They were to be joined at Hamilton by other bands, but the support failed to turn up and they retired ingloriously back to Glasgow. See Mackinnon, *Union of England and Scotland*, pp. 310–13.

[3] J. Pierce (Defoe supplies the initial in Nos. 80 and 82) cannot be identified with assurance. Dottin (*Defoe*, pp. 139 and 165) takes him to be that shadowy J. Pierce who in 1704 fled to the North on being charged with complicity in the publication of *Legion's Humble Address to the Lords*. That identification is plausible. Since Defoe himself was probably the author of the *Address*. and was certainly suspected of being such (J. W. to Harley, *H.M.C. Portland*, iv. 93), the exile would have been no stranger to him. And Defoe's sympathy for one who had suffered in an old cause of his own could have prompted him to employ Pierce in Government service, thereby placing the fugitive in a position to 'merit a pardon for what has past'. Andrew Lang, writing earlier than Dottin, argued that 'Pierce' was a pseudonym for John Ker of Kersland, the 'amusingly unscrupulous professional spy' (*History of Scotland*, Edinburgh, 1907, iv. 124–31). Lang notes that Ker was sent to the West of Scotland to soothe the people there and to prevent their joining the Highland Jacobites for a march on Edinburgh, and that Defoe's 'Pierce' was sent on a like mission. Lang further points out that Ker later inclined away from the Government and towards the Squadrone, and that 'Pierce' later abandoned Defoe, who explained that someone else had 'Employ'd him Out of my way' (p. 207). 'Pierce' may have been John Ker, but these parallels are neither numerous enough nor remarkable enough to invite confidence in the identification. For other mention of Pierce in these letters, see Nos. 80, 81, 82, and 97.

self, I sent him with my servant and horses with some heads of Reasons if possible to Open their Eyes.

He is Very well known among them and Very Acceptable to their ministers who are the firebrands, and I hope may be servicable to Cool the people if he scapes the first fury, but I Confess myself in pain for him.

He is Sincerely Zealous for the publick and will merit a pardon for what has past if he performs this service whether he has success or no.

The parliamt has this Day past an act[1] to Repeal the act of security and Discharge the Musters and Appearing in Arms that were made lawfull before. I shall not fail to give you an Account of Every step on both sides.

I am, Sir, Your Most Obedt Servt

D F

Nov. 30. 1706

MS.: Duke of Portland, Defoe Papers, 1 ff. 94–95. *Pub.*: *H.M.C. Portland*, iv. 362. *Address*: 'To The Right Honble Robert Harley Esqr., Principall Secretary of State.' *Endorsed*: 'Edenburg Nov: 30: 1706, R̸ Dec 6' and 'Mr De Foe.'

71. [*To* ROBERT HARLEY]. *5–7 December 1706*[2]

Sir

In My last[3] I gave a perticular of the Encreasing Rabble at Glasgow, which Grew to That hight That the Magistrates and honest Townsmen Press't for Some Soldiers to be sent with all speed, and Finly[4] One of the Leaders of the Mob boasted he would be at Edinburgh in Two dayes.

You will please to Observ this Finly is [a][5] mean, scandalous scoundrell fellow Carryed Arms in Dumbartons Regimt and a profess't Jacobite, and I believ that is One Reason the Cameronian people tho' Equally Dissaffected would not Joyn him, at least not So as to March from Glasgow or from their Other Towns.

[1] See *History of the Union*, p. 282.

[2] Though this letter is dated 7 Dec., all of it except the last four paragraphs was written on 5 Dec., the day upon which Parliament debated the malt tax and upon which the Dutch fleet arrived. See *History of the Union*, pp. 389–91, and *H.M.C. Mar and Kellie*, p. 351.

[3] Apparently missing.

[4] For an account of Finlay's attempt to march on Edinburgh, see *History of the Union*, pp. 274–9.

[5] Omitted in MS.

I Think I Noted In my last how the prudence of the Dutchess Dowagr of Hamilton prevented their assembling at Hamilton,[1] and I am Sorry to Tell your Honr that 13 Ministers of parishes in their severll pulpits Read the paper handed about for their assembling. They Excuse it here by saying it was Onely a legall summons for the people to Muster and Exercise as by the Act of Security they might do and by Custome Used to do, But—I say no More. Their best Friends here are Asham'd of it— They did not Meet it seems, for the Dss of Hamilton haveing Recd the proclamation and act of Parliamt[2] sent Ordrs to all the places in her Country & perticularly to her Own Tenants not to Meet Upon any Terms, and perticularly Threatned her Own Tenants with Dispossessing them if they presumed to Appear in Arms— Had his Grace the Duke behav'd like this Matters had not Come thus far.

Wednsday night, the Detachmt of Dragoons which went from hence with the Horse Grenadiers of the Guards, and a second Detachmt who Marcht out of Fife by way of sterling bridge, were Ordred to March all night with the Uttmost Expedition to Glasgow. We had sevll Reports of Action happening between them and that the Mob haveing taken posession of the Castle at Glasgo had kill'd severall of the Dragoons, But This is Contradicted.[3]

Tis True they have kept a Court of Guard in the Bishops house, which is the Remain of an Old Castle, but I Can not think they will Defend themselves there. We Expect the Event here with Great Impatience.

The Parliamt have been to day on the Article of the Malt Tax, and have made a Determination which I like the Worst of any thing they have done, Not that I think it Materiall in its Nature, but that tis an Absolute breaking In Upon the Articles, and to me a breach of the Equallity which is the foundation of the Union.

They put it first whether scotland should be Exempt from it for a Certain Time or for Ever, and Carryed it Onely for a Certain time, by a Majority of 30. Then after a long Debate it was put whether the Time should be for 7 yeares as in the Salt

---

[1] The Dowager Duchess of Hamilton was no friend to the Union, but she may have been following out the inscrutable policies of her son, who at the last moment decided against bringing the crisis to a trial at arms. See *Lockhart Papers*, i. 199–201.

[2] Which suspended the right of mustering.

[3] Finlay and his accomplice, one Montgomery, were arrested by the troops, but there were no casualties (*History of the Union*, p. 278).

or *Dureing the war*, and with Great Difficulty it was Carry'd for the latter, and this was so nice a Turn that the House was Equally Divided and My Ld Chancellors Vote Carryed it.[1]

I Need not Tell you Sir the long Argumt to prove that scotland Can Not bear this Tax. The Onely Argumt I saw of any force Was this, that the Malt here is Very Ordinary and does not produce Equall with the English—but when I alleag'd two things to the Gentlemen here, 1: why then do you demand Equall bounty on Exportation, and 2: that the Malt in England Used Onely for Distilling is worse than theirs and pays the full, they knew Not what to say.

I Can not help saying that these Tumults and Terrors have brought all this Mischiefs on and tis Impossible to Avoid the Amendments— I hope Some Expedient will be found in England to bear with them for the yet Greater benefit of the wholl, and that her Majtie will be the Great Intercessor between the Nations that these things shall not break a Treaty of so much Consequence.

> I am, Sir, Your Most Obedt Servt
> D F

The Dutch fleet is just Arriv'd and with them near 200 men, officers and servants for Recruits which is some help to us here.

Edinb. Dec. 7th 1706

The Above was written, but by a Misstake kept too late for the last post for which I ask your pardon but make Amends in part for it by adding that this short war is God be praised at an End. The Detachment of Dragoons are Come back from Glasgow And while I am writeing This they are Marching by the Door with Finly and Montgomery the Two Leaders of the Glasgow Rabble who they seiz'd in Glasgow with out any Resistance and all Things are Restord There, and by this stroke I hope all is at an End.

The Church also begin to Face about again. I Wish they had been Wise Enough to have done it sooner.

Last night They Concluded upon a Letter in the Comission of the Assembly to be written to the severall presbyteries to Exhort Them to Use Their Endeavours in Their severall Districts to perswade the people to peace and to prevent all Tumults and Disorders.[2]

[1] See *History of the Union*, pp. 389–91.
[2] For the text of the letter see the *Review* for 17 Dec. 1706.

The Draught is not finished but I hope to have a Coppy of it against Next post.

I am, Sir, Your Most Obedt Servt
D F

MS.: Duke of Portland, Defoe Papers, 1 ff. 99–100. *Pub.*: *H.M.C. Portland*, iv. 364–5. *Address*: none. *Endorsed*: 'Edenburg Dec: 7: 1706, R̶ Dec: 15.'

72. *To* ROBERT HARLEY. *7 December 1706*

Sir

The Enclosed[1] was wrott at Three Essayes, and yet I am Obliged to add a fourth.

Since all the proceeding of the Forces at Glasgow of which you See the Issue in the Enclosed, The Mob has been up there Again as furious as Ever. I Confess I thought it a wrong step to let the Dragoons quitt the Town Again so soon.

As soon as they were Come Away the Rabble Rose again and Took all the Magistrates prisoners and Declared that if their Two men[2] were not Restored and sent home Again they would Treat the Magistrates just in the same Manner as they should be Treated.

They Took the Parol of some of them and let them go to Edinburgh to Sollicit and they were here as Soon as the prisonrs. What the Issue of their Sollicitations will be I know not, but I suppose they will Force the Govornmt to Hang these Two Men and to send the Dragoons back again. Of Every Thing that Occurs you will Depend Upon an Exact Account.

My Ld H . . . . x[3] has not given the Return his Ldship promised my Bro:[4] to the Letter I sent so I have not wrott since, but whoever I write you may Sir Depend Entirely on my Absolutely Concealing that any Thing but my Own Affaires Drov me hither.[5]

I am, Sir, Your faithfull and Obedt Servt
D F

Dec. 7. 1706

If you please to Convey to me in a Letter the Draught of your

---

[1] The preceding letter.
[2] Finlay and Montgomery.
[3] Halifax. See p. 147.
[4] Robert Davis, Defoe's brother-in-law.
[5] In the *Review* for 21 Jan. 1706–7, Defoe maintained that he had worked to bring about the Union 'unsent, unemploy'd, *and then any one will grant,* not only unrewarded, but unsupported'. See also *History of the Union*, p. 213.

Coat of Arms I will Onely Use it to Make you a small present of the Manufacture of this Country.[1]

MS.: Duke of Portland, Defoe Papers, 1 ff. 101–2. *Pub.*: *H.M.C. Portland*, iv. 365–6. *Address*: 'To The Right Honble Robert Harley Esqr., Her Majties Principall Secreta of State, Present.' *Endorsed*: 'Edenburgh Dec. 7: 1706, R Dec: 13.'

73. [*To* ROBERT HARLEY]. *9 December 1706*

Sir

I sent you an Account Last Post of the Takeing of Finley And Montgomery, the Two Ringleaders of the Glasgow Rabble and their bringing into the Castle here.

They had no Sooner brought them away but the Rabble Rose again there, took the Magistrates prisoners and sent some of them hither, Assuring them if they did not procure their Two men again they would burn their houses &c. The foolish men, frighted with the Rabble, were here as soon as the prisoners.

They have been I hear to day before the Council who as they Very well Deserv, bid them go home and take better Care of the peace of the Citty, (for that must be Ownd) had they Timely done their Duty these Rabbles had been suppresst before they Came to a head. I suppose these foolish people will Force the Govornmt to hange these Two Miserables.

Finley behaves Very Haughty and Positiv, Declares himself a Jacobite, Talks of Dying, and I believ Expects no other.

The Other I hear has a pen and Ink allowd him and Perhaps may Tell some Tales. The Committee of Council have been Three times (or the Ld Register[2] from them) to Examine them. What has pass't there I presume you will not Expect I should be able to Accquaint you of.

The Committee of whom I have often hinted, have been to day on the salt— The Other party Insist on haveing 10s per Barrll instead of 8s 4d Drawback on white Herring.

I was sent for, and took upon me to Oppose it. First I Convinc't them Even by their Own Accounts that 8s 4d which is allowd in England was 1s 8d more than the salt Came to which Curd the fish, and was Clear gain to the Importer. Then I Undertook to prove that on a New Demand, the same Drawback being allow'd in England would Encrease Our fishing so

---

[1] The present probably was to be a piece of linen with Harley's arms interwoven (Sutherland, *Defoe*, pp. 164–5).

[2] Sir James Murray, Lord Philiphaugh.

much as to make us Rivall them and perhaps supplant them in all the streights Trade, and so lessen the Encouragemt of their fishery, which was Much of it Expected from England.[1]

They are Come to no Conclusion yet, but I am to attend again to morrow and to give in my Reasons in writeing and my Calculation of the Duty and the Drawback.

I Obtain Coppy of their Resolution or Report Rather on the Customes, which is pretty Enough and I believ will please you. They are all Very honest hearty Gentlemen and Zealously for the Union.

I am your Humble and Earnest Petitioner not to let it be known that you have this Coppy from me. It would so lessen my Esteem among them that I should be Very ill used by them and no more Consulted with on any Occasion.

I have also Estimates of the Respectiv Customes on Goods here to which I am to Draw farther Replyes and to present them at the next Sitting.

These things take me up some time, and Indeed made me lose the post for my Last Letter for which I again Humbly ask your Pardon.

If you will please to give me any hints in the things Now before them, and whether you Approve my Endeavouring to lessen their Amendments, it will be Very Usefull and Encourageing In this matter to me perticularly.

I am printing a Single sheet Entituled a Letter to the Glasgow men[2] but which I presume may be usefull to all the rest to Open their Eyes a Little. It is not out of the press to night so shall not be able to Enclose it till next post.

Mr Bell Sir writes me I must write to you for farther Ordrs if I make any more Demand on him— I have not yet made any Demand nor shall not as long as I have any thing left— But then if you do not permitt me to do it I shall pass my Time Very ill here and be Worse as to Returne. I hope you will please to approv both of my work and of the Expence when I Rendr you my Account, and that in the mean Time you will please to Recall me in Time when you do not think Fitt to subsist me any Longer.

I have I Confess spent you Sir a great Deal of Money here and tis the most Expensiv place I was Ever in. But Indeed Sir that

[1] The problem is clearly explained in the *Review* for 4 Jan. 1706–7. See also *History of the Union*, pp. 416–18.
[2] *A Letter to the Glasgow Men* was also printed in the *Review* for 2 Jan. 1706–7.

has not been my Expence; I have layd out myself and your Money in the True Service I Cam here for And I flatter my Self I have been Usefull— I Earnestly wrot to you Sir to be limited in my Expences, and I would Not have Exceed[ed],[1] and I have not been the larger for the liberty you have given me.

I have had £75 and a Horse of Mr Bell[2] and I have just 13 guineas left, about 6 of which I propose to lay Out for the Effectuall spreading this letter at Glasgow and Over all the West, and therefore purpose to print about 2500 of them and send them to Glasgow, Lanerk, Hamilton, sterlin and Dumfreis.

I beg Sir you will please to signifye your mind about Expences and if you think me too forward you need but a word to Restrain me; Ile stop Immediately. Otherwise I am Every Day saying something in print that Exposes these people here and Encourages the thing.

I Earnestly Entreat your Thoughts about the salt, the draw backs I mean, and about the Committees Report, and am

Sir, Your Most Obedt Servt
D F

Edinb. Dec. 9. 1706

MS.: Duke of Portland, Defoe Papers, 1 ff. 103–4. *Pub.*: *H.M.C. Portland*, iv. 366–7. *Address*: none. *Endorsed*: 'Edenburg Dec: 9: 1706.'

74. *To* ROBERT HARLEY. *12 December 1706*

Sir

Since my Last Nothing Materiall has happened. The house Sitts Dilligently on the Report which I sent you last post.[3]

The Glasgow Magistrates Recd a Checq from the Governmt as they Deserv'ed (for Really they have been too Accessary to all this mischief) and are sent home and there is no More done with the prisoners yet.

The paper I mentioned in my last About the Glasgow men I send you Enclosed. Tis a plain but Course Expostulation and they Flatter me it has done a great Deal of service here.

---

[1] Omitted in MS.

[2] On 4 Jan. 1706–7, Bell sent Harley the following statement (Duke of Portland, Harley Papers, xxiv f. 5; pub. in *H.M.C. Portland*, iv. 378):

8tobr 2,	Paid Mr D F	£40:17:6d
9mbr	Paid Ditto In Edenb	£52:10:6
xmbr	Paid Do In Edenb	£10:00:0
		£103:08:00

[3] Concerning customs duties. See *History of the Union*, pp. 399–409.

I forsee Sir a great Debate will Arise here about settling a Court of Appeals and I Enclose you a paper on that head.[1] I Wish I Could have your Opinion on the subject because I fear some thing to be offred here that may be Erroneous in fundamentalls (Viz)

A Court of Appeal in scotland will be Insisted upon to be Establisht here.

If it be Composed of Peers they will object for they Dare Not Trust their Own Lds. If of Commons how will it Consist with the Lords being the soveraign Judicature. If there is no Court of Appeals atall they will Either be forced up to England with their Causes, which will be Intollerable, or they will have the Lds of the session be a soveraign Judicature, which seems still worse.[2]

I may do much in stateing this Case, haveing some Notions of the matter which I Digested before I thought of Comeing hither—but I Entreat your Directions in this Case as far as you think Convenient, and am

Sir, Your Most Obedt Servt
D F

Edinb. Dec. 12. 1706

The post is Miscarryed to day. The weather is so bad and snows so great there is no Travailing.

The parliamt have granted to day an Equivalent to the Breeders or keepers of sheep for their Not Exporting wooll to France and Other parts. I suppose they are to pay it themselves.[3]

MS.: Duke of Portland, Defoe Papers, 1 ff. 105–6. *Pub.*: *H.M.C. Portland*, iv. 368. *Address*: 'To The Right Honble Robt Harley Esqr., Her Majties Principall secrets of State, Present.' *Endorsed*: 'Mr De Foe.'

75. *To* ROBERT HARLEY. *14 December 1706*

Sir

This post affords me Very Little Matter worth a Letter. The Parliamt has not Sat Since Thursday,[4] and the Commissionr being Each day in the Comittee in person I have not been sent for.

[1] A six-page tract entitled *A Letter to a Member of Parliament, upon the 19th Article of the Treaty of Union between the Two Kingdomes of Scotland and England: December 4th 1706.*
[2] This question of appellate jurisdiction is reviewed in A. V. Dicey and R. S. Rait, *Thoughts on the Union between England and Scotland*, 1920, pp. 191–200.
[3] See *History of the Union*, pp. 403–9.
[4] i.e. 12 Dec.

The present Close Debates[1] are about the Drawbacks on Salt and an Encouragemt of 20*s* per last[2] on Exporting fish, which they will allow to the Merchant Out of the Money from England.[3]

The hopes of Tumults and Noise being Over, the Designs are now if possible to Argue them into something that they think may shock England. I am as Watchfull in this as I can Upon all Occasions.

The Rabble at Glasgow are not yet quiet tho' not so Dangerously Uneasy as before. However, the Govornmt has thot fitt to Ordr a Detachmt of Foot and Dragoons to March thither to protect the Magistrates.

                 I am, Sir, Your Most Humble and Obedt Servt
                                     D F

Edinb. Dec. 14. 1706.

By the Enclosed[4] you will see a little more of the Temper of the West.

MS.: Duke of Portland, Defoe Papers, 1 ff. 107–8. *Pub.*: *H.M.C. Portland*, iv. 368. *Address*: 'To The Right Honble Robert Harley Esqr., Her Majties Principall Secreta of State, Present.' *Endorsed*: 'Edenburg Dec: 14: 1706, R̶ Dec: 20:'

76. [*To* ROBERT HARLEY]. *16 December 1706*

Sir

I have not the honor of any from you lately. The Treaty goes on here in parliament pretty well; my Fear is the Clogging it with Amendments.

As I hinted in My last the Rabbles and Noise of the party have push't them Upon Amendments and there was no possibillity to Avoid it; Now the Dilligence of the party is Employ'd if possible to bring Them to Agree to Such Amendments as they know the English Can not Complye with. Thus the Party would fain have Drawn them into an Allowance for Exporting Wooll.

I Told Them it was Declareing Against the Union, and They had as good Do Nothing. Even the Comittee, some of them Too Much Intrested, Seemd to stagger in it but at last Came to Resolv against it and to have a Satisfaction to the sheep masters in the Room of it.

---

[1] In the Committee.   [2] i.e. 12 barrels.
[3] The Equivalent.   [4] Missing.

The 6th Article is past to day with an addition of the Drawback on Fish 20*s* per last and a license to Salt the provisions for ships on Inland Trade with Their Own Salt, paying English Duty.[1]

I Confess the Alterations are Numerous and Confused but I Take them hitherto to be Not Very Considerable and None of them Fatall to the Union in Generall.

Here is a Church Dispute started in private by some Ministers to me for they take me for Their Friend, and I am so, More to their Intrest then their Mannagemt; but it is serious and Considerable, and I Entreat your private Judgemt for my Governmt, for a Committee of the assembly are to meet me privately Upon it.

Their request is honest and if I Can have a favourable Answer they will Depend much on it and it will Reconcile a Great many to the Union, and they believ I have Intrest Enough in England to Lay it before the Queen and before such great people (they do not guess who) as may be of service to Them.

If The Union goes on, say they, The Queen is Declared Queen of Great Brittain, The Coronation Oath must be altred,[2] and the subjects must Renew their Oath.

If the Oath be Imposed Upon us, the Ministers half of us will be Turn'd Out of Our liveings. 1) We Can not swear to a Queen of Brittain as On the foot of the Union, for that is swearing to Episcopall Magistracy and swearing to the Union— Now tho' we Can Accquiesce and be passive in a Union with Prelacy, yet to swear to it is an Active subjection and we Can not do it; Our Nationall Oath[3] is Direct upon us and we must be Undone Rather than submitt to it— We have sworn to the Queen and we will keep it Inviolably to the last Drop—but the Other is Against Our Consciences and we Can not do it. Nay if as Queen of scotland her Majtie should Require us to take the same

---

[1] See *History of the Union,* pp. 410–15.
[2] At the request of the Commission of the General Assembly, a change in the Coronation Oath had been agreed upon whereby the sovereign should swear to maintain the rights and privileges of the Church of Scotland as well as those of the Church of England (Mathieson, *Scotland and the Union,* pp. 183–4).
[3] 'The National Covenant had disallowed the civil power of Churchmen, and the Solemn League, besides abjuring prelacy, had pledged its subscribers to labour for the reformation of the Church of England; and, in view of these engagements, it was contended that the nation could not unite with, and so recognise the institutions of, a kingdom whose Church was Episcopal, and in whose Parliament twenty-six Bishops had seats' (Mathieson, op. cit., pp. 180–1).

Individual Oath of Alleigeance Over again we Could not do it, for haveing sworn allready, to do it again would be Multiplying Oaths, which we hold sinfull and Could no more do it than Marry or baptise Twice Over.

The Next thing is the Abjuration Oath. If this be Imposed Upon them in the Terms as Now Worded in England, there are not ten Ministers of the Kirk will hold their places and the Confusion will be Incredible.

The Case is This—The Oath Expressly sayes, or the Act for I have them Not here, That the Successor must Conform to the Church of England. Now for them to Abjure any successor but such as shall be of the Church of England is to Joyn in Excludeing their Own Church from the succession—which they say is Not Reasonable, nor Can they In Conscience Complye; but They are Content No person shall succeed that is not a protestant, and they Desire the Generall Term Protestant May be Allow'd or Elce they Can Never Abjure.[1]

Thus Sir I have stated their Questions. I Assure you the persons proposeing them are Sober, Wise and judicious, friends to the Union and sollicitous for the Generall quiet, hearty, Zealous promoters of her Majties Intrest, and the succession, But Scrupulous to a Nicety about Oaths, Episcopacy and such things as those.

I give you their Own words, and as near as I Can, do not Alter— I beseech you assist me with your thoughts. I kno' Nothing in this Country in which I may be able to Render her Majtie Equall service as in this, and the Turn it will give to the Opinion of the preasts will be Unexpected—and Indeed their Mannagemt has done Incredible Injury to the Case.

Some Medium I hope will be found Out and I beg your thoughts whether it may not be in England Rather than here, because to do it here would start such a Cloud of scruples as will allarm all the Clergy here and Especially in the West, and may Endanger a Reall Commotion—

The people who have broke this to me are few and have promised to keep it private if possible to have it Remedyed, and if it be, you Gain the wholl body of Ministers at a blow.

You will pardon my warm way of Expressing it. I Confess

---

[1] This objection had been raised previously by the Commission of the Assembly but was not countenanced by the Scottish Parliament. The question came up six years later in the British Parliament, but no change in the oath was allowed (Mathieson, *Scotland and the Union*, pp. 203–4).

I am Concern'd in my thoughts that some way may be found
Out to mak them Easye.

I am, Sir, Your Most Obedt Servt
D F

Edinb. Dec. 16. 1706

MS.: Duke of Portland, Defoe Papers, 1 ff. 109–10. *Pub.*: *H.M.C. Portland*, iv. 368–70. *Address*: none. *Endorsed*: 'Edenburg Dec: 16: 1706, R̸ Dec: 23:'

77. *To* ROBERT HARLEY. *17 December 1706*

Sir

Since the Enclosed[1] we Are Inform'd the Dragoons who We
Thot went to Lye in Glasgow to keep the Peace there have been
to Apprehend Some Persons, who Upon the Confessions of The
Two Prisoners they have here are Accused of being principalls
in the Tumults There.

We are told they have Taken Seaven. Who they are I Can
Not yet Learn, but a Party of Dragoons being Detach't this
Day, we suppose it is to Reciev the prisoners and bring them
hither.[2]

My Messenger[3] is not yet Return'd from the West. We hear
the people have been gathering a little in Galloway and the
West but Nothing Considerable.

I Again Recommend the Case Enclosed to your Thoughts
and Am

Sir, Your Most Obedt Servt
D F

Edinb. Dec. 17. 1706

MS.: Duke of Portland, Defoe Papers, 1 ff. 111–12. *Pub.*: *H.M.C. Portland*, iv. 370. *Address*: 'To The Right Honble Robert Harley Esqr., Her Majties Principal Secreta of State, Present.' *Endorsed*: 'Edenburg Dec: 17: 1706, R̸ Dec: 23:'

78. [*To* ROBERT HARLEY]. *19 December 1706*

Sir

I wrott you a Long letter last post,[4] Relateing to the Kirk
and the Uneasyness of the Ministers. I Doubt my Account
was Something Confusd.

I have Since Converst more Closely with Them on That head
And Not to Run Out in Perticulars, The Summe of the Matter
is as Foll'

[1] The preceding letter.   [2] See *History of the Union*, p. 280.
[3] Pierce. See p. 163.   [4] No. 76.

1. The Union *as Such* They are Not Against and Some of Them profess to be Very Willing to Come into it but they Complain They are Treated haughtily and at first Something Rudely.

The Overture Or Act of Security for the Church[1] was hurryed Up Onely among a few. Large Amendments and Long Considerations are in hand On Accounts of Trade, Taxes &c., but Matters of Religion Are hurryed On too fast, the Comission Thin and the Members Not Come Up,[2] and all their Motions or Demands, public or Private, Recd with haughtyness and Contempt.

As to the Bishops,[3] they are Not Enclin'd to Any Opposition On that Account, Other than by the formallity of a Protest Or Declaration, to Satisfye their Consciences as to submitting to Episcopall Legislation.

From This short Abridgement I Crave your Pardon for the Freedome of giveing my Opinion.

These Are a Refractory, Scrupulous and Positive people. It is in the power of the Govornmt to Inflame Them to the last Degree, and were the Design their Destruction, they might Easyly be Driven into the Agency of their Own Ruin.

On the Other hand if they are Mannag'd with a Little Lenity And Tenderness, if used kindly, you may yet have Them heart and hand for the Union—And I Can Not but Say it is yet worth while and Not too Late.

I know the Moderation of your Honrs Principles, and as it is Agreeable Not Onely to the Intrest but Inclination of her Majtie with all her people, So I Can Not but Repeat it, That a little of that Gentleness Exercised here instead of what has been a little too warm would Quench all this fire.

If it be Needfull for me to Descend to Some perticulars perhaps Nice Enough for the Govornmt of This Matter, your Ordrs shall be Observd On the first Notice by

Your Most Humble Servt

D F

I had this Day again the honor to Dine with the Comittee at the Ld Cessnocks.[4]

---

[1] The Act of Security for the Church of Scotland had been passed on 12 Nov. The text is reprinted in *History of the Union*, pp. 541–3.

[2] By February so many members had drifted away that the Commission was unable to muster a quorum (Mathieson, *Scotland and the Union*, p. 186).

[3] In the English House of Lords.

[4] See p. 159, n. 3.

The Occasion was the Debate to Come on this Day in Parliamt about the Salt Tax.

The Motion they Expect is Either a Totall Exemption from the Duty as Insupportable to the poor, or a lengthning Out the Term of Seaven years to a longer Time.

The Case I Doubt will go hard. I See no Argumt has any Room on the Other Side, the people being So posesst of the Burthen that the word Insupportable is in Every Mouth and they Run away with it without any Consideration.[1]

However, I proposed to Examin what Quantity of Salt per head the people Could Expend and So to Considr whether it was Really Insupportable or no. It happend to be a New thought to them and I was amaz'd to hear Even the Gentlemen themselves Guess that the People Consum'd 2 Bushell English Measure per head per Annum, and it was an Equall Surprize to Them when On a stricter Examination they Came all to be Convinc't that less than Two Pecks scots Measure, which is not quite 1 1/2 peck English, was the Uttmost they Expended—and My Ld Cessnock by Calling his Servants found his family of 24 did not Use 2 Pecks Each per Annum Not Reckoning Children nor strangers.

On this foot they Think themselves Furnisht for the Debate at least better than they were before.

But Just as they were prepareing to go Into the house they Are all in a Surprize at an Unhappy Accident which happening This Morning kept the Commissionr back till Near One a Clock, a Duell fought in the Park this Morning between the Duke of Argyle and The E of Crawford.[2]

The Quarrell it seems was Triffling, from a Bottle. I have Not yet the perticulars, but am Told the Duke of Queensb'ry haveing Some Notice of their Resolution Took Their Parols not to fight—how they have Thot fitt to break thro' that Engagemt I kno' Not yet.

They have neither Much harm, So the Hurry[3] of it is the most. Wll Kerr, Brother to the E of Roxburgh,[4] Was with the E of Crawford, and Ld Delorain[5] with the Duke.

The Dragoons have brought severall prisoners in this after noon From Glasgow and Hamilton, Among which Are some of

---

[1] See *History of the Union*, pp. 425–30.

[2] John Lindsey (d. 1713), nineteenth Earl of Crawford, was Colonel of the Horse Grenadier Guards.   [3] i.e. agitation.

[4] Roxburgh was a leader of the Squadrone.

[5] Henry Scott (1676–1730), later Earl of Deloraine.

the Duke of Hamiltons Servants. Their Names and perticulars shall be in My Next.

I am, Sir, Your Most Obedt Servt
D F

Edinburgh, Dec. 19. 1706

The house have not gone thorow the Clause of the Salt to day.

MS.: Duke of Portland, Defoe Papers, 1 ff. 113–14. *Pub.*: *H.M.C. Portland*, iv. 370–1. *Address*: none. *Endorsed*: 'Edenburg Dec: 19: 1706, R̶ Dec: 25:'

79. *To* ROBERT HARLEY. *21 December 1706*

Sir

I Doubt I Throng you with Letters, The Variety here affording Every Day Fresh Matter.

The Debate about the Salt I Wrott you in my Last is Not yet Come on, The house haveing been Embroild on Another head Vizt the Draw back on Pork and Beef.

This is an Article long Plotted to hamper the Cause if Possible. The Committee had Unwarily Reported the Beef and Pork in One Article— I must Acknowlege there Seem'd some Reason in their Demand on pork of which they have a large and Encreasing Trade from Aberdeen Only to Italy, Leghorn and Genoa, and they say ship't off 1000 barrells there this last year, and as the pork being fed with Corn is a great Article of the Consumtion of Corn, I the sooner Came in to it, which Mr Paterson[1] pretended[2] to give me a Caution for after wards as if I had put it into their heads.

But tis a Sign to me how little he Convert with the Gentlemen Concern'd, Since it was allways in their Mouths Every time I was with them from the first Discourse of the Salt Tax.

But this bringing the Beef in is a most Ridiculous thing Since tho' they have the same thing Now and a bounty paid too boot, they do not nor Can Export Ten Barrells of beef a year for sale, One year with Another.[3]

If Mr P . . . . n Represents any branch of this thing as above in My Prejudice he does me wrong, and I beg leav to be favourably Construed and heard to it.

I must Confess I am Sometimes shock't in my Thoughts at the

---

[1] William Paterson, banker and projector, at this time financial adviser to the managers of the Union Treaty. For a letter from Defoe to Paterson see No. 2.
[2] i.e. presumed.
[3] See *H.M.C. Mar and Kellie*, pp. 359–60, and *History of the Union*, pp. 421–3.

Multitude of Amendments here, tho' this is a most Insignificant thing in it self, neither kingdome Exporting any quantity of Beef for Sale.

However, the party boast of a Victory and say they have secur'd the Union from being Ever finished, and yet they Carryed this but by One Voice, and that was *Seaton of Pittmeddon*,[1] an honest whig too, and for the Union but byassd in this Case.

This Discovers Sir what I wrott you before, that the present Design was to load the Treaty with Such amendments As they think will Ruine it in its Consequences, and This is the Onely Card left to play.

The affair of Crawford and Argile[2] Made more Noise Then Mischief and is all Over, but the Duke has not got any Reputation by it. I Earnestly Crave your Thots on My Last.

I am, Sir, Your Most Obedt Servt
D F

Edinb. Dec. 21. 1706

MS.: Duke of Portland, Defoe Papers, 1 ff. 115–16. *Pub.*: *H.M.C. Portland*, iv. 371–2. *Address*: 'To The Right Honble Robert Harley Esqr., Her Majties Principall Secreta of State, Present.'

80. *To* ROBERT HARLEY. *24 December 1706*

Sir

This Unhappy Debate about the Draw back on Beef and Pork has held them here all this Week. The Case was Thus. The Committe had Unhappily Voted it together, No Draw back on Pork or Beef Exported for Sale.

When it Came to the house the Draw back on Pork Appear'd So Reasonable there was no withstanding it, and The Vote being wholl, the beef went with it.

Every body Laughs at the Demand of a Draw back for beef when scotland Exports none for Sale to any part of the World, but This Triffle being Carry'd made the party Very Chearfull Thinking they had Gaind Some Ground, but all This prov'd their loss, for the Very folly of the Vote brought this addition to it this Day Vizt That This should be Subject to the Parliamt of Brittain—which was Carryed to the Infinite Mortification of The party.[3]

[1] William Seton (d. 1744), later second baronet, was M.P. for Aberdeen and had been a Commissioner of the Union Treaty.
[2] See the preceding letter. [3] See *History of the Union*, pp. 423–5.

I hear Nothing More About the prisoners. There are Three more in the Castle and Two belonging to the Dutchess of Hamilton in the Town.

Since my last I have had a long Account from Mr J. P.[1] whom I hinted to what purpose, and when, I sent into the West. He has been at Dumfries and in the highlands, has been with John Hepburn[2] the Cameronian Minister, and with Some of the Most Resolute of That Party, and I hope has been Very Servicable to Cooling and Calming the Minds of an Ignorant and Deluded people, and I must do him that Justice I believ has been Very Usefull. I have a large Account from him which I had sent you this night— But I Confess myself in Some Disordr to night, The Account of the Death of my Father[3] Comeing just as I was writeing this.

　　　　　　　　I am, Sir, Your Most Obedt Servt
　　　　　　　　　　　　　　　　　D F

Edinb. Dec. 24. 1706

Tis Very Long Since I had any Account from you whether mine Come to hand.

Enclosed is the Vote pass't to day about the Salt.[4]

MS.: Duke of Portland, Defoe Papers, 1 ff. 117–18. *Pub.*: *H.M.C. Portland*, iv. 372–3. *Address*: 'To The Right Honble Robert Harley Esqr., Her Majties Principall secreta of State, Present.'

81. *To* ROBERT HARLEY. *26 December 1706*

Sir

I am Unhappy in all This Negotiation That your More Important Affairs Permit you Not Sometimes to Cast an Eye This way and spare me the Consolation of a Line or two.

I Accquainted you in My Last I had a Letter from Our

[1] Pierce. See p. 163, n. 3.

[2] See p. 150, n. 5.

[3] James Foe was about 76 years old at the time of his death. For some notice of his estate see G. A. Aitken, 'Defoe's Wife', *Contemporary Review*, lvii (1890), 233.

[4] The enclosure, written in a hand other than Defoe's, and entitled 'My Ld Registers clause (approven)', runs as follows:

> And with proportionall Drawbacks & allowances as in England with this exception, That Scotland after these seven years shall remain exempted from the duety of two shills & four pence a bushell on home salt Imposed by an act Made in England in the Ninth & tenth of K. Wm the third of England, And if the parlat of Great Brittain shall at or before the expireing of the said seven years substitute any other ffund in place of the said 2 sh & 4 d of excise on the Bushell of home salt, scotland shall after the said seven years beare a proportion of the sd ffund and have an equivalent in the terms of the treaty.

Itinerant[1] which I had Not Then Time to Abstract; I Must Acknowlege he has Succeeded there beyond Expectation, and has Done Such Service there as No Man in scotland but himself Could have done. Nay he has Gone where No Man but himself Durst go at this Time.

He has been at Dumfreis, in the Mountaines of Galloway, in the Dales, and Allmost Every where. He has been with Mr John Hepburn The Cameronian Bishop, spent Three dayes with him, and with his Disciples, heard him preach without Intermission near 7 houres, to a Vast Congregation Severall of which Came 24 Miles on foot to hear him.[2] He has Opened his Eyes in Severall things, and he shows us he has been Missrepresented in Severall Others, and he Authourizes me to assure you there is No Danger from him, Unless some New Artifice Succeed to Inflame them.[3]

Some persons of Quallity here, and Sincere for the Union, haveing the knowlege of his being there, have been with me for This Two or Three Dayes pressing me to write to perswade him to stay there longer, being all Convinc't of the Suitableness of The person, and the Servicableness of the Design, for tis publick here that he is in Galloway, and 'tis the Onely place from whence any Reall Danger is Apprehended.

Indeed Sir Nothing Restraines me in this Case but the Article of Expence, and haveing Said the Needfull on that head I Can Not add, for it is Not for me to Dictate to you.

If I had my Own to Carry me thro' this affair I would not say a word and I fear I am too plain— Tis hard Sir if the Endeavour we Use here (and shall I Say it, the hazard of Our lives, for in both Cases that has been Evident) in Pushing on faithfully and Sincerely a Cause of this Concern should not be supported by the Govornmt—and Nothing has more prescrib'd[4]

---

[1] Pierce.

[2] Eighteen years later, Defoe found another use for Pierce's report: 'Here we [ostensibly Defoe, the Duke of Queensberry, and 'a Darbyshire Gentleman'] were surpriz'd with a Sight, which is not now so frequent in *Scotland* as it has been formerly, I mean one of their Field Meetings, where one Mr. *John Hepburn*, an old Cameronian, preach'd to an Auditory of near 7000 People, all sitting in Rows on the steep Side of a green Hill, and the Preacher in a little Pulpit made under a Tent at the Foot of the Hill; he held his Auditory, with not above an Intermission of half an Hour, almost seven Hours; and many of the poor People had come fifteen or sixteen Miles to hear him, and had all the Way to go home again on Foot' (*Tour thro' Britain*, ii. 730).

[3] By now, Hepburn was working secretly in the interests of the Government (Mackinnon, *Union of England and Scotland*, p. 315).

[4] i.e. restricted or restrained.

me than when you Were pleased to say it Comes from your self.

I Earnestly Entreat your Approbation of what I am doing, and a word or two about supplye, for without it 'tis Impossible for me to Render you the Service I strive for. I am and shall be as spareing as is possible— Earnestly begging a line from you, I Am

Sir, Your Most Obedt Servt

D F

Dec. 26. 1706

MS.: Duke of Portland, Defoe Papers, 1 ff. 120–1. *Pub.*: *H.M.C. Portland*, iv. 373–4. *Address*: 'To The Right Honble Robert Harley Esqr., Her Majties Principal Secreta of State, Present.' *Endorsed*: 'Edenb. Dec: 26: 1706, R̷ Jan: 3: 1706/7, Came a post too late.'

82. *To* ROBERT HARLEY. [*27–28*] *December 1706*

Sir

My Last was the 26th. What the parliamt has done in the salt Tax I Enclosed you and that Clause is since past.[1]

I am Very Sorry to see things Run So heavy here. But I am some times afraid the worst is not past here yet.

The Court[2] here is Very Uneasy and I Doubt not but there is some Cause for it— I have Accquainted you of the Appearances of Mobs and Tumults and I hope they are Over—but it has been Observ'd that Unusuall Concourse of strangers and Highlanders are Resorted to Town in these few weeks. At the Ferrys of Leith and Queens Ferry Unusuall Numbers of Men Armed and horses have been seen to Come Over, and some Circular Letters have been Discovred sent privately about.

This makes honest people here Very Uneasye, and I must Own I am not without just Apprehensions.

Yesterday there was a great Council at the Abbey and to day the parliamt Met—there was no Bussiness done but to forme the Enclosed Proclamation,[3] which pass't not without Great Opposition and a protest with a number of adherers.[4]

Tis Certain there are some Secret Designs on foot; what they are Time and providence alone Can Discover.

[1] See *History of the Union*, pp. 425–30.
[2] The Scottish Ministry.
[3] Missing. The proclamation was directed against 'tumultuary and irregular meetings and convocations'; it is reprinted in *History of the Union*, pp. 658–9.
[4] See *History of the Union*, pp. 435–6.

In this Criticall Juncture J P[1] is Returnd. I Can not attempt to give you the hystory of his Journey in perticular, but tis a Most Unaccountable thing to think how the Jacobite subtillty had Imposed Upon the Ignorant people there and brought them to be Ready to Joyn with allmost any body to Raise a Disturbance. Hepburn the Minister, tho' Mad man Enough, Declares against Tumult and Arms, and J P Sayes there is no fear there. The worst people are about Hamilton and that Side of the Country, and principally because they have the worst Engines About them, and are Dayly Deluded by the party of that family.

Finly[2] tho' a prisoner in the Castle Openly Drinks King James the 8th health—and tis as good a thing as he can do. I have made Mr J P Write word of it into Galloway.[3]

And to let you kno' Sir that I leav no stone Unturnd in this work, I have procur'd Letters from Some Dissenting Ministers in England to Mest Jno Hepburn and to some of his principall Neighbours to quallifye and perswade him not to peace Onely but to perswade his people to the like.

After all Sir I Assure you tis a Very Criticall Juncture and things are Ripening apace. It will be Either a Union or all Confusion in a few weeks more.

Nothing afflicts me so much as not to hear from you or have the least hint what Measures to take. I Resolve not to stir, while I Can with any tollerable Safety be here Either in publick or private—but if any Disturbance happens I shall have an ill post.

My Ld Leven[4] has appeard to day by a Friend plainly to me to Desyre the Return of Mr J P. They are sensible he has done Service there, nor is there a man in Town Dare go there but him—and they are Very Jealous of those people.

Upon these Repeated sollicitations we have Agreed he shall go Imediately— Indeed I Expected they would have Considred that he Could not be Out a month with himself and Two horses, for my servant goes with him, and spend for Ought they know his Own Money— However there was not the least Mention of it— So I have furnish't him for the Journey Out [   ][5]

---

[1] Pierce.   [2] See p. 166.
[3] For the benefit of the bitterly anti-Jacobite Cameronians.
[4] David Melville (1660–1728), third Earl of Leven, was Commander-in-Chief of the Scottish forces. Defoe and Leven were later brought together by Godolphin. See p. 254, n. 2.
[5] MS. torn.

little stock left— I have Said Enough of that affair—and beg your pardon for it. I am Satisfyed you will do what you think Needfull.[1] I Accquiesce and Am

Sir Your Most Obedt Servt
D F

Dec. [28]th[2] 1706

The above was wrott yesterday. The Consternation here Encreases, and I see Every honest man loaded with Concern Even in their Countenances. They say there are above 100 strangers come in to Town to day.

The sherrif Deput of Lanerk,[3] that is Deputy Lieutt, Issued Out Circular letters for assembling. They say he sent 69 Letters.

I have Removd my Lodging for I have been Openly Threatened to be the first Sacrifize—

MS.: Duke of Portland, Defoe Papers, 1 ff. 122–3. *Pub.*: *H.M.C. Portland*, iv. 374–5. *Address*: 'To The Right Honble Robert Harley Esqr., Her Majties Principll Secretary of State, Present.' *Endorsed*: 'Edenburg Dec: 28: 1706, R̸ Jan 2.'

83. *To* JOHN FRANSHAM.[4] *28 December 1706*

Sir,

I have been several times going to give you some account of my being in this part of the world and some abstract of affairs here as what I thought would be both usefull and diverting to you and our friends in your parts.

I have been here three months and in a most difficult time. The Treaty of an Union has been receiv'd here with a different gust from what we in England expected, and indeed from what any rational people might expect.

The Kirk at first seem'd very ready to comply with it, and Mr Roswell and Mr Taylor,[5] two dissenting Ministers from

---

[1] On 4 Jan., two days after this letter reached London, Godolphin wrote Harley: 'I think there is not much to be said upon your Scotch letters more than to ask you what should be given to D F' (*H.M.C. Bath*, i. 152).

[2] Defoe first wrote '27', but changed the '7' into an '8', probably upon adding the postscript.

[3] Probably Andrew Hay of Craignethan.   [4] See p. 64, n. 2.

[5] 'Mr. [Samuel] Roswell, a young Presbyterian minister, is returned from Scotland, whither he went some months since with another Presbyterian minister, Mr. [Christopher] Taylor, who continues there with Mr. [John] Shut, a councillor of Lincoln's Inn. They were in no deputation, but Mr. Shut being a creature of the Lord Wharton, it is not doubted but his and their charges are defrayed by others. The Presbyterian ministers here would not write as a body, but several of them wrote to those of their acquaintance in Scotland in favour of the Union'

London who were here before me did their endeavour to answer all scruples, and indeed I was in hopes they had effectually answer'd the end of their coming.

But we soon found an alteration, and I must acknowledge chiefly from some hot men in the Assembly who when they came to Town set all in a Flame.

The Jacobite Interest had done their best before, and possest the people with their Trade and a multitude of wild chimera's, and one Mr. Hodges[1] wrote a Book full of Invectives against the Union and the English Nation, which being sent from England was industriously spread over the whole Kingdom.

But when these discontents met with proportion'd encouragement from the Ministers a louder cry was added to it that the Church was in danger—tis hard to describe the fury of the people here. The Treaters[2] went in danger of their Lives and Sir Patrick Johnson, late Ld Provost and till then the peoples Darling, was assaulted in his House by the Rabble and had not the Guards reliev'd him before they broke the Door I believe he had been a second De Wit.[3]

I thought myself in no danger having offer'd nothing to any body offensive, but the name of an Englishman had been sufficient and mine much more. However, some Friends here that thought me in more danger than I thought myself secur'd me and I began to think of comeing to England again.

But the Government brought the Forces into the City and took such precautions that this Tumult was appeas'd and something of peace restor'd. I call it something of peace for really it was but a something, for the people on all occasions exprest their Inveteracy and that in a most furious manner when they durst. If the Commissioner at any time staid at the parliament House later than ordinary so as to come down in the dark he was allways insulted with Stones and Dirt and Curses, the Guards hurt with stones from the tops of Houses, and once one of his Gentlemen beaten very cruelly in the Street.[4]

All this while Duke Hamilton was Huzza'd and followed with the Blessings and prayers of the crowd following his coach every day.

(*News-letter* [?], in *H.M.C. Portland*, viii. 253). See also Edmund Calamy, *An Historical Account of My Own Life*, 1830, ii. 44–45.   [1] See p. 141, n. 2.
   [2] The Commissioners who had framed the Treaty were derisively so called, contemporary pronunciation allowing for a pun on 'treater' and 'traitor'.
   [3] Jan De Witt, Dutch statesman, was torn to pieces by a mob in 1672.
   [4] Cf. No. 65.

In this manner they have gone on in parliament just as Nehemiah did with the Wall of Jerusalem with the sword in one hand and the mattock in the other.[1]

The Country follow'd this Example and in Glascow the Rabble have excersiz'd all manner of Insolencies to their Magistrates and to every body else that appear'd for the Union till at last they carried it up to open Rebellion and a Body of men march'd to an appointed Rendezvous, but the Country not being so hasty as they, that Plott has miscarried and a detachment of Dragoons sent against them have taken 5 of their principals who are now safe in the Castle.[2]

Great endeavours have been since used to inflame the presbyterians in the West and a party of them did once in arms march 24 miles to Dumfries and solemnly burn the articles at the Market-Cross there and after that posted a protest against the union up upon the Cross.[3]

Some endeavours have been us'd to open the eies of these deluded people and perhaps I might have told you particulars but I am not writing to set out myself. I shall only tell you I have done all my share and with better success than I expected.

Things are cooler now everywhere, though yet there are some apprehensions in the West, and if our Friends[4] should be so mad as to joyn the Jacobite party the strength here is too weak to oppose them and I wish that they be not drawn in.

During these agitations the parliament and Government go on vigorously enough at least considering the Ferment of the Country, how they are every day bullyed and worried with pamphlets, Addresses, Representations and protests. There is indeed a happy Majority in the House but it is next to miraculous that they are not . . .[5] and hurried into dispair of success and so to give up the cause.

They are now pursuing the articles and examining the particulars. The plot of the party now is if possible to push them upon some amendments in the articles such as they think England will not nor cannot comply with and so break all to pieces in England.

Indeed this project has had but too much success and having had the honour to be allways sent for to the Committee to

[1] Neh. iv. 13–18.
[2] See Nos. 70 to 75.
[3] See p. 146.
[4] The Cameronians. See 'Miscellanea' in the *Review* for 14 Dec. 1706.
[5] 'A word omitted here in the MS' (Norgate's note).

whom these amendments were referr'd I have had the good fortune to break their measures in two particulars vizt the Bounty on Corn and the proportion of the Excise.[1]

Thus far things are now carryed. The proceedings of the Kirk are more calm and regular but the presbyteries in the Country act with no manner of consideration and an address the other day from the presbytery of Hamilton to the parliament narrowly escap'd in parliament being censur'd as seditious and being burnt by the Hangman and I must own it deserv'd it.[2]

I endeavour in the Review as I suppose you will see to put the best Face on the proceedings of the Kirk and to distinguish between their actions as a Body and the actions of their Members in order to prevent the ill use will be made of these things among our high Flyers in England.[3] Thus according to my poor Talent I endeavour to reconcile you to these people and by all possible means keep up the character of their management tho' I must own tis a very difficult task.

I cannot enlarge. I dare not prophecy the Event but tis pity the two Nations should be divided any longer. This people are a Sober, Religious and Gallant Nation, the country good, the Soil in most places capable of vast improvements and nothing wanting but English Stocks, English Art and English Trade to make us all one great people.

The Court are just now in apprehensions of more Tumults, great concourse of people being observed to come arm'd to the Town.

> I am Sir your Friend & Servt
> D. FOE.

Edinburgh Dec. 28, 1706.

MS.: untraced. *Pub.*: Francis Norgate, 'Correspondence between De Foe and John Fransham, of Norwich', *Notes and Queries*, 5 S, iii (1875), 283–4. *Address*: none recorded.

84. *To* ROBERT HARLEY. *2 January 1706/7*

Sir

I Wrott you at Large last post. The feares we were then in Vanish apace. I have Incognito gotten into the Company of Some of the people who Came here on the Design I mentioned. They Own the Design was to have Gone in a body to the

---

[1] See Nos. 61, 62, 67, and 69.
[2] The Address appears in *History of the Union*, pp. 627–8.
[3] See p. 151, n. 3, and in addition the *Reviews* for 3, 5, and 17 Dec. 1706.

Commissioner and Then to the parliamt and Demanded Answers to their petitions— They do not Deny that if the people had taken that Occasion to have Risen, they would not have been displeased, nor I suppose backward to Encourage them all they Could. But I do not find they were Very forward to Venture their Own heads in the Fray;—and this Baulks all their Designs, for I Observ they are like the Pharisees in the Gospell, that bound heavy Burthens on Other Mens shoulders but would not Touch them &c.[1]

Some of them I Understand are gone away again, and Indeed the Dearness of this place, where people Now pay from 2*s* to 5*s* a night for Nasty Lodgings, Will Soon Make them Weary of their attendance, And their private Discourse is of addressing the Queen. I was Glad when I heard that, but Can not Imagin what they can ask of her Majtie or what they can have the face to say for their Cause.

The Union Mean time proceeds Apace and this day[2] they past the 16, 17, and 18th Articles, about Coin, weights and Measures.

I wrott you at large about the Kirk. I hope, tho' you do not think Fitt to Replye to me, you will take that Case in thought. They are now on an act to be proposed to the house, to put a Test upon all English men Enjoying places in scotland, Equivalent to that in England.[3]

If nothing better Can be found Out for me I Could Wish you will please to Settle me here after the Union. Perhaps I might do her Majtie a Service of One Sort while I was in an office of a Different Face, but of that hereafter.

I am, Sir, Your Most Obedt Servt
D F

Jan. 2. 1706[4]

MS.: Duke of Portland, Defoe Papers, I ff. 124–5. *Pub.*: *H.M.C. Portland*, iv. 376–7. *Address*: 'To The Right Honble Robert Harley Esqr., Her Majties Principall Secreta of State, Present.'

---

[1] Leaders of the attempt were Atholl and Fletcher. See Mackinnon, *Union of England and Scotland*, pp. 318–19. Defoe alludes to Luke, xi. 46.

[2] See n. 4 below.

[3] The Act of Security did not absolve Scotsmen from taking the Sacramental Test as a prerequisite to their holding public office in England. It was therefore proposed that Englishmen should be required to meet a Kirk Test before holding public posts in Scotland. The Scottish Parliament rejected the proposal. See *History of the Union*, pp. 341–2, and 447.

[4] The letter is so dated, but Articles 16, 17, and 18, mentioned as having been passed 'this day', were actually passed on 31 Dec. Defoe is not likely to have been

85. *To* ROBERT HARLEY. *4 January 1706/7*

Sir

I wrott you last post, That the Apprehension We were Under here began to Vanish. The Day began to shine after all The Nights of Cloud and Darkness We have had here.

The Crowd of Strangers lessens Amain. They had, as I am Informd by Some of Their Own friends, Three private Meetings and One Generall Meeting to Consult what to do.

D. Hamilton proposed to his people to wait on the Comisr and beg him to give Them Time to address the Queen, but the Difficulty was how to get to him. No Single Man would do it, and to go in a body as they Designed, they knew they would not be Admitted.

I am Told that in One of Their Meetings Some Force was proposed but they found themselves too weak for the attempt.

At their Generall Meeting it was offred to Draw up a Petition or address to the Queen; To Offer the Succession and an Expedient for the Union, or at least for a Delay, but the D of Athol told them his Men would not Come into the succession, so that Vanisht— Then a protest was proposed In which was to be Express't their Detestation of the Union in Terms Bitter Enough, their being Imposed Upon in the parliamt, the Guards and power of the Court and the Bribes of English Money haveing frighted or Debaucht the Parliamt from their Duty, That they are betraid, bought and Sold, and are to be Enslav'd to the English.[1]

I am promised a Sight of the Drafft proposed; if I Can get it, I shall not fail to Transmitt it per Next.

In This Little scheme of their Affaires I have Acted a *True spy* to you, for by an Unexpected success I have Obtaind a Converse with Some Gentlemen belonging to the D of Gordon[2] who are Very Frank, and I Dare say the perticulars Above are Unknown to the Commissioner himself. Their Assembly broke Up without any Conclusion.

I Can Not help giveing you the Satisfaction of Letting you

careless in reporting this kind of fact; he probably did write the letter on the day the Articles were passed, 31 Dec. But he sometimes missed the post, and if he did so in this instance, he may have dated the letter just before belatedly posting it. Bell received it in Newcastle on 4 Jan. (*H.M.C. Portland*, iv. 377), and Defoe himself refers to it on 4 Jan. as having been sent 'last post'. The posts ran three times a week.

[1] See *Lockhart Papers*, i. 201–5.
[2] George Gordon (1643–1716), first Duke of Gordon, was a Jacobite.

kno' Sir that I believ the bussiness as good as Over here, and if I may yet beg a line from you Sir it should be for your Orders when to Leave this place or how to Govern my Self.

I Confess Sir I have had an Uneasy Post here Undr so Many frequent Feares of Murther, Tumult, Rabble, &c, but I Resolv Not to be Uneasy in Any of your Commands.

My Chief Uneasyness [has been the want][1] of Now and Then a line from you, without which I am in So Many Doubts whether my letters Reach your hand, whether my Measures here please you and the like, that Indeed Sir It is Very Discourageing at this Distance.

I shall Very Impatiently wait your Directions About My stay here or Comeing Away. If you please to Ordr me away, my former Sollicitation for a supply Ends with a small Ordr for Travailing Charge—and I Say This to Convince you Sir that I have Never Sollicited for any thing but the Absolutely Necessary Dissburses, and am Very forward to put a stop to them.

I Think you will Expect me to attend your Ordrs for staying or Goeing, and I shall do So, as a Duty to the Service, but when I See my Self Uncapable of More Service I shall think Very Much of the Charge.

The 19th Article[2] was past yesterday with Some Amendmts Relateing to their Own Courts &c which England will not be Much Concern'd in. To day They Sitt on private bussiness, and I believ about 14 dayes more will End the session and I May give you Joy of the Union.

I am, Sir, Your Most Obedt Servt
D F

Edinb. Jana. 4. 1706

MS.: Duke of Portland, Defoe Papers, 1 ff. 126–7. *Pub.*: *H.M.C. Portland*, iv. 378–9. *Address*: 'To The Right Honble Robert Harley Esqr., Her Majties Principall Secreta of State, Present.' *Endorsed*: 'Edenburg, R̲ Jan: 10.'

86. *To* ROBERT HARLEY. *6 January 1706/7*

Sir

I have little to say to Day but to Confirm what my Last hinted, That all the feares of the Matter is Now Over on this Side and The Angus men &c. are Most of them Dropt away as Silently as they Came.[3]

---

[1] MS. torn; words in brackets are supplied.
[2] Concerning Scottish Courts of Justice. See *History of the Union*, pp. 450–2.
[3] See No. 84.

I wrott you Earnestly Sir last post for your Ordrs About my Goeing Or staying when the Union is Over here, and I Repeat my Request on that head, but am to Accquaint you They press me here to stay a few weeks after, to Quiet peoples minds about it.

I am to leave that Wholly to you Sir, by whose breath I Would Direct all my Measures on this head, and therefore Again most Earnestly Entreat your thoughts on that subject.

I am, Your Most Obedt Servt
D F

Edinb. Jana. 6. 1706.

They have begun to day on the 22d Article.

MS.: Duke of Portland, Defoe Papers, 1 ff. 128–9. *Pub.*: *H.M.C. Portland,* iv. 379. *Address*: 'To The Right Honble Robert Harley Esqr., Her Majties Principal Secreta of State, Present.'

87. *To* Robert Harley. *9 January 1706/7*

Sir

I hope I may Now give you Joy of the Union, The 22d Article[1] haveing past last Tuesday night by a Majority of 40 Voices.

Yesterday The house Sat But did No bussiness but Quarrell— The Duke of Athol had made a formall protest Against the Vote of the Day before. So had Severall Others as you will I presume See by The Minutes.

The D of Argile Said it[2] was Indecent, Illegall and Iregular, the Duke of Athol Defended it and Reflected On the D of Argile, and words Rise at last to a loss of all Decency on both sides giveing and Returning the Lye in the Open Assembly— The house took it Up and Made them both Give Their Words to stand by the Decision of the E of Marschall, E of Leven, Genll, and Ld Errol, Constable, or to be Committed, So I hope tis at an End.

There is Some Expectation of Another ill Naturd paper from the Church About an Oath to be Imposed Upon Englishmen here,[3] and haveing the honor to wait on the Comissionr last Night I find his grace is Something Apprehensiv of it; I have

[1] Which limited the number of Scottish representatives in the Parliament of Great Britain; it was passed on 7 Jan. (*History of the Union*, pp. 460–3).
[2] That is, the protest, not the Act.
[3] See p. 188, n. 3.

Since been with Some of the Ministers and am Not Out of hopes of getting it stop't.

Yesterday was a Day of Disaster and scotland has Lost One of the best Men in the Nation, I mean as to Publick Matters, My Ld Stair. He was in the house and Made an Extraordinary speech on the Debate on the 22d Article, and was found Dead in his bed in the Morning. He was Alive at 4 a Clock and spoke to his Lady, Went to sleep Again and Wak't No More in This state— He is Generally Lamented, and had he Dyed a little Sooner Would ha' been Very Much Wanted in the house, where he was One of the Most Usefull Members in the Grand affair.[1]

I am, Your Most Obedt Servt
D F

Jana 9. 1707, for So they Write
here from New year Day.[2]

MS.: Duke of Portland, Defoe Papers, 1 ff. 130–1. *Pub.*: *H.M.C. Portland*, iv. 380. *Address*: 'To The Right Honble Robert Harley Esqr., Her Majties Principal Secreta of State, Present.'

88. *To* ROBERT HARLEY. *11 January 1706/7*

Sir

I Wrott you Last post the Account of the broil in the Parliamt on the protests, and of the suddan Death of the E of stair.

The house have Since been Taken up Upon the proposall I hinted of an Oath &c, which is Thrown Out.

It was Hatch't in a private Cabal of parsons and proposed to the Commission, but the Ministers Were prevaild on to Refuse it and I hope I may say without Vanity I have been Usefull in that part.

The rejecting it there stab'd it to the heart, and tho' it was Offred in parliamt it the sooner sunk there.[3]

The Ministers presst hard for an Explanation of the Clause in the Abjuration Oath binding the successor to be in the Comunion of the C of E—and Indeed it seems to me So Rationall that I Can not but think they Ought to have it. Not that Ever a presbyterian king is likely to Come, but it would be hard to make the Ministers abjure a prince for being of their Own

---

[1] John Dalrymple (1648–1707), first Earl of Stair, best known today for the part he played in the massacre of Glencoe, had been a Commissioner of the Union.
[2] In Scotland the new year was reckoned from 1 Jan.
[3] See p. 188, n. 3.

perswasion; and England, that Dispenses with the Quakers Takeing it atall and Accepts their Affirmation for an Oath, will Never Scruple this—and if not done half the ministers in scotland, and some Sincere friends to the Union and who have been Very servicable in it, will be Turn'd Out of their places, which will make here Intollerable Confusions.[1]

One line Sir from you to the Commissionr here would soften all this, and I perswade my Self you will be sencible of the Necessity.

The Council are Sitting to Day on that Article of the Kirks Representation Respecting the Encourageing papists, the Number of popish priests &c.[2]

I am, Sir, Your Most Obedt Servt
D F

Edinb. Jan. 11. 1707

MS.: Duke of Portland, Defoe Papers, 1 ff. 132–3. *Pub.*: *H.M.C. Portland*, iv. 380. *Address*: 'To The Right Honble Robert Harley Esqr., Her Majties Principall Secreta of State, Present.'

89. *To* ROBERT HARLEY. *16 January 1706/7*

Sir

I am Now with Joy to Accquaint you That the Treaty of Union Recd the Touch of the scepter this day and an Universall Joy of the Friends of both Nations Runs thro' the Citty.

The Church has made some struggles, but they are faint and Opposed by the most worthy, Learned and to be Vallued of their Number, who Deserv Regard, and Mr Carstares[3] in perticular Merits Great Consideration on that account.

[1] This change in the Abjuration Oath had been requested by the Commission of Assembly in its six-point petition of the previous November, but Parliament had refused to incorporate the provision into the Act of Security for the Church. Later, an effort was made in the united Parliament to alter the oath, but the Houses could not agree and the attempt failed (Mathieson, *Scotland and the Union*, pp. 183–4 and 203–4).

[2] Probably the 'humble representation and petition' of 14 Nov. 1706, published in the *Review* for 5 Dec.

[3] William Carstares (1649–1715), Principal of Edinburgh University and the most influential ecclesiastic in Scotland, had furthered the Union by counselling its political managers and by softening the opposition of the Scottish clergy (Mackinnon, *Union of England and Scotland*, pp. 297–8). For a letter from Carstares to Defoe, see No. 200.

It is not my bussiness to Recomend persons. I Wait now your Instructions whether to stay or Come away, and am

Sir, Your Most Obedt Servt

D F

Edinb. Jan. 16. 1707

MS.: Duke of Portland, Defoe Papers, 1 ff. 134–5. *Pub.*: *H.M.C. Portland*, iv. 382–3. *Address*: 'To The Right Honble Robert Harley Esqr., Principall Secreta of State, Present.' *Endorsed*: 'Mr De Foe.'

90. *To* ROBERT HARLEY. *17 January 1706/7*

Sir

Since the papers I lately sent you I have printed here Two Essayes.[1] One I Enclose you here; The Other shall be sent The Next post.

The Bussiness Seems Now to be Over, But the Dissatisfactions of the kirk begin to Reviv On the Two following Occasions, which I Think tis Very Needfull to Accquaint you with.

The kirk, Especially the Ministers, Mov'd for an Explanation of the Abjuration Oath, the Thing I formerly hinted—[2] but no Notice was taken of it, Nor of the following.

Just at the breaking Up of the Parliamt, They Supplicated again Against the Clause which leaves the C of England to make any Act they shall see fitt for their Own Settlemt, and that it shall Implicitly be past without being Reconsidred here.[3]

Tis True, as they alleage, the Church may bring in some things Inconsistent with or Invasiv of the Church here, or the Dissenters in England, and 'tis past of Course, and Thus they make the people Very Uneasy about here.

Tis True also that if the C of E should make an act the Most Reasonable in the world and it should be brought hither to be

[1] The one was probably *A Fifth Essay at Removing National Prejudices; with a Reply to Some Authors Who Have Printed Their Objections against an Union with England*; the other probably *Two Great Questions Considered, Being a Sixth Essay at Removing National Prejudices against the Union*. Both were published in January (Lee, *Life*, i. xxxiii).

[2] See No. 88.

[3] According to the Act of Security for the Church of Scotland, 'the Parliament of England may provide for the security of the Church of England as they think expedient, to take place within the bounds of the said kingdom of England' (*History of the Union*, p. 543). The Scottish Parliament thereby ratified in advance whatever the English Parliament might insert into the Treaty for the security of the Church of England. The Commission of Assembly protested that to allow such blank powers to the English Parliament might be to jeopardize the security of the Kirk. The protest had no effect. See Mathieson, *Scotland and the Union*, pp. 185–6.

Confirm'd, the wholl Nation would Crye Out Murther, and the Clergy Roar Out prelacy and the Covenant.

You will pardon my freedom Sir of Expression; they are a Restless, Uneasy people, but Tender Usage and Cool Counsels may Mannage Them, and you are too Much Master of Such Measures to Need that I add any Thing on that head.

I Enclose you also a peice like *a post Hume* birth brought to light just after the work was Over.[1]

What posess't the Man is hard to guess, Since he has Ever Since I have been here, and before, profess't himself for the Union, and often in my hearing Declared the Church Could Not be Safe without it.

But this is an Instance of the Change in Temper I Mention'd above. The Man is a worthy Good Man, popular in Character, a great preacher, and, which you will think strange by his poetry, a Man of witt, a good judge, and of a Clear head: In short Sir he is in himself the Very Reverse of the pamphletts— What Dark Interval has posest him at such a juncture is Every mans surprize to know.

But tis most Surprizeing to see with what Greedyness the Town Runs with him.

I shall Take him to task in the best manner I Can but tis a Tender point, and as I have studiously preservd an Esteem with all his friends, and which I have found Very much to the purpose in what I have been Doeing here, So I must use him wondrous Gently and shall Onely take him to task for his falling on the English Dissenters, which Indeed Everybody blames him for.

I shall by next post Transmitt you the Coppy of what I Say on him and anything Elce that Occurs, Mean Time Referring to my last.

I am, Sir, Your Most Obedt Servt
D F

Edinb. Jana. 17. 1707

P S There was a hard pull in the Commission of the Assembly on the 14. and 15. to obtain a Remonstrance to the parliamt

---

[1] Missing, but doubtless it was James Webster's *Lawful Prejudices against an Incorporating Union with England; or, Some Modest Considerations on the Sinfulness of This Union, and the Danger Following from It to the Church of Scotland.* For the progress of Defoe's controversy with Webster, see Nos. 91, 93, and 99; and Wilson, *Life,* ii. 491–6. Webster was minister of the Tolbooth Church in Edinburgh (*Fasti Ecclesiæ Scoticanæ,* i. 123–4).

against the things above noted, but it was Carryed in the Negativ.

MS.: Duke of Portland, Defoe Papers, 1 ff. 136–7. *Pub.*: *H.M.C. Portland*, iv. 383. *Address*: 'To The Right Honble Robert Harley Esqr., Her Majties Principal Secreta of State, Present.' *Endorsed*: 'Mr. De Foe.'

91. *To* ROBERT HARLEY. *27 January 1706/7*

Sir

I Can Not but Return my humble Acknowlegements for the Honr of your Letter of the 21th.[1] It is my Singular Joy That the Constant Accounts I have Sent have been to your Satisfaction. Indeed I have been Very Sad On the Account of my haveing had No Line for Now Eight Weeks, and fear'd my Self forgotten.

I Confess there seems Sir Equall Occasion of Some body here Now as before and Indeed if a person were Constantly here, provided he had No publick Mission, it would be Very Usefull.

The Implacable parsons are Unsufferably Insolent and Now They flye in the Face of Every body, Friend and Foe, and The Coals are blow'd on all Occasions by the Others. I sent you the last letter The Attempt of One Webster, a minister, against the Dissenters, I here Send my Answer to him.[2] They are Now laying their heads to Defame the Dissenters to Rendr them Suspected to the people.

It is in Vain to go about to Excuse these people; they are proud, passionate, Ignorant and Jealous. I have hitherto kept my Self Unsuspected, have whisprd and Caused it to be spread that I am fled hither for Debt and Can not Return, And this perticularly that they may not suspect me. Under this Reproach, tho' I get some Scandal, yet I Effectually secure my Self against Suspicion.

Now I give Out I am goeing to write the hystory of the Union in folio, and have got warrants to Search the Registers and parliamt books and have begun a Subscription for it. I Tell them it will Cost me a years Time to write it.[3]

Then I Treat with the Commission to Make them a New Ver-

[1] Missing.

[2] Missing; but it was *The Dissenters in England Vindicated from Some Reflections in a Late Pamphlet Called Lawful Prejudices, or, the Sinfulness of the Union.*

[3] Defoe announced his intention of writing the *History* in the *Review* for 24 Dec. 1706, declared that the work was in progress in the issue for 21 Jan. 1706–7, and advertised for subscribers in that of 29 Mar. 1707. The work took longer than he expected and did not appear until 1709.

sion of the Psalms, and that Ile lock my Self up in the College 2 year for the performance—by these things Sir I Effectually Amuse them and I am perfectly unsuspected.

Then I am Setting Weavers to work to make linen, and I talk of Manufactures and Employing the poor,[1] and if that Thrives I am to Settle here and bring my Family Down and the like, by which Triffles I Serv the Great End Viz/ a Concealmt.

I Would be Glad Sir you would please to Consider the Case I Wrott about the Abjuration Oath, which is Very hard Upon them.[2]

I Humbly Thank you Sir for Representing Favourably my poor Endeavours for the Service here. If her Majtie was Informd of the Circumstances of my Family, from whom I have been So long absent, & whom I Effectually stript just before by my surrendr;[3] I perswade my Self it would Move her Royall Goodness to some Compassion. I Need but Represent it to you Sir. I leav the Rest to your Self, but must Own to you I am Distress't in my Mind on their Account. I ask your Pardon for Runing Out on that here.

The present affair Sir is about Settling the Representation here,[4] which they have in part agreed as you will see by the Minutes— Tis Now strongly Contended to keep Out the Eldest sons of Noble men from the house,[5] and the house are now Sitting upon it. The Barrons struggle hard for it, and the Nobillity to get them in.

I am to Thank you Sir for your hint of a Supply. Indeed I have been Expensiv, but I Dare Say the Money I have laid Out is Expended to the Very Directest End you Desire it.

But I am Now attended with a New Disaster. Mr B . . . ,[6] who is my Onely Resource, is Gone to London & I suppose will kiss your hand Ere this Reaches you. He is a Capable, faithfull and Judicious Gentleman. I suppose Sir if you Direct him he may

---

[1] 'I have told them of Linen Manufactures, and I have now above 100 poor Families at Work by my Procuring and Direction, for the making such Sorts of Linen, and in such Manner as never was made here before, and as no Person in the Trade will believe, could be made here, till they see it' (*Review*, 29 Mar. 1707). See also Sutherland, *Defoe*, pp. 164–5.

[2] See No. 88.

[3] He refers to his bankruptcy of the previous summer. See Nos. 50 and 51.

[4] That is, the manner of selecting the 45 Members of the Commons and the 16 peers who were to represent Scotland in the united Parliament.

[5] It was feared that the powerful Scottish nobility, limited to 16 seats in the House of Lords, might compensate by getting their sons elected to the Commons, and hence perhaps control the Scottish representation in the new Parliament. See *History of the Union*, p. 496. [6] John Bell.

supply as well in London as here, and hope he will wait on your Ordrs for that affair.

I am, Sir, Your Most Obedt Servt

D F

Edinb. Jan. 27. 1707

They have Carryed it in the house for the admitting the sons of the Nobillity—but it was by Dexterous Mannagement. They had a Majority of 14 onely & the people Rail at it abominably, but that wi[ll be] Over—[1]

MS.: Duke of Portland, Defoe Papers, I ff. 138–9. *Pub.*: *H.M.C. Portland*, iv. 385–6. *Address*: 'To The Right Honble Robert Harley Esqr., Principall Secreta of State, Present.'

92. *To* ROBERT HARLEY. *2 February 1706/7*

Sir

I Omitted writeing the last post perfectly for Want of Subject—being at present Entirely Taken up in Meer Cavil and Continuall Dispute with the Clamorous Clergy.

If I have done any Service Since I Came hither I Think it is Now, for These Men are Really the Boutefeus[2] of the Nation, and If they Talk against the Union Every body will do so also.

However, I have Pick't Out Some who are for it; a Very Very few I have brought Over; and I have So Sett these against the Other That like Sathans kingdome Divided against it self the Furious Temper Can not Stand.

These Reconcild parsons begin to Call the Other Mad Men, and they Call these Apostates, and the people Divide just as their Leaders, but Peace will prevail and I hope gets ground.

I hope the affair shall Not Come Down again for Amendments. If it does, the Latter part will be worse than the beginning and I shall be Sincerely affraid of it, Severall of the Best men being gone or Goeing, Some into the Country, some to England. Nothing Ought therefore to be More Avoided than its Comeing back hither for Amendmts. I Thought it Meet to hint this Sir, because I See the party Seem to promise themselves something of hopes in Difficultyes to be Raised in England that shall Occasion Its being brot hither again Clog'd with Something proper to be Dislik't here.

There is Also One Criticall Day here yet, which I Apprehend will Put Them into Some Confusion, but as tis Wisely Deferr'd

[1] See *History of the Union*, p. 494.   [2] i.e. *boutefeux* (firebrands).

to the last, So if the Treaty does Not Come Down again, the breach it will Make Can Not be fatall—and This is when They Come to Name the persons for the first Representativ.

The Partys here, the Temper of the persons, the Circumstances and the forms Rendr it Impossible to Avoid a brush when this Comes on the Stage. But if This should be first Entered on and Amendments from England Come after—Pardon my freedome Sir, It will Endanger breaking the wholl affair.

On these and Severall Other Accounts I Thought it my Duty to give This hint Tho' I question Not but your own Judgement will agree—That it is Very Necessary To keep it if possible from a Returne hither, And Indeed So Necessary that the Summe of the Affair will Seem to Depend Upon it—

If This Can be Avoided Sir, the heat of the Ministers will Abate, and One kind thing Done for Them, *I Mean that of the Oath*, which I hinted before[1] and (which you were pleased to Tell me in your Last you would Consider of) all would be Easy and a Little Mannagemt would Reconcile Them all, or at least take off the Edge of their Discontent.

Indeed Sir Would her Majtie afford the Charge or Grant me a Very Moderate Request, I kno' No way in the World I Could Serv her Intrest More in Than Makeing Onely a Trip to London, and then Come Down and spend a year at least Among a people Unaccquainted with Peace, Moderation or Temper—but of That hereafter. I ask your Pardon for This freedome, and Am

Sir, Your Most Obedt Servt
D F

Sir

Since the Above I am Surpriz'd with the Accounts we have here of your Sudden Illness—[2] God almighty in Mercy to These yet Unsettled Nations preserv a life So Necessary to Their Imediate felicity— Indeed Sir, I have often Thot to use the Liberty you are pleasd to grant me On that head.

Tho' the Vigour of your Mind quallifyes you for Uncommon Burthens, yet Sir We have *all these Treasures in Earthen Vessells*. Tis a New Turn to the Text but I presume it will hold— The body Sir is Not Made for wonders. And when I hint That Denying your Self Needfull and Regular houres of Rest will Disorder the best Constitution in the world, I speak Sir my Own Imedi-

---

[1] See pp. 173 and 192.   [2] Cf. Edward to Abigail Harley, *H.M.C. Portland*, iv. 384.

ate Experience, who haveing Dispised sleep, houres, and Rules, have broke in Upon a perfectly Establish't health, which No Distresses, Disasters, Jails or Mellancholly Could Ever hurt before— I Beseech you Sir, Pitty your Country in the spareing your Self For a work So Few but you are able to go thorow.

Idem ut supra

Edinb. Feb. 2. 1707

MS.: Duke of Portland, Defoe Papers, 1 ff. 140–1. *Pub.*: *H.M.C. Portland*, iv. 387–8. *Address*: 'To The Right Honble Robert Harley Esqr., Her Majties Principall Secreta of State, Present.' *Endorsed*: 'Edenburg Feb: 2: 1706, R̸ Feb: 10:'

93. *To* ROBERT HARLEY. [*13 February 1706/7*][1]

Sir

If I have Omitted my Constant advices to you it has been Undr the Very Uneasy Reports spread here both of your first illness and After of a Relapse, and Severall flying Reports have Allarm'd me with the Account of your being Dead.

I Will Not Trouble you with my Concern on that Score. The loss to the wholl Island is what I hope God in his Mercy to them will Not Afflict Them with in Many yeares.

My Close Concealing my Accquaintance with, Much less Employment from you Sir Rendred it Impossible to kno' any Thing from Other than Common Intelligence, But haveing a Letter from Mr Bell[2] this day that he had the honor to wait on you the 8th and No Mention of your Indisposition Revives my hopes of your health and Renews my Very pleasant Labour of thus Conversing with you.

I Wrott you a Large Letter last week,[3] but Cautious of the Case of your health, Sent it to Mr Bell, who I hope will do me the honour to put it Safe into your Own hands.

The Town Rings here with a Report that the Test act is Repeal'd as far as Concerns the Dissenters, but the Various manner of its being Told here makes me Doubtfull;[4] I should

---

[1] This undated letter was assigned to 23 Feb. by the editor of *H.M.C. Portland*, iv, but that date cannot be correct. Defoe here writes that members of the united Parliament were being chosen 'This Very Day'. That election was held on 13 Feb. (*History of the Union*, pp. 507–8; and *H.M.C. Mar and Kellie*, pp. 373–7). This correction also clears up the meaning of 'the Other letter' mentioned in the opening of No. 94.
[2] Missing.   [3] Missing.
[4] 'This day [11 Feb.] a committee of lords examined several masters of coffee houses and news writers, for inserting in their letters that the house of peers had repealed the sacramental test act; and some of them will be prosecuted for the same' (Luttrell, *Brief Relation*, vi. 137).

Improve[1] it to the Uttmost Advantage here Against Presbyterian Jealousies, if I had the Certainty of Fact; however, as it is I begin to make Some of them blush at their suspicions of English Sincerity.

We are Surpriz'd here with an Account that the Wholl Treaty has Passt [the][2] Committee of the house of Commons. It is So Good News that I Can Not but suspend my Expectations till a Confirmation Arrives of So Valluable a thing.[3]

I Troubled you with an Invectiv by Mr Webster here against the English Dissenters.[4] I have had another Railing bitter pamphlet on the same head from him,[5] but So taken up with ill language, scurillous personall Railery, and little Sence that I Can not think it worth giveing you the Trouble of it.

Raillery and ill Manners have just the Same Effect here as in Other places Vizt to Sink the Character and Reputation of the Author.

The parliamt have now before them the severall Requests of the Commission for plantation of kirks and Valuation of Teinds, as they Call them here, Or Tiths as with us.

This Very Day they are Upon Nameing the Members for the first parliamt, the Quarrellsome work I hinted in my Last. The Peers as Expected are as folls, but I do not yet hear they are Determined in the house.

D of Queensberry	E of sutherland
Ld Chancellor[6]	E of Roxburgh
2 secretarys of state[7]	E Rothess[9]
Marquis of Tweedale	E of Glasgow
Marq: of Montrose, Lord Presidt of the Council	E of Stair
	Viscount Duplin[10]
Marq of Louthain[8]	Ld Ross[11]
	the Others not Named

The people are strangely Irritated here and there is a spirit of Bitterness and Slander gone Out among them.

[1] i.e. turn it to good account.
[2] MS. torn.
[3] The Treaty passed the Committee of the whole House on 8 Feb. (*J.H.C.* xv. 282).
[4] *Lawful Prejudices against an Incorporating Union.* See p. 195, n. 1.
[5] *The Author of the Lawful Prejudices against an Incorporating Union Defended. In Answer to a Pamphlet Intitled 'The Dissenters in England Vindicated'.* See Wilson, *Life*, ii. 493.
[6] The Earl of Seafield.   [7] The Earl of Mar and the Earl of Loudon.
[8] i.e. Lothian.   [9] Not elected.
[10] Not elected.   [11] Not elected.

The Mob are a Machine; the Jacobites have wound them up to a Pitch and Nothing but Time, Mannagemt, Temper and success Can Reduce them to the proper Medium. They must be let Run Down Gradually or they precipitate at Once into all Manner of Confusion.

I have had severall Letters and some hints, I guess, from the Other Newly alter'd part of an office Near you Sir, which I long to give you the hystory of if you please to Command it.[1] I presume you will Suffer nothing of that to be to my prejudice, and permit me the freedome of takeing your honour for the Concealmt from all Eyes or Eares but your Own.

I am Not to be pumpt or Sounded, and yet would be Glad to have a hint from you Where I should be wary and where not. Perhaps here may be no Need of Caution. I believ you are all in the True Intrest and if I may be Open I would be Glad to kno'.

I have little Sir in this world to boast of but my fidelity, and as that is to you before all the World, so I Entreat a hint from you whether I may be free in Case of Such Suggestions as—We hope he[2] is Not Dropt—Tis hard if the persons who *say they Employ him* do not stand by him. Pray let me kno' if you are in anything Uneasy, and the like:

These *if Right* are kind things, and to one Circumstanced like me should be Improvd, but *if wrong* Sir I thank God Can have No Influence on me, who as before have neither hands to act, Mouth to speak, nor purse to Reciev favours but as you Direct.

I humbly Entreat your hints for my Conduct and as frequent Orders as your affaires will permitt.

[Your Most][3] Humble & Obedient Servt
D F

MS.: Duke of Portland, Defoe Papers, 1 ff. 146–7. *Pub.*: *H.M.C. Portland*, iv. 389–90. *Address*: 'To The Right Honble Robert Harley Esqr., Her Majties Principall Secreta of State, Present.' *Endorsed*: 'Edenburg Feb: 13: 1706/7, R̸ Feb: 19:'

[1] Alterations in office were numerous at this time; the Whigs were moving into the ascendancy. The wording here suggests that Defoe refers to the office of the other Secretary of State, to which the Whig Earl of Sunderland had been appointed in December, replacing the Tory Sir Charles Hedges. Although Defoe's intentional obscurity still hides the identity of his correspondent, it may have been Sunderland himself. Another member of the Junto, Halifax, had written to Defoe a short time before (pp. 147 and 167), and Sunderland was certainly in touch with Defoe in the following year (Nos. 129 and 130). If Sunderland was the correspondent here referred to, Defoe's diffidence in mentioning the matter can be attributed to his awareness that Harley and Sunderland heartily disliked one another.   [2] i.e. Defoe.   [3] MS. torn.

94. *To* ROBERT HARLEY. *13 February 1706/7*

Sir

I had Closed the Other letter[1] before the Parliamt was Over—
and gave you an Account of Names but by Guess from the
Common Opinion.

Since that, the Wholl is finish't and Very happily without any
Broil, and the True list of the Names is On the Other Side,[2] To
which I Referr, and am

Sir, Your Most Obedt Servt

D F

Ed. feb. 13. 1707

MS.: Duke of Portland, Defoe Papers, 1 ff. 142–3. *Pub.*: *H.M.C. Portland*,
iv. 388. *Address*: 'To The Right Honble Robert Harley Esqr., Her Majties
Principall Secreta of State, Present.' *Endorsed*: 'Edenburg Feb: 13: 1706,
R̸ Feb: 19:'

95. *To* SIDNEY GODOLPHIN, EARL OF GODOLPHIN.[3]
22 February 1706/7

May it Please your Lordship

I Most Humbly Crave your Ldships Pardon for Presuming
to write to your Ldship at This Distance, But hearing of the Very
Unhappy Illness of Mr Secretary Harley, and The Subject of my
writeing Concerning More Perticular your Ldships Part in the
Governmt, I Mean the Revenue, I Thought it My Duty to Lay
The following Case before your Lordship.

Your Ldship knows well That in This place There is an Open
Trade with France.[4] And as This Trade is Very Considerable,
So on the Prospect of a Union I perciev There are Severall
wheels at work to Lay schemes of Private Trade From Hence

---

[1] The preceding one.
[2] Defoe wrote this note on the back of the list of representatives, which is in
another hand. For the names, see *History of the Union*, pp. 507–8.
[3] Sidney Godolphin (1645–1712), recently created first Earl of Godolphin, was
Lord Treasurer and head of the Ministry. In 1703 he had agreed with Harley that
Defoe might be made useful to the Government and had obtained his release from
Newgate. Since that time he had been continually aware of Defoe's activities, for
Harley forwarded to him many of Defoe's reports, a practice that probably accounts for the absence of many of them from Harley's own papers. Defoe dedicated
his anonymous *High Church Legion* (1705) to Godolphin, and celebrated him in
many other writings. After Harley's fall from office in 1708, Defoe transferred his
services to Godolphin and acted as his agent until 1710, when Godolphin left
office and Harley returned. For Defoe's other surviving letters to Godolphin, see
Nos. 128 and 131.
[4] Which in England was prohibited on account of the war.

for England; Some of which I May get Insight Enough into to Accquaint your Ldship both of Time, place and person, if your Ldship Commands me to Search Farther into it.

But the Main Perticular I give your Ldship This Trouble Upon is this. Here Are Great Commissions from London allready for the Buying up Wines and Brandys On the Supposition That They shall be Freely Convey'd to England after the Union, and That England will Not So far Disoblige Scotland at first as to Obstruct it—[1] Tis true An Obstruction of That kind would do Some harm here at first, as it will be Improved—But if They are Assured of a Liberty, as I find the Merchants of London Encourage Them in it,[2] your Ldship Will Find the Inconvenience Very Great and the Quantity before the first of May Incredible: Here Was Three ships Entred last week and all the Wines are bought up, and I am Informed There Are Eight More at the *Orcades* Waiting to Come in—and This place is Unusually and Prodigiously Full of English Money at This Time.

I Need Not Trouble your Ldship with any Notes of the Consequence of This, and how Easily 20 or 30 Thousand pounds Duty shall be avoided by The Merchants in This Case, the best Wines being Now Sold here for 11*l* per Hogshd, Brandys at about 13*l*, and So of Other Things.

Nor shall I presume to Offer my Thoughts of Expedients in This Case Without your Ldships Imediate Command, Onely Presume to Lay it before your Lordship as what I Thought for her Majties Service, for which I Humbly Ask your Ldships Pardon.

> I am, May it Please your Ldship
> Your Ldships Most Humble & Obedient Servt
> De Foe

Edinb. Feb. 22° 1707

P S If your Ldships Commands Directs me to Note the

---

[1] Since the Union was not to become effective until 1 May, Scotland's import duties, which were lower than England's, were not yet superseded. And after 1 May commodities could cross the border from Scotland to England without paying any duty. Merchants in Scotland, whether Scotsmen or Englishmen, were quick to see here the opportunity for profit. They began importing large quantities of commodities, at low duties, against the day when they could ship them into England, duty free, and hence undersell the importers in England. See Mackinnon, *Union of England and Scotland*, pp. 356–8.

[2] Only those London merchants who were able to participate in the scheme encouraged the subterfuge; it was far from being countenanced by the great number who stood to suffer from the unfair competition.

Quantities of Wines bought and by whom in London, I suppose it may Not be Difficult, & perhaps where Lodg'd.

MS.: Duke of Portland, Defoe Papers, 1 ff. 144–5. *Pub.*: *H.M.C. Portland*, iv. 388–9. *Address*: 'To The Right Honble The Ld High Treasurer of England, Humbly Present.'

96. *To* ROBERT HARLEY. *4 March 1706/7*

Sir

My Last[1] Represented my Feares of The Returning The Treaty hither On Account of The Oxford Clause.[2]

Tis Very Mysterious to us why That Affair was not Included in the Act of Security For the Church, and I fear it was kept in Petto as an Ambuscade against the Bill.

I Will not Despair of Any Thing but it is a New Danger here and some good Friends to the Affair Seem Under great Apprehensions.

Indeed here are Disgusts and Dissatisfactions among The great Ones which give Room to Apprehend an ill Effect of any Thing to be brought before them Again.

Some Are Disgusted, as I Wrott before, That They are Not in The Brittish List, Others at Want of Places. But I Can Not but Observ, *Tho' by The by,* The Equivalent is the Main Disgust. Many had swallowd Large Morsells of it in Expectation, and I Daresay Little Enough of it should go as Designd, if it were in the Mannagemt of Some people.[3]

As it is, Every body Saies The Nobillity will . . .[4] it, and That the Onely hope is, they will Fall Out about shareing it, which is likely Enough.

The persons who They say are Uneasy begin to Complain Loudly, and if the Temper and Moderation of the Commis-

---

[1] Missing.

[2] On 22 Feb. William Bromley, M.P. for Oxford University, had moved that there be added to the Union Treaty a clause providing that Oxford and Cambridge were to 'continue for ever as they now are by Law established'. But any addition to the Treaty, except for the Act of Security for the Church of England (which Scotland had ratified in advance), would require that the Treaty again be placed before the Scottish Estates, a risk that the Unionists were anxious to avoid. Bromley's motion was defeated (*J.H.C.* xv. 307).

[3] The Equivalent had been reckoned at almost £400,000, of which a considerable proportion was to go to individuals: stockholders in the ill-fated Darien Company, creditors of the Scottish Government, the Commissioners who had conducted the Treaty negotiations of the previous year, those who had sat in the inconclusive Commission of 1702, persons who should suffer losses as a result of the Union, and the like. See Hume Brown, *Union of England and Scotland*, Oxford, 1914, pp. 134–5.   [4] Thus in MS.

sioner,[1] who indeed is the Soul of This wholl Affair, does Not help it, I Doubt least They may Come to Calling One another some Names, which the by standrs may be apt to say are True on both Sides.

Tho' I write my Apprehensions of Things, yet Sir I shall Not be Discouragd From my small Endeavours, and wait your farther Instructions.

I am, Sir, Your Most Obedient Servt

D F

Edinb. March. 4 1707

MS.: Duke of Portland, Defoe Papers, 1 ff. 148–9. *Pub.*: *H.M.C. Portland*, iv. 391. *Address*: 'To The Right Honble Robert Harley Esqr., Principall Secretary of State, Present.'

97. *To* ROBERT HARLEY. *10 March 1706/7*

Sir

I have Now I hope the Satisfaction of Seeing the fruit of all This Mischief, the Effect of all The Labouring, Fighting, Mobbings, &c. Viz: Union, and while I write This the Guns are Fireing from the Castle and My Man brings me Up the Queens speech.[2]

Methinks *Nunc Dimitis* Comes Now in My head and in writing to you Sir I should Say, Now let me Depart from hence for My Eyes have Seen the Conclusion.

I Confess Sir I believ I might be Servicable here a long Time yet. But Sir Every body is Gone Up to Sollicit their Own Fortunes, and Some to be Rewarded for what I have Done— while I, Depending on your Concern for me and her Majties Goodness, am wholly Unsollicitous in that Affair.

I Wrott Earnestly to you and to my Ld Treasurer about the Import of Wine and Brandy.[3] 3 ships More Came in yesterday and 10 more are at hand, and 200 Tun of Brandy is Sent for from Holland.

If it shall pass into England why shall your honor Not Permit me to buy you a Ton of Rich Claret here which I May do as Cheap as you buy a hhd[4] and Ile Take my hazard that it shall be Extraordinary on My Own Risq.

J P[5] is This Day Gone for England. He has been at first Usefull

---

[1] The Duke of Queensberry.

[2] The Act of Union received the Royal Assent on 6 Mar. (*J.H.C.* xv. 326–7).

[3] See No. 95 for Defoe's report to Godolphin; no previous letter to Harley on the subject survives.

[4] Hogshead.　　　　　　　　　　　　　　[5] Pierce. See p. 163, n. 3.

to me, but Since, Some who were fond of haveing an Agent here Employ'd him Out of my way, of which More hereafter.[1] I have Not Recomended him to you.

I am Now On the Old Doctrine of Peace, and her Majties speech[2] is My happy Text, and I please my Self in Telling your honor it Gains Ground— I have been Invited to Glasgow, where I Must have been Torn to peices if I had Gone before, but I Think to Venture a Round Thither and to St Andrews and spend Every Minute to the best Issue I Can, That the Charge I have put you to Sir May Not be ill laid Out. And Now I am Impatient for your Ordrs which way to Steer my Course, which I Entreat I may have the honor of as Soon as possible.

Your Most Obedt Servt
D F

March. 10. 1707

MS.: Duke of Portland, Defoe Papers, 1 ff. 150–1. *Pub.*: *H.M.C. Portland*, iv. 392. *Address*: 'To The Right Honble Robert Harley Esqr., Principall Secreta of State, Present.'

98. *To* JOHN BELL. *18 March 1706/7*

Sir

Your Ordring me to write no More to you at London left me at Some loss for a post or Two & I wrott to Mrs Bell to Direct as formerly by Sir Tho: T.[3]

I am Glad your stay in London is Somewhat longer and perticularly for the Conveyance of the Enclosed.[4]

When you Wait on Mr Secr. Again, Giving My Humble Duty to him, be pleased to Move him in The following Cases.

I have been Extremly Desirous to Choose Out One Ton of Rare Claret here for his Own Table, and As we are all assured that it will Come Free into England, & all the World are buying it up, the Goodness and the Cheapness makes me Earnest to have his Commission, Considering I may buy him a Ton as Cheap as his honor Inform'd me he gave for One hhd in London, and This Trade being my Old bussiness,[5] I perswade my Self my palat Can Not be Decieved in What will please him.

[1] But no further particulars of Pierce's defection have come to light.

[2] See *J.H.C.* xv. 326–7.

[3] Perhaps Sir Thomas Trevor, Chief Justice of the Common Pleas and a Commissioner of the Treaty of Union, who stood within Harley's circle.

[4] The following letter.

[5] 'I have sold many a Tun of as good *French Claret* as is in the World' (*Review*, 3 Apr. 1711). See also Sutherland, *Defoe*, pp. 28–29.

My Other Request is that he would be pleased to let me have a short Quartering of his Arms in Ordr to make him a small present of this Countrys Manufacture.[1] Perhaps it may be to the Honor of Scotland and to his Own Very Good likeing.

In this Sir you will perticularly Oblige me and I shall at large Informe you of Perticulars as to the Manufacture when I see you.

As to my Comeing up, I have neither Feet to Travail Nor Tongue to say when but as I Reciev Orders from him whom you have the honor to Converse with, and if you will make it your perticular Request to Obtain me the favour of a letter, I shall place it to the Account of the Many Favors Recd of you by

Sir, Your Most Humble Servt
D F

Edinb. Mar. 18. 1707

There Comes a packett with this, which is said to be Enclosed but it was too Large.

MS.: Duke of Portland, Defoe Papers, 1 ff. 152–3. *Pub.*: *H.M.C. Portland*, iv .394. *Address*: 'To John Bell Esqr., at Wm Carr's Esqr. Chambr, in Lincolns Inn, London.'

99. *To* ROBERT HARLEY. *18 March 1706/7*

Sir

I have Not wrot So Constantly as Usuall, haveing Nothing Materiall to Communicate but private bills in parliamt, Horse Races at Leith, Fire in the City, and Such things, which are not worth Disturbing your Thoughts with.

To Tell you my Ld Hoptons Horse won the plate, that a fire burnt Three or four houses and 5 people, that the parliamt have been busy about a quarrell between the Doctors and Surgeons (*Knaves all*) to Determine which shall have the Greatest privilege to kill people and be paid for it, These things will be so far from Informing you Sir that they will Not So Much as Divert you.

Indeed should I Tell you the story of Ecclesiastic Frenzy in these parts, and Draw a scheme of North Country Bigotry, I Could make you Merry in spight of your Most Serious Concern for the public peace.

I Find there is Bigotry without popery, and Gods priests Ride Upon Gods people as well as the Inferior Clergye of less Pure Churches. Certainly Sir the Clergy here have More to Account for here than in Other places, where the Customary slavery of

[1] Cf. pp. 167–8.

Other Nations is Inverted but is Every jot as Fatall as there. The priests lead aside Silly women, these Silly women more Silly men. The women are the Instructors, And the Men are Meer Machins wound Up just as the spring goes at home.

Thus as the Velocity of Motion Doubles and Encreases as tis Remote from its Center, So if the priest be Chagrine at the Union, the good Wife Rails at it and the Husband Grows Mad— This Sir has put a Notion into my head which if Ever I were to write a book should take up a good part of it. I have heard of the Circulation of the blood, and Great Discoveries have been made of late on that head. I think it would be Very Instructing to write an Essay Upon the Circulation of the brain, In which Case more wonders would be found Out in this Clear air here than Could be hoped for Even in a journey to the Moon.[1]

Youl pardon me Sir this Excursion. Indeed the Morall of it all is Instructing. The Ministry here strangely Influence the people, and the Conflict between Mr Webster[2] and I here has Discovred more of it than I Could have Imagind was possible.

His attempt has had Two Very Fatall Designs in it, tho' I thank God I Can without Vanity Say I have Defeated him in both.

1. To Argue the Sinfullness of the Union as a breach of the Nationall Covenant and Inflame the people on that Account.

2. To represent the Dissenters as No friends of the Kirk and Not fit to be Depended Upon, & So break the Generall Friendship of the Nations.

Thus One design was to Inflame, the Other to Divide.

To his first[3] I printed a short peice[4] to prove the Nationall Covenant was so far from being broken that it was not atall Concern'd in the Treaty.

He Cryed fire at this, Said I had Blasphem'd the Covenant, that Every body Ought to shun my Company, that if I Came into his Church while he was preaching or praying he would stop and proceed no farther till I was Removed.

---

[1] In 1705 Defoe had written four pieces concerning the world in the Moon: (1) *The Consolidator; or, Memoirs of Sundry Transactions from the World in the Moon. Translated from the Lunar Language*, (2) *A Journey to the World in the Moon*, (3) *A Letter from the Man in the Moon, to the Author of the True Born English-man*, and (4) *A Second and More Strange Journey to the World in the Moon*.

[2] James Webster, minister at the Tolbooth Church in Edinburgh. See p. 195, n. 1.

[3] Probably *The Covenants Displayed*, Edinburgh, 1707 (*Fasti Ecclesiæ Scoticanæ*, i. 124).

[4] *Two Great Questions Considered: I, What Is the Obligation of Parliaments to the Addresses or Petitions of the People, and What the Duty of Addressers? II, Whether the Obligation of the Covenant, or Other National Engagements, Is Concerned in the Treaty of Union? Being a Sixth Essay at Removing National Prejudices against the Union.*

But when he saw the best Ministers in the City my Constant friends and Visitants it put him Distracted, and he Goes about Railing at my Moralls, Calls me Drunkard, Swearer, blasphemer and I kno' not what, for which he has the pleasure of seeing himself laught at.

To his second peice[1] I published Three Tracts. 1. A sheet Called the Dissenters Vindicated &c,[2] which I sent your honor Long Since. To this he Replyed with little but Ill Language which made his Own friends Blush for him.

I had printed a Replye to him Bitter Enough, But when I Considred my bussiness here was Peace, Reconciliation and Temper, I thought it was better to use him Gently, and as to his railing it did me no harm, that wise men Would see the beauty of Moderation, and bearing Reproach was better than Returning it, Especially haveing my Eye to the work before me. So I suppresst the book[3] and wrott another, which I Call *a short View of the state of the Protestant Religion in Brittain as it is professt by the Episcopall Church in England, the Presbyterian Church in Scotland, and the Dissenters in both.*[4]

Here Omitting to Mention the Man, I have as Clearly as I Can, stated the Case and the Differences Among us all, how farr We Ought to Agree, & how behave where we Can not.

This has gotten me a Compleat Victory and the Moderate Men of the Clergy Come Every Day to thank me for it. I have sent it you Sir Enclosed by this post tho' 'tis Rather too Bulky for a Letter, & I Recommend it to your Reading, and its Author to your Concern when at this Distance too likely to be forgotten.

As I Told your honor in my last[5] my Design, if you Approve it, to stay till I see the Issue of the Genll Assembly,[6] So I Entreat your Orders about it. I Must Own tis too Much in the power of the Ministers here to Ruin the Peace of this Nation, and this Makes me think the Meeting of the Generall assembly here a Thing of more Consequence than Otherwise it would be at This

---

[1] *Lawful Prejudices against an Incorporating Union, or, Some Modest Considerations on the Sinfulness of the Union.*

[2] *The Dissenters in England Vindicated from Some Reflections in a Late Pamphlet Called Lawful Prejudices, or, the Sinfulness of the Union.* Defoe had sent Harley a copy on 27 Jan. (p. 196 n. 2).

[3] It was to have been entitled *Passion and Prejudice the Support of One Another, and Both Destructive to the Happiness of the Nation* (Wilson, *Life*, ii. 494).

[4] Defoe omits a word of the title, which actually begins, *A Short View of the Present State. . . .* The pamphlet appeared in March (Dottin, *Defoe*, p. 813) and was reprinted in London under the rather confusing title (see n. 2 above), *The Dissenters Vindicated; or, a Short View of the Present State of the Protestant Religion in Britain. . . .*

[5] Missing.   [6] Which was to convene on 8 Apr.

Time, & I Repeat my humble Motion that their session May be as short as May be.

I am in Nothing more Unhappy in this affair than that your Extraordinary Affairs permitt you to favor me but Very Seldome with your Directions, and Methinks I look too much a Voluntier in the Service. However Sir, I Resolve to Omitt Nothing I Can do, and I Doubt you find I spare no Charge to Carry On the work I am Upon in the best Manner I Can, and to push the Great work of Reconciling the minds of this People to One Another and to the Union.

To This purpose I have in the Review, which I humbly beg you will please to Cast your Eye on, begun a long Series of Discourses on the Reciprocall Duties of the Two Nations One to Another after the Union.[1]

In my Mannagemt here I am a perfect Emissary. I act the Old part of Cardinall Richlieu. I have my spyes and my Pensioners In Every place, and I Confess tis the Easyest thing in the World to hire people here to betray their friends.

I have spies in the Commission, in the parliament, and in the assembly, and Undr pretence of writeing my hystory[2] I have Every Thing told me.

I am in Dayly Conferences with the Ministers, who are Members of the Assembly, and hope they will Come More Moderately Enclin'd than was Expected.

They now Solicit me to write to my friends in England Among the Dissenters to Assure them that they are not Concernd in the scandal Raisd on them by Webster, which I shall do— In all things I labour to Reduce them to Temper and Union of affection both with England and with One Another, and Indeed I think my work is harder and More perplexing Now than it was at first. In all which I study to approve my Self to your Judgement, that haveing put you to a Very Great Expence, that Expence is faithfully Applyed and not Intrusted with an Unprofitable Servant.

I am, Sir, Your Most Obedt Servt
D F

Edinb. Mar. 18. 1707

I Entreat your Directions about a Ton of Wine.[3]

MS.: Duke of Portland, Defoe Papers, 1 ff. 154–7. *Pub.*: *H.M.C. Portland*,

[1] The series begins with the issue for 1 Apr.
[2] Cf. p. 196. Subscriptions for *History of the Union* were opened in the *Review* for 29 Mar. 1707. [3] See No. 97.

iv. 394–6. *Address*: 'To The Right Honble Robert Harley Esqr., Her Majties Principall Secreta of State, Present.' *Endorsed*: 'Edenburg Mar: 18: 1706/7, R̸ Mar: 25 1707.'

100. *To* ROBERT HARLEY. *25 March 1707*

Sir

I have Now Seen the Finishing of This happy Work. The Union has been Confirmd as they Call it here, That is, pro-claim'd at the Cross, and This Day the Parliament is at An End and all is Over.

I have wrott your honor my Thoughts of staying to see The Assembly Meet, and act my part Among them, then to make a Tour to Glasgow, Aberdeen, and St Andrews to preach Peace & Good Manners to the preachers of Truth[1] and Sedition, for Such some of them are.

When I signifye my Design tis allways subjected to your Opinion & in hopes of your Direction, in want of which I am Obliged to Satisfye my Self with a Negative allowance and take your Not forbidding me for an Order.

I Entreat you Sir to favour me with your Approbation of my Measures, or your Ordrs, and Withall to Signifye to me what Course I shall steer next.

           I am, Sir, Your Most Obedt Servt
                               D FOE

Edinb. March 25. 1707

I hear the Bill for Secureing the Right of printed Coppyes is stopt.[2] I beg of you Sir in your Respect to Encouragemt of Letters and Dilligence in Learning to give it your help.

At the Closeing the Parliamt the Commissr Made a short speech which I presume you will have a Coppy of.[3]

And I Can Not but Observ that a Motion was Made to Recomend Mr Paterson to her Majtie,[4] and if my Labour had Not been allways to Conceal my Self I might have had the same honour—but I have No body to Recommend me Sir but your

---

[1] Thus in the MS.

[2] In 1706 the booksellers had petitioned for an Act of Parliament to give them adequate remedies against piratical publishers. The claims of the booksellers to perpetual copyright had been countenanced by the old Licensing Act, but that Act had expired in 1695, and the Trade was now without any real security. This petition of 1706, like a similar one of 1703, brought no success; but a third overture, in 1709, resulted in the famous copyright statute of Queen Anne. See Defoe's *Essay on the Regulation of the Press*, ed. J. R. Moore, Oxford: Luttrell Society, 1948.

[3] See *History of the Union*, p. 526.   [4] See *History of the Union*, p. 525.

Self, to whom I leav it. I am Sure he has the Credit of a good stock in the Face and is Applauded for some things I Actually did in the Committee.[1] I beg Sir I may not however be forgotten.

MS.: Duke of Portland, Defoe Papers, 1 ff. 158–9. *Pub.*: *H.M.C. Portland*, iv. 396–7. *Address*: 'To The Right Honble Robert Harley Esqr., Her Majties Principall Secreta of State, Present.' *Endorsed*: 'Edenburg Mar: 25: 1707, R̷ Mar: 31:'

101. *To* ROBERT HARLEY. *3 April 1707*
Sir

Mr Bell being Come from London has I Doubt Stopt the Delivery of My last.[2] I have at present Nothing Materiall to Write. We are prepareing for the Genll Assembly, and tho' I hope well, yet I am Now Busyer than Ever, but it is a Nice point to Act, and the Parsons here are Unaccountable people, Humorous, Jealous, Partiall, Censorious, Haughty, Insolent, and Above all Monstrously Ignorant.

I shall Omitt Nothing I Can to Influence those of them that Are *Come-at-able*, and hope for a Good Issue and a short Sitting.

The Great Men are posting to London for places and Honours, Every Man full of his Own Merit, and affraid of Every One Near him. I Never Saw So Much Trick, sham, pride, Jealousy, and Cutting of Friends Throats as there is Among the Noble men. I presume Sir you will soon see the Effects of it at London. I Wish some of Our Friends had Not so much hand in it.

Last Night I Waited on the Comissionr[3] to Wish him a good Journey and Take my Leav. He Recd Me Very Obligeingly. He is pleased to Say More of my small Services here than I have a face to repeat, and has promised to Recommend me to the Queen and to My Ld Treasurer. If his Grace be Sincere Sir, I Can not Miss to Meet with Some help when tis Joyn'd with your prevaling Assistance.

I shall no more Afflict you with Sollicitations for your Ordrs. I proceed by my Own Undirected judgemt, Giveing you a Constant Account, and Am forced to take your Long Silence for a Tacit professing your Satisfaction.[4] If I Flatter my Self in a Mistake I am Doubly Unhappy.

[1] 'I know some, that are gone to *London* to sollicit the Reward of what they have had no hand in. I might have said, are gone to claim the Merit, of what I have been the single Author of' (*Review*, 29 Mar. 1707).
[2] Missing. It was returned from London to Newcastle and thence to London again (Bell to Harley, *H.M.C. Portland*, iv. 402).
[3] The Duke of Queensberry.
[4] Harley had last written on 21 Jan. (p. 196).

I am spending your Money a Little Freer than Ordinary On the Occasion of the Assembly, but tis from my Sence of the Danger if it Miscarryes, and I have some Engines at work Among the Ministers. In short, Money Will do anything here.

Some Angry Men are Chosen, but the Rancor of the Temper is Abated Exceedingly and I hope shall More Abate, to which Nothing shall be wanting in

Your Most Obedt Servt
D F

Edinb. Aprill 3. 1707

After the Assembly I Entreat your Ordrs what to do.

P S The Commissr Sets Out for London this Day.

MS.: Duke of Portland, Defoe Papers, 1 ff. 160–1. *Pub.*: *H.M.C. Portland*, iv. 398. *Address*: 'To The Right Honble Robert Harley Esqr., Principal Secreta of State, Present.' *Endorsed*: 'Edenburg Apr: 3: 1707, Ŗ Apr: 9:'

102. *To* ROBERT HARLEY. *12 April 1707*

Sir

I have the Satisfaction of writeing you that the Assembly goes on here with all Manner of Calmness and quietness, Contrary to the hopes of Some and I must Own Contrary to my Apprehensions. I have Not failed In plying them hard with Arguments and perswasions in Print,[1] in Discourse, and by Other Instruments which I have Employ'd. I will not presume to say I have been anything in the success, but I have done my Duty.

The Hottest of the Clergy are Extreamly Coold by this surprizeing Alteration, and some of them Are Very much Asham'd of their Former behavior. I Converse not much with them that Are for it, For they Need Not the Physitian, but I single Out the Opposers, and am Dayly and allmost Hourly in their little Clubs and Caballs. They begin to Sollicit me Now not to Represent them to their Dissadvantage In England, And Value Themselves Upon their Negativ behavior, What they did Not do to Excuse themselves from the blame of what they Did.

And Now Sir I Entreat your Directions how to steer my Course.

I have been Long here without a word or hint how to Govern my Self, But Now it Seems Absolutely Necessary to have some

[1] Perhaps *A Voice from the South; or, an Address from Some Protestant Dissenters in England to the Kirk of Scotland,* published in Edinburgh, and reprinted in the *Reviews* for 10 and 15 May 1707.

Orders and I Humbly Recommend it to you Sir to Determine for me what Course I shall Take.

I did propose a small Circle here Among the Clergy to Cultivate the Good Temper that Appeares among Them and then to Leav this Country. But I have No Satisfaction in Undertakeing any Thing without your Ordrs. I Entreat One line Sir for my Governmt whether to go, or stay here, or Come for Engld, for without your Directions I am a Meer Image without life, soul or Action.

I am, Your Most Obedt Servt
D F

Edinb. Aprll 12. 1707

MS.: Duke of Portland, Defoe Papers, 1 ff. 162–3. *Pub.*: *H.M.C. Portland*, iv. 400–1. *Address*: 'To The Right Honble Robert Harley Esqr., Principall Secretary of State, Present.'

103. *To* ROBERT HARLEY. *22 April 1707*

Sir

I presume you will Now have Notice That the assembly is Up, and all Things grow better That way Every Day. The Address will Come away to Night and The E of Glasgow In the Morning.[1]

I am much at a Loss how to Mannage My Self About the Affair of Trade here.[2] What the Cort in England Seemd to Desire Was, as I Thot, to allow Some Latitude, and Now by her Majties speech it looks quite Another way—[3] But as to the thing it self I Crave leav to Note

If no Exception be Made for the scots It will make ill blood here, and they Talk loudly here that the Union is Broke before it is begun.

If an Exception be made, the End will be Defeated and all Manner of Doors are Open'd to Perjury by Transferring of Property and Innumerable frauds.

And after all, the Quantity brought in is but small Compar'd to what is Talked off— I Could Do some Service in this if I knew what the Measures are— The wholl Fleet is but 42 sail at most.[4]

---

[1] See Glasgow to Mar, *H.M.C. Mar and Kellie*, p. 388. Glasgow had been Commissioner of the Assembly.

[2] London merchants had petitioned the House of Commons to prohibit the importation into England of the tons of commodities that scheming dealers had brought into Scotland with a view to landing them duty-free in England after 1 May. See p. 204, n. 1.

[3] See *J.H.C.* xv. 385.   [4] See the *Review* for 1 May 1707.

The foundation laid here for Clandestine Trade is beyond all this fatall to both the Revenue and to Trade, and As I am let into Some of it, I am the More Moved, Nor Do I see any possibility of Wholly preventing it without an Army of Officers.

I am too farr to offer schemes for this here. I have said Enough to sollicit you to Think of me, and shall Not press you On that head Onely thus far. His Grace the D of Queensberry Gave me his word and his hand to Recommend me to Her Majtie, and I perswade my Self will second any Motion you Will please to Make for me.[1]

I Am Inform'd, I kno' Not How true, that My Ld S. . . .[2] is No Friend to me On an Occasion which Concerns your Self; the perticulars I Referr till I have the Honor to see you.[3]

> I am, Sir, Your Most Humble and Obedt Servt
> D F

Edinb. Aprll 22. 1707

MS.: Duke of Portland, Defoe Papers, 1 ff. 164–5. *Pub.*: *H.M.C. Portland*, iv. 402–3. *Address*: 'To The Right Honble Robert Harley Esqr., Principall Secretary of State, Present.'

104. *To* ROBERT HARLEY. *24 April 1707*

Sir

I Can Not write to you Now without Concern and I fear heartily The Unravelling all we have been Doeing.

The New Votes of the house of Commons makes the most Unaccountable Fermentation here That if the Next News does not Cool it, I shall Need No New Orders from England about staying Or Returning, for Really Sir here will be No staying here for me nor hardly any English man.[4]

---

[1] See p. 224, n. 1.

[2] Perhaps Sunderland, the other Secretary of State.

[3] The particulars remain unknown.

[4] On 7 Apr. the Commons had passed a Bill for the purpose of preventing 'the mischiefs of a fraudulent practice, in obtaining drawbacks for goods carried from England to Scotland, in order to be brought back again, and in carrying goods from foreign parts into Scotland, in order to be [be] brought into England, without paying the English duties' (*History of the Union*, p. 570). See p. 204, n. 1. The Lords had rejected this Bill on the grounds that it violated the Union Treaty. But such was the outcry of London merchants, who demanded protection against the threatened flood of duty-free imports, that the Queen prorogued Parliament for three days, so that the ferment might be reduced and the measure introduced again. On 19 Apr. the Commons passed a similar Bill, upon which the Lords had not yet taken action (they later rejected it). Harley had supported both Bills and had contributed a clause making their provisions retroactive (Earl Stanhope, *History of England Comprising the Reign of Queen Anne*, 1870, pp. 286–7). Defoe's account of the Parliamentary proceedings appears in the *Review* for 20 May 1707.

The Importation of all their Goods to England free of Dutyes is they say Expressly Capitulated in the Article of free Communication, and the English Ought to have known the Consequence of the Intervall as well as they— The Vote of the House they say is Directly Against the Union, and they talk of Meeting and Declareing the Union Broke—

I Dare not write to you the Murmurs of the people, and My worst Missfortune is that I Can make no Answer to it, and tho' I thought my Reputation Establish't here yet I must Confess this shocks it. They Come Crowding about me Reproaching me Every hour with What I have said of the Honour and justice of the English Parliament.

Ay Ay, Sayes One of them, Now you see how we are to be served! And what we Are to Expect from a Brittish Parliament! How Early they begin with us, and what Usage we are to have when Ever Our Advantage Clashes with their Intrest.

I am Exceedingly Harrass't and Fateagu'd with them and I know Not what to Answer because I Do not know what the Measures Are.

I Tell them (tho' I kno' nothing of it yet) that there will be an Exception for scots men,[1] and have printed the Clause of the last Act with Some Remarks,[2] shown the Necessity of the preventing the Abuses About Tobacco and the Drawbacks,[3] and I Endeavour to Buoy them up with hopes. But Tis a strange Hurry[4] they Are in, and if something is Not Done to Cool and Satisfye them I acknowlege I Apprehend the Consequences.

Here's One Gentleman that shows a letter from London as he sayes by a parliamt Man—which saies that Even those scots who shall be Excepted shall be Obliged to Come to London to prove the property of their Goods, and the Difficultyes at the Custome house will be Chargeable and Vexatious so that the Exception to the scots Will signifye little.

I Entreat you Sir to Consider these things & give me a hint

---

[1] Neither of the Bills passed in the Commons was intended to affect the legitimate trade of genuine Scottish merchants. Both were aimed chiefly at the machinations of foreign speculators. The second Bill appears to have contained a clause specifically exempting Scottish traders, but that news did not reach Scotland until later. See the *Review* for 31 May 1707.

[2] The publication has not been identified.

[3] English importers had sent thousands of hogsheads of tobacco across the border into Scotland, and, having thereby drawn back most of the duty they had originally paid on it, now planned to reimport it duty free. This practice would have been prohibited under the two Bills previously mentioned. See the *Reviews* for 22 May and 14 June 1707.   [4] i.e. agitation.

What I must say to Defend the Case and make the people Easy.

I am, Your Most Obedt Servt

D F

Aprill 24. 1707

This Early Ferment is Very Unseasonable.

MS.: Duke of Portland, Defoe Papers, 1 ff. 166–7. *Pub.*: *H.M.C. Portland*, iv. 403. *Address*: 'To The Right Honble Robert Harley Esqr., Principall Secreta of State, Prest.'

105. *To* ROBERT HARLEY. *25 April 1707*

Sir

I Write to you Now Upon a Very Odd and Unhappy Occasion. I shall Say little to the Fact, but Referr to the Enclosed.[1] But My Appollogyes are to you Sir for gieving you the Trouble of it.

By the Manner of the Letter you will See I have Obtain'd Upon the Clergy here Every whitt as Much as I have Represented to you, for This was a great Opposer of the Union. I would have gladly Rac'd[2] Out his Compliments Upon me as what No way become me to be the Messenger of but I Could not send you the Letter Blotted.

You See Sir what a Charge I have laid Upon me, which I knew not how to Dispense with, and as I am Directed to Send it to you and the Arichbiship, I Enclose a short Letter to his Grace that you may at your Pleasure Deliver it your Self or Send it to his Grace without Accquainting him that It Came thro' your hands.

The Case is Indeed Horrid and Becomes her Majties Justice, But the Secret History of it is This. 1/ The Murtherer[3] is Grandson to the E of Melvill and a Near Relation to the E of Leven,

---

[1] Missing.   [2] i.e. erased.

[3] Robert Balfour (d. 1757), later fifth Baron Balfour of Burleigh, had murdered an Inverkeithing schoolteacher named Henry Stenhouse (Luttrell, *Brief Relation*, vi. 367). Balfour had courted a young woman of his father's household, who had refused him on account of the difference in their stations. When the affair came to light, the two were separated for a while; but Balfour swore that if the girl married during this separation, he would kill the person she married. 'After some Time', wrote Defoe of the affair, 'the *Young Master* (so they call the eldest Son of a Lord, while his Father is living) *of* Burleigh, returns from his Travels, and enquiring for the young Woman, and being told she was marry'd, and to whom, retaining his hellish Resolution he rides away to the Town, and up to the School Door, and calling for the Schoolmaster, the innocent Man came out to him unarm'd in a Gown and Slippers; when, after asking if he was such a one, and flying out in some hard Words upon him, he drew his Pistol, and shot the poor Man dead upon the Spot,

and Tis Very Much feared My Ld Leven should Intercede for him. 2/ Her Majties Exemplar Justice will be Very Gratefull to the Country here, who have an Exceeding Resentment of the Fact; and to the Burgh of Innerkeithin is preparing an Address to her Majtie for a proclamation and Reward for Aprehending him. 3/ He has behav'd himself So Notoriously Impudently Since the Murther as gives a Generall Abhorrence of him, and to Pardon him will form a Sad Prejudice Among the people here.

I shall not Presume to give my Opinion here, but have laid it before you as the Minister has been pleased to Command me.

As to Other Matters I Refer to My Last, and waiting your Commands

I am, Sir, Your Most Obedt Servt

D F

Aprll 26. 1707

I am Sorry to Tell you Sir that My Friends Write me word I shall stay here till I am Forgott.

If you Think Fitt to Deliver the Enclosed you will be pleased to Cause Coppie the Letter and Seal the Outer One.

MS.: Duke of Portland, Defoe Papers, 1 ff. 168–9. *Pub.*: *H.M.C. Portland*, iv. 404. *Address*: 'To The Right Honble Robert Harley Esqr., Principall Secretary of State, Present.'

106. To ROBERT HARLEY. *15 May 1707*

Glasgow May 15. 1707

Sir

I hope your Charity will Determine for me that Something Extraordinary has Restraind my writeing Thus Long—I found by a Suddain stop of my Letters that some were Opened, some Intercepted, and three letters [Current][1] to my Wife Came not to hand Till a long Time after the Course.

This Sir, and This Onely, Interrupted my Conversing with you in the Usuall Manner, which was my pleasure as well as my Duty, Till I saw The Course of Letters Clear and Found the stop of Letters was onely Delay, tho' I knew not nor yet know where.

I stayed in Edinburgh Till the Assembly broke up, and after that the Commission, and after that the synod of Louthain, in all which I have perhaps been more Jealous than Needed, but riding away in the open Day, and no body daring to meddle with him. . . . This Tragedy, and its Circumstances, I think, merits to be recorded, and the rather, because most of the Circumstances came within the Verge of my Knowledge, and I was upon the Spot when it was done' (*Tour thro' Britain*, ii. 773).

[1] MS. has 'Currr^t'.

I allwayes thought the Cautious part the safest in these Cases, tho' it were too Much; Since Over Caution may Do harm but Too little Can do no Good.

After I Saw all Clear of the priests, I thought to ha' Travaild a Little as I hinted to you formerly, but I am posted here to Bully a Clamarous people, and as I Mention'd I think in my last, if the Parliamt had not Dropt the Drawback bill[1] I must ha' fled this Country and Come away without your Commission, which I should ha' been Very loth to ha' Done.

It is scarce possible to Describe to you the Disgust that affair gave here and what Use was made of it—and as I am posted here On the Frontiers, I Could not Breath *hardly* for the Importunate Queries of the Friends to the Union What would become of them, and what the Parliamt would do with them, and the like.

I Won't perplex you with these Country Impertinences On that head. I Write this Onely to satisfye you how I have been Employed here for some Time.

Now the Main affair is Over, Now they are frighted afresh with the Accounts they say Come from London that Notwithstanding this, the Custome house Officers will stop their Goods.[2]

Sir I have not had the Honor of a line from you a long while. I Humbly Entreat a hint or Two in this affair what to say and what to Do, for I am at a Great loss how to Answer, and Indeed in the Generall how to behave my Self. Nor Do I yet kno' whether my Negotiating pleases you or Not, being to Act wholly my Own judgement in Every Case.

I am Now to Offer Another thing. I am at the City of Glasgow and Unless I Reciev your Contrary Directions I Design to Take a short Tour and Come back hither and stay a week or 10 Days here.

---

[1] That is, the Act whereby the House of Commons, with Harley's active support, had sought to break up the current schemes to cheat the customs. To be sure, the Bill had been aimed chiefly at non-Scottish speculators, and had exempted from its provisions the legitimate traffic of honest Scottish traders. But even these latter, though presumably they would be gainers by a law that would strangle their dishonest competitors, rejoiced when the Bill failed in the Lords, for under its provisions they were to be called upon to prove their good faith before the London customs officials, an expensive and vexatious procedure. See *History of the Union*, pp. 570–3, and 687–9.

[2] The account proved correct. In June a fleet of 40 vessels from Scotland attempted to land their goods at London. Customs officials seized the ships, refused to allow them to be unloaded, and treated their crews as smugglers. But eventually, after prolonged clamour and vexation on both sides, the goods were landed, and no duty upon them was ever collected (Mackinnon, *Union of England and Scotland*, pp. 358–60).

You will be sure Matters are Changed that I Dare to show my Face here where it had been Death to have been known but a few Months Agoe.

I am Acting my Part with the Magistrates and the Ministers. For the Rest I Do not Concern my Self. I am Argueing the Great Concern England has shown for them in Letting Fall the Drawback bill, and pressing them to Suitable Returns of Duty and Moderation—and I am pleased to Tell your honour I am heard in it, And that I think I am Doeing More Service Now than Ever Since I Came into this Country.

And here I beg your Leav to Give One hint— There Are Officers sent Down to the Customes and Excise. I make no Complaints Nor Do I say there is yet any Cause, but I Humbly Move that who Ever Are sent may be Commanded to use all the Courtisye, Civillity and Calmness possible here. Nothing Elce Can Oblige This Surly, Haughty, Vain Humour of the poorest and Meanest people.

I have been often Mov'd on This head, tho' the Gentlemn should be in the Right and it Consists with Their Duty, yet if They have any Regard to the Nature and Temper of Things and Folks they Must wink, Abate, and bear with Circumstances. In short Sir, This people May be Drawn; the Contrary I Need Not Mention.

I have Now Another Thing to Mention Sir. Mr Bell is Gone Again to London and he will Accquaint you I have been No Good husband for you— Indeed I hinted the Measures I Took about the Assembly, of which I was Really heartily afraid, put me to No small Expence—[1] But I have been forced Since to supply in part Family Demands, My Long Absence Makeing it Absolutely Necessary and Indeed Impossible to Avoid— I shall be sorry to have your Censure in This as Invadeing your bounty, but I hope your Honor will prevail to have an honest and I hope Faithfull Engine supported while Abroad— However, I Thot it my Duty to Inform you of it, For I will not have (No Not bread) Without your Knowlege, and will Desist when Ever you summons Me away.

I am to Dine On wednesday with The Presbytry of Dumfermling,[2] and the Next week at that of St Andrews, and shall then Come back hither. I Can not help Expressing my Joy at the

---

[1] See p. 214.
[2] That is, on 21 May; but his letter from Stirling on that day (No. 107) does not mention Dunfermline.

Visible success of my Negotiateing here—and Tho' I am Alone
too little for it, yet I think Nothing More Needfull than this
work, for this Is a Fermented and Implacable Nation.

I am, Your Most Obedt Humble Servt

D F

MS.: Duke of Portland, Defoe Papers, 1 ff. 170–1. *Pub.*: *H.M.C. Portland*,
iv. 407–8. *Address*: 'To The Right Honble Robert Harley Esqr., Her Majties
Principall Secreta of State, Present.'

107. *To* ROBERT HARLEY. *21 May 1707*

Sterling May 21. 1707

Sir

My Last was from Glasgow of the 15. I am Now at sterling, in
the Circuit I hinted to you before. I gave you an Account of my
Self at Large in My last, to which I Referr.

I Can not but think my Self Olig'd to Lay The state of Things
before you as Clearly as Possible, and if for want of your Commands Explicitly Guiding me I Err in My Conduct, I hope for
your pardon—Since it is Impossible for me to Judge at a Distance what is your pleasure, being So Absolutely Destitute of
your Directions in this Affair.

The Country here was Very Easy On Account of the Union
and I began to boast my Self of the happy success—But Two
things have given so Much Disgust here that I am Amaz'd to
See how Soon These people are to be turned about to Extremes.

Dyer in his Letter Sayes The Lawyers have found Out a
Method to stop the French Goods without breaking the Union,
and this is spread Over the wholl Kingdome, being printed
Again in the Edinb. Gazette.

Now Sir as to this affair I Remember I formerly hinted to you
My Thots, and had Some publick Notice been then Concerted
and the Court here took some Measures to ha' Corresponding
with it Discouraged the Import, I believ much of The Mischief
might have been Prevented, but that is past.[1]

My Humble Conclusions form'd from Serious Observation
here Are That 1/ If a Generall stop be Made you put The wholl
Nation here Distracted, 2/ With a partiall stop They will be
Very well pleased.

I Explain my Self Thus.

To stop or Seize Our Goods who are scots Men[2] is highly

[1] Defoe had given both Harley and Godolphin early warning that schemes to
cheat the customs were afoot. See Nos. 95 and 97.
[2] That is, as distinct from English, Dutch, and other foreign speculators.

Injurious to us, As Our Market here is Destroy'd by The Flux of Goods brought in by The English on a prospect of Trade to England, who when they shall be Obliged to Sell here will Glut the Markett and lower the Price, and so you Ruin us for what is your Own fault, which is Not fair.

In This part Indeed they seem to have Reason, for if The stop be Generall The Case will be Very Miserable here with a Great Many, and the Clamour Intollerable.

2 They Say if Their Goods are stopt The Union is Directly broken and the Article of a Free Intercourse of Trade Destroyed.

And Indeed this to me Seems Evident too, and the Exception in the house of Commons[1] Imply's as Much, and This is what I am So Earnest for Direction about.

I am Clear however That the Importations of Forreigners and English Ought to be stop't, and tho' Concealing and Transposeing properties May be practised, yet you will find it something Easyer to Discover properties here than in England, Especially Considering the Entries are allready Made without any Caution and the proprietors in Most Cases Discovred, And I have Made some Observations that in Their season will be Usefull that way.

I am also to Assure you Sir that if this Medium be Agreed On, It will Give an Universall Satisfaction here, for 1st They Can Not pretend any breach of the Union, and 2dly their pride is fully Gratifyed as well as their purse, and they all Crye Out Tis just to stop the Encroachments of Strangers.

I Ask your pardon for thus freely giveing my thoughts, and as I kno' you put the stress upon the giveing just Satisfaction to the subject, I presume it my Duty to give you the Sence of the Country.

This is the scheme I have also followd in speaking to Dyers News paper,[2] and I Endeavour as 1st to allow what they Claim as to their Own Goods, so to shew the Reasonableness of stopping Others, In which I hope I am Right, and Entreat a hint if I am Not, but I am sure I am Right as to the people here in prepareing them to Accquiesce in all the proceedings, but just as farr as Touches their seperate propertys.

I Am Inform'd Sir the Custome house is Settled for this Country. Is there No Room for an Absent Servant to be ad-

---

[1] Cf. p. 217, n. 1, and p. 220, n. 1, for the exemption of bona fide Scottish trader to which Defoe here alludes.
[2] In the *Review* for 3 June.

mitted?[1] I formerly hinted that a Generall Survey Such as Dr Davenant[2] has in England would be of Great service here, and I am perswaded if I had the honour to Accquaint my Ld Treasurer of the steps I formerly hinted About Clandestine Trade,[3] which some have Taken and Are makeing large provision for, his Ldship would find such an Employmt Absolutely Necessary, Considering the Infinite Creeks and Coves here in which Frauds will be Carryed on, and where tis Impossible without an Army of Officers to prevent it.[4]

My Brother[5] writes me he has had the Honor to see you and you were pleased to Say My Ld Treasurer had Mentioned Me in the Matter of the Settlement here— I have No body to Recommend me but your Self, Save That the D of Queensberry promised Me to Recomend Me to My Ld Treasurer & to The Queen also.[6]

I Repeat my humble Entreaty to you to be thoughtfull of Me that I may No Longer be Thus Chargable to you.

I am, Your Obedt Servt

D F

MS.: Duke of Portland, Defoe Papers, 1 ff. 172–3. *Pub.*: *H.M.C. Portland*, iv. 411–13. *Address*: 'To The Right Honble Robert Harley Esqr., Principall Secretary of State, Present.'

108. *To* ROBERT HARLEY. *23 May 1707*

Sir

My Last to you from Sterling Gave you My scheme of the Nationall Discontents here about the Wine & Brandy. I Mentioned Two things but spoke to One Onely.

The Next is The Affair of the Equivalent. —And why is Not the Equivalent Come Down, sayes the Country Man. You were to pay it by the 1st of May, and you have broke the Union in

---

[1] A week earlier Godolphin had written to Harley: 'I have been this morning endeavering to fix the Custom house Officers for Scotland. Mr Henley is named for one, & there is a blank Left for the Secry; I have Not yett ventured to propose de Foe for fear I shd never gett him to goe down with Mr Lowndes, unless it bee recommended from you' (Duke of Portland, Harley Papers, xxiv f. 72). Defoe later said that Harley did recommend him to Godolphin, and that Godolphin offered him a post in Scotland, but that both ministers persuaded him to decline the appointment in order to remain in the secret service (p. 331).

[2] Charles Davenant (1656–1714), son of Sir William D'Avenant, was Inspector General of Imports and Exports.

[3] See No. 95.

[4] See *History of the Union*, pp. 577–8.

[5] His brother-in-law, Robert Davis.

[6] See No. 101.

that—and where is it all this while?[1] Now the Treaty is finished you do what you please with us, and Thus we shall be Used in Everything. This in them is Very serious Language—

Great advantage is made Indeed of this, not so much pretending it shall not be pd, but that time is not kept with them, and Agreements not performed, and we have a story whispred here that D Hamilton Came the first of May in the Night and protested at the Cross of Edinb that the Union was broke. I do not I Confess believ the thing, but these Reports Joyned with the Want of the Money makes a great Deal of Ill blood here and Does Unspeakable harm.

The Governmt knows how to Apply Suitable Remedyes to these Mischiefs, and I Doubt not will do so, but I thought it my Duty to hint my Observations.

The Apprehensions of the people here at the stop of their Goods is Very Great, and I Confess if that matter is not Clear'd up and the property of scots men Set Free, together with some Settled Method how the property of scots men may be ascertaind and Determined, the Discontents will Run too high and I Apprehend New Tumults Very Much.

I have spoke my mind freely in print in the Review,[2] and printed One here[3] to shew the Justice of preventing Frauds, but I must with it Own, and Indeed my own judgment joyns in it, and I believ yours also, that the True property of scots Men should be admitted free.[4]

I wish I had but Two lines from you Sir to Direct me in this Affair. Tis Really a Difficult time here, and I think more so than when the Union was in Agitation, for the wholl Nation is in a Ferment About the French Goods and the Equivalent.

[1] Although no actual date had been set for payment of the Equivalent, the Scots expected to receive it as soon as the Union became effective. In spite of the continued outcry, the money did not reach Edinburgh until 5 Aug.

[2] See especially the issues for 3, 17, and 20 May. He continued his remarks in those for 31 May, and 3, 5, 10, 12, 14, and 17 June.

[3] He seems to say that he had printed a special issue of the *Review* for his Scottish readers. No such issue for this period is known. The regular Edinburgh edition of the *Review* had not yet been established.

[4] To prevent frauds but still to allow the legitimate exports of honest Scottish traders had been the purpose of the Bills backed by Harley and passed by the House of Commons. But Godolphin had thought the measure impracticable, and the House of Lords had thought it illegal. Since the attempted legislation was now dead, there was no legal bar to the exports, whether honest or fraudulent. But rejection of the Bills had not allayed apprehension in Scotland: London merchants were still clamouring against the threatened deluge; Dyer had announced that 'the Lawyers' had discovered a way to prevent entry (p. 222); and the London customs officials might (and indeed did) refuse to permit the goods to be landed.

I might do you much more Service Sir if I had but Now and then a letter of proper hints from your Self— I kno' you are in a Hurry[1] and I lament the Occasion, but Indeed Sir things here are of Consequence, and a little Disorder here Would give things a bad aspect and have too great an Influence on Credit, Trade, Funds and all those things: The Matter therefore Mourns to be settled. I beg your Excuse for the liberty I Take, which I think my Duty.

I am, Your Most Obedt Servt
D F

At Wemyss May. 23. 1707

MS.: Duke of Portland, Defoe Papers, 1 ff. 174–5. *Pub.*: *H.M.C. Portland*, iv. 413–14. *Address*: 'To The Right Honble Robert Harley Esqr., Principall Secreta of State, Present.' *Endorsed*: 'Wemys, May 23: 1707, R̸ May 30: 7 days.'

109. *To* ROBERT HARLEY. *10* [*June*] *1707*

Sir

I Wrott you last post. I have Nothing to Add worth your Note. The Weather haveing been favourable I am Travailing thro' the Towns and Disputeing with The Rigid and Refractory Clergy who are the worst Enemies of the Union. I act all This Sir of my Own head, for haveing No Direction From you I am loth to be Idle and live upon your Expence without forwarding the Work I Came hither About, and I hope you will believ me that I Do my uttmost not to be So Expensive as I am sensible I am, without persuing the True End of the Charge.

I am Not able to say any thing More to what I have formerly Hinted about my self; I kno' absent and Forgotten are frequently synonimous. I have no Dependence but on your Self, but Sir while I see Men as *Rigby, Isaacson* &c.[2] in Commission, I Can Not but hope you will Cause me to be Remembred.

[1] Harley was more agitated than Defoe perhaps knew. The old days of the Triumvirate and coalition government were drawing to a close, and Harley, the moderate Tory, was getting ever further out of step with a Cabinet that was turning steadily Whig. He had opposed the appointment of Sunderland, now an embarrassing colleague in the other Secretaryship. He had differed with Godolphin over the Drawback Bill and, in backing it in the Commons, had found himself in alliance with the Tories. Mrs. Masham was about to come upon the scene, and through her influence with the Queen, Harley would soon be seeking to oust Godolphin and take over the white staff himself. This aim, and its method, would alienate both the Churchills. The struggle was now beginning which was to end in the following February with Harley's dismissal from the Government.

[2] 'Sir Alexander Rigby, John Henley, and James Isaacson, esqs., and sir Robert Dixon and Mr. Boile (brother to the earl of Glasco) are appointed commissioners

I formerly hinted my proposall of a Survey of the Out ports[1] and still wish for it—but if not, the Accompta or Comptr of the Accounts, things I pretend to be Master of, would be suitable for me. I Thro' my Self wholly On your Concern for me, and perswade my Self while you are my Intercessor I Can not be Denyed.

Your Most Obedt Servt
D F

May. 10. 1707[2]

MS.: Duke of Portland, Defoe Papers, 1 ff. 176–7. *Pub.*: *H.M.C. Portland*, iv. 417–18. *Address*: 'To The Right Honble Robert Harley Esqr., Principall Secretary of State, Present.' *Endorsed*: 'D: F: dated May 10: 1707, by mistake for June 10:, R̃ here 17:'

110. ROBERT HARLEY *to* DEFOE. *12 June 1707*

June 12 1707

Sir

I have received your Letters very constantly, and I cannot think that any one has miscarried.[3] I am sure I have taken care to represent your services in the best light from time to time where it may do you service; and I hope I have not been an unprofitable Servant: I Am very sorry that You or your humble Servant should bear Reproach for doing what others could not, or would not do, but it has been often so. I have set up my Rest,[4] and therefore it is not in their power to disappoint me. I count upon all that impotent malice, inveterate spleen can do, by mis-representations and notorious forgeries, to do me hurt. I am prepared for all. And the wrath is greater agt me because their Weakness as well as villanous Arts happen to be detected; And if God Spares me Life; I think I Shall be able to pull off the Mask from the reall Atheists & pretended Patriots—but too much of this now.

You are in the right to put the D: of Queensberrie in mind of You;[5] repeat it again; It will Serve to cover your friends in doing You justice; I need give You only a hint: As to more particulars,

of the customes in Scotland; their salaries 400*l* per ann. each' (Luttrell, *Brief Relation*, vi. 173).

[1] That is, Scottish ports other than Edinburgh.
[2] See the endorsement.
[3] Defoe had suspected that his letters were being intercepted. See p. 219.
[4] That is, he has made his resolution and is resolved to stand by it.
[5] See pp. 213, 216, and 224.

I desire You will write a Letter to Ld Treasurer (inclose it to me) proposing Your own Service & where You can be most use-full.[1] *He* thinks surveyor of one of the Ports. If that meets with Your Approbation, propose that, or any other Alternative; the Sooner the Better.

I cannot let this Letter pass without a few words upon the point of Trade: The true State of the matter is this: Upon the View of the Union; Dutch, Jews, Swedes, Danes &c Struck into the Notion of bringing in Goods before May 1, which arose from one certain Gentlemans[2] giving great Commissions, think-ing to have Swallowed all the profit; This set every body a gog to get the pence; The malicious World Reports & Names the Men & Summs of Money ventured by those in both Houses, but be sure You do not believe that, for it is impossible that persons of all Sorts, Colours & pretences can be such Knaves— And what has passed Since is only Accidental, which the Men of the World interpret to very wrong Ends. However, the House of Commons would have rescued Us from the Scandall & obliged Scotland; They had contrived to make the Cheats do Justice, and at the same time indulged the Scots with an Opportunity of getting clear and honestly 150000£ to Speak with the least—but Satan hindred—. The Scots, but I should more truly Say one person only,[2] Solicited agt their Own Nation under pretence of the Union, Whereas there is nothing plainer can be said in words (for any Case which is contingent & is to happen) than the words of the Union against the practice: What is more, no one Lawier of Credit would ever pretend to Stand by the con-trary Opinion, but it was hoped that power, Faction & Noise, which are the Same, together with fear of Offending Scotland whom they hop'd to enrage, would bear the Cheats out in this barefaced fraud. When they found that a middle way was dis-covered, to indulge the Scots & make the others pay, then they were Surprised, and to hinder it all the tools were to be used— Acheronta Movebo—What was the present End You know, what is to come God knows; but this is certain, if our Scots Friends knew what a sweet Morsel these people have taken out of their Mouths, they would turn their rage the right way.

I will add but two things more; those Goods (tho' they should

---

[1] Defoe had made such proposals in No. 107 and again in No. 109, though Harley had not yet received the latter. Defoe now followed Harley's suggestion and wrote to Godolphin. The correspondence is missing, but see Godolphin to Harley, 7 Aug. 1707, *H.M.C. Bath*, i. 177.   [2] Unidentified.

come in quickly) will come to no market, And the next thing is that the Wine, Brandys & other Goods of the Growth & Manufacture of the Kingdom of France are intirely forbidden here, and can no way be brought in either before or since the Union but as Prize Goods, & then the Duty is fixed high, and this is as plain as A.B.C.

You will excuse me for being so large upon a head which is so Copious, and as extensive as the vast Volumes of Cheat & Knavery; but You will quickly guess at the true State of Affairs relating to this matter by these short hints. I think it will be for Your own Service as well as the public that You consider what method is the best to prevent future frauds in the Customes & to Allay the heats of Our New Friends, & Send it as soon as you can in writing.

I desire You will Send me an Account of what Money You have received from Mr Bell; and the times when. He being now in Town I am clearing with him, & L. T. Says it is not fit you should be longer at my Charge, which I hope is for Your Good.

I am most really Sir Yours

MS.: Duke of Portland, Defoe Papers, 1 ff. 178–9; a copy, unsigned, but in the handwriting of Harley. *Pub.*: *H.M.C. Portland*, iv. 418–19. *Endorsed*: 'Copy, June 12: 1707, to D: F:, inclosd to Mr Bell.'

111. *To* ROBERT HARLEY. *8 July 1707*

Sir

I Gave you Some of my Thoughts last post[1] and Some Instances of Jacobite Insolence. I Can Not but Accquaint you of what I Think not without ground gives a Great Many Sober people a Great Uneasyness and I must Acknowlege has Some Appearance of Mischief in it.

The Intollerable boldness of the Jacobite party in the Northern Highlands is Such Now, And in some of the Lowland provinces also in the North, that Unless Some speedy Care is Taken to prevent Their Disorders The Consequences Can not but be fatall.[2]

About 14 days Since, they Rabbled the wholl synod of Ross and Maltreated the Ministers, and this by a Made Rabble of Men Disguised in Womens Cloths, of which Complaint haveing been Made to the Council I presume you have a perticular.[3]

[1] Missing.
[2] Nathaniel Hooke, emissary of the King of France, had secretly visited Scotland during the spring, and had strengthened the hopes of the Jacobites that the French would support them in an uprising to break the Union and bring in the Pretender.
[3] For a detailed account of the incident, see the *Reviews* for 26 July and 14 Aug. 1707.

But the Thing I Perticularly Instance Now is that The Duke of Athol, who Now makes himself the head of the Discontented party, has Appointed his Great Hunting.[1] I have not Learnt the precise Day, but the Ld Sinclear[2] & sevll Other of the popish and Jacobite Gentlemen on Fife Side where I Now Am Are allready Gone to it, who are known to be no sports men Nor Ever Used to Go— The Jacobites Report Their K Ja. VIII will be On show quickly, some report he is Arriv'd Incog., but all Agree there is some Mischief in hand—and the Forces here are So Contemptible that if any Commotion happen they Can Do Nothing.

After all Sir, the secret Talk Among Some of their Privadoes is That They have 30000 Men[3] Ready at a word—and Good people Are Very Uneasy.

But the perticular Reason why I write this is The Easyness of the attempt supposeing a party of these Desperate people should offer to Surprize the Equivalent, and it is but this Day that I strangely had an Occasion to hear Something like it whispred as it Comes Directly from some that kno' more than Every body Imagin.[4]

I Thought it my Duty to hint this Sir. Tis a Doubtfull Time here and Such a bait would flush the Wholl party and push them Headlong into Generall Confusion.

If you think it may Conduce to the publick Service, I shall willingly hazard my Self to go North and Make my Self Master of as Much of these Mysteries of Iniquity as Can be Obtaind, in Order to give you Seasonable Intelligence. If you Approve it your Ordrs should Come by the Very Next post.

> I am, Sir, Your Most Obedt Servt
>
> D F

July 8. 1707

MS.: Duke of Portland, Defoe Papers, 1 ff. 180–1. *Pub.*: *H.M.C. Portland*, iv. 425. *Address*: 'To The Right Honble Robert Harley Esqr., Her Majties Principall Secreta of State, Present.' *Endorsed*: 'D: F July 8: 1707, R̸ July 16.'

[1] See Forster to Harley, *H.M.C. Portland*, iv. 449–50.
[2] Henry St. Clair of Herdmanston (1660–1723), tenth Baron Sinclair.
[3] In his report to the King of France, Hooke also set the number of potential rebels at 30,000 (Mackinnon, *Union of England and Scotland*, pp. 387–8).
[4] To ensure safe delivery of the Equivalent to Edinburgh Castle, a convoy was ordered to accompany the wagons during the journey. On 15 July Leven wrote to Mar, 'The party is to consist of one hundred and twentie dragouns under the command of Lewtenant-Collonel Dowglas, and under him two captanes and three subalterns, which I think more then sufficient, yet I am told sume are grumbling that it is so weak' (*H.M.C. Mar and Kellie*, p. 404).

112. *To* ROBERT HARLEY. *19 July 1707*

Sir

I am Sorry to Say that I look Now as One Entirely forgott, That haveing the honour to be sent hither, and Not thinking it my Duty to Abandone my post without your Orders, have now neither Capascity to stay Nor orders to Come Away.

The Commrs of the Customes are Sitting Every Day and Filling Up the places with persons as Usuall supplyed with More Friends than Merit— I have been in hopes from what you were pleased to hint to me that I should be Thought of—[1] I Entreat you will please to Interpose your Intrest on that Account which I Doubt not would be Effectuall— If Nothing be to be Expected, It is a Favour I perswade my Self you will not Deny me, to let me have a hint from you Sir and a help to Returne me to Serv you some other way.

I Gave you an Item, of a Design to Surprize the Equivalent. Were it Reall or not I thot it my Duty to Communicate it to you. I believ their heart will fail them. However, I Took this Method in which I believ I did not Amiss, that I Effectually spread a Report that there was such a Design—which I believ will make half the Country Go Out to Meet it, and quite make the attempt Impracticable.

Ignorance and prejudice has Raised a Clamour against the Exchecqr Bills that they say are Comeing.[2] I had wrott half a sheet to Explain the advantages of them and their answering Money in their Effect on Trade, but I am Run too low to print, for there is no printing here but at an Expence. I shall Disperse some written Coppies, that I may Continue to do what service I Can when straightned from Doeing what I might.

I Fear Sometimes you have thot me too Chargable here, but if you will permit me to give you a scheme of my way of liveing and what I have been Doeing, I perswade my Self you will be Convinced I have not missapplyed neither the Time Nor the Money.

I am I Confess impatient to have Some Directions what to Do and how to Govern myself, and Entreat your pardon for my Importunity.

It has been Reported they are Discontent here at the Many English who Come hither for places,[3] but that I think is a

[1] See No. 110.
[2] Of the Equivalent as finally delivered in Edinburgh, only a quarter was in gold; the rest was in Exchequer bills.   [3] See *Lockhart Papers*, i. 223-4.

Groundless Report— But One thing I Ought to Note—It gives a very great Distast here that the Officers of the Excise are Obliged to Gauge on the sabbath Day.

It would be also a Caution Needfull to be given that the English officers should not Frequent the Jacobite Conventicles, which will soon Rendr not them Onely Odious, but So Encourage them that they will think themselves supported or at least Approved by the English Governmt.

These hints Sir I thought Needfull to give you the Trouble of.

I am, Sir, Your Most Obedt Servt

D F

Edinb. July 19. 1707

MS.: Duke of Portland, Defoe Papers, 1 ff. 182–3. *Pub.*: *H.M.C. Portland*, iv. 427–8. *Address*: 'To The Right Honble Robert Harley Esqr., Principle Secreta of State, Present.'

113. [*To* ROBERT HARLEY]. *5 August 1707*

Sir

My Last long Letter Prevented The Enclosed[1] and withall Supposeing It had been Sent you in a Public Manner— We are Told here That My Lord Marr has Suppresst the Address, and They Are Very Angry with him here for it.[2]

Notice has been Sent from Some Merchants in London to Their Principalls here That all Their ships will be Confiscate and Their Goods spoiled, and That Their Seamen Are all presst or, *As I Tell them is More likely*, Run Away For fear of Pressing.

The Merchants here have *They Say* Sent Ordrs to Their Friends in England To give No Security[3]—but to Demand Their Goods and if not Delivred to give bills of Parcels[4] to the Officers Who Detain Them and to Sue Them for the Money— If This be So, it Must be by procurment from London, That

[1] A printed Petition from the Scottish merchants whose ships had been seized by the London customs authorities, requesting the Convention of Royal Burghs to intercede with the Government for their relief. The Convention had accordingly drawn up an Address to the Queen, the text of which is copied, in a hand other than Defoe's, on the back of the Petition. On the printed side, Defoe wrote: 'This is the petition of the merchants on which the address on the other side is founded.' This enclosure no longer accompanies the letter, but see *H.M.C. Portland*, viii. 354. Both the Petition and the Address are printed in *History of the Union*, pp. 683–5.

[2] Mar, in London, delayed presenting the Address of the Royal Burghs (*H.M.C. Mar and Kellie*, p. 411).

[3] Ships were to be allowed to unload provided the owner gave security that he would abide by whatever decision Parliament might eventually reach (Mackinnon, *Union of England and Scotland*, p. 359).

[4] That is, itemized statements.

Method being Unknown here—and The persons I believ are Wa. Stuart, Tho. Coots[1] &c, who are the Principall Merchants in London Concern'd in This Affair, with Mr Elliot[2] in Round Court, Lace Man—if These Could be Made Easy This wholl affair might be Closed.

Now They begin to be Convinc't here That if the First Bill[3] had past in Parliamt, Scotland had been Safe and Also gainers, and they blame the Scots Merchants for Opposeing it; a short hint Sir How to Behave in This Affair would give me a great help. Indeed the Jacobite Party make Great Use of it, and it Does an Unspeakable Injury as to the Tempers of the people, which began Very Much to Abate in Their Ill Influences but Now Encrease Again.

The Brewers are Now Goeing Mad in Their Turns.[4] I hinted the Case in My last.[5] Severall of Them gave Over work, and the Servants finding Others did Not, Went yesterday in a Tumult to Those houses That were at work and Put Out Their fires and let Their Liquor Run about house, and The Like Disorder today also— Where It Will End I Can Not yet foresee.

I Entreat the hand of the Enclosed may Not be Seen, because I Obtain'd it by a private Correspondence which it will be Necessary to keep up, and being a known hand it would be both Unfaithfull to him and Entirely Close the Door of my Intelligence On That Side if I should Not Conceal him.

I am, Sir, Your Most Faithfull Obedient Servt
DE FOE

Edinb. Aug. 5. 1707

The Equivalent is Safely Lodg'd in the Castle This Night.

MS.: Duke of Portland, Defoe Papers, 1 f. 184. *Pub.*: *H.M.C. Portland*, iv. 430. *Address*: none.

114. [*To* ROBERT HARLEY]. *7 August 1707*

Sir

I Wrott you in my Last that The Equivalent was Arrived in the Castle— I think it my Duty to give you a Destinct account

---

[1] Walter Stuart and Thomas Coutts were prominent Scottish merchants resident in London. Both had been principals in the Darien enterprise and had been named in the Act establishing the Darien Company. Coutts was a member of the family which later became famous in banking.
[2] William Elliot (mentioned by Cranstoun to Cunningham, *H.M.C. Portland*, iv. 284).   [3] See p. 216, n. 4.
[4] See *History of the Union*, pp. 582–3.   [5] Missing.

of The Circumstance of That Affair here, I mean with Respect to The Humours of the people.

I Must Confess the ill blood Occasion'd by This is Such, and So Much has it Revived the Old Heats, That were the Union Now to be Transacted it would be Impossible—

I am Never Sir you kno' for Searching an Evill to be Amazed at it, but to Applye The Remedyes.

The Capitall Quarrell is at the Bills Come Down.[1] Were the people here that are to Reciev it Men of Trade, or were there any Such thing as paper Credit here, or were the Bank here in hands that were not Secret Enemies to the Publick good, Or had the bills had a Running Intrest Upon them—This Matter had been better.

But as it is, pardon me to foul my Paper with Some of their Langguage. Tis Necessary you should kno' it tho' you have the happyness to be Remote from it and Out of its Reach.

First at England in Genll, Did we not say they would do what they pleased with us when they had us in their power? Did not Mr Hodges[2] Tell us they were a Tricking, faith breaking Nation, and Now We have given Ourselves up, Now they Unmask, now they begin with us— Others, Ay and they begin Early too. One would ha' Thought that in Policy they might ha' Dealt Smoothly with us at first, but now we see how we are to be Treated. They Contemn us so Much that they do Not Think it worth while to wheedle us.

Of The Bills— Heres the English Money that was to Circulate Among Us and Encourage Our Trade, and Now Tis Come in bitts of paper. What are their Banks and Exchequers to us. Our Gentlemen Carry them Down to pay their Heretable Debts with and who Do they Think will Discharge their lands for Bitts of Paper that if they will be paid must be sent 400 mile or more to get the money where those people have neither Friend Nor Correspondent.

I Confess Sir I am Tyred with Filling your Eares with these Things. But Really The Gent. of the Bank have been Much in the wrong— If they had Expected their bills should have been made Currant, they should have brought sealed Notes with Intrest and Sett up a small Cash here to Answr them, Some-

---

[1] Of the sum sent to Edinburgh, three-quarters was in Exchequer bills. See No. 125.

[2] James Hodges, author of *The Rights and Interests of the Two British Monarchies.* See p. 141, n. 2.

thing like the subscription for Circulateing Excheqr Notes. Credit you kno' well Sir is what Can Not be Forced. It is a Meer Consequence of Wanting No Credit. He that Can have his Money when he will, will Refuse it and let it lye or Take paper for it—But he That is ask't to stay For his Money will Certainly Demand it.

If The Bank therefore has Done this They have put their Reputation On the Tenters and stretched it farther than it will goe. The Prudence of which is at their Own Door.

I Write this Sir On Takeing it for Granted what I suppose is True, that the Bank has Thus Sent their Bills to Offer in payment, And I am Glad to hear the people lay it On the Bank Rather Than On the Governmt.

I am to have a Meeting in a Day or Two with the four Gentlemen who Come from Engld, Sir Jno Cope &c,[1] who it Seems Desire a private Conference with me On this head. I am Not Sencible I Can Do them Much Service, but I shall Tell them heartily and Frankly what they have before them.

It is most Certain if they Offer any man a Bill Till Some Other step is Taken to make the people Easy it will be Refused, and if One be Refused all the Rest Are Wast paper.[2]

In The last Letter I hinted the Arrivall of the Carriges. It is not to be Described the Fury and Indignation of the people On the Sight of it, Cursing Their Own Guards that brought it in, stoneing the Poor Fellows That Drew the Waggons, Nay the Very Horses. I Saw One of the Waggon Drivers Wounded with a stone On the Face which if it had not Glanced On his shoulder First I believ had Certainly Killed him— They Call it the Price of their Country and the poor people Are Incens'd by the Subtill Jacobites and too much by some of the Presb. Ministers—that they go along the streets Curseing the Very English Nation.

This is a Mellancholly story Sir, but I Thot it was Necessary you should be Informd how it stands.

Till the Matter of the bills, and of the Wine and brandy is

[1] Cope was a member of the Bank of England and one of the four London merchants appointed by the Queen to the Scottish Commission which was to manage the distribution of the Equivalent. See *History of the Union*, pp. 586–7.

[2] As a matter of fact, the Commissioners of the Equivalent protected the reputation of the Exchequer bills by sending to London for £50,000 in gold, and, thus fortified, offered payment in gold to all who were reluctant to accept paper. This accommodation, together with the willingness of several large stock-holders in the African Company to accept the bills, soon restored public confidence. See Mackinnon, *Union of England and Scotland*, p. 360.

adjusted, There Can be no Temper Expected here. I hope something may be Done after ward— It must be Time and Mannagemt which must bring them to themselves again— Mean time I Omitt no Occasion of Throwing Water Upon this Flame but Can not honestly boast of any Success. I mean just Now, I hope better.

I am, Sir, Your Most Obedt Servt
D F

Augt. 7. 1707

MS.: Duke of Portland, Defoe Papers, 1 ff. 186–7. *Pub.*: *H.M.C. Portland*, iv. 430–2. *Address*: none. *Endorsed*: 'Edenburg Aug: 7 1707, R̸ Aug: 18, Equivalent.'

115. [*To* ROBERT HARLEY]. *9 August 1707*

Sir

I am in hopes myne Come Constantly to your hand and Therefore I Repeat Nothing of what I have wrott; My Own Case I leav wholly with you, and Doubt not but My Ld Treasr Will be pleased with the Choice I have Made, of being Servicable Rather Than Proffiting of his Ldships Goodness.[1] I Referr That wholly to his Ldships Direction, Onely Pray the Return with his Ldships farther Ordrs as Soon as may Consist with Convenience.

I am Not to be Discourag'd Either with Dangers or Difficultys in This work. I kno' That the more Disordred they are here, The more Need of what I am Upon; and Therefore when I give his Ldship a Very Mellancholly Account of Things,[2] it is Neither to Enhance his Opinion of my Services nor to Suggest that I am Either weary Or Affraid of the Undertakeing;—and I speak This Now because I Really am goeing to give you a Very Mellancholly Account of Things—

The Ferment Runs Every Day higher here, and the ill blood

---

[1] Four years later he reminded Harley, then Earl of Oxford, 'Your Ldpp knows and I Presume Remembers That when your Ldpp Honord me with your Recommendation to The Late Ld Treasurer, My Lord Offred Me a Very Good Post in Scotland and afterward Offred me to be Comissionr of The Customes There, and That I did Not Refuse Those Offers, but it being your Opinion as well as his Ldpps That I Might be More Servicable in a Private Capascity, I Chose Rather to Depend Upon her Majties Goodness That I Might be Most Servicable, Than to Secure My Family a Maintenance and be Rendred Uncapable to serve her Majties Intrest' (pp. 331–2). Defoe continued to send reports to Harley, but his subsistence allowance was now to come from Godolphin (p. 242).

[2] On 14 Aug. Godolphin wrote to Harley: 'I don't like D F's letter, but I have often observed that he gives you the worst side of the picture' (*H.M.C. Bath*, i. 178).

of This people is So much Encreased that There is No speaking among them but with the Uttmost Caution—Not but that I am apt Freely Enough to speak, but if I should give way to Talking in Cases which would Move the patientest Man On Earth to lose his Temper, I should Deprive my Self of the Opportunity of Doeing Good Another Time.

I Therefore hear all Their ill language, and Onely Desire them to have Patience, till they see the End of things, and to Moderate as well as I Can, but 'Tis a Fitt of Lunacy Just Now and when the spirits Are Evaporated it will Cool Again.

I hinted to you a Sermon Preached at a Communion by Mr John Anderson[1] of St Andrews—last Sabbath he preached Again at the Gray Fryers Kirk in this City—his Text Hosea. 7. v. 8. *Ephraim is a Cake Not Turn'd. Strangers have Devour'd her strength and she knew it Not.* Here he Railed at and Abused the English Nation, Denounc't Gods Judgemt Against the people for Uniteing with a Perjur'd and a Godless people as he Call'd them—and In short flew in the Face of The Union and of the Governmt in Such a Manner as Really is Unsufferable—

He has in Conversation the Same stile, and Goes up and Down Enflameing and Enrageing the people— He is a bold, popular Man, and thereby the more Mischievous.

I have Taken No Notice of it Other than Gently in Discourse, for Really it is not the Time to Do it just Now—But if the Governmt here had a hint given them That her Majtie has an Account of and is Displeased &c at Such Dealing, And they Directed My Ld Advocate[2] to send for and Reprove him Gently, perhaps it might Give a Check to his Raillery—and as that is the Common Method here of Treating their ministers It will make No New Motion.

This Man is Really a Fatall Instrumt at this Time because he is Esteemd a Good Man.

I shall not Trouble you with the Artifices of the Jacobites to Enflame these things, How Men were Employd to Go about the streets and Crye Out Upon scotland, and Call the Brewers Men scotch Rogues, and scotch Dogs, just as passing in the streets, and so make the people Believ it was the English Excise men, and such like Methods to Exasperate the people Against them, which makes the poor Fellows afraid to go About their bussiness.

[1] Not to be confused with the better-known John Anderson, minister at this time at Dumbarton and later at Glasgow. See *Fasti Ecclesiæ Scoticanæ*, v. 234.
[2] Sir James Stewart.

In this Ferment We are Now, and Till the affair of the ships is Over, it will be No Otherwise.

My Fear of it is its Encreaseing and Refounding a Nationll Aversion, which is the Great thing we hoped the Union would have worne off—and which the Ministers in perticular do now Especially strive to spread in the Minds of the people, and which if it goes On will be past Cure.

I must Confess I Never Saw a Nation So Universally Wild and so Readily Embraceing Everything that may Exasperate them. They Are Ripe for Every Mischief, and if Some Generall step to their Satisfaction is not Taken, *I do not yet foresee how*, they will Certainly Precipitate themselves into some Violent thing or Other On the first Occasion that Offers.

It Seems a perfect Gang-green On the Tempers, And like the Genll Method of Such Exasperations, it Reconciles smaller things to promote this Greater— Different Intrests, Differing partys, all Joyn in a Universall Clamour—and the Very whiggs Declare Openly they will Joyn with France or King James or any body Rather than be Insulted as they Call it by the English —Tis the Happyest thing in the World that the Union is finisht. Were it to act Now it would be all Confusion and Distraction.

I have nothing to Say Sir in This Relation but that it is Much short of the Fact— I wish heartily some Medium may be found Out in the Case of the Wines—stop of the ships, and perticularly the Impressing their Men—for tho' I hope things will Cool then, yet Really Such Heats as These are Dangerous in Takeing too Deep Root.

I Thot my Self Oblig'd to give you This Account. I ask your Pardon for its Length, and am

> Your Most Obedt Servt
> D F

Augt. 9. 1707

MS.: Duke of Portland, Defoe Papers, 1 ff. 188–9. *Pub.*: *H.M.C. Portland*, iv. 432–3. *Address*: none. *Endorsed*: 'Edenburg Aug: 9: 1707, R̸ Aug: 19:'

116. [*To* ROBERT HARLEY]. *19 August 1707*

Sir

I am Glad to Tell you The Affair of the Wines &c, which we are Told Are Delivred Seems to Abate here—[1] and This Clamarous Party Are Now Turning their Tongues to Other Subjects.

[1] For the arrangement under which the Scottish merchants were allowed to unload their cargoes in London, see *History of the Union*, p. 573.

I Can not Say they Rail less, but I have the Comfort to be able better to Defend any Case and better to Understand Any Other Case Than That.

Two Cases Now Occupy Their Gall which I Thot it my Duty to Signifye to you. The Great Quantitys of Goods Run here, as Well Openly and Insolently as Secretly, I hinted at before: In Ordr to Make themselves Amends Upon The Merchants and Come at a Compleat Discovery, The Commissionrs have Sumon'd in Generall all the Merchts, as well those Suspected as Not, to Come in and Swear whether they have not Defrauded the Queen of her Customes and to Tell upon Oath How Much Since the 1st of May.

Now I am Not Saying This is against Their Law for Really They have Such a Barbarous Law,[1] being a Remnant of the Old Suppresst Tyrrany.

Nor Am I Debateing Sir Whether the Queen shall get Money by this Prosecution yea or No, for Certainly if prosecuted the Queen must get 2000o*l* or Multitudes Must be perjured or be Undone and Unable to pay.

But Sir I Humbly Represent to my Ld Treasurer That a Rigorous prosecution of this Case will be attended with Infinite Murmurs and Discontents, and Serve more to that fatall Design of Alienateing this people from the Governmt and the Union Than all that Money Can Countervail.

1st The Kirk Exclaim and Say This is practiseing that Old Abhorr'd Custome of Multiplyeing Oaths, which Tends to perjury &c; That it is leading people to Destruction by forcing them to perjure themselves or be Ruind, which Multitudes Can Not Resist; That however Such a Law is in Force, it is Against the Law of Nations, in which it is Every where A Maxim Nemo Tenetur Seipsum Accusare; That This Law has Rarely if Ever been Practised and is not Now in Any Christian Country, and the like.

2. The people Say This is the First Test of the Moderation of the British Governmt, in which tis Apparent The Subjects of Scotland Are to Meet with Nothing but Severity; That Tis Against the Union, in which all the Subjects are to Enjoy Equallitys in Trade, Mutuall Restrictions &c; That the Sub-

---

[1] 'By our law all merchants are oblidged within three moneths after importation to depone if they have imported any goods to this kingdome without paying the duties, and in there oaths to condescend upon the particular goods so imported' (Seafield to Mar, 31 July 1707, *H.M.C. Mar and Kellie*, p. 409).

jects of England Can Not be Thus Purged, And all Laws to produce an Inequallity are to be Repealed; That this has been a Time of as it were an Inter-regnum in Trade and Unusuall Libertys May have been Taken; That This is a Design to punish the Conscientous offendour and let the Hardened Sinner Escape; That This will be of no Use any Farther, for it will put them Upon Measures in which the Nicest and Most Scrupulous will be Able to swear for the Future—&c.

I act in This I hope the part My Ld[1] Means I should act Vizt to Accquaint his Ldship what Measures here may work ill, and what not; & have No Other prospect in it. I am Sencible this proceeding Makes great additions to the ill Temper here, which Really Sir is too great all ready Not to Merit a Great Deal of Caution.

If this Matter were pusht Now to Extremety I Can Not Express the Confusion it would Make here, For Really half the Nation are in the Crime—[2] But Measures to prevent it May better be Used to all Extremeties than Retrospects, Especially On the foot of this Exploded Law.

The Debate by Council In the Excheqr Court here was Very Long, and yesterday the Lords Adjourn'd it to the Third Wednesday in November, and This Makes me lay it before you Sir That My Ld May be judge whether it will Not Rather be held as a Rod to Awe them, than Otherwise.

The Next Thing I Note is the Council here Settling Justices or Comissions of the Peace,[3] in which I Doubt they Distinguish too Much Such as were not for the Union, Tho' some of them being Men of Temper and Honour Are at the Same Time Well affected to the Government, and being Gentlemen of Absolute Superiourity in their Severall Countryes, it will be a Little too much Dishonour to them and perfectly alienate them to see their Vassalls in the Commission and themselves subjected and left out.

---

[1] Godolphin.

[2] An indignant delegation had protested to the Scottish Lord Chancellor that 'above 1,000 people had been summoned to compear before the Exchequer for runing of goods', but this number was an exaggeration. See Seafield to Mar, 31 July 1707, *H.M.C. Mar and Kellie*, p. 409.

[3] Scotland's traditional hereditary jurisdictions were plentiful, but they were not properly distributed for efficient handling of the new flood of smuggling cases. If the revenue was to be collected effectively, the courts would have to be more numerous and more widely scattered. The Scottish Privy Council met this need by establishing Justices of the Peace in localities lacking ready access to other courts. See J. H. Burton, *History of Scotland*, 1897–1901, viii. 210.

This Matter the Constitution of Things here Makes to Differ from England, and in Such Case the Law and Course of Justice will be Obstructed, Since those Vassalls Dare not and Will not Act without the Authourity of their Chiefs, Tho' they were of Greater Estates Than their Chief.

These Things I Humbly Offer as my Own Observations. If it be your pleasure I May lay before you Some Names wherein this is perticularly Mischeivous.

I should be Glad to kno' if my Answr to My Ld T . . . . rs Letter Reach't your hands,[1] and if possible see my Self Delivred from the present Circumstance I am in here, which I Need Not Explain to you Sir. I ask your Pardon and am

Sir, Your Most Obedt Servt

D F

Edinb. Augt 19. 1707

MS.: Duke of Portland, Defoe Papers, 1 ff. 190–1. *Pub.*: *H.M.C. Portland*, iv. 435–6. *Address*: none. *Endorsed*: 'Edenburg Aug: 19: 1707, R̸ Aug: 26.'

117. *To* ROBERT HARLEY. *11 September 1707*

Sir

You have Allways Allow'd me The Freedome of a plain and Direct Stateing things to you. If I Should Not do it Now I should Not be just to you, Much less Faithfull to My Self; and I Entreat your Pardon for This from the True and Necessary part of it.

If I Were where I have had the honor to be Sir, in your Parlour, Telling you my Own Case, and what a Posture my Affaires are in here, it would be too Moveing a Story; you Could Not, I am Perswaded, *pardon my Vanity*, you have too much Concerne for me and too much Generosity in your Nature, you Could Not bear it— I have allwayes Sir been bred like a Man, I Would Say a Gentleman if Circumstances Did Not of late Alter that Denomination, and tho' my Missfortunes and Enemies have Reduced me, yet I allwayes struggled with the World So as Never to want, till Now— Again Sir I had the honour to Come hither in a Figure Suitable to your Design, whom I have the honor to Serv; while you Supply'd me Sir, I Can Appeal to him that knows all things, I Faithfully Serv'd. I baulk't No Cases, I Appeard in print when Others Dared not to Open Their

[1] The letter had been received and passed on to Godolphin (see Godolphin to Harley, 7 Aug. 1707, *H.M.C. Bath*, i. 177).

Mouths, and without boasting I Ran as Much Risq of my life as a Grenadr in storming a Counterscarp;—It is Now five Months since you were pleased to Withdraw your Supply;[1]—and yet I had Never your Ordr to Return;—I knew My Duty better Than to quitt my post without your Command; But Really Sir if you supposed, I had lay'd up a Bank Out of your former, It is my Great Missfortune That Such a Mistake happens; I Depended too much on your Goodness to withold any Reasonable Expence, to form a Magazine for my Last Resort.

Tis true I spent you a Large Summe. But you will Remember how often I Entreated your Restraint in that Case, and perticular Directions, but as left to my liberty, I acted as I Concluded I Ought to Do, Pushing Every work as Thoro'ly as I Could,—And in stead of Forming a Magazine for My Self. If you were to See Me Now, Entertaind of Courtisy, without Subsistence, allmost Grown shabby in Cloths, Dejected &c, what I Care Not to Mention; you would be Mov'd to hasten My Relief, in a Manner Suitable to that Regard you were Allways pleased to show for me.

I Was Sir Just on the brink of Returning, and that of Meer Necessity, when Like life From the Dead I Recd your last, with My Ld Treasurers Letter;[2] But Sir Hitherto, his Ldships Goodness to Me, Seems like Messages from an Army to a Town besieged, That Relief is Comeing; which heartns and Encourages the Famished Garrison, but Does not Feed them; and at Last They Are Obliged to Surrender for want, when perhaps One week would ha' Delivred them.

What shall I farther liken my Case to? Tis like a Man hang'd, Upon an Appeal, with the Queens Pardon in his Pocket; Tis Really the Most Disscourageing Circumstance that Ever I was in; I Need Not Tell you Sir that this is Not a place to Get Money in.[3] Pen and Ink and Printing will Do Nothing here. Men Do Not live here by Their Witts— When I look on my present Condition, and Reflect that I am Thus, with my Ld T . . . . s Letter promiseing Me an Allowance for Subsistence in My Pocket, and Offring me Comfortable Things, Tis a Very Mortifying Thought that I have Not One friend in the World

---

[1] He had received £40 in April (Bell to Harley, *H.M.C. Portland*, iv. 402).

[2] Neither letter has come to light.

[3] Cf. the rosy accounts of his business dealings reported in the *Review* for 29 Mar. 1707.

to Support me Till his Ldship shall think Fitt to begin That allowance.

The prayer of this Petition Sir is Very Brief, That I may be helped to wait, or that you will please Sir to Move my Ld T . . . r That Since his Ldship has thought Fitt to Encourage Me to Expect Assistance in Order to Serve the Governmt in this place;—his Ldship will be pleased to Make Such steps Towards it, as may prevent My being Oblig'd to abandone an Employ of Such Consequence, to My Own Ruine and the loss of the Capascity I am Now in of Doeing his Ldship Service.

I Need Say No More to Move you to This Sir. I entreat a speedy Reply and Supply to

Sir, Your Faithfull Tho' Discouragd Servt
D F

Sept. 11. 1707

MS.: Duke of Portland, Defoe Papers, 1 ff. 192–3. *Pub.*: *H.M.C. Portland*, iv. 444–5. *Address*: 'To The Right Honble Robert Harley Esqr., Principall Secreta of State, Present.' *Endorsed*: 'Edenburg, Sept: 11: 1707, R̸ Sept.: 17.'

118. *To* ROBERT HARLEY. *18 September 1707*

Sir

My Impatience Urged me to Write a Long and Importunate Letter Two Posts Agoe. I would Not be Construed that I Doubt your Concern for me, but fear you Are Not Sencible of my Incapacity of Waiting As I am Circumstanc'd in This Remote place.

I Do Not in the Least Doubt but you will So far Carry On what in your Meer Goodness to Me you have begun, As to Move My Ld T . . . . r to Remembr me, and I will be Easy in Depending On it, That I shall Not be Obliged to Make a Dishonble Retreat from a place where I have work't my Self Into a Capascity of Serving both Countryes; I Therefore Give you No More Trouble of That Sort Tho' hard press't &c.—

It would be of Service if I Could kno' perticularly how the Affair of the Wines stands, that I might Mannage the Clamor of the people here as Much to Advantage as possible; you will Depend Safely On its being Cautiously Used.

We are Taken Up with a Discourse of Severll people Landed in the West of scotland From France, and Capt Murray[1] is Apprehended. The Council Are Sitting On it to Day and I

[1] Robert Murray, a Jacobite emissary from St. Germains. See Gassion to Harley, *H.M.C. Portland*, iv. 456–7.

Doubt not you Will be Rightly Accquainted with the perticulars. I hope There is Nothing Dangerous in Agitation yet, But I Must Own and have Often Thought to hint it; The humors of That party Are at present Undr Such fermentation, So Encouraged by the successes of The French, and So Unhappily Back't by the Common Disgust, that should the K of France but support them, *Not with Men for they Need them Not,* but should he send About 200 Officers, Arms and Amunition, Artillery &c. to furnish them, & about 100000 Crowns in Money, he might soon Get Together 12 or 15000 stout fellows & Do a great Deal of Mischief. Nor is it so Much the Inclination of the Men As the Money Disperst among the Landlords, the Lairds, & Jacobite Gentry That would bring them in and The Men Follow of Course.

I Confess this would be a Very Fatall Diversion As things stand here Now, and I hint it because tis a juncture in which it would be of Worse Consequence than Ever with Respect to Other parts of the World.[1]

I am, Sir, Your Most Obedt Servt
D F

Sept. 18. 1707

MS.: Duke of Portland, Defoe Papers, 1 ff. 194–5. *Pub.*: *H.M.C. Portland,* iv. 449. *Address*: 'To The Right Honble Robert Harley Esqr., Principal Secreta of State, Present.'

119. *To* ROBERT HARLEY. *29 September 1707*

Sir

When I Read Over Sometimes My Ld Tr . . . . s Letter which I Carry in My Pocket, I Think 'tis Impossible I should be in the Case I am, Since Therein his Ldship Mentions That he knows my Necessitys.

I Can not but Think it hard to be left So in a Strange place, and where I speak with Out Vanity I had Made my Self Capable of Doing Ten Times More Service than I or any Ten Can do by New Measures; Why the Service as well as the Man is So forgotten is Not for me to Enquire.

I Bless God Sir I have Never been Driven to Importunitys with My Friends, and were I in England, tho' I have Miss-

[1] The war had been going badly all the year. Almanza had been lost, and with it all hope of taking Spain; the elaborate design to capture Toulon had met with dismal failure; and Marlborough had neither won a battle nor captured any place of importance. While Britain, the Netherlands, and Austria sank into divisions and jealousies, the fortunes of France and Spain had steadily risen.

fortunes that Crush me, yet I shall Never be So Reduc't as to sollicit Bread, and Sue for Subsistence:

I kno' Sir it is your Supposition that They will Supply me, for you Never would have left me to This, I have too much Experience of your Concern for me. I Humbly Entreat But This Last Favour As the *Coup de Grace* to send me Out of This Torture; Give me your Ordr to Come Away: Ile Ever be your faithfull and Sincere Servt whether Subsisted Or Not. Ile be the Constant Friend of your Family And Intrest, in Meer Remembrance of your past Care of me; It is Sir my Aversion to quit a post I am plac't in by your Ordr and which without your Ordr I Ought not to abandonne; but Sir the Bravest Garrison May be starv'd Out, and It is my Duty to Tell you when I Am Not able to hold out Any Longer.

I had a letter from my Bro: who Tells me you Ordred him to Write to me I should be Supply'd[1] and I had Resolv'd to Come Away the last week but for That letter; I Will make hard shift Till if you please I may have a line in Answer to this. I kno' My Ld T . . . . r will be at New Markett,[2] and if I am left to his Return Tis Impossible for me to wait.

If I do not Come away this Month The Roads will be Impassable, and to Subsist here of my Self the Winter is not for me to pretend to.

Besides Sir If My Ld had Answd his Own Letter and I had Gone On here, I Would ha' proposed my Makeing a Trip up, tho' I had Come post back Again, and had Convinc't you of what Use it had been for me to ha' been Among Our scots Members at the Meeting of the Parliamt.[3]

I beseech you Sir to Believ me that Nothing but Necessity Can oblige me to This; had I been in a Condition, I Would have Conquer'd all Delays with a patience should ha' forc't My Ld to Remember— But it is Not with me as it has been And I Can hold Out No Longer. And tis a Double Affliction to me to Tell you so.

I am, Sir, Your Most Obedt Servt
DE FOE

Wemyss, Sept. 29. 1707

To morrow The Synod of Fi[fe me]ets.[4] I have been Very

---

[1] Davis's letter to Defoe is missing; for his plea to Harley on behalf of Defoe, see *H.M.C. Portland*, iv. 450.   [2] For the races.
[3] The first Parliament of Great Britain was to convene on 23 Oct.
[4] MS. torn.

busye Among the Ministers there for 14 Dayes past—for This I have found to be a Maxim for Mannageing here, If you will form any Thing here it must be by The Ministers— I am Invited to Dine with The Presbytry of *Kircaldy* to day, being the Day before the Synod, And shall have the honor to sit in The Synod the Next Day and Hear all their proceedings; and which is More Than Ever was allow'd to a stranger, have Liberty to give my Opinion in any Case, *tho' Not to Vote, That Can not be*. But you may Judge Sir by This whether I am Not Come a length to Render me Capable to Serve the Intrest, & Tis Great Pity it should be all blasted at Once.

MS.: Duke of Portland, Defoe Papers, 1 ff. 196–7. *Pub.*: *H.M.C. Portland*, iv. 453. *Address*: 'To The Right Honble Robert Harley Esqr., Principall Secreta of State, Present.'

120. *To* ROBERT HARLEY. *31 October 1707*

Sir

According to your Ordr & Directions I wrott to my Ld Treasurer and This Day I had the honor of a Letter From his Ldship in which his Ldship Not Thinking proper to Ordr any person On whom I May Draw, proposes my Bro: whom I sent with my Letter.

Still Sir, My Lord Neither Directs Me when to Draw or how Much. I had Sollicited his Ldship That in Consideration of my Circumstances, family &c, and That I had No Subsistence the Last half year, that his Ldship would give me leav to Draw Something, Leaving the Summe and Time to his Ldship.

Now his Ldship Ordrs me to Draw by my Brother but Gives Me No Ordr Either as to Summe or Time, Trying My Modesty in a manner I Dare Not Venture On.

I am Sir your Humble Petitioner that you will please to Move in my Favour for The advance of That half year— I have Not Dissembled when I have Wrott you of the Difficulties I have been in, And have gotten into Some Debt both here and On Family Account,[1] and if my Ld please to give his Allowance that Retrospect he shall Never find Me Craveing— I have been all the While Upon the spott and Sincerely Dilligent in the Grand work. I leav it to your Goodness and hope you will prevail by your powerfull Intercession.

What my Ld is pleased to give my Brother I have Ordred him to bring forthwith to you, Entreating you will please to give

[1] His daughter Martha had died two weeks earlier.

him your Letter to Mr Bell to Answr it to me, for the Exchecqr
bills have So Supplyed all Exchanges from London Hither, it is
Impossible to Remitt hither, by which you will Observe Sir That
the project of bringing Those bills hither has Answerd No End
here, Not One of Them passing in Paymt but being Imediately
Sent for England, and Even for that Are Now Sold at 2 and
3 per Ct Discount, But of This hereafter.[1]

It is my Humble Opinion That the best way to Make me
Truly Usefull in The affair I am Upon is to have me be 8 Month
here and 3 Months in London Each year, And the One Month
Travailing between, Goeing Various Roads, I shall perhaps do
More Service in Than all the Rest.

I have hinted the Same Thing to his Ldship, and if your
Opinion Concurrs I Could Wish to be Comeing forward Ere
the wayes Are too Deep, and That I may be here Again before
The Assembly Sitts, which is in March.

I Humbly Referr all This to your favour, and Am

Your Most Obedient Thankfull Servt
D F

Octo. 31. 1707

I formerly gave you The Trouble of a Letter About the Mastr
of Burleigh who barbarously Murthered an Inocent poor Man
without Any.[2] Tis a Surprizeing Thing to See That Mad Man
Come home Again, and Goes Unmolested about the Country
Insulting and Threatning the people, & boast he has the Queens
Remission or pardon in his pockett.[3]

MS.: Duke of Portland, Defoe Papers, 1 ff. 198–9. *Pub.*: *H.M.C. Portland*,
iv. 458. *Address*: 'To The Right Honble Robert Harley Esqr., Principall
Secreta of State, Present.' *Endorsed*: 'Edenburg Oct 31: 1707, R Nov: 7:'

121. *To* ROBERT HARLEY. *28 November 1707*

Sir

I have Not the honor of any from you Since My Last, But
I have an Account from Mr Bell That he has your Ordr to
Furnish me with One hundred pound and This post has
Accordingly Remitted it hither— And as This gives New life to
my Affaires, So Sir in Three or Four Dayes I Purpose to Set Out

[1] See No. 125.
[2] Thus in MS.
[3] See No. 105. Balfour was finally brought to trial, but not until 1709. He was
sentenced to death, but escaped from the Tolbooth by changing clothes with his
sister. The sentence was never executed.

for London, and hope to Kiss your hand, and Acknowlege My Engagemts to your Constant Goodness in a Few Dayes, Tho' The shortness of the Dayes and badness of the Way will Make me Longer On The Road Than I would be.

I have little to advise of here. The Vote of Takeing off the Noli prosequi from the Scots Merchants pleases Very well,[1] and My Ld Havershams speech is Laught at by Every body.[2] I am Sorry My being So far off will make me late in giveing my Ld his Due praise, but I shall be Out of his Debt This post.[3]

I am your Most Humble Petitioner to give My Sincerest Acknowlegemt and The Fullest Expressions of Duty and Gratitude That a Mind Deeply Sencible of his bounty Can Imagin to My Ld Treasurer.

As I Come forward I shall Continue to Accquaint my Self of the Circumstances of Every place & The state of Things, and shall do my Self the honor to write On all Occasions.

I am, Sir, Your Most Obedt Servt
D F

Edinb. Novemb. 28. 1707

MS.: Duke of Portland, Defoe Papers, 1 ff. 200–1. *Pub.*: *H.M.C. Portland*, iv. 461. *Address*: 'To The Right Honble Robert Harley Esqr., Principall Secreta of State, Present.'

122. *To* JOHN FRANSHAM.[4] *20 December 1707*

Mr. Fransham,

It is a long time since I had the least hint from any body that you or any of my Friends in Norwich were in the Land of the Living.

I take this occasion to let you know that your old Friend and humble Servt is yet alive in Spite of Scotch Mobs, Swedish Monarchs[5] or Bullying Jacobites and is going to London to

---

[1] Under writs of *devenirunt*, the Scottish traders had been permitted to recover the goods previously seized by the London customs officials but were liable for the duties thereon if the Crown should decide to prosecute. See Luttrell, *Brief Relation*, vi. 237.

[2] Lord Haversham had recounted in the House of Lords the woes and vexations of the nation and had warned that the only remedy lay in changing the Ministry (*Parliamentary History*, xiv. 598–600).

[3] Defoe composed a satirical *Review* against Haversham, in which, through mocking applause of the latter's speech, he defended the statesmanship of Godolphin, Harley, and Sunderland. The paper appeared nine days later, on 6 Dec. The allusion is useful as an example of the lag between the time a *Review* was composed in Edinburgh and the time it was published in London.   [4] See p. 64, n. 2.

[5] On 23 Sept. Luttrell had written: 'The Suedish envoy has complained against D'Foe for reflecting on his master in his reviews of the 9th and 28th of August, and

shew his Face to the worst of his Enemies and bid them defiance.

I took the freedom to write to you from the antient Kingdome
and suppose you receiv'd it[1] but never had the favour of a
return which made me suppose you thought the charge of that
correspondence not worth while.

I should be glad to hear you are well and if it pleases you now
and then to exchange a Scribble as usual with

Your very humble Servt
D. FOE

Gainsbro' Dec. 20, 1707

MS.: untraced. *Pub.*: Francis Norgate, 'Correspondence between De Foe
and John Fransham, of Norwich,' *Notes and Queries*, 5 S, iii (1875), 284.
Address: none recorded.

123. [*To* ROBERT HARLEY]. *5 January 1707/8*

Sir

I have been in Town five Days, but have kept my Self
Incognito, being willing to have My Ld Treasurrs Commands
how to Dispose my Self before I Took any Step of My Own— In
Ordr to This I Sent by my Bro: as I Thot it my Duty to Accquaint
his Ldpp That I attended his Ldpps Pleasure, but have Not yet
had the Honor of his Ldpps Answer.

I Give you This Trouble to Entreat your Intercession with his
Ldpp for an Audience, Since I shall Not be Able to Continue
Long Conceald, And I have No hand to Act or Tongue to speak
Now but by his Ldpps Directions, to whom I Resolv to be Not
Onely a Faithfull but a punctuall Servt. I Ask your Pardon for
This, and Am

Sir, Your Most Obedt Servt
DE FOE

Kingsland[2] Jan. 5. 1707

MS.: Duke of Portland, Defoe Papers, 1 f. 202. *Pub.*: *H.M.C. Portland*, iv.
473. *Address*: none.

2 of September' (*Brief Relation*, vi. 215). He later added that an order had been
sent to Scotland for taking Defoe into custody (vi. 216). Dyer's *News-letter* gleefully
announced that Defoe was to be bound hand and foot and turned over to the
insulted Swedes (Lee, *Life*, 1. [143]). Defoe answered with *Dyers News Examined as
to His Sweddish Memorial against the Review*, Edinburgh; *De Foe's Answer to Dyer's
Scandalous News Letter*, Edinburgh; and the *Review* for 6 Nov. 1707. The matter
thereafter dropped out of sight.

[1] Probably No. 83.
[2] See p. 96, n. 5.

124. *To* ROBERT HARLEY. *10 February 1707/8*

Sir

The Report which fills the Mouths of your Enemies of your being No Longer Sec. of State[1] Allarm'd me a Little I Confess, And Perticularly Brot me to Wait Upon you this Night. Others Sir Compliment you On The Accession of your Good fortune. I Sir Desire to be The Servant of your Worst Dayes, And yet Upon My word Sir I kno' Not whether to Congratulate or Condole. I Think Verily you are Delivred From a Fateague which Never Answer'd the Harrassing you in Such a Manner and the Wasting your Houres in the Service of Those That Understand Not how to Vallue or Reward in proportion to Merit.

Perticularly you Are Delivred from Envy, and I perswade my Self you Are Removed from a Tottering Party That you may Not share in Their Fall.

My Bussiness Sir was Onely in Duty and Gratitude to Offer my Self to you Against all your Enemies. My sphere is Low, but I Distinguish No body when I am speaking of The ill Treatmt of One I am Engag'd to as to you in The Bonds of an Invviolable Duty. I Entreat you Sir to Use me in Any Thing in which I may Serve you, and that More Freely Than when I might be Supposed following your Riseing Fortunes. Tis also my Opinion you are still Riseing— I Wish you as Successfull as I believ you Unshaken by This storm.

I am, Your Most Obedit faithfull Servt

[signature torn off]

feb. 10. 1707

I shall wait On you To Morro' Evening as by your Ordr.

MS.: Duke of Portland, Defoe Papers, 1 ff. 204–5. *Pub.*: *H.M.C. Portland*, iv. 477. *Address*: 'To The Right Honble Robert Harley Esqr., Principall Secreta of State, Present.' *Endorsed*: 'Mr De Foe.'

[1] Harley, backed by St. John and aided by Mrs. Masham, had persuaded the Queen to look with favour on the idea of forming a moderate Tory Government. Godolphin and Marlborough, on the other hand, had capitulated completely to the Whigs. Further co-operation of the two wings within the Cabinet now became impossible; it would have to be either Godolphin's Ministry or Harley's, one or the other. In the first week of February, the Queen made her choice. In spite of the shadow cast upon Harley by the Greg scandal, she elected to drop Godolphin and give Harley his way. But when Godolphin resigned, Marlborough, incensed at what he called 'the treacherous proceedings of Mr. Secretary Harley', resigned too. Even so, a Cabinet meeting was called on Sunday the 8th, the Queen in attendance and Harley prepared to manage its proceedings. But the members refused to transact any business 'as neither the General nor the Treasurer were there'. To end the resulting confusion, Harley and St. John resigned; and Marlborough and Godolphin, Tories or no, returned to a Government now unequivocally Whig. See G. M. Trevelyan, *Ramillies and the Union with Scotland*, 1932, pp. 326–9.

125. *To* ROBERT HARLEY, *20 February 1707/8*

Sir

In Obedience to your Commands I Send you Enclosed The state of the Case in scotland Between the Bank and The People in the Payment of The Equivalent.[1]

I shall allwayes be Glad of an Opportunity to Rendr you Service in This or any Thing in My Power, Sincerely Wishing you Deliverance from all your Enemyes.

I am, Your Most Oblig'd Humble Servt
D F

feb. 20. 1707

[Enclosure]

Of The Paying The Equivalent in Excheq Bills

By The Treaty The Scots were to be paid The Equivalent in Money and The affrican Debt[2] in Perticular was to have Intrest Till it was paid. In all Our Discourses For the Union, Prints without Doors and speeches within, it was an Argumt Used to Inforce the Union Vizt the Great Advantage Scotland would Reap by 400000*l* stock Imediately brot to them Circulateing in specie and Encourageing Commerce &c.

When it Came to be paid 100000*l* Onely was brot in Money & the Rest in Bills. It is True they sent for 50000 more because they saw plainly they Could not do without it.

It is True They did not Force any body to take them. But the Methods used to put them off were a force in Effect and Inconsistent with the Nature of the Union, and farr from that study & Care for the Good of Scotland which was so Much promised and pretended to.

1. Those whose Money was Due were as Much as they Durst Delayed to bring them to take bills, while those that Would Accept them were paid before They were Due.

2. Every One was askt to Take them and prest as far as possible when any person had power or Influence Upon them.

---

[1] The editor of *H.M.C. Portland*, iv, suggested that this letter was written from Edinburgh, and some biographers have therefore concluded that Defoe had left London and was back in Edinburgh by 20 Feb. But Harley's endorsement indicates that the letter must have been written in or near London, and No. 128 shows that Defoe did not return to Edinburgh until the middle of April.

[2] That is, the losses suffered by subscribers to the 'Darien Company', the correct name of which was 'The Company for Trading with Africa and the Indies'.

But the Sending them was Unjust, and the bills in themselves a Fraud put upon the Nation by the Bank.

1st. Because they were payable no where but in London, Nor was there any Such thing as a Runing Cash Set up to Circulate them, which at first might Easily ha' been Done.

2. Because They had no Intrest upon them to the person Recieveing them, whereas by the Treaty Intrest was Due till the money was Recd.

3. The Bank Engrosst the Intrest plac't on the bills by Parliament and put their Credit upon the Scots, which to them was Good for nothing.

4. Whereas Every man that Recd them Could neither have his money in Scotland nor Intrest till paid for they were of no use to any but such as wanted to Remitt to London, which to be sure they would not do with out a Consideration & so they Came to a discount Imediately.

5. No man Could send them Safely to London for neither Coppying them or Wittness of sending them Could secure them but if they miscarryed by post the Money was lost, No second or third bill being to be had as in the Case of bills of Exchange.

Thus the Recievor was Imposed Upon—Scotland Cheated being supplyed with paper not Cash, and the Articles broke in Not giveing Intrest Till paid as by the Treaty.

And after all the End was not Answerd here neither Viz/ of Makeing the bills Circulate in Scotland and Extending the Credit of the Bank, Since they Imediately Dissappeared in Scotland and not One of them is now to be seen, whereas had the Intrest been Running On Upon them One half of them had Remaind there both to the advantage of Scotland and also of the Bank.[1]

MS.: the letter, Duke of Portland, Defoe Papers, 1 ff. 206–7. *Pub.*: *H.M.C. Portland*, iv. 477. *Address*: 'To The Right Honble Robert Harley Esqr., Present.' *Endorsed*: 'Mr De Foe.' The enclosure, Duke of Portland, Harley Papers, 39 ff. 352–3. Hitherto unpublished. *Address*: 'To The Right Honble Robert Harley Esqr., Present.' *Endorsed*: 'concerning paying the equivalent in Scotland, R̸ Feb: 21: 1707/8.'

[1] The substance of these remarks, somewhat enlarged upon, appears in *History of the Union*, pp. 590–2.

126. To THOMAS BOWREY.[1] [*9 March 1707/8?*][2]

Tuesday night

Sir

I have yours of the 8th Instt in which you Desire a Meeting with me to Advise &c. On something you have to propose.

You Can Not Take it ill Sir That being wholly a stranger to you And My Self a Person Not without Enemyes,[3] I make Some little stipulations before hand, after which I shall show all Readyness to give you The best advice or Assistance I Can.

If Sir you please to Communicate in Writeing Anything of the bussiness you Design to propose to me by which I may judge whether I am able to Render you any Service or not.[4]

Or If you please to Call as you Come to the Exchange at Waits Coffee house in Bell yard in Grace Church street and let the Mistress of the House know when and where you would meet and but in the least give a knowlege of your person, I will wait on you as you shall Direct.

[1] Thomas Bowrey (1650?–1713), Younger Brother of Trinity House, had been a seafaring man in his younger days and was now a London trader and shipowner. Bowrey had owned part of the cargo of the *Worcester* when that ship was seized by the Scots in 1704, a retaliatory act that culminated in the notorious 'Captain Greene Affair'. For years he busied himself in continual efforts to recoup the losses suffered by himself and his partners in that unfortunate and politically explosive incident. Defoe told the story of the *Worcester* in his *History of the Union*, pp. 78–83. Later, both Defoe and Bowrey advised and encouraged Harley during the formation of the South Sea Company (Nos. 168, 169, and 170; and Brit. Mus., Add. MSS. 28,140). See also J. R. Moore, *Defoe in the Pillory and Other Studies*, Bloomington, Indiana, 1939, pp. 147–54.

[2] This letter was written on the 'Tuesday night' preceding what Defoe in the following letter calls 'March 14. 1708.' Was the year 1707–8 or 1708–9? Ordinarily one would incline towards 1708–9, for Defoe usually reckoned the year from 25 Mar. But if the two Bowrey letters belong to 1708–9, then this first one must have been written on Tuesday the 8th, and its first sentence, acknowledging Bowrey's 'of the 8th', sounds odd. Would Defoe have used that phrase if he was himself writing on the 8th? If, however, one assumes that by '1708' Defoe meant 1707–8, the difficulty disappears. In that year 'Tuesday night' would have been 9 Mar., and the opening of this letter is what we might expect. See A. W. Secord, 'Defoe in Stoke Newington', *PMLA*, lxvi (1951), 214–15.

[3] His London enemies are mentioned but not identified in No. 122.

[4] Accompanying the MS. letters are some notes on Juan Fernandez in Bowrey's hand. Sir Richard Temple wrote that 'the business about which Bowrey wished to see Defoe was no doubt concerning the island of Juan Fernandez' (*Notes and Queries*, clx [1931], 39). But there is no evidence that Bowrey's notes have anything to do with his request for the interview. His business with Defoe remains unknown.

You will Excuse my being thus Cautious, for which I shall give you Very sufficient Reasons when I see you. Interim I am

Sir, Your Most Humble Servt

DE FOE

MS.: Dr. Henry C. Hutchins, New Haven, Conn. *Pub.*: R. C. Temple, 'Daniel Defoe and Thomas Bowrey', *Notes and Queries*, clx (1931), 39. *Address*: 'To Mr Tho: Bowrey, In Marine Square Near Goodmans Fields.'

127. *To* THOMAS BOWREY. *14 March* [*1707/8?*][1]

Sir

I Wrott you a line Or Two last week in Answer to yours and being wholly a stranger to you Desir'd a word Or Two of your affair.

But I Am So Well Satisfyed Since in your Character, That Hearing you have been Indisposed I give you This trouble to Let you kno', I shall be Very Ready to Meet you where you please, in Ordr to do you Any Service I am Capable of,—and if your Illness Continues So as to Make your Comeing Abroad Inconvenient, Tho' I have not a great Deal of Time to Spare, yet Rather Than your bussiness you have to propose should Suffer by Delay, Il make No Difficulty to Wait on you at your House.

I am, Sir, Your Very Humble Servt

DE FOE

Newington March 14. 1708

MS.: Dr. Henry C. Hutchins, New Haven, Conn. *Pub.*: R. C. Temple, 'Daniel Defoe and Thomas Bowrey', *Notes and Queries*, clx (1931), 39. *Address*: none.

128. [*To* SIDNEY GODOLPHIN, EARL OF GODOLPHIN].[2]
20 April 1708

My Lord

I forbear to Trouble your Ldpp with any Account of the Severest Journey That Ever man had, Onely as it will I hope

---

[1] See p. 253, n. 2.

[2] On the advice of the fallen Harley, Defoe had applied to Lord Treasurer Godolphin for a continuance of employment in the service of the Government. Godolphin had received him kindly, arranged for the continuance, and presented him 'for the second time' to the Queen (*Appeal to Hononr and Justice*, in *Later Stuart Tracts*, pp. 78–79). Although Defoe's subsequent correspondence with Godolphin is almost entirely lost, his new duties were presumably similar to the old— to act as an intelligence agent, especially in the North. Scotland was far from calm, and the attempted invasion by the Pretender had been beaten off only a few days before Defoe set out from London for his return. He took with him the following

be my Most Just Excuse to your Ldpp For being So long On the Road; The Continued Rains for the First Eight dayes, and the Depth of The Wayes all the length, Made it Almost Impossible for me to Come faster, Rideing my Own horse, One of which I have been Oblig'd to Leave behind Me.[1] I am the More Concern'd at it because I do Not Use to be a slow Messenger, And hope your Ldpp shall Not find me a slothfull Servt.

The Assembly had been Sat Down Two days when I Came,[2] So I Need Not Accquaint your Ldpp That Mr Carstares[3] was Chosen Moderator. But I May Note That it may be Taken by your Ldpp as a Signall of The Good Temper here, That people are pleased Generally with the Election of That Gentleman, Tho' they Never liked him before; His Moderate principles, his Temper and Caution, were allways offensiv to Those that Could Not Imitate him.

I Need Not give your Ldpp his Character, But Crave leav to add Her Majtie has in him a Faithfull and Above most Men here a Capable subject.

I Have Made but Few Observations yet, but I Think by what I have Observ'd I find The Ministers in better Temper Than Formerly, and the forbearing to Offer the Abjuration Oath to them has this Good Effect, That it Deprives those That would ha' Clamour'd, and Love it, of their Expected Occasion.[4]

I am pressed by a private Message to Visit my Ld Beilhaven in the Castle.[5] I have been in Doubt whether I should go or No, but as I Can Not Tell the Occasion, and am sure I shall Either

note from Godolphin, dated 22 Mar., to the Earl of Leven: 'My Lord, I give your lordship the trouble of this letter by the bearer, Mr. De Foe, only to recommend him to your protection as a person employed for the queens service in Scotland relating to the revenue, etc., by, my lord, your lordships most humble and obedient servant, Godolphin' (Sir William Fraser, *The Melvilles, Earls of Melville, and the Leslies, Earls of Leven*, Edinburgh, 1890, ii. 217).

[1] The horse fell lame at Coventry and had to be replaced. The incident gave rise later to a printed attack on Defoe's honesty entitled, *A Hue and Cry after Daniel Foe and His Coventry-Beast*, 1711, to which Defoe replied in the *Review* for 10 May 1711.

[2] The Assembly convened on 15 Apr. (Glasgow to Mar, *H.M.C. Mar and Kellie*, p. 437).

[3] See p. 193, n. 3.

[4] See Carstares to Harley, *H.M.C. Portland*, x. 351.

[5] Belhaven had been unjustly charged with complicity in the recent attempt to restore the Pretender. Defoe visited his former adversary, came to like him, and at the time of his death wrote a generous vindication of his character in the *Review* for 10 July 1708. Included in that eulogy, and in the *Review* for 15 July, are fragments of their correspondence, none of which otherwise survives.

Make a Right Use of it, or no Use at all, I Purpose to see his Ldpp, And shall Not fail to let your Ldpp kno', if it be worth while, what his Mighty bussiness Can be. I shall not fail on all Occasions to Accquaint your Ldpp with Every Thing that Appeares worth your Ldpps Note.

> I am, May it Please your Ldpp
> Your Ldpps Most Obedt Servt
> DE FOE

Edinb. Aprll 20th 1708

MS.: Lt.-Col. F. D. E. Fremantle, Bedwell Lodge, Hatfield, Herts. *Pub.*: Wright (1931), pp. 153–4. *Address*: none.

129. *To* CHARLES SPENCER, EARL OF SUNDERLAND.[1]
20 May 1708

According to your Lordship's orders to apply myself to your Lordship by Mr. Shute,[2] I did the first post after my arrival here write at large to him, to which I humbly refer. But, my Lord, according to the liberty I humbly crav'd of your Lordship, and which I had your Lordshipp's permission in, I entreat your Lordshipp's pardon and patiences while I lay before your Lordshipp impartially and in a manner I care not to trust but with your Lordshipp the particular observations I have made on the state of this miserable nation I am in. I cease troubling your Lordshipp with apologies and circumlocutions. I kno nothing can be more agreeable to your Lordshipp or more useful to the publick services than plain, naked, and unbyasst accounts both of persons and things, and your Lordshipp shall always find me endeavouring to act the honest rather than the artfull part in my accounts. I know, my Lord, all the accounts are full of the steadyness of the people here, especially the Presbyterians, and of those more particularly the west, and it is very true in the gross that it is so, nor is it without its uses to magnifye those reports, and much noise I have made about it myself, and much more praise I give them for it here, which I find they are fondest to hear who are most conscious they do not merit it. But, my Lord, when I view more narrowly the past

[1] Charles Spencer (1674–1722), third Earl of Sunderland, son-in-law of the Duke of Marlborough, and member of the Whig Junto, was Secretary of State for the Southern Department. When he was dismissed from office in 1710, Defoe eulogized him in three issues of the *Review* (17, 20, and 22 June). For later relations between Defoe and Sunderland, see Nos. 233, 234, and 238.

[2] John Shute (1678–1734), later Lord Barrington, was a Commissioner of the Customs and a political emissary of the Whigs.

circumstances of the invasion,[1] when I see how much of the present principle has its foundation in the success, how it was procured, how shallow it lyes in the affection of the people, how little of the out-of-humour principle is removed by it, how blind, how prejudiced, and how much averse to English government a large party even of our friends are here, I cannot but say the bauk the French have received here is a double deliverance, and it is yet unknown in the greatest part of Britain what in this success we are delivered from. I am not treating now, my Lord, of the Jacobite interest here; for though it be in its turn formidable, yet it is visible, it is known, it is to be provided against by open measures, viz., forces and the iron hands of the law. But, my Lord, these poor honest but ill-natured imposed upon people are to be managed another way. They really merit the compassion of the Government, as they are ignorant, abused by others, and led by a certain je ne sçay quoy of temper into violent extremes; yet I must acknowledge they merit some concern from the Government. I mean as to keeping them within bounds, and this with respect to publick safety. It is most certain, my Lord, that there are party here who have always served themselves of this infirmity of these people, and, the Government having no agents among them, have wheedled them into several excesses, of which the tumult at Glasgow was a manifest example.[2] The diligence of this party, my Lord, is but too successful, and has but too much matter to work upon. In the affair of the Union, they influenced them by a great varyety of suggestions needless to repeat to your Lordshipp; the radicated aversion to Episcopacy and to the English were the toppicks then. The like aversions to the Union are the foundation now, and I am sorry to say, my Lord, this aversion to the Union had politickly enough been improv'd by that party 'till it had wrought the poor people up to a kind of neutrallity, a thing as fatal itself as a direct opposition, and it began to be the general answer in the case of the invasion. That it was the effect of this Union, that it lay between the English and the French, and let them fight it out. There was nothing for the honest people, as they call themselves, to do in it. While they were encreasing in this temper of neutrallity, and perhaps were come to a greater

---

[1] In March the French had attempted unsuccessfully to land the Pretender and 5,000 troops near Edinburgh in the expectation of rousing the Jacobite countryside, placing James on the throne, and breaking the Union.

[2] See *History of the Union*, pp. 266–80.

hight in it than your Lordshipp would imagine possible, the French appeared. What temper then began to shew itself, there was so little time between the appearing of the French and Sir Geo. Bing, *being but one afternoon*, that little judgment can be made, and yet here are honest people to be found who speak of it with concern enough. Now my Lord, as I am far from accusing this people, so I think your Lordshipp, who I kno will make a prudent use of it, ought to be informed of the most exact and nicest part of this affair, and to kno who are the friends of Her Majesty's interest, and who the friends of her prosperity only. Two things have effectually turned the scale here. Success principally and the diligence of the Ministers. And I take the liberty to assure your Lordshipp that the strength of Her Majesty's interest in this country depends upon the Ministers, of which I have opportunity to give your Lordshipp other instances hereafter. But in this case it is remarkable to observe what diligence they used to awaken the abused people, going from house to house and engageing them under their hands and opening their eyes to the delusion they had been under, 'till in some parishes where they had been ready to stone their ministers for praying for the Queen they became the most forward against the enemy. And yet, my Lord, these are the men who will refuse the Abjuration,[1] and tho' firm in Her Majesty's interest yet can not get over their scruples on that account; from whence, and my observation of the Jacobites complying with the Abjuration, I humbly offer your Lordshipp this Northern Paradox, that her Majesty is in danger from those that take the Abjuration and safe in those that refuse it. I am not pleading merit when I take the freedom to assure your Lordshipp I am not idle, and I hope not unsuccessfull in clearing up the doubts and opening the eyes of these good but out-of-humour people. Here is now a new scene of office opened, viz., of elections of members for the Parliament, and in this there are some perfect novelties of conduct, *mysteria politica*, that are hard to understand. The Squadron, and as they call them here the Court party, acting against one another.[2] My Lord, I own I may at this distance

[1] See No. 88.

[2] The first general election for Scottish Members to a British Parliament was to be held in June. (Scottish representatives to the first Parliament of Great Britain, which had met during the previous winter, had been elected by the Estates.) The English Whigs, directed by Sunderland, were seeking to capture the entire Scottish representation. They won the support of Hamilton, arranged for the release of the Jacobites suspected of complicity in the 'invasion', and tightened their relations with the Squadrone (Mathieson, *Scotland and the Union*, p. 288). For the 'Court'

take wrong aim, but if the gentlemen called the Squadrone here act from a right principle, then the best meaning people here are quite wrong; for there is certainly an error in design or in conduct, that party now setting up Tories on the foot of their party in several places against the honestest gentlemen and truest Whigs in the nation. I am cautious of enlarging on this head, 'till if possible your Lordshipp will be pleased to signifye either directly, if I may obtain that honour, or by any hand that your Lordshipp think fit, that this reaches your Lordshipp's hands. According to what I hinted to your Lordshipp I have writt of this [to]¹ my Lord T——r, yet I humbly refer to your Lordshipp my former entreaty that your Lordshipp will be pleased not to communicate to my Lord the favours I have received from your Lordshipp, least perhaps it may cool the inclination my Lord T——r has been pleased to express of doeing something for me. I presume that Her Majesty's interest is the same in the hands of my Lord T——r, and your Lordshipp, and that it can not be offensive to either that I give equal hints of things of this nature; nor have I any reason for the caution but what I nakedly and honestly give your Lordshipp, for which I beg your Lordshipp's pardon, and am, may it please your Lordshipp, your Lordshipp's most humble and obedient servant.

D E F O E

Edinburgh, May 20, 1708²

MS.: untraced. *Pub.*: *H.M.C. Eighth Report*, Pt. 1, 1881, pp. 48–49. *Address*: none recorded; the *Eighth Report* names Sunderland as the addressee.

130. *To* CHARLES SPENCER, EARL OF SUNDERLAND.³
25 May 1708

My Lord

I have Endeavord to Pay the Debt of Correspondence to your Ldpp by the Method your Ldpp Directed, Viz: by Mr shute,⁴ but have not the favor of a line from him, to Signifye The Receipt of it, which Makes me fear it is Not Come to his hand.

view of these machinations, see the letters of Godolphin, the Queen, Mar, and Nairne in *H.M.C. Mar and Kellie*, pp. 445–54. For Defoe's remarks on the confused state of Scottish political parties, see the *Reviews* for 22 and 24 June 1708.

¹ *H.M.C.* editor's brackets.

² Date supplied from caption in *H.M.C. Eighth Report*.

³ *H.M.C. Eighth Report* names Sunderland as the addressee. Later, dealers who handled the MS. came somehow to describe it as being addressed to Godolphin; but the text is sufficient evidence that the Lord Treasurer, who is prominently mentioned therein, cannot have been the addressee.

⁴ See p. 256, n. 2.

Yet I Could Not Satisfye my Self with Neglecting My Duty to your Ldpp on So Weak an Excuse, and therefore Resolv'd to write Directly to your Ldpp; and On This head I Wrott your Ldpp the Enclosed.[1]

Now you will Pardon My Weakness my Ld in This. Were I keeping a Foul, and False Correspondence between this part and England; or Serving Two masters, which would in Effect be betraying One, I should want to Engage Either Side to Secresie; But my Ld, My strait is of Another kind, and I find No Remedy for it but in An Open, Candid, and honest stateing the Case to your Ldpp, and Depending On your Ldpps Generous Care for me, of which I have had Sufficient Testimoney.

I have Since my Comeing hither from Time to Time Given My Ld Treasurr an Account of affaires here, in Such a Manner, as I perswade my Self shall be, Exact as to Truth of Fact, usefull to His Ldpp, and For the Good and Advantage Even of this Country too; and I have the honour and Satisfaction of his Ldpps Approveing my thots on those things.

I have No Reason to Doubt but his Ldpp Finding me faithfull, and Capable, will as he shall Think I Merit, Considr Either my Services or Circumstances; and I leav that Entirely to God and his Ldpps Goodness.

But when I write to your Ldpp as per the Enclosed, and Sollicit your Ldpp not to Comunicate the Secret of my writeing to your Ldpp, which looks as if Something Clandestine was acting, a thing which in all my life I Thank God I have abhorrd, it has shock't my Sending it without this Explanation, and that has kept me from forwarding it for Some Dayes.

I Doubt not but my Ld T . . . . r may have Comunicated to your Ldpp what I have wrott, and I kno' your Ldpp and my Ld T . . . r are in One Intrest, and both Entirely in the Intrest of England, the Same Intrest of Truth, Liberty, & Peace, which all Good Men love, and Equally Honour your Ldpps for; and Therefore all my Caution my Ld in this Case (shall I acknowledge it) has been my Own Intrest, a Thing Till Now I Confess I Never Persued, and My Distress has been Ever, I hope your Ldpp will not Let it be said I speak it with more Ingenuity than Discretion; That My Ld T . . . . r supposeing your Ldpp Supports me, I Should Decline what otherwise his Ldpp may Design to Do for me, Or your Ldpp Supposeing my Ld T . . . . r —&c., Vice Versa. I need say no More, but begging your

---

[1] The preceding letter.

Ldpps Pardon I Venture the Enclosed, and layeing my Self at your Ldpps Feet, Recomend me Onely for So Much Tenderness in this Case, as your Ldpp shall Think I Merit:

I have but One humble Petition to Close This Matter with, that if it be Acceptable to your Ldpp that I should Continue to Represent the affaires of this Country to your Ldpp, in the best Manner I Can, your Ldpp will be pleased, Either by a Servant, *if Not doeing me the Honor of a Line from your Ldpp,* Directed to Robt Davis[1] at the post house in Edinb. to signifye in two Words the Receipt of this and what Elce your Ldpp pleases to Command.

  Your Ldpps Most Obliged Humble and Obedient Servt
DE FOE

Edinb. May. 25. 1708

P S I have Some Other things of Consequence to Comunicate to your Ldpp after I have the honor to kno' that this Comes Safe to your Ldpps hands.

MS.: The Rosenbach Company, Philadelphia and New York. *Pub.*: *H.M.C. Eighth Report*, Pt. 1, 1881, p. 49. *Address*: none.

131. *To* SIDNEY GODOLPHIN, EARL OF GODOLPHIN.
3 August 1708

My Lord

In My Last I Noted to your Ldpp the good Use I hope I have been Makeing of the humour of the people, here Raised by the Two public Acts of the Governmt, *One* the Proclamation for a Thanksgiving,[2] *the Other* the letter to the Royal Burghs, Expressing the Care Taken of their ships, persuant to which the ship *Norwich* is Come in From the Bar of Tinmo[3] to Convoy their ships thither for London or the Baltick.

I Think Verily Such small things as these will in Time bring This People to Much better Temper, than they have Ever yet shown, & I shall not Cease to Improve it all I Can to Their Conviction.

I Have Often Hinted to your Ldpp that the Squadr.[4] have Really Little or no Intrest here. I think tis Discovred More

---

[1] Defoe's brother-in-law.

[2] A public thanksgiving for the victory at Oudenarde and for the defeat of the attempted invasion of Scotland was appointed for 19 Aug.

[3] Tynemouth.

[4] The Squadrone Volante, now allied with the extreme Whigs against Godolphin (*Review,* 14 Sept. 1712).

Evidently in this, than in Any thing, that One May Perciev A kind of Uneasyness Among the best Sort of People here, least they should carry their Point in England; which Apprehensions Chiefly Rise from the Generall Notion they spread Among the people here, that All the Whigs in England are With Them; and that The queen must Come undr *their Mannagemt*, as they Rudely Call it; and which they gather from Letters, which they basely shew'd About here, of which I formerly hinted Something to your Ldpp; both of things and Persons.

Now They Talk Loudly of a Letter from the Earl of Orkeney[1] From the Army which Reflects Upon the D of Marlbro' with Respect to Delays Since the Battail; and in which They Say, there is an Expression to This Purpose, That at last there is a Detachmt Sent to the Frontiers, of about 15000 Men, but if it had been 5000 More, he Could have gone to the Gates of Paris with them, But Complains they Are both *too few*, and Sent *too late*;[2] I am in hopes to Obtain all the perticulars of the Letter, for they Make Nothing a Secret here, and this Insolence, My Ld, Makes the people here Apprehensiv; for while I have assur'd your Ldpp they have no Intrest, and Are Not beloved here, it is a Very just Consequence, that while Their Success is in prospect, they will be feared in proportion, and Indeed the honestest and best and Most Sencible people here, Are affraid of them, and Very Uneasy About them.

On the Other hand, it is Not Very Easy to Express to your Ldpp, what Use They Make of this Letter, and How they Vallue themselves Upon it; And I am Confident (According to what I formerly Noted to your Ldpp of that Gent. Upon whom They Depend Very Much for Makeing a Party by him in the Army)[3] —I say I am Confident they shall Never Want a Missrepresenter of his Graces proceedings On Every Occasion,— This I thot Very Proper to Lay before your Ldpp, for his Graces perticular Service.

They Made Their Cavils at the Victory[4] a Great while Their

---

[1] George Hamilton (1666–1737), first Earl of Orkney, Lieutenant-General under Marlborough, and Scottish representative peer, had been prominent in the recent victory at Oudenarde.

[2] This passage has been used as evidence that after the battle of Oudenarde, Orkney 'advocated, in opposition to Marlborough, an immediate advance on Paris' (*D.N.B.*). But Marlborough too wanted to march on Paris; it was Prince Eugene who opposed the plan and persuaded Marlborough to abandon it (G. M. Trevelyan, *Ramillies and the Union with Scotland*, 1932, pp. 366–8).

[3] Probably the Duke of Argyll.

[4] Defoe reported some of these 'cavils' in the *Reviews* for 29 and 31 July 1708.

shift, and Now that grows stale, Now they Are Raiseing Exceptions to the Conduct of the Duke, and both Carry On the Same Cause.

And here My Ld I Crave Leav to Offer your Ldpp Another Observation Purely My Own, and your Ldpp will be judge whether it be just or Not. It Seems at This Time My Lord Very prejudiciall, that The public News Men Perticularly the Dayly Courant, and the Post boys, and a post script[1] by the flyeing post, Are Suffred to Translate the Blusters and Form'd storys, which the Paris Gazette, the Mercure Gallant, and Gazette a la Main, spread Over the World.

Without Question My Lord, it would be of No little Use if *a True Account* of Things as we have them, Could be allowed to be printed *in Paris*, and it is Most Certainly of Use to them, that the Glosses they put on their Actions, and which Serve to Delude and Hoodwink their Own people, should be spread Among us; where they want Not Emissarys to Make a Use of them, Pernicious Enough to the publick peace.

I Remember Some yeares ago an Attempt was Made to Translate the Paris Gazette, and I was Offred an Annuall Summe to do it, but it was Supprest by the Governmt; Now My Ld your Ldpp will allow, that the Governmt in Vain Supprest the publication of that paper, if the Dayly Courant shall in Every paper Translate Such paragraphs as Serv their Cause; —for the Author and proprietors of that paper Are known to be of that Party.[2]

If it be Objected that those papers Can Not be Suppresst, I shall presume to Say of my Own knowledge—They are a Club of 20 Booksellers, who are Concern'd in that paper, and whose Aim is the Gain of it, and if Mr Secretary does but Send for the Author, and Reprimand him for the printing the French News,[3] and Threatn him, Tho' they will not Refrain in Respect to the Governmt, they will for Fear of prosecution, which would both Ruine their paper and Sink the profit of it:—and if Once the Messengr of the press leaves word at the publishers, that the Governmt has Ordred him to prevent the publication, to

---

[1] The *Flying Post* appeared on Tuesday, Thursday, and Saturday mornings; its *Postscript*, a supplement containing the latest news, appeared on the evenings of those days (Stanley Morison, *The English Newspaper*, Cambridge, 1932, p. 68).

[2] The *Daily Courant*, often attacked in the *Review*, was edited by Samuel Buckley, who was a Whig. In later years Defoe and Buckley co-operated in supporting the Whig Ministry of Lord Townshend (No. 234).

[3] When Harley was Secretary he seems to have taken some such action against Buckley. See *H.M.C. Portland*, viii. 245.

prosecute &c., tho' that prosecution would Not do Much, they would Imediately submit, from the Apprehension, and if they did Not it would Ruin their paper.

In One of the last Flyeing Posts which I saw here, They have News from Ghent That all things were Very plentifull and Cheap in the French Camp, and that their Army Encreased Every Day;—when Our Advices from the Army at the Same Time, published that the Enemy were Very Much streightned in their quarters & Found it hard to Subsist.

At least My Ld, this makes the people believ, that the Governmt According to The French Mode, Orders wrong Accounts of Things to be spread abroad, and that these are the Onely True Accounts. I Need Not Observe to your Ldpp what Irreparable Mischiefs this brings Among us here; And how Usefull it is to them Especially at This Time while a Party Among the people are So busy Endeavouring to put false Representations Upon Every public Action. I submitt this Thought to your Ldpps Observation and Am

May it Please your Ldpp

Your Ldpps Most Obedt And Faithfull Servt

DE FOE

Edinb. Augt 3. 1708

May it please your Ldpp

I Humbly Ask your Ldpps pardon, for Offering to Remind your Ldpp of My former Request; I Confess I Ought Not to be Impatient But the just Concern which I have layd before your Ldpp for a Desolate family, and Considering I have No Advocate but your Ldpps Meer Goodness to me, these Are powerfull Motives:

I have layn My Ld at the Pool for Deliverance a long Time, But have Ever Wanted the Help Needfull when the Moment for Cure happend; I Most Humbly Seek your Ldpps Help: which with the breath of your Mouth Can Restore the Disstresses of your faithfull Servant, who shall Ever Dedicate his life, and strength, to your Ldpps Intrest and Service.

I Am ut supra

D F

MS.: Yale University Library. *Pub.*: *H.M.C. Eighth Report*, Pt. 1, 1881, p. 44. *Address*: none. *Endorsed*: 'De Foe to the Lord Treasurer, Aug. 3: 1708.'

132. *To* LIEUTENANT-GENERAL JAMES STANHOPE.[1]
8 March 1709/10

Sir,

As it is my misfortune not to have the honour to be known to you, so at this time it may be some loss to the public interest in the affair of Sacheverell, which you are managing (pardon me the word) with so much applause.[2]

I was moved to give you this trouble, Sir, upon my being informed you had sent for some *Reviews* to furnish something of the Doctor's character. But, as I will not deceive you, Sir, in what I am writing, so neither will I in the person writing, and therefore, after asking your pardon for the rudeness of this, I have plainly subscribed my name.

Nothing, Sir, has witheld me from blackening and exposing this insolent priest but a nicety of honour, that I thought it dishonourable to strike him when he was down, or to fall on when he had other enemies to engage. But since his defence is made of false suggestions as to his being for the Revolution, and his character is part of his applause among this rabble, and particularly since I find it necessary to represent him right to those who are his Judges, I chose rather to be impertinent, which I ask your pardon for, than that you should not be let a little way into his character, to the truth of which I will at any time appear and produce sufficient testimony, at the same time running the venture of the indignation of the Doctor and his rabble, with which I am severely and openly threatened.

First, Sir, as to his morals, I do not say there are Members in your House who have been drunk with him a hundred times,

---

[1] James Stanhope (1673–1721), later first Earl Stanhope, was at this time Lieutenant-General, Commander-in-Chief of the British Forces in Spain, M.P. for Cockermouth, and one of the managers appointed by the Commons to conduct the prosecution of Dr. Henry Sacheverell. For later relations between Defoe and Stanhope, see Nos. 233 to 238.

[2] On 27 Feb. had begun the famous trial of Sacheverell, extreme High Churchman and enemy of Whigs, Dissenters, and moderate Tories, who had preached an inflammatory sermon on the previous 5 Nov. To reassert the doctrine of nonresistance on the anniversary of William's landing at Torbay had seemed to the Whig Ministry a seditious threatening of the whole Revolution Settlement and Protestant Succession. No one followed the trial with more interest than did Defoe. Sacheverell had been a principal target of his *Shortest Way with the Dissenters* in 1702. Defoe had been severely punished for a merely ironical statement of the extreme High-Church position. Should Sacheverell now escape punishment for a literal statement of that same position? Defoe's printed attacks on Sacheverell are numerous. See especially the *Reviews* between Dec. 1709 and Apr. 1710, *A Letter from Captain Tom to the Mobb*, 1710, and *A Speech without Doors*, 1710.

and can say enough of that to you, because I know it would be said to press gentlemen to betray conversation. But if you please to converse with Mr. Duckett,[1] a Member of your House, or with Coll. Oughton[2] of the Guards, they will (especially the first) furnish you abundantly on that head (or at least can). Then, Sir, as to his favouring the Revolution, that he has drunk King James's health upon his knees. That he has spoken so scandalously of the Government, that some strangers have asked him if he had taken the oath to the Queen, and being answered by him that he had, have expostulated with him how it was possible either that talking in that manner he could take the oath, or that taking the oath he could talk in that manner.

And lastly (as to the Revolution also) I shall name you two persons: Samuel Eberall of Birmingham,[3] and the minister of Birmingham (I think his name is Smith,[4] but can come to a certain knowledge of the name),—these can make proof even to conviction that in their hearing he said with an oath in the late King William's reign—He (Sacheverell) believed that he (the King) would come to be *De-Witted* and that he hoped he would live to see it.[5]

These words Mr. Eberall affirms he heard him speak and will justify that fact in his tooth. And these things I thought it my duty to acquaint you of, that you may make such use of them as you shall see cause. If I had the honour to know you, Sir, I might give you larger accounts, and if you think it for your service I shall do it when ever you please.

Asking your pardon again for this freedom,

I am, Sir, your most humble and obedient servant,

DE FOE

Newington Near Hackney, March 8, 1709

MS.: missing. *Pub.*: (with excisions) Earl Stanhope, *History of England Comprising the Reign of Queen Anne until the Peace of Utrecht*, 1870, pp. 549–51; (as here given) G. M. Trevelyan, *The Peace and the Protestant Succession*, 1934, pp. 332–3. *Address*: none recorded.

[1] George Duckett, M.P. for Calne. See p. 111, n. 2.
[2] Adolphus Oughton, later M.P. for Coventry, Baronet, and Brigadier-General.
[3] See 'Miscellanea' in the *Review* for 13 Apr. 1710.
[4] I find no record of this name among the Birmingham clergy of the period.
[5] See the *Reviews* for 9 Mar. and 22 July 1710.

133. *To* THOMAS WHARTON, EARL OF WHARTON.[1]
7 April 1710

My Lord

As This is written from a Sincere Principle of Duty, and Respect to your Ldpp, and a just Concern for that honest Cause your Ldpp is So heartily Embark'd in, I hope your Ldpp will Pardon The forwardness and presumtion of The attempt, tho' you Should Not Accept of the Hint.

I am Not goeing to Offer to your Ldpp any Thing that wants Proof or that shuns Sufficient Enquiry. I would Not have Insulted a Person of your Ldpps Character in that Manner. The Design is Not to Speak in the Dark, but to assist Truth to Come into the Light, and offer Something to your Ldpp, for your Ldpps farther and More perticular Enquiry, and Service, and Therefore My Lord I shall Neither Conceal from your Ldpp the Story, Nor who it is That writes it.

I have My Lord Repeated Importunitys from Some people in the North, Men of Honesty and Friends to your Ldpps Intrest, to Accquaint your Ldpp of The following affair. Their Onely Mistake is that they Suppose I have the honor to be known to your Ldpp, which is Their Error as it is my Missfortune, and My Not haveing that honour is the Occasion of My Makeing So Much preamble to your Ldpp, Contrary to My Custome in the World, and for which I ask your Ldpps Pardon.

The Story is This

There is One Cooper[2] a Clergye Man of or Near Leeds, who if Fame Sayes True, is Now or has been Lately, Applying himself to your Ldpp Either to be Entertaind in your Ldpps Service, or to Obtain your Ldpps Favour, and Recomendation to Some Liveing, Or Some Other way to be Employ'd or advanced by your Ldpp; And perticularly it is alleaged that he gets himself Recomended to your Ldpp as a Low Church Man or a

---

[1] Wharton (1648–1715), Member of the Junto and Lord Lieutenant of Ireland, had returned to England in order to push the impeachment of Sacheverell.

No addressee is named in the MS., but the text itself is doubtless sufficient to show that the letter was intended for Wharton. William Hutchinson (1732–1814), the topographer and antiquarian, owned a mass of correspondence addressed to Wharton, among the writers of which appears the name of Defoe (*Gentleman's Magazine*, lxxxiv [1814], 516). This letter may have been in Hutchinson's collection; at least no other letter from Defoe to Wharton is known.

[2] Unidentified, but Cooper may be one of the persons criticized in a letter deploring the conduct of certain Yorkshire clergymen which Defoe had printed in the *Review* for 1 Dec. 1709.

Moderate Man, and as persecuted and Turn'd Out by The Vicar On Account of his Moderation &c.—

Now My Lord The bussiness of This Letter is To give your Ldpp a True Account of the Moralls and Manners of This Man, That your Ldpp May be Inform'd from Unquestioned Authourityes what kind of Person he is; And No body Then questions but your Ldpp knows what Measures to Take Either That the Church May Not be ill Serv'd and Further Reproach't, or your Ldpps Recomendation Dishonour'd, by the Most Scandalous person alive.

And My Lord That your Ldpp May Not Depend Upon My Single Authourity I shall Give your Ldpp his Brief Character in the Words I Recd it, and the persons shall at any Time be produced for your Ldpps Farther Satisfaction.

From Leeds March. 22.

This Scandalous priest his Name is Cooper, he was Seen in the Very Act, Debauching a woman On a Sunday Morning, and perticularly being to Administer the Sacrament the Same Day, and Did also Actually administer the Sacramt in Our Church That Same day (call'd the Old Church in Leeds). Perjury in Severall Cases can be proved Against him, and that in Severall places he has been Discarded as a Common Drunkard, and for his being a Common Swearer Our wholl Town will wittness it.

For these Crymes Our Vicar[1] Turned him Out, and Deny'd him his pulpit, Upon which he is fled to My Ld Wharton for prefermt, and we are told my Lord has given him hopes of a liveing &c.

Thus far my Authors. There is More in My Letters, but I presume This is Enough to prevent your Ldpps being Imposed Upon—and This I Thought it My Duty to Lay before your Ldpp. If your Ldpp pleases to hear any More, or that I should Make farther Enquiry about it, in That, or any Thing Elce for your Ldpps Service I shall Esteem it My Honor to Reciev your Ldpps Commands.

I am May it Please your Ldpp
Your Ldpps Most Humble and Obedient Servt
DE FOE

From Newington Near Hackney
Aprll 7th 1710

MS.: Hyde Collection, Four Oaks Farm, Somerville, New Jersey. *Pub.*: Wilson, *Life*, iii. 121–2. *Address*: none.

[1] John Killingbeck, B.D.

134. *To* JOHN DYER.[1] *17 June 1710*

Mr Dyer

I have your Letter. I am Rather glad to find you put it upon the Tryall who was Aggressor, than justifye a Thing which I am Sure you can Not Approve, and in this I assure you I am farr from Injuring you, and Referr you to The Time when long Since you wrott I was fled from Justice, One Sammon being Taken up for printing a libell,[2] and I being Then on a Journey, Nor the least Charge Against me for being Concern'd in it, by any body but your Letter:— Also Many Unkind personall Reflections on me in your Letter, when I was in Scotland, On the Affair of the Union,[3] and I Assure you when My papers had Not in the Least Mentioned you, and These I Referr to Time and Date for the proof of.

I mention This Onely in Defence of My Last Letter, in which I Said no More of it than to let you See I did Not Merit Such Treatment, and Could Nevertheless be Content to Render any Service to you Tho' I Thot my Self hardly Used.

But to State the Matter fairly between you and I, as writeing for Differing Intrests, and So possibly Comeing Under an Unavoidable Necessity of Jarring in Severall Cases; I am Ready to Make a fair Truce of Honour with you, (Viz) That if what Either party are doeing, or Sayeing, that May Clash with the party we are for, and Urge us to speak, it shall be done without Nameing Eithers Name and without personall Reflections; and Thus we May Differ Still, and yet preserv both the Christian and The Gentleman.

This I Think is an Offer, may Satisfye you I have not been

---

[1] John Dyer, author of the Tory *News-letter* and one of the least responsible of the Queen Anne journalists, had often been attacked by Defoe for both his politics and his inaccuracies. For Defoe's opinion of his adversary before the 'truce' here suggested, see for instance the *Review* for 9 Feb. 1709–10. Dyer wrote his news in accordance with the tastes and opinions of his subscribers and was even suspected of issuing two letters, one Tory and the other Whig (Drummond to Harley, 10 Nov. 1710, *H.M.C. Portland*, iv. 627). His reputation for truth was such that Vellum, in Addison's *The Drummer*, is confident that his master is alive 'because the news of his death was first published in Dyer's Letter' (ii. 1).

[2] In the autumn of 1704 Dyer had written: 'The Weaver [Sammon or Sammen] in Spittlefields that was taken up for dispersing a poem call'd the Address [*Legion's Humble Address to the Lords*] is admitted to Bail by my Ld C. Just. Holt, but his Tenant Mr De Foe is absconded so that a Messenger can't get to speak with him notwithstanding he falsly asserts the contrary in his Review.' See No. 21.

[3] In Sept. 1707, when the Swedish ambassador had taken exception to Defoe's remarks in the *Review*, Dyer had written that Defoe was to be bound hand and foot and turned over to the Swedes (Lee, *Life*, i. [143]).

Desirous of giveing just Offence to you, Neither would I to any Man, however I may Differ from him; and I See no Reason why I should affront a Mans person because I do Not Joyn with him in principle. I please my Self with being the first proposer of So fair a Treaty with you, because I believ as you can Not Denye its being Very Honble, So it is not the less So, in Comeing first from me, who I believ Could Convince you of My haveing been the first, and the Most ill Treated—for Farther proof of which I Referr you to your letters, at the Time I was Threatned by The Envoy of the king of Sweden.

However Mr Dyer, This is a Method Which may End what is past, and prevent what is future; and if Refused, the future part I am Sure can Not Lye at my Door.

As to your Letter, your proposall is So agreeable to me That Truly without it I Could Not have Taken the Thing attall, for it would ha' been a Trouble Intollerable both to you as well as me, to Take your Letter Every post, first From you and then Send it to the post house.[1]

Your Method of Sending to the black box, is just what I Design'd to propose, and Mr shaw will Doubtless Take it of you;[2] if you Think it Needfull for me to speak to him, it shall be Done— What I want to kno', is Onely the Charge, and that you will ordr it Constantly to be sent, Upon hinting whereof I shall Send you The Names— Wishing you Success in all things (your Opinions of the Governmt Excepted)

I am, Your Humble Servt
DE FOE

Newington June. 17. 1710

MS.: Brit. Mus., Add. MSS. 7001 ff. 460–1. *Pub.*: George Chalmers, *Life of Daniel De Foe*, 1785, pp. xiii–xiv. *Address*: 'To Mr J Dyer in Shoe Lane.'

135. [*To* ROBERT HARLEY]. *17 July 1710*

Sir

I can Not but Think that Now is The Time to find Out and Improve Those blessed Mediums of This Nations happyness,

---

[1] In the absence of Dyer's letters and his proposals, this and the following paragraph are obscure. Dottin offers this conjecture: 'De Foe usa d'un autre procédé pour désarmer le plus redoutable de ses adversaires, le journaliste tory Dyer. Celui-ci avait besoin, pour répandre en province sa *Lettre de Nouvelles*, de dépositaires sérieux; De Foe lui offrit ceux de la *Revue*, proposant ainsi d'établir sous sa direction de véritables messageries' (*Defoe*, p. 191).

[2] Neither the black box nor Shaw can be identified.

which lye between The wild Extremes of all Partyes, and which I know you have long Wisht for.[1]

I kno' Sir you are blest with Principles of Peace and Concern for your Country and a True Tast of its Liberty, and Intrest, which are Now Sadly Embarrast.

My Lot (in which your Favour was My Introduction) has been So Much abroad, That I have had but a Small View of Things; yet I have Room Enough to See and Lament Preposterous Conduct On Every Side. I can Not but hope That Heaven has yet Reserv'd you to be the Restorer of your Country by yet bringing Exasperated Parties and the Respective Mad-Men to Their Politick Sences, And Healing the Breaches on both Sides which have Thus wounded The Nation.

If I can be Usefull to So Good a work without the Least View of private advantage I should be Very Glad, and for This Reason I presume to Renew the Liberty of Writeing to you which was Once My honour and Advantage, and which I hope I have done Nothing to forfeit.

My Personall Obligations to you are Very Great, and Can Not be forgotten by me. It would be a Double honour to Me to have my Gratitude Mixt with the Service of My Country.

If you please to Admitt a short Conference On These heads, That honour to me May at Least Issue in My being Rendred More Able to Guide My Self to the publick advantage, which is what I Sincerely Desire to Make The End of all my Actions, and shall Esteem it My Singular advantage to Take Right Measures by your Direction.

I am, Sir, Your Very Much Obliged
Faithfull and Obedient Servt
DE FOE

July. 17. 1710

P S If I May have the honor of a line or any Ordr by your Servt, The bearer shall attend for it as you Shall please to Direct. Be pleased Sir to Direct it To A. Goldsmith[2] as Usuall.

MS.: Duke of Portland, Defoe Papers, 1 f. 208. *Pub.*: *H.M.C. Portland*, iv. 550–1. *Address*: none.

[1] In this period of intense political activity and turmoil at Court, the Queen, encouraged on the one hand by public sentiment and on the other by Harley, Shrewsbury, and Abigail Masham, was forming her new Cabinet, dropping her Whig advisers one by one in favour of Tories. The change was as yet far from complete, but Sunderland had been replaced in June, Godolphin was about to be dismissed, and the fortunes of Harley and the Tories were obviously ascending.

[2] Defoe's pseudonym.

136. [*To* ROBERT HARLEY]. *28 July 1710*

Sir

Since I had the honor of Seeing you, I can Assure you by Experience, I find, That Accquainting Some people They are Not all to be Devoured, and Eaten up—will have all the Effect upon Them Could be wish't for; Assureing Them That Moderate Councils are at the Bottom of all These Things, That the Old Mad Party are Not Comeing in; That his Grace the D of S . . . . . y¹ and your Self &c. Are at the head of This Mannagemt and That Neither have been Mov'd however ill Treated to forsake The Principles you allways Own'd, That Tolleration, Succession or Union are Not Struck at, and They May be Easy as to the Nations Libertys. These Things Make Strong Impressions, and Well Improved May bring all to Rights again.

I Wish for an Occasion to Discourse Farther on These heads when your Leisure will Permitt me That Favour, when I have Also Something to Offer about Ways and Means to prevent the Ruine of the public Credit; and Raise Things Again in Spight of Some peoples Endeavor to Run them Down, In which if I can do any Service I shall Think my Self happy.² I should Enlarge, but Rather Referr it to Discourse, and shall call on your Servt my Self to Reciev your Commands as to Time, promiseing My Self when I have That Honor Again I shall Not break away So Rudely as I did last.

I am, Sir, Your Most Obedt Servt
D F

July. 28. 1710

MS.: Duke of Portland, Defoe Papers, 1 f. 210. *Pub.*: *H.M.C. Portland*, iv. 552–3. *Address*: none.

¹ Charles Talbot (1660–1718), first Duke of Shrewsbury, a Moderate, was Lord Chamberlain. His appointment to that office in the previous April had been the first of the series of changes which by September was to produce a Tory Ministry. 'Yet even now Harley desired not High Toryism but those moderate policies, by the promise of which he had drawn Shrewsbury, Somerset and Newcastle into the plot to overthrow Godolphin and the Junto. On this basis Defoe, who had been serving the Whig Ministry, returned to his old allegiance to Harley as the true "moderate" ' (G. M. Trevelyan, *The Peace and the Protestant Succession*, 1934, p. 67).
² In June City financiers had warned the Queen that if the Ministry was changed, 'all credit would be gone, stock fall, and the Bank be ruined' (Harley to Arthur Moore, *H.M.C. Portland*, iv. 545). A month later, when the dismissal of Sunderland and rumours of a dissolution of Parliament had caused stocks to fall, the alarmed Defoe sprang to the breach, and in a series of *Reviews* running from 13 July to 17 Aug. exhorted, bantered, reassured, and wheedled the public in an effort to restore confidence and stability.

137. [To ROBERT HARLEY]. *12 August 1710*

Sir

I can Not but heartily Congratulate you On the happy Recovery of your Honors and Trusts in The Governmt.[1] Her Majtie is Perticularly just in placeing you in This Station, where you had been So Coursly Treated.

It is with a Satisfaction Sir That I can Not Express, That I See you Thus Establish'd Again; And it was Allways with Regret That when you Met with ill Treatment I found My Self left and Oblig'd by Circumstances to Continue in The Service of your Enemyes.

And Now Sir Tho' I am Sunk by The Change, And kno' Not yet whether I shall find help in it or No, yet I not Onely Rejoyce in the Thing, but shall Convince you I do So, by Publickly Appearing to Defend and Reconcile Things if possible to Open the Eys of a wilfully blind and prejudic't Party.

In Ordr to This Sir, I shall wait on you in The Evening with those sheets I shewed you, finished from the press,[2] and to Lay before you Some Measures I am Takeing to Serve That Honest Principle, which I kno' you Espouse at a Time So Nice, and when Every Man Thinks 'tis in his Power to wound the Government, Thro' the Sides of The Treasury, and to Run Down Their Masters by Running Down The Public Credit.

I Have Two or Three Times Set Pen to Paper to Move you Sir in My Own Case, yet Can Not put on Assurance Enough to do it, Believing Also your Own Generosity, and The former Goodness I have had Such Experience of, will Move you in My behalf.

Providence Sir Seems to Cast me back Upon you (I write that with Joy) and Layes me at your Door; at the Very Juncture when She blesses you with The Means of doeing For me, what your Bounty shall prompt to.

But Sir in Recomending My Self to you, I would fain have an Eye to your Service. I would Not be an *Invalid*, and My hope is, That as you were pleased to Recommend Me to Another, As One That Could be Made Usefull, and who it was worth while

[1] On 8 Aug. Godolphin had been dismissed from the Treasurership. On the 10th Harley was appointed Chancellor of the Exchequer and in the following May he became Lord Treasurer. In the interim the office of Lord Treasurer remained vacant.

[2] Perhaps his *Essay upon Publick Credit*, which was published on 23 Aug. (Lee, *Life*, i. xxxvi).

to Encourage;[1] The Same Argumt will Move you to Entertain The Man your Self, Since your Merit, and The Voice of the Nation, place you in The Same Point, in which you were pleased to present me to Another.

I Cease to press you Upon This head— I shall Study to Make my Self Usefull, and Leav The Rest wholly to your Goodness.

I am, Sir, Your Most Humble & Faithfull Servt

DE FOE

Augt. 12. 1710

MS.: Duke of Portland, Defoe Papers, 1 ff. 212–13. *Pub.*: *H.M.C. Portland*, iv. 562–3. *Address*: none. *Endorsed*: 'Mr D: F:, Augu: 12: 1710.'

138. [*To* ROBERT HARLEY]. *2 September 1710*

Sir

What you were pleased to Say to me Relateing to my Own Perticular, The last time I had the honour to wait on you, has So much goodness in it, and Especially So Much concern for me, that it Extorts my Acknowlegements, tho' I am a man Entirely Void of Ceremoney; That you will be pleased to Move her Majtie on My behalf Sir, I must look upon as an Assurance, That it shall be done; knowing The Queen will Denye Nothing to your Intercession, Especlly when back't with Such Argumts as I hope My Case affords, Such as a Man Entirely Given up to, and I had almost Said Ruin'd in her Majties Service.

I will Say Nothing of being Capable of Serving, willing, faithfull, and in the Affair of the Union Successfull; I leav That Sir to your kindness in Recomending; If I would Move her Majtie in any Part of it, Twould be of a wife, and Six Children[2] allmost Grown up, and Perfectly Unprovided for, After haveing been Stript Naked in That Jayl from whence you Sir were Once pleased to Redeem Me.[3]

What I have Enjoy'd (And that too had its Originall in your kindness) has Constantly gone in Expensiv Travelling, Maintaining Usefull Intelligence abroad, family Subsistance, and a little Clearing of Encumbring Circumstances, Tho' far from finishing that Unhappy work.

This Sir Makes The Step which I Mentioned to you of Almost half a year past Distress me, More Than I am willing to

---

[1] He here alludes to the transfer of his services from Harley to Godolphin after the former had been dismissed from the Cabinet in 1708. See *Appeal to Honour and Justice*, in *Later Stuart Tracts*, pp. 78–79.

[2] Hannah, Daniel, Benjamin, Maria, Henrietta, and Sophia.

[3] See p. 3, n. 2.

Mention,[1] And Really These Things too Much Dissable the Very Capascity of Serving Usefully, and is a great Reason why I Move in This Matter with More Assureance, haveing No Reason Sir to Expect from you any Thing but as it May Render me Servicable to you. Tis with too Much Experience Sir That I Express to you That the Anxieties and Impatience of Perplext Circumstances lessen the Very Capascity of Service, Sink the spirits, and leave Neither the hands Free, or The head Clear, for any Valluable Performance.

I Entreat your Pardon for This Importunate writeing. You May Judge Sir of The Importuneing Circumstance by the Importunity it Self, which you will Easily believ is too Irksome to me, if The Occasion did Not Urge it.

And yet Sir what Ever was the Necessity, I would Not Press upon your Goodness, which has hitherto Allways Prevented[2] me, If I did Not Perswade My Self, That being Once Made Easy, I Might have Some little Merit, to Render the Queens bounty to Me, and yours Also, Rationall; I would Not be an Invalid, and hope still I May Render you Some Service, That may Save me from the Scandall of an Unprofitable Servant; yet I forbear to promise for my Self, Onely This Sir, That I shall Serv both with Principle, and Inclination; which I can Not Say has been So Clear to me, Since I have been Out of your Service, as it was before, and is Now.[3]

I am Convinc't And Thorowly Assur'd, you Sir have in View the True Intrest of your Country, and Think it an Unaccountable blindness, That hides it From Some, who Ought to See it as well as I; This Made me Apply my Self to you, before I Saw your present happy Restoration in View, or indeed Expected it; which Cleares me of worshiping your Fortunes Rather Than your Person; I Perswade my Self Sir it shall be in My Power to assist the honest, but prejudiced people of both Kingdomes, to kno' Their Intrest, and Their Friends, better Than Hitherto They have done: This I Applye My Self to, with all my Might, and begin to Meet with Unexpected Success;[4] But shall Ever be

---

[1] The 'step' remains unexplained.   [2] i.e. anticipated.

[3] Harley, though nominally a Tory, was a professed Moderate who shared Defoe's distaste for faction and extreme measures. It was Harley's moderation, not his Toryism, that Defoe was so willing to support 'with Principle, and Inclination'.

[4] Although the *Review* had supported the tottering Whigs through the weeks of uncertainty, it was by now assuring the public that the new Ministry, regardless of its political colouring, would carry out the national programme very much as the Whigs would have done. See, for instance, the issues for 17, 20, and 22 June

backward in Magnifying My Own Merit, and therefore I Refrain to Say any More of That.

I have Sir Since I have Serv'd (as you kno') Established a Generall Correspondence, and at Some Charge Maintain'd it, by which I have a Fixt Intelligence (I May Say) all Over Brittain, But Especially in the North. I Confess it Grievs me to Think of Letting it Fall, Because I can Not fail of Rendring it Very Usefull to your Service, On Every Occasion, and shall the Next Time I have the honor to wait on you show you a Proof of it.

I Humbly Ask your Pardon for This Long and Pressing Letter. I will no More be Importunate, but Resolving to have my Entire Dependence Upon you, Endeavor to Convince you That I am Entirely

Sir, Your Faithfull Obedient
and Greatly Obliged Servt
DE FOE

Sept. 2. 1710

MS.: Duke of Portland, Defoe Papers, 1 ff. 214–15. *Pub.*: *H.M.C. Portland*, iv. 581–2. *Address*: none. *Endorsed*: 'Mr Goldsmith, Sept: 2: 1710.'

139. [*To* ROBERT HARLEY]. *5 September 1710*

Sir

I would fain be Rendring you Some Service in Returne for the favours I dayly Reciev from you, and This Makes me give you Frequent Troubles of This Nature.

I am Not Insensible That to bring a Certain Party of People to a Sence of Things, (Viz) to be Sensible of Their Need of Friends, and to kno' them, as also to kno' how to Use Them, is a Materiall work, and a Thing which by Degrees May be brought to pass, Tho' it must Not be attempted abruptly and hastily. The people are Out of humour and Allarm'd, and to speak to Them in the Public Paper I write, would be to do no good atall. Yet They should be Spoken to; Even just as Solomon Directs of a Certain kind of People, to whom we should *Answer* and *Answer Not*.

I am Vain of Saying Sir The first Step I Took has been Successfull and has done More Service Than I Expected, in which The Town does me too much Honour, in Supposeing it

and 19, 22, 24, and 26 Aug. 1710. The Whig journalists were furious at Defoe's shift towards support of the new Ministry. See John Oldmixon, *History of England*, 1735, p. 456.

well Enough done to be your Own. I Mean the Essay Upon Credit.[1]

If you Think it proper, I would Offer Another Piece of The Same kind; which I would Call an Essay Upon Loans;[2] in which I Think it May be of Some Service, to Take a Certain people a little off of a Notion, That They can bring The governmt to do what They please, by Refuseing to Advance Their Money; Layeing No Weight Upon The Advantages The lenders Make, and what Need They stand in of Funds. This Sir I promise My Self shall Tend to lessen the Vanity of Some people, who still fancy The Governmt Must be obliged to Change hands Again Merely to Oblige Them, if They do but Exert Themselves by keeping back Their Money.

After This Sir, I Would Offer *an Essay upon Banks*,[3] in which I Would attempt to bring Those Men of Paper to kno' Themselves a little, by shewing how well the Government can do without The Bank, and how ill The Bank can do without the Government. These Things Sir are the Effects of My Constant Study to Render my Self Usefull, in the Low Sphere in which I act; and I Humbly Offer them for your Approbation.

Enclosed I Give you The papers I Mentioned formerly About Edinburgh, and The proposall as I formerly Layd it before the Late Lord Treasurer; I Lay Them before you Sir That you May be Rightly Apprised of That Matter, when the Pick-Pocket proposall of a Dock at Leith shall Come to be Debated,[4] and Doubt not you will be Convinc't That my Scheme is Equally of Service to Scotland, and Onely Saves her Majtie Thirty Thousand Pound in her Pocket; I shall give you farther hints of This kind, when Ever you shall judge it Seasonable.

I am, Sir, Your Most Humble and Obedient Servt

DE FOE

Sept. 5. 1710

Anothr paper of Insolent Queries Appears about To day, and a Most Impudt Ballad[5]— Sure There are printers of These Things and I Fancy I kno' Them too.

---

[1] Three editions and a Dutch translation appeared during the year. A century later the pamphlet was still attributed to Harley in *Somers Tracts*, 2nd ed., vol. xiii, 1815.

[2] Defoe's *Essay upon Loans* appeared on 21 Oct. (Lee, *Life*, i. xxxvi).

[3] No such pamphlet is known.

[4] In April the Corporation of Edinburgh had petitioned the Queen to order the erection of a wet dock and a dry dock at Leith. See J. C. Irons, *Leith and its Antiquities*, Edinburgh, n.d., ii. 146–7.

[5] The paper was probably a broadsheet entitled *Queries* (Brit. Mus., 816. m. 1. [12]), defending the Whig Ministry. Defoe answered it in a broadsheet, not

[Enclosure]¹

Of Improvemts in Scotland

I Lay it down as a foundation Principle upon which all the following Proposals will Depend, That it is the great Interest of England to Study & Promote the Prosperity and Encrease of Scotland.

By the Encrease of Scotland I mean Encrease of wealth and People, And that is Only to be brought about by Encrease of Trade which brings home wealth and Encrease of Employment for the People to keep them at home.

The People of Scotland do not fly abroad and help to People all Europe because this Country is not Equally Fruitfull and Habitable with other Places, but because want of employment at home for the People makes it more difficult for them to Subsist, and therefore they fly abroad.²

If employment for the Poor may be found out, and encouragemt given by raising the Price of Labour and encreaseing Wages, the People will Stay at home. Nay, People will flock thither from foreign Parts, & Scotland may be made as populous as other Nations

If the Number of People Encreased, the Consumption of Provisions would Increase, and as the Value of Labour and rate of Labour shall rise, the Price of Provisions would Rise, and by Consequence land will be Improved and the Estates of Landed men will rise in Proportion.

Improvements Then being Confin'd to these Heads may be Farther Considered—

Improvemts of Trade: By Navigation and foreign Commerce
By Manufacturing and Employing the Poor

hitherto attributed to him, entitled *Counter-Queries* (Brit. Mus., 1850. c. 5. [33]). The 'impudent Ballad' cannot be identified; among the possibilities is *A New Ballad, to the Tune of Fair Rosamond* (Brit. Mus., Cup. 645. e. 1. [26]). Swift wrote that 'every day some ballad comes out reflecting on the ministry' (*Journal to Stella*, ii. 394).

¹ The enclosure consists of two units. The first, which includes 'Of Improvemts in Scotland', 'The Proposall', and 'Of the Advantages of this to Scotland', is written in a hand other than Defoe's, and bears on the back of the last page Defoe's endorsement: 'The Generall Proposall'. The second, which includes the remainder of the enclosure, is in Defoe's hand and bears his endorsement: 'The Perticular Proposall of the Town of Edinburgh stated.'

² Scotland, not yet recovered from the hungry years of King William's time, had suffered a renewal of crop failure and famine in 1709.

of Land: By altering the methods of Husbandry
in Scotland
By planting, Encloseing & mending
the Lands
By Grafting & Dary keeping, a method
which would soon bring Scotland
to Plenty & Quite alter the Miserable Lives of the Poor Tenantry

Of all these I have Some thing to offer, but in my Present
Proposall I Confine my Self to Navall Improvemts, in which I
take upon me to Say Scotland is as Capable of being Improved
as any Nation in the world, notwithstanding the present De-
ficiency of Materialls.

And which is Still more to the Present Purpose, I alledge that
in this one affair of Navigation The Governmt of Britain have
the Greatest opportunity Imaginable to make a Present Immediate advance in the Improveing & encourageing Scotland
(viz):

First, for Building and Repairing Ships, and Here I cannot but
observe that it was a very great mistake in the Commissioners
of the Customs in Scotland when they Obtain'd my Lord
Treasurers Order to Build Three Small Frigates to Cruise upon
the Coast to preserve the Trade,[1] That they Should Send for an
English builder to Contract for them, and then give him leave
to goe back into England & build them at New Castle, whereas,
by a Workman (I carryed down there and) who has Since built
them Severall Smaller Boats, it Has appeared it May even
Under the Present Discouragemts and Scarcity of Materials be
very well Perform'd in Scotland.

Again, the Encrease of Building would encourage the Import-
ing Materialls and in Time the Produceing them in Scotland,
Particularly Hemp for Cordage & planting Timber for the
Work, & So make the work Cheap.

But all men kno' that in Holland They have neither Timber
nor Iron, Hemp or Plank or Pitch or Tar or any Materialls, and
Yet that they are the greatest Builders in the World.

And all men kno' That whether it be from Archangell or from
the east Country, From Swedeland or from Norway, Scotland
Lyes nearer & more Convenient For the Importing Navall
Stores Then Holland, Nor do they want the most proper things

---

[1] In Jan. 1708. See *Calendar of Treasury Books, 1708*, pp. 81–82.

to export for the Purchase of those Stores, I mean Herrings, and which in its Course would be a Considerable advance to the fishery of Scotland, which otherwise I confess I never promised much from. But of these things Hereafter.

In Order to Push This advantageous proposall of Encourageing Scotland to build, fitt out and repair Her Own Shipping, it seems the Government have an Oppertunity to Give an Introduction to it and that with such Force as shall (tho' it may be Some Charge at First) most Infallibly put Scotland in such a Posture as for ever after to be able to Do it without Help, and Perhaps not Build for Her Self only but for Her Neighbours also, and this is most the Substance of my proposall.

The Proposall

The Short of my Proposall is to erect a Yard with Docks, Store houses, Launches, Wayes and the Like for building, Laying up, Fitting and repairing of Ships in Scotland Such as is now at Plymmouth, Portsmouth &c For the Use of the Navy, and then to appoint a certain Squadron of Her Majties ships to have their winter Station and be Laid up there.

It Seems Proper Here to examine Three Things.

1 The Occasion of it to England and its advantages Here in Order to make it please the English.

2/ The Practicableness and Charge, and in that a farther explaining the Particulars.

3 The Advantages to Scotland.

As to England, Two Things prove the Occasion or indeed the Necessity of this Proposall.

1/ That Since this War with France, The Navall Power of our Enemy Lying to the west of us, it was found So Dangerous to our Trade to have no Port in the west &c where our Ships might winter that the Governmt was oblig'd at Prodigious expence to erect a Dock and Yards at Plymouth, Tho the place was So improper that the Dock is Cut by force out of a Firm Solid Rock. But without it Our Navall affairs were Perfectly impotent. And if the French were powerfull in the Channel, as Sometimes they were, and Lay between Our Ships and their winter Ports, Our Squadrons Could not come Home, but were oblig'd to Lye in the Roads of Falmouth, Plymouth &c and not to be repair'd or refitted, and So became Useless for the Next Summer. Or if they waited till the Enemy was Retired, they Came Home in the

Winter and were exposed to Storms and Tempests by which they were Lost and Destroyed, all which is now remydyed by the Yards and Stores being Placed at Plymouth, by which we have alwayes a Number of men of war there, ready to Protect our Trade and to Join on occasion with the Grand fleet, who alwayes come that way.

2/ There was the like want of a Dock &c to the Northward in the Late wars with the Dutch, and for the very Same Reason. King Charles the 2nd was So Sencible of it that Haveing no Port capable of receiveing the men of war farther North than the Humber, the King built the Cittadell of Hull, and Design'd a Station there for Layeing up a Squadron, and we found a Prodigious Disadvantage in the want of it, the Dutch getting frequently between us and our Northern Trade in Such a manner That our Commerce with the Baltique was almost wholly Cut off, & our Coal Trade So Stopt that no Ships dared to Stir but with very Strong Squadrons for Convoy, whereas Had we then Had a Squadron of men of war in the Firth, there had been a Retreat for our East Land Fleets and Norway and Russia Fleets, where they would have been protected and at Convenient Times brought Home with a Strong Convoy.

These are, I Humbly Suppose, Sufficient precedents to prove the necessity and usefulness of the thing. It is true we all Hope there is no Probability of a Dutch war. But we are always to Provide, and be in Ready posture for all Events.[1]

The Explaining the Proposall is next, which would require a long Discourse, but I shall contract it, reserving a farther explication to a farther Occasion.

By a Station of Men of War in Scotland I mean

That Such a Certain number of men of [war][2] as the Government Shall think needfull for the Security of our Northern Trade in Time of war Should be appointed to winter in Scotland in Time of peace.

That at Some Proper place in the Firth of Forth (and I am not to Seek for the place) a yard may be Erected with Dry Docks for repairing, Launches for building, and wayes for Graveing and Washing the men of War.

That Offices and Store Houses be built for Layeing up and

---

[1] England, though allied with the Dutch in this and the previous war against Louis, had fought the Dutch three times within the past sixty years and was at this time in uneasy relations with them again.

[2] MS. has 'men'.

Secureing the Sails, rigging, ammunition &c for the Said Ships, with Victualling Offices for provisions, that they may be entirely Fitted Out to Sea.

That Navall Stores be furnish'd from the Proper Countryes, & Sufficient Quantityes Laid in for all Occasions.

That Rope Walks and all Necessaryes be built and Provided for makeing all Sorts of Cables and Cordage, with Encouragemts for Planting Timber and Hemp, Flax &c for Supplyes.

In Short, that all things be modell'd according to the Usage of the Navy for the Effectuall furnishing and Supplying about 14 men of war of the fourth and fifth Rate, or as many as the Governmt shall appoint, and for building or rebuilding as occasion may require.

And above all, that it may be in Such a Place in the Firth as, if Possible, may be Secured from the Insults of an Enemy, and in Particular as Cannot be bombarded, for which proposalls shall be offered when needfull.

Of the Advantages of this to Scotland

It would be very Long to Enter into all the Particular advantages, But without Enlarging on the Heads, they will be Such as these.

1/ The Expending and Circulateing a very great Summ of money every year in Scotland, and especially in the first erecting the Yards.

2/ The Employing a great number of people in the Necessary Works Constantly attending an Undertakeing of Such Consequence, Such as Carpenters, Caulkers, Labourers &c about the repairing and building Ships; Carvers, Painters, Joyners, blockmakers, anchorsmiths, rope makers, and a Multitude of Trades which depend upon the fitting out Ships.

3/ The breeding Seamen and Encourageing them to Stay at Home in scotland, of which a Certain Number would be alwayes Entertain'd in Pay, and the youth of Scotland would have a kind of School to Initiate them into the needfull Arts of Building and Navigating Ships, The Said men of War being alwayes Mann'd from Scotland.

4/ Encrease of Shipping and Trade for Importing the navall Stores for these things, and Encrease of business for goods to export.

5/ Consumption of Provisions, encrease of wages to the Poor, encrease of Labour, and by Consequence detaining the people at Home, and by all these Improveing the Land.

6/ Security to the Trade of Scotland in Time of War. Such a Strength being kept at their Own doors as will be always able to Protect them from Pyrates and Sea Robbers, whereas at this time there is not a Gun Can be fired at an Enemy in all the Firth. But all the Shipping there Lyes exposed to every rover, and it Seems Something Wonderfull that in all this War the French Have not Swept the whole firth and even burnt the Very Town of Leith, which they might Frequently Have done but with 2 men of war and a Bomb Ketch.

The State of The Case of Docks &c at Leith

The First Proposall Being Made for Docks, yards &c. and The Town of Edinburgh projecting Great Advantages to Themselves, without any View of the public profitt, They Petition the Queen and Council for Docks, yards &c. in the River or Haven of Leith.

Which Proposall of Theirs being Enquir'd into will be found

1. Deficient to the Main proposall of Layeing Up a Squadron of Men of War.

2. Impracticable in its Nature by The Scituation and Other Circumstances of The place.

3. Calculated Onely for the private Advantage of the City of Edinburgh, without any View of the Public Good.

Their Proposall Consists of a Projected Wet Dock and Enlargeing The Harbour and Peir of Leith, by which They propose to bring in any of The Men of war to Refitt &c.

Objection:

1. Tis Humbly Suggested That if all This were done, The Port of Leith can Not be Capable of Bringing in a Squadron, and of all The Necessary yards, Buildings, &c. which are Required to That Purpose; They do Not propose it, Nor is There Room for The work on the spot they Lay out for it.

2. The Expence which They propose, being at Least 40 or 50 Thousand pound, will Seem to be ill Lay'd Out Onely for bringing in Now and Then a ship to Refitt, Seeing There is allready Room Enough for all The shipping The place does or Can be Expected to Employ.

3. The few ships of war Requisit to Guard the Trade in Time of This war can Not be Worth while to Expend So large Sums

for Refitting Them; in Time of peace None Are Required. And for Layeing Them up, Their proposall is Not Calculated for it.

But Supposeing They would Lay up a Squadron in Scotland, The Port of Leith Can Not be Capable On Sundry Accounts.

1. The Hazard of Bringing Men of war into a Peir or Narrow Haven, which has allways been Avoided in the Navy Upon any Account whatsoever; and The Perticular Difficulties of The Pier of Leith with Respect to a Dangerous Bar, shoal water, and Storms of wind &c. Make it On all Accounts too great a hazard for the Queens ships.

2. All The while They are within the Harbour and Out of the Wett Dock They Must Lye a ground at Low water, which has on all Occasions been judg'd Inconvenient, and Carefully Avoided in The Navy.

3. The Onely Piece of Ground Practicable for a wett dock and where it is proposed has These Inconveniences.

   1. That being just on the Edge of the shore, which is all a Sand, it is Not probable it can Retaine the water, But it will Drayn Out with the Ebb and leave the ships a ground Every Tide.
   2. That Lyeing just on the Edge of The Firth, it is Exposed to an Enemy and May be bombarded at Pleasure.
   3. It is believed That it is Impracticable to have a Depth of water to Bring The Queens ships into it.

But Suppose all These Things Could be Answer'd, This Seems Meerly Calculated for the Advantage of The City of Edinb without any View of the Public Good, Since Nature has allready Made a wet Dock of The Firth it Self above The Queens Ferry; and There can be None Made like it, So That to Make one at Leith can have no pretence but to help the City of Edinburgh; which if her Majtie Thinks Fitt to do by Giveing Them fourty Thousand pounds Out of her Pocket and Letting The Dock Alone, it shall be Much More to the Publick Advantage.[1]

The advantages of The Firth for Laying Up The ships[2]

1. For at Least Eight Mile in Length From the Narrow Passage as high as Alloway, The Seat of The Earle of Marr, The Channel is Safe, The Ground Good, Land lockt From storms, and Safe for Rideing The ships.

[1] Nevertheless, the docks were built at Leith, though not until 1717–20.
[2] Defoe here anticipates Rosyth Naval Base, built two centuries later.

2. There is a Full Depth of water From Six fathoms to Eighteen fathom at Low water For The breadth, in Most places, of a Mile, So That the ships have Roome to Wind Upon the flood and Ebb, and Ride Clear of One Another in Case of Fire.

3. A Small Charge will Fortifye The Mouth of the Passage at the Queensferry, The Island of Inch Garve Lyeing in The Middle, and The Main Channell Not half a Mile Broad On Either Side, yet Deep and Safe, in Some places 30 to 40 Fathom water, So That No ships can pass but Must Come Under The Command of The Batterys on both Sides.

4. No Enemy Can Come Near to Bombard Them or to Burn the Storehouses and yards, Unless They Bring a land Force to Go on shore and March Round.

Thus The work will be better done and all the Charges Saved.

MS.: Duke of Portland, Defoe Papers, 1 ff. 216–25. *Pub.*: *H.M.C. Portland*, iv. 584–90. *Address*: none.

140. [*To* ROBERT HARLEY]. *12 September 1710*

Sir

Since I waited On you last I have farther Enquir'd into the Scots Mission I hinted to you; and Find it goes forward. The Gentleman[1] has Signify'd his Goeing to his Congregation. The Occasion, as I Noted, is Purely (So farr as Appeares) the affair of the College.

I am Sir Very well Assur'd of the Good Disposition of the Ministers of Scotland to the Queen, and to a quiet peacible behavior, and am Very Sorry to See any Attempts to Infuse Groundless Jealousys into Their heads. Wherefore Sir, as the best Service I can Render her Majtie on This Occasion, I shall (if you Approve of it) Apply my Self, to Weaken the Councils of Achitophell, and preposess the Ministers There, with whom my Intrest I believ is So good, That he shall be able to do Little Mischief.

This I did before in the Case of Mr Callamy,[2] and with Such

[1] Probably Joshua Oldfield (1656–1729), dissenting minister at Globe Alley, Southwark, who visited Edinburgh at about this time. Oldfield, famous in his day as a Presbyterian preacher, teacher, and controversialist, had been the first pastor of the dissenting congregation at Tooting, a congregation said to have been formed there in the 1680's by Defoe (Thompson MS., Records of Nonconformity 10, pp. 295–6, in Dr. Williams's Library, London).
[2] Edmund Calamy (1671–1732), the biographer of nonconformity, was at this time dissenting minister at Westminster. In the previous year he had travelled in Scotland, where he had made the acquaintance of many among the Scottish clergy. See his *Historical Account of My Own Life*, 1830, ii. 144–220.

Success That to This day, he has Not been able to Maintain a Correspondence There. And This I do, Not to prejudice Them on Either hand. But I have a Double View in it, and both I hope Very honest and Very Usefull.

First, I would prevent Them Makeing the honest poor people in Scotland Uneasy to Themselves, As I Think Our Dissenters here now are, without any Cause.

Secondly, I would prevent Their being Uneasy to the Government, which Now God be praisd They are Not, but if Fermented From Hence May be.

I am Really Concern'd, to See Our people Dilligently Spread, and Others Eagerly Reciev, the Greatest Absurdities, by which They would Make Their Disgusts at the late Changes appear Rationall; Such as the favouring a French Intrest, and Countenancing The pretender—Terrifying the poor Ignorant People with Notions of Popery, and of Persecution, as if Our Safety was Not in her Majtie, but in her Servants; and The Queen Could Not Govern us but by Such hands as we lik'd of.

This Sir I Apply my Self to Expose as Ridiculous; and in all the Correspondence I keep up, which is Now all Over Brittain, I Dilligently Counter act this folly.

I Relate This Sir, Not to Vallue my Self Upon my Service, but to have your Approbation of it, That I may Not Ignorantly Or Officiously Take Much pains and do No Service.

I kno' the Gentlemen are busye, Spreading Jealousies Among all the Country People, and I may Trace Some of their Methods too; if to Set the people Right in Their Notions, if to prevent The Malignity of Nationall Jealousy, if to keep up in the Minds of her Majties Subjects Their Zeal and Affection to the person as well as to the Government of Their Soveraign, be any Service to her Majtie, be of any Moment, I flatter my Self I shall be Made usefull, Especially in Scotland and the North of England.

Matters of Credit, and Oppressing the public affairs by Refuseing to lend Money, and withdrawing the Assistance Their Duty as well as Intrest Demands, is the Great Consequence of These Discontents, and No Doubt is The Great Design in propogateing This Uneasy Temper. To This Sir I shall not fail to Applye the best Remedy I can by Exposing first the Mallice, and Then the folly of it.

You See Sir in This a Specimen of Party Fury, and how Difficult it is to Struggle with the follys of Men, but I hope Time and a little Experience will Make Our people wiser. I ask your Pardon for The length of This, and am

Sir, Your Most Humble and Obedt Servant

DE FOE

Sept. 12. 1710

MS.: Duke of Portland, Defoe Papers, 1 ff. 226–7. *Pub.*: *H.M.C. Portland*, iv. 593–4. *Address*: none. *Endorsed*: 'Mr Goldsmith Sept: 12 1710, R̸ Sept: 13:'

141. [*To* ROBERT HARLEY]. *21 September 1710*

Sir

The Joy I Conciev'd when you were Pleas'd to Signifye to me That Her Majtie has Directed the Affair in My Favour,[1] Moves Me Sir in the Humblest Manner to Applye my Self to you in Two Cases.

First Sir, That the Sence I have of her Majties Goodness May be Represented in the best Manner Possible to her Majtie, So as becomes a Subject Under the Strongest Tyes of Duty and Gratitude.

And Secondly Sir, That you would be pleased to Furnish the Occasion how I May Render her Majtie Such Service, as May at least Testifye for me That This Bounty is Not wrong Plac't.

I do Not pretend to be Able to Merit So Much Favor; yet the Meanest Capacity can allways do Something. There is a Difference between Not being Worthy, and being Unworthy. I hope I Need Not assure you Sir That I will slip no Opportunity of Service, but Sir It is wholly in your Self to make me Usefull, and as the Favor Comes by your Intercession, So the Power of Serving Depends Upon your Assistance in Directing.

I Remembr your Discourse About the Approaching Dissolution.[2] I would Humbly Offer it to your Consideration Whether you Think I may Not do Some Service in the Country for a Month or Two. I Mean in the North, to Argue with, perswade, and bring to Their Temper and Eye-Sight a Certain people who are but too Apt to Reciev Impressions from Some here who want both.

I do Not propose it as Matter of Charge. I shall Submitt that to you. I shall Endeavour Rather to be too backward Than too forward on That Account. But I humbly Offer it as my Opinion Onely That at This Juncture It May be of More Service Than

---

[1] Harley had promised to recommend Defoe to the Queen, doubtless concerning a renewal of his service to the Government (p. 274).
[2] Parliament was dissolved on this same day.

perhaps it would be possible at another Time; I Can Not but Remembr Sir, The Journey I Once went on Such an Occasion, I mean at the Last Election, By your Ordr, In which I had Such Success That I can hardly Wish More upon like Occasion.[1] I Submit it wholly to you Sir, and shall Chearfully obey your Ordrs in it One way Or Other.

             I am, Sir, Your Most Humble and Obedt
             [remainder, including signature, torn off]

Sept. 21. 1710

MS.: Duke of Portland, Defoe Papers, 1 ff. 228–9. *Pub.*: *H.M.C. Portland*, iv. 597. *Address*: none. *Endorsed*: 'Mr Goldsmith, Sept: 21: 1710.'

142. [*To* Robert Harley]. *29 September 1710*

Sir

Tho' This is Sooner Than the Time I had your Ordrs to attend, I Could Not but give you This Trouble to Cover The Enclosed.[2]

This is Another Street Letter, Said to be Taken up in the Night. I will not presume to Anticipate your Thoughts of These Things; To me They Appear Very Naked and Undresst. The design Appeares Villainous (Viz) To Draw Innocent Persons into Suggested Plots &c. 'Tis the Easyest thing in the world to Cause Trayterous Letters to be written to any person, and Then prompt the Intercepting Them. The Thing therefore, as it is a Vile and Most Absurd Method, So 'tis withall So foolish and So ill Set Out, That the Mischief Seems Taken away and The Mischievous Design Onely left; For Surely in Vain is the Net spread in The Sight of Any Bird.

As to the Comeing of the Pretender, The Vain Scarecrow is too Visible: I kno' Not whether if Ever we should wish for him, it should Not be Now, and That an Invasion Might Set us to Rights. Then we should See the falsity of The Clamours and Noise of a Party. And Many of Those who are Reproacht with being for him, would have an Opportunity to wipe off That Scandall by Discovering The persons who Really are So: It is True the Experiment Might be Costly, but a knave Discoverd is Cheap bought, Almost at any price.

If This Method be Used with Success, I Expect Next

---

[1] Defoe refers to the election of 1705, during which he canvassed much of England for Harley. During the election of 1708 Defoe was in Scotland.
[2] Missing.

Counterfeit Letters and Treasonable papers to be Convey'd into houses and Then be Searcht for, Letters sent and Then Intercepted, Innocent Men to be Suspected and Then to be fully Accused; and all the Wicked Things That can be, past for Current Law Among us— I hope her Majtie will Take a Right View of these Things, and will protect her faithfull Servants from The Snares Thus Laid for Their Honour and Safety.

There May be Other Ends in Spreading These Letters which without Doors a man can Not See. I must Confess I See nothing in Them to be Apprehensiv of. They Tend indeed to Encrease Jealousys Among The people and Make Them Affraid of One Another, but They are So Weak, So Much Malice with So little witt, That I Think There is Not Much to fear from Them.

I kno' Sir you will abate me The Ceremony of Thanks For the Favour done Me.[1] The best Acknowlegemts I can Make Either to her Majtie The Originall, or your Self the Means, of My Support, is a Vigrous Application to what is the Duty of Every honest Man (Viz) To promote The Generall Peace, and Upon all Occasions to Persue The best Intrest both of her Majtie and her People, which is The Union of all Their hearts in her Service; This I Take to be the best Method to oblige you, and the best way to shew The Sence I have both of My Duty and Obligation, and in This I shall Not be wanting.

This is a day of City Hurry. I Could ha' been Very Glad to have Seen A Haughty, Proud, and (I must Own I Think) Empty Man Defeated; and a Man of Peace, Temper, and Modesty in his Room; but I foresee Right Measures are Not Taken for it, So if it should happen I must Acknowlege my Self Deciev'd.[2]

This is a day when Men of Peace and Patience are The Onely Usefull people Either for themselves or the Governmt; But how few Such are to be found! The Zeal of Parties has Eaten Them up, and Men Seem heated for Their Countries Mischief, as if They were to Feel no share of her Ruin when it should Come to pass.

I am Prepareing Sir to Reciev your Commands, and perswade My Self you will Agree in This that the Sooner I am

[1] On 27 Sept. he had been paid £100 from the Secret Service funds (Laurence Hanson, *Government and the Press*, 1936, p. 96).

[2] Sir Gilbert Heathcote (1651?–1733), chief founder of the New East India Company, member of the first board of directors of the Bank of England, and a leading Whig financier, was a candidate for the office of Lord Mayor and, as Defoe predicted, was elected. In the previous June Heathcote had attempted to coerce the Queen into retaining Sunderland by prophesying a fall in credit if the Minister was dropped (Harley to Arthur Moore, *H.M.C. Portland*, iv. 545).

There[1] The More Service I May do: The Gentleman of Letters and Degrees[2] who I formerly hinted to you Sir was Goeing Northward is Sett Out.

I am, Sir, Your Most Humble
And Most Obedt Servt
[signature torn off]

Sept 29° 1710.

MS.: Duke of Portland, Defoe Papers, 1 ff. 230–1. *Pub.*: *H.M.C. Portland*, iv. 602–3. *Address*: none.

143. [*To* ROBERT HARLEY]. *10 October 1710*

Sir

Tho' I am to Attend in the Evening According to your Ordr, yet I Could not Delay Sending you an Account (which I Recd Last Night after I had the honor of Seeing you) of the Elections of Magistrats for the City of Edinburgh.

Adam Brown, Ld Provost—Lord Mayor.

William Hutchinson, Archibald Cockbourn, John Hay, Thomas Dundass, Bailies.

John Duncan, Lord Dean of Guild, Le Mesme Avec Le Provost de Merchands au Paris.

William Dundass, Treasurer or Chamberlain.

I Referr Their Characters Till Evening, Onely hint to you Sir, That they are all but Two My Very Perticular Accquaintances,[3] which will I believ give Me Occasion of Influencing Them Very Much for her Majties Service.

I am Sir, Your Most Humble and Obedt
[remainder, including signature, torn off]

Octob. 10. 1710

MS.: Duke of Portland, Defoe Papers, 1 ff. 232–3. *Pub.*: *H.M.C. Portland*, v. 612. *Address*: none. *Endorsed*: 'Edenburgh, Octo: 10: 1710.'

[1] Scotland, for which he was shortly to set out.
[2] Probably Joshua Oldfield (p. 285, n. 1), who had received an honorary doctorate from Edinburgh University in the previous year. See Dunton, 'A Narrative of the Scotch Commencement', and 'The Dissenting Doctors', *Life and Errors*, ii. 678–729.
[3] Among those with whom Defoe was acquainted were Adam Brown and John Duncan. 'Both were members of the Edinburgh Society for the Reformation of Manners and were present with Defoe at many of the meetings held between April and November, 1707. It was John Duncan who proposed Defoe for membership in the Society' (C. E. Burch, 'Defoe and the Edinburgh Society for the Reformation of Manners', *Review of English Studies*, xvi [1940], 312).

144. [*To* ROBERT HARLEY]. [*c. 21 October 1710*]

Queries for Mannagemt

1/ Whether the Generall Design be not to Inform and advise
The people of her Majties Resolutions, as well in These Changes
of Things as any Other that shall happen, to Continue to
Maintain—

1 The Union in all its Parts
2 The Church in all its Just Rights and Established priveleges

And to Discourage and Disscountenance Intrusions[1] and Innovations, That her Majtie will protect and Defend Their Revolution Establishment and Take all Occasions to Encourage And
protect Their Commerce and the Improvemt of their Country.

2/ Whether I am Not to Apply my Self on all Occasions to
Calm and Make Easy The Minds of people there, Filld with
Jealousies and Feares, and On Every Opportunity to Detect the
false Accounts Imposed Upon Them from Hence whether by
writeing, Printing or Conversation, That the Poison of a Factious
spirit May Not Spread Among them Nor the people be Irritated
and Exasperated Against the Public Administration of Affaires
here as if Calculated for Their Destruction.

3/ In Matters of Election whether of the Commons or Peers,
by all Such Methods as shall Offer (for tis Impossible to prescribe Them here) to forward the Intrest and Choice of Such
Men whose Tempers are Most Moderate and best Enclind &c.
and as plainly as Circumstances will admitt, to Discourage The
Contrary.

4/ From Time to Time to give Such Intelligence of Things
and Persons as May be for her Majties Service.

5/ To Settle and Continue Such Correspondence in Every
Part, whether the Same allready Settled, or Such as May be
proper, for an Exact Intelligence in all parts after this Journey
May be Over.

MS.: Duke of Portland, Defoe Papers, 1 ff. 234–5. *Pub.*: *H.M.C. Portland*,
iv. 616. *Address*: none. *Endorsed*: 'Queries, Mr Goldsmith, Octob: 21 1710.'

145. [*To* ROBERT HARLEY]. *16 November 1710*

Sir

The stop I Met with at New Castle prevented My Arriveing
here Till the Day before The Election of Peers.[2] I kno' I Need

[1] 'The settlement of a minister of the Church of Scotland contrary to the will or
without the consent of the congregation' (*O.E.D.*).
[2] He must have arrived, then, on 9 Nov.

Not give you a List of Their Names. Some Observations on the Conduct of the Parties on both Sides I shall Comunicate in My Next, being Not Sufficiently furnish'd for That work at So short Notice.

I find the people here Allarm'd Very Much, but willing to hope Every Thing shall not Isue So bad as The Embassador[1] of a Certain Party whom you kno' was here before Me had Suggested. They Seem Surpriz'd when They hear that Moderate Thoughts Remain Among Those of whose Mannagement They had Recd Such formidable Ideas. I flatter my Self her Majtie shall be Successfully as well as Faithfully Serv'd in The Great work of quieting The Minds of her Subjects in This Part of Britain, and Really I find a Disposition here, Especially Among the Most Judicious both of Ministers and people, to Rest Upon the Assurances of her Majties preserving Their libertys, and to leav all Other Things to her Royall Justice; The Church here is Their Great Concern. This being Untouch'd They will be The Easyest part of the Nation in Other Cases.

This is the foundation I am building Upon, and Indeed Sir I find as Many Endeavours to Embroil Them here and Disorder the heads of the people as I did in the Time of the Treaty, Tho' I hope Easyer to be Defeated— I presume Confuteing these and Informing the people here of Their True Intrest and a little of Their Duty May be Acceptable Service to her Majtie, and May Answer the End of My stay here, and in this I shall Not fail, and shall More Constantly Now Inform you of what Occurs.

I presume you have an Account of what I Did at N Castle in Answer to Mine. I am Very Sorry to write That the Gentleman I Sent My Last by From Thence is No More to be Confided in, of which I shall Give a Larger Account Among Other Things in My Next.[2]

> I am, Sir, Your Most Obedient Servt
> [symbol]

Edinb. Nov. 16. 1710

MS.: Duke of Portland, Defoe Papers, 1 ff. 236–7. *Pub.*: *H.M.C. Portland*, iv. 629. *Address*: none. *Endorsed*: 'Eden, Mr Guilot Nov: 16 1710.'

[1] Probably Joshua Oldfield (p. 285, n. 1).

[2] For some explanation of the differences that had arisen between Defoe and John Bell, the Newcastle postmaster through whom Harley communicated with his agents in Scotland, see pp. 296–7.

146. [*To* Robert Harley]. *18 November 1710*

Sir

I wrot you briefly last Post but One.[1] I have been in Close Conference Since that with men of all Parties. Indeed the Scenes here have as great a Variety as can be Imagin'd, differing not Onely from themselves but from things of the like Nature in England in a most Extraordinary Manner. This Moves me to be the more Perticular, believing it Very Much for her Majties Service to give you a Succinct Account of the humours of men and Parties, and of their Conduct in the present juncture.

The whigs here are bauk'd in their Elecctions of the Peers, of whom I Need Not Give you the Names Tho' they are in the Enclosed list.[2] How Unhappily the Severall Parties behave in this Case shall be my first Remark.

The Torys (as we call them in England) are here a Differing kind of People from Ours of that Denomination, being Universally Jacobite, and so above board as to Own it; in the last of which they Certainly show more honesty than Discretion. It is so Open a thing and So much the Mode of the Place to Own the pretender, Drink his health, and Talk most Insolently of his being Restored, that I think it my Duty to Represent this to you Sir for her Majties Service, and that with the greatest Concern.

You will wonder when I shall Repeat to you an absurdity of a Nature which One Would think Uncapable of Deludeing any body (Viz) that the 233 [Queen][3] should have been privately

---

[1] Apparently an error; the posts ran thrice weekly and the preceding letter is dated 16 Nov.

[2] Missing. The election of the peers was a triumph for the Government, all sixteen of whose candidates were chosen (*H.M.C. Portland*, x. 351).

[3] The cipher used here appears also in Nos. 148 and 150. The numbers are not deciphered in any of the three manuscripts, and I have not found the key among either Harley's papers or the many keys preserved in the Public Record Office. All three letters were first deciphered by the editor of *H.M.C. Portland*, iv, J. J. Cartwright, with whose solutions I concur in all but two instances. The meanings of many of the symbols can be inferred from the context, and these clues are sufficient to indicate the scheme of the cipher: a selection of words and names was placed in roughly alphabetical order, the alphabetized list was then numbered, and each number was then used as a symbol for the word or name to which it corresponded. Another of Harley's correspondents was using a somewhat similar scheme at this time. 'I am at a great loss in writing to you for want of the cipher; to serve in the meantime I sent you a list of a certain set of men from Stamford, number them beginning the first with 17, and so on' (Mar to Harley, 1 Nov. 1710, *H.M.C. Portland*, x. 347). Knowledge of Defoe's scheme does not, of course, by itself enable one to reconstruct the list, but since the arrangement of that list was both alphabetical and numerical, and since the context yields the meaning of

Resolved to dissolve the 253 [succession] and to Restore 214 [the Pretender], being Chagrin, Pensiv and in Conscience Uneasy at his being So long and so much Injur'd—and Not Onely So, but that 233 [the Queen] will Resign In favour of the said 214 [Pretender].

I had not Mention'd this, for I would not Trouble you with Triffles, if I did not See a Strange Use made of it here to Encourage the profest Jacobits and to Impose upon the poor highlanders and Other People in the Country, who do not look for their Saviours Comeing with half the Assurance as they do for that of the 214 [Pretender]. I doubt not Sir but you will Think it proper in its Season to represent this to her Majtie, Since the Encouragemt of the Jacobites in the New Turn of Affaires is the great Argument which the other people make Use of to Make their Quarell at the late Changes become Popular.

In the late Election, the Conduct of the D of 60 [Argyll], the E of 163 [Islay], and the Earle of 194 [Mar][1] is Very Perticular, and Either their Instructions were to use no Temper or they discovred most Impolitick Openess. Many that were willing to Come into Measures Exclaim'd Openly Upon the Impudence of those Gentlemen—who Treated them with Mennaces and Contempt on the One hand, and Declared Openly the Quallification of those to be Chosen, which is Now called the Test upon which the Peers were Closeted by those two above (Viz) their agreeing to Impeach 140 [Godolphin] and 193 [Marlborough].[2] Nor did the Impudence End there, but On all Occasions to Say in So Many Words They had her Majties Orders to Choose Such and Such and it must be don: This was So abandonning all Reserves, that it has disgusted the Generallity, and has Put them Upon Measures of Uniteing, which may shut the door

many of the numbers, the remaining numbers by interpolation can be assigned to more or less limited areas of the alphabet. Speculation on their meaning is thereby guided and controlled.

[1] Argyll, Islay, and Mar helped choose the Government's candidates for seats in the House of Lords and largely managed their election (*H.M.C. Portland*, x. 346–51). John Campbell (1680–1743), second Duke of Argyll, had quarrelled with Marlborough and thrown in his lot with the Tories; but he was no Jacobite, as Mar was to learn at Sheriffmuir in 1715. Archibald Campbell (1682–1761), first and only Earl of Islay, Argyll's brother and successor, was Extraordinary Lord of Session and Lord Justice General. He soon turned in violent opposition against the Tory Government he was at this time serving. John Erskine (1675–1732), sixth or eleventh Earl of Mar, had been Secretary of State (of Scotland) and was now a Privy Councillor. He joined the Jacobites in 1715 and was defeated by Argyll at Sheriffmuir. For Defoe's opinion of these three, see his *Atalantis Major*, Edinburgh, 1711, pp. 16–23.

[2] Leaders of the fallen Ministry. See Defoe's *Atalantis Major*, pp. 26–27.

upon all future Measures, what Ever the Occasion may be; Prudence Will never let a Wise man Play a game So as he can Never play it again. But these Gentlemen have not onely don So, but Exposed their Measures So Openly that had a Proposall 260 [Stair] made been Closed with,[1] all the Mannage of 60 [Argyll] and 194 [Mar] had been Dissappointed, and the Success of this Election is Oweing to the Cowardice, not good will, of 182 [Leven], 138 [Glasgow], with Seafield,[2] Hyndford and [   ],[3] and not atall to the Wisdom and Conduct of 60 [Argyll] and 194 [Mar], who Certainly lost themselves More in this than Any man would have thot Possible for men of their Character, Especially 194 [Mar], to have done, and was within a Triffle of spoiling all their Work.

Now they have Returnd their Number, it were to be Wished they Could have Avoided a few who are Declar'd profest Jacobites, Such as 197 [Marischal], Kilsyth, Blantire, Hume &c.[4] who are known to aim in all they do at the Pretender, and whose being Now Chosen has many ill Effects here What Ever may be as to Over-ruleing them in England, I mean as to Encreasing the Insolence of Jacobitisme in the North, where its Strength is far from being Contemptible, and the Rendring the work of Makeing the other people Easy far more difficult than it might Otherwise have been.

It was Very Remarkable that when My Ld 163 [Islay] attempted Some of the 100 [clergy] of this City to assure them of the good Intentions of the 233 [Queen], and Resolutions not to Invade their Church, the Circumstance of Nameing Jacobite Peers as the Express order from 233 [the Queen] to be Chosen

---

[1] John Dalrymple (1673–1747), second Earl of Stair, representative peer in the first Union Parliament and commander of a brigade at Oudenarde, resisted the tactics of Argyll and Mar. Defoe thought that 'had the other Lords been advised by this gallant Gentleman, they had broke all their [i.e. Argyll's and Mar's] Schemes; but they were not all united in their Resolutions, or equally determined in their Measures' (*Atalantis Major*, p. 28).

[2] David Leslie, formerly Melville (1660–1728), third Earl of Leven, Commander-in-Chief of the Forces in Scotland; David Boyle (1666–1733), first Earl of Glasgow, representative peer and Lord Clerk Register; and James Ogilvy (1664–1730), first Earl of Seafield and later fourth Earl of Findlater, formerly Secretary of State and Lord Chancellor. These three, together with Stair, at first resolved to stand for election, but later withdrew from candidacy.

[3] Left blank in MS.

[4] William Keith (*c.* 1664–1712), ninth Earl Marischal, and William Livingston (1650–1733), third Viscount Kilsyth, had been arrested after the threatened invasion of 1708, and Kilsyth was later to join Mar in the insurrection of 1715. Alexander Home, or Hume (d. 1720), seventh Earl of Home, was a cautious Jacobite. He was not molested in 1708, and was imprisoned but briefly in 1715.

was Retorted as a bad token for them to rest upon, and the famous Tale of the Hangman of Edinb. was Told him by One Mr Miller¹ of Kirkliston (Viz) How he used, when he had any man to Execcute, to Encourage them, and bid them not fear, not fear, till he Got them Up the ladder and So Turnd them off.²

I hint this Sir to Confirm my Censure of the Conduct aforesaid as Imprudent and as what has rendred the quieting these people, which was Easy before, Very Difficult now.

I would not lay down my Opinion of things too Positively; therefore I Cease to Enlarge on the affair of this Mannagement —How the whig lords behave, how the Squadroni and old Court Unite,³ what Measures they took then and are Takeing Now, with Some Observations on both shall be the Subject of my Next— Mean Time Sir I should be Made Easy if I had the Honour to know if these Accounts Come Safe to hand, being Unexpectedly Depriv'd of the Opportunity of Conveying by Mr Bell, whom I can not think of Trusting in this affair Unless I have again your Commands to do so.⁴

I am, Sir, Your Most Humble faithfull and Obedient Servt
C. GUILOT

Nov. 18. 1710

MS.: (in Defoe's hand, though disguised): Duke of Portland, Defoe Papers, 1 ff. 238–9. *Pub.*: *H.M.C. Portland*, iv. 629–31. *Address*: none. *Endorsed*: 'Claude Guilot Eden: Nov: 18 1710, R̷ Nov: 27:'

147. [*To* ROBERT HARLEY]. *21 November 1710*
Sir

I am Unhappily in Some Perplexity about the Conveying my letters as well as my other Circumstances in this Place, and this Causes me giveing you this Trouble by the Ordinary Post. I Subjoyn my humble Request that I may Reciev a line or Two Signifyeing that my letters Arriv; and also that my proceedings are to your Satisfaction, if according to my hopes I have the honor to Answer your Expectation.

I had the Honor of your Credit to Mr J Bell Restricting me to Twenty Pound, which he Readily Complyed with, but Imediately made my haveing that Credit and Waiting there for

¹ Thomas Miller, minister.
² Defoe tells the story of John White, the Edinburgh hangman, in the *Review* for 30 Nov. 1710 and in *Atalantis Major*, pp. 22–23.
³ The Squadrone, ignored by the Government in the election, now found common cause with the old Court Party that had supported the Godolphin Ministry.
⁴ See the following letter.

it Public all Over the Town, Haveing himself Espoused a Contrary Intrest to what he Supposed me Acting for, of which I shall add more largely when I am assured my letters Arriv Safe to your hand.

This Causes me (However straightned) to offer no farther desire of Supply that way, Chooseing Rather to struggle with my Own Circumstances than to hazard the Service.

I kno' Sir, If you think fitt to Continue me here any Time, you will not Abbandonne me in your Service; and as for Methods of Supply, if you please to Order me any Support here, I may Draw it in *this hand* and *Name* Safely and Entirely Conceal'd on your Self or any Person you shall please to Appoint.

If you do me the Honor to leav me to judge whether I am More Usefull in staying here or not, I must Confess I think I can in no spot of Ground in Britain Render her Majtie like Service (tho' in this I speak against my Own Intrest and affairs). I Mean for a Month or two yet longer, Since these people are Infinitely prejudiced and alarm'd, and yet not So Tenatious and ill Temperd as I Expected, and will be Soon Restored and Recovred to their Temper.

I Humbly lay my Own Circumstance before you, but Submitt it Entirely to your goodness whose Concern for me has allwayes been beyond my Merit. I Most Humbly and Earnestly Entreat for a line signifying the Receipt of my letters, Since I can not write with Equall freedome while I am Uncertain whether what I write Comes Safe to your hands.

I am, Sir, Your Most Humble
and most Obedient Servt
C GUILOT

Novemb. 21. 1710

P S I have written at large last Post, directed to Mr Bateman.[1]

MS. (in Defoe's hand, though disguised): Duke of Portland, Defoe Papers, I ff. 240–1. *Pub.*: *H.M.C. Portland*, iv. 631–2. *Address*: none. *Endorsed*: 'C. Guilot Eden Nov: 21: 1710, R̸ Nov: 27:'

148. [*To* ROBERT HARLEY]. *25 November 1710*
Sir
    I wrott you at large the Observations I had made on the

---

[1] Probably Thomas Bateman, an associate of Harley's, who later became Comptroller of the Coal Duty.

Conduct of Our Great men here. I am not the best judge of the reasons of things, but the Consequences Seem Obvious and any Man may determine of them.

On this Account Sir I Presume to assure you, that the Unwary Openess which I Gave you my thoughts about in my last, has done a great deal of hurt here, in Raiseing the jealousies and Uneasiness of this people, who were Very much Inclined to accquiesce before in her Majties prudence and Relye on the assurances Given of the Royall Protection.

The Queen (they Say) has allways adhered to the Law, and never Carryed it with a High hand, But the D of 60 [Argyll] Destroy'd the Very appearance of Liberty in producing a list, and Openly telling the Peers, The Queen Would have those Men Chosen. It is not my bussiness Sir to make Coments—Her Majtie Will judge whether this was her pleasure. The best I can Say to them is that they can not Suppose her Majtie gave his Grace Instructions to treat the Peers in that Manner, but that the 60 [Duke of Argyll] might be a little Warm; That Perhaps her Majtie Might have Seen Such a list, and appear Satisfyed in the persons, but that her Majtie would Command them to Choose Such and no other, was not Probable.[1] In this Sir, If I do wrong I shall be Very Unhappy, Since I do it as the Onely Means of quieting the Uneasy People, which I take to be Very Much her Majties Intrest.

I shall go on to Accquaint you with this part as the Perticulars Offer, But for the Present I can not Avoid Representing One thing to you, which as it Concerns the Public Peace Here, I believ it my Duty to Lay before her Majtie.

The Uneasyness the people are Under here on the Affair above Said is not little, Especially att the Returning four of the Number Profestly 161 [Jacobite].[2] But they are now farther allarmd at the Confident assurances given them, of a Change in the Great Officers here, Perticularly the military Government.

I perswade my Self you will believ me Sir, that I have No Intrest to make or Persons to Serv. I am no biggot to a Party, Much less to Persons. But when her Majtie shall be Inform'd of the Temper of her people here, and of the Imediate Consequences of a Change, I Doubt not my Notion of that Matter

---

[1] The Queen did, in fact, make known her preferences, though 'upon a promise of secresy' (Islay's letter of 9 Nov. 1710, *H.M.C. Portland*, iv. 625–6).

[2] Marischal, Kilsyth, Blantyre, and Home.

Will appear to have Some Weight in it, at least Enough to Excuse me in the Mentioning it.

1st/ Sir, be it that Some (Worthless Enough) May have the Cheif hand in the affair—yet to Take it from them and leave it to the Next in Course may not mend the matter, or to put it into the hand of any of the Same Party, May not be Worth the broil Such a Remove will make among them.

2nd/ To Give the millitary Power here, which indeed is the Supreme (till the Country is a little more Accquainted With the Civill), to the New Party, who the people by the Needless and Unseasonable Conduct aforesaid are So Jealous of, is to put them into Infinite Confusions and make the Uneasinesses past any Private mans Remedy.

3/ To let in the Tory Party or indeed those who would be called the Episcopall Party into the Millitary Commands, is to put the Pretender in Actuall Posession of this Part of the Island.

I humbly ask your Pardon for Representing this So Positively, yet I am not able to See any Medium. I Would not Reflect on any of her Majties Episcopall Subjects, But Certainely if they are in her Intrest they act the most Impolitic Part in the World, for they will not So much as Say it themselves; nor in all my knowlege of things and persons in this Part of Brittain did I Ever See, or know, or find any Other man that has Seen or known any One Man who was Purely Episcopall and not also Jacobite,[1] avowedly So, Except a Very few under the ministry of Some of the Episcopall ministers who are continued in their Churches by the Presbyterian Government.

I Cease Sir to go on with my Notes on this till I See how the disposition of the people shall hold, for these things Vary as Every New Notion Comes on. But I must Offer you One farther hint Sir of my Own, which I Submit to your Charity because I think it Acting beyond my Sphere—I do not love to be officious, But if you would please to give me leave, I could Name Two or three Persons who while they are in are Rendred Suspected to the New Juncto here, and who Perhaps may be kept off from them, whereas their being Displac'd will make them Popular and place them at the head of a Party which it is Very Much her Majties Intrest to keep down, and which can Never be better kept Down than by Rendring them Suspected to One another— I shall Explain my Self farther If I may Obtain

[1] Of this observation Defoe was so confident as to publish it in the *Reviews* for 28 Nov. and 7 Dec. 1710.

your Commands and Som hint that my letters Come to your hands.[1]

I am, Sir, Your Most Obedient Servt
C GUILOT

Edinb. Novembr 25 1710

Any letter Directed to Mr Wm Clift at Mr Walter Ross's to be left at Mr David Monroe in Edinb Will come to my hand. The Number of Such Names is to make it Secure.[2]

MS. (in Defoe's hand, though disguised): Duke of Portland, Defoe Papers, 1 ff. 242–3. *Pub.*: *H.M.C. Portland*, iv. 633–4. *Address*: none. *Endorsed*: 'Mr Guilot Edenburg, Nov: 25: 1710 Ṛ Dec: 1.'

149. [To ROBERT HARLEY]. 3 December 1710

Sir

I have been So Anxious About the Safe Conveying of My Letters, haveing Not had the honor of the Least hint from your Self, That I Convey This Enclosed by a Trusty Friend, as well That I May be Sure of its Comeing to your hand, as That I may Reciev if you please One line for my Direction whether to stay here or Returne, and whether what I am doeing here, is for your Service and to your Satisfaction.

It is a Dissaster to me That I lost the Occasion of writeing by Mr Bell, whose Conduct I Observ'd to you Renders him Suspected to me.[3]

What Ever you please Sir to do me The Honor to Direct, Either by word or by writeing, will be faithfully Convey'd to me by Mr young,[4] the bearer, a faithfull and honest Man, and On whom I can So farr Depend or I would Not have Entrusted him.

I am, Sir, Your Most Humble and Obedt Servt
D F

Edinb. Decembr 3. 1710

I Wrot a long Letter this Night Directed to Mr Tho: Bateman[5] to which I Humbly Referr.

MS.: Duke of Portland, Defoe Papers, 1 ff. 244–5. *Pub.*: *H.M.C. Portland*, iv. 638. *Address*: none. *Endorsed*: 'Edenburg Dec: 3:: 1710, Ṛ Dec: 13:'

[1] No further explanation appears.
[2] The three persons—if persons they were—remain unidentified.
[3] See pp. 296–7.
[4] Unidentified.
[5] See p. 297, n. 1. The letter has not come to light.

150. [*To* ROBERT HARLEY]. *6 December 1710*

Sir

I Wrott you Two letters the last Post, One to Mr Bateman and One in Cover to a faithfull friend to Convey if possible to your Self and Reciv Some Notice of your haveing Recd Mine, for which I have been Indeed Very Anxious, and also to Reciev your further Commands.

The Notice here Sir that in 212 [Parliament] you have Personally Spoken Against 214 [the Pretender][1] has fixed the Character I have had the Honor to Spread here of your Steddy Zeal for the Revolution, and Confirmed what I hinted in My last that Lieutt Generall Maitland[2] had Avouch'd Publickly in your just Defence (Vizt): that No Man in Britain was a Greater Prop to the Constitution than your Self.

I was Very Glad to have So Good an Assistant in So great a piece of Justice to you Sir, who I think have Recd So Much Injury from Some, from whom you have Merited much better, and the Rather because it directly Contradicted what Dr Oldfield[3] had been bussy here in Spreading both of your Self and Even of your Great Mistress the Queen her Self.

Now the joy begins to be Visible among the honest people who were and still are firm to her Majties Person as Well as Governmt, but were Terrifyed with the Absurd Notions of all being to be Given up to the 214 [Pretender] Even by 233 [the Queen] her Self. It is not strange that a Thing So Ridiculous Should prevail if the assurance of those who Reported it were Considred, and that they had Obtain to be Sent up to 212 [Parliament], where they had peremptorily Said it should be don.

This Sir will Satisfye her Majtie That the Intrest of the Pretender is too great here to be Slighted, and that Nothing but Discouragements of it from her Self can keep them in bounds; but if her Majtie Pleases on any Occasion to Express her being pleased with the Zeal of her Subjects Against the Pretender, it Would strike them here as with a blast from Heaven, and Weaken his Intrest More than an army of 10000 Men Could do.

As to the people here, I mean the presbyterians, they Come heartily into Her Majties Intrest. Neither do they Relish the Chagrin of Our 288 [Whigs] in 116 [England]. The Ambas-

[1] See *Parliamentary History*, vi. 930.
[2] James Maitland, Commander of Fort William.
[3] See p. 285, n. 1.

sador¹ who has Resided here from the 106 [Dissenters], and who
has left his Mission here for 249 [Southwark],² is gone back re
Infecta, and his Negotiations have Made less Impression than indeed I Expected. In Short Sir, Nothing but the 214 [Pretender]
and Encroachments of 109 [Episcopacy]³ can make them Uneasy. I Endeavour to Assure them, and Shall hereafter Give
you Some Account of Mediums to preserv her Majties Intrest
here and yet make all but the 161 [Jacobites] Easy also.

I am, Sir, Your Most Obliged Servt
C Guilot

117 [Edinburgh] Decemb. 6. 1710

MS. (in Defoe's hand, though disguised): Duke of Portland, Defoe
Papers, 1 ff. 246–7. *Pub.*: *H.M.C. Portland*, iv. 641–2. *Address*: none. *Endorsed*:
'Edenburg Dece: 6, R̶ Dece: 16.'

151. [To Robert Harley]. 18 December 1710

Sir

I have wrott Frequently Since My Comeing hither. I hope
they are all Arrived. I had Determin'd to Leave this Place Some
days Since, Unless your Commands had prevented me, believing it more Usefull to Tender my Service Nearer your hand.
But the Unusuall Tempests, Storms and floods have Made the
Country Impracticable, So that there is No Passing the Country
Without Iminent Danger.

The Accounts last Post from England Seem to Make my
Stay here, tho' Otherwise accidentall, Very Usefull. Some
Private Letters have Alarm'd the Poor people here with a
Story That an attempt is to be Made Upon their Church in
the Case of Greenshields⁴ and in the Article of Patronages. The

¹ Probably Oldfield.
² Cartwright (see p. 293, n. 3) supplies 'secret service', which seems hardly
appropriate for so distinguished a dissenting minister as Oldfield; the word,
whatever it is, probably begins with 's', and Oldfield was minister at Southwark.
³ Cartwright supplies 'clergy', as a result of misreading the number as '100'.
But the number is clearly '109', which points to a word beginning with 'd' or 'e',
and the context suggests 'episcopacy'. See n. 4.
⁴ Use of the English liturgy had been growing among the Episcopal congregations in Scotland. These congregations, though protected by no act of toleration,
had caused no great resentment so long as their services differed little from those
of the parish kirk, but as they turned more and more to the Prayer Book and other
liturgical devices, they began to alarm the Establishment. And when, in 1709, the
Rev. James Greenshields set up an Episcopal meeting-house at the very door of
St. Giles's, Edinburgh, and there ostentatiously employed the English liturgy, his
boldness could hardly pass unchallenged; he was prosecuted and imprisoned. But
the affair did not end there, for Greenshields in a move that yet further alarmed
and exasperated the Scottish churchmen appealed his case to the 'prelatic' House of

first Tends to a Tolleration, the other to a Direct Invasion of the Constitution of the Church and, as they Say, The Union.[1]

Whether This be fact or no I can Give them No Answer as to that, but as I have all along perswaded them that No Evill is Designd Against them in all these alterations, and have Satisfyed them So Well that they began to be Very Easy; So I assure them Now, that her Majtie is So Tender of the Union that they May be assured Nothing will be done of any kind that shall any Way Encroach Upon it.

I Would Vallue my Self upon my haveing Some Influence upon things and persons here if I was pleading My Own Merit, but when I have an Argumt So Well founded as this of her Majties Royall Promise, I think it Very Much more to my advantage to Say I Rather Improve that forcible Argumt than perswade them by my Influence. The Queens promise in her late Speech,[2] This I Insist upon, and the people Depend upon it Very Much.

It is Not my bussiness Sir to Debate here the Reasons for or against A Tolleration here. I Presume from what you were pleased to Say to me, that you agree with Me in this, that this is not a proper Season, and I Crave leav to add that what Ever Some people may pretend, it is Not the Aim of the Dissenters[3] here, Nor do they Desire it.

However, I wave This Now. I Conciev my proper Work here is to Calm and quiet the minds of the people here, Reconcile them to her Majties Measures, and keep them Easy—of this I hope I can Give you a good Account, and am Very Thankfull for my Success.

I Fear indeed their Uneasyness from these New allarms, and Wish I knew what Answer to Give, but it is My Misfortune to act wholly by my Own judgement. If I am Defficient I Shall the Rather hope for your Pardon, but if I had the Honor of

Lords, a tribunal whose very jurisdiction over Scotland they denied. There the matter lay at this moment. Scottish resentment ran even higher when in Mar. 1710–11 the House of Lords gave judgement in favour of Greenshields. For Defoe's comments on the question see the *Reviews* for 4, 6, 8, and 11 Oct. 1709, and his *Greenshields out of Prison and Toleration Settled in Scotland*, 1710.

[1] These fears were well founded. By 1712 Parliament had passed a Toleration Act to protect Scottish Episcopalians and had restored to the old patrons the right of presentation. Both changes grew out of the Greenshields affair.

[2] On 29 Nov. the Queen had assured both Houses of Parliament: 'I shall employ none, but such, as are heartily for the Protestant Succession in the House of Hanover; the Interest of which Family no Person can be more truly concerned for, than myself' (*J.H.C.* xvi. 403).

[3] That is, the Episcopalian Dissenters from the Church of Scotland.

your Instructions I should act with more Effect as well as with
More Courage.

I am, Sir, Your Most Obedient faithfull Servant

C GUILOT

Edinb. Decemb. 18. 1710

MS. (in Defoe's hand, though disguised): Duke of Portland, Defoe Papers,
1 ff. 248–9. *Pub.*: *H.M.C. Portland*, iv. 646–7. *Address*: none. *Endorsed*:
'Cl. Guilot Dece: 18 1710, R̸ Dece: 28:'

152. JOSEPH BUTTON[1] *to* DEFOE. [*c. 25 December*] *1710*

Sir

Yours of the 23 Inst I recd, but had Sent you before 400
Pa[ ]² prophesies.³ I knew there were Severall Errata's in't
but did [not?] think it worth while to amend; however when
I've sold these [ ] I've already done, & do more, shall both
correct and print [ ] addenda's. If you don't Sell those sent,
pray return 'em [ ]. In the Gazette of Thursday Xbr 21 there
is Something of Sir [ ] Cunningham.⁴ I suppose that is it you
wou'd ha' printed. There is [ ] in that you sent last, & you say
it is in that paper—

As to the Man & boy, I can't tell what to say in the Matter.
If you can get a boy, perhaps now this Saywell⁵ is bad & lo[w?]

---

¹ Joseph Button was a bookseller on Tyne Bridge, Newcastle, and publisher of
the *Newcastle Gazette*.
² The right-hand margin of the MS. is badly worn; the affected parts are
represented by brackets.
³ The 'prophesies' cannot be identified, but see p. 305, n. 1, below and also
Defoe's reference to 'the Northern Prophecy' which he saw 'in *Scotland* in *November*
last' (*Review*, 26 Apr. 1711).
⁴ Cunningham is unidentified; no copy of either the *Newcastle Gazette* or the
New Edinburgh Gazette for 21 Dec. is known to survive. C. E. Burch identified this
person as Sir Alexander Cunningham, Advocate, and maintained that Sir Alexander
had failed to appear before the Presbytery of Edinburgh to answer a charge of
adultery and that Defoe was interested in publicizing that defection ('Defoe and
the Edinburgh Society for the Reformation of Manners', *Review of English Studies*,
xvi [1940], 306–12). But even though Cunningham's first name is worn away in
the MS., enough of the initial remains to suggest that whoever he was his Christian
name probably did not begin with 'A'. Furthermore, the whole case for identifying
Button's Cunningham as Sir Alexander rests ultimately on a printed notice of 1711
concerning the failure to appear before the Presbytery of 'Sir Alexander C—ing
of C—ter', which for some reason has been taken to mean Sir Alexander Cunningham. But 'Sir Alexander C—ing of C—ter' is clearly quite another person, Sir
Alexander Cumming of Culter; the printed notice therefore does not concern any
Cunningham at all, and is hence quite irrelevant to the present question.
⁵ The *Newcastle Gazette* was 'Printed by *J. Saywell*, for *J. Button*, Bookseller on
the Bridge.'

in Pockett & in debt would be willing for the Money to Instruct him.

But than Who must he be bound to? It must be to your selfe [for?] I can neither make him free of London nor Edinburgh— & another [thing?] these fellows have so disgusted & tired my wife that I don't know how I sha[ll] please her in bringing any More. I'm for haveing these two fell[ows] out of the house as soon as possible, & in order to it have desired [them] to look out Lodgeings &c.

When you do Bickerstaff[1] I wou'd not ha' you fright all people as you say you will; perhaps the Governmt may call us in question for intimidateing her Majesties good subjects—

Who woud ha' thought but the Provost,[2] who I heard you say was [your?] very good friend, wou'd ha' given you the advertisemt else it shou'd [ ] been Sent.

Mr Moody[3] hase your steell[4] & 3*d* per pound & he pay Carriage. 5 [ ] are shipt aboard the same old wife your pickles are in & directed for [your?] Brother Davis.[5] Your specticles hase been mended many daies ago & [are?] lyeing by me. If you'll ha' 'em sent, they shall.

I hear nothing of the paper you Say you ordered from London. [ ] a happy Xmas, I am

Your friend & Servt
JOS: BUTTON

[ ][6] 1710

MS.: National Library of Scotland, 1717 f. 16. The MS. was found loose in a copy of the *Newcastle Gazette* for 23–25 Dec. 1710. *Pub.*: James Maidment, *Analecta Scotica*, Second Series, Edinburgh, 1837, pp. 79–80. *Address*: 'To Daniel D Foe Esqr., in Edinburgh, post pd 3*d*, but one Sheet.'

153. [*To* ROBERT HARLEY]. *26 December 1710*

Sir

I have Constantly written to you by the Same Conveyance as this, and have given you an Exact Account of Every thing Materiall in this Part. I am Perticularly Unhappy in not haveing the least hint any way whether mine Come to hand or no, which Restrains me very much in my writeing, fearing what

[1] According to the title-page, Defoe's *British Visions, or Isaac Bickerstaff Senior: Being Twelve Prophecies for the Year 1711* was 'Printed First in the North, and Now Reprinted at London.' See the *Review* for 28 Apr. 1711.
[2] Adam Brown.　　　　　　[3] Unidentified.
[4] The reading is dubious.　　[5] Robert Davis, Defoe's brother-in-law.
[6] MS. torn.

hands it may fall into and knowing the jealousy and temper of the people I have to do with.

I think Sir I may boast to you of my little Mannagemt in this Place, where the people are brought to be perfectly Easy in her Majties Measures and have a full Confidence in her Majties Concern for the Generall Good. I might assume the Words *I have brought them to this*, but I leave that to your Charity.

I have done my Self the honour On all Occasions to do Justice to her Majties Measures in the late Changes, in Answer to the Clamour of Some Certain people which had Reached thus far, and which began to Spread here, both Against your Self and against Other of her Majties faithfull Servants, and in this I have the happyness to assure you Sir there is none of that Noise heard here; but the Dependance of the Honestest people here, is On your Zeal for the Libertys of your Country and her Majties justice to the Constitution, and when They hear of Some let in to posts of Trust and Power whose former Measures they have Reason to Apprehend, They Frequently Conclude Their Safety Depends upon Her Majtie and the Councils of Mr H . . . .

This is the Plain and True state of the Temper here. I hope you will not Suspect I flatter My Self in it; if it were Otherwise I know my Duty better than to Conceal it.

Here have been Two Vile Ill Natur'd Pamphlets prepared, both of which have fallen into My hands in Manuscript, and I think I have prevented both their Printing. The first Was advertised in the Gazette here and Called the Scots atalantis.[1] The Printer being My Accquaintance, I got a Sight of it but Could not get a Coppie. However, I Warnd him Against Venturing to print it, upon his Refuseing which, the Author Sent for it Again, and he knows not the Messenger. It was full of Invectives Against the Queen and Governmt, the Parliamt, and Especially the Members Sent from hence to the Peers. It had Some Banter on the Lord Glennochy[2] and Some Satyr upon familys which Appear'd meer Scotish, but Otherwise it Seemd to be done in England, or at least by Some hand that had been lately there. The Messengr said he that sent the advertisemt was a Lord, and Gave the Printer 2. 6*d* for putting it in the first Time, and paid him for a Second, but on My Warning the Printer he Refused to put in the Second, and they have never

---

[1] In such issues as I have been able to find of the *Scots Postman, or the New Edinburgh Gazette*, there is no mention of the *Scots Atalantis*.

[2] John Campbell (1662–1752), son of the Earl of Breadalbane.

yet Sent to kno' the Reason, but I suppose on his Returning the Coppy, they care not to be So Much known as to Reciev the Money back.

The Other Pamphlet is called *Atalantis Major*; and is a Bitter Invective against the D of Argyle, the E of Mar, and the Election of the Peers. It is Certainly Written by Some English man, and I have Some Guess at the Man, but dare not be positive.[1] I have hitherto kept this also from the Press, and believ it will be Impossible for them to get it printed here after the Measures I have Taken. The Party I Got it of pretends the Coppy Came from England, but I am of Another Opinion. I shall Trouble you no farther about it because if possible I can get it Coppyed, I will Transmit the Coppy by Next post, for I have the Originall in My hand. They Expect I shall Encourage and assist them in the Mannageing it, and Till I can Take a Coppy I shall not Undeciev them.

I beg your favourable Construction of My Conduct in an Age So Nice as this, and hope On all Occasions to Approve my Self to be

Sir, Your faithfull Humble and Obedient Servt
C GUILOT

Edinb. Decembr. 26. 1710

MS. (in Defoe's hand, though disguised): Duke of Portland, Defoe Papers I ff. 250–1. *Pub.*: *H.M.C. Portland*, iv. 647–8. *Address*: none. *Endorsed*: 'Mr Guilot Dec: 26 1710.'

154. [*To* ROBERT HARLEY]. *1 January 1710/11*

Sir

I am humbly to Ask your Pardon that I have not been able to Send you yet the Coppy of the Book which in my last I Gave you Notice of, yet I have with Some Difficulty and meerly by force prevented its goeing to the press. I Shall yet in a few days Compass an Opportunity to get it Coppyed.

I am Very Anxious About my letters, yet I presume to give you hints of what Occurrs here. The Concern of the people here has been quieted as I formerly Noted, but a New Suggestion Rises Now of Some Mischief awaiting them from the Case of Greenshields, whose Petition and Appeal lyes Now before the

---

[1] But of course Defoe himself is now known to have been the author of *Atalantis Major*, which was published early in the following year (Lee, *Life*, i. xxxvi). Note the outrageous equivocations in the last two paragraphs. There is no evidence that Harley penetrated the deception.

house of Lords, and whose wholl Case has from its beginning threatned them here with that formidable Creature, a Tolleration.[1]

I have Sir with your license allways Taken So Much freedome in My Layeing these things before you as to State Rather the Intrest of the Governmt than the Merits of the Cause, but here I think both Argue Against Countenancing this attempt— I am No biggot, and farther yet from a friend to Coertions of any kind. But Sir, The Liberty Obtaind here by Connivance is So great, the people that will Accept of a Tolleration Except without Oaths to the Governmt So few,[2] the Design of Seeking it So Manifestly a plot upon the public peace, and the Consequences apparently So Distracting to the people here, who are Now So happily Easy Under all her Majties Measures, that I Can not but in Duty to her Majtie and in Obedience to the Orders you were pleased to give me Accquaint you of the Case, And humbly Offer it to your Consideration whether at Least this may be a Time for it.

There is Another Affair Relateing to Justices Imposeing the Oaths to the Ministers which Requires a little your Thots when at Leisure, and which I shall be better quallifyed to lay before you in a post or Two.

I have been So long here without your Commands Either to stay or to Remove, That Indeed I had presum'd to Come Away, had the Roads been Passable,[3] my Circumstances also Unhappily Dissabling me to Subsist longer, without your Goodness had been Extended as Usuall for my Support.

I Can Not but presume to hint (however Remote to My present sphere), the Time for Ways and Means being at hand, that a Contrivance of Some people in England to prevent the Governmt in the Article of Funds, has Gone that length as they are Very sure of Success.

I am at a loss how to Express My Self on this head, but I

---

[1] See p. 302, n. 4. By 1 Mar. the House of Lords had tried the Greenshields case and had held 'that the said Sentence of the Magistrates of *Edinburgh*, and the Decree of the Lords of Session in *North Britain*, made against the said *James Greenshields*, shall be, and they are hereby, reversed' (*J.H.L.* xix. 240). An Act of Toleration, protecting Scottish Episcopalians, was passed in 1712.

[2] 'As staunch adherents of the Pretender, the majority of them [the Episcopal clergy] were deprived by their political principles of sharing in the benefits of a toleration, qualified by an oath of abjuration' (Mackinnon, *Union of England and Scotland*, p. 419).

[3] 'This moneth and the last, yea, almost these ten weeks, we have had the most excessive rains and tempestouse winds that I ever was witness to' (Wodrow, *Analecta*, i. 312).

humbly Lay it before you, whether it shall be Expedient for her Majties Service, to Lay funds and Venture their filling *by loans,* or Rather, to think of Means to Raise the sums within the Time, which no Doubt, Notwithstanding pretences of Poverty, bad News abroad, and Divisions at home, May be Effected. My Anxiety on this head proceeds from My knowledge of the Design above to bank the funds, and My Sence of the Consequence of Such a Dissappointment.

I am, Sir, Your Most Humble and Obedient Servt
DE F

Edinb. Jan. 1. 1710

MS. (in Defoe's hand, though disguised): Duke of Portland, Defoe Papers, 1 ff. 252–3. *Pub.*: *H.M.C. Portland,* iv. 650–1. *Address*: none. *Endorsed*: 'Cl. Guilot Janu: 1: 1710/11, R̷ Janu: 8:'

155. [*To* ROBERT HARLEY]. 9 *January 1710/11*

Sir

I have Since my last had Occasion of doeing I hope Some little Service here, The Commission of the assembly haveing been Sitting for this Week past; I have been forward to Accquaint you Every Time I write of the Good Disposition of the people here and Especially how Well the Ministers behave. Yet at this time, the Numbers Met being Great, they were not without Some hot Spirits who had Diverse projects and made Several Essays to bring the Meeting into Some Heats: first they were for an Address to the queen in which they would have been Glad to Introduce Some Uneasy things about Greenshields, about Tolleration, and about Invasion of Churches in the North. But with Some help they have been put off from this.

Then they were for appointing a fast, and had that Design Gone On, it Might have been hard to have kept them from bringing in Some Odd reasons for a fast, for fear of haveing No Good Reasons to Give. But the News of Our loss in spain[1] falling in, Some Moved for a fast upon that Account, which had Some Reall foundation; but then the Gentlemen that had a worse Design in it Dropt their Motion and So the wholl fell to the ground for that Time.[2]

There fell an Unhappy Jarr in their Way of a rabble upon a

[1] The Allies had suffered a bad season in Spain, and on 9 Dec. Vendôme had defeated and captured General Stanhope and 4,000 British troops at Brihuega.

[2] That the Queen should be asked to set the fast 'was thought unfitt'; the Commission therefore left the matter to the individual Presbyteries. See Wodrow, *Analecta,* i. 315.

Number of their Ministers in a Presbytry Meeting in Angus; in which many of the Ministers were Stoned and Beaten.[1] This is put in a way of process in the Criminall Court, and at that they are Something Pacifyed. The Gentlemen of that Country have Really Acted too Imprudently in it, and thereby given them advantages Against them which they Need Not have done.

Last Night the Commission Rose again and the Ministers are Most of them Disperst; and I am Glad to Write in this Time of Uneasyness that they parted So Well.

I am, Sir, Your Most Humble & Obedient Servt
C GUILOT

Edinb. Jan. 9. 1710

MS. (in Defoe's hand, though disguised) : Duke of Portland, Defoe Papers, 1 ff. 254–5. *Pub.*: *H.M.C. Portland*, iv. 652–3. *Address*: none. *Endorsed*: 'Mr Guilot Eden: Janu: 9 1710/11, ℞ Janu: 18:'

156. [*To* ROBERT HARLEY]. *13 February 1710/11*

Sir

Tho' I Confess the honour you are Pleased to do me in Frequent and long Audience is Very Great, yet Sir, Considering The weight of Public Affaires which Lyes on your hands, and The Sevll Things which after so long Absence[2] I have to Give you an Account of, Some of which if Not all May be of Importance; I thought it my Duty to Save as Much as possible your Time and Trouble by Minuting Down Thus the heads of Things, That you May please to call for Such first as you find Most proper, and Such as you please may be after lay'd before you in writeing.

1st Of The Temper of the People in Scotland, Their Temper when I came There, Their Temper when I left Them, what uneasynesses They have left, and how they May be kept Easy.

Of The Affaires of the Church, Greenshields,[3] Tolleration, Common prayer, Intrusion and the Rabbles upon their Presbytrys in the North.

Of The Mission of Dr O,[4] The Breaking up of all Correspondence between Them and The Dissenters in London, and of

[1] See Wodrow, *Analecta*, i. 315.
[2] He had been absent from London since the preceding November.
[3] See p. 302, n. 4.
[4] Joshua Oldfield. See p. 285, n. 1.

Their New Agent,[1] The Commissions Motion for a Correspondence &c.[2]

The State of the Civill and Millitary administration There, with Characters of Persons And Conduct as They Respect The late Changes.

Of The State of the Debate between Johnston and Hamilton or Between the Merchants and The Trades in The Election for Edinb.[3]

Of The Project Pushing on by Sir Pat. Johnston at the Expence of the City of Edinb. for a Dock &c. at Leith—[4]

Of The Raiseing Men in The Highlands and The Directing Genll Maitland to That Work.[5]

Of The Assembly, Their last Division and How Cool'd,[6] about a Medium for quieting Them in the Nicety of Appointing Fasts &c,[7] about a Comissioner,[8] and about her Maj' letter to Their Next Meeting.

Of all These Perticulars I May have Severall Things to lay before you, Usefull and proper for your Observation in your Mannageing That Difficult people in the North.

In Matters Relateing to England, I Humbly Crave leave to Offer That if [you][9] Think it proper I should Turn My Thoughts That way, I May have Something to Say On the following Subjects.

Credit and of Proper Means for Filling The Lottery[10] which I

[1] In January Wodrow had written: 'The bussiness of sending up some to agent the Churche's business at London is yet delayed as unfitt, and soe I think it will be delayed till the nixt Assembly' (*Analecta*, i. 315). In the meantime Defoe himself seems to have been acting as agent to the Kirk. One reason for his wishing not to return immediately to Scotland was 'least on My Suddain Return, They May Think They want a Correspondent here, and Return to the Notion of Settling Some Other Agent' (p. 320).

[2] 'About the end of this moneth [Dec. 1710] we had a meeting of Correspondents at Glasgou, for all the Presbitrys of the Synod. . . . It was wished that some would, in a sheet that might be spread throu the country, expose the hazard and danger we are in from the Pretender and Popery, and the hazard of the English Service, and we wer appointed to meet the last Wensday of January' (Wodrow, *Analecta*, i. 313).

[3] See *H.M.C. Portland*, x. 159.

[4] See No. 139, enclosure.

[5] See *H.M.C. Portland*, x. 374.

[6] See R. H. Story, *William Carstares*, 1894, p. 320.

[7] See Story, op. cit., p. 325.

[8] Defoe's nominations for the office of Commissioner to the General Assembly appear in the following letter.

[9] MS. has 'your'.

[10] As a device for raising public funds the Lottery had been abandoned in 1699, but had been revived by the Commons in 1710. Defoe points out some defects of the scheme in the *Reviews* for 19 Apr. and 31 July 1711.

hear Allready Some people please Themselves with Expectation of Seeing Dissappointed.

Funds, and Therein of a Clause in the Coal Duty[1] which Very Much Sinks the Revenue.

Post office, and Some Circumstances which May Enlarge That Duty.[2]

Stamp Office, and Some Perticulars of Encreasing That Duty, with Some brief hints of Other Funds which, if you Approve Of, May be Enlarg'd Upon afterward.

Affrican Company, and How to Make Them Usefull to advance a Sum of Money on Their New proposall which is Now prepareing.[3]

French Trade, and how it May be Opened Most to advantage both of the Nation and of the Revenue.[4]

I ask your Pardon for the Length of This, and hope it is Not Impertinent. I shall wait your Commands On which of These Things to begin, That I May be as little Troublesome and as Much usefull as possible.

I am, Sir, Your Most Humble and Obedient Servt
DE FOE

Feb. 13. 1710

Sir

Haveing Given you So long a Diversion Allready, I Should have forborne Sayeing any Thing of the Unpleasant Part. But a Long and Expensive Journey, Family Importunitys, and all the *et Cetera's* that Make a Dependant allways Importunate; These Sir force me, in spight of Blushes, to Remind you of The usuall Period being past of That Relief, which by what Ever hand I Recd it, was Originally Owing to your Goodness.[5]

I shall Venture to Say Nothing of Merit but This, That as I Resolve to have an Entire Dependance On your hand Sir, So I

---

[1] The coal duties were at present paying for the rebuilding of St. Paul's, and were being looked to as a source of funds for building 50 new churches in London.

[2] A re-examination of the whole postal system was under way. The resulting Act for Establishing a General Post Office received the royal assent in the following May (*J.H.C.* xvi. 668).

[3] The Company, all but ruined by the war, was attempting to reorganize itself (*J.H.C.* xvi. 522).

[4] Although the war continued, a movement was afoot to allow the importation of wine from France (*J.H.C.* xvi. 556). Defoe had never favoured the prohibition of trade with France, war or no war (*Review*, 25 Feb., and 6 and 10 Mar. 1711).

[5] According to the Secret Service accounts, he had received £50 as of 27 Dec., but this may have been required to satisfy Edinburgh obligations. See Laurence Hanson, *Government and the Press*, 1936, p. 96.

would Gladly be made Usefull, That I May Not be an Unprofitable Servant.

I am, Sir, and Ever Shall be
Your Most faithfull and Obedt Servt
DE FOE

MS.: Duke of Portland, Defoe papers, 1 ff. 256–7. *Pub.*: *H.M.C. Portland*,
iv. 659–60. *Address*: none. *Endorsed*: 'Mr Claude Guilot, Febr: 13: 1710/11,
℞ Febr: 14:'

157. [*To* ROBERT HARLEY]. *19 February 1710/11*
Sir

In Obedience to your Comands, I have Applyed My Self
More Perticularly to Think of a Proper Person to Serve her
Majtie as Commissionr to the Genll Assembly, and in Ordr Sir to
Represent Things with More Clearness, I have with the best of
My Judgment, Drawn Out short Descriptions, or Characters of
the Persons, That Seem proper for That Charge; which I beg
Leave to Lay before you for Observation, with This Exception
Onely, That These Characters are more Perticularly Confind to
Their Conduct in the Affair before you, Their Temper, Intrest,
and Acceptableness with the people *There*, and The Governmt
here, Since, as I Conciev, a person May be fitt and Acceptable on
One Side, and Not On the Other, But That the present Case
is to find One if possible That May be So to both.

From Hence Sir, I Conclude The wholl Squadroni Utterly
Unquallifyed, as a Set of Men Tho' Otherwise Well Enough
with the Kirk, yet Unfitt for the Queens Intrest to Consist with;
and This Sir is the Onely Objection I have to My Lord Polwarth,[1]
who would Otherwise be a Man without Exception, both for
Sence, Moderation, and Agreeableness to both Sides, and perhaps were Some Method Used with him, Might be Seperated
From Them:—This Also Removes My Ld Yester[2] from My
Thoughts, Tho' he has also No Intrest among the Ministers,
which is an aditionall Exception.

I Come Next to the Persons you were Pleased to Name, and

---

[1] Alexander Hume-Campbell (1675–1740), later Earl of Marchmont, now
styled Lord Polwarth, was elevated to the Bench as Lord Cessnock, supported the
Union Treaty, and served as a member of the Committee on the Equivalents.
Defoe was acquainted with him (pp. 159 and 176).

[2] John Hay (before 1670–1715), eldest son of the Marquess of Tweeddale.

which I humbly Objected Against, as First the Marquiss of Annandale,[1] and (Second) the Marquis of Louthain.[2] The first is of No Reputation on Either Side, because Steady to None. Nor would the Ministers have any Confidence in him, Or Come into any Thing he should propose,— The Second has Made himself Odious by Scandalous Vices, and Imorrallitys; Sordid Covetousness, and Some Things So Offensive, That it Might be Some question, Whether They would Not Rather Think of Delateing him for Scandal, Than Recieving him as a Commissioner.

If I did Not Think it my Duty Sir to Lay Every Thing Nakedly before you, I should Not go Such a length in Characters, Especially of Men you were pleased to Name, But I hope The Necessity of Giveing you a Clear View of Things, will Excuse Me.

It is Really Not the Easyest Thing, in a place where a Church is So Generally Abandonn'd of her Nobillity, to find a Man who will Suit both Sides of The present Circumstance; yet I shall Name a few of Such, as I Think May be Depended Upon.

The Earle of Polewarth (Except as before Excepted).

The Earle of Loudon.[3] I do Not Take his Character to be So Clear with the Church, as I Take him to have a True View of her Majties Intrest, and yet to be without any Visible Objection on the Side of the Kirk also.

The Earle of Hyndford.[4] I Think a person without Exception, but Doubt if he would Serve.

The Earle of Buchan.[5] I Think without Exception also Perfectly Agreeable to the Ministers, and yet to be Mannag'd; He

[1] William Johnstone (1664–1721), first Marquis of Annandale, had opposed the Union but was a representative peer in the first Union Parliament. In spite of Defoe's objection, Annandale was appointed Commissioner.

[2] William Kerr (1661–1722), second Marquess of Lothian, supported the Union, in 1707 became Lieutenant-General, and in 1708 was elected representative peer but was unseated on a petition. According to Macky, Lothian 'is brave in his Person, loves his Country and his Bottle; a *thorough Libertine*; very handsom, Black, with a fine Eye' (*Memoirs of the Secret Services of John Macky, Esq.*, 1733, p. 198).

[3] Hugh Campbell (d. 1731), third Earl of Loudon, had been Keeper of the Great Seal of Scotland since 1708, and was a representative peer both now and for the rest of his life.

[4] James Carmichael (d. 1737), second Earl of Hyndford, who had succeeded to the title of his eminent father in the previous September, was a Brigadier-General.

[5] David Erskine (1672–1745), first Earl of Buchan, a zealous Whig, had been Governor of Blackness Castle from 1702 to 1707 but had lost that and all his other offices as a consequence of having opposed the Union. The Governorship was restored in 1710, and he served as representative peer from 1715 to 1734. Buchan later learned of Defoe's recommendation (see No. 163). Defoe's grandson, David Erskine Baker (b. 1730), was named after the Earl, who was the child's godfather (Wilson, *Life*, iii. 647).

parted From The Squadroni in the Affair of the Union, and was
Dissoblig'd by The last Ministry in Voteing Against the Court,
for which My Lord Marr quarrelled [with][1] him; and he lost
the Governmt of Blackness Castle. They Report him to be Hott—
but I Think I Could Answer for him on That head. He is a
person of Great Integrity and Understanding, and I believ Can
do More with the Ministers Than Any Noble Man in Scotland.

The Earl of Weymiss.[2] I can Not Say for his Steadyness So
Much, but he stands well Enough with the Ministers, and is
Generally Belov'd.

There is another Person which for Ought I kno' Might be
able to Mannage both Sides Very Well, if Other Circumstances
will admitt. This is The Old Lord Advocate;[3] But I Doubt his
being Tractable to Measures, and is Immoderately Politick.

The Onely Person I Think Remaining That both Sides would
Trust is the Earle of Stair,[4] of whom There is Onely This Objection, his late Engagemt with The Squadroni.

I Humbly lay These Thoughts before you in Ordr to be farther
Discours't of Tomorrow, when I shall attend According to your
Commands.

Sir

I Can Not Close without Some Acknowlegemt (Tho' Small in
Proportion) of your Constant Bounty to me; The Small Return
I can Make Sir, is a Steady adhering to your Intrest and Service,
and a Dependence On your Goodness; That her Majties Bounty
to me and your Perticular Favors May Not be ill placed.

It is allways with Regrett That I Mention My Own Case to
you, and your Goodness has been allways Perticular in Preventing My Blushes on That Account. This Makes me Remembr
with Thankfullness, How you were pleased to Anticipate my
feares, by Telling Me your Last bounty (which I am Now
Acknowleging) was Not Part of her Majties Appointment; This
Sir Doubles my Thanks and Makes me Earnest to Merit (as
Much as Possible) So Much Goodness. I Most Humbly beg The

[1] Omitted in MS.
[2] David Wemyss (d. 1720), third Earl of Wemyss, was a supporter of the Union
and had sat in the first Union Parliament as a representative peer.
[3] Sir James Stewart (1635–1713) had been Lord Advocate from 1692 to 1709,
and in spite of his age was to be reappointed to that office in 1711. He was a
staunch Presbyterian and had opposed the Union, though not actively.
[4] John Dalrymple (d. 1747), second Earl of Stair, was a representative peer in
the first Union Parliament, commanded a brigade at Oudenarde, and became
Lieutenant-General in 1710.

Continuance of your Favour and Goodness, which I shall Study Never to forfeit.

I am, Sir, Your Most faithfull Obedt Servt

DE FOE

Feb. 19. 1710

MS.: Duke of Portland, Defoe Papers, 1 ff. 258–9. *Pub.*: *H.M.C. Portland*, iv. 661–2. *Address*: none. *Endorsed*: 'Cl. Guilot, Febr: 19: 1710/11.'

158. [*To* ROBERT HARLEY]. *26 February 1710/11*

Sir

Tho' the Other Accounts I am prepareing Seem Interrupted by This,[1] yet I Thought it my Duty to have my Eyes About me here also, as well as my Thoughts Intent Upon Scotland.

I have had but Little Time Since My Return to look among Our old Friends The whigs, and Therefore Could Say but Little when you were pleased to ask me of Them.

I am Sorry to be Witness to So Much of The weakness of Those I Thought would have before Now have been Wiser. When I came Among Some of My Oldest Accquaintance, They would hardly Converse with me Because as They Said I had fallen Upon Them in My Review for Runing Down Credit.[2] Yet I had Not Discourst half an hour before They Discovred themselves. One Said he Used to Pay Six Thousand Pounds in Upon Every Land Tax but Now had Not Paid in a farthing, Another had Constantly Discounted Navy bills but would Meddle with No More of Them, a Third would keep his Money by him Seaven year before he would Trust The Governmt with a Farthing, And the like. And yet These Gentlemen would Not have it Said That They Run Down Public Credit.

They Now Set up to Run Down and Discourage The Lottery[3] and Say Tis a Cheat; That The prizes Carry a shew of Smaller Odds Than the last but are but Triffles Except a Few, and They Inferiour to the Other; That the Fund is Confused and Uncertain, and The Summe Suppositious; That the Summe Appropriated in Perticular is Defficient by a great Deal besides the Charge of Mannagemt of which No Notice is Taken.

By This Last I perciev the Calculator I Gave you Notice of[4]

[1] Defoe presumably had visited Harley on the 20th, and apparently had received at that time orders to prepare reports on some of the subjects mentioned in No. 156.
[2] See especially the issues for 16, 18, 21, and 23 Nov. 1710.
[3] For the plan of the Lottery, see John Ashton, *A History of English Lotteries*, 1893, pp. 52–53. For some of Defoe's views upon it, see the *Reviews* for 19 Apr. and 31 July 1711.   [4] Unidentified.

Comes From Them and has been Among Them— I am Sorry to
See The Weakness of These people, and indeed Not More so
That I am Apprehensive of The Mischief They Can do, as That
No Men Are So Inconsiderable but They May do Some Hurt.
Sir if you Think it May be of any Service, I Humbly Offer my
Thoughts, That a Small Tract may be written, about the Size of
The Essay Upon Credit;[1] and with The Same Secresie; to Ex-
plain The Lottery it Self, and Answer a little The Coffee house
Clamour of ill Men, and Make Some of Them blush— It May be
So ordred as to be Disposed all Over England, and Into Scot-
land, principally Among Those people who are Most Influenced
by These people, and I am Verily Perswaded will be Mighty
Usefull at This Time.[2]

I hope your Charity will prevent any Suspicion That I do
This to Make a Charge. You are too Generous to me Sir to have
any Such Thought Enter into My heart; My wholl Design is
to Render Some Good Service if Possible to Merit and Make
Rationall The Bounty I do Reciev; and if it Cost Me Twenty
Pound Out of My Pocket, I shall Rejoyce to have done any
Thing if possible to Restore These wild People to the Govern-
ments Intrest, and The Rest (as well I May) I Referr to your
Self.

           I am, Sir, Your Most Humble and Obedt Servt
                           DE FOE

Feb. 26. 1710

MS.: Duke of Portland, Defoe Papers, I ff. 260–1. *Pub.*: *H.M.C. Portland*,
iv. 662–3. *Address*: none. *Endorsed*: 'Mr D: Feb: 26: 1710/11, R̵ Febr: 27.'

159. [*To* ROBERT HARLEY]. *2 March 1710/11*

Sir

I am Very Sorry to write to you On This Occasion, And
Indeed Never Thought the affair Could ha' been Carryed This
Length—Especially Considering what Assurances were given by
her Majties Express Direction at the Time of The Union.[3]

---

[1] Which Defoe had published anonymously in the previous August.

[2] Apparently Harley did not concur; Defoe is not known to have written such a
pamphlet. It would not have been needed anyhow, for the Lottery was filled by
13 Mar. (Luttrell, *Brief Relation*, vi. 701).

[3] On the previous day the House of Lords had considered the appeal of Greenshields (p. 302, n. 4), reversed the decision of the Scottish Courts, and thereby
opened the way for the Toleration Act of the following year. Defoe criticized the
decision of the Lords in the *Review* for 8 Mar., and reprehended Greenshields in
the *Reviews* for 17 and 22 Mar.

I am the More Concern'd, because of the Quiet, and Good Temper Things were brought to There, and The Difficulty There has been Ever Since, as well as at the Treaty, to bring it to That pass; which had Never been, had Not her Majtie been Very Faithfully Serv'd, by Some who perhaps have not themselves been heard of.

But it is Not a Time to look back. The bussiness is how to prevent the Mischief That will Other Wise Follow, which According to your Order Sir I have been Applying My Self to.

The First Step I have Thought of is, to Let Them kno', and Make Them if possible Satisfy'd in the Belief of it, That This part has not been Concerted by The Court; That her Majtie was Surpris'd at it, and Very Much Concern'd to hear how it was Carryed; That all the Queens Servts (Except &c.) were Ordred to Oppose it; and That her Majtie will do any Reasonable Thing to prevent The Evill Consequences of it.[1]

This Sir I Hint, because I have for These Three yeares past, Given Them Repeated assurances (and I presume by her Majties Especiall Direction) That The Queen would upon all Such Occasions, Take Them into her Protection; and prevent, as farr as possible, The Encroachments and Invasions which The Rest of That Party might push Them Upon. And This was Confirm'd by Letters From the Ministers of State at That Time and by Her Majties Express Command, Approveing of the proceedings of the Magistrates Against This Greenshields,[2] whose behavior was Not Insolent Onely to the kirkmen and Ecclesiastic judicatories, which he Contemn'd; but Even to the Magistrates and Indeed to the Magistracy it Self; and This Sir is Indeed One of the Worst Things I Apprehend as the Consequence of This, That if The Magistrates of the Capitall City May be Insulted, as They were Then, and I fear will be again on This Occasion; The Little Civil Governmt There is in scotland will be Lost, and The Matter will be Decided in Every place by Tumults and Rabbles;—which Tho' Mischievous Every where, will be worse There, and will Never End without blood, to the Destruction of her Majties Authourity and bringing all Things into Confusion.

For This Reason Sir I Most Humbly propose, That if her Majtie Thinks Fitt, These Two steps, or Such Other as Shall Appear Reasonable, May be Taken.

---

[1] Harley and his close colleagues had indeed opposed the measure. See *Lockhart Papers*, i. 346–7.

[2] See Wodrow, *Analecta*, i. 211–12.

1st *As before*, to quiet Them Gradually, with Assurances That the Queen will Protect Their Church, in all its just Rights, and Encourage No Innovations &c, and let Them have (as before) private hints, That the Queen was Not pleased with or Concern'd in the past Transaction of the Peers. And This if you please May be My Province.

2. To Restrain (by Mannagemt on the Other hand) The Insolcnce of Those, who Think themselves Let loose by This Victory to Offer New Affronts to the people There; and to Invade Either Their Civill or Religious Rights.

These Two Things I Humbly Offer my Thoughts in, in Obedience to your Commands, As what I Concieve to be The Onely Method to quiet Them Under the First Surprises, and I Doubt Not but Time and Application May Reconcile Things better; But if the Other Side Gentlemen go on to Renew Their Insulting of The Magistrates, and of the kirk; and Set up the Common prayer book as it were by Authourity, I Dread The Consequences, and am allmost Assured The Rabble will Tear them to peices, The Consequence of which I Need Not Insist on to you Sir.

And yet Sir I Dare Say, were quiet Calm Steps Taken, Even That formidable Creature the Liturgy would *in Time* Come to be a Native of Scotland; But by Violence The Aversions will Encrease.

The proposall Sir I Humbly offer here, I Make the Rather, because The Ministers There, in whom you kno' Much of the peoples Conduct is Resolved, have been Ever Since the Union perswaded, That Their Safety Depends More Upon her Majties Personall Veracity and Pious adhereing to her Royall Word in The Assurances Given Them of her Gracious protection, Than in any Security by The Constitution of The Treaty—and This will Not Onely Confirm That Opinion, which I have allways Cultivated Among Them, But farther Endear her Majtie to Them.

At the Same Time, Her Majtie May So Hold the Ballance Between Them, That They May No More Oppress The Episcopall men, Than They May Invade The Establishmt, and I shall lay before her Majtie a Scheme of Such a Temperament when Ever you please to Command it.

I Shall Omit Nothing in This juncture, That May Contribute to heal This Breach, and to Restore Things There; And if you Think Sir *My Goeing* May Contribute any Thing to Makeing

319

Them Easy, I am allways at your Disposall:—'Tho if you please to Accept my Thoughts upon That, I humbly Suggest, It May Not be So Usefull just Now, as Some Time hence; least on My Suddain Return, They May Think They want a Correspondent here, and Return to the Notion of Settling Some Other Agent, By which I May loose the Opportunity (Not the Office, for That is of Not a penney Advantage) of Serving her Majties Intrest with Them.[1]

I shall attend in the Evening, According to your Commands, in Ordr to Reciev what Instructions you please to Give in This Affair; and beg, if you please, That I May Reciev Them This Night, because, as you were pleased to Say you would Not have it Delay'd Longer Than Next post, I would have Time Enough to write to all the parts where I Correspond, which is Seaven or Eight; That if possible The Antidote May Spread as far as The Poison, and as fast.

> I am, Sir, Your Most Humble Faithfull
> And Obedient Servt
>> [signature torn off]

March. 2. 1710

MS.: Duke of Portland, Defoe Papers, 1 ff. 262–3. *Pub.*: *H.M.C. Portland*, iv. 663–5. *Address*: none. *Endorsed*: 'Scotland, Mr Guilot, March. 2: 1710/11.'

160. *[To* ROBERT HARLEY]. *3 March 1710/11*

Sir

I am Really Perplexing you with Letters on The Occasion of This New Affair of Scotland, But hope My Zeal for The Service will Excuse My Impertinence.

I have had My Thoughts Very Intent Upon The Thing it Self, and have been up all Night writeing Letters Upon the Subject, According to My Proposall and your Commands: But a New Thought Offring it Self, I Could Not but Lay it before you Sir for your Approbation, and This is whether if a Small pamphlett of 2 or 3 sheets at Most were written to Allay the feares and Lessen the Surprize of the people There, to Dispose Them to Consider Calmly of Things, and a Little Encourage Them—whether you may not Think it Usefull at Such a juncture as This, and follow it with a Second at Some Distance of Time, to Improve and Applye the first.

This Sir I Can Send from Hence in Manuscript, and print it at Edinb: and privately Convey Them Among The Ministers all

[1] See p. 311, n. 1.

Over scotland, and I am perswaded, Submitting it at the Same Time to your Commands, That it May do a Very Great Service.[1]

I am Sorry to Mention The Expence, and should not if My Unhappy Craveing Circumstances would bear it. But as I Entirely Submitt that to your Self, So Sir I shall go the Uttmost Length I Can without a Demand; But if I speak my Own Sence, I Think if it Came to 30 or 40 or 50 pound, it would be well plac't, and May do More Service just Now Than Modesty will let me Name. But I forbear to Urge my Own Opinion. I shall attend in the Evening According to your Command.

I am, Sir, Your Most Obedt Servt
DE FOE

March 3. 1710

MS.: Duke of Portland, Defoe Papers, 1 ff. 264–5. *Pub.*: *H.M.C. Portland* iv. 665. *Address*: none. *Endorsed*: 'Edenburg, March 3: 1710/11.'

161. [?   ][2] *to* DEFOE. *24 March 1710/11*

24th March 1711

Memorial Anent the power and priviledge of presenting ministers in Scotland

Before the reformation the power of presentation of ministers belonged to the Patrons who were bound to present a fitt qualified person upon any vacancy in the Church, with this distinction That the Laick patron was bound to present Such a fitt person to the Bishop within four months of the Vacancy, And if ane Ecclesiastick Patron, within Six months, which time was computed from their knowledge of the vacancy, and the reason of the distinction of the time was because if the Laick Patron did present ane unfitt person he had liberty to present ane other, but if the Ecclesiastick Patron, to whom the qualifications of the person were presumed to have been knowen, did present ane unfitt person he did forfault his priviledge for that time. Lib. 1 Reg. Maj. cap 2. parag. 3d and 4th.[3]

The Patron's right did arryse either from the donation of the Subject which was the Subsistence of the Ecclesiastick person, or from building the Church, or from the donation of the ground

[1] If Defoe wrote such a pamphlet, it has not been identified.
[2] No covering letter at present accompanies the MS. and the handwriting is unidentified.
[3] The citation refers to *Regiam Majestatem*, which was compiled by Sir John Skene in 1607. See *Regiam Majestatem and Quoniam Attachiamenta*, ed. Lord Cooper, Edinburgh: Stair Society, 1947, p. 61.

wherupon the Church was built, conform to the knowen rule Patronum faciunt dos, edificatio fundus; and before the reformation where no Patron was knowen the Pope claimed the right as universall Patron, though many of our Kings of Scotland did both question and deny them that priviledge.

Though the Patrons had allwayes this power of presentation, yet the institution and collation or admission was allwayes lodged in the hands of Churchmen, to whom also the power of presentation belonged jure devoluto when the Patrons did not present a fitt person within the Space appointed by Law.

Before the reformation the power and priviledge of institution, collation or admission, and priviledge of presentation jure devoluto, was lodged in the hands of the Bishop or Archbishop as Sd is. But after the reformation Scotland haveing reformed by Presbiters, and the Church government then consisting of Presbiters divided into Presbitries, Provinciall, and Generall assemblies, and each Presbitrie and Provinciall assemblie haveing a Superintendant, and there being ane appeal from the Presbitry to the Provinciall, and from the Provinciall to the Generall assembly, By the 7th act i. parl James the 6,[1] the examination and admission of Ministers in Scotland was lodged in the hands of these Churchmen, and the Patrons bound to present a qualified person within Six months from their knowledge of the Vacancy to the Superintendent of the bounds or those haveing commission from the Presbiters within that bounds. And in case of refusall to admitt the person so presented, there was ane appeal to the Superintendant and the Provinciall assembly and from them to the Nationall assembly. And in case the Patron did not present a fitt person within the Space forsaid, the power of presentation as well as admission did belong to the Superintendant and Presbiters within the bounds where the benefice lay.

The Patrons had the power of retaining and disposing of the whole fruits of the benefice dureing the Vacancy by the act ii5. parl. 12. James 6,[2] yea even after Episcopacy was restored by K. James the 6th anno 1606. As appears by the 1st act parl. 2i James 6.[3]

By the introduction of Episcopacy the time forsaid, the power

---

[1] See *Acts of the Parliament of Scotland*, 1814–44, iii. 23. The references offered by Defoe's correspondent require identification because they are based on a system of numbering different from that of the editions now considered standard.

[2] Ibid. iii. 542–3.

[3] Ibid. iv. 469.

of admission of ministers and presentation jure devoluto was lodged in the hands of the Bishops and Archbishops from the act forsaid and other acts of parliament James the 6th.

After the reformation the Abbacies and Priories were erected into temporall Lordships and the Lords of erection had the right to the tyths and were Patrons of the Churches within these Benefices, whereby and with the Patronages that belonged to Laick Patrons before the reformation very few patronages were reserved to the Croun, and of these few a pairt did accress to the Bishops from the establishing of Episcopacy by K. Ja. 6th.

King Charles the 1st upon his accession to the Croun, from the information of the prejudice to the Croun by these erections of Church lands, teynds,[1] and patronages, did make a revocation of all alienations of the Croun in order to resume the same, quherupon ensued four submissions and surrenders, one by the Lords of Erection, another by the Titulars of the teynds,[2] a third by the Clergy and a fourth by the Royall Burrows[3] and decreets arbitrall qhen ratified in the parliament 1633. And by which decreets the Lords of erection were to get ten years purchase for the rents, fewdueties, superiorities and patronages, and to retain the same ay and while they be redeemed, but this reversion of Kirklands is rescinded by the iith act Q. Anne anno 1707,[4] and the reversion renunced & discharged for ever, but prejudice of her majesties right of superiority of the erections and services and casualties arryseing therefrom.

This revocation made a great noyse in Scotland and was the first thing that gave ryse to those troubles that ensued during that good King's life, Presbyterian government haveing been restored in anno 40.

By the 20th act anno 1644 Charles the 1st,[5] Patrons are ordained to apply the rents and fruits of the benefices dureing the vacancy for pious uses within the paroch by the advice and consent of the severall Presbitries, and where the Presbytries have the power of planting kirks in place of the Patrons, they are to apply the same for pious uses within the paroch by the advice and consent of the Heritors and Parochiners, and by the

---

[1] i.e. tithes.

[2] The titulars of the teynds were lay lords who had obtained the right to receive tithes formerly payable to the Church.

[3] The four submissions are printed in a separately paged section following p. 522 of *The Laws and Acts of Parliament*, ed. Sir Thomas Murray of Glendook, Edinburgh, 1681.

[4] *Acts of the Parliament of Scotland*, 1814–44, xi. 431.

[5] Ibid. vi. 128–9.

39th act anno 1649, Charles the 1st,[1] all presentations by
Patrons are made void, and the Patrons to have the heritable
right to the superplus tyths over and above the provisions to the
Minister and without prejudice to the Titulars or tacksmen of
their prior right thereto.

These acts were repealled upon King Charles the 2d's restauration, and the restauration of Episcopacy anno 1661, but
by the 52. act parl. 1st Charles the 2d and the 23d act 3d sess.
of the same parliament[2] the Vacand stipends are to be applyed
for pious uses.

Upon the late Happy revolution Episcopacy was abolished,
and the Presbyterian church government reestablished in Scotland upon the foot of the claim of right and grievances, and by
the 23d act anno 1690 K. Wm and Q. Mary[3] the power of presentation is taken from the Patrons and lodged in the hands of
the Heritors and Elders except as to the Royall Burrows where
it is lodged in the Magistrats, Toun Councill and Kirk session
of the burgh and in the hands of the Presbitry jure devoluto,
and for ane equivalent of this right of presentation the Patrons
are to be payed 600 mks by the Heritors and have a right to the
superplus teynds over and above the provisions to the Ministers
where the teynds were not heritably disponed, and with a priviledge to the Heritors to buy those teynds which did so accress
to the Patron at the rate of six years purchase, and by the 26th
act anno 1693 parl. K. Wm & Q. Mary[4] this right to the superplus teynds in favour of Patrons in lieu of their right of presentation is extended to personages and other benefices, and by the
6th act of her majestie Q. Anne anno 1707[5] The Presbyterian
Church goverment in Scotland in it's doctrine, discipline and
worship and whole acts relative thereto are ratified and to be
held and observed in all time comeing as a fundamental and
essentiall condition of the Union.

From what is said it's manifest:

1° That while Presbitry obtained in Scotland, the power of
admission of Ministers was allwayes lodged in the hands of the
Presbitry, and even the power of presentation conform to their
book of discipline and the laws dureing Presbiterian government to be lodged in the hands of the Heritors and Elders,
which seems also more equitable and conform to the practise of

---

[1] *Acts of the Parliament of Scotland*, 1814–44, vi. 411–13.
[2] Ibid. vii. 303 and 18–19. [3] Ibid. ix. 196–7.
[4] Ibid. ix. 304–5. [5] Ibid. xi. 402–3.

the Primative Church, That those who are to reap the benefit and success of the Gosple ministry should have the choyse and call of the Minister, than one Single person who probably neither is to reside in the p[aroch][1] nor injoy the fruits of his ministry.

2° This point seems now to be established by the Union as being a pairt of the disciplin, form and practise of Presbiterian Church government ratified and made ane essentiall pairt of the Treaty of Union as Sd is.

3° The Patrons have ane equivalent by their right to the superplus tyths in manner forsaid & all Heritors and proprietors of teyths have the priviledge of purchasing them at ane easie rate in manner above exprest.

4° By these acts all the teynds are with the burden of suteable provisions to the Ministers, and upon application to the Lords of the Commission they accordingly get suteable provisions and augmentations forth of the teynds quhich prevents those simoniacall pactions quhich were in use to be interposed and adhibit betwixt the Patron and the person he presented.

For what is promised in sum it's manifest that the resumption of patronages and repealling the former acts must necessarly infer a great prejudice to all the pairties concerned above exprest, and seems inconsistant with the Presbiterian Church Government in Scotland ratified and made ane essential pairt of the Treaty of Union as Said is.

As to the [City] of Edr the teynds pertaining to them were by K. Charles [the] first's letter ordained to continue in the same state they were in before his revocation and quhich was ratified in the parliament 1633. And the Magrats, Toun Councill and Kirksessions were allwayes in use [to] present their Ministers, and the Magrats and Toun Councill even in time of Episcopacy had right of presentation by the payment of the Stipends, the building and repairing the Churches, and all the tittles that constitut a patron, and since Episcopacy and patronages were abolished the power of presentation lodged in manner forsaid.

MS.: Duke of Portland, Harley Papers, xlviii ff. 1071–3. Hitherto unpublished. *Address*: 'Daniel Defoe Esquire, at Newington near London.' *Endorsed* (not by Defoe): 'Memoriall Anent the Power and priviledge of presenting ministers in Scotland, 1711.'

---

[1] MS. torn. Bracketed words from here to the end have been supplied.

162. [*To* ROBERT HARLEY]. *25 April 1711*

Sir

Tho' I am Comforted with the Sight of your Personall Safety, which No Man has More Reason to be Thankfull for Than my Self, yet when I See the wonders of Providence in your Preservation, and Reflect Upon what Depends Upon your life, I Confess I am Silent with Astonishment.[1]

These Sir are Some of The wayes God is Pleased to Take to Vindicate The being and Power of his Governing Attribute in The world, and by Invincible Demonstrations to Conquer The Influences of The Devill in the hearts of Men— When The Endeavours They use to blott Out the Prints of his being which Nature left on That blank leaf The Soul Grow strong, and they Perswade Themselves There Either is no God Or That he is Not the Agent of his Own productions, This Secret Wittness Whispers *Thou Fool* in Their hearts; and The Conviction can Not be withstood.

The Same Testimony Sir That he is Pleas'd to Give of himself in Thus Directing The Actions of Men, as it is a Wittness to his Providence, Prescience and his Descending to The Governmt of his Creation, So it can Not without gross absurdity but Argue That an Eternall Wisdome and Goodness is Concern'd in That Governmt. From This I Inferr to the present Case That the Singular Discoveries of That wisdom, *for Example* in Eminent Deliverances, prove That there is Some End and Design in Every One of Those Deliverances, as well as in the other Events of his Providence.

It can Not be That (in your Case in Perticulr) Wise and Righteous Providence should Distinguish its Self in Sacrifizeing One life and preserving Another, Abandoning a wretch to Rage and Desperation, Directing him to Reach Out a Murthering hand pointed at That life it was forbidden to Touch, and which it should Onely hurt, but Not Destroy.

Why was he Permitted to Assault, and Not Permitted to Effect his Design; what Armour Guarded The Precious Part;

---

[1] Harley had just recovered from the consequences of a wound inflicted upon him six weeks earlier by Antoine de Guiscard. The assailant was an exiled Frenchman who, after having served the Godolphin Ministry against France, had more recently entered into a treasonable correspondence with the enemy. While under examination by a Committee of the Privy Council he had suddenly whipped out a penknife and stabbed Harley in the breast. The wound was not serious, but the affair was dramatic enough to arouse for Harley a popular sympathy that resulted in his elevation to the peerage and Lord Treasurership.

what Restrain'd The point; why Directed just to The Onely
Little Solid part That was in The wounded place, But to bear
Wittness to This Glorious Truth, That Verily There is a God
That Governs The Earth, That The Hairs of Our head are
Numbred, and Not a Sparrow falls to the Ground &c.

Yet This is Not all, nor is it the End of my Goeing Thus out
of My Way Sir in this Manner of Discourse—But *The Why* is
The Thing I Dwell upon, why a life Thus Cloth'd with Wonders
and Cover'd with Mercy—But because The Same hand That
Thus Guarded your life Sir From Evill by its Imediate power,
has Some Great work for you to do, which Must be done, Must
be done by you, and For which, as he has Furnish'd you Above
Others, So he will preserv you till it be Compleatly Finished.
Nor can it be Doubted But as your preservation beares a proportion to The greatness of The worke you have to do, So The
work beares a due proportion to the Greatness of The Deliverance.

May The Same hand Still Guard you, The Same Goodness
protect you. May you be filled with Wisdome and Counsell For
The great Things Heaven has Reserv'd you for, and as I Doubt
Not your Eyes are up to him who has bid us if We want wisdome
to ask it of him; So I am Perswaded he has Not placed The
Weight of This Great Nations affaires on your Shoulders, and
Thus Miraculously Preserv'd your life, But he will (for his Works
like himself are all Perfect) He Will Compleat what he has
Purposed to Do For us, by your hand; to his Own Glory and
The Great Honour of The Instrumt also—and Great is your
happyness That They are Joyn'd to gether.

The Subject Sir is So Moveing, My weakness Betrays it Self
and I am Forced to break off, Onely Prayeing That The life
Thus Sav'd by wonders May be Dedicated to him That has
preserv'd it, That it may be Employ'd for, blesst by, and
Directed From himself, That Heaven May have the Praise,
This Nation The Benefit, and your Self The Open, Comfortable
Reward from him That Sees in Secret. Amen.

Your Most faithfull Sincere
Humble and Obedient Servt
[signature torn off]

Aprill 25. 1711

P.S. I began this Letter Sir with a Design of bussiness, but
my Thoughts are too full So that I am forc't to adjourn it, for

which I ask your Pardon. If your Leisure permits, I would Gladly Wait on Thursday Evening for half an hours Audience, or any Other Time you please to Direct.

MS.: Duke of Portland, Defoe Papers, 1 ff. 266–7. Hitherto unpublished. *Address*: none. *Endorsed*: 'Mr Goldsmith, Apri: 25 1711.'

163. *To* DAVID ERSKINE, EARL OF BUCHAN.[1]
29 May 1711

My Lord,

I have had the honour of your Ldpps Letter of the 12º ultimo so long that indeed I blush to Date my answer the 26º May.[2] I could indeed make some excuses, but I choose to own it a Fault, because I will not lessen the vallue of your Ldpps remission.

Your Ldpp does me too much honor in acknowleging good wishes instead of Services, and bestowing on a Late and Unsuccessfull proposall of mine, the weight due to a reall and effectuall Piece of Service;[3] this generous Principle of your Ldpps however Lays an obligation on me, to watch for any opportunity that may offer, of Layeing reall obligations on a hand so bountifull in accepting. And your Ldpp may be assur'd I shall Lose no occasion.

The Person with whom I endeavoured to Plant your intrest has been strangely taken up since I had that occasion (viz.) First in suffering the operation of the Surgeons to heal the wound of the assassine and since in accumulateing Honours from Parliamt Queen and People.

On Thursday[4] evening her Majtie created him Earl Mortimer Earle of Oxford and Lord Harley of Wigmore and we expect that to-morrow in Council he will have the white staff given him by the Queen herself and be Declar'd Ld High Treasurer.

I writ this yesterday and this Day May 29 he is made Ld

---

[1] See p. 314, n. 5. The identity of the addressee rests upon the statement of George Chalmers, who printed about a third of the letter and said of it: 'Lord Buchan was so obliging as to communicate the subjoined extract of a letter to his Lordship's grandfather, the Earl of Buchan, from De Foe, dated the 29th of May 1711' (*Life of Daniel De Foe*, 1790, p. 33).

[2] Probably an error for 28 May. See the fifth paragraph.

[3] In February Defoe had recommended Buchan for consideration as Lord Commissioner to the General Assembly of the Church of Scotland (pp. 314–15). Harley had appointed Annandale instead.

[4] But 'Thursday' was the 24th, and Harley was elevated on the 23rd. Defoe seems to have lost track of the correct day of the week; all three *Reviews* for that week are similarly misdated, e.g. 'Thursday May 23. 1711.'

High Treasurer of Britain and Carryed the white staff before the queen this morning to the Chappell.

Your Ldpp will easily believ the hurry there too great to make any Motions at this time. But you may assure yourself (my Lord) nothing shall be wanting to represent either yourself or your affaires to your Ldpps greatest advantage, and I hint by the way that no man is Fitter to move in such a case than the Duke of Newcastle[1] whom your Ldpp mentiond. When ever your Ldpp resolves to attempt the thing I shall be glad to have notice that I may take a proper season to mention it to advantage.

I am, May it Please your Ldpp,
Your Ldpps most Humble & obedient servant
DE FOE

Newington, May 29, 1711

MS.: untraced. *Pub.*: Fred W. Joy, 'Autograph Letter of Daniel De Foe', *Notes and Queries*, 6 S, ix (1884), 65. *Address*: none recorded.

164. [*To* ROBERT HARLEY, EARL OF OXFORD].
7 June 1711

My Lord

In Obedience to your Ldpps Commands I have here Enclosed an Abstract[2] of the Papers I Recieved From Scotland which Relate to The Late Tumult in the City and the Breach between The Magistrates of Edinb. and the Custome house Officers.[3]

It is Not for me to Offer any Thoughts on This Affair, But to Lay before your Ldpp The Matter of Fact in Generall. Your Ldpp will Easily See whether the Custome house Officers have been in The Right. My Account has Sevll Little aggravations in it and Recriminations on the Characters of the Officers (which Indeed are Not Very Good),[4] But These as Less Material and Comeing From but One party I Omit.

[1] John Holles (1662–1711), Duke of Newcastle, was Lord Privy Seal. A moderate Whig, Newcastle had joined with Harley in overthrowing the old Ministry in 1710, and was now supporting him against St. John.

[2] Missing.

[3] The altercation seems to have arisen over the failure of the local authorities to assist the customs officers, especially when the latter tried to prevent the illegal entry of French wines. See John Scrope to Oxford, 13 July 1711, *H.M.C. Portland*, x. 386.

[4] For further remarks on the character of English officials in Scotland, see the *Review* for 5 Feb. 1711–12.

My Lord

As I am big with Severall Things of This kind to Lay before your Ldpp which the happy Hurryes you have been Taken up with have Deprived Me of the Opportunity of, and as I kno' the Inconvenience of Troubling your Ldpp with Tedious preambles which Come from that Country, I beg leav to Lay Things Down in heads, That your Ldpp May Command The Perticulars of Such first as are Most Usefull.

1. The Composition Made by The heritors of *Old Deer* (where The Great Rable Now undr prosecution before the Justiciary in scotland was begun)[1] As the First Fruits of The happy Conclusion of the Generll assembly.

2. A great Uneasyness of the Ministers for Fear of The Printing The Bible being given Exclusively to a Sett of Men, who They Say are Not Enemy's Onely to Their Church, But not Orthodox in the principles of Religion, by which They judge Erroneous and Clandestine Coppys of the Bible May be Dispersed in The Highlands and Disputes about the Translation of the Scriptures be Commenced among the Common people.[2]

3. A Dispute Between the Commissrs of Excise and The Garrison of Innerlochy which will be Brought before your Ldpp and of which I have all the Perticulars to Apprise your Ldpp of before hand.[3]

4. A Case of the Earle of Hyndfords Dragoons.[4]

---

[1] In the previous spring the Jacobite heritors of Old Deer, Aberdeenshire, caused a 'Riot, Tumult, and horrid Rabble upon the Ministers, going in a Peaceable, Legal, and Judicial manner, according to the Laws, and according to their Duty, to plant a Minister in a Church Vacant by the Death of the former Minister' (*Review*, 8 May 1711). Defoe was so much concerned at this affront to the Kirk that he doubled the number of pages in the *Review* just cited in order to reprint the entire indictment against the rabblers. See also the *Review* for 9 June 1711, and Wodrow, *Analecta*, i. 328–9.

[2] Defoe here attempts a service for his Edinburgh associate Mrs. Agnes Campbell Anderson, printer of his *History of the Union*, a number of his pamphlets, and the Edinburgh edition of the *Review*. Under a patent granted in 1671 to her husband, since deceased, she held a practical monopoly on the printing of the Bible. But her privilege was due to expire on 12 May 1712, and a syndicate was now attempting to prevent the renewal of her patent and to gain the reversion for themselves. This 'Sett of Men', John Baskett, James Watson, and Robert Freebairn, could hardly have been considered by the Church of Scotland as reassuringly orthodox. Baskett was an Englishman, Watson was thought to be a Roman Catholic, and Freebairn was a Jacobite who later joined in the insurrection of 1715 and then became printer to the Pretender. Nevertheless, Defoe's plea failed. The syndicate won the patent on 11 Aug. 1711. See Nos. 169 and 176; and W. J. Couper, 'Mrs. Anderson and the Royal Prerogative in Printing', *Proceedings of the Royal Philosophical Society of Glasgow*, xlviii (1918), 79–102.   [3] No account of this dispute has come to light.

[4] Harley was at present receiving nominations for a captaincy recently vacated in Hyndford's Regiment (*H.M.C. Portland*, x. 193, 376, and 438).

5. The Case of Dalziel the Privateer and the Merchants of Aberdeen.[1]

6. A proposall of Improvemt of the Duty of Excise.

These and Sevll Other Cases as your Ldpp pleases to Command Shall be Lay'd before your Ldpp More at Large. I Shall attend On Monday Evening According to your Ldpps Ordr.

I am, May it Please your Ldpp
Your Ldpps Most Humble & Obedt Servt
[signature torn off]

June. 7. 1711

MS.: Duke of Portland, Defoe Papers, 2 ff. 1–2. *Pub.*: *H.M.C. Portland,* v. 4–5. *Address*: none. *Endorsed*: 'Claude Guilot, June 7: 1711.'

165. [*To* ROBERT HARLEY, EARL OF OXFORD].
19 June 1711

My Lord

I am Very Unhappy Not in My Private Affaires Onely, which are Mellancholly, and Ruinous, from the Discontinuance of your Favor, But in Not haveing The Occasion and Honor of Layeing before your Ldpp Severall Matters of Importance Relateing to the Publick.[2]

I had Once My Lord The honor of your Promise That if I did any Thing Offensive you would be your Self my Reprover, and would not be Dissobliged Till I had first your Mind for my Governmt. God is My Wittness if I knew any Thing in which I Should Dissplease your Ldpp I would Avoid it Dilligently. If my Lord I am Not So Usefull a Servant as I would be, I hope I have been Usefull, and still May be So, and it must be want of Opportunity Not fidellity or Dilligence if it is Otherwise.

I Humbly Lay my Case at your Ldpps Feet. Your Ldpp knows and I Presume Remembers That when your Ldpp Honord me with your Recommendation to The Late Ld Treasurer, My Lord Offred Me a Very Good Post in Scotland and afterward Offred me to be Comissionr of The Customes There, and That I did Not Refuse Those Offers, but it being your Opinion as well as his Ldpps That I Might be More Servicable in a Private Capascity, I Chose Rather to Depend Upon her Majties Goodness That I Might be Most Servicable, Than to

[1] No other mention of this 'case' has been discovered.

[2] 'By this time Harley had found a new friend and pamphleteer in Swift. Defoe could not have been ignorant of the friendship of the two men, and of the work that Swift was doing for the Ministry; it was common knowledge' (Sutherland, *Defoe*, pp. 184–5).

Secure My Family a Maintenance and be Rendred Uncapable to serve her Majties Intrest.[1]

Since My Lord I had The honor of Returning into your Ldpps Service and Protection, your Ldpp was pleased to Speak for me to her Majtie and to Assure me her Majtie had been pleased to Appoint the Paymt of My Pension, and your Ldpp had the Goodness to Supply me The first quarter. Had I Not My Lord The Importuneing Circumstance of a Large Family, a Wife and Six Children, I could Serve your Ldpp Twenty year without the Least Supply Rather Than Thus press upon your Goodness, But my Lord—My Weakness Permits me to Say No More. A Family Often Ruin'd and Now Depending Upon your Ldpps Goodness presses me beyond Measure. I humbly Ask your Ldpps Pardon for it.

May it Please your Ldpp

I am your Dayly Petitioner for an Opportunity in but Six words to Lay before your Ldpp Some Things Relateing to New Uneasynesses in Scotland,

Something Relateing to The Trade to the South Seas,[2] which abundance speak Evill of because They do Not Understand,

And something Relateing to The Poor keel men at New Castle whose Oppressions Seem Reserved for your Ldpps hand to put an End to—[3] I beg a few Minutes at your Leisure, and Am

My Lord, Your Ldpps Most Humble & Obedient Servt

[signature torn off]

June. 19. 1711

MS.: Duke of Portland, Defoe Papers, 2 ff. 3–4. *Pub.*: *H.M.C. Portland*, v. 13–14. *Address*: none. *Endorsed*: 'Claude Guilot, June 19: 1711.'

166. [*To* Robert Harley, Earl of Oxford].
26 June 1711

My Lord

I am backward to Trouble your Ldpp at Such a Time of Hurry as This, yet I Thought it my Duty to Lay before you in

---

[1] See p. 236.   [2] See Nos. 168, 170, and 171.

[3] After years of voluntary contribution the coal-barge men ('keelmen') of Newcastle had erected a hospital for the support of their needy, aged, and destitute. But because the institution had been mismanaged they were now petitioning the Crown for a charter of incorporation under which they themselves could take direct control of the foundation. Their petition was opposed, however, by the magistrates, hoastmen (who controlled the sale of coal), and fitters (coal-brokers) of Newcastle, who hoped themselves to get control of the institution and hence strengthen their grip on the keelmen. Defoe fought stoutly against this threat. See p. 369 and the *Reviews* for 12, 14, and 16 Feb. 1711–12. On 29 Mar. 1712 the Commons decided in favour of the keelmen (*J.H.C.* xvii. 160).

Generalls Onely what Seems Necessary for your Ldpp to be Inform'd of Since My Last.

As 1st, The Affair of the Provost and Magistrates of Edinb. with The Custome house Officers; of which I Enclosed an Abstract According to your Ldpps Commands;[1] The Magistrates Say They have Recd Some Threatning Message or letter On That Occasion Telling Them they Shall be Sent for up to answer before the Council for Their behavior to the Custome house Men. This They Believ Neither your Ldpp or Her Majtie has been Made Accquainted with and Desire your Ldpps Protection, of which I shall Give your Ldpp a Farther Account when I may have the honor to wait on you.

The Next is The Constant feares of The Good people of the North about The Pretender and The French Squadron,[2] Occasioned Rather by The Insults and Openess off the Jacobite Party There Than any Intelligence of The Thing, which Feares are Encreased They Say by The Naked Condition of Scotland as to Troops, haveing No Troops That Can be Drawn into the Field but One Battalion of Foot and Three Regimts of Dragoons, One of which is but half a Regimt.

I hinted Something Also About the Millitary Governmt in Scotland and the affair of Superiourities[3] which, however Weighty at This Time, I adjourn Till I have your Ldpps Commands.

I would Gladly have Spoken Six words to your Ldpp on the Subject of the South Sea Affaire, in which I Perswade My Self I May do Some Service in print.[4]

> I am, May it Please your Ldpp
> Your Most Humble & Obedt Servt

June. 26. 1711   DE FOE

MS.: Duke of Portland, Defoe Papers, 2 f. 5. *Pub.*: *H.M.C. Portland*, v. 22. *Address*: none.

[1] See p. 329.

[2] As far back as February Wodrow had written: 'We have the alarame of a neu invasion from France, which I have been expecting nou of long time' (*Analecta*, i. 321).

[3] The Union Treaty guaranteed the continuance of superiorities, which, in Defoe's definition, were 'the rights of vassalage which the gentry of Scotland have over the people; which, as it is extended, gives the chiefs and heads of clans, lairds, and heretors, such an absolute dominion over both the persons and goods of the poor subjected people, as seems perfectly inconsistent both with peace and improvement of Scotland in particular, or of any free nation in general' (*History of the Union*, p. 458).

[4] See Nos. 168, 170, and 171; and the *Reviews* for 28 and 30 June; 3, 7, 12, 17, 19, and 26 July; 7 and 30 Aug.

167. [*To* ROBERT HARLEY, EARL OF OXFORD].
13 July 1711

My Lord

I can No way Express My humble Thankfullness to your Ldpp for The Relief which The Return of your Goodness and Bounty has been to Me Unless I should give you The Trouble of a Sad Account of The Anxietys and perplexitys which The Late Interruption of her Majties Appointmt had brought me to, first by The late Ld T . . . . r, who On the Change left me Desolate without the Arrear;[1] and Next by The Dissaster on your Ldpp,[2] which for a long Time gave me a Dark View of the Nations Ruine, as well as my Own: These Things (My Lord) had brought me Very Low, and as a Sinking Family is Thus Raised Again (Especially in hope) by your hand, in Proportion to That Deliverance is My Sence of your Bounty.

But my Lord as words can Not Describe This, I Extreamly wish for an Occasion to Render my Self Usefull, as The best Method to shew my Self Gratefull, and According to The Freedome your Ldpp was allways pleased to allow me, I shall Endeavour to shew my fidellity to your Intrest, and Zeal for the Public Service, as The best way to Serve and Oblige your Ldpp: —In Ordr to This, and in Obedience to your Ldpps Commands of Putting My Thoughts into writeing, I am Now Applying My Self to State to your Ldpp Some heads of Observation, which I hope May be Usefull, on Some Transactions More Imediately before your Ldpp— I shall Sett down The heads here, and Enlarge on Them in Their Ordr, as I Think They May be Seasonable and Servicable.

Yet I am your Ldpps Humble Petitioner That you will be pleased, Some-times, when Leisure May admitt, to Continue Me the Liberty of a personall Conference as Usuall, as well to Explain my Self on Such Things as are Needfull, as to Reciev Such Hints From your Ldpp in Public Matters as your Ldpp shall See Meet to Comunicate for my Direction.

The Heads I Crave Leave first to Lay before your Ldpp as More Imediately for your Service are

1. The affair of a Third Secretary for Public Affaires,[3] with

---

[1] Godolphin's dismissal had taken place in the previous August.

[2] The stabbing of Harley by Guiscard in the previous March.

[3] After the Union the two English Secretaries of State had been joined by a third, in charge of Scottish affairs. The Duke of Queensberry had held the post until his death, a week earlier, on 6 July.

334

Some Remarks Upon the State of The Civil Governmt in Scotland.

2. The New Undertaking of the Trade to the South-Seas, and How it May be put in Terms not to Give The spaniards any Umbrage and yet carry as good a Face and be as Effectuall at home as if it were otherwise.

3. Some Observations On The Miscarriage of The Customes in Scotld and Schemes of a Better Mannagemt.

4. Some Proposalls (if your Ldpp pleases to allow me That Liberty) for Improvemt of The Revenue and Raiseing Money in England Against The Next year.

I forbear to Trouble your Ldpp with a Multitude of heads. Other Things Remain in Petto, but I begin with These as well because I Think Them Most Usefull as because I gather From your hints to me in your Last Discourse That These Things will be Acceptable to your Ldpp. I Mean the Three First.

I am, May it Please your Ldpp

Your Ldpps Most Humble & Obedt Servt

[signature torn off]

July. 13. 1711

[Enclosure]

May it Please your Ldpp

On The affair of a Third Secretary &c I Need Say The less Because I Observ My Thoughts on That head happily Agree with your Ldpps Judgemt.[1]

As a Third Office was Erected Upon The Union with Scotland, and fill'd with a Native of that Country, It became Insensibly to Seem an Office Peculiar to Scotland and for Scottish affaires, which has allready been attended with Sevll Inconveniences and is Threatned with More.

1. It became The Center of The Hungry Sollicitations Naturall to That Country, and Mightily Encreased and Encouraged Them, by which Her Majtie would in Time be Under a Constant Painfull Opperation From a poor, Craveing and Importunate people; who had so Easy a Method of Obtaining Requests, That it Made Them Invite One Another to be Allways Requesting; and Every Desire Granted, procured a Multi-

---

[1] Harley did not want a third Secretary. The post remained vacant for two years, during which Scottish affairs were managed by Bolingbroke, Northern Secretary of State. The office was renewed in 1713 with the appointment of the Earl of Mar.

335

plication of Petitions; Till in Time That Office would have been a True Court of Requests. A Certain Clark in That Office, who has Resided in scotland, and is There still, has Made his Market of prepareing, Solliciting, and handing forward bussiness of This Nature, has his Office in Edinb., and Gives Methods, Instructions and Recomendations to the office here, As if it were his Bussiness to prompt people On Every Triffle to Seek Redress and Supply from the Queen. Her Majties Goodness and Bounty (Tho' Great) Must be at Last Exhausted by Continued Craveings, and Cases Really Moveing will Suffer by The Constant Clamour and Sollicitation of a Multitude.

2. What Ever Secretary Succeeds must be a Scots man. They Seem to Claim it as a Right— This (first) keeps up a kind of a Form of Seperate Mannagemt, which being Destroy'd by Union, all Vestiges of The Seperate State of Things Ought to Dye with it, and the Very Remembrance if possible be Taken away; Scotland No More Requires a Secretary Than Yorkshire or Wales, Nor (the Clamour of Petitions Expected) can it Supply bussiness for an Office with Two Clarks. As to Needfull Petitions, her Majties Eares will allwayes be Open to her Subjects just Requests, and private Persons may Sollicit Their Own Cases, as the English did before, whereas a Scotish Secreatary is No Other Than a Scottish Sollicitor. This I kno' The D of Queensberry allways Complain'd of and I have heard his Grace Say it was The Burthen of his Office, yet he Could Deny Nobody.

If a New Scots Secretary Succeeds he has a New Throng of Dependents who hang about him as if he had the wholl kingdome to Give, and I kno' The Names of Some who have Entertain'd Thoughts of This Very Office Some Time past, and have kept back Their Craveing Friends from Pushing Their Requests till They should be in power to act for them, when They have promised to do Mighty Things for Them.

If a Third Secretary Should be put in (and Not a Scots man) They themselves would be The First who would Crye Out There was No Occasion for the Office.

The addition of Bussiness from Scotland (Petitions Onely Excepted as before) Seems to be No argument at all, Since That Bussiness Seems So little as that it can Not be an Employ for any One Clark in the Other Offices, and when it is promiscuously Mannaged Among them all, will not be felt at all.

The Signet May have a little Office for it in Either of the

Other Offices, or in The Signet Office here, or by it Self, of which a proposall may be Lay'd down by it Self.[1]

3. The Very Appointing A Scots Secretary has Severall Inconveniences in it. 1./ It keeps up a Faction in Scotland, and Forms a Party To Support the Intrest of That Person, as also another to Supplant him, So That Instead of his Secureing the quiet of The people he is *Ipso facto* The Means of Disquieting and Dividing them. (2) He Constitutes himself a kind of a Governour of Scotland, Since he becomes quietly and Gradually (Whether with or without Design) the Medium of all Transactions between her Majtie and The people of Scotland, and Makes those people More Depending on him than perhaps is fit for any perticular person on That Side to boast of.

4. It Seems to Lay a foundation of a Custome which in Time will plead prescription and be Claim'd by Posterity as a Right, and No Time can be So proper to Crush it as while (The Thing being young) No Such Claim can be made.

5. It Layes The Crown Under a Constant and Needless Expence.

There might be Many Other Reasons Given for This, But These Seem Sufficient— There Seems to be No Objection but the Discontenting The Scots, to which I answer

The People will Soon be Easy, Since They can Assign No Injury They Reciev as a Reason why They should be Dissatisfyed.

The Clamour will be Onely Among those who Expect the Office, which Requires No Other Answer Than This—They can Not Desire the queen should do it Onely to find them an Employment—A Pension if her Majtie Sees it Reasonable is an Equivalent to that.

As to the Power They Want by The Office, The Very Reason why They Desire it is a Strong Argument against her Majties bestowing it.

All which is Humbly Submitted to your Ldpp
By your Ldpps Most Obedt Servt
[signature torn off]

MS.: Duke of Portland, Defoe Papers, 2 ff. 11–14. *Pub.*: *H.M.C. Portland,* v. 44–47. *Address*: none. *Endorsed*: 'Mr Goldsmith July 13 1711, R̰ July 14:'

[1] Even after the Union, Scotland had retained its own Great Seal and its own Signet. The latter had been in the custody of the late Duke of Queensberry.

168. [*To* Robert Harley, Earl of Oxford].
17 July 1711

My Lord

In Persuance of your Ldpps Orders of Putting My Thoughts in writeing on the Subject of The Trade to the South-Seas,[1] I have Enclosed to your Ldpp a Short General which I humbly offer to your Ldpp. I have put a Stop to what I was Saying in Print[2] Till I may kno' if my Thoughts are of any Consideration in your Ldpps Judgemt, and because I would Not by Distinguishing too Nicely, Discourage the Thing in Generll; I Shall go on to draw up my Notions as Succinct as possible, and Then attend your Ldpp, If I may have The Honr, to know how far my scheme May be agreeable.

I kno' well how Much is at Stake upon This Affair, and how well pleased Some would be (Meerly on your Ldpps Perticular Account) to have it Misscarry; I Perswade My Self what I have Offred here is the best way to Dissappoint Them; as it Shall leave Least Possibillity of a Misscarriage, and Lay Less Weight on That perticular Than Now Seems to Lye Upon it. I Shall be glad to Make This So Clear as That your Ldpp May have the Same Opinion of it.

I am, May it Please your Ldpp
Your Ldpps Most Humble
[remainder, including signature, torn off]

July. 17. 1711

[1] On 3 May the Commons had given official approval to Harley's proposal for establishing a South Sea Company (*J.H.C.* xvi. 680–1). The scheme combined two purposes: to reduce the national debt and to expand trade. The new corporation was to relieve the Treasury by assuming almost ten million pounds of the national debt; the creditors to whom this debt was owed were to receive the equivalent in shares of the Company's stock plus interest at 6 per cent. In return the Company was to receive a monopoly of British trade to the South Seas, by which was meant primarily the Spanish possessions in the Americas. The Company was chartered in the following September, received the coveted Asiento in 1713, and prospered until 1720. In that year it incorporated into its own capital the entire national debt, a move that set off a wild frenzy of speculation. In Aug. 1720 shares reached 1,000 per cent.; in September the bubble broke. The Company retained its privileges, however, until 1807. Defoe has sometimes been pointed to as the originator of some parts of the scheme; actually he seems to have been sceptical about it. The one idea that he probably did originate and that he certainly did believe in—the planting of British colonies in Chile and Patagonia—was not adopted. See J. R. Moore, 'Defoe and the South Sea Company', *Boston* (Massachusetts) *Public Library Quarterly*, v (1953), 175–88.

[2] See p. 333, n. 4.

[Enclosure]

May it Please your Ldpp

The Present Difficulty in the Affair of The South-Sea-Trade Seems to Consist in The Notion of what we call *a Free-Trade*, and The Dissatisfactions That Some people are Industrious to Spread, Arise from the Differing Construction which people put upon The Thing called a Free-Trade and The Insuperable Difficulties which Seem to attend it.

All our Merchants kno' That the Spaniards (I mean by Spaniards the Governmt of Old Spain) in whatsoever Circumstance Considred, whether in Peace or war, Undr Philip of Bourbon or Cha: of Austria,[1] will Never be brought to Consent to a Generall liberty of Commerce with any Collony or Settlement the English may Make on the Coast of America.

By *a Liberty of Commerce* I Mean, just as your Ldpp was pleased to Explain it to Me (Viz) That Such Collony or Settlement should be as The Magasin or warehouse of English goods, which, instead of being Landed in Old spain (paying 23 per Ct Customes There, Then Registring in The Contractation house at Sevill,[2] and paying Duty again There, and the Effects of the Galleons, which is The Return, paying an Indulto[3] of 4 to 8 per Ct to the king), shall Come Directly from England Custome Free, and be admitted into all the Spanish dominions in America.

This My Lord is what I Grant, and what Every body in Town who knows the Trade Say, The Spaniards will Not be brought to. I Need Not Trouble your Ldpp with Other Reasons Than This, That Really *Old spain* is Ruined if They do, and The Indies (Farther Than barely The Revenue of Them to the Public) are Lost And of no Vallue to Them (Comparitively speaking) if They should.

On The Other hand, The Very Pretence of This Undertakeing will Make a handle to the French Intrest, will speak Loud in Spain in Favour of king Philip; Since king Charles has by Contract Given Them away to The English, who *as They Say* are to Enjoy The America Trade for Ever, whereas the French, with Specious pretences of Protecting The Indies Now from The

---

[1] The rivals over whose claims to the Crown of Spain the war was being fought.
[2] The *Casa de Contractacion* at Seville regulated the sailing and loading of the two annual fleets which traded between Cadiz and Spanish America. The Cartagena fleet was called the 'galleons', the Vera Cruz fleet the 'flota'. See the *Review* for 3 July 1711, and Ruth Bourne, *Queen Anne's Navy in the West Indies*, New Haven, Connecticut, 1939, pp. 139–44.
[3] Import duty.

Enemies of Spain, Promise to quit all pretensions to the Trade in Time of peace; and Entirely to withdraw and Recall all Their Merchants and all Their people from Thence.[1]

I Need not hint to your Ldpp That the people who Are Enemies to the project On Account of your Ldpps Concern in Proposeing it, Think They have Gain'd a great Point in haveing So Specious and, as they Think, Unanswerable Argumts Against the probabillity and Practicablness of the Design, and how They give Out boldly That it is an Inconsistency in it Self and Must Therefore of Meer Necessity Misscarry and Come to Nothing.

But My Lord if My Thoughts of this Affair Are Agreeable to your Ldpp, I am of Opinion I Might state This Undertakeing So That it Might Neither Give Umbrage to the Spaniards Abroad, Or appear Impracticable or Inconsiderable to Our people at home. I shall Onely Lay it Down in Generalls here, but Shall Enlarge on it in Perticular and in Print when first the heads of it have passed your Ldpps Opinion.

1. There Seems to be No Necessity of Putting This Term *A Free Trade* into the Proposall, for the Reasons following

> 1st. It is This Onely can Give any Pretence to the French and Jealousie to the Spaniards.
>
> 2. It is This Onely which Creates Difficulties and Raises Suspicions and Doubts of the Success in England, to the Discredit of The Design.

2. The Thing will in Some Degree be a Consequence without a Public Claim to it, in which Lyes The greatest part of The Inconvenience, And The Assiento will be Naturally the Companys.[2]

3. Tho' we Should have no Such Thing as a Freedome of Commerce with the Spaniards, yet will a Settlement on the spanish Continent of America, Especially in Such places as May be Named, be of Sufficient Consequence to justifye The prudence of the wholl Undertakeing, Give a Credit to the

---

[1] See the *Reviews* for 5 and 7 July.

[2] Defoe seems to mean that since the Asiento carried with it the half-recognized right to smuggle commodities, the South Sea Company would enjoy some degree of free trade without making a public issue of the matter. Harley already assumed that France, as part of the price of peace, would be compelled to surrender to Britain the Asiento, the exclusive privilege of supplying slaves to Spanish America. See G. M. Trevelyan, *Blenheim*, 1930, p. 139, and *The Peace and the Protestant Succession*, 1934, pp. 123-4.

Design and Answer all the Ends of a *South-Sea* Company Tho' Their Stock was to Contain the Capitall of The wholl Subscription.

A Scheme of which Shall be Lay'd before your Ldpp when Ever you please to Direct it.

I Presume Two Great Ends Must be Answerd in The Proposall

1st. Respecting The Governmt, That a Debt of Nine Millions be at Once Satisfyed and the Governmt Eased of So Great a Demand.

2°. That the Creditors for That Debt may Reciev Some advantage above Their Six per Cent That may be So Considerable as to Raise Their Actions, and Make them gainers by Their Subscription.

This I Presume Shall better be done by Setting Forth what The Company May and Shall do which is Feizible and probbable, Than by Pretending to Something Impracticable or at Least improbable, which Opens the Mouths of Malecontents and Gives The Enemies of The Design an advantage— Especially Considering That the Probable adventure Shall be Sufficient both to Encourage The Undertakeing and Answer The greatest Reasonable Expectation.

All which is Humbly Submitted to your Ldpp &c.

MS.: Duke of Portland, Defoe Papers, 2 ff. 7–10. *Pub.*: *H.M.C. Portland,* v. 50–52. *Address*: none.

169. [*To* ROBERT HARLEY, EARL OF OXFORD].
20 *July 1711*

My Lord

Among Severall Other Things which with your Ldpps Approbation I have had The Honor to Lay before your Ldpp, I have Taken the Freedome to Mention a Dispute which I fear is Now without your Ldpps Interposition Comeing to a Very Unhappy Period; This is My Lord The Changeing The Authourity of Printing The Bible in Scotland, From the hands who have Now with Generall Approbation been Entrusted with it for Many yeares.[1]

My Lord, if it were The Intrests of the Persons Only who were Concern'd, Tho' I See The Ruine of Many Families Lyes

[1] See p. 330, n. 2.

in it also; yet it were No bussiness of Mine to Mention it to your Ldpp, who are better judge Than to Need any hints from Me, and I better kno' My Duty Than to Meddle with it.

But (My Lord) as I have the honor of your Commands to Represent Such Things to your Ldpp as May or May Not be for the Public Good and for her Majties Service in Scotland; and as I have had Frequent Letters from the Ministers there, Expressing Their Apprehensions and Uneasyness at the Mischiefs which May (and I doubt indeed will) follow Putting the Printing of The Bible into hands who (*as They Say*) Are Professt Enemies to the Church of Scotland and Contrary in Principle to Orthodox Religion in Generall—I Thought it My Duty humbly to Move your Ldpp, That if possible a Stop May be put in the Secretarys Office to Such grant;[1] Till your Ldpp May have from better hands Than Mine, a True Account of The Disorders which May attend it.

I Doubt Not but Mr Carstaires and Those Other Ministers whom your Ldpp knows to be Judicious, as well as Zealous for the Peace of her Majties Subjects, will give your Ldpp the Same Account;[2] and also That when your Ldpp shall Examine The Merits of the Cause, I Mean as to the Public Peace, This Ordr (which I hear has just Now been Obtain'd,[3] without any address to your Ldpp)[4] will pass a farther Test from your judgemt Than has yet been Thought Needfull: I Humbly ask your Ldpps Pardon for This Representation, which I do purely on Account of the Satisfaction of That Unhappy People, who I foresee will be Most Uneasy on this Account. In Any Other Respect I am Perfectly Dissintrested On One Side or Other.

I am, May it Please your Ldpp
Your Ldpps Most Humble and Obedt Servt
DE FOE

July 20. 1711

MS.: Duke of Portland, Defoe Papers, 2 f. 15. *Pub.*: *H.M.C. Portland*, v. 57–58. *Address*: none.

[1] But Scottish affairs were now in the hands of St. John, who showed no inclination to keep the monopoly out of the hands of Freebairn and his associates. See Stewart to Carstares, 27 Nov. 1711, *H.M.C. Portland*, v. 123.

[2] Carstares later forwarded to Harley a letter from James Stewart which mentioned the affair; but Carstares, at least at that time, did not seem to be much concerned (*H.M.C. Portland*, v. 122–3).

[3] The patent was granted on 11 Aug. (W. J. Couper, *James Watson, King's Printer*, Glasgow, 1910, p. 16).

[4] Closing parenthesis omitted in MS.

170. [*To* ROBERT HARLEY, EARL OF OXFORD].
[*c. 20 July 1711*]¹

May it Please your Ldpp

What is allready offred to your Ldpp on Account of The Trade to The South-Seas being on the Supposition of The Impossibillity of Obtaining a Free-Trade with The Spaniards in America, It Remaines to Enquire whether The Proposall of the Said Trade May Not be Made On a foundation as Effectuall and a Prospect Every way as advantageous and Encourageing, yet at the Same Time Not Lyable to Those Objections which Some people So Dilligently Improve to make the world Uneasy and to lessen the Vallue of the Undertakeing.

If This can be done, The Reputation of The proposall And by consequence of the Proposer, which is what Those people aim at, Seems to be better Secured, and any Uncertainty which may afterwards appear in Circumstances will not be placed to The Account of the Undertakeing in Generall.

I beg leave to Explain My Self Thus

That all proposalls for the Carrying On a Trade To The South-Seas Should be made So That the Substance or Main Stress of The Design May Turn Upon Makeing a Settlement or Colloney (or Severall Such) On the Continent of America; and Supporting it by The Governmt for Improvement—Not Layeing any (or Not So great) weight on an Imediate Commerce Thro' the Spanish Dominions (which people have allready a Notion can not be Obtained) as On the Reall advantages of haveing an English Collony on the Continent of America, and in the Midst of The Gold, Silver and Other productions with which The Spaniards have So Enrich't Themselves, and which The English are Much more capable to Improve Than They.

On This Foundation So Much May be Said, and The Objections against it will be So Few, So weak, and So Easily Confuted; That it is humbly Conciev'd it will Soon gain an Universall Approbation.

---

¹ Though undated, this letter may be assigned to the period between 17 and 23 July. The opening sentence clearly refers to No. 168 (17 July) and the concluding sentence looks ahead to No. 171 (23 July). Furthermore, No. 171 mentions 'Two Papers' on the South Seas 'allready Sent your Ldpp', that is, this letter and No. 168.

No Man can Object against The advantages of a Collony provided The place be well Chosen; and Even Those places in which the spaniards Could Make little or no advantage Shall be Infinitely profitable to us; Since England is quallifyed to Grow Rich Even where The Spanish Settlement would Perish and Starv; Because we Are posest of So many Other Collonys which would be Their Support.

Thus we have Improved Barbadoes, Upon which There Now Subsists So Many Souls, which if it were in The Governmt of the spaniards would Eat up one Another; The place being in No Capascity to Support and Feed Them, whereas by Constant Supplys from Our plantations on The Main land Provisions of all Sorts are often as Cheap as in Newengland, New York, &c. From whence They Come.[1]

That a Settlement Made in America would be Infinitely advantageous to England Tho' there were to be no Free Trade with the Spaniards, is Easy to prove. Nor will The people be hard to Take in the Notion of it and Understand it. The advantages are Manifest and May be handsomely Enlarg'd on. If New England, N York &c. and Our Collonys on the North, where The spaniards Thought it Not worth while to plant, and where meer husbandry and labour has brought The Inhabitants to Such a Degree of wealth and Strength, have Brought So great a Trade; Planting On the South and West of America, where the Soil and Country is So Naturally Rich, and Gold and Silver is the Imediate Return, will Much Sooner and with Much More Ease Make The Trade Great and The plantation flourish.

The advantage of Private Trade with the Spaniards will also be a Constant addition as it is Now at Jamaica and Much More, Since Tho' The Spaniards will Not Open Their Ports and Markets for us to Sell, we Shall allways have an Open Port and Market for Them to buy.

To Carry on Such a proposall and Make it More Intelligible, I Humbly Suggest That Schemes of Proper Places for Such Settlements, with Their Respective advantages of Trade May be Lay'd before your Ldpp and if Approved by your Ldpp May be Made Public—That people may be Taken off From Amuseing Themselves about Difficultys and Impossibillitys and May be Led to a probable View of The Thing which May be Intelligible and Encourageing, which Schemes I Shall Humbly Lay

[1] Cf. Defoe's *Plan of the English Commerce*, Shakespeare Head edition, pp. 231–2.

before your Ldpp when Ever your Ldpp shall please to Command Me.

> All which is Humbly Submitted to your Ldpp
> By your Ldpps Most Humble & Obedt Servt
> D F

MS.: Duke of Portland, Defoe Papers, 2 ff. 23–24. *Pub.*: *H.M.C. Portland*, v. 66–68. *Address*: none.

171. [*To* ROBERT HARLEY, EARL OF OXFORD].
23 *July 1711*

My Lord

The Two Papers[1] I have allready Sent your Ldpp were Onely The Thoughts in Generll which in Obedience to your Commands I have Reduc'd to form on the South Sea Expedition. I here Offer to your Ldpp a Scheme for The Practise. I hope it May Not be less acceptable to your Ldpp for That it has been formerly proposed, Since I can Assure your Ldpp No Eye Ever Saw The Drafft Except his Late Majtie and The Earle of Portland,[2] and The Originalls were allways in My Own hand; Till my Lord Nottinghams fury forced me to Burn Them with Other papers to keep Them Out of his hands.[3]

They are here Rough and Indigested, But if your Ldpp Approves any of Them in The Gross I shall Single it Out to put it in a Dress more Suitable for your Service. Mean Time I shall go On to Lay The Remaining Schemes before your Ldpp.

> I am, May it Please your Ldpp
> Your Ldpps Most Humble and Obedient
> [remainder, including signature, torn off]

July. 23. 1711

[Enclosure]

May it Please your Ldpp

In Persuance of a Proposall for a Settlement Upon The Coast of America, as well in the *North* as in the *South Seas*;[4] which May

---

[1] Nos. 168 and 170.

[2] William Bentinck (1648–1709), first Earl of Portland, had been one of King William's most trusted advisers.

[3] In 1703, at the time when Defoe was under prosecution for his *Shortest Way with the Dissenters*.

[4] That is, on the Atlantic as well as the Pacific coasts of South America. Although the Government did not adopt his proposal, Defoe did not wholly abandon the idea. He revived it in 1720 in his *Historical Account of the Voyages and Adventures of Sir Walter Raleigh*, and in 1724 in the second part of his *New Voyage Round the World*.

be Effectuall for the Establishing a Trade, whether with the Spaniards or no, and Every way Suitable to the present Undertakeing and Encourageing to the Subscribers, I Humbly Lay before your Lordshipp The Severall Schemes Following, Some of Them being The Same which I had the Honor by his Majties perticular Order to Lay before him at the beginning of This war, And which the Said king Approved Very well, and had Not Death prevented him, had been Then Put in Practice. I present your Ldpp Onely The Heads, and Shall Enlarge on any of The Perticulars as you shall please to Direct.

> 1. A Proposall for Seizing, Posessing, and forming an English Collony on The kingdome of Chili in the South Part of America[1]

The Kingdome of Chili is Perticularly Proper for an English Collony, Because by The Scituation And Other Properties it is More Adapted For Commerce, Planting, and Inhabiting, which are The Three Articles Especially to be Considred.

1. It Lyes between The Latitude of 27 and 45 Degrees,[2] in a Climate So Tempered both for the Constitution of English bodyes and The production of Necessary Fruits for life, That all Sorts of provisions, Corn, Cattle and Fruits, may be Raised by Themselves Especially in The Southern parts; and the wholl Country Lyeing Upon the Coast, Such Things are with Ease Carryed to the More Northern parts, which are Hotter and More Unfruitfull. The want of which Fruitfullness and Temper of Clime was Evidently The Ruine of The Design at Darien—[3]

2. The Collonys of the Spaniards being So Remote,[4] and The Countries between Them and Chili being Part under The Line it Self, and all The way between The Tropicks, it will be Impracticable for Them to March by Land to Attack Our Collony, and by Sea it is Supposed we may be allways too strong For any attempt They can Make in That Part of The world.

---

[1] Under Article 6 of the Grand Alliance, 'Pourront le Roi de la Grande-Bretagne, & les Seigneurs États Generaux, conquérir à force d'Armes, selon qu'ils auront concerté entr'eux, pour l'utilité & la commodité de la Navigation & du Commerce de leur Sujets, les Païs & les Villes que les Espagnols ont dans les Indes, & tout ce qu'ils pourront y prendre fera pour eux, & leur demeurera' (G. M. Trevelyan, ed. *Select Documents for Queen Anne's Reign*, Cambridge, 1929, p. 7).

[2] Approximately correct for the Chile of Defoe's time.

[3] 'Where our Brethren of *Scotland* fix'd a Colony [1698–1700], which if we had Encouraged, might by this Time have been an excellent Footing for the *South-Sea* Trade' (*Review*, 3 July 1711).

[4] That is, their populous colonies, in the Caribbean area.

3. This Country as being too Remote, The Spaniards as if They had been Sated and Glutted with the Wealth of Peru, Never Entirely Conquer'd; by which Means tho' They did posess The Coast, yet the Natives Remain, and Are Very Numerous, Hateing The Spaniards, and willing to Reciev any Nation That are likely to Deliver Them from The slavery They are Undr to the Cruell and Tyrannic Temper of the Said spaniards.[1]

4. These Natives are a foundation of Commerce, because They Go Cloathed, and would Generally Cloth Themselves, if They Could Obtain Manufactures. They Inhabite Chiefly The Hill Country and the Sierra Cordilliera or Mountains of Andes, From whence They bring Gold and Skins of Beasts for Exchange of Goods.

5. By Means of These Natives a Correspondence of Commerce will of Course be Carryed on with The people of Peru, and by Consequence with the Spaniards On the other Side of the Mountains, From whence They have a Navigation to the Rio de la Plata and the Cityes Le Conception and de Beuenos Ayres, and which Country The spaniards call *des Valegas* or The Valleys, From whence to the North They have a Clear plain Country to The Cityes of Potosi and La Plata in The Country of Peru— This will be a Private Trade [among][2] The Natives—[3]

6. The Plenty of Gold in Chili Exceeds That on the Coast of Guinea in Affrick,[4] and The spaniards, who bring Great Quantitys From Thence, would have much more if Their Improvident Pride would Permit Them to Encourage The Natives to bring it in, But The Treachery and Cruelty with which They Treat the *Chileans* has Ruin'd That Trade.

The Best Place for a Capitall City and Collony in This kingdome of Chili, is at the Port of *Baldavia* as we call it; But More Properly *Valdivia*, called So by The Spanish Generll of That Name[5] who Planted Here—Being an Excellent Port, a good Harbour, and Three fresh Rivers falling into it; haveing a Navigation allmost up to *St Jago* North,[6] and *Villa Rica* East, a Considerable way into the Country.

Here The Climate is good, The Country Fruitfull, The Natives Courteous and Tractable, and The Wealth of the Place in Gold Incredible.

[1] Cf. Defoe's *New Voyage Round the World*, Aitken ed., pp. 185–7.
[2] MS. defective.   [3] Cf. *New Voyage Round the World*, pp. 194–5.
[4] Cf. ibid. pp. 216–17.
[5] Pedro de Valdivia (1500?–53).
[6] An error. From Valdivia, no river runs anywhere near to Santiago.

The Soil here will Encourage The Industry of Our People, who will Settle and plant, produceing Rice, Cocoa, Wine, Exceeding Rich and Pleasant, and on the North Side Sugar and spices in abundance, but Especially Gold and Salt peter.

The Air here is pleasant, Agreeable, and Healthy. The Mountains of Andes being Exceeding high, The winds from Their Tops keep The air Cool; and on the Other side The breezes from the Sea keep it Moist and Moderate; and being in the Latitude of 39 to 40 Degrees, it Answers to Our Collony of Carolina, which is Esteemed the Most Healthy of all Our Collonys in the North Parts of America.[1]

Both to the North and South of This, are Severall Other Ports Very Proper for Settling smaller Collonys, preserving The Center of Strength and Commerce at Valdivia, Both for Safety and Strength of Shipping.

> 2. To Secure Our Passage to This Collony, as well as to Supply the Collony it Self with Corne and Cattle in Case of Need, and Also For the Refreshment and perhaps wintering of Our Men and Ships in Their passage to or from the Collony both Goeing and Comeing, The passage thro' The Straights of Magellan being Sometimes Found Impracticable

It is Next Humbly Proposed That a Previous Settlement be made on the South East Coast of America, Between The *Rio-de-la-Plata* and The Mouth of The Straights of Magellan, where Our Ships may all Touch In Their Passage Out and home; whither Convoys may Go with Them, and Meet Others Comeing home and bring them back.

It is Observed That by The Accounts of all That have gone on shore here, The Country is adapted For Corn and Pasture in Especiall Manner, being a plain Country Covered well with good Grass, Vast Downs and Valleys for Feeding, and Rich Marly Ground for plowing, Very Little wood, And Very Good Rivers; So That This Country may be a Magasin for Supplying The *Chilean* Collony with all Manner of Provisions, and For Supporting The Navigation against The Length of The Voiage.[2]

Also a Communication May be Made by Land From This Collony to Chili, which will not be Above 360 Miles, which

---

[1] Cf. *New Voyage Round the World*, pp. 241–2.
[2] Cf. ibid. pp. 271–4, 292–3, and 342.

(Especially For Intelligence) May be Easily performed, The Voiage by Sea being at the Same Time Near 2000 Miles.[1]

This Collony I Propose to be on the Coast Between The River *De la Plata* and The Fretum Magellanicum, but Especially from Cape Redondo to St Julien and Near the Mouth of *Rio-Camarones*, which River is Navigable within 200 Miles of Valdivia, and Rises Out of the *Andes* aforesaid.

All The Sea Coast here and The Banks of This River have been Discovred and Appear to be Excellent Land to breed and Feed Cattle, Sow Corn, and Establish a Collony.

It Seems That a Collony on The Coast of Chili Could not be So well Maintained as by The Assistance of Such a Sister Collony in The North Seas.

But Especially This Northern Collony may be Usefull to The Navigation, The Voiage to The Other Coast being So Very Long, and in Time, Barks being Built there for the Currency of The Trade Between Them, The European Navigation May End here, and The Goods be Respectively Carryed and Fetch't in sloops and Barqs of Their Own.

If any Ships Lose Their Passage in The Straights, They may Come back and winter here, Or Unlade here and Return, which is Most proper by Reason of The Exchange of The Seasons, Their Winter being Our Summer, So That the Season Most Improper to pass The Straights in is the Most proper to Come to England in.

A Post being Established From Hence to Chili in 7 or 8 dayes, advices May Come to England in about four Months, One Time with another, Very often in Three Months or Ten weeks.

The Collony on the North Side is Not Appointed Nearer The Mouth of the Straights because The Climate is Reckoned Too Cold, The Air Inclement, and The Country Not atall Fruitfull or capable of Improvemt.

All which is Humbly Submitted to your Ldpps judgemt
By your Ldpps Most Humble and Obedient Se[rvt]
[signature torn off]

MS.: Duke of Portland, Defoe Papers, 2 ff. 17–22. *Pub.*: *H.M.C. Portland*, v. 58–61. *Address*: none. *Endorsed*: 'Mr Guilot July 23: 1711, R July 24: South Sea.'

[1] Cf. *New Voyage Round the World*, pp. 275–6.

172. T. P.[1] *to* DEFOE. *15 August* [*1711*]

Ed. Aug. 15

My Dear D Foe

You revivd me by your last when you tell me that our Scots Tories are sent doune with disgrace and have scarce gott a footmans wages for their blind service.[2] I am also glad to hear that my freind R: Cuningham has the greatest interest of any Scots man with the Treasurer.[3] I desyre no other State Secretary; we'll feed the better when he rules the roast.

I hope worthy Mr Carstairs is at London by this time. His cheife errand as I am told is to preserve Montrose and Levin.[4] God grant him Success. Be sure to keep up the alarm about the Medal.[5] Rippeth hath done us Knights Service in England.[6] I hear Mr Dundass will be at the press againe about the medal.[7] That may affoord you some work for your happy pen.[8] I hope in a short time to see all matters at rights againe. I See a letter from R: Cuninghame where in he tells that there are great differences arisen among our great men, and that the Duke of

---

[1] Unidentified.

[2] Parliament had risen in June, and the Scottish members had returned home disgruntled at having received neither attention nor places from the Government. See Wodrow, *Analecta*, i. 348 and 365–6.

[3] Robert Cunningham seems to have been one of Harley's agents. See *H.M.C. Portland*, iv and v, *passim*.

[4] Carstares, leading figure in the Church of Scotland, had gone to London chiefly in the hope of persuading the Government to prevent the restoration of Toleration and Patronage in Scotland. Montrose was Keeper of the Privy Seal of Scotland and Leven was Commander-in-Chief of the Forces in Scotland. Both were Whigs, and both were eventually dropped from office, Leven in 1712, Montrose in 1713.

[5] In June the Jacobite Duchess of Gordon had presented to the Scottish Faculty of Advocates a silver medal showing on one side the head of the Pretender with the legend *Cujus est,* and on the other a map of Britain with the word *Reddite.* This gift the Faculty accepted. The London Government demanded an investigation, whereupon the Faculty rejected the medal and professed their devotion to the Protestant Succession. See the *Review* for 31 July, and G. W. T. Omond, *The Lord Advocates of Scotland,* Edinburgh, 1883, i. 291–5.

[6] George Ridpath, Whig author, had publicized the acceptance of the medal in the *Flying Post.*

[7] James Dundas the younger, of Arniston, had spoken in favour of receiving the medal, and had later defended his position in a tract entitled, *The Faculty of Advocates' Loyalty, in a Letter to the Queen's Most Excellent Majesty, by One of the Dean of Faculty's Council.* He was eventually charged with sedition, but the case was abandoned.

[8] Defoe entered the lists with his satirical pamphlet entitled, *A Speech for Mr. D[unda]sse Younger of Arnistown, if He Should Be Impeach'd for H[igh] T[reason] for What He Said and Did about the Pretender's Medal,* 1711.

Salsbury[1] (as I remember) has left the Court, and that the Tories will In a short time ruin themselves. It were no Smal misfortune if our great man[2] were as good at keeping in himself as he is in turning out others. Let heaven never be stow upon him that blessing. Pray let me hear from you frequently, by which ye'll much oblige

Your affectionate Comrade
T: P:

MS.: Duke of Portland, Harley Papers, vol. xxviii (unfoliated). *Pub.*: *H.M.C. Portland*, v. 72–73. *Address*: none.

173. [*To* ROBERT HARLEY, EARL OF OXFORD].
24 August 1711

My Lord

It was my great Missfortune to Miss the Moment of your Ldpps Leisure when I had the honour of your Last Appointment, and as what I Offred in My Last[3] was as I Thought Very Much for the public Service, I Mean my goeing Northward, So I have wisht Earnestly for your Ldpps Opinion, According to which I Desire to govern all my Steps in these Affairs. I have been Interrupted by Indisposition in My Attendance on your Ldpp, which I hope I Shall Now be able to Retriev. I Humbly beg your Ldpp to believ I have no End in My proposall but to preserv the Intrest and Correspondence which I First Fixed there by your Command, and which I hope allways to Improve and Employ with your Approbation for her Majties Service, and Indeed for the Service and Intrest of That people, who want Nothing So Much as to kno' what is Their True Intrest, and How much Their Intrest and Their Duty to her Majtie Are Twisted together and built upon One Foundation, And a little to be warned From Joyning in with Some honest but weak people here whom your Ldpp Needs not to have me Describe.

I can not Close This without Sending your Ldpp a Printed paper[4] which is a Test of the Forwardness and boldness of a Party Among us. I make no Comments on the Subject but Shall accquaint your Ldpp of the Manner how I obtain'd it when I

---

[1] There was no Duke of Salisbury, and the earl of that title was not of age. The correspondent perhaps meant the Duke of Somerset, who was at this time on bad terms with Harley and St. John, and who left the Government a few months later.
[2] Perhaps the Earl of Mar.
[3] Missing.
[4] Missing.

shall have the honor to wait on you, which I Shall attend for as usuall Every Evening.

I am, May it Please your Ldpp
Your Ldpps Most Humble & Obedt Servt
DE FOE

Augt. 24. 1711

MS.: Duke of Portland, Defoe Papers, 2 f. 25. *Pub.*: *H.M.C. Portland*, v. 75. *Address*: none.

174. [*To* ROBERT HARLEY, EARL OF OXFORD].
27 August 1711

My Lord

I had Not Given your Ldpp This Trouble, being So Near the Appointment I have of attending your Ldpp; but On the Occasion of what you were pleased to Observe to me of The Magistrates of Edinb. Not doeing Their Duty in The Case of The Virulent Pamphlets published There by Dundass and Others.[1]

My Lord, I Humbly Take this Occasion to Represent to your Ldpp That the Madness and Insolence of The Jacobites in Scotland is come to That hight That The Magistrates are Dispirited and Aw'd by them, and in Generall This has been Obtained by those people asserting on all Occasions that The Governmt is with them and Supports Them, allows and Countenances them.

I Doubt not but They will go on till they Force the Governmt to Resent, But (My Lord) it wants but Little of Their believing Not Onely That they will not but That they Dare Not Strike.

On the Other hand My Lord, The Magistrates are Intimidated. The Provost and Bailys are honest, but They want Some Encouragemt from your Ldpp or the Queen That They Shall be protected and Countenanc'd by her Majtie in the Discharge of Their Duty; I Need Not Trouble your Ldpp with the Accounts I have From Severall hands of this, and how The Jacobite Party boast themselves of it; yet I can Not but with A plaineness which I hope your Ldpp will allow to be my Duty, Observ to your Ldpp That there are Unhappily a Party Among us, who I Need Not Name, both There as well as here, who Take great pains from These Things to posess the Minds of The People

[1] See p. 350, n. 7. A month later the Lord Advocate, Sir David Dalrymple, was dismissed from office for failure to deal appropriately with Dundas and the affair of the medal. See G. W. T. Omond, *The Lord Advocates of Scotland*, Edinburgh, 1883, i. 294–5.

That the Ministry are Not in the Revolution Intrest; That the
Ends of all These Things are The Dissolution of the Establishmt,
and The Bringing in the pretender; That the Ministry aim at
Overturning the Union, The Succession, and the Constitution;
It is not Needfull to hint to your Ldpp who these Things are
pointed at; Nor is it Sufficient to Render it Doubtfull to Say tis
aim'd at Their Benefactor, and They can not be So Ingrate;
There are people had Rather the Vessell Should Sink, Tho'
they Run the Risq of Shipwreck in it, Than That their Own
Pilots should Not Steer; These are the Men your Ldpp Must
Save against Their wills, and (like Heaven to us all) Must do
Good to, while They do Evill to you.

But (my Lord) There are Some Honest Men yet, whose Eyes
are Open; who abhorr the Faction and Ingratitude of the
Other; and who, being True and Firm to your Ldpp and to the
Government, should (Pardon me That Arrogance my Lord) be
Cherished and Encouraged; I Mean *Should*, in Order to keep
up The Governmts Intrest, and Ballance the Mad Men on both
Sides: One of My Letters from Scotland, from a Man True to
the Queens Intrest and to the best Measures of Preserving it, has
the following Expressions which I beg Leav to Quote in This
Case.

The Narrativ of the Act of the Faculty, a Coppy of which
was Sent to the Queen, if Narrowly Enquir'd into, will be
found Not to Give a full or True account of Matter of Fact; but
it passes, *cum Ceteris Erroribus.* If the Governmt shall let this
Affair of the Medall drop thro' their Fingers, what the Jacobites on One hand Give Out, That the Government is on
Their Side, and what the Squad.[1] gives Out on the Other
hand, That the Ministry is for The Pretender, will be So farr
Confirm'd to the people, That all honest Men and Friends to
the Queen, and the present Ministry, will be Silenc'd; and
all That you or any Man can Say, Will Never be able to
Remove the Jealousies of it Out of the peoples thoughts.

Thus far my Letter.

My Unfeigned Zeal for your Ldpps Person and Intrest, and
the Sence of Many Obligations I Lye Under to Espouse both,
Makes me Importunate with your Ldpp That both These Sorts
of people, whose Aims point, *One* at the Person, Crown, and

[1] The Squadrone, ignored by the Government in the elections of the previous
autumn, were in opposition.

Governmt of The Queen, and The Other at your Ldpps Person and Administration, may Reciev Their Respective Dissappointments, and This is One Reason why I Moved to your Ldpp my goeing North, Neither the place or people makeing it Desirable; but That I might be where I may Render you Most Service.

I Humbly Lay This Matter before your Ldpp, That the Insolence of a Party in Scotland May be Suppresst, her Majties Faithfull Friends and Servants Encouraged, and a Weak, foolish, Out-of-Temper Party here, and There also, be Effectually Dissappointed.

> I am, May it Please your Ldpp
> Your Ldpps Most Humble and Obedt Servt
> [signature torn off]

Augt. 27. 1711

MS.: Duke of Portland, Defoe Papers, 2 ff. 27–28. *Pub.*: *H.M.C. Portland*, v. 77–78. *Address*: none.

175. [*To* Robert Harley, Earl of Oxford].
3 September 1711

My Lord

Seeing your Ldpp was pleased to Approve My goeing North, I Thought it My Duty to Lay before your Ldpp Some Thoughts of Mine Relateing to Affaires There as They Occurr from My Constant advices from persons of Probity and judgement On the place as well as From My Own Observation.

The Erecting a Form of Governmt Among Them as an Equivalent for the Loss of the Privy Council[1] (The Dissolving of which was no Token of the skill of Our late Mannagers) is Doubtless My Lord a Thought calculated for the health of That place. The Choice of Persons and the Conduct of Those Persons when Chosen Seems to be Now The Onely Nicety in the Case.

There are Three Partys in Scotland which your Ldpp will Observ Influence Affaires and who will come under your Consideration.

1st. The Jacobite Party, whether Popish or Episcopall Matters Little. These Fancy they have Now a Crisis to Push Their Intrest

---

[1] The Scottish Privy Council had been abolished in 1708. The only compensation for that loss of governmental power in Scotland had been the establishment there of the English system of Justices of the Peace. Harley's proposal for an 'equivalent', whatever it was, did not materialize.

in That the juncture is Favourable to Them, and That the Governmt (at least) has Some Need of Them. They act Now barefaced, Furious, and Insolent, Even to the Amazemt of the honest people, who are Terrifyed and Discouraged at The Insolence of The Jacobites; These I presume are to be a little Check'd or Elce The Governmt it Self will be Insulted.

2. The Hot Presbyterians called The Squadroni—These Are by a kind of Principle allwayes against the Court, Right or wrong. They were So in king Williams Time, And were So in The Last Ministry, and Are So Still; and Are indeed worthy to be lay'd Aside by Every Party that purpose to keep the Governmt in bounds.

3. There are a Third kind, which indeed Are the Generallity of The People, who Tho' they are Presbyterian yet go upon Right principles of Government, are Entirely in the present Intrest, hearty to the Queen and Easy undr her administration; Onely Jealous of The Great Favour the Jacobite Party Meet with Least Sometime or Other They get The Power into Their hand in Scotland to pull Down The kirk.

It is Observable The Squadroni Never had any Ruleing Intrest with these, Nor indeed Are Many of The Nobillity with Them, who are Rather Divided between the Jacobites and The Squadroni. But The Ministers are Generally of These, and by The Ministers They are kept Right. These are The people who indeed are The Stay of her Majties Intrest in Scotland. The Little Intrest the Squadroni have with these Appeared in the Great struggle at the last Election but One,[1] when These stuck all to the Court whigs against The Other and Threw Them Out Every wherc.

These are The people which I humbly Move it is her Majties Intrest to preserv, to keep Them Easy and Safe, for These May be Depended Upon in all Extremeties whether of Invasion from Abroad or Partys at home. They will allways Appear on her Majties Part against all Sides— These My Lord Are The people I allways Acted by, These Made The Union, and These keep the Ballance in Their hands So as you will Never find any hot Measures or Furious Motions while They are Encouraged.

If I go Thither I shall give your Ldpp a View of who Among the Nobillity are well with These people and who Not, That in the scheme your Ldpp is Layeing, Such Regard May be had to These people as May Consist with her Majties Service, and

[1] The election of 1708.

That all Such steps May if possible be Avoided as May Tend to Make these Jealous or Uneasye.

The Nobillity of Scotland My Lord are an Odd kind of People, to Say no More of Them. There are Some of Them May Deserv Favour who Should hardly be admitted to any Power; Others (which is Very Strange) it May be Requisite to Entrust with Power who yet hardly Merit The Governmts Favour; and Others yet Merit to be Entirely Neglected and are Neither proper for Favour or Power; and Most of This Varyety Arises From The posture these people stand in with Respect to the kirk, which I Explain to your Ldpp Thus.

Some of the Nobillity are Men of worth, honour and Principles, and as Such Merit her Majties Favour. But to put Them in Power would put all in Confusion, as They onely Are Episcopall in judgement and can not bear with the Establishmt which is Presbyterian, So That Neither would They be Easy to the Presbyterians nor The Presbyterians be Easy under them.

Some of The Nobillity, however worthless in Themselves, and hardly worth any of her Majties Favour, yet as They Are in the Intrest of The well Enclyn'd people abovenamed and of Principles Conforming to the public Service, and withall have Som Considerable Intrest in and Influence upon The best people, are The best Objects for the Trust of Power.

Some of The Nobillity again for Many and known Reasons are Dangerous to her Majtie and The administration, and are Neither Quallifyed for Favour or Power, but to be Continually Forming squadrons of Malecontents and Disquieting the Governmt.

If it May be for your Ldpps Service, I shall Give you lists of Names to These Classes and The just Characters of The Persons. However, Thus Much I Thought it My Duty to Represent to your Ldpp while your Scheme for Governmt May be young and in Embrio, and while perhaps The Persons are not fix't upon in your Thoughts.

> I am, May it Please your Ldpp
> Your Most Humble and Obedt Servt
> [signature torn off]

Septembr. 3. 1711

P S I shall attend Wednsday Evening According to your Ldpps Command.

MS.: Duke of Portland, Defoe Papers, 2 ff. 29–30. *Pub.*: *H.M.C. Portland*, v. 82–84. *Address*: none. *Endorsed*: 'Mr Goldsmith Sept: 3, 1711.'

176. [*To* ROBERT HARLEY, EARL OF OXFORD].
7 September 1711

My Lord

It is with Concern That I give your Ldpp Frequent Trouble of Letters on The affair of Scotland. My Last was Long and I hope Acceptable to your Ldpp; I had Not given your Ldpp This farther Trouble But on Recieving advices from Thence of a Grant which it Seems is Come down Thither And passed The Seals (One Letter Says Stopped at The Seals) to Take away The Privelege of Printing the Bible From the present Posessor Mrs Anderson and Give it to Others.[1]

I formerly hinted Much of This by Letter to your Ldpp;[2] I did Not Say More, least your Ldpp Should think me Solliciting Private Intrests and Cases; But I hope your Ldpp will believ me to Regard, as well as to know, My Duty better; My Study, and the Reason of My pleading with your Ldpp in these or Such Cases, is to Remove or prevent as Much as possible all Grounds of Jealousy, Discontent, and Uneasyness from those people who are True Friends to the Governmt, and to your Ldpps administration; and which I Take it to be good Service to both to keep Right;—and This My Lord The More by how much the Friends of the Pretender go on with too much Success to Divide, Disturb and Intimidate Them, Rendring Them Jealous and Fearfull of Designs to Overthrow Their Kirk and Constitution.

In This Case My Lord They are Made Very Uneasy, and I have a long Representation or adress to her Majtie From the Printers against this Grant to be presented to her Majtie. The Coppy [is][3] in My hands. The Originall is to be brought me and which I shall Lay before your Ldpp also.[4]

The Uneasyness of the Other people is Expresst, Or Rather Abridgd, into Two heads

1. They Say The Printing of The Bible is put into the Hands Of One Papist,[5] One Nonjuror,[6] and a wholl Scocyety of Men

---

[1] See p. 330, n. 2. Baskett, Watson, and Freebairn had obtained the patent in August; it passed the seals in October. Their champion seems to have been St. John (Stewart to Carstares, *H.M.C. Portland*, v. 123).

[2] See Nos. 164 and 169.   [3] MS. torn.

[4] Harley received two petitions in favour of Mrs. Anderson (Duke of Portland, Harley Papers, li ff. 1864–5 and 1866).

[5] James Watson, called 'Popish Watson' (W. J. Couper, *James Watson, King's Printer*, Glasgow, 1910, pp. 4–5). Watson had printed, perhaps piratically, some of Defoe's pamphlets in 1705 (Lee, *Life*, i. 104).

[6] Robert Freebairn, who joined the Jacobite insurrection in 1715 and became printer to the Pretender (W. J. Couper, op. cit., pp. 16–17).

Declared Enemyes to The Church of Scotland and to the Revolution.

2. That the Grant is Illegall in its Nature,[1] Inconsistent with The Union, Invades private Right and The known Liberty of The Subject.

These being heads on which Loud Clamours may be Raised, I Thought it My Duty to Lay before your Ldpp; Not presumeing to Say any thing of My Own thoughts One way or Other, But humbly to Recomend to your Ldpp, as I have done all along, the Occasion There is to keep those honest, weak people as Easy as possible by Such Methods as your Ldpp shall Think proper.

I have Persuant to your Ldpps Commands Put my Self in a Posture for Travailling into Scotland; If your Ldpp pleases to Suffer me to go while The Weather and Roads are Tollerable, it will be a great Favour, The year Declining Appace.

I have One Humble Request to Subjoyn to This Relateing to My attending your Ldpp in the Morning, as by your Ldpps Appointment for tomorrow—It is my Honor and a Privelege No Man Vallues more, That your Ldpp admitts me to wait on you at any Time, and if your Ldpp Commands my Attendance in Public I shall Thankfully Obey. But as my being able to Serve your Ldpp and Her Majties Intrest Consists Much On My being Concealed, I Humbly Submit it to your Ldpp whether I should not Rather Attend in an Evening.[2] I Say no More, Leaving the Rest Entirely to your Ldpps wisdome and Direction, Onely begging leav to Attend this Evening Rather Than to morrow Morning, till I have your Farther Commands.

> I am, May it please your Ldpp
> Your Most Humble and Obedt Servant
> [signature torn off]

Sept. 7. 1711

MS.: Duke of Portland, Defoe Papers, 2 ff. 31–32. *Pub.*: *H.M.C. Portland*, v. 87–88. *Address*: none. *Endorsed*: 'Mr. Goldsmith, Sept: 7: 1711.'

[1] 'Certain irregularities and illegalities in the 1711 patent were alleged—that, *e.g.* it had been obtained while the Anderson patent was still running, that Freebairn had never qualified according to law for holding it, and that it transgressed certain Scottish Acts' (W. J. Couper, op. cit., p. 16).

[2] Now, as before, Defoe was charged with being 'under the Direction of a much greater Man than himself', and was inviting his traducers 'to prove I write under the Direction of any Man alive, or ever would submit to do so' (*Review*, 11 Oct. 1711).

177. [*To* Robert Harley, Earl of Oxford].
15 September 1711

My Lord

In Obedience to your Ldpps Command I have Applyed My Thoughts Seriously to The Affair of a Commander in Chief in Scotland.¹ Your Ldpps proposition is, What Person May be Thought of who May be Easy to the Kirk, or Rather, who the Kirk Party May be Easy with, who is Untainted with Jacobitisme.

It is Not for me my Lord to Give Characters here. The question Principally Lyes on The Character The Kirk Gives of The Person, Or how the Person Stands with the Kirk &c.

I have Rumaged The wholl List of The Nobillity for a Man, and it is hard to Find Them But Either They are Tainted with Jacobitisme, or Embarkt with the Squadroni, Or Uncapable and Improper for The Employ, And Therefore before I Mention Perticular Men, I ask your Ldpps Leave to Make Two Proposalls for your Consideration as an Alternative.

1. That a Person May have The Title of The Employ who is Or is Likely to be allways Abroad, and May be Especially kept abroad; And the Queen Appoint a Person Under him to Command— This I Humbly Offer For two Reasons: 1.) Because Appointing Either The E of Orkney² or Some Such Experienc'd Officer to be Commandr, The Strife of Competitours would Cease, and 2.) Then her Majtie May Give The Sub-Command to Lieut Generall Maitland,³ a Man Acceptable to all Partyes, A Hearty Friend to the Present Establishmt, both Governmt and Ministry; No Bigot, yet Perfectly Well with The kirk, and who None would Object Against, Nor the Oldest Souldier in the Army Think it below him to Serve Under him.

Or if (without the Ceremony of a Commander in Chief

---

¹ The present Commander-in-Chief, the Earl of Leven, was a Whig. He was dismissed in the following summer and was succeeded by Argyll.

² George Hamilton (1666–1737), first Earl of Orkney, brother of the Duke of Hamilton, had fought at the Boyne, Steinkirk, Blenheim, Liège, Ramillies, Oudenarde, and Malplaquet. Although independent command was not especially congenial to his talent, he was an admirable subordinate and was now Marlborough's General of the Foot in Flanders. Orkney was a representative peer and was later to become Governor of Virginia.

³ Defoe seems to have been personally acquainted with James Maitland, who had long commanded Fort William. See Defoe, *Memoirs of the Church of Scotland*, 1717, pp. 245–6.

abroad) he had The wholl Trust, I am Perswaded Not a Man in Scotland Would be Uneasy, Tho' he be not a Noble man.

2. My Second Proposall is, to have no Commander in Chief atall—Any More Than a Third Secretary,[1] or a Privy Council,[2] or a Commander in Chief for Yorkshire, But to Let the Eldest Officer Command, Takeing it as it happens, and The Custome and Usage of The Army Directs.

I am Not Now Giveing My Reasons, but Barely Proposeing to your Ldpps Consideration. Onely I Crave Leav to Offer This, as what I aim at all along in Every Thing I propose (Viz) The Takeing Away Every Thing That keeps up a Faction or a Strife of Partys Among Them. This is what I have my Eye Upon in both These. I Referr My Explanations till your Ldpp shall have Perused The Generall proposall.

I am, May it Please your Ldpp
Your Ldpps Most Humble and Obedt Servt
[symbol]

Sept. 15. 1711

MS.: Duke of Portland, Defoe Papers, 2 ff. 33–34. *Pub.*: *H.M.C. Portland*, v. 90–91. *Address*: none. *Endorsed*: 'Mr Goldsmith, R̃ Sept: 18, 1711, Scotland.'

178. [*To* ROBERT HARLEY, EARL OF OXFORD].
16 October 1711

My Lord

As it has allways been my Study to be where, and be doeing what, may Render me most Usefull, So I allways think it my Duty to Signifye it to your Ldpp when and where I May be capable of doeing any Service; This Occasions me humbly to Move your Ldpp at This Time: I acknowledge it is But little my Low Station is Capable of, But if Ever I was, or Ever Shall be capable of Rendring your Ldpp any Service, If I have any foresight into Things, Now is the juncture; when The Minds of The People, Fluctuating and Stormy like The Sea, Listen to

---

[1] The office of Secretary of State for Scotland, established after the Union, had been abandoned on the death of the Duke of Queensberry in the previous summer.
[2] The Scottish Privy Council had been abolished in 1708. Cf. p. 354, n. 1.

Every Wicked Inflamer and Would Listen also to Calm and Cool admonitions if Given with Temper and Sincerity.[1]

I have My Lord Humbly addressed your Ldpp and Constantly attended in Order to Obtain your Approbation of my thoughts on This head, being Affraid to be Officious, yet hitherto I go Unsent; your Ldpps Leisure Not Permitting My Audience. This however is a great Missfortune to me, and My Enemies, who Reproach me (as they think) with being Under your Ldpps Direction, Labour to Suppress Me for what I do Not Enjoy The Honor of.

My Lord I am Perswaded, and This makes me bold to Move your Ldpp, That I am yet able to Conquer the Obstinacy of a hot but Deluded Party and at least to take off the Edge of That Venemous spirit that has Infected Them. I Onely Humbly Entreat your Ldpps Approbation and Protection So far as I do my Duty Therein. I have Represented My Case to your Ldpp; I add Nothing to it but [that I][2] have Irritated and Exasperated The Party So Much by but Gently Refuseing to Declare for [their refr]actory and Unpeacable Measures; That Unless your Ldpp pleases to Take me into your Protection, and Afford me The Usuall Support your Own Goodness Lay'd the Foundation of, *I shall One day Fall by The hand of This Saul*. Pardon me My Lord The Allusion, But The Case is So farr gone That I Could Not Refrain This hint.

The present Case I beg of your Ldpp is Onely whether a warm Application to The Opening the peoples Eyes in The Affair of Peace, in which They are goeing Mad, will be Acceptable to your Ldpp, in which as my Own principle agrees and The Public Service Requires, So I Humbly Suggest your Ldpps Service also Very Much Consists.

---

[1] The great subject of agitation at this time was the Peace. Conversations between the British and the French had been in progress for more than a year, and by now St. John and Torcy had reached a preliminary agreement. Favourable as the terms were to Britain, they were not so favourable as to please the Whigs, whose inordinate demands had blocked peace in 1709. 'The Whig party are furious against a Peace', wrote Swift on the 24th, 'and every day some ballad comes out reflecting on the ministry on that account. The secretary St. John has seized on a dozen booksellers and publishers, into his messengers hands. Some of the foreign ministers have published the Preliminaries agreed on here between France and England; and the people rail at them as insufficient to treat a Peace upon' (*Journal to Stella*, ii. 394). To defend the Government came runs of pamphlets by both Swift and Defoe. Swift's most telling contribution, published on 27 Nov., was his *Conduct of the Allies*. Defoe had already published, on 6 Oct., his *Reasons Why This Nation Ought to Put a Speedy End to This Expensive War*, now in its third edition; and he continued to state the case for peace in succeeding pamphlets and in numerous *Reviews*.

[2] MS. torn; this and the following bracketed reading are conjectural.

There are Some Measures for This which I would lay before your Ldpp also, if I had the honour of half an hour of your Leisure. I shall attend This Evening as your Ldpp was pleased to Ordr me, in hopes of Admittance.

I am, May it Please your Ldpp

Your Ldpps Most Humble and Obedt Servt

[DE]¹ FOE

Octo. 16. 1711

P S. I hope your Ldpp does not forget that I had Success in as hard a Case in Scotland.²

MS.: Duke of Portland, Defoe Papers, 2 ff. 35–36. *Pub.*: *H.M.C. Portland*, v. 101–2. *Address*: none. *Endorsed*: 'Mr Goldsmith Octo: 16, 1711.'

179. [*To* ROBERT HARLEY, EARL OF OXFORD].

30 November 1711

My Lord

In Obedience to your Ldpps Command I here Enclose The Receipt which I had to Signe and have Filled Up the blank with the Date. I do not Exactly Remember whether your Ldpps Order was to Send The Same Signed or a Coppy written by me, but if I have Mistaken I Shall not Fail to Rectify it on your first Command; Suitable My Lord to the Extremetys My Last³ gave your Ldpp an Account I am Reduced to, is My Humble Thankfull Return to your Ldpps goodness and Her Majties Bounty.

I Believ My Lord I Need not give your Ldpp an Account how I am Treated in Print by The Observator⁴ for Espouseing The just article of Peace, and how he is (and I have been Offred to be) Supported, and by who. I am Far from Mentioning it as Merit; but to Let your Ldpp kno' your Enemyes and The Fury They Act with; The assurance They pretend to of Breaking all her Majties Measures abroad Makes Their Friends Perfectly Insolent, and The Feares Least They should, Terrifyes on the other hand.

¹ MS. torn.
² In helping overcome opposition to the Union in 1706 and 1707.
³ Missing.
⁴ In three *Observators* between 28 Nov. and 5 Dec., George Ridpath, the Whig journalist, attacked not only Defoe's political affiliations but his personal character as well. Defoe took up the challenge in the *Reviews* of 1, 4, 6, and 29 Dec. 1711, and 5 Jan. 1712. In 1713 Ridpath helped bring about Defoe's arrest for writing the ironical *Reasons against the Succession of the House of Hanover* and two other pamphlets on the succession (see No. 204). In July 1714 Defoe retaliated by helping William Hurt bring out a continuation of Ridpath's *Flying Post* after that paper had been removed to another printer (see p. 446).

I have my Lord Openly Declared against and Opposed Them, my Own Principle Concurring with my Duty to your Ldpp Therein; and as my Entire Dependence is That I Shall not be left Unsupported in The prosecution of That Duty; This gives Me Confidence with all humillity to Represent my Condition to your Ldpp, and How if Ever This Party Prevail I am to Expect No Quarter Or Favour, and in the Mean Time am Onely Supported by This Bounty of her Majtie, which is all Owing to your Ldpps Goodness, and The Arrear whereof has So Much Reduced me.

I Long for an Occasion to Lay before your Ldpp The Madness and Rage of your Enemies, And Something Also of The Feares of your Friends; God Give your Ldpp Wisdome and Courage, Faithfullness to himself, and Success to Dissappoint Them all.

I shall go on to Discharge My Duty in Opposition to all The Madness of The Age, Recomending Onely My Self and Family to your Goodness, which I can Not but hope will not Decrease to me for my steady adhereing, however weakly, to your Ldpps and The Nations Intrest.

> I am, May it Please your Ldpp
> Your Ldpps Most Humble and Obedient Servt
> DE FOE

Novembr 30. 1711

MS.: Duke of Portland, Defoe Papers, 2 f. 37. *Pub.*: *H.M.C. Portland*, v. 118–19. *Address*: none.

180. [*To* ROBERT HARLEY, EARL OF OXFORD].
20 December 1711

My Lord

I confess my Self So much Surprized with the Perticulars which your Ldpp did me the honor to Communicate to Me On Tuesday of the Conduct of a Set of Men with Respect to the Dissenters,[1] That I could not Express my Self on Severall Things

---

[1] The Whigs, dissatisfied with the terms of peace drawn up by the Government, had offered to abandon their old friends and supporters the Dissenters and vote for an act forbidding occasional conformity, if the Government in return would acquiesce to Whig wishes for a reconstruction of the Ministry and a revision of the peace terms. This overture Harley had rejected. But the Whigs found their man in Nottingham, high Tory and former Secretary of State, who was not a member of the present Ministry. Through Nottingham, the Whigs got the House of Lords to declare to no peace under the present terms; and through the Whigs, Nottingham got his cherished Occasional Conformity Bill through the Lords (*J.H.L.* xix. 345). The Commons passed the Bill two days later, the day of this letter. Defoe never condoned the practice of occasional conformity, but he denounced this betrayal

Needfull to be Observ'd to your Ldpp on the Occasion, which Defect According to the Freedome your Ldpp is pleased to Allow me, I Supply in This Manner.

And first My Lord, in the Midst of My Real and just Concern for The Intrest of the Dissenters which I look upon as Ruind; I can Not but look up with Thankfullness in your Ldpps behalf That The Mouths of your Enemies Are Most Effectually Stopt in Offring to Lay the Reproach of Their Dissaster Upon your Ldpp, which is Most Aparently the Effect of an Implacable but I hope Impotent Aversion to your Ldpp and of a Manifest Resolution to Injure and Insult you:

Had it Not been too late to Retriev The Injury, I should have Rejoyc't also in behalf of The Dissenters; That The Idols They adored have Appear'd capable of So Mean a Step, as to Sell The Party That Ventur'd Their Safety on The Leaky bottom of a Supposed Zeal, into Perpetuall Tory bondage, to form a New Interest for The Supporting Their Party Designs; but my Lord This Joy is like Singing a Psalm at a Funerall, too Sad to be Sonorous.[1]

May it Please your Ldpp

As your Ldpp has for the Sake of a Little Sincerity, borne with a great Deal of Course and Unpolish't plainess from me; Indulgeing a Freedome which I have No Title to but from your Own Goodness; So I beg your Ldpp to bear with One Humble Motion in behalf of an Intrest, which I kno' your Ldpp has been Patron of, which has been Vallued by you, and which Tho' the Usage of Some of The People to your Ldpp has been Inexcusable, yet I am Fully Perswaded your Ldpp has still at Heart; I Mean that of The Dissenters.[2]

There Remains but One Point between Them and The Fate of Their wholl Cause (Viz) her Majties Passing Or Not Passing The bill; I kno' The Negativ is Not without its hazard, and Many Watch The advantage; But My Lord Her Majtie has Sollemnly Pass't her Royall Promise to the Dissenters, to

of the Dissenters in the *Reviews* of 20, 22, and 25 Dec., and in *An Essay on the History of Parties and Persecution in Britain*, which appeared on 22 Dec. according to the *Review* of that date.

[1] The Whigs and the Dissenters had been in alliance ever since the time of Charles II, and in spite of the present short lapse, were to be again until the time of Victoria.

[2] Though now Church of England and Tory, Harley came of nonconformist stock, and had attended the dissenting academy at Sheriffhales (H. McLachlan, *English Education under the Test Acts*, Manchester, 1931, p. 49).

Preserv The Tolleration Inviolable. I kno' My Duty too well to Enter On any Argumt on the Consistency of Passing This bill, with The keeping this Promise; yet I could not Satisfye my Self, Neither in Duty to the Dissenters Intrest, or The Imediate Intrest of your Ldpp, without Humbly Moveing your Ldpp in This Case (Viz) How Effectually it would bind to your Intrest, and to her Majties Person and Governmt, and to your just Measures, The wholl body of The Dissenters, and Low Church men also, who are as ill Pleased as any; How Effectually it would bring in Those Very People who have Suffred This Chicane of a Party to be pass't upon them; and Are Rageing with shame and Confusion at what They have done; How Effectually it would Rivet your Ldpp in the hearts of all Good Men, Silence passt Unjust Clamours, and Powerfully Establish your Ldpp as The protector of Liberty, The Patron of justice, and The true Refuge of an Injur'd people: All This I firmly believ, with a blessing From Heaven, would be The Consequence, if her Majtie in Maintenance of her Sacred Promise aforesaid, May be advised to Refuse This Bill.[1]

God Allmighty give your Ldpp Wisdome, and Council from himself, to Direct in an Affair of So Nice but Important Consequence, So as May Issue in his Glory, your Own blessing, and an Innocent Peoples Deliverance. Asking Pardon for This freedom,

I am, May it Please your Ldpp
Your Ldpps Most Humble and Obedt Servt
DE FOE

Decemb. 20. 1711

MS.: Duke of Portland, Defoe Papers, 2 ff. 39–40. *Pub.*: *H.M.C. Portland*, v. 130–1. *Address*: none.

181. [*To* ROBERT HARLEY, EARL OF OXFORD].
10 January 1711/12

My Lord

When I am Thanking your Ldpp for the Continuance of a Bounty I can Not Merit, I Blame My Self for the Importunities I have Used. But I hope for your Ldpps Pardon when I Consider That Really The Treatmt I meet with from a poor Enraged People[2] whose True Intrest I believ I Serve, Seems to Recommend Me to your Ldpps Compassion— God Grant your

[1] In the *Review* for 22 Dec. Defoe begged the Queen to reject the measure, but the Bill received the royal assent on that same day.   [2] The Dissenters.

Ldpp Victory Over This New Posession, for however I May Fare while your Ldpp holds the Reins; I am Sure to Sink if any Thing happen to The prejudice of your Intrest:

I have Not the Fewest yeares Over my head[1] of any Man That Observes these Things, And I have Seen Many of these Court Revolutions, But of all The Outed Parties That Ever were Seen, at least in the Last 50 yeares, None Ever push't with So much Fury at The Governmt who have Dissmiss't them as These have done. Nothing but down Right Takeing Arms can be like This, and I am Perswaded Onely want of Power Restrains from the worst Sort of Violence.

God That Directs your Ldpp I hope in all Things, has Moved you No doubt to Take This Most Necessary step of Deposeing The Idol Man,[2] who Coveted to Set himself up as The head of a Party, and by whom They pretended[3] to Make Themselves Formidable. All wise men Own the Necessity, and Applaud The Wisdome of This step, and if it be Needfull for her Majties Safety to go on, I believ no Man can Think Amiss That those who Eat her Majties Bread, should (when a Threatning behaviour Demands Such a Course) be left to kno' the want of it.

The Small Tract[4] which I hinted to your Ldpp in My Last[5] I Send herewith, and as your Ldpp was pleased to Ask me if no way Might be found Out to Open The Eyes of These poor Deluded people The Dissenters; I doubt Not My Lord but the Fury and Precipitation of Their Old Supporters[6] will be a proper Means, and The Exposeing it for That purpose I make my bussiness in Ordr to help on Their Conviction. Nor Shall all Their Fury at me Cause me to Cease This Method, which I Take to be The best Service to your Ldpp which lyes in My Power.

I am, May it Please your Ldpp &c

[symbol]

Jan. 10. 1711

I Omit my Name by your Ldpps Ordr

MS.: Duke of Portland, Defoe Papers, 2 f. 41. *Pub.*: *H.M.C. Portland*, v. 137. *Address*: none.

[1] He was about 51 years old.

[2] Prompted by Harley and St. John, the Queen to the consternation of the Whigs had dismissed the Duke of Marlborough from all his employments on 31 Dec.

[3] i.e. aspired, endeavoured.

[4] Probably his *Essay on the History of Parties and Persecution in Britain*, published on 22 Dec., in which he denounced the Occasional Conformity Bill as a violation of the toleration promised the Dissenters.

[5] Missing.　　　　　　　　　　　　　　　　　　　　[6] The Whigs.

182. [*To* ROBERT HARLEY, EARL OF OXFORD].

24 January 1711/12

My Lord

In My Last[1] I hinted to your Ldpp Something I would Lay before your Ldpp which I Thot Transacting Against her Majties Intrest in Scotland, but I confess to your Ldpp I did not Suppose So Near breaking Out, and in This Manner.[2]

In Duty to your Ldpp I can Not but humbly Represent That This Step, which Amounts to no less Than a Setting up The Common Prayer book on One hand and a Tolleration of Episcopacy on The Other, will, besides The Unhappy Consequences which are Easy to foresee, Effectually Lose The wholl body of The presbyterians From her Majties Intrest in That Kingdome, who till now have kept Steady and have not Mingled with the Common Discontents of the Dissenters here, Or of the whigs on Either part, And I Humbly beseech your Ldpp to Think Whether on the Other hand The Episcopal Party (not jacobite) in That place are Able to Stand her Majtie in Any Stead in the Room of it.

I Am Not Arguing The affair of Religion One way or Other, but Nothing Seems More Evident Than that her Majties Intrest There is founded Onely on The Presbyterian Party and she has Very Few Other Friends There.[3]

Farther My Ld I beg Leav to Suggest That the Snare Lay'd in This bill to Involv in Ruin a Poor, hot and Furious but well Meaning people is Very Visible, and the Gentlemen who kno' that No Act of Parliamt can Restrain the Zealous people in This Case Depend upon Embroiling Them as Formerly with the Governmt and bringing Them into blood, which I fear will be Unavoidable. Nor will The Liturgy Ever be Set up in Scotland (The poor, Subjected Clans of highland Slaves Excepted) but by Force, Persecution, and all the Unhappy Consequences of Arms; I Entreat in the humblest Manner your Ldpps Leave to

---

[1] Missing.

[2] On 21 Jan. the Commons had given leave that a Bill be brought in 'to prevent the disturbing those of the Episcopal Communion in that Part of *Great Britain* called *Scotland*, in the Exercise of their religious Worship, and in the Use of the Liturgy of the Church of England' (*J.H.C.* xvii. 33). The alarmed Commission of the General Assembly of the Church of Scotland protested that the Bill contravened the Act of Security of their Church, and their deputation in London, headed by Carstares, placed their petition before the Queen. Defoe warned his readers of the dangers of the proposed legislation in the *Reviews* for 26 Jan. and 2 and 5 Feb. 1711–12. Nevertheless, the so-called Toleration Act became law on 3 Mar. (*J.H.C.* xvii. 123).   [3] Cf. No. 175.

Remind your Ldpp of This Very Objection, Made by the poor, jealous people at the Time of the Union, which I did my Self the honor frequently to Signifye to your Ldpp at That Time, and which I had your Ldpps License then to Assure Them They Should not have Need to fear.[1]

I have frequently Recomended The poor, warm people There as on Many Accounts to be borne with and Pityed; and Capable on Many Occasions to Render her Majtie Good Service; and Their Readyness in the last affair of The Invasion[2] Testifyes for Them, and Recomends Them to her Majties Compassion; When These Episcopall people who Appear Now So Zealous for the English Liturgy (and My Ld Lyon[3] most Especially) Openly shew'd Themselves Ready to Embrace a popish Pretender.

I pray God This be not a Plot to Deprive her Majtie of The Assistance and Service of So Considerable a part of her faithfull Subjects; and to make Them a constant Uneasyness to the Governmt, and The Governmt to Them.

I can Not but Apprehend The Fatal Consequence of This to the Peace of Scotland, and as your Ldpp has been pleased to give me Leave with Freedome and Faithfullness to Lay Such Things at your Feet, I could not Omit it; I Lament the Obstinacy of a Party Among us which Make Such Things Necessary, But My Lord The Poor people of Scotland have had no share in Them, and Resolv'd to adhere to her Majtie in all her Just Measures.

I kno' if any help be for Them with Man, it is in your Ldpp. I pray God Make your Ldpp The happy Instrumt to Save Them from the Ruine Evidently before Them.

I have Much of This Affair to add but I am loth to Offend your Ldpp with My Importunities; I Shall attend your Ldpps Leisure to Mention it More Fully. I Humbly ask your Ldpps Pardon for So Much Freedome and Am

May it Please your Ldpp
Your Ldpps Most Humble and Obedient Servt
[symbol]

Jana. 24. 1711

MS.: Duke of Portland, Defoe Papers, 2 ff. 43–44. *Pub.*: *H.M.C. Portland*, v. 139–40. *Address*: none. *Endorsed*: 'Scotland, Goldsmith, Jana: 24: 1711/12.'

[1] See Defoe's letters of Nov. and Dec. 1706.
[2] The invasion of Mar. 1708, when the French attempted to land the Pretender.
[3] Sir Alexander Erskine (1663–1727), Lyon King of Arms and M.P. for Fifeshire, was one of the three persons who prepared the Toleration Bill. He was a Jacobite, and joined Mar in the insurrection of 1715.

183. [*To* ROBERT HARLEY, EARL OF OXFORD].
14 February 1711/12

My Lord

I Reproach my Self with The Answer I gave your Ldpp when you were pleased to Ask me if I had any Thing Perticular to Offer, Because I Fully purposed to have Represented a Perticular Case of the Poor keel men of New Castle, which I Once Offred formerly to your Ldpp,[1] and who are Now like to have the Governmt and Mannagemt of Their Own Charity Subjected to The Fitters and Magistrates; by which a New foundation also will be Lay'd to Influence and Enslave The poor Men, and Thereby Again Make a Monopoly of the Coal Trade.

There is So Much Justice and Charity in The Case That I Perswade my Self your Ldpp will be pleased with Appearing in behalf of a Thousand Families of poor and Injured Men, who None but God and your Ldpp can Now Deliver; If your Ldpp pleases to give me Leav I would Gladly Lay an Abstract of The Case before you; It being in a Few days to pass the house of Commons.[2]

I have had Severall People Frequently comeing to me for advice in Little projects which They offer afterwards to your Ldpp as I Suppose in The Treasury office, and I have not Troubled your Ldpp with any of Them because I have Thought Few of Them worth your Notice. But There is One who offers a proposall for Raiseing The Revenue of Excise, as he Sayes, about 60000*l* per Annum without any Additionall Charge— I Confess I Thought his design well Lay'd, and Encouraged him for That Reason to proceed. The Mans Name is Finch,[3] an honest man of Good Character, by Trade a Brewer. If your Ldpp pleases to call for Such a Name, I believ his Petition or Memoriall is in the Office; or if it May be for your Ldpps Service, I Shall Lay his scheme before your Ldpp, First Assureing your Ldpp I have No Concern or Intrest Directly or Indirectly in it, Onely as I Thought it my Duty to Lay any

[1] See p. 332. Before Parliament now was the petition of the Newcastle barge-men for a charter of incorporation whereby they might take direct control of their hospital. Defoe supported their cause in the *Reviews* for 12 and 14 Feb.

[2] The Commons decided in favour of the keel-men on 29 Mar. (*J.H.C.* xvii. 160).

[3] Perhaps Robert Finch, who had made a similar proposal before. See *Calendar of Treasury Papers, 1702–1707*, p. 302.

Thing before your Ldpp which I Thought Might be for the public good.

May it Please your Ldpp

I Would on My Own Account Gladly have Represented Some Things Relateing to the Press.[1] I have allways Expresst my Self Ready to Lay down My pen when it shall Cease to be any Longer Usefull to your Ldpp, yet I would humbly hope your Ldpp will not look upon me as an Invalid, If I should be Lay'd by as to printing; Believing That Generall Intrest and Correspondence I have Settled, Especially in The North, shall allways be Capable of being Improved for your Service.

Indeed My Ld as I am Used by the whigs and Dissenters for writeing & Printing, because I can not go Their Length, and Dare to write what does not please Them, It can be Nothing but The hopes I have That I am Some way Usefull To your Ldpp That Supports me; and tho' I forbear to Trouble your Ldpp with it, as Not worth your Notice, yet in The Generall it may Suffize to Say, The Persecution and Reproach I Meet with from Them is Turn'd to Personall Mischief, Raiseing Creditors, Reviveing old prosecutions, and Open Endeavors to Ruine and Disstress me.

But My Lord as This Drives me the More into your Protection, and your Goodness has been pleased to Support me, I have not failed, With the Uttmost Force I have had, to Detect The Arts and shifts of a Party, and Open The Eyes of Those who would Otherwise be blinded by Their popular Clamour, and it is My happyness That this is Perfectly Agreeable to My judgemt and Principle as I hope it is to your Ldpps Service. I Therefore Lay My Self att your Ldpps Feet, Entirely Depending On your Goodness for my Support, and I Openly Defye and Contemn the fury of a Party Baffled by Their Own Ungovernd Heat.

I Sincerely Lament The Case of Scotland.[2] I See The Neces-

---

[1] As pamphlet and newspaper wars became more and more acrimonious, the Ministry became increasingly disturbed. On 17 Jan. the Queen had invited the Commons 'to observe how great License is taken in publishing false and scandalous Libels', and had recommended that they 'find a Remedy equal to the Mischief' (*J.H.C.* xvii. 27). The warning sounded ominous to Defoe and he now feared a general suppression of the party press of both sides, including of course the *Review*. By April the Commons were deliberating upon the Stamp Act, which became law in the following August. See the *Reviews* for 24 Jan., 7 Feb., and 26 and 29 Apr. 1712; and *Journal to Stella*, ii. 553–4.

[2] The Bill for granting a toleration to Episcopal Dissenters in Scotland had passed the Commons and was now before the Lords. See the *Reviews* for 2 and 5 Feb.

sity of Giveing way to the Current and can heartily blame those who have Driven Things to Such Extremeties; But I Dread The Consequences in Scotland; I do not fail to Temper and Perswade The warm people There to Calm Their Thoughts and keep Themselves quiet; and were There to be no Aggressors, More might be done. But I fear The Fury of the Jacobite party will Drive the Other into Excesses.

If my health would Permit me, I should Tender my Service to Spend the Summer Now at hand Among Them, And if your Ldpp shall Think me Usefull, Nothing but Utter Dissabillity shall Detain me, for I Perswade my Self I may do Something among Them which Every One can Not—But all That, and My Self, my Fortunes and hopes, Are at your Ldpps absolute Command and Direction.[1]

> I am, May it Please your Ldpp
> Your Ldpps Most Humble and Obedient Servt
> [symbol]

Feb. 14. 1711

P. S. I shall attend on Saturday Morning, According to your Ldpps Command.

MS.: Duke of Portland, Defoe Papers, 2 ff. 45–46. *Pub.*: *H.M.C. Portland*, v. 143–4. *Address*: none. *Endorsed*: 'Mr Goldsmith, Febr: 14: 1711/12.'

184. [*To* Robert Harley, Earl of Oxford].
5 April 1712

My Lord

My last[2] Seems to Make this Necessary. The Evill I Then hinted at about the Stamp Office I wait an Opportunity to Lay before your Ldpp.

I could not but Represent to your Ldpp how The party Among us, who are So Famous for pushing their Own dissasters, as well as those of their Country, please Themselves with the hope of haveing broke all the Ministry's Measures; and that they have, as they think, put an End to the Treaty of Peace:[3] Were They alone to Suffer by a war, it were Pity but They

---

[1] He did not go north until the autumn (Nos. 193, 194, and 195).

[2] Missing.

[3] In February Swift had written: 'The Lds have voted an Adress to the Qu, to tell her they are not satisfyed with the K. of France's Offers. The Whigs brought it in of a sudden, and the Court could not prevent it, and therefore did not oppose it. The H. of Lds is too strong in Whigs notwithstanding the new Creations' (*Journal to Stella*, ii. 489–90). At Utrecht the peace negotiations were dragging intolerably, and elicited from Defoe a long series of exasperated *Reviews*. See especially the biting issue for 1 Apr.

Should be Fill'd with Their Own ways;[1] It is Evedent They desire the war Onely as They Envy your Ldpp the Glory of The peace, and as they think it Gratifyes The Party They foolishly call Their Friends: Honest Men hope Still your Ldpps prudence will Baffle all the plots they carry on Against the Generall good, and That the Peace So Needfull to a bleeding Nation Shall not be So slightly Rejected.

It is a Sort of pleasant tho' Mellancholly Contradiction to hear These Men Rail at the peace in One breath and at the New Taxes with the Next, as if we were to Carry On the war without Money; as if they could have a War Renewed and a Stop put to The Raiseing Money at the Same Time. The Contrary must be One of the ways to Convince them who are Their Friends, Those who would Take off the burthen or those who would bind it On and Encrease it till the Nation Sinks undr it.

These Things perswade us all to peace if Our Eyes were Open, but who shall cure a Nation born blind!

I long Impatiently to Represent to your Ldpp Some Very Materiall things Relateing to Scotland; I am full of Feares for The public peace on That Side,[2] and as I kno' The hardships put Upon Them there, Are Against your Ldpps Mind and Against The Queens Intrest, I am Studious to find out Mediums to keep both sides Easy, and if your Ldpp pleases at Leisure to Enter on Some Measures for That good work, I Shall hope it may not be too late, Especially if Something May be done before The assembly meets.[3]

I Apply my Self with constant and Dilligent Endeavour to stem the Torrent of Clamour and Dissaffection both here and [There],[4] and Tho' the Success may Not Answer, I hope The Labour and the Labourer Shall be Accepted by your Ldpp, and This Supports me Under The worst Treatment (Among them) That Ever man Met with.

I am, May it Please your Ldpp
Your Ldpps Most Obedt &c.
[symbol]

Aprill. 5. 1712

MS.: Duke of Portland, Defoe Papers, 2 ff. 47–48. *Pub.*: *H.M.C. Portland,* v. 160–1. *Address*: none. *Endorsed*: 'Mr. De Foe.'

[1] See Prov. xiv. 14.   [2] See p. 367, n. 2.
[3] The General Assembly of the Church of Scotland was to convene on 1 May.
[4] MS. torn.

185. [*To* ROBERT HARLEY, EARL OF OXFORD].
17 April 1712

My Lord

I am to ask Pardon for a Mistake I thought my Self Uncapable of (Viz:) That haveing written to your Ldpp last Night for Cover of The Enclosed, and Given The letter to a Servt to Carry, I Found The Receipt on My Table left Out. I have left it without Date because your Ldpp So Ordred before.[1] I Humbly Ask your Ldpps pardon for the Mistake And am

> May it Please your Ldpp
> Your Most Humble and Obedt Servt
> [symbol]

Aprill. 17. 1712

MS.: Duke of Portland, Defoe Papers, 2 f. 49. *Pub.*: *H.M.C. Portland*, v. 165. *Address*: none.

186. [*To* ROBERT HARLEY, EARL OF OXFORD].
29 April 1712

My Lord

I can Not Pay The Debt I owe to your Ldpps goodness a better way Then by faithfully and Impartially Representing things to, as well as from, your Ldpp in This Nice and Difficult Time.

It was Wisely Observ'd by your Ldpp the Last Time I had the honor to wait on you That There might Come a Time when the Dissenters Might better be Talked to Than They can Now; It is an Unhappy Truth, that The Temper of those honest men is yet So Ruffled at the Loss of their Politick Intrest,[2] That it Threatns their Religious, and I find too Many of them willing Enough to Sacrifize the Latter, to Retriev the former.

This Makes me, I Confess, not atall Regrett that they Are Ruin'd in their Politick Intrest; hopeing Still that Their Religious Intrest Shall be Established by it; and when all the Dissenters in Masq are Drop't from Them, and Nothing but meer Conscientious Nonconformity Remains, I Doubt not your

---

[1] Neither the receipt nor the letter has survived. According to the Secret Service accounts, Defoe had received £100 on 24 Feb. and a like sum on 6 Mar. (Laurence Hanson, *Government and the Press*, 1936, p. 96). But Harley's request for undated receipts suggests that the entries were being manipulated and hence throws some suspicion on the accuracy of the Secret Service accounts.

[2] See p. 363, n. 1.

Ldpp will become their protector as you have allways been of Honest principles and Honest Men.

Mean Time God Deliver your Ldpp from a New Doctrine in Politicks which I suppose is Taught them by their Old Masters (Viz) that The Ministry Ought to be prompted and push't On to all Immoderate Councils That They May be Overthrown by Them.[1] If this be Borrowd from The practise of the Late Ld Sunderland with King James, to which they Say we Owe the Revolution,[2] I can Onely Say to Them—*We like the Treason, But &c.*[3]

I Apply my Self to Represent to the Dissenters the ground they have lost and the Injury they have done Themselves by joyning into Parties and Meddling with Politicks, and to let them See, that being beaten off from these Things with loss, and much wounded in the Scuffle, The Onely way they have left to Retriev their Figure in the world is to become a Religious body as they were at first, and by Layeing Aside Politicall Views and Party makeing, Remove Effectually from Their Enemys the pretence, and From others the Reall Apprehensions, of their being Dangerous to the Church.[4]

Perhaps your Ldpp, Than whom None knows The Temper of the Men better, May believ my Success Improbable; But I hope yet a Time for their Illumination May Come, And I perswade my Self your Ldpp is So Much their Friend Still, Tho' Amidst a Thousand provocations, as that you would be Glad to See it.

I Trouble your Ldpp with Nothing Relateing to Scotland because The Success[5] of the assembly is So Near.[6]

I am, May it Please your Ldpp
Your Ldpps Most Humble and Obedient Servt
[symbol]

Aprill 29. 1712

MS.: Duke of Portland, Defoe Papers, 2 f. 51. *Pub.*: *H.M.C. Portland*, v. 166–7. *Address*: none.

[1] Cf. Defoe, *Eleven Opinions about Mr. H[arle]y*, 1711, p. 30.

[2] Robert Spencer (1640–1702), second Earl of Sunderland, was thought to have beguiled King James into disaster by treacherously advising him to take those steps that ruined him; but see F. C. Turner, *James II*, New York, 1948, p. 304.

[3] 'We Love the Treason, but we Hate the Traytor' (Sir Roger L'Estrange, *Fables of Æsop and Other Mythologists*, 1708, p. 210).

[4] This counsel to the Dissenters Defoe expanded in the *Reviews* for 1 and 10 May; in *The Present State of the Parties in Great Britain*, 1712, pp. 338–52; and in *Wise as Serpents: Being an Enquiry into the Present State of the Dissenters*, 1712.

[5] i.e. outcome, result.   [6] See p. 372, n. 2.

187. [*To* ROBERT HARLEY, EARL OF OXFORD].
27 May 1712

My Lord

Tho' my Observations in This Letter Should not be just, yet
My Zeal for your Ldpps Intrest and the Public Good Shall
plead I hope with your Ldpp if it Should Not be According to
knowlege.

The Article published yesterday in The post-Script to the
flying Post (Viz) *that when the Genlls of The Confederates were
Resolv'd to Attack The Enemy, The British Generall pull'd Out the
Queens Ordr Not to fight Or Undertake a Siege,* Occasions This.[1]

This My Lord is told in Such a Manner and Recd with Such
a Temper as Raises a Mighty popular Clamour, and does
Much Mischief Thro' the Nation.

If The Fact is Not True, I Need Not hint to your Ldpp what
Resentmt The publishing it calls for from the Governmt, for
tho' I am None of Those who prompt the Missfortunes of My
Neighbours, yet Governmts as well as private Men Sometimes
find it Necessary to do themselves justice.[2]

On The Other hand, if The Thing be Fact, I can Not but
Think it Recieves Such a Compleat Justification in practise,
from the Constant Conduct of the Dutch, of The Imperialists,
and Other Confederates, and There Are Such justifyable
Reasons to be given for Such a Conduct at This Time; That
Might I Reciev The least Remote hint from your Ldpp, Something Might Easily be Said without doores, that would Take off
all the Edge of The popular Surprize Some people Think They
have Rais'd in the Nation, and Turn all the Mischief Against
Themselves. If your Ldpp please but to hint your Commands to
Mr Read[3] by a Single *yes* or *No*, it is Enough to be Understood
by me, and shall be Imediately Obey'd, I hope to your Ldpps
Satisfaction. I Mean by *yes* or *No* Onely whether *yes* or *No* Such
a Historicall Deduction of practise From Our Idolised Allies
May be Usefull at this Time to do her Majtie Justice and
to Checq The Loud Clamours of a Party who watch for all

---

[1] On 10 May St. John had secretly issued the notorious 'Restraining Orders',
under which Ormonde, then commanding in Flanders, was instructed to avoid
engaging in any siege, or hazarding a battle, until he received further orders from
the Queen. When Ormonde consequently refused to join Eugene in attacking
Villars, the secret could no longer be kept, and by now all London knew the story.
[2] The *Flying Post* was written by George Ridpath and printed by William Hurt.
In the following September the embarrassed Government finally arrested them
(Laurence Hanson, *Government and the Press*, 1936, p. 63).
[3] Probably Michael Read, Harley's porter. See p. 132, n. 3.

Occasions to Enflame us;[1] I Humbly Ask your Ldpps pardon for This Motion, and Am

> May it Please your Ldpp
> Your Ldpps Most Humble and Obedient Servt
> [symbol]

May 27. 1712

MS.: Duke of Portland, Defoe Papers, 2 f. 53. *Pub.*: *H.M.C. Portland*, v. 177–8. *Address*: none.

188. [*To* ROBERT HARLEY, EARL OF OXFORD].
5 June 1712

My Lord

I am humbly to Ask your Ldpps Pardon That the Enclosed books have been So long Comeing Out; But the Case proves Longer Than I Expected to Make it.

The Sincerity of My Design is My Appology to your Ldpp for the Performance. It[2] is written without Doores, and for The Use of Those Cheifly, who kno' Nothing but without Doores. I hope it May be Usefull to Undeciev an abused people, and Let Them see How The wholl Nation was Forming into One Tribe of Issachar,[3] and Taught to Couch Under The Tyranny of Our Neighbours; to bear what Burthen was Imposed Upon them by Those who allways took care by Loading us to Ease Themselves.

I Send also another book to your Ldpp in Answer to The Dutch Memorialls,[4] in all which your Ldpp will perciev an Honest but Art-less Design of Opening the Eyes of a people So Imposed Upon, and So Tenacious of Their Own Mistakes, as Leads Them to a world of Troublesome and Dangerous Excesses.

Your Ldpps Goodness will pass The Errors of performance; it is My Satisfaction to be Serving your Intrest and doeing the

---

[1] Harley seems to have concurred; see the following letter.

[2] Probably his *Reasons against Fighting. Being an Enquiry into This Great Debate, whether It Is Safe for Her Majesty, or Her Ministry, to Venture an Engagement with the French, Considering the Present Behaviour of the Allies.* The tract was published two days later.   [3] See Gen. xxx. 1–21.

[4] Earlier in the year the Commons had expressed their dissatisfaction with the conduct of the Dutch in a number of resolutions, and in a long Representation which they placed before the Queen. The Dutch replied to these charges in a Memorial, which they sent to the Queen, and part of which was published in the *Daily Courant.* See *Bishop Burnet's History of His Own Time*, Oxford, 1823, vi. 105–6, and *Somers Tracts*, xiii. 154–73. Defoe replied to the Dutch Memorial in a tract, probably the one here mentioned, entitled *A Farther Search into the Conduct of the Allies, and the Late Ministry, as to Peace and War. Containing Also a Reply to the Several Letters and Memorials of the States-General.*

people good together; I am farr from Exciting the people against The Dutch, and believ it is not the Governments View to Injure or to Break with The Dutch; but it Seems Necessary, and I believ it is your Ldpps Aim, to have the Dutch Friends and Not Masters; Confederates not Governours; and to keep us from a Dutch as well as a French Mannagement.

I Shall go on to Open the Eyes of The Injur'd people in These The More Chearfully if My Servicc in it is Approved and Accepted by your Ldpp.

I am, May it Please your Ldpp
Your Faithfull Obedt Servt
[symbol]

June. 5. 1712

MS.: Duke of Portland, Defoe Papers, 2 f. 54. *Pub.*: *H.M.C. Portland*, v. 180. *Address*: none.

189. [*To* ROBERT HARLEY, EARL OF OXFORD].
16 June 1712

My Lord

My Attending The Other day was Principally to Congratulate your Ldpp On the Successes of your Late Mannagemt On Account of the Peace,[1] and to have given your Ldpp an Account of The Influence it has Among The partys; How Many of The Wisest begin to Open Their Eyes and be Easy; while The Rest Rather Rage that they can do no Mischief, Than hope to Obstruct your Ldpps Measures.

Withall I purposed to have Accquainted your Ldpp with an Extraordinary Congress of The Squadroni just Now at Edinburgh;[2] whether the affair they Meet about be worth your Ldpps Notice Or not, is Not My province. The avow'd Occasion is (as I hear but do not assert) to Consult The advocate,[3] and Other Lawyers, About The form of An Association &c, and also to Consider how to Act at the Ensueing Election of a Peer in the Room of Ld Mareschall;[4] This I Thought it my Duty to Lay before your Ldpp, and Shall be able to Send More perticulars as they go On.

[1] On 6 June the Queen had acquainted Parliament with the terms upon which peace was being negotiated. The Commons immediately approved an Address expressing their satisfaction. On the 7th the Lords overcame Whig opposition and did likewise (*J.H.C.* xvii. 258–60; *J.H.L.* xix. 471–2, 474).
[2] Cf. Balmerino to Mar, 11 June (*H.M.C. Portland*, v. 183).
[3] Sir James Stewart.
[4] Marischal had died on 27 May. In the following August the Scottish peers chose as his successor the Earl of Seafield.

If your Ldpp would be pleased to Allow me So Much Freedome, I would Express My Apprehensions from the Warmth of his grace of Argyle in his New Command,[1] Unless he be Restraind by your Ldpps Authourity:— A Middle way, with Temper and Prudence, May yet preserv the Peace of That Country and Cultivate her Majties Intrest There; But Alas it is No slander On his grace to Suggest, That These are Not the Greatest part of his Graces Character:[2] The Onely Security of that Uneasy people, is in your Ldpps Wisdome, and This Makes me Officiously Lay these things So Often before you, for which I Humbly Ask your Ldpps Pardon and Am

May it please your Ldpp
Your Ldpps Most Humble and Obedt servt
[symbol]

June. 16. 1712

MS.: Duke of Portland, Defoe Papers, 2 f. 56. *Pub.*: *H.M.C. Portland*, v. 183. *Address*: none.

190. [*To* Robert Harley, Earl of Oxford].
19 August 1712[3]

My Lord

The Notice your Ldpp was pleased to take of My Mellancholly Case, Stated in The preface to the Review,[4] and The goodness wherewith you were pleased to Express it to me, Make Deep Impressions On a Mind fixt to your Ldpp by So Many Obligations.

At The Same time (My Lord) That I profess Not to plead it as Merit, I acknowlege it is to My Honour, That The Indignity and Reproach cast on me by These Unhappy People,[5] is Levell'd at your Ldpp;[6] and Providence Haveing placed you out of Their Reach (May it Ever be So!), They fall upon him

[1] Argyll had been appointed Commander-in-Chief of the Forces in Scotland on 2 June.
[2] For Defoe's estimate of Argyll, see his *Atalantis Major*, 1711, pp. 17–18.
[3] Misdated 18 Aug. in *H.M.C. Portland*, v.
[4] See the Preface to vol. viii, wherein Defoe, now apparently in ill health, deplores the machinations of his enemies and the ingratitude of his friends.
[5] The Dissenters.
[6] 'The Dissenting Ministers at London doe stick very closse to the old Ministry, and will not leave the juncto Whiggs in ane ace. They oppose the Treasurer in evry thing, and look on him as ane apostate from them, and a dissembler' (Wodrow, *Analecta*, i. 341).

They can hurt, to Shew Their Rage at your Ldpp who They Can not; as The Dog Bites The stone Flung at him, Not Dareing Or not able to Touch The Hand That throws it.

I Endeavor to practise The great work of Resignation Under The Injurious Treatmt I Reciev, Submitting it to his Disposall who in a like Occasion (Tho' of higher Moment) Bad shimei Curse, But left him not Unrewarded.[1]

It is My Satisfaction, that as Their Rage is a Testimoney to The Weight and to the Conviction of what I Say, So your Ldpp is pleased to Approve my Service, and thereby add a Weight to it, which I have not Modesty Little Enough to Think it Deserves.

God and your Ldpp are witnesses for me Against This Generation, in That your Goodness to me was founded On No Principles of Bribery and Corruption, but a generous Compassion to a Man Oppressed by Power without a Crime, and Abandon'd, *Even Then*, by Those he Sacrifized himself to Serve.[2]

The Same Witnesses Are a Testemony for me that My Services (However Small) are founded Rather *and indeed Entirely* on a Deep Sence of Duty, and Gratitude for That Early goodness, Than on any View That I can Merit what may be to Come.

Your Ldpp has allways acted with Me On Such foundations of Meer abstracted Bounty and Goodness, That it has Not So Much as Suggested The Least Expectation on your part That I Should act This way or That, Leaving me at full Liberty to Persue My Own Reason and Principle; And above all Enableing Me to Declare my Innocence In the Black Charge of Bribery.

What Ever your Ldpp has done for me, you Never So much as Intimated, (tho' Ever So Remotely) That you Expected from me The Least Byass in what I should write, or That her Majties Bounty to me was Intended to Guide my Opinion; Your Ldpp has too Much Honour in your principle to look That way, Or to Think me worth your Notice, if I Could have been So Moved; and How would These people blush Should I Own to Them, That Her Majties Bounty, which I Now Enjoy,

---

[1] See 2 Sam. xvi. 5–14.
[2] In 1703, when *The Shortest Way with the Dissenters* had landed Defoe in Newgate, he was condemned and abandoned by his fellow Dissenters, and was eventually delivered not by those whom he had sought to defend but by Harley.

was procur'd for me by your Ldpps Intercession, Even Under The Administration of your Ldpps Worst Enemyes.[1]

This Fills me with Peace Under all Their Clamour, That I Serv a Master who Scorns the Service of a Mercenary Conscience; and who at the Same Time That he does me good, leaves me full Liberty to Obey the Dictates of My Own principles; This My Lord Gives Me Room to Declare, as I do in Print Every day, That I am Neither Employ'd, Dictated to, or Rewarded for, or in, what I write by any Person Undr Heaven;[2] And I Make This Acknowlegement with Thankfullness to your Ldpp, and as a Testimony to your great Goodness to me; That your Ldpp Never lay'd The least Injunction on Me of One kind or Other To Write or Not to write This or That in any Case whatsoever.

It is However my great Satisfaction, That what first is founded on principle and Reason, agreeable to Conscience, Equity, and The good of my Country (ay, and to These Unhappy peoples Intrest too, if They Understood their Intrests), is at the Same Time Agreeable to your Ldpp, and That while I am Rendring your Ldpp Service, I am Dischargeing The Debt of justice to Truth and Liberty, The great Principles on which I hope I shall Never Cease to Act; and which while I persue I am allwayes Sure to please and Oblige your Ldpp.[3]

I Most Humbly Ask your Ldpps Pardon for This Excursion. A Heart Oppress't as Mine by Publick Reproach (without Guilt) must Needs be Full; and as I am Driven by The Torrent Upon a More Entire Dependance On your Ldpp, So have I No Humane Appeal But to your Self; However, I Cease to Enlarge on This Unpleasant Subject, haveing yet a farther Humble application to Make, for which I have Still More Reason to ask Pardon.

May it Please your Ldpp

I Hinted to your Ldpp My Desire to Take a Journey North.[4] I will not Dissemble So farr with your Ldpp as Not to Own,

---

[1] In the autumn of 1707, a few months before his fall from the Ministry, Harley had persuaded Godolphin to settle upon Defoe an allowance for subsistence (p. 242).

[2] In the *Review* for 26 July he had offered a hundred guineas to the author of *The Medley* if the latter could prove that Defoe had ever received either direction or reward for writing his paper.

[3] For a comment on the claims made by Defoe in this letter, see Sutherland, *Defoe*, pp. 190–2.

[4] See p. 371.

That a Little Bussiness part of the way, and withall The Direction of Physitians for my goeing to The Bath in Derbyshire,[1] Joyn in to Make me Desirous of goeing— But I am perswaded also I may be More Usefull to your Ldpp in a small Circuit On That Side at This Time; as well for Counteracting the Measures taken to Distract the Country, as for Calming and quieting the Minds of the poor preposess't people, Than Ever I was yet; and as The Juncture for Such a bussiness Seems proper, and Leisure at home agrees, I am your Ldpps Humble Petitioner for Leave.

But my Ld I am yet Straightn'd in The Rest of My Petition. Your Ldpps Goodness to Me is too great to allow me the Least Sollicitation for farther Favours than I Enjoy; Nor My Lord Am I Representing the Expence of My Journey (For which your Ldpp had allways the Goodness to make me Large Allowance); But I am forced by Importuneing Circumstances to Remind your Ldpp That of That Allowance Or Appointment which by your Ldpps Intercession and Her Majties Goodness I Enjoy, There are Two quarters behind, which Insensibly (*Except to me*) Elapsed Dureing The Mellancholly Intervall, when your Ldpp was Hurt and Things Unsettled.[2]

I Say no More! I am a Very Mean Advocate in My Own Case, and had Rather My Circumstances Should Silently Move your Tenderness and Compassion, Than That by Importunity I should be forward and Craveing; God has Cast me on your Ldpps Goodness So Entirely, That he Seems to Direct me Thereby to a More close Application than Ever to your Intrest and Service; for Sure, when Ever I shall be Depriv'd Of your Ldpps favour or assistance, if This party can Make me Miserable They will Not fail to do it to the Uttmost.

I am, May it please your Ldpp
Your Most Humble Obedt Servt
[symbol]

Augt 19. 1712

MS.: Duke of Portland, Defoe Papers, 2 ff. 57–58. *Pub.*: *H.M.C. Portland*, v. 212–14. *Address*: none. *Endorsed*: 'Msr Guilot Augu: 19 1712.'

[1] Perhaps the warm springs at Matlock or Buxton, both of which he visited at some time. See *Tour thro' Britain*, ii. 567 and 573–
[2] See p. 326, n. 1.

191. [*To* Robert Harley, Earl of Oxford].

27 August 1712

My Lord

According to your Ldpps Order I have Enclosed an Exact Coppie of The Letter which I Recd from Scotland So farr as Relates to the Thing I Mentioned to your Ldpp.

As (my Lord) I Accquainted your Ldpp with The Name of The Person From whom I Recd The Said Account,[1] I Take This Occasion to assure your Ldpp, That The Character of That Gentleman is Such as May Recomend him Upon all Occasions to your Intrest and Favour; and as may Render him perticularly Usefull to your Ldpp in Case The Squadroni Take any Measures against the Governmt; of all which by This Means a Constant True account of Every step may be Obtaind: —More is not proper to Say Till Occasion makes it for your Ldpps Service, But This I Thought perticularly Needfull, That your Ldpp May allways kno' who may be Depended Upon, and who not.

> I am, May it Please your Ldpp
> Your Ldpps Most Humble & Obedt Servt
> [symbol]

Augt 27. 1712

[Enclosure]

Sir

——We have had in This Country a great Confluence of people about 5 Miles from the Earl of Hyndfords Seat of Caermichell,[2] who on Thursday the 25th of July to the Number of about 8 or 9000 people[3] met in the fields on Occasion of Recieving the Sacrament the Sabbath following. Preparatory to the Sacrament, The Sd Thursday was their fast when, in the first place, They Sollemnly Renew'd the Covenant, tho' they thot fitt to Exclude that part of it which Mentions the Governmt and Establish't Church. They then went On publickly Confessing their Sins, Tho I believ they Confessed not the Greatest of them. Among Other Sins they Insisted on the Crime of hearing and Joyning with the present Ministers and the Kirk.

---

[1] Defoe's correspondent cannot now be identified.

[2] Those assembled were Cameronians; they met at Auchensauch Hill in Lanarkshire.

[3] Probably an exaggeration. Wodrow reported that 'some say one thousand, some say seventeen hundred' (*Analecta*, ii. 76).

At This Rate They spent Three whole dayes, Most of them lyeing all night on the Hills and on the Ground Till the Sabbath following, when the Sacrament was administred to them. Before which, pronouncing as is Usuall The Commination,[1] They publickly Excommunicated Her Majtie by Name, The wholl British Parliament, and all the Establish't Kirk Ministers. One Mr McMillan[2] is their Leader, being an Ordaind Minister but Deposed by the Assembly, and he has One Mr Neil[3] for his assistant, who was Never Ordaind. What Carryes off these poor people So much at this Time is the Apprehensions They are Under that their Ministers will take the Abjuration.[4]

They had no Arms, nor do I See that they have any thoughts of Disturbing the peace; but you kno' Some people who May in Time Make Some use of Such a Thing, Especially if their Numbers Encrease;[5] and it would be well if The Governmt would please to post Some Troops at hand, to be Some Awe to Those who hope for Some advantage from The poor peoples folly—

MS.: Duke of Portland, Defoe Papers, 2 ff. 59–61. *Pub.*: *H.M.C. Portland*, v. 217. *Address*: none. *Endorsed*: 'Guilot, Scotland, R̃ Augu: 28: 1712.'

192. [*To* Robert Harley, Earl of Oxford].
3 September 1712

My Lord
Since I had the honor to Accquaint your Ldpp of The affair in Scotland I have had Sevll Concurring Accounts, both of the

[1] The liturgical office consisting of a recital of God's anger and judgement against sinners.
[2] John MacMillan (1670–1753), founder of the Reformed Presbyterian Church, was ordained in 1701 and deposed by the Presbytery two years later for 'disorderly and schismatical practices', but his local popularity enabled him to hold both his church and his manse. Since 1706 he had acted as spiritual director of 'the Remnant'. His followers were called 'MacMillanites' until 1743; thereafter they became the 'Reformed Presbytery'.
[3] John Neil, or Neal, or MacNeil, or M'Kneilly. See Wodrow, *Analecta*, ii. 77.
[4] As required under the Toleration Act of the previous March.
[5] For an account of MacMillan's meeting, see Wodrow, *Analecta*, ii. 75–78; for Defoe's comment on 'the Auchensauch Wark', see the *Review* for 30 Aug. 1712. In September Wodrow wrote: 'I hear some private letters from London bear, that the end of the last moneth, or beginning of this, the Treasurer called for De Foe, and told him he heard of ane insurrection in Scotland, meaning Mr M'Millan's meeting at Douglasse, and ordered him to write to Scotland, and inform himself about it, and write some reveues upon it. I'le be fond to see them, when they come out' (*Analecta*, ii. 89).

fact and Subsequent Circumstances, But do not find There has been any More Assemblyes of the Nature of That I formerly gave account of.

But (My Lord) as The Encrease of That Party to the Degree Mentioned was Not Without Some Extraordinary Application of Emessaries and bussy people who Dilligently foment The Popular Notions of That poor Distracted people, So if Those Leaders are Not in Some Manner Discouraged Or Removed From Them, There May be Many ill Consequences to be Apprehended.

I believ your Ldpp Knows I am an Enemy to all Coercions in Matters of Religion or (and indeed more Especially) of Enthusiasme, and am Convinc't That there is No way So Effectuall to Confirm and Encrease This Disorder, Than to fall upon Them with Force and put the Laws in Execution Severely Upon Them. But Some Method May in your Ldpps Wisdome be perhaps thought of to Take from Them That Poor Ignorant Incendiary who Now Leads Them into all These Wild Things.[1]

This (my Lord) I Say The Rather because all my Accounts agree That he goes about Increasing The Evill, and Confirming The poor people in Their Notions with Too Much Success, and will Certainly at Last precipitate Them into Some Mischeivous Thing to Their Own Ruine, and To The Injury of The public.

If your Ldpp Thinks Fit to Approve The Design I had of a private Tour to The border, I Would have gone Incognito Among Some of these people, and have Given your Ldpp a More Exact and Impartiall Account both of the people and of The Reasons of Their New Appearance; and perhaps have found out Some of The Persons also, whom I can not but Think it is Very Much for the Service of The Governmt to Discover.

I hope your Ldpp is Fully Satisfyed That I have no Other View in This part Than The public Service. As for my perticular Journey, which I am undr a little Necessity of Takeing into Darby Shire, if your Ldpp does not Approve of the Other, I Shall Onely beg leav for about a Fortnight, and Shall not fail, God willing, to be here again in That Time.

I do Confess it has been Upon my Mind That I might be Usefull in The Country Upon Many Accounts, but I Submit

---

[1] John MacMillan. See the preceding letter.

That and My Self wholly to your Ldpps Direction, Onely beg
Again your License for the Small Step above, And Am,
Your Ldpps Most Humble and Obedient Servant
[symbol]
September 3. 1712

I Send here One of Their Distracted papers On Occasion of
The public Fast—[1]

MS.: Duke of Portland, Defoe Papers, 2 ff. 62–63. *Pub.*: *H.M.C. Portland*,
v. 218–19. *Address*: none. *Endorsed*: 'Guilot Sept: 4: 1712.'

193. [*To* ROBERT HARLEY, EARL OF OXFORD].
20 September 1712

My Lord
I had Not been So long before I paid my Duty to your Ldpp,
but That I have been for Some Time Out of the Reach of the
post. But as I Shall Now Continue to give your Ldpp a full
account of what Ever Occurrs Worth your Ldpps Notice, So I
can Not Omit a few hints of what is allready passt.

Meeting with an Accidental Invitation and My Curiosity
joyning in, I went from Sturbrige Fair (which[2] I had Made My
first Stage) Towards Lyn, where Resolveing to be Incognito, I
found I had Room for Many Speculations. Here My Ld (Asking
your License to jest a little with what is indeed the Nations
Dissaster) I found my Self Out of her Majties Dominions, and
in the Capital City of the Terretorys of king Walpole.[3]

Here I have Seen what I confess it is Difficult to Express, and
what I could not have thought had been in The Nature, Much
less in The practise, of protestants or English Subjects. Here I
have Seen with Some Horrour The Spirit of Parties in its
highest Extraction. How her Majtie is Treated Among them,
would fill any Man who Makes Loyalty and Duty to his

[1] Missing. The Commission of the Assembly had not dared propose a national
fast for Scotland lest the proposal offend the Government. See Wodrow, *Analecta*,
ii. 74.
[2] In the MS. the opening parenthesis precedes 'I went'.
[3] Robert Walpole (1676–1745), later Prime Minister, entered the Commons in
1701 and soon rose to leadership among the Whigs. In 1705 he was appointed to
the Council of Prince George, Lord High Admiral; in 1708 he became Secretary
at War; and in 1710 he was named Secretary of the Navy. Upon the change of
Ministry in 1710, he was dismissed from his places, and in 1712 he was found guilty
of venality in the Army Office, expelled from the House, and committed to the
Tower. While there, he was once more returned for Lynn, but the Commons
declared his election void. He was released in July 1712 and was at this time
regarded by the Whigs as a martyr and hero.

Soveraign a Principle with Indignation, any Man who Vallues the peace and Tranquillity of his Country with abhorrence, and Any Man that has his Sences in Excercise with Contempt and Aversion.

If They do This in The Green Tree, what Shall They do in The Drye! The Deciple is Not above his Lord; if her Majtie is Thus Treated Among Them, your Ldpp and all That Serve her Majtie and Their Country faithfully Share most Plentifully of Their Rage, in a Manner I blush for Them too Much to Relate. But your Ldpp has Learnt from a Superiour Pattern, To Pity and Contemn the Madness of The people. God Almighty who has placed her Majtie and all her faithfull Servants Out of The Reach of Their hands Be praised for the Safety Enjoy'd by it.

Your Ldpp Can Not doubt But where A Party with Such a Temper Seem to prevail, and have what they call a Leading Intrest, The people, Smothered with the Smoke or Mist of Their Delusions, Suffer a generall Inflamation and are Made Lunatick with the Madness of their Leaders. What Strange Things they are Made to believ, what wild Inconsistent Notions they have Infused into the Minds of One Another, what preposterous, Ridiculous, Incongruous things Take up their heads, is Incredible, and but for the Novelty of Them Are not worth Repeating. Such as, That The queen is For The Pretender, The Ministry Under The Protection of France, That Popery is to be Tollerated, That as Soon as a Peace is Declared The War with the Dutch will be proclaimed, That The French are to keep their Trade to the South Seas, That the people will be brought to address the Queen Not to Interrupt the Heredetary Right of The Royall Line Since The Heir is willing to Abjure popery, and The like.

As far (my Lord) as Consisted with my Resolution of keeping Incognito, which I have Effectually Done, and which I Thought Necessary on Many Accounts, I have Layd the foundation of Undecieving the poor people in these things and have Effectually Convinc't The Dissenting Minister[1] and Two Leading Men Among the Dissenters, who with Astonishment look back upon The Delusions they have been Under, and who I doubt not will in A Short Time Undeciev Many More.

I Find my Lord The Countrys Every where Share of The Generall Distemper, Tho' not with the Same warmth; An

---

[1] Probably John Rastrick, Presbyterian minister in Spinner Lane (Alexander Gordon, *Freedom after Ejection*, Manchester, 1917, p. 337).

Inclination to Moderation Appeares Among The best men Every where, but the poison is Unhappily Spread from London, and Especially Among the Dissenters, who are made Every where to Believ That the Ministry is for The pretender, and That French Governmt and Popery is the Design; Wherever I Converse with Them I find Them posest with The Very Same Notions, which is an Evedence that it is a Concerted Measure of The party to Spread Such Things thro' the Country.

I also find it less Difficult than I Expected, to Open The Eyes of The Honest and well Meaning, and that They are Eager and Forward to be better Inform'd, and hope I may not be an Unprofitable Servant That way, So farr as This Short Journey will Extend; I wish proper persons were on the like Occasion in Other parts. I am Perswaded your Ldpp would Soon find a good Effect from it.

I am, May it please your Ldpp
[symbol]

Lincoln Sept. 20. 1712

MS.: Duke of Portland, Defoe Papers, 2 ff. 64–65. *Pub.*: *H.M.C. Portland*, v. 223–5. *Address*: none. *Endorsed*: 'Claude Guilot, Sept: 20: 1712, R̸ Octo 1:'

194. [*To* ROBERT HARLEY, EARL OF OXFORD].
3 October 1712

My Lord

Mr Milton in his Paradise lost in the   th[1] Book (it is I think) brings in Adam Listening with wonder and Astonishmt at the Account The Angell Gives him of The Great and strange Things which Shall happen in The world; and of The attempts Sathan Shall make to Ruine and Delude his posterity— Comparing Those Great Things with these Small, I Could not but Think of That Description when I found The poor Country people here Wondring and Astonished when they look back into The Notions and falsities They had been posess't with, and find That It was all Delusion and a Ridiculous Cheat put upon them by a Party.

How did an honest Country Minister stand Amazed when I would Not Agree That my Ld Wharton was a Most Pious, Devote Christian:[2] *Sure I have liv'd in a Wood*, Said a Very Sensible and Considerable Man at Gainsbro' when he heard

[1] Left blank in MS. See Books xi and xii.
[2] Thomas Wharton (1648–1715), first Earl and later first Marquess of Wharton, reputedly the greatest rake of his day.

That The late Juncto had Ever push'd at the Lord Treasurer Godolphin and The Duke of Marlboro'; and Said all the Wicked Things of Them That have been Said Since, and That they Joyn'd with Jacobites to Throw them Out; If I Ventur'd to Say The Queen was Not a Jacobite, or That the Ministry were protestants, That The Pretender was not Just comeing ashore and The like, tis hardly Possible to Tell your Ldpp how the people Listen with a kind of Amazemt, which Testifyes (1) how glad they are to hear it is So, and (2) how they wonder at The Delusions They have been Undr before.

I am Now My Lord Reach't to NewCastle where (Except Lyn) I find the posessions I have hinted at The most Riveted of any place I have been at, and principally Occasioned by Two Dissenting Ministers who have been at London, and Convers't at the Amsterdam and Hamlin's Coffee houses,[1] and who Came down with Such a fraight of the Ridiculous Things Mentioned in My Last, That I Confess I am Amaz'd to See good Men Satisfye themselves in Drinking in Such Delusions and Spreading them Among Others.

There are (My Lord) besides these, Inumerable Storys Spread Among the Common people in Prejudice of the Queen and of the present Mannagemt as to the Peace, and perticularly That The queen will have The Dutch give up their Barrier in Flanders, That the French are to Carry On their Trade to the South Seas,[2] and the like, and Tho' the Nature and the public Accounts of things plainly Contradict this, yet it is hard to Open their Eyes.

The Jacobite party on the Other hand, behave with So Much Imprudent Assurance that Terrefyes the poor people with the Apprehensions of the pretender, and tho' they Ought to See That the queen and the Ministry are the Onely Security they have left against the Jacobite Faction, yet the Other party blindly perswade Them, that The Queen and The Ministry are Their Enemies and That their Onely Danger is where Their Safety Indeed can Onely be.

Ile Trouble your Ldpp No More with these Follies. My Stay Among them is So Small as can not go farr in Turning Such a Stream, but I Endeavour to Undeciev the most Reasonable and Moderate and leave Them to work upon the Rest.

---

[1] Defoe derided the 'Coffee-House States-men' in the *Review* for 16 Aug. 1712.
[2] The Asiento had been in the hands of France since 1701, when Louis had compelled Spain to grant it to a French company.

The great floods have hindred my Travelling for Some Time, The like Rains, Especially on the border, haveing not been known a long Time. God Direct your Ldpp to Heal the breaches Made Among us by a wretched party who, however They Rage Against your Person, have nothing to hope for but from your Wisdome and prudence; and who like Children must be Saved against the Struggles of their Own passions; Surely if your Ldpp is Once Made the Instrument to Save Them from Their Feares, and From the Pretender, and to Secure Their Religion and Libertys, *As I hope*, Even Their Deliverance Must be a Burthen, it will load them with So Many Blushes and Self Reproaches at what is past. I am,

May it please your Ldpp
Your Most Humble & Obedient
[remainder frayed away]

Newcastle Octob. 3. 1712

MS.: Duke of Portland, Defoe Papers, 2 ff. 66–67. *Pub.*: *H.M.C. Portland*, v. 231–2. *Address*: none. *Endorsed*: 'Cl. Guilot, Newcastle Octo: 3 1712.'

195. [*To* ROBERT HARLEY, EARL OF OXFORD].
October 1712

My Lord

Since My Last I have been Out of the Reach of any post Road, which has hindred my Writeing to your Ldpp. I am Now Return'd From a land of Distraction and Confusion[1] and Indeed am at a loss how to Describe it to your Ldpp. The best Thing I can Say of it is That I hope it is an Uneasyness That will not Imediately Give the Governmt any Disturbance; I say Imediately Onely because I fear it will hereafter.

I find in the West and South part Many of the Ministers would Take the Oath[2] but The people are So Enraged at Them That They Dare not, and This puts the poor Men to an Inextricable Difficulty, So That They are like to be Martyrs for a principle which they do Not hold. I perswaded Some of Them to qualifye privately, and Continue preaching as if They had not qualifyed.

In Edinburgh There are Onely Four Ministers who will

[1] Scotland.
[2] The Oath of Abjuration, now required of the Scottish clergy.

Refuse. These are Mr Webster[1] of The Tol-booth Kirk, Mr Flint[2] of The Old Kirk, Mr Hart[3] of the Grey Fryers, and Mr Miller[4] (an English man) of Lady Yesters Kirk. Mr Hart I am in hopes will Complye.

I find The Squadroni Exceeding bussy in prompting Evry thing which Appeares Malecontent, and They Seem pleased at the Breach This Makes, as They Think it prepares The Minds of the people for Something Worse; and I can Not Say They Endeavour to Reconcile The people to the Oath but Rather The Contrary, Tho' they Take it themselves.

There is a Manifest Distrust and Division between Those they call The last Court whiggs[5] and The Squadroni, and it were to be Wished some Measures were Thought On to keep Them from Joyning, and I Mention it the Rather because I See it is So Easie to be done (Viz) by Takeing off but One Man,[6] who your Ldpp May have with a Word. I Referr The Rest Till I have the honor to attend your Ldpp.

It is for me Onely to Represent Dangers to your Ldpp, Not to presume to prescribe Remedies, and Therefore I do not Descend to any Methods to be Taken with those poor Distressed people. If They Merit any thing it is The Governmts Pity; but I fear They Shall Some Time or Other put Themselves out of The way of her Majties Clemency; They are Entirely Naked and Defenceless, and yet so provokeing That I See not how the Governmt can long preserv its Authourity without Some Method of Restraint Upon them.

I am allarm'd at my Comeing into the Conversible part of the world Again with an Account of your Ldpps Indisposition.[7]

[1] James Webster, who had carried on a pamphlet war with Defoe in 1707. See Nos. 90, 91, 93, and 99.
[2] John Flint (d. 1730) had been a protégé of the Cameronians before they disowned him. He was now assigned to West St. Giles, but he may have preached also at Old Kirk, where the pulpit was temporarily vacant (*Fasti Ecclesiæ Scoticanæ*, i. 71 and 143).
[3] James Hart (1663–1729) had been at Old Greyfriars since 1702. He had opposed the Union and had denounced Carstares for supporting it (*Fasti Ecclesiæ Scoticanæ*, i. 40). For Hart's relations with Defoe in 1714–15, see J. R. Moore, 'Defoe and the Rev. James Hart', *Philological Quarterly*, xix (1940), 404–9.
[4] William Miller, or Millar (d. 1732), later became Dean of the Chapel Royal (*Fasti Ecclesiæ Scoticanæ*, i. 46).
[5] That is, the 'New Whigs', who had supported the previous Ministry, as distinct from the 'Old Whigs', who had opposed Godolphin and Marlborough and who were already in some degree of alliance with the Squadrone. See the *Review* for 14 Sept. 1712.
[6] Unidentified.
[7] Harley had had 'an ugly fit of the Rheumatism' (*Journal to Stella*, ii. 561).

God preserv a life on which So Much of the Nations Safety Depends. Your Ldpp Might have the Satisfaction here of Seeing those people who are poisoned with Prejudices from the City Tremble at The Thoughts of That Persons being Removed who they kno' not how to Vallue when alive. They acknowlege That when They look beyond your Ldpp They See Nothing but Confusion; yet it is Not Among Their Mercys to See The hand That does Them good.

I Struggle in My Mean station with This Delusion, But in Some places with more Success than in Others. I am,

> May it Please your Ldpp
> Your Most Humble and Obedt Servt
> [symbol]

New Castle Octob. [ ]¹ 1712

MS.: Duke of Portland, Defoe Papers, 2 ff. 68–69. *Pub.*: *H.M.C. Portland*, v. 242–3. *Address*: none. *Endorsed*: 'Newcastle, R̸ Nov: 10: 1712.'

196. [*To* ROBERT HARLEY, EARL OF OXFORD].
7 January 1712/13

My Lord

Your Ldpps Indisposition² is Not Onely My Missfortune But the Nations, And I yet believ The Time will come when your Enemyes will Acknowlege it, Tho' for So long as Heaven Permits, Sathan Hinders.

The Earnest Desire I had to have Lay'd before your Ldpp a brief Account of My long Journey has Made Me too Importunate; and My Own Circumstances, which I can Not hide from your Ldpp On whom Providence and a Cruel Party have Made me More Than Ever Entirly Depending, have Concurr'd, and I Most Humbly ask your Ldpps Pardon.

But a Perticular Speciall Affair Moves me Now to Applye to your Ldpp in a Case From the Company of Brass Manufacturers; who have been with me to State Their Affair, and which I may Lay before your Ldpp previous to Their Public Application.

---

¹ Left blank in MS.
² On 30 Dec. Swift wrote: 'I calld this Evening at Ld Treasrs, and sate with him 2 hours; he has been cupped for a cold, & has been very ill' (*Journal to Stella*, ii. 590).

They Say They Are Able to Serv the Governmt So as to Save a Great Summ in the Vallue of Copper for the Coinage of Farthings; which they hear is Now Undr Direction. They do not Offer at the Coining Part, but at Furnishing Copper Ready wrought for the Work.[1]

It is My Zeal for her Majties Intrest, which I kno' your Ldpp Makes your Own, which Makes me Mention This; and Shall be Very glad to have been So Officious if your Ldpp finds it, as They alleage, Fitt to be Accepted; assureing your Ldpp I have no Other Intrest in it. I am,

May it Please your Ldpp
Your Ldpps Most Humble & Obedt Servt
[symbol]

Jan. 7th 1712

MS.: Duke of Portland, Defoe Papers, 2 f. 70. *Pub.*: *H.M.C. Portland*, v. 260. *Address*: none.

197. [*To* ROBERT HARLEY, EARL OF OXFORD].
15 January 1712/13

My Lord

The Affliction it is to me to have Lost the Favour of being Admitted to your Ldpp as Usuall I can Not Express. If I were Conscious of haveing Dishonoured That favour Or done Any thing to Offend your Ldpp, I should kno' that I Ought to Expect it as a just Punishment.[2]

I Humbly Ask leav to Claim your Ldpps Promise to Me, Made long Agoe, That if in any thing I Incurr'd your Dislike, or Displeased you, I should kno' it first from your Self: No Man Alive would if Occasion permitted, Serv your Ldpp with a More Dissintrested Zeal, at More hazard, or perhaps So Much, from a Sincere Principle of affection to your Intrest. Shall I Say (My

[1] The project was probably that of Charles Tunnah and William Dale, who wished to supply a cheap artificial metal for the coinage of farthings and half-pence. The scheme was referred to the Mint but was rejected by Craven Peyton and Sir Isaac Newton (*Calendar of Treasury Papers, 1708–1714,* pp. 546–7).

[2] By now, Harley was completely recovered from his illness, had been up and about for ten days, and presumably could have received Defoe had he wished to do so. But during the preceding year or so, Harley had developed close ties with Swift, who was now writing what we know as *The History of the Four Last Years of the Queen,* and who was enjoying almost daily access to the Treasurer (*Journal to Stella,* ii. 596–603). Sutherland has suggested that Harley's growing preference for Swift may have been at least one cause for Defoe's present melancholy (*Defoe,* pp. 184–5).

Lord) No Man has been Used like me by this Furious Age, For Openly Avowing My Self in your Intrest, tho' My Services are but small.

I am not Saying (My Lord) what I have been able to do. I am not Either Vain to boast Or Reflecting; But What I have a will and Inclination to do, I may; and with the Greatest Humillity I Say, *No Man has More*. But when I Speake of the Treatment I Meet with in the World for Even but a Will to Render My Self Usefull to your Intrests, There my Lord I Suffer, as if I had been More your Ldpps Instrument Than I have Vanity to Suppose I was Ever Capable of.

The Disstresses I am Reduc't to by This, tho' they plead Nothing with your Ldpp by way of Demand, yet They Claim your Pity and Compassion, Because They Oppress me on a Supposition of My haveing The honour of Serving your Ldpp.

At Least my Lord, I would Humbly hope The Popular Hatred Incur'd by Me for Opposeing This Enrag'd Party Should not be a ground to Lose me your Favour, which would Cause Them to Triumph Over My Disstress.

I kno' your Ldpps Goodness, and have had long Experience of it. I kno' the being Ruin'd for adhereing to principle and The True Entrest of the Nation, which your Ldpp Allways made your Own, Can Not Dissoblige you. Nor does any Man Suffer (My Unhappy Case Excepted) for Faithfully Espouseing her Majties Intrest without being Otherwise Comforted.

While your Ldpp was pleased to be The Instrument of her Majties Bounty to me I Chearfully Fac't Them all, But if I lose That Relief I must Fall Under Their hands who have no Mercy, and be as Miserable as they can Wish.

Nothing but an Extremety of this kind Could Oblige me to Expose my Case So Much. But were it possible to Describe The Treatment I have from These people, and the Circumstances I am Reduc't to by it, Unless your Ldpp on whom Under God I Depend [to][1] Deliver and Support me, It would Move your Compassion beyond what I can hope for.

I most Humbly Entreat your Ldpps Favour, That her Majties Bounty, which I have Enjoy'd by your Goodness and Intercession, May not be stopped, Since being Malitiously Depriv'd of all bussiness and Other Subsistance by the Party fury of your Ldpps as Well as my Enemyes, I Shall be Reduc't

---

[1] Omitted in MS.

to the Uttmost Distress if I am Depriv'd of your Ldpps assistance.[1] I am,

Your Ldpps Most Humble
and Most Obedt Servt
[symbol]

Jan. 15. 1712

MS.: Duke of Portland, Defoe Papers, 2 ff. 72–73. *Pub.*: *H.M.C. Portland*, v. 263–4. *Address*: none.

198. [*To* ROBERT HARLEY, EARL OF OXFORD].

My Lord   *19 January 1712/13*

What your Ldpp was pleased to Say to Me about the Distraction of a Party is Nothing but what I have Seen with great Regret, and what I have Long waited an Occasion to Lay before your Ldpp.

It is This (My Lord) which I have Lamented in My Own Case, That haveing No Assurance of Support Or of your Ldpps Favour, I have Not Dared to Tell Them So plainly as I would do, and as They Deserv, how They Prevent her Majtie and your Ldpp doeing Even Themselves the Good you would do Them, and as far as in Them lyes, do The Nation all The Mischief They Are able.

It is my Missfortune to be what I Never was, Especially in a just Cause (Viz) a Coward, and Affraid to be at the Mercy of Furious and Foolish Party-Men, Meerly For want of That Capascity of Standing, which My Confidence in your Ldpps Goodness Ought to Furnish me with. I Humbly Lay My Self at your Ldpps Feet with This Resolution, That These wicked Designs shall Never want a due Reproof, and For My Self I will Still Depend Upon your Goodness, That you will not Suffer a Mean Servant to Perish in The Defence of his Country And your Ldpp.

The attempt if possible to Raise a Mob to Insult The French Ambassador, On pretence of Importing wrought Silks, French wines, &c. Custome Free,[2] This I purposed to Accquaint your

---

[1] Defoe apparently received his money, for on 1 Apr., when he again reminds Harley that the date for making the quarterly payment is 'a few days past', he does not mention any other arrearage (p. 402).

[2] On 2 Jan. Louis, Duc d'Aumont, had arrived in London, but soon afterward the parish constables had to be summoned to protect his house, 'for the People had got Intelligence, that his Domesticks had brought over and run Wines, Silks, and other Goods, which they sold, as they could well afford, at cheaper Rates than the *English* Tradesmen could do' (John Oldmixon, *History of England*, 1735, p. 527). Defoe maintained that the duke was innocent and that the story was 'forged and

Ldpp of, and how bussy They have been in Spittle Fields to That purpose— As to his Exellency Importing a great Many Bales of Jesuits and Priests, a Sort of Goods Contraband, This, however Ridiculous here, They Make great Use of in the Country, and print Libells about it Stuff't with all The Simple and Absurd Stuff in the world, yet it Takes with Their Party.

The Distraction Runs Now (My Lord) to Such a hight That They are not Backward to Own That Horrid Principle of *The Worse The Better*, and That all Our Safety Now Lyes in bringing All Things into Confusion. They Say Openly They Desire The Ministry would bring in The Pretender, and That Enflameing the Nation is The Onely way to Deliver Them.

To This End Their Incendiary The Flyeing post goes on with Such a kind of Unsufferable Insolence, and They Triumph So in The Ministrys Forbearance, That Really he does a Very great Deal of Mischief. They Openly Boast The Governmt Can Not Touch him, That Four Informations Are Layd indeed but The Ministry Dare Not Trye Them, That They Are Ready for Them, Let Them begin when They will, and The like. This My Lord No Government Can bear, and I am Sure The Late Ministry did Not bear it.[1]

There is No Doubt my Lord Any jury in England would bring in That paper a libell. Inumerable passages are to be found in it which They blush at Themselves, and I could give your Ldpp abundant Assurance That if The Fellow were push't he will Never Screen the Author long. I kno' him to be No Man of Sence or Principle.

I Never was forward to prompt any Mans Fate or Dissaster. I Believ your Ldpp knows it is Not My Temper. But Never Governmt was Insulted in Such a Manner, and Never Cause was So kept alive by The Scandall and Ribaldry of So Insolent an Author.

calculated for no other End, than to amuse the Spittle-fields Men, and dissatisfie the Rabble, that some Mischief might follow' (*Review*, 24 Jan. 1712–13). Mischief did follow; on 26 Jan. the duke's house burned down, perhaps fired by incendiaries (*Journal to Stella*, ii. 608 and 610–11).

[1] In the previous October Swift had complained: 'These devils of Grubstreet rogues, that write the *Flying-Post* and *Medley* in one paper, will not be quiet. They are always mauling lord treasurer, lord Bolingbroke, and me. We have the dog under prosecution, but Bolingbroke is not active enough; but I hope to swinge him. He is a Scotch rogue, one Ridpath. They get out on bail, and write on. We take them again, and get fresh bail; and so it goes round' (*Journal to Stella*, ii. 568–9). In Feb. 1713 Ridpath was found guilty of writing libels and fled to France; in June, William Hurt, his printer, was found guilty of publishing a seditious pamphlet and was severely punished (Abe Beyer), *Political State*, July 1713, vi. 79).

I have Many Other Things to Lay before your Ldpp, but I wait The Time when your Ldpp will admitt me, and shall attend to Morrow According to your Commands. I am,

Your Ldpps Most Humble & Obedt Servt
[symbol]

Jan. 19. 1712

MS.: Duke of Portland, Defoe Papers, 2 f. 74. *Pub.*: *H.M.C. Portland*, v. 264–5. *Address*: none.

199. [*To* Robert Harley, Earl of Oxford].
23 January 1712/13

My Lord

I had Not given your Ldpp The Trouble of my calling last Night but (as I Understood your Servant) by your Ldpps Command, and Ask Pardon For The Mistake.

At the Severall Times I have had the honor to See your Ldpp (your Leisure Not Admitting Me to Give you The Trouble) I have forborn Offring The Enclosed proposall.[1] I Thought it Might be Improper to Delay it Longer, Least as The people alleage, it be of Reall Service to the Government, That benefitt Should be also Delay'd: It Relates to a petition which I Enclosed Some Dayes Ago From the Brass Company to Supply with Copper Plates for Coinage.[2] If it be of Public Use, I Shall be glad to have Comunicated it; if Not, I hope for your Ldpps Pardon; They will Applye in The Ordinary way by Petition to your Ldpp, and My Laying it before your Ldpp Thus was in Ordr to have stated The Thing for your Immediate Information in Case your Ldpp had found it Needfull.

I am, May it please your Ldpp
Your Most Obedt Humble and Faithfull Servt
[symbol]

Jan. 23. 1712

MS.: Duke of Portland, Defoe Papers, 2 f. 76. *Pub.*: *H.M.C. Portland*, v. 265. *Address*: none.

200. William Carstares[3] *to* Defoe. *10 February 1712/13*

Edr Feb: 10. 1713

Sir

I am heartlie glad to hear that you are safe at London, and shall be glad to hear too that you find the heat of parties so farr

---

[1] Missing.   [2] See No. 196.   [3] See p. 193, n. 3.

at least abated, as that they will allow themselves calmlie to consider what may be for the publick safetie and quiet.

As for us here, our matters are in such a posture as it is hard to frame a Judgment of them; they seem to be in a suspence till it be seen what course the Parltt will steer. But our Jacobits are unaccountable in their bold and foolish actings in some places and, as I am informed, they seem to be much displeased with our great friend,[1] which I must say doeth not much grieve me. I only wish he might have more of support and encouragement from men of another kidney, for I have a great honour and true concern for him and doe allways attend him with my best wishes.

My great design Sir in troubling you with these lines is earnestlie to desire that when at any time you see our noble friend you would take occasion to putt him in mind of my brother in law Major Coult,[2] who you know hath been long an Officer, is a gentleman of true merit and worth and Justlie esteemed as such here, and is of untainted integritie. He had an Act to be Major of the Castle of Edr. and additional pay before the Union which is of late retranched, though her Matie hath been pleased to continue to some others the advantages they had before the Union though they were not allowed by the English establishment. That noble person when I was at London did show an inclination to doe some kindnesse to Major Coult, and I hope he may yet doe something for him both as to renewing his Commission as Major and restoreing his additional pay, if reasonablie putt in mind of him. I know Sir, I may with confidence leave this affair to your discreet mannagement. I trouble you with my heartie respects to your Lady and the young Ladies your daughters, not forgetting your sons;[3] believe me to be without complement

Sir, your most faithfull humble servant
W Carstares

MS.: Duke of Portland, Harley Papers, xlix f. 1213. *Pub.*: *H.M.C. Portland*, x. 288–9. *Address*: 'To Daniel De Foe Esqr.'

201. [*To* Robert Harley, Earl of Oxford].
14 February 1712/13

My Lord

In My last[4] I Mentioned The Usefullness and Service Severall ways of Some Measures for Seperateing The Squadroni in Scot-

---

[1] Harley.　　　　[2] Maj. James Coult (*H.M.C. Portland*, x. 473–4).
[3] Defoe's children living at this time were Hannah, Maria, Henrietta, Sophia, Daniel, and Benjamin Norton.　　　　[4] Missing.

land. I could not Refrain (tho' I hope to Attend your Ldpp on Monday According to your Command) Giveing a Short Account to your Ldpp of The Restless attempt of The Distracted people here to Carry on Their professt Aversion to her Majties Measures.

More Especially That Their present View is to allarm and Amuse The Common people with Terrible Dismall Apprehensions of Popery and The Pretender.

Under The first head They are Now Spreading it Over the Countrys That The papists Are Arming and Prepareing for a Generall Massacre, That Inumerable Numbers of Priests and Irish Papists are Come Over, *and The like*, with which They Really Amuse The poor people and Render Them Very Uneasie, Especially in The Country.

Of Their Suggestions About The Pretender I Shall give your Ldpp a Farther Account, but for the present Humbly Lay before your Ldpp a Paragraph or Two Coppyed Out of a letter I Recd Last post Out of Lincoln Shire which I Thought Very Necessary to Accquaint your Ldpp of, and is as folls

We Are Very Much Disturb'd here with the News Our friends write us from London and with The Paper called The flying Post, which Has been Sent Enclosed like a Circular letter Over all This Country, Suggesting Very strange and Unaccountable Things, which almost Sink us, and had we not Some hopes That These Things are not True in Fact but Meer Entities of his Own Brain, it would quite Overwhelm us.

The first is the Affair of Mr Lewis which has made So much Noise in Town and Country. The Substance of The story he Takes Out of the Dayly Courant. I Wish you would Explain That affair to us, for he Insinuates a Direct Correspondence by it between Our Court and That of St Germans.[1]

The Next Relates to the New Treaty of Barrier and Succession, Concerning which The Flying-Post Tells us That

---

[1] One Charles Skelton, an officer in the French service, had been permitted to return to England under a licence that had passed the Privy Seal and for which Skelton therefore wished to thank Erasmus Lewis, secretary to the Earl of Dartmouth. But Skelton, through a confusion of the names, called upon not Erasmus Lewis but Henry Lewis, or Levi, who immediately thereafter spread the news abroad that Skelton's reason for seeking out Erasmus Lewis was to bring him greetings from St. Germains. The story was without foundation, but the Whigs made capital of the supposed correspondence between the English Ministry and the Pretender's Court. See *Journal to Stella*, ii. 609, and Abel Boyer, *Political State*, Jan. 1712–13, v. 46–47.

what Ever Our Danger Shall be, The Dutch are Come Under Obligation Never to come to Our Assistance Till The Government Or Ministry That Shall then be Shall Send for Them, and this they Represent as Effectually Tyeing Up the hands of the Dutch to leav us to the Mercy of a Jacobite Ministry.[1]

Another Story he Tells us is of a Design in The Next Parliamt to Settle the Succession So as The Queen Shall leav it by will to whom She Pleases, and This is Much Magnifyed by private letters From . . . . . & *.[2]

Another Story by the Sd letter is That The Ministry Design to Compliment The Freeholders and Landed Men by Takeing off The Land Tax Entirely and Laying a Settled and Excessiv load Upon stock, and That a Vast Loan to The Queen is to be Made Upon That Fund, The Ministry Designing for Their Secret purposes to get all the Money in The Nation into Their hands.

These Are Dismall stories I must Own, but what Very Much Supports me is That I believ Them to be Most if not all of Them False. If these Men have no grounds for what they write I Think They are Very ill Suffred, Not Onely as Causing Very Unreasonable but Very Anxious, perplexing Thoughts in the breasts of the best people, but as Endeavouring thus to Support a Cause That Never Till Now wanted Lyes and Chimericall Contrivances for a Refuge, and also putting those Things into The heads of Our Enemyes which perhaps They Never thot of before.

I Could not But Lay These Things before your Ldpp, who Alone is able to Correct The Insolence of These people, who are Justly called Incendiaries. I Do Not fail to Use My Uttmost Endeavours in all places to Undeciev The people and Expose These wicked Designs. But what is The Uttmost So Mean a

[1] Though stated in terms disadvantageous to the Ministry, this account was fundamentally true. Under the old Barrier Treaty of 1709, drawn up by the Whig Ministry, the Dutch were required not merely to support the Hanoverian Succession but to take military action on their own initiative should that Succession ever appear endangered. Swift had pointed out that this obligation 'put it out of the Power of our own Legislature to change our Succession, without the Consent of that Prince or State who is guarantee; however our Posterity may hereafter, by the Tyranny and Oppression of any succeeding Princes, be reduced to the fatal Necessity of breaking in upon the excellent and happy Settlement now in force' (*Conduct of the Allies*, in *Prose Works*, ed. Herbert Davis, vi. 27). Under the new Barrier Treaty, drawn up by the present Ministry and signed in January, that agreement was changed. Now the Dutch were to intervene in favour of the Hanoverian Succession only if called upon to do so. See Abel Boyer, *Political State* Jan. 1712–13, v. 78.   [2] Thus in MS.

hand can do! Your Ldpp can Applye The More Imediate Cure.[1]
My Author is a Dissenting Minister, but One of Differing Notions
and Temper from these people. I Humbly Lay this Matter at
your Ldpps feet, and am

> May it please your Ldpp
> Your Most Humble & Obedt Servt
> [symbol]

Feb 14. 1712

MS.: Duke of Portland, Defoe Papers, 2 ff. 78–79. *Pub.*: *H.M.C. Portland*,
v. 266–7. *Address*: none. *Endorsed*: 'Cl: Guilot, Febr: 14 1712/13, R̸ Febr: 15.'

202. [*To* ROBERT HARLEY, EARL OF OXFORD].
1 April 1713

My Lord
    The last Time I had the honour to See your Ldpp was Upon
The Case which I had Lay'd before your Ldpp of Clark[2] of Darby
Shire, and the Clamours of The foolish People on That Occasion.
Had Not the Accident of which I Shall Speak presently Inter-
ven'd, I had waited on your Ldpp to Relate The Victory I
Gain'd Upon that Occasion; when I came to Talk with those
people Again, How Mute and Asham'd they stood, when I ask'd
them If they Could Name Me any One Man to whom your
Ldpp had allow'd the Liberty of Selling a Civil Employmt?
And when they Could not Say they could Name any, I ask'd
how then they could Say this was a Singling Out a Dissenter?
And where the Dissenter was who *Even Since the late act*[3] had been
Prosecuted, tho' I Nam'd them Severall who kept Posts in the
Publick Offices and Were Seen at The Meeting houses Every
day, and Some who went Railing about in Coffee houses all The
week at That Very Governmt whose bread they Eat.
    After That, I Saw the Man himself. I Convinc't him that his
Friends as he thot them were far from doeing him any Service in
the Noise They Made; and That if those Things Were prompted
by his Complaints, I could liken his Case to Nothing So Readily
as that of Adonijah in the Text;[4] who Not Content with haveing
been spar'd by Solomon, Ask'd a foolish Favour against his Own
life; I Told him if these things Came to the Governments Eares,

---

[1] That is, by suppressing Ridpath of the *Flying Post*, who was to come to trial
on the 19th (John Oldmixon, *History of England*, 1735, pp. 525–6).
[2] Unidentified.
[3] The Occasional Conformity Act of 1712, under which any holder of public
office who attended a conventicle, whether he occasionally conformed or not, was
to lose his post and pay a fine of £40.
[4] 1 Kings ii. 13–25.

he Ought to Think it an Unusuall Clemency if he was Permited to Enjoy what he had. The Man I believ was Satisfyed he was in the wrong, and as I Hear is Since Gone home, and I Suppose your Ldpp will be Troubled No More with him.

I had Lay'd Some Other Things before your Lordpp but am Oblig'd to Excuse my Self On The Following Occasion—I have Often Troubled your Ldpp with long Complaints of the hardships I Meet with from an Angry Party Upon their Notions of My being in the Intrest of the Ministry and Entertain'd by your Ldpp, and Tho' I have not the Merit of Rendring your Ldpp Any Services Worth Nameing, yet the Fury with which These Men Treat me is proportion'd to the greatest, and Indeed they honor Me in their Malice as if I was Capable to Serv your Ldpp More Than I can pretend to, tho' I Rather Judge They Show by it what Treatment Not your Ldpp Onely but all Her Majties faithfull Servants and best Friends should Meet with if This party had the Power.

However My Lord, I Never Thought that Party Resentment could have stoopt So low as to Persue it to private Injury till I was Surprised, as I was Comeing from home to have attended Upon your Ldpp last Monday Seven night,[1] and Was Taken up by an Escape Warrant.

This sleeping Lyon had been Retired into the Country where the Creditor liv'd (at Yaremouth)[2] Ever Since the year That by your Ldpps Favour And Appointmt I Travelled a journey into The West,[3] and when (which I Ought Never to forget) your Ldpp was pleased to Concern your Self for my preservation from it.

It had Never More stirr'd had not a private Set of Men here in Meer Revenge prompted and Even Sollicited the person to stirr Now, Assureing him That I had Great Favours &c. which I am Satisfyed they knew Nothing off, but believing that Such a process would Effectually Ruine and Destroy Me.

May it please your Ldpp

Tho' I do Humbly Complain in this Manner, and am Indeed in Great Danger of being Quite Overwhelm'd by this Dissaster; yet I am Not Representing it to your Ldpp to Plead for Unusuall Favors. Your Ldpps Goodness to me has allways called for my Thankfullness, and left no Room for Encroachments Unless

---

[1] That is, on 23 Mar.
[2] For other mention of Yarmouth creditors, see pp. 115 and 123.
[3] In 1705.

with the Uttmost breach of Modesty, which I hope is not in My Nature.

However Unhappy this May Render me, I Struggle to Submit to it with That Resignation that becomes me. I have yet kept it from Comeing Abroad, and am striveing to bring it to Some Accomodation if possible.[1]

If your Ldpp will allow me in a Case of Such Extremety Humbly to Mention, That the Usuall Period of her Majties Bounty being a few days past, and which your Ldpps goodness would have allow'd me to Move (tho' this had not happend), If, I Say, your Ldpp will be pleased to grant me that help at This Time, I shall hope to Dissentangl my Self without a public blow to My affaires.

I Would have Conceald this Dissaster from your Ldpp, haveing too often spoke of My Own Circumstances, but I fear'd My being So long absent might cause your Ldpp to Think me Defficient in My Duty.[2]

The youth that brings This is My Son, and Shall attend if your Ldpp please to Permit it, to bring Any Return your Ldpp pleases to grant me to This Request—

With the Humblest Submission to your Ldpps pleasure, I ask Pardon for this Motion, and Tho' Now Distress't by a Faction Rather than a Creditor; I shall allways Endeavour to Approve my Self, at what Ever hazard

Your Ldpps Most Humble faithfull
and Obedt Servt

primo Aprl 1713   [symbol]

MS.: Duke of Portland, Defoe Papers, 2 ff. 80–81. *Pub.*: *H.M.C. Portland*, v. 274–5. *Address*: none.

[1] Defoe's trouble eventually came to light, and in the following January, Henry Martin, one of the editors of the *British Merchant*, the Whig rival of Defoe's *Mercator*, alleged that Defoe had been taken up on a warrant for £1,500 and had paid that sum the next day. Martin went on to ask why, since Defoe had £1,500 for writing *Mercator*, he should wait to be arrested before paying his debt. Under the pseudonym of 'Geoffry Backstroke', Defoe replied: 'To this Charge Mr. D'Foe says, That it is true he had the Disaster to have such a Warrant executed upon him, and for such a Sum; but, that Mr. Martin's Informer has LYED almost in every part of it; for that, *first of all*, the Payment was not the next Day, nor till after eleven Days Confinement: (2.) That instead of paying 1500*l.* the Creditor accepted 150*l.* and of that but 25 in Money: And (3.) That this was some Months before the *MERCATOR* was ever thought of. For the Truth of all which, Mr. D'Foe referr'd us to the Attorney employ'd against him, who was Mr. Evans in Fleetstreet, who he says is a Man of so much Justice as not to deny the Particulars' (*Mercator*, No. 101, 14 Jan. 1713–14).

[2] He must have still been in custody; he was arrested on 23 Mar. (p. 401) and was held for eleven days (n. 1 above).

203. [*To* ROBERT HARLEY, EARL OF OXFORD].
11 April 1713

My Lord

It was to pay the Duty of My Acknowlegemt to your great goodness to Me in My Late affliction[1] that I waited the Other day On your Ldpp, tho indeed Not in Condition to have come Abroad. And being still indisposed, I beg leav to Lay Some Thoughts before your Ldpp which I believ of Moment Enough to Merit Som Consideration.

The Affaires in Scotland, tho' yet quiet, Stand Very Tottering, and The Public peace Seems to Turn upon Very Nice and Criticall Points; The Division of The Ministers Among themselves, I mean as *Jurant* And *Non jurant*, Tends to a Wide Breach, and in The Approaching Assembly may probably appear ill Enough stated. The *Non jurant* behave with Rage and want of Charity to the *Jurant*, and Are back't by The people, who Especially in the West Treat the last with Insolence, Contempt, and Scarcely keep the Peace with them, Universally forsakeing the Churches where They preach, and Refuseing to hear them.[2]

Hitherto the Clemency of the governmt in forbearing to prosecute the Penal part of the act keeps them quiet as to Outrage and Violence. What Medium to find Out to keep them So Still Deserves the Governmts Imediate Care.

I kno' Some will Offer to your Ldpp a proposall to bring in a Clause or bill to grant longer Time &c. for the Takeing the Oaths;[3] I Confess My Lord I do not See that will be any Expedient, because They will Naturally Contemn a grace that They do not Seek. That longer Time Must Some time or Other

---

[1] See the preceding letter.

[2] Under the Toleration Act of 3 Mar. 1711–12, both the Episcopal and Presbyterian clergy in Scotland were required to take the Oath of Abjuration. Though the Presbyterian ministers were willing enough to disown the Pretender and to support the Hanoverian Succession, they were reluctant to take the Oath for several reasons. It violated the Union Treaty (which had exempted members of the Kirk from taking any oaths inconsistent with their national establishment); it interfered with their spiritual independence (by requiring them to pray, during divine service, for the Queen and for Sophia); it implied that officers of the Church were on the same level as officers of the State; and, in binding the juror to accept the English Act of Settlement, it automatically committed Scottish jurors to the rejection of any monarch who might in future belong to their own Established Church. See Wodrow, *Analecta*, ii. 109–14.

[3] According to law, the oaths were to have been taken by 1 Nov. 1712. That a later date should be established had been suggested to Harley by Carstares (*H.M.C. Portland*, x. 285–6).

Expire. If *when it Expires* the Law is not prosecuted, they will Conclude the Government Either Approves their Contempt of it or is Not in a Condition to Resent it.

If The Last, The Ministers who have shown Their Wisdome and Loyalty to the Government by Complyeing Will Really want her Majties protection from the Rabbles, and Those poor wild people will bring her Majtie to a Necessity of useing Rough Means with Them On That Account.

If On the Other hand when the given Time *Expires* Those who Refuse The Oath Now Refuse it Still, As it is Certain They will, and The government allows or Commands the putting the Law in Excecution; those Ministers go Imediately to the Hills as they call it, Set up Field Conventicles, and all the people Run after Them: If They are not Suppresst *then*, They will grow formidable to the Peace, Insolent to the Governmt, and Upon Occasion Dangerous; If They are, *Then* Follows a Crye of Persecution, and They'l all Run to Arms as if on Purpose to Dye for Religion.

Pardon me (My Lord) The freedom of Thus Stateing the affair of those people, which I do with a True Zeal both for Their good and Her Majties Intrest, Humbly adding My Thoughts Thus.

That Tho' it is True the Governmt Seems Obliged to protect and as much as possible to Encourage Those who have Complyed with the Laws, yet Since it is Many Wayes Inconvenient to press too Warmly the Excecution of Those Laws, It Seems better That those Ministers May yet labour Under Some Dissadvantages Than that the Public Peace be Endangerd.

On the Other hand My Lord, it May not be forgotten that if the Non jurant Ministers (I Mean Presbyterian all the way)[1] are prosecuted to a Dissposessing them of their liveing, a great Many of Them will Flock into England and Up to London, and what flames they will blow up Among a poor Distracted Sett of people here your Ldpp knows Very Well.

Upon The whole My Lord, The affair Seems to Turn Upon this Single point, which your Ldpps wisdom will Determine: whether The proposall of a longer Time with the Hazard of the Inconveniences above Named is best, Or whether keeping the Law as a Rod Over Their heads, The Excecution May not be Delay'd Meerly as an act of Clemency and Forbearance, the

---

[1] Nearly all of the Scottish Episcopal clergy were Jacobites and hence nonjurors.

Certanty of its being Execcuted as well as the Reasons being Not known.

I am, &c

[symbol]

Aprill 11. 1713

I Was goeing on with this My Lord, when the Occasion Expresst in the Cover to This¹ broke me off, and I Was fearfull They would have Taken this from me.

MS.: Duke of Portland, Defoe Papers, 2 f. 82. *Pub.*: *H.M.C. Portland*, v. 277–8. *Address*: none.

204. [*To* ROBERT HARLEY, EARL OF OXFORD]. *12 April 1713*

My Lord

I am Really Asham'd to Lay before your Ldpp So Scandalous an Account of a party of Men (who Ought to know better), as I must do in Stateing my affair to your Ldpp.

The Persons, the Pretences, and the Design are Equally foolish and Malitious.

The Persons Are Benson, Burnet, and Redpath; all Three Under prosecution from the Governmt for Scandalous pamphlets, the first for the Letter to Sir Jac. Banks, The Second for a Book called a *Certain Discourse*, The last for his flying Post.²

¹ The following letter.
² William Benson (1682–1754), a Whig, had been Sheriff of Wiltshire and was later to succeed Sir Christopher Wren as Surveyor-General. The pamphlet which embroiled him with the Government was *A Letter to Sir J[acob] B[anks], by Birth a Swede, but Naturaliz'd, and a M[embe]r of the Present P[arliamen]t*, of which Swift wrote: 'The Queen Her self is no longer spared; witness the Libel published some Days ago under the Title of *A Letter to* Sir Jacob Banks, where the Reflections upon Her Sacred Majesty are much more plain and direct, than ever the *Examiner* thought fit to publish against the most obnoxious Persons in a *Ministry*, discarded for endeavouring the Ruin of their Prince and Country' (*Examiner* No. 30, 1 Mar. 1710–11). Benson is criticized in Defoe's *Tour thro' Britain*, i. 365–6.
Thomas Burnet (1694–1753), son of the Bishop of Salisbury, was an active Whig pamphleteer who was later to become a Justice of the Court of Common Pleas. In 1712 he had defended Marlborough in a pamphlet entitled, *A Certain Information of a Certain Discourse, that Happen'd at a Certain Gentleman's House in a Certain County*. Bolingbroke had proceeded against him and Burnet was at this time free under bail (Abel Boyer, *Political State*, Jan. 1712–13, v. 63–64). In 1715, following Burnet's publication of *The Necessity of Impeaching the Late Ministry*, Defoe defended Harley and attacked Burnet in three pamphlets, (1) *A Letter to a Merry Young Gentleman, Intituled Tho. Burnet, Esq.*, (2) *Burnet and Bradbury, or the Confederacy of the Press and the Pulpit for the Blood of the Last Ministry*, and (3) *Some Reasons Offer'd by the Late Ministry, in Defence of Their Administration*. For a sketch of Burnet, see D. Nichol Smith, ed. *The Letters of Thomas Burnet to George Duckett 1712–1722*, Oxford: Roxburghe Club, 1914, pp. xxi–xxxvii.
George Ridpath (d. 1726) was author of the Whig *Flying Post*, which Defoe had

The Pretences Are Sevll, Some too simple to Name, But they were heard to Say that they had all been prosecuted and the Review had a full Liberty, but They would bring him in whether the Ministry would or no.

The book which Angers Them, is Entituled Reasons Against the Hannover Succession,[1] where There Own Topicks of the Allyes being Disobliged by the Peace, and France being a Power Irresistible, and Our fatall Heats at home are Ironically Lay'd Down as Reasons why We Should think no More of the Succession &c. But all the Rest of the book are Clear and professt Banters upon The Pretender.

The perticular in all most grievous is That in all I Say, I Never would Allow that the Queen and The Ministry were in the Intrest of the Pretender, which however I Think Now her Majties speech[2] must make them Asham'd of.

As to Their Design, I Find their first Notion is, that The book is Treason, and That therefore My Ld Chief Justice should Refuse Bail, and Commit me to Newgate; which I am Some times Apprehensiv my Lord May be weak and warm Enough to do,[3] and In that, I Can not but beg your Ldpps Interposition.

Their Next Design is Visibly an Insult upon the Ministry, Pretending that the Governmt Neglecting to prosecute for an

---

been urging Harley to suppress (pp. 395 and 400). Ridpath had already been found guilty of libel, was at this time free on bail under a bill of exceptions, and was soon to flee the country. For a Whig account of his prosecution, see John Oldmixon, *History of England*, 1735, pp. 525–7. For Defoe's jeering farewell to him, see the *Review* for 7 May 1713.

[1] The complaint of Defoe's three enemies was actually based on three of his pamphlets, all dealing with the Succession. In February had appeared *Reasons against the Succession of the House of Hanover*; in March, *And What if the Pretender Should Come? Or, Some Considerations of the Advantages and Real Consequences of the Pretender's Possessing the Crown of Great Britain*; and in April, *An Answer to a Question That Nobody Thinks of, viz. But What if the Queen Should Die?* Alarming as these titles sound, the first two tracts are ironical throughout and the third is merely a solemn warning that a succession will some day occur and that Englishmen must turn their attention seriously to that certainty. But Defoe's indiscreet titles had given a handle to his Whig enemies, and Benson, aided by his two colleagues, 'spar'd neither Pains nor Expence on this Occasion, and in a few Days he got into his own Possession the Original Manuscripts of all those three pamphlets, written in *D. Foe's* own Hand, or rather Hands, for they were every one of them different; but all the three being prov'd by one of the Printer's Servants, before the Lord Chief Justice *Parker*, to be the Hand-writing of *D. Foe*, his Lordship granted a Warrant to take him up; which being done, tho' not without much Trouble and Charge, his Lordship committed him to *Newgate*' (John Oldmixon, op. cit., p. 509). See the *Reviews* of 16 and 18 Apr. 1713, and G. A. Aitken, 'Defoe in Trouble: More State Papers', *The Athenaeum*, 12 Jan. 1895, p. 50.

[2] Delivered to both Houses on 9 Apr. (*J.H.C.* xvii. 278).

[3] Lord Chief Justice Sir Thomas Parker was a Whig.

affront upon the House of Hannover, They would Officiously shew their Zeal, and also to let the Ministry see they will prosecute who they please in the Governmts Name, whether The Ministry will or no.

I forbear to Trouble your Ldpp with the Contradictions in this attempt. The Town begins to be Asham'd of it allready, for the whiggs (not Seeing the Satyr upon themselves in it) were all pleased with the book, and Now they give Out that the prosecution was for the Scurrillous paper called The Ambassadress's Speech.[1]

I Think I Need Say no More to your Ldpp, than give the Names of the Persons and the Manner of their goeing to Work, as a Test of the Design; Onely Hinting Again to your Ldpp as a Reason for The Manner of writeing in all these books, the Necessity There has been to give a Turn in all I Wrot, which should gratifye Some of the Weaknesses of those poor people, to Detect the Rest.

I Believ the greatest Injury they can do me is the Expence and the Surprise. *The first* the wound which your Ldpp knows I had So lately[2] makes me ill able to bear. *The last* I hope will wear off.

I Humbly beg your Ldpps Protection, and Such Directions from the Secretarys Office, as may be thot proper by your Ldpp to make my Ld Chief Justice Easye tomorrow, when I am brought before him:[3] The Rest I Referr to Such Measures as The Nature of the Thing shall Direct afterwards; and as your Ldpp shall think proper. I am

> Your Ldpps Most Obedt Humble & Faithfull Servt
>
> [symbol]

Aprll 12. 1713

MS.: Duke of Portland, Defoe Papers, 2 f. 84. *Pub.*: *H.M.C. Portland*, v. 278–9. *Address*: none.

205. [*To* ROBERT HARLEY, EARL OF OXFORD].
14 April 1713

My Lord

I had Not gone home to My Family before I had come like the *Tenth Leper* to pay my Duty and acknowlegemts to your Ldpp, had not my Case made me Unfitt to See your Ldpp;

---

[1] Which Defoe disavowed and denounced in the *Review* for 7 May 1713. See *Journal to Stella*, ii. 644.

[2] The necessity of settling with the Yarmouth creditor. See No. 202.

[3] He was deliberately arrested on Saturday so that he would be unable to arrange bail and would therefore be forced to remain in prison until Monday. This letter was written on Sunday and hence presumably from Newgate.

Harrass'd by The Treatment I Recd; So Hoarse with a Cold Taken in Their hands That I can Not Speak to be heard; But, however, Effectually Cheer'd and Reviv'd by your Ldpps Most Seasonable and happy Deliverance.[1]

This My Lord is The Third Time I am Rescued from Misery and A jail by your Ldpps Generous and Uncommon Goodness;[2] and This is the goodness for which the Gratitude of This Age Would have me, Against principle, Conscience, Honour, and Gratitude, Maltreat and Abuse you, and for Refuseing which They fall upon me in This Manner.

But I am bound to your Ldpp in bands too strong, and Am Sure, Unless God and Nature Abandonne me together, it is Impossible I can forbear to Serv your Ldpps person and Intrest, while I live; at what Hazard Soever.

I Should be Unjust (my Lord) to Mr Borrett[3] if I did not Accquaint your Ldpp, That he Excecuted your Ldpps Orders So Wisely, with So Much Caution, So Much Indifference, and yet with So just an Authority; That no Suggestion Could be made of his being Directed, and yet The End was Imediately Answerd; and I was Set Free, Giveing Two Sufficient Bail for 800*l*[4] and my Self £800.

I Shall Take up no Room in This Letter with any Thing but my humble Thanks and Acknowlegemt of So Seasonable a Deliverance, Except it be Humbly to beg your Ldpp, That Mr Borrett may Watch what progress They may pretend to Make in The prosecution of This foolish attempt (to Say no worse of it).

I am, with the Uttmost Duty and Humillity
My Lord, your Ldpps Most Obedient Servt
Newington Aprill 14. 1713   [symbol]

MS.: Duke of Portland, Defoe Papers, 2 ff. 85–86. *Pub.*: *H.M.C. Portland*, v. 281–2. *Address*: none. *Endorsed*: 'Mr Goldsmith, Apr: 14: 1713.'

[1] He had been admitted to bail on Monday, 13 Apr. (*Review*, 18 Apr.).

[2] In 1703 Harley had delivered Defoe from Newgate for writing *The Shortest Way with the Dissenters* (No. 5), and earlier in the present month had enabled him to placate his Yarmouth creditor and hence again obtain release from confinement.

[3] William Borrett, Solicitor to the Treasury, had approved Defoe's bail (John Oldmixon, *History of England*, 1735, p. 509). Borrett had played a part in the arrest of Defoe in 1703 (*Calendar of Treasury Books*, xix. 408–9) and had secretly investigated the management of Defoe's *Review* in 1708 (D. H. Stevens, *Party Politics and English Journalism 1702–1742*, Chicago, 1916, p. 51).

[4] His two friends were John Grantham, printer, and Thomas Warner, publisher, who bound themselves for £400 each (John Oldmixon, op. cit., p. 510). Neither was involved in the pamphlets, which were printed by Richard Janeway and published by John Baker (P.R.O., S.P. 34/21/242–5).

206. [*To* Robert Harley, Earl of Oxford].
19 April 1713

My Lord

I attended on Saturday and also the Evening before to have Layd before your Ldpp Some farther Perticulars of This Affair of Mine which has given your Ldpp So Much Trouble and Made So Much Noise in The world.[1]

Tho' My Lord by your Ldpps Assistance I believ The Mischief of This attempt will be Effectually prevented, yet The Perticulars of it Every day discover Themselves More and More, and let us into a View of the Originall Design, which Design, least my present Indisposition should prevent My attendance tomorrow Morning According to your Ldpps Command, I beg leav to Give Some View of, together with a Method which I Humbly Offer, to Render Their Dissappointment More Effectuall, and More Mortifying to Them Than Ordinary.

The Design My Ld has Many branches, and if I may Use So much freedome, I think they are all weak, foolish, and yet Malicious to a Degree.

1. Their Design is Aim'd at your Ldpp and Her Majties Intrest, to let the Nation See how formidable Their Faction is, and That They Could Overthro' any Man who dared Oppose Them, in Spight of her Majties Favour and protection.

2. They aim at makeing a Discovery to the Nation, who are or are not in your Ldpps Service, So that Their falling upon me Must as They Thought Infallibly Answer Their End One way or Other; for That if the Ministry *did not* protect me, They knew they Should Oppress and Sink me by The Partiallity and Favour of my Ld Chief justice (whose Conduct has been Really wonderfull in it),[2] And if your Ldpp *Did* protect me, Then They Gaind the Other point by publishing, First, That I Was Secretly Entertaind and Employd by your Ldpp, which hitherto They have made Much Noise of, but Could Never prove; and

---

[1] Defoe's troubles were gleefully publicized in the *Flying Post* and the *Post Boy* for 16 Apr. (Lee, *Life*, i. 210–11), and in an anonymous tract entitled *Judas Discover'd and Catched at Last: or Daniel de Foe in Lob's Pound. Being a full and True Account of the Apprehending and Taking of Mr. Daniel de Foe on Saturday Last, for High-Treason against the Queen and Government.*

[2] Defoe's criticisms of the conduct of his case appeared in the *Reviews* for 16 and 18 Apr., and gave such offence to Lord Chief Justice Parker that the Court held Defoe guilty of libel and committed him to the Queen's Bench prison. Upon apologizing to the Court, he was released from jail—for the third time in this month. See the identical *Reviews* for 28 Apr. and 5 May, and Lee, *Life*, i. 211–12.

Secondly, That your Ldpp should Oppose a prosecution which Seemd to be in behalf of the House of Hanover.

They have a Third End in all This (Viz) Meerly to shew an Insult upon the Ministry, of which I Need Say no More here.

In all These things I Think I may Venture to Say They shall be Effectually Dissappointed if my Following proposall be Approv'd by your Ldpp; and yet they shall Never Know that your Ldpp has any way Thought it Worth your Notice, or any way in the least Concern'd your Self in it—

Mr Borret My Lord Mannag'd himself with So Much Prudence and good Conduct, That they are Perfectly Amused, and make no Guess upon what foundation he acted: And this because he Came (not as Concerning himself in haveing Me delivred or in Giveing Bail but) As haveing good Satisfaction That the Bail which I had Ready was Sufficient (*as They Really were*), Tho' had he not Appeared, the best Bail I Could have produced, would have been Rejected.

After I was Bailed, My Ld Chief justice call'd Mr Borret Aside and Asked him if the Governmt would prosecute This De Foe. Mr Borret answerd he knew Nothing of that atall, Upon which his Ldpp Said he would write to my Lord Bollingbrook to kno', as I Suppose he has done.[1]

---

[1] Parker's letter (P.R.O., S.P. 34/21/241), dated from Serjeant's Inn on 15 Apr., runs as follows:

My Lord,

    I have had a Complaint laid before me upon Oath against severall Libells, one intituled 'Reasons against The Succession of the House of Hanover with an Enquiry How far the Abdication of King James supposing it to be Legal ought to affect the Person of the Pretender' which has had four Editions, a second intituled, 'And what if the Pretender shou'd come, or some Considerations of the Advantages and reall Consequences of the Pretenders possessing the Crown of Great Britain' which has had two Editions, a Third call'd An Answer to a Question that no body thinks of viz 'But What if the Queen should die?' I have taken up and bound to appeare the first day of the Term Danl De Foe who appeares to be the Author of them, and to have sent great Numbers of some of them in to the North. The Printer and Publisher have given Information of the Author, and have likewise readily brought in their Servants to give Evidence against him; however, I have bound them over likewise that they may be sure to be forth coming. The person that made the first Complaint is fully bent upon prosequuting for these libells. However, I send them and the Informations against De Foe to Your Lordship *believing that probably Your Lordship will think it for the Honour of her Maty and the Ministry that directions be given to the Attorny Generall to prosequute at her Maties charge and that the reason why it has not been done already, is that such Scribbles have not faln within Your Lordships notice.* The very Titles of two of them are libellous and seditious, and neare Treason; And the third sawcy. They contain Arguments to make out that the Pretender has a Title to the Crown and that the Advantages of his Reign will be greater than what we now enjoy under her most sacred Maty (whom God long preserve); tis of much less

The Design of This my Lord is, That if The Secretarys Decline it, This Mr Benson will bring an Information On purpose to Trye if I can Obtain a Stop to be put to Their Proceedings by *Noli Pros*, which will give Them an Occasion of Plentifull Railing, which is what They Desire.

Now My Lord The Governmt May Effectually prevent this if a Seeming prosecution be actually begun (Onely I must Depend upon your Ldpp That it be not pushed On) and an Information Ordred against me.[1]

1. This prevents Their stirring in any Separate prosecution Effectually.
2. The True Reason for not prosecuting it may be want of good Evedence, which Really will be wanting.
3. They have no Reason to Examin why the Governmt does or does not prosecute after an Information is layd.

All This while, Ile Complain Loudly of the Oppression. Ile Petition (I mean in Print) to be brought to Tryall; and shall have abundant Room to Expose Them for attacking me in a Thing they can not make Out; and Thus the pretence of being protected by your Ldpp or the Ministry will be quite Taken away.

May it please your Ldpp

If There is any Defect in This scheme which I can not foresee, I Humbly Referr it to your Ldpps Wisdome; The Reason of My proposeing it is purely to Dissappoint Them in That Part of Their Malitious Design, which is Pointed at your Ldpps Person and Administration; For There is no Doubt but haveing a Full stop Put to Their Rage by your Ldpps Authourity, would be much more for my Safety, as well as Reputation; Perticularly

moment to mention after that, the Attacking the protestant Succession, and the many insinuations reflecting upon those now in her Maties Service and in power, and tending to make her Maties Subjects uneasy. There is in some parts a Mixture of what They call banter which seems design'd to screen the rest, and to make way for a pretence of an innocent intention, To which I shall say no more at present than that these are not Subjects to be play'd with. I was in hopes to have sent along with these, an Account that I had taken up William Pittis the Author of another Pamphlet call'd Jus sacrum, concerning which a like Complaint was laid before me at the same time, But I have not yet been able to lay hold of him. However, the Information against him and one of the Books comes along with the others. . . .

Your Lordships most humble & obedt Servt
T: PARKER

[1] This scheme was put into practice, but the Government prosecution thus begun was not dropped, and in the following October Defoe was ordered to plead (Nos. 213 and 214). He escaped trial only by means of a royal pardon (No. 216).

as it would Make Them Cautious of Falling Upon me Again; But My Lord I See who This Bullet is shot at, and if They do This in The green Tree, what would They do in the Drye? May your Ldpp be Ever Preserv'd from Their Rage: Myne be The wounds and The hazard, of whatever kind; and May My station be between your Ldpp and all your Dangers, in The worst attempts of your Enemies, Even to a *Guiscards knife.*[1]

I am Sorry My Lord This foolish Affair has Interrupted me in Those Things of Much greater Consequence, which I had just begun to Lay before your Ldpp, of the affaires of Scotland; where The assembly Approaches;[2] and where The Establishing the Troops,[3] and The Approaching Election[4] offred me Many Things Very Needfull for your Ldpp to kno'; The first of which I was writeing, when the Furies Came upon me, and which I Sent away to your Ldpp Unfinished, and without Takeing a Coppie.[5]

I shall Endeavour (being a little Composed Now) to begin where I brake off, and go on to Those Things I Conciev are for your Service. As to This Affair, I leave my Self Entirely in your Ldpps Disposall, with the Greatest Tranquillity Imaginable, Resting on That Goodness for my protection of which I have had Such Constant Experience.

I am, May it Please your Ldpp
Your Ldpps Most Obedt &c
[symbol]

Aprill 19. 1713

P S If I am able to Come Out of Doors, I will not fail to attend according to your Ldpps Command.

MS.: Duke of Portland, Defoe Papers, 2 ff. 87–88. *Pub.*: *H.M.C. Portland*, v. 283–4. *Address*: none. *Endorsed*: 'Mr. Goldsmith, Apr 19 1713.'

207. [*To* ROBERT HARLEY, EARL OF OXFORD].
18 July 1713

My Lord
I am Among Those who look on The Times with Grief and Indignation, to See the Violence and Rage of a Party Drive men who at the Same time Make a profession of Religion and call Themselves Christians to Such Dreadfull Extreams, That

---

[1] See No. 162.   [2] The General Assembly was to convene on 30 Apr.
[3] The advent of peace made necessary a re-establishment of the regular Forces, ncluding those of Scotland. See Abel Boyer, *Political State*, Apr. 1713, v. 262.
[4] A General Election, required by the Triennial Act, was to be held in August and September.   [5] No. 203.

the Ruine of Their Country, and Of all That Should be Dear to honest Men, is of No Vallue when in Competition with their Party Designs.

To See These men Act The Same Injurious Extravagant Things, which They allways condemn'd in Others; and while They Reproach The Ministry For Joyning with Jacobites to keep Them Out; They Plainly Confess They would Joyn with any Men and in Any Measures to get in.

The Scots however weak and Misled are honester Then these, Even in That folly of Rejecting the Thanksgiveing;[1] for These Mock men in keeping The day while They Insult those who Appointed it; and Mock God in Meeting to Give him thanks for The Peace while They Curse The Peace in their Hearts which they Seem to give Thanks for.

It is with Horror I Mention to your Ldpp Their Treatment of The Queen. How Visibly they discover in Their Very Faces a Secret Satisfaction at any Indisposition Her Majtie may Suffer, Eagerly Enlarge The Account, and Report Every Triffle of That kind to be Fatall; as if her Majties Dangers, which makes an honest Mans Heart Sink at the Very Thought of them, were Their Pleasure. They Appear Dissapointed when They find The Hellish hopes are but Imaginary and The Confusions they Expect Are Delay'd.

God Allmighty for Ever Dissappoint Them and Grant Her Majtie may Out live Not So Much the Men but The Temper; and May See The Spirit of Faction and Fury allay'd and all Our Storms Calm'd in a generall Peace both at home and Abroad.

I hope your Ldpp will believ I am not an Idle Spectator of These Things, and Tho' I was backward to Trouble your Ldpp while The Hurry[2] of the house lasted,[3] I can Not but Renew My humble Petition to your Ldpp, That I may be Directed in My Opposeing these Things, in Such Manner and place as I May be Most Usefull.

> I am, May it Please your Ldpp
> Your Most Humble and Obedt Servt
> [symbol]

July. 18. 1713

MS.: Duke of Portland, Defoe Papers, 2 ff. 89–90. *Pub.*: *H.M.C. Portland*, v. 305–6. *Address*: none. *Endorsed*: 'Mr Goldsmith, July 18: 1713, faction.'

[1] Although 16 June had been set as the day upon which Scotland should formally give thanks for the Peace, the Scots for the most part ignored the occasion. See *Correspondence of the Rev. Robert Wodrow*, Edinburgh, 1842, i. 476–9.

[2] i.e. commotion.　　　　　[3] The session had ended on the 16th.

208. [*To* ROBERT HARLEY, EARL OF OXFORD].

1 August 1713

My Lord

As no Man That has any Sence of Duty to her Majtie or Regard to his Country Can look on The Conduct of Some People[1] Among us without Just Indignation, So (My Lord) I That have all my Life been brought up among and Conversant with Those People profess my Self Amazed at Them.

I allways Thot *However Mistaken* They Meant well, acted From Principle, and lookt up, as well as about Them, in The Measures They Took; But I am Astonished to See Them Implacable, Outrageous, and Flying to all Those abhorr'd Methods of Compassing Their Own Designs, which They allways Censur'd and Condemn'd in Others.

This and The Indefatigable Application with which They are just Now working at Their Scheme for a New Election,[2] and what They promise Themselves, and Good Men fear in Case of Their Success, Makes me Renew My address to your Ldpp with This Humble Question (Viz) *Can I Render your Ldpp and Her Majties Intrest No Service On This Nice Occasion?*

Your Ldpps Indisposition[3] is Not an Affliction to your Faithfull Servants Onely, but to all Honest Men, and a loss to the whole Nation; My Loss in it is not worth Naming, tho' to Me Very Heavy; but I Omit Troubling your Ldpp with my Missfortunes.

I Hope I have not been an Unprofitable Servant in the New Undertakeing which I am Embarkt in.[4] But I would willingly be Farther Usefull According to My Duty, and For This Reason I attend The First Occasion I may have to Lay before your Ldpp, Such Thoughts as I hope May be for your Service, On This Occasion.

I am, May it Please your Ldpp
Your Ldpps Most Humble and Obedt Servt

Augt 1. 1713   [symbol]

MS.: Duke of Portland, Defoe Papers, 2 f. 91. *Pub.*: H.M.C. *Portland*, v. 314–15. *Address*: none.

[1] The Dissenters.   [2] A General Election was about to take place.

[3] Harley was just recovering from a two-weeks' illness (Lewis to Swift, *Correspondence of Jonathan Swift*, ed. F. E. Ball, ii. 57).

[4] The *Review* had come to an end on 11 June, and on 26 May there had appeared the first issue of *Mercator*, a periodical which supported the commercial policies of the Ministry. Defoe was a principal contributor to the new publication, and during the last months of its lifetime, in the following year, apparently carried it on single-handed. See p. 441; *Appeal to Honour and Justice*, in *Later Stuart Tracts*, p. 101; and Laurence Hanson, *Government and the Press*, 1936, pp. 100–1.

209. [*To* Robert Harley, Earl of Oxford].
9 October 1713

My Lord

I had Not Sent again So Soon to your Ldpp, haveing your Orders to Attend to Morrow, but on This Extraordinary Occasion.

I am Surprized My Lord with Notice given Me From Mr Borret[1] That Notwithstanding all That has been Said, and your Ldpps Orders to him, They are proceeding Formally Against me On Account of The Old affair of the Three Pamphlets,[2] and That if your Ldpp is Not pleased to Interpose, I shall be Made a Sacrifize to a Party who would Sacrifiz your Ldpp and The queen also, if it Lay in Their Power.

I can Not forget That your Ldpp was pleased to assure me of your Protection, and That I should Reciev No Prejudice by This affair. Indeed my Lord I have no Other Guilt Than is Included in My Zeal for your Ldpps Intrest and her Majties Service, and Their Rage at Me is founded Purely on my Serving the publick And it would be Very hard if I Should fall by The hand of That Very Government I am Serving.

The Attorney Genll[3] Sends me Word I must Petition The Queen, and That there is No Other way to be Effectually safe but to Obtain her Majties Pardon, and Sayes This Must be Lay'd before your Ldpp Imediately.

I have no Other Method but to doe as Directed, and have Therefore Sent a Petition,[4] which I Humbly beg your Ldpps help in, Haveing No Other Protection Against These Furious Men, Than your Ldpps Intercession and her Majties Clemency. Mr Moore[5] has promised to be The bearer of my Petition to your Ldpp.

They have Sent to me to day to Take out a Coppie of The Information, which is a Charge together with the Following which I am no way able to Support.

> I am, May it Please your Ldpp
> Your Ldpps Most Humble & Obedt Servt
> [symbol]

Octob. 9. 1713

MS.: Duke of Portland, Defoe Papers, 2 ff. 95–96. *Pub.*: *H.M.C. Portland*, v. 345–6. *Address*: none.

[1] See p. 408, n. 3.   [2] See p. 406, n. 1.   [3] Sir Edward Northey.
[4] Defoe's petition is preserved among the papers in P.R.O., S.P. 34/37.
[5] Arthur Moore, Bolingbroke's financial adviser, who was in charge of *Mercator* (Laurence Hanson, *Government and the Press*, 1936, p. 100).

210. [*To* Robert Harley, Earl of Oxford].
16 October 1713

My Lord

If a Stranger were to Make a judgement from The Hurry the Town is in at this juncture, and from The Rage and Elevation of a Set of Deluded People on the Success they promise themselves in the City Election; He would Conclude The Summe of Affaires Depended upon These Four Members, and That The Fate of The Governmt was Determined By The City Election.[1]

Altho' My Lord The Victory, if they Should gain it, May be of Much less Consequence Than they Imagine; yet I hope it will Assist her Majties Friends to Apply themselves to the giveing Some Needfull Check to This Insolence, which is Really Come to Such a hight That it Calls aloud for The just Resentment of the Governmt.

Were The House of Hannover to kno' how They are Thrown in The Face of Every Honest Man Upon all Disputes of This Nature, They would Easily See that Nothing Can Weaken Their True Intrest More Than to Make Them a Terrour to the People who They are to Govern. To have English Liberty Aw'd with the Apprehension of The Successor, is to Make That Successor Odious as well as Terrible and Arm Mens Minds with Aversions to Them; and by Consequence put Them upon Considering whether They Ought to admit or Oppose Them.[2]

I kno' your Ldpp is Sensible what These Men drive at, and I hope are Sufficiently Prepared to dissappoint Them: The Shibboleth of Trade[3] is Now artfully put into the Mouths of the people, and The Parliament will be Throng'd with Clamarous Petitions on The Subject; if Some Vigorous and Speedy

---

[1] In the London election for Members of Parliament, held on 12 Oct., the Whigs had set up four merchants to oppose the four Tory members. When the Sheriffs declared the election won by the Tories, the Whigs demanded a poll, which was now in acrimonious progress. The Tories were eventually seated, though not until the dispute had raged for a full month. The Whig candidates were John Ward, Thomas Scawen, Robert Heysham, and Peter Godfrey; the victors, Sir Richard Hoare, Sir William Withers, Sir John Cass, and Sir George Newland. See Abel Boyer, *Political State*, Nov. 1713, vi. 385–91.

[2] Cf. Defoe's *Letter to the Dissenters*, 1713, pp. 23–24.

[3] Bolingbroke's Treaty of Commerce with France, which would have encouraged and facilitated trade between England and France, had been defeated in the Commons on 18 June by a vote of 194 to 185. The Whigs had led the opposition and had won over enough votes from their rivals to give them their first important victory since their fall in 1710. But the question was still being agitated in a pamphlet war.

Resolution does not Repulse Them at first, They promise Themselves to put The whole Nation in the Same Ferment They have don The City.

I have Many Expedients to Offer your Ldpp on This affair, if your Ldpp would be pleased to Admit me at Proper Times to Attend for That purpose; No question but Some Wayes May be proposed to put a stop to This Fury.

I Shall Attend in the Evening as by your Ldpps Command, and Humbly Acknowlege in the Mean Time your Ldpps Goodness in Delivering Me From The Danger I was in,[1] by which I hope I shall with greater Composure Applye my Self to your Service.

I am, May it Please your Ldpp
Your Ldpps Most Humble and Obedt Servt
[symbol]

Octob. 16. 1713

MS.: Duke of Portland, Defoe Papers, 2 f. 93. *Pub.*: *H.M.C. Portland*, v. 348. *Address*: none.

211. [*To* Robert Harley, Earl of Oxford].
19 October 1713

My Lord

Haveing your Ldpps Commands to Think on the Expedients I Mentioned in My Last with Relation to The French Trade, which Occasions Such a Hurry in the Nation at This Time, I presume to Offer a Few Generlls preliminary to farther Thoughts on That affair, which if your Ldpp Gives me Leave to attend at your Leisure I Would Gladly Explain My Self upon.

It is Most Certain The Party are fallen into This Clamour about Trade Not from Their Zeal for Our Commerce but for a Handle, and to Raise a Party Against the Ministry.

Suppose Then (Tho' it is hoped it May be Otherwise) There Should be Some Difficulty in or Room to Doubt of Carrying The Bill against Them, or of doeing it So Easily as might be desired.

Q. May Not The Ministry proceed by Another Method, and if The bill can not be brought down to the Trade, Bring the Trade up to The Bill.

By This Means the Treaty Shall be Made Effectuall without bringing the Bill in atall,[2] and in One Sessions More, or perhaps

[1] See the preceding letter.
[2] As a matter of fact, the Bill was never again brought before Parliament.

The Same Session, The Very Portugall Merchants Themselves Shall beg to have the bill brought in,[1] and The Ministry in the Mean Time Not Run the Risq of Recieving any Affront From The Party; *to Their Eternall Mortification* and Dissappointmt.

My Lord I was Loth to Communicate This to Any Till your Ldpp had Given Me your Leave to do So, and had Determined whether it has Weight in it or no. I am Perswaded it will be an Effectuall step to put a check to This Broil, and if your Ldpp Approves it I Shall Endeavour to give your Ldpp a full Satisfaction in The Methods, and Shall attend to morrow in the Evening to your Ldpps Command.

I beg your Ldpps leave to Mention Once More My Own Affair, Mr Borret Giveing me still Reason to fear, That if it be not Effectually done before The Term, I may be still Insulted by This Enraged party:[2] If your Ldpp was to kno' how I am Treated by Them, your Own known Generous Principles would Move you to Pity and to Protect a faithfull Servant from a Generation of Men who have Neither Justice or Compassion.

I Humbly also Lay before your Ldpp my Other Circumstance, The quarter being Expired Some Time, and haveing No Subsistence but in your Goodness and her Majties Bounty, haveing also Recd Not One Penny On the Other affair which your Ldpp knows of,[3] which Encreases my Importunity, for which I Humbly ask your Ldpps Pardon.

I am, May it please your Ldpp
Your Ldpps Most faithfull Humble and Obedt Servt
[symbol]

Octob. 19. 1713

MS.: Duke of Portland, Defoe Papers, 2 f. 97. *Pub.*: *H.M.C. Portland*, v. 349–50. *Address*: none.

212. [*To* ROBERT HARLEY, EARL OF OXFORD].
[*c. 22 October 1713*]

My Lord

Nothing is More plain than that The Disputes upon the Subject of the Commerce with France, are Carryed on, Not Meerly

---

[1] Under the Methuen Treaty of 1703, Portuguese wines were imported into England at a duty one-third lower than that laid upon French wines. The traders with Portugal naturally opposed the Treaty of Commerce with France, which, by equalizing the duties, would have deprived them of their advantage, and which, by depressing the English market for Portuguese wines, would have thereby depressed the Portuguese market for English woollens.

[2] See No. 209.   [3] Probably the publication of *Mercator*.

as a Dispute about Trade, which Most of The people Now So hot about it Understand little of, But as an Arrow Shot at The present administration, a handle taken hold of, and an Opportunity which They think is given Them, to Raise a Tumult against the Ministry, and Enflame The People.

It had been to be Wish't That The Ministry had Layed less Stress, or at least Seemed to do So, upon This Affair at First; But Rather Lay'd it before Them as a Thing Indifferent to The Ministry, whether it was accepted or Refused;[1] Then There is Reason to believ, they would Soon have Desired the Trade, because Those who Understood Trade would have Seen The loss of it, and Those who did Not would have been left Out of The Question.

It May So happen Still, that The Clamour of the Rabbles They have Raised May Prevail to preposess the Members and Make it doubtfull.

If The Ministry are Not Certain to Carry it Thro' both houses, The better way Seems to be to Lay it Aside at First and Not bring it to The question till Some Other Steps may be Taken which May Let Men See Their Mistake, and bring those Very Men to Seek it, who Now Oppose it.

Two Sorts of Men began The Opposition against The Bill. All That have followed are come into it as a Party Question, not as a Tradeing Question.

1. The Portugall Merchants, On The Account of The Trade They Drive in Portugall Wine, in which their Argumts are Specious[2] with Respect to our woolln Manufactures, but Not of any Weight in The Generll Argumt of Commerce.[3]

2. The Dutch, of whom This is to be Said in few words, They are Very Desirous that we Should be Excluded the French Trade That they may Carry it On themselves.[4]

That The Dutch are against Our Trade with France is in it Self a Reason why We Ought to Open that Trade, and More Need Not be Said to it.

That the Portugall Merchants are against it is plainly Opposeing a Private Intrest to a public Good.

---

[1] This indeed had been Harley's own attitude toward the Treaty of Commerce. See Strafford to Peter Wentworth, *Wentworth Papers*, p. 338.
[2] i.e. fair enough.   [3] See Abel Boyer, *Political State*, May 1713, v. 333.
[4] See Bolingbroke to Harley, *H.M.C. Portland*, v. 299–300.

Supposeing Then That the Ministry Find it Reasonable to Lay aside The Debate for a Few dayes, and be pleased to let Them Suppose it was quite Lay'd aside and look't Upon by The Ministry as a Thing Indifferent to Them whether it pass't or no.

In The Mean Time, as The house of Course Comes to Consider of wayes and Means For Raiseing Money, Silently Among Other Things Some of the Following Dutyes May be proposed: a Duty on all Forreign wrought Silks Except French, The Duty of which is high Enough allready; a Duty On Wines of Galitia, Leghorne called Florence, Portugall, and Mallaga.

All The Weavers, Turkey and East India Merchants, will Come into the First, and The Opposition to The Last will be but from a Few Private Merchants.

This is what I call bringing the Trade up to The Bill. For as I Conciev, The Treaty does not Oblige The English to Take off Or not to Lay On any Dutyes on French Goods, Provided That Our Dutyes on Other Goods of The like quallity are The Same.

When The Portugall Merchants Shall See The house Resolved to Lay higher Dutyes on Their Trade, They will Choose The Bill of Commerce Rather than The high Dutyes for Many Reasons.

First, because Such additionall Dutyes Streighten Them in Their Trade, Requiring Greater stocks to Carry it On. (2). Lessen The Consumption in Generall and (3). The French Wines Will out Sell them Much More in proportion when both are at a high Price Than when both were Lower.

It will at The Same Time be Easie to bring in a Clause, to Take off the Eight Pounds per Ton upon French wine formerly Spoken of;[1] and The French and Portugall wines Shall be Brought Very Near a *Par*.

Thus The Portugall Merchants will be put to a Full stand, and The Letter of the Treaty of Commerce be Exactly Complyed with, in Makeing The Dutyes Equall.

I am perswaded Makeing a Motion Towards it, Or but passing a Vote for it in the House, first, before The bill of Commerce is proposed, would Effectually bring all The Portugall and Italian Merchants Over to The bill, and bring them to beg For One, to Avoid the Other.

---

[1] In the fourth year of William and Mary, an additional duty of £8 per tun had been imposed on French wines, over and above the regular duty. See Defoe's *Letter from a Member of the House of Commons to his Friend in the Country*, 1713, pp. 13–14.

The Objections From the Portugall Treaty,[1] and The Threats of prohibiting Our Trade in Portugall, are all to be Answerd another Way; Her Majtie is Not without Means in her Own hands to keep the king of Portugall in Temper, or to bring him to Reason if he Should pretend to Resent it;[2] and if Not, The Merchants have themselves to blame for the Consequences; who would Make The Portugall Wine trade a Monopoly, and Oblige The Governmt to Support an Exclusive Trade to Some of her Majties Subjects, to The Injury of The Rest.

By The Same Method The Dutyes on wrought Silks will be brought to An Equallity, So That The Dutch, who Now Enjoy a great Trade with us by the Excludeing The French, will Either Come to an Equallity with the French, or Not Import any Silks atall, which Our Weavers will have No Reason to Repine at.

Note: The Dutch have great Reason to desire the Dutyes on French alamodes and Lustrings[3] Should Remaine, because They have all That Trade Now in their Own hands; and Run them on shore here in Such quantities as has quite Overthrown The English Manufacture of Alamodes and Lustrings.

The Linen, and Paper, Canvas, Sail-Cloth, Dowlasses[4] &c. will all admit the Same Method, and with This advantage, That The Manufacturing The like Goods in Scotland, Ireland, and The North of England, will be Thereby Encouraged.

But There is great Reason to believ, That a quietly beginning the Method above with The Silk and The Wine will at Once allay all the Clamours at the Bill of Commerce; and bring all The Merchants Over to Submit to it.

The question of how Much The Said Dutyes should be is Reserved to a Callculation of the proportion between the Dutyes allready Charg'd on both Sides.

All which is Humbly Submitted &c.

MS.: Duke of Portland, Defoe Papers, 2 ff. 99–102; unsigned, but in the handwriting of Defoe. *Pub.*: *H.M.C. Portland*, v. 351–3. *Address*: none. *Endorsed*: 'Commerce, Proposal of an accommodation, R̶ Octo: 22: 1713.'

[1] The Methuen Treaty would be violated if, as Defoe proposed, the duty on Portuguese wine were raised to equal that on French wine. See G. M. Trevelyan, *Blenheim*, 1930, p. 300.

[2] Now that Spain was governed by a Bourbon king, Portugal was in no position to forego the protection of her powerful English ally.

[3] Two kinds of silk fabric.

[4] Coarse linen.

213. [*To* ROBERT HARLEY, EARL OF OXFORD].
26 October 1713

My Lord

If I had not Enemyes who have Neither Justice or Compassion I Should Not Importune your Ldpp in this Manner.

It was my great Dissaster That I had not the honor to See your Ldpp when I Attended This Evening, Mr Borret giveing Me Notice That The Attor. Genll,[1] Timerous and Cautious to a Fault, has Ordred a Rule for me to plead, and That if The Pardon be not Obtain'd before I am Obliged to plead, I Shall Still be brought upon The Stage.[2]

This Makes me Apply my Self Again to your Ldpp, begging your Protection, and That Such dispatch may be Used as That my Enemyes May Not Triumph, and your Ldpps good Design for my Delivrance be Frustrated by The Delay; Mr Borret will attend to Give your Ldpp an Account of the Danger if your Ldpp pleases, when at the Treasury, to call for him to That purpose.

> I Am, May it please your Ldpp
> Your Most Humble & Obedt Servt
> [symbol]

Octob. 26. 1713

MS.: Duke of Portland, Defoe Papers, 2 f. 103. *Pub.*: *H.M.C. Portland*, v. 355. *Address*: none.

214. [*To* ROBERT HARLEY, EARL OF OXFORD].
28 October 1713

My Lord

I had your Ldpps Command to Attend This Evening, and Considering of what Importance it is To Me to Lay my Case before your Ldpp, Nothing could have hindred me but an Indisposition So Violent as has Obliged me to be Carryed home and lay all bussiness aside.

Yet my Lord I can not go, without Humbly Repeating my Importunitys to your Ldpp in The affair of my deliverance, Mr Borret again assureing me That if it be Delayed a Very little longer It will be my Ruine. I have no hope but in your Ldpps

---

[1] Sir Edward Northey.   [2] See No. 209.

Goodness, and Humbly Entreat your Ldpp I may not be forgotten till it may be too late to help me.

    I am, May it please your Ldpp
        Your Most Humble & Obedt but Distresst Servt
                      [symbol]

Octob. 28. 1713

MS.: Duke of Portland, Defoe Papers, 2 f. 105. *Pub.*: *H.M.C. Portland*, v. 355. *Address*: none.

215. [*To* ROBERT HARLEY, EARL OF OXFORD].
31 October 1713

My Lord
    It is Time that I Should Mention Something to your Ldpp besides my Own affaires, and Let My fate Rest upon your Ldpps pleasure, as my Prosperity does on your Goodness and Bounty.

    I Gave your Ldpp Some hints[1] for a Method to Reduce These Clamours against The bill of Commerce, Supposeing Those Clamours Should grow So Loud as to Make it Reasonable not to hazard the debate in Parliament.

    But as Things Seem to look with a better Face, and The Case appeares with its True Shape on, It Occurrs to me, and This I thought worth your Ldpps Notice, That it is Very Needfull to apply by all possible Means to Open the Eyes of all The Governments Friends to This Perticular, which Indeed too Many have been Perswaded not to See (Viz) That The dispute about Trade is but a Circumstance, An Excressence grown Out of The Generall Party Broil; Taken hold of as They would have done of Any thing Elce That had Offred; as Men Drowning Take hold of One Another and Drown the Faster; But That the Quarrell is Individually the Same as before, and They who will be Amused with the Clamour of a Party without Enquireing into The True design, Really Make that Design Effectuall, and Assist that Party to Destroy themselves and the government together; And Those (I Say) who will be Amused with this Artifice, Ought to Remember, it is Not Trade That they are Voteing For; but The Queen and Ministry, against Rage and Disorder.

    This My Lord is what, if your Ldpp Approves my thoughts, I Shall Applye my Self to;[2] and wish that all Men who have

[1] See No. 212.   [2] See *Mercator* for 3–5 Nov. 1713.

any Zeal for her Majties Service would do The Same; and I The Rather Mention it, because I See There is Room for the Arguments on This head; and People do begin to See it allready, tho' Not Sufficiently.

I have also Compil'd a Letter to The Dissenters,[1] of which I had a hint from your Ldpp, and Tho' I may Not Reach The Scheme of your Ldpps Thoughts; yet I am hopefull it May have Some Effect upon Them; Onely I would hint a Thing to your Ldpp without the Least View to my Own Intrest (Viz) They have Taken of Late Such Measures to stiffle Every thing that is not for their Turn by Clamouring at it in their flyeing Post and by their New Corresponding Letters, that Nothing Can be Spread into the Country but by Force of Mannagemt, and Indeed No printer will now print at his Own Charge, which is the Reason The world is Over-run with their Pamphlets, which they disperse privately Two or three Editions at a Time, and No Man stirrs a hand to Oppose Them because They Must do it at Their Own hazard and Expence.

I have done what Lay in My Power, But your Ldpp knows by Other ways the Extent of My strength is too small. However, I lay this before your Ldpp without any Respect to My Self, Humbly Recomending it to your Ldpp because Tho' the thing it Self is small, The Mischief they do is not Inconsiderable.

I am, May it Please your Ldpp
Your Ldpps Most Humble and Obedient Servt
[symbol]

Octob. 31. 1713

MS.: Duke of Portland, Defoe Papers, 2 ff. 107–8. *Pub.*: *H.M.C. Portland*, v. 355–6. *Address*: none.

216. [*To* ROBERT HARLEY, EARL OF OXFORD].
18 November 1713

My Lord

My Sence of your Ldpps Goodness to me in This Unhappy Affair[2] is too great for me to Express; it must be Testifyed in Duty Rather Than words.

---

[1] The pamphlet, entitled *A Letter to the Dissenters*, appeared on 3 Dec. (*Mercator*, 1–3 Dec. 1713). Its object was to withdraw the Dissenters from their association with the Whigs, to gain their support for the Government rather than for a party, and to warn them that their present conduct might result in future severities. For the reaction to it of one Dissenter, see Edmund Calamy, *An Historical Account of My Own Life*, 1830, ii. 274–7.

[2] See Nos. 209, 213, and 214.

But my Lord It still leaves me in A Difficulty too Great for me, without The farther help of your Ldpp as to The Expence of The Pardon, which is too great for me; Your Ldpp was pleased to Say That Mr Borret Should do that part and I humbly beg he may have your Ldpps Ordr on That Account, because he Seems to Say he is Not Empowred.

I Fear also Mr Attorney May So Contract and limit the Pardon as to leave Room to a Mallitious Party to Fall on me Again; I Was in hopes Like a Receipt in Full it should have Ballanc't all accounts, and I doubt not If your Ldpp Sees fit it May be So still.[1]

I am, May it Please your Ldpp
Your Ldpps Most Obedt Servt
[symbol]

Novemb. 18. 1713

MS.: Duke of Portland, Defoe Papers, 2 f. 109. *Pub.*: *H.M.C. Portland*, v. 359. *Address*: none.

217. [*To* ROBERT HARLEY, EARL OF OXFORD].
26 November 1713

My Lord

No Man That has a Reall Concern in your Prosperity but Must Condole with you in This Second Stab So Near your heart.[2]

But you (My Lord), That have allways made The publick Cares So Much Superiour to your Private Intrests, will with the More Ease heal all The wounds of This Kind with That Soveraign Specifick, That Truly Noble and Sublime Remedy, I Mean *Resignation.*

I know I Need but Name it to your Ldpp; who have long Since Made it your Guide, and by which you have been Led thro' The Various Changes of Life to That Eminent Greatness, for which wicked Men Envy you.

Yet I Thought it My Duty, and The Duty of Respect, to

---

[1] Northey's draft of a warrant for Defoe's pardon, dated 17 Nov., may be found among the papers in P.R.O., S.P. 34/37. It concludes: 'Our Will and Pleasure therefore is that You prepare a Bill for Our Royal Signature to pass Our Great Seal containing Our Gracious and free pardon unto him the Said Daniel De Foe of the Offences aforementioned, and of all Indictments, Convictions, Pains, Penalties, and Forfeitures incurred thereby, And You are to insert therein all such apt and beneficial Clauses as You shall judge requisite to make this Our intended Pardon more full, valid, and effectual.'

[2] Harley's eldest daughter, Elizabeth, Marchioness of Carmarthen, had died on the 20th.

Make Such a Hint, in the stead of a Compliment of Condoleance, which I hope your Ldpp Will accept, and Pardon The Officious forwardness of

May it Please your Ldpp
Your Ldpps Faithfull and Obedt Servt
[symbol]

Novemb. 26. 1713

MS.: Duke of Portland, Defoe Papers, 2 f. 111. *Pub.*: *H.M.C. Portland*, v. 361. *Address*: none.

218. [*To* ROBERT HARLEY, EARL OF OXFORD].
7 December 1713

My Lord
  I have forborn Troubling your Ldpp as much as possible, being Very Sencible I Ought to do So.
  I presented your Ldpp a Small tract about the Dissenters.[1] The hint is your Ldpps Own, But Ought to have had a better workman, for So good a foundation deserv'd a Compleat Building. Yet I have the Satisfaction of Seeing Some good Effects from it allready, and Some men begin to be Convinc't.
  I Never Sollicited your Ldpp for any thing in My life, however great my pressures have been, with So much Earnestness as I would beg your Ldpp to Enable me to Make This Little book Extensive, That in Spight of The arts used here to check and Stiffle it, I might Make it be Seen Among the Country Dissenters. I am Verily Perswaded it would do more Service Than any Single Thing of its kind, at least That I Ever Perform'd.
  I am not Seeking private advantage, and will be Contented to Reap None by it, but I See The Contrivance of a Set of Men Among us, if possible, to Suppress it, and Especially to Send None into The Country.
  It Seems hard That the most Virulent Inflameing Writeings, Such as are not fit to be Read in a Civiliz'd Nation, are privately Sent all Over the Nation at a public Contributed Charge,[2] thereby to poison and posess the People.
  But my Lord if a Word is written in behalf of the Governmt it is not Onely left upon the Authors hands at his Own loss, but the Service honestly Intended is Rendred abortive and The True End not Answered.

[1] See p. 424, n. 1.   [2] i.e. under the frank of Whig M.P.s.

Would your Ldpp give me leav There are Very Few dissenters in England but Should See This little Tract, and should also be Told who have Endeavourd to keep it From them and why.

Pardon me my Lord That I Seem to put So much Value upon this Small piece. I do hope it is a word in Season, and am Sure There is Need of Something to be done to allay the Spirits of an honest but Misguided people.

Were it in my Power My Lord, my Zeal for The public good would make me do this and More, But my Case is Such, as I can Neither bear to Relate, Or forbear to Lament. I Cease my Complaint however Now, because I am Moveing your Ldpp in an Affair That I flatter my Self is an Opportunity of doeing Good to a body of Men who May yet be made Usefull both to The Governmt and Themselves, and Tis on that Account I am bold to Importunate your Ldpp and No Other.

> I am, May it please your Ldpp
> Your Ldpps Most Humble & Obedt Servt
> [symbol]

Decemb. 7. 1713

MS.: Duke of Portland, Defoe Papers, 2 f. 113. *Pub.*: *H.M.C. Portland,* v. 371–2. *Address*: none.

219. [*To* ROBERT HARLEY, EARL OF OXFORD].
25 December 1713

My Lord

I hope your Servts accquainted your Ldpp That I attended last Night and The Evening before according to your Command.

I Mention it That your Ldpp May Not Think me wanting in duty in Not attending This Evening, being Confin'd by a Violent Cold.

I assure your Ldpp I have Imediately apply'd good part of your Ldpps Last bounty to the Use I proposed it.[1] I am Vain of The honor They do the letter to the Dissenters in Nameing your Ldpp to be the Author of it.[2] But More yet am I Vain with the Success I hope That Little work has among The wisest and best of The Dissenters. I have Caused it to be Reprinted in Little[3] to be Convey'd as proposed Over The West, and have Ordred

---

[1] Probably to the dissemination of *A Letter to the Dissenters.*
[2] See Edmund Calamy, *An Historical Account of My Own Life,* 1830, ii. 277.
[3] A 16mo edition dated 1714 was published in Dublin (W. T. Morgan, *Bibliography of British History 1700–1715,* Bloomington, Indiana, 1934–42, ii. 383).

it to be printed at New Castle and Edinburgh.[1] Perhaps it may Mutatis Mutandis be Many wayes usefull in Scotland as well as here.

Either My Lord These Men Must alter Their Conduct to the Governmt or the Governmt Must alter its Conduct to Them. There is a Time when Clemency becomes Criminall, and when Justice Must Exert it Self or Suffer a Contempt Dangerous Even to Governmt it Self.

> I am, May it please your Ldpp
> Your Ldpps Most Humble & Obedt Servt
> [symbol]

Decemb. 25. 1713

MS.: Duke of Portland, Defoe Papers, 2 f. 115. *Pub.*: *H.M.C. Portland*, v. 374–5. *Address*: none.

220. [*To* ROBERT HARLEY, EARL OF OXFORD].
30 December 1713

My Lord

In my Last I hinted Something of The Necessity There was for The Governmt to Exert it Self, So far as May Tend to Checq of The Fury of a Party who grow Insolent by The Indulgence of their Superiours.

It is No New Temper; *These Things thou didst and I kept Silence* &c.[2] was a Complaint mov'd Even from Heaven it Self, by The Insolence of Men.

God knows My Lord I would be The last in This Nation, who Should prompt Justice, Especially On The Men I Mean; But We Restrain Our Children From playing with Gunpowder Least They blast Themselves and blow up The house.

It has been with Amazemt That I have Observ'd These Men On the late Surprise of Her Majties Indisposition,[3] and it Fills Every honest faithfull Subject of her Majtie with Indignation to See These men Brighten Their Faces and Betray a Secret Satisfaction at The appearance of That Danger which Every Good Man Trembled at. And Now How Do they feign a joy at her Majties Recovery, which any One May See is Rather a Visible Dissappointment to them.

[1] No Newcastle or Edinburgh edition has come to light. The title does not appear in Richard Welford, 'Early Newcastle Typography, 1639–1800', *Archaeologia Aeliana*, 3rd series, iii (1907), 1–134.

[2] Psalms, l, 21.

[3] The Queen had been extremely ill at Christmas time (*H.M.C. Portland*, v. 374–5).

In like Manner My Lord, Upon the Little Disorder at Canterbury Among the Marines; How did They Magnifye it to Such a Degree as if half the kingdome had been in Arms! What Joy did They Express at The hopes of Seeing Some blood Shed among us! And how do they appear disspleased at the Dissappointment.[1]

I Need Say No more Than this to prove to your Ldpp, That This Spirit of Rage and Fury is gone too Far for The Clemency and Moderation of the Administration to have any Effect upon. And The Mercy of the Governmt to them, is but like a little water Cast on a great fire, which makes it Burn with the More Fury.

It is True My Lord When we call For Fire From Heaven &c. We kno' not what spirit We are of, But my Lord Resentmt in an Injur'd Insulted Governmt is as Necessary to The publick Safety as Correction is in a Family.

What I Say proceeds from what I See dayly in That Conduct of a party who have Vowed the Destruction of The present administration, and who Own Themselves not to be Obliged or Won by The Tenderest Usage in The World.

God Deliver Her Majtie and all her faithfull Servants Out of their hands.

> I am, May it please your Ldpp
> Your Ldpps Most Humble & Obedt Servt
> [symbol]

Dec. 30. 1713

MS.: Duke of Portland, Defoe Papers, 2 f. 117. *Pub.*: *H.M.C. Portland*, v. 376. *Address*: none.

221. [*To* ROBERT HARLEY, EARL OF OXFORD]. *19 February 1713/14*

My Lord
It is Impossible but with The Uttmost Indignation to hear and Converse among the Constant Indecencys and Furious Excursions of The people here, who Set Themselves in Opposition to her Majtie and all That are Faithfull to her Intrest, and Sometimes I Suspect my Self whether I do not Really Complain to your Ldpp Rather to give Room to The Resentment Than to Inform your Ldpp of The Fact.

Sure My Lord, Justice Vested with Legall Power will not

---

[1] Details of the disorder at Canterbury have not come to light.

allwayes Suffer; If The Governmt Never Exerts it Self The Friends of The Government will not be Protected.

The New Champion of The Party, Mr Steel,[1] is Now to Trye an Experimt Upon The Ministry and shall Set up to make Speeches in The house and Print them[2] That the Mallice of the Party may be Gratifyed and The Ministry be Bullyed in as Publick a Manner as possible.

If my Lord The Virulent writeings of this Man May Not be Voted Seditious, None Ever May, and if Thereupon he May be Expell'd, it would Suppress and Discourage The Party and break all Their New Measures,[3] But if not, The Mischiefs which will follow will be Inumerable: They are prepard for his Loseing his Election of stock-bridge[4] and Mr Hampden has the Town of Wendover Or Berwick to put him into,[5] But if he may be Expell'd it would break all Their projects at Once.

My Ld, It is far from me to Move your Ldpp to personall Resentmts. It is The party Not the Man, and I See Such black Designs in Their View That if possible They will Run things up to blood and Confusion.

Mr steel (as they Say) is to Move for Calling Over The D. of

---

[1] Richard Steele (1672–1729) had taken his seat in the Commons on the 16th. In the previous summer he had resigned his pension so that he might more freely oppose the Government, and his post in the Stamp Office so that he might enter Parliament. Since that time he had attacked the Ministry in the *Guardian*, in *The Importance of Dunkirk Considered*, in the *Englishman*, and in *The Crisis*. His chief charges had been that the Government had failed to require the demolition of Dunkirk and had allowed the Protestant Succession to be placed in danger. Steele's arguments in the *Guardian* against the Treaty of Commerce had been answered gently and respectfully by Defoe in four issues of *Mercator* from 29 Sept. to 6 Oct. 1713.

[2] Though Steele's first speech, in support of Hanmer for Speaker, consisted of only a few lines, yet it was published in quarto (G. A. Aitken, *Life of Richard Steele*, 1889, ii. 9).

[3] This proposal did not originate with Defoe. Steele's expulsion was predicted— even before his election—in the *Examiner* for 21 Aug. 1713; it was suggested in a pamphlet entitled *Reasons Concerning the Immediate Demolishing of Dunkirk: Being a Serious Enquiry into the State and Condition of That Affair*, published on 12 Sept. 1713; and it was mentioned as being 'design'd' in a letter from Peter Wentworth dated 13 Sept. 1713 (*Wentworth Papers*, p. 354).

[4] Steele had been returned for Stockbridge in Hampshire, a notoriously corrupt borough. On 3 Mar. his election was challenged on grounds of bribery and was referred to the Committee of Privilege and Election (*J.H.C.* xvii. 480). The Ministry, however, were reluctant to await the outcome of this case and decided to speed Steele's expulsion by attacking his writings (Aitken, op. cit. ii. 12).

[5] Richard Hampden of the Whig Hampdens of Buckinghamshire had been returned for both Wendover and Berwick-upon-Tweed, and hence would relinquish one seat or the other. On 3 Mar. he gave up Wendover, to which General James Stanhope was elected a few days before Steele's expulsion. See *J.H.C.* xvii. 477, and Abel Boyer, *Political State*, Mar. 1714, vii. 249.

Cambrige[1] and if they Could Draw that young Gentleman into Their Measures They would show themselves quickly, for they are not asham'd to Say They want Onely a head to Make a begining.

I have No Excuse to Make for This Freedom My Ld but my Zeal for her Majties Safety and The Nations peace. The Ferment is So Great that they want Nothing but power and Believ that [they][2] do not want That; and This Makes them Unsufferably Insolent. God Deliver your Ldpp and all her Majties faithfull Servants Out of their hands.

I Am May it please your Ldpp
Your Ldpps Most Obedient Servt
[symbol]

Feb. 19. 1713

MS.: Duke of Portland, Defoe Papers, 2 ff. 119–20. *Pub.*: *H.M.C. Portland* v. 384–5. *Address*: none.

222. [*To* ROBERT HARLEY, EARL OF OXFORD].
2 March 1713/14

My Lord

I believ your Ldpp is Not atall Surpris'd at The Unexampled Fury of the Party. Their public Conduct has Threatn'd This[3] a Long while. As the Justice of your Ldpps Cause will Not Suffer any discouragemt Either from the Growing Enemies or which is Worse Unsteaddy Friends of the Administration, So it Puts me in Mind of The words of Henry the IIII of France to his

[1] As Duke of Cambridge, the young Electoral Prince of Hanover, later George II, had the legal right to be summoned to his seat in the Lords. The Hanoverian party in England, both Whig and Tory, believed that his presence in England would strengthen the chances of an orderly and peaceful succession should the ailing Queen suddenly die. In April Baron Schütz, the Hanoverian agent, demanded the writ. The Queen issued it, but with such great reluctance that the Prince was advised not to come over.

[2] Omitted in MS.

[3] On this day, Wharton and Devonshire had taken action in the House of Lords against *The Publick Spirit of the Whigs*, the anonymous pamphlet in which Swift attacked Steele's *The Crisis* and incidentally derided the Scottish peers in the upper House. The Lords had resolved 'that the said Pamphlet is a false, malicious, and factious Libel, highly dishonourable to the *Scotch* nation, tending to the Destruction of the Constitution, and most injurious to Her Majesty' (*J.H.L.* xix. 628). On the same day, the Lords ordered into custody John Morphew, publisher of Swift's pamphlet, and on the following day ordered the Black Rod to seize John Barber, the printer (*J.H.L.* xix. 630). On 15 Mar. a reward of £300 was offered for the discovery of the author; 'but nevertheless', as Abel Boyer put it, 'JONATHAN, the most *scandalous* and most *flagitious* of all *Libellers*, being under the Wings of some great Men, escaped Discovery and Punishment' (*Political State*, Mar. 1713–14, vii. 223). See also Boyer, op. cit. vii. 215–23, and *Parliamentary History*, vi. 1259–65.

Predecessor Hen III when he Seem'd Amaz'd at The Rage of The Guises and of The Parisians and ask'd him what Course was left to Take; But One Sir, Said the King of Navarr. What's That Cousin, Sd Hen. III. To CONQUER, Reply'd The Great Henry, and Accordingly he attack't The Enemy and Delivred him.[1]

Your Ldpp has but One way left with These Men. They Must be Conquer'd; Or The Nation is Undone, The Queen Undone, and all her Majties Faithfull Friends and Servants Sacrifiz'd to a Rageing and Mercyless Party.

I Presume your Ldpp is Not destitute Either of Means or Council. You have The Fountain of Honour, The strength and The Right on your Side. All Legall steps are justifyable in Such a Case. If a slack Rein is held Now, They will Run down all before Them. Clemency and Kindness will prevail No More with Men that Can be Ingratefull, or justice and Reason with Men who Resolv to play the Bully.

They Openly Declare That They have Thrown away the Scabbard, and as They Expect, So They will Give, no Quarter.

They have begun their attack where they found an advantage. I am Sorry That Gentleman[2] layd himself So Open to them; But my Lord They have by this step pointed the way Out and Told what Ought to be done to The most Insolent Pamphlet writer[3] that Ever was permitted to go Unpunishd. I hope the Occasion will appear of Too Much Moment to be Overslippd Tho' they pretend to Give no Time for it. God Deliver your Ldpp From the hands of these Violent and Unreasonable Men.

I am, May it please your Ldpp

Your Ldpps Most Humble and Obedt Servt

[symbol]

March. 2. 1713

MS.: Duke of Portland, Defoe Papers, 2 ff. 121–2. *Pub.*: *H.M.C. Portland*, v. 388. *Address*: none.

[1] The anecdote appears in H. C. Davila, *History of the Civil Wars of France*, 1678, bk. x, p. 402; a copy of this book is listed in the sale catalogue of the combined libraries of Defoe and Philip Farewell (G. A. Aitken, 'Defoe's Library', *The Athenaeum*, 1 June 1895, p. 706).
[2] Swift. Defoe may have deplored the attack on much of *The Publick Spirit of the Whigs*, but he himself objected to that part of the pamphlet which maligned the Scottish nobility. He replied to Swift's jeers in a pamphlet entitled, *The Scots Nation and Union Vindicated; from the Reflections Cast on Them, in an Infamous Libel, Entitl'd the Publick Spirit of the Whigs*, 1714.
[3] Steele.

223. [*To* ROBERT HARLEY, EARL OF OXFORD].
[*c. 10 March 1713/14*]

Collection of Scandal

In The Late[1] Guardian

Many Repetitions of That Insolence Upon The Queen in Three Guardians Successively (Vizt) *The People of Britain Expect Dunkirk to be Imediately Demolished.*[2]

This Repeated Severall Times and wickedly Paraphrased in The flying Post.

The First English-Man[3]

In The Letter Signed Richard steel where he Falls upon The Examiner There are Diverse Threatning Speeches to The Ministers of state but Concealed Under The Generall Head of a Certain Lord.

In The last English Man[4]

Pa 3. The following words.

'*That the Honour and Intrest* of the Queen *and* her *Love of her people hath been Sacrifiz'd to a Scandal.*'[5]

The Examples he Gives of these are as follows *ibid*

1. The Blackning and Ridiculeing the Noblest Parts of her Reign.

2. Inhumane usage of her Old Servants.

3. The life of The Queen doubtfull.

In The Same page he Subjoyns The following Question as folls:

Whether it be for The Queens Honour to have One half of her peoples affections alienated From her by studyed provocations.[6]

1 This Insinuates That the Queen has alienated half her peoples affections By studyed Provocations, for if Those Provocations Were from any One Elce why should it alienate our affections From The Queen.

---

[1] The *Guardian* had ceased with No. 175, the issue for 1 Oct. 1713.

[2] The demand had appeared not in three successive issues but rather thrice in one issue, No. 128, 7 Aug. 1713.

[3] The first issue of Steele's *Englishman* had appeared on 6 Oct. 1713.

[4] The final issue of the *Englishman*, No. 57, had appeared as a quarto pamphlet on 15 Feb. 1714.

[5] *The Englishman: Being the Close of the Paper So Called*, in *Tracts and Pamphlets by Richard Steele*, ed. Rae Blanchard, Baltimore, 1944, p. 189. Defoe's quotations from Steele are not always strictly literal.

[6] *Tracts and Pamphlets by Richard Steele*, p. 189.

2 This Supposes half The peoples affections alienated from her Majtie, which is Malitious and Scandalous to the highest Degree, and God be praised False also.

3 It is a Charge upon The administration as studying to Provoke The People and Consequently is a Reall stirring up and provokeing the people Against The Governmt, which is Sedition and of the worst kind.

Page 17 he has These words

One might Very Lately have Said—The Dignity and Authourity of Parliaments Could not be better strengthened Than by placeing a Despotick power in the Soveraign.[1]

This he has warily Express'd but he Ought to have proved That Such a Principle has been allowed and Encouraged by the Government for he Sayes Expressly a Man would be Thought to Argue Very well who Said So.

Pa. 18 and also Page 10, The Following Expressions Concerning The Demolishing Dunkirk

'The Queens Garrison is Exposed by Levelling the works to the Mercy of The French And The Mole and Harbour which were first to be demolished stand as They did The Terrour of Great Britain.'[2]

Before this, Page 10, He Sayes, 'At This Day it (Dunkirk) is in a More Dangerous Condition as to England Than it was when I wrot about the Importance of it,[3] for I Insisted on the Demolition of the Mole and Harbour, and Instead of That They have Exactly, as if Mr Tugghe's Memorial[4] had been the Direction in This Case, Demolished The Works, and left The Harbour, its sluices, and all its Accesses, that Concern us, Our Trade, and Our Safety, in Good Condition.'[5]

The Seditious Design of this is Evedent, and The Falshood of it is Manifesst; in That The Accesses, as he Calls Them, to The Mole were The Risbank and Forts, which Guarded The Access to The Said Harbour From us, which are all Demolished, and The Harbour till it is filled up is left Open and Defenceless, Except by The Citadelle, which was in her Majties posession.

---

[1] *Tracts and Pamphlets by Richard Steele*, p. 207.

[2] Ibid., p. 208.

[3] Steele's *Importance of Dunkirk Consider'd* had appeared in Sept. 1713.

[4] Tugghe, Deputy from the Magistrates of Dunkirk, in July 1713, presented a Memorial to the Queen, asking that the harbour and mole be spared (Abel Boyer, *Political State*, July 1713, vi. 52–62).

[5] *Tracts and Pamphlets by Richard Steele*, p. 196. For the Dunkirk affair, see J. R. Moore, 'Defoe, Steele, and the Demolition of Dunkirk', *Huntington Library Quarterly*, viii (1950), 279–302.

To Say The Mole and Harbour stand as they did, when they are stript of Their Defence which Rendred them Safe, is Very absurd.

Pa. 22. He has The Following abominable Reflection upon The Queen

'I Wish Thirdly That his Electorall highness of Hannover would be So Gratefull to Signifye to all The World The perfect Good Understanding he has with The Court of England in as plain Terms as her Majtie was pleased to Declare She had with That house on her part.'¹

This is The Most Malicious, Undutifull and Reproachfull Thing he Could possibly Say of the Queen; Suggesting That her Majties haveing Declar'd it was of No Weight, nor Ought not to be Depended upon by her people without a Voucher From The Elector of Hannover.

In The Crisis²

Pa 1 of The Dedication to The Clergy³

He Endeavours to perswade The Clergy to preach Sedition and uses Arguments to press the Necessity, Dictateing Arrogantly and scandalously to The Ministers of the Church of England to Recommend what he has Collected both in Their Sermons and writeings.

The body of his book Consists Onely of Quotations and Reciteings of Acts of Parliament, But—

In his Seasonable Remarks on The Said Quotations he has The following Expressions

Pa 27.

'One can not but Think that Our Popish and Jacobite Party who have been of Late So bold both in Writeing and Speaking Against the Settlement of the Crown of Great Britain in The Protestant line Must have Some Unaccountable Encouragement for their Support.'⁴

Here is a plain Insinuation of The Danger of the Succession under her Majties administration.

In The Same Page he Sayes

'Let me Inform Every Briton That Loves his Queen, Religion, laws and Liberties it is his Duty to Appear boldly in Their

---

¹ *Tracts and Pamphlets by Richard Steele*, p. 212.
² *The Crisis* had appeared in Jan. 1713-14.
³ *Tracts and Pamphlets by Richard Steele*, pp. 129-33.
⁴ Ibid., p. 169.

Defence, and Detect and SEIZE Those (Jacobites) Enemies to his Country wherever he Finds Them.'[1]

Here he puts The Civil Justice into The hands of the Rabble and Empowers them to fall upon who They please under The pretence of Their being Jacobites.

Pa. 29. He asks a question Relateing to The Settlemt of Our Peace which Implyes a Strong Negation (Viz)

'Where are The Marks of a Lasting Security'[2]

Insinuating That Our Settlement is without any Visible Security for Our posterity.

Pa. 31. After a fulsome Harangue upon The Conduct of The Duke of Marlbro' he Sayes

'The Reputation of The Duke of Marlebro' Could not well be Impair'd without Sullying The Glory of Great Britain it Self.'

'The Minds of the Common People Against all Common Sence are Debauched with Impressions of The Dukes Affectation of Prolonging the War for his Own Glory.'

'That The Duke of Marlbro' was not permitted to Enjoy the Fruits of his Glorious Labour.'[3]

Here he acknowleges Takeing Away his Employmt as an Injury to The Duke; and That prolonging The War was the Fruit of his Glorious Labour; which he Expected but was not Permitted to Enjoy.

Pa. 31. Speaking of The Peace he Sayes

'The house of Bourbon is at This Juncture become More Formidable and bids Fairer for an Universall Monarchy and to Engross the whole Trade of Europe Than it did before The War.'[4]

This [is][5] a Most False and Therefore Scandalous Suggestion and Inconsistent with what he had been Saying before of The Glories and Conquests of The D of Marlbro' and with what he had printed of the Importance of Dunkirk and of France being Removd 2 or 300 Miles From us by The Demolishing Dunkirk.[6]

Ibid

'The Brittish in the Midst of The Enemies Garrisons withdraw themselves from The Confederates.'[7]

---

[1] *Tracts and Pamphlets by Richard Steele*, p. 169.
[2] Ibid., p. 171. Steele has 'what' instead of 'where'.
[3] Ibid., p. 173.   [4] Ibid., p. 174.   [5] Omitted in MS.
[6] See *The Importance of Dunkirk Consider'd*, in *Tracts and Pamphlets by Richard Steele*, p. 103.
[7] *Tracts and Pamphlets by Richard Steele*, p. 174.

This was False in Fact for when The D of Ormond Withdrew, The Confederates had not advanc't from Their First Encampment and had all Their Own Garrisons in Their Reer, and were Superiour to The Enemy as Appear'd by Their Attacking Quesnoy, and Might have Continued So if by a Fatall Arrogance They had not in Contempt of Their Enemy Exposed Themselves in the Most Unsoldierlike Manner in the World, which was their Ruin at Landrecy.[1]

P 31 and 32. Speaking of Dunkirk he Sayes Thus

'Which They have begun Contemptuously and Arbitrarily (to Demolish) Their Own Way. The Mole and Harbour which Onely are Dreadfull to us are yet Untouch't and just Suspicions Given That They Will Ever be.'[2]

This Needs No Comment. It is in Every Sentence Most Scandalous, false and Seditious.

P 32. Speaking of Portugall he Says

'Portugall has Onely at Present a Suspension of Arms for its Security.'[3]

This is upon The Queen also, who has Engaged to Get Reasonable Satisfaction for Portugall as Well as for the Rest of her Allyes, which Engagemt he here Calls No Security.[4]

Pa. 33. Speaking of The Catalognians He Sayes

'Drawn into The War by The Encouragemt of The Maritime Powers—Now abandon'd and Exposed.'[5]

Insinuateing That her Majtie both Drew the Catalans into The Snare of the War and has basely and Unrighteously abandon'd and Exposed Them.[6]

P. 33. Speaking of The present state of The French kings affaires he adds

'What have Great Britain to hope From But The Mercy of France.'[7]

Here he Represents his Country as Given up to France and bound hand and Foot, lyeing at the Mercy of The French king.

The Remainder of The whole book is an Incongruous[8] unadapted discourse On The Danger of The Pretender, Insinuating That we have no present Security Against him but in the

---

[1] See Winston S. Churchill, *Marlborough*, 1933–8, vi. 556–61.
[2] *Tracts and Pamphlets by Richard Steele*, p. 174.   [3] Ibid., p. 175.
[4] See G. M. Trevelyan, *The Peace and the Protestant Succession*, 1934, pp. 225–6.
[5] *Tracts and Pamphlets by Richard Steele*, p. 175.
[6] See G. M. Trevelyan, op. cit., pp. 226–8.
[7] *Tracts and Pamphlets by Richard Steele*, p. 176.
[8] MS. has 'Inongruous'.

Severall Laws and Acts of Parliament which he had Recited, Never once Suggesting what Farther Security humane Wit Can Invent or proposeing any Thing To that End; But allowing That her Majties Zeal for The Safety of her Subjects is No Manner of Security &c.

The Next book Observable is The *Neck or Nothing* of which They have printed Six Thousand and Many whereof are Sent down into Scotland. The Author, John Dunton.[1]

But The whole book is Such a Continued Rhapsody of Scandal and Raillery That it Seems Enough to Name it, and to Collect from it would be to Transcribe it from One End to the Other, for it is but One Continued Breath of slander and Scurrillity on The administration, Calling The Ministry Vile Names and Charging The Queens faithfull Servants with Treason, Robbery, Drunkness and all Manner of Crimes.

This it is hardly worth while to Lay before The Ministry Except Onely to Observe how pleasing Such Scandalous Things are Among us.

MS.: Duke of Portland, Defoe Papers, 2 ff. 123–32; unsigned, but in the handwriting of Defoe. *Pub.*: *H.M.C. Portland*, v. 392–5. *Address*: none. *Endorsed*: 'Heads of scandal, R March: 10: 1713/14.'

224. [*To* Robert Harley, Earl of Oxford]. *11 March 1713/14*

My Lord

After what is printed This day in The Flying Post I Think Nothing can be So Insolent, but her Majtie May Expect it

---

[1] Dunton's *Neck or Nothing*, 1713, had already been subjected to Swift's lash in *The Publick Spirit of the Whigs*. John Dunton (1659–1733), bookseller, projector, Whig hackney writer, and author of *The Life and Errors of John Dunton*, had long been acquainted with Defoe and though appreciative of his abilities had taken offence at some of his actions. Upon the death of Samuel Annesley, Dunton's father-in-law and Defoe's pastor, Dunton published Defoe's *Character of the Late Dr. Samuel Annesley, by Way of Elegy*, 1697; but when Defoe reprinted the piece without permission in his *True Collection* of 1703, Dunton resented what he considered a breach of copyright (*Life and Errors*, 1818, i. 180–1, and ii. 424). Again, Dunton had charged that his monthly *Athenian Oracle*, which undertook to answer questions submitted by the public, had been ruined by the competition when Defoe set up the same practice in his *Review* (*Life and Errors*, ii. 423–4). And by now, of course, Defoe was unpopular with all extreme Whigs of Dunton's kind. When, in April, Defoe published his *Reasons for Im[peaching] the L[or]d H[igh] T[reasure]r and Some Others of the P[resent] M[inistry]*, Dunton replied to him in *The Impeachment, &c., &c.* (Lee, *Life*, i. 227). In 1717 Dunton seems to have proposed that Defoe join him in publishing a weekly paper to be called the *Hanover Spy*, but nothing came of the proposal (Lee, *Life*, i. 274–5).

From These Men; And if The house does not Think Fit to Resent it, They will neither do justice to her Majtie or to her Subjects who They Represent.

The Supposition That the Printer[1] is in Prison Tho' in Reality he is at full Liberty is it Seems The Encouragemt to This Offence; as if a Man Under Conviction of One Crime Could not Commit Another; But Neither is The Man Concern'd but the Party, who Insultingly Say The Printer has the Protection of a jail and That The Government can not Come at it Nor Suppress it.

I am far From Prompting justice but No faithfull Subject can be Satisfyed to See justice Thus affronted, and I Move your Ldpp The Rather because I See This as a forerunner of Greater Insults under the Same protection.

I Hear the whole Town Crye out of this Insolence as the Most Unparalelld affront to The Person and Honour of her Majtie That Ever Subject was permitted Unpunished to be Guilty of. My Zeal Carrys me too Far. I Humbly ask your Ldpps Pardon.

The words I Speak of and which I Humbly Referr your Ldpp to are in The first 26 lines of The Third Paragraph, The Second Col. Flying Post No. 3462, March 11.[2] I presume I Need not Send The paper, haveing it not at hand.

I am, May it please your Ldpp
Your Ldpps Most Humble & Obedt Servt

Ma: 11. 1713   [symbol]

MS.: Duke of Portland, Defoe Papers, 2 f. 133. *Pub.*: *H.M.C. Portland*, v. 395–6. No address.

225. [*To* ROBERT HARLEY, EARL OF OXFORD].
21 May 1714

My Lord

Last Nights Conversation Could not but afford Many Usefull Remarks to Me, and I Thought it My Duty to Mention to your

[1] In June 1713 William Hurt, printer of the *Flying Post*, had been sentenced for printing *The Br[iti]sh Embassadress's Speech to the French King* (Laurence Hanson, *Government and the Press*, 1936, p. 63).

[2] The gist of the passage is that 'we were lately told from the Throne that those who represent the Hanover Succession to be *in Danger under her Majesty's Administration*, are a Faction, and no Friends either to her Majesty or to that Succession', and that therefore 'a Man of profound Duty and Loyalty will, whatever he thinks, for the future never open his Lips about the Danger of the Protestant Succession, till he hears that the Pretender is come again with a French Fleet into the Frith of Edinburg, or into the Mouth of the Thames . . . .'

Ldpp again my Observations on that part of it which Relates To The Dissenters.

First The Bill depending about The dissenters Schools, which I fear will pass;[1] It is True My Lord The Conduct of The Dissenters has call'd for More Than this, and This may Remind them of a hint I gave Them in *The Letter*, whether They Enjoy'd No Favours from her Majties Bounty which They might not Forfeit by Their present behaviour.[2]

I doubt not but Their Pretended Friends the Whigs, will give them up in this, as they did in the Occasionall Bill;[3] and which is Worse, They will Give Themselves up too, Rather Than not Carry On Their Party Mischief; I Pity Them, but I can not Recommend The Intrest of Posterity to your Ldpps Compassion; As to Their Accademies, if there had Never been any, I kno' not but Theyr Intrest had been as Good, and Fewer beggars and Drones had been bred up for Ministers Among Them:[4] But for The Schooles for Common Introduction[5] of Children, I think Their Loss will be Irreparable.[6] It is True, That They will have schooles still; They will be No More Illegall Than before; but it Seems hard upon the Nation in Generll to make Laws which it will be Necessary to Break, Like That of the late Abjuration Oath act in scotland.[7]

---

[1] On this day, Sir William Wyndham had laid before the Commons Bolingbroke's Schism Bill, designed to bring about the eventual extirpation of Dissent by destroying the Dissenters' schools and academies (*J.H.C.* xvii. 636). Bolingbroke intended that the Bill, in addition to its avowed purpose, should serve a political end, by embarrassing his rival Harley, the would-be patron of the Dissenters, and by rallying the disunited Tories into a solid front with himself at the head. To Harley the Bill was both politically and morally obnoxious, but he was by now in no position to venture opposition in public to a measure so warmly supported by the Queen and the Party. The Bill passed, to become effective on 1 Aug. The death of the Queen on that date, and the consequent fall of the Tories, averted rigid enforcement of the Act, and it was repealed in 1719. See Defoe, *Secret History of the White Staff*, 1714, pp. 31–33; David Bogue and James Bennett, *History of Dissenters*, 1808–12, i. 267–77; and G. M. Trevelyan, *The Peace and the Protestant Succession*, 1934, pp. 279–84.

[2] In *A Letter to the Dissenters*, 1713, p. 20, Defoe had warned his brethren that 'their Schools and Seminaries [are] allow'd them, though by Law they may and ought to be suppressed'.

[3] See p. 363, n. 1.

[4] For Defoe's strictures on the Dissenters' academies, see his *Present State of the Parties in Great Britain*, 1712, pp. 295–6 and 315–17. Defoe himself attended such an academy at Newington Green (*More Short Ways with the Dissenters*, in *Works*, 1705, ii. 276).   [5] Thus in MS.

[6] The Bill was eventually amended to allow the Dissenters to provide instruction for their children in reading, writing, arithmetic, and practical mathematics (*Parliamentary History*, vi. 1355–6).

[7] See p. 403, n. 2.

The Dissenters have Now Leisure to Reflect upon Their In-
dolence and Supine Negligence, who at the Revolution when
They Obtain'd the Tolleration, Took no Thought for The Education of their Posterity, or a Succession of Ministers to Preach to
Them; Neither of which would Then have been denyed them
at That Time.[1]

I am Prepareing to put Them in Mind of Their Duty and
Intrest in the Present juncture, and if (as I hope) I have Room
to Morrow when According to your Command I shall attend
your Ldpp, I purpose to Give your Ldpp Some Account of it:[2]
I am in Great want also to Lay before you Something about the
Mercator,[3] and if it May Please your Ldpp to have That Paper
Made More usefull, I Mean to More Purposes Than its Single
Originall design, I have Some Thoughts to Lay before your
Ldpp on That head.

I Hope your Ldpp is made Accquainted That Mr M...,[4]
who first Set me upon that work, and Undertook The Support
of it, has Declined any Consideration for it Ever Since Lady day
Last; So That I perform it wholly without any Appointmt for
it, or benefit by it; which I do Singly as I hope it is of Service,
and That it may be agreeable to your Ldpp to have it Continued;
Tho' my Circumstances render it hard to me to do So because
it is Expensive to me. But I Lay it all and my Self at your Ldpps
Feet.

> I am, May it Please your Ldpp
> Your Ldpps Most Humble and Obedt Servt
> [symbol]

May. 21. 1714

MS.: Duke of Portland, Defoe Papers, 2 ff. 135–6. *Pub.*: *H.M.C. Portland,*
v. 444–5. *Address*: none. *Endorsed*: 'Mr Goldsmith, May 21: 1714.'

226. [*To* ROBERT HARLEY, EARL OF OXFORD].
23 June 1714

My Lord

Tho' I have Not been able to pay my Duty to your Ldpp as
Usuall by Reason of a lameness which has long Confin'd me,
yet I Could not Refrain writeing on the following Occasions.

[1] Cf. Defoe, *Wise as Serpents*, 1712, pp. 14–15.
[2] This perhaps refers to *The Weakest Go to the Wall*, which he published a short
time later.
[3] See p. 414, n. 4.
[4] Arthur Moore, Commissioner of Trade, and Bolingbroke's financial adviser.

Tho' I go not abroad, yet I find Ever Since the Depending bill against the Dissenters[1] There has been a Certain Set of Men, Appointed no doubt, who make it their bussiness Among the Dissenters to Talk in a New Dialect (Viz) That Things are Now Comeing to a Crisis, That Men had as Good lose Their Lives as their Libertyes and Their Religion, That these Were The Onely Two Things which made The Revolution, That There is a Time when Men Can bear No Longer, That we Ought to Resist Such Violence, That Our Children will be Taken from us Next and put to Charity Schooles, That we had better begin at first while we have Some Friends and Means to help Our Selves Than stay till we are quite Ruin'd and till Matters become Irretrievable—

There is Much More in The discourses of these men. I hope and Believ My Lord That the Main body of the dissenters are wiser Than to be Influenced by Such speeches to any thing Undutifull and Unquiet, and if they should, which I should be Very Sorry For, I know it would End in Their Ruine.

But That there are Some who would Gladly bring them into Some Such Snare, Nay tho' it were to Their Ruine, So it might but Give Some shock to the Public Tranquillity, This I Make no Doubt of, and Therefore I Thot it might not be Improper to Represent it to your Ldpp.

> I am, May it Please your Ldpp
> Your Ldpps Most Obedt Servt
> [symbol]

June. 23. 1714

MS.: Duke of Portland, Defoe Papers, 2 f. 137. *Pub.*: *H.M.C. Portland*, v. 461–2. *Address*: none.

227. [*To* ROBERT HARLEY, EARL OF OXFORD].
26 July 1714

My Lord

I humbly Thank your Ldpp for your Order to me to Send a Reciept for the Usuall Summ on my perticular Account,[2] which I have done Enclosed,[3] and Shall attend my Self in the Evening.

---

[1] See p. 440, n. 1. The Bill as amended by the Lords passed the Commons on the day of this letter, and received the royal assent two days later, 25 June (*J.H.C.* xvii. 697–8 and 701).

[2] He had received £100 on this day (Laurence Hanson, *Government and the Press*, 1936, p. 96).

[3] For 'Enclosed', Defoe had first written 'by The Bearer'.

I am My Lord Capable of Judgeing but by Outsides of Things, and of knowing Little but without doores, but my Lord when I See Those who Owe Their Fortunes to your Ldpp, and who have pretended So Much, face About upon Their Benefactor, It can Not but Move me to Lay Their Conduct before you.

When I See with what assurance They Tell the world how Capable they are to act without your help; when I kno' The Time They Could not have stood an hour without you, This Tells me Their Folly and Treachery at the Same Time.[1]

But My Lord, when They Speak of their haveing Power with the Queen to disposess and Succeed your Ldpp, I must Confess it Amazes me, as Well to Think whether Such a thing Can be, as what Ruine The Nation will be Exposed to if it should.

I hope still your Ldpp, who has been Victorious Over worse Enemyes than These, will Easily Baffle their projects; if Not I Think it my Duty to Repeat my assurances of my following your Worst Fortunes, and of being, fall it foul or fair, your Constant, faithfull and Steddy as Well as Humble and Obedt Servt.

[symbol]

July. 26. 1714

MS.: Duke of Portland, Defoe Papers, 2 f. 139. *Pub.*: *H.M.C. Portland*, v. 475–6. *Address*: none.

228. [*To* ROBERT HARLEY, EARL OF OXFORD].
3 August 1714

My Lord

The Surprissing Turn given by The Imediate hand of Providence to the State of things[2] Since my Last has been the Reason

---

[1] By now, Bolingbroke, Harcourt, Lady Masham, and their faction were within a few hours of achieving their goal of persuading the Queen to dismiss Harley from office. Swift had already advised him to resign. Erasmus Lewis had 'long thought his parts decayed'. The Queen no longer trusted him, and complained that 'he neglected all business; that he was seldom to be understood; that when he did explain himself, she could not depend upon the truth of what he said; that he never came to her at the time she appointed; that he often came drunk; that lastly, to crown all, he behaved himself toward her with ill manner, indecency, and disrespect' (*Correspondence of Jonathan Swift*, ed. F. E. Ball, 1910–14, ii. 199, 202, and 223). Harley still clung by a thread, but 'by the 23rd July all hope was over' (Keith Feiling, *History of the Tory Party*, Oxford, 1924, p. 474). On the day following that of this letter, he was dismissed.

[2] Queen Anne had died on 1 Aug., and a few hours later King George had been proclaimed. The Queen's last official act had been to appoint a successor to Harley: Shrewsbury was now Lord Treasurer.

why I have not Persued what I was upon for Vindicateing your Ldpps person and Conduct and Exposeing your Enemyes as I had proposed to your Ldpp and which was actually in the Press and part of it Printed off.[1]

The Change of affaires Necessarily working a Change in The judgement Men Make of things, I thot It my duty to Take my Measures from your Ldpp, and from the farther Turns in The publick administration which a Little Time may produce.

I Give your Ldpp the Trouble of This Onely to Let your Ldpp See that I am Not Unmindfull of my duty, and that your Service and Intrest, which was allways at My heart, is still So as much as Ever, and will Remain So at all Times.

I can not Omitt My humble and Thankfull Mention of your Ldpps Goodness to me, when I had last the honor to attend you, when you Were pleased to give me assurance of the Continuance of your favour and Bounty. It Remains that I Endeavour to Merit your goodness, or at Least to Convince your Ldpp That I am willing to do So, by a Constant adhereing to your Intrest and Service to the Uttmost.

    I am, May it Please your Ldpp
       Your Ldpps Most Obliged Humble & Obedt Servant
                         [symbol]
August. 3. 1714

MS.: Duke of Portland, Defoe Papers, 2 f. 141. *Pub.*: *H.M.C. Portland*, v. 482. *Address*: none.

229. [*To* ROBERT HARLEY, EARL OF OXFORD].
26 August 1714

My Lord

It is not That I have been Either Negligent Or Unmindfull Either of your Ldpps Intrest or my Own Obligation, That I have not Sooner offred to your Ldpp what I formerly Proposed for your Service.[2] But I hope in a Few dayes by Convinceing proofs to shew your Ldpp what my Zeal for your Intrest will allwayes dictate to me. Indeed my Lord, the juncture has been So Nice I hardly could Tell which way to direct words So to Suit the Fluctuating Tempers of the people, as Not to do harm instead of Good; If I press'd Moderation and a Return to Charity and Temper, Our Outrageous people presently call it

[1] Perhaps an early form of Defoe's *Secret History of the White Staff.* See p. 445, n. 1.
[2] Probably the vindication mentioned in the preceding letter.

fear of punishmt and The Law, and They begin to be calling for Fire from Heaven allready Not knowing what Spirit they are of; Alas how Sick will They be of their New king if he will not Gratifye their Revenge and make war upon half his people.

In this difficulty My Lord I find the way to Talk with them is by Little and Little, gaining upon their Furious Tempers by Inches. This therefore is but an Introduction[1] and Speaks all upon Generalls, and will be followed with Another and Another as things present; and as the Distinction between your Ldpps administration and That which would have follow'd is absolutely Necessary, My Next will state That part more Clearly Than any thing Seems to have done yet, I mean within the Reach of Common Observation.

I Humbly Referr the Tract herewith Lay'd before your Ldpp to your Charity, on Account of the Goodness of the design.[2] I shall go on to do Every thing that I Can See the least Room to Suppose may be of Service, haveing Neither Thought or Judgemt but what is fully Employed to find out Methods how I may Render my Self Usefull and Servicable to your Ldpp, to whom I am bound by So many Obligations.

I am, May it please your Ldpp
Your Most Humble & Obedient Servt
[symbol]

Augt. 26. 1714

MS.: Duke of Portland, Defoe Papers, 2 f. 143. *Pub.*: *H.M.C. Portland*, v. 490. *Address*: none.

230. [*To* ROBERT HARLEY, EARL OF OXFORD].
31 August 1714

My Lord

I had not given your Ldpp The trouble of any of the Little Ruffles I meet with in The world, if it were not That I See

---

[1] This 'Introduction' may well be Defoe's defence of Harley which was published anonymously in October under the title, *The Secret History of the White Staff, Being an Account of Affairs under the Conduct of the Late Ministers, and of What Might Probably Have Happened if Her Majesty Had Not Died*. It was followed on 27 Oct. by Part II, and on 29 Jan. 1714–15 by Part III (Lee, *Life*, i. xxxix).

[2] Since the printed pamphlet did not appear until October, Defoe may here be referring to the manuscript. Harley probably collaborated to some extent, for the tract as published contains details that Defoe could hardly have obtained from anyone else. Indeed, Harley was thought by some to be the author. See the anonymous *Considerations upon the Secret History of the White Staff*, p. [5]. Later, both Harley and Defoe publicly denied having had any part in *The Secret History* (*London Gazette*, 19 July 1715, and *Appeal to Honour and Justice*, in *Later Stuart Tracts*, p. 101).

allwayes Som little Stroaks of Malice (in Every Thing that pushes at me) pointing at your Ldpp who they would fain Think they affront when they fall upon me.

This makes it Necessary for me to Lay before your Ldpp a brief hystory of Fact in a Broil which I have just Now upon my hands, which would not be Otherwise worth your hearing.

It has been long That I have been Endeavouring to Take off the Virulence and Rage of the Flying Post.[1] Mr Moore[2] has been wittness to the Design and to Some of the Measures I took for it, which were Unsuccessfull.

After Some Time an Occasion Offred me which I Thought might be Improv'd Effectually to Overthrow it; The Old Author Redpath Quarrell'd with his Printer Hurt and Takes the Paper From him; Hurt Sets up for himself and applyes himself to a Certain Author to write it for him, but being Not Able to get any One to Publish it, he lost ground.[3]

It Occurr'd to me That To Support Hurt would be the Onely Way to bring the paper it Self Out of Redpaths hand, and to this Intent I frequently at his Request Sent him paragraphs of forreign News but Declin'd Medling with home Matters.

The publisher Recd a letter Very Unhappily for me and finding it full of Reflections desir'd it to be Softn'd as he calld it, and Sends it to me. I left out indeed a great Deal of Scandalous Stuff that was in it but added Nothing and Sent it back. This they have printed from my hand, and I am Charg'd as the Author of the Letter, am Sent for by a warrant and held to Bail.[4]

---

[1] See pp. 395, 400, and 439.

[2] Arthur Moore, with whom Defoe had been associated in publishing the now-abandoned *Mercator*.

[3] George Ridpath had been a fugitive since late in the previous April, but apparently kept control of the *Flying Post* through local agents. In July these agents had transferred the printing of his paper from William Hurt to Robert Tookey, but Hurt had continued to publish a paper, retaining the title and format of Ridpath's *Flying Post*. The two papers of the same name appeared from 27 July until 21 Sept., after which Hurt seems to have abandoned the game. See Lee, *Life*, i. 230–1; *C.B.E.L.* ii. 707; and Stanley Morison, *The English Newspaper*, Cambridge, 1932, pp. 69–70.

[4] The letter as rewritten by Defoe had appeared in the *Flying Post* on 19 Aug. Two days later, Hurt, the printer, and Baker, the publisher, were taken up and their papers seized. The offending letter was found to be in Defoe's handwriting, and he was arrested on the 28th (Dottin, *Defoe*, pp. 222–3). Some years later, when Defoe was engaged in the hazardous game of editing and writing for Tory journals so as to make them inoffensive to his Whig employers, he took care to destroy his manuscript copy (G. A. Aitken, 'Defoe and Mist's "Weekly Journal" ' *The Athenaeum*, 26 Aug. 1893, p. 287).

The use They make of this is that I have Insulted my Ld Anglesey and that your Ldpp has Employd me to do So.[1] God knows that all I did in it was to prevent their Printing Severall Scandalous Reflections on his Ldpp which I therefore struck quite out and Wrot the Rest Over again; I Humbly beg your Ldpps Intercession with my Ld Anglesey in this Matter, assureing his Ldpp I Never knew any thing in this Matter Other than the Above and did nothing in it but with Design to Serve his Ldpp.

> I am, May it Please your Ldpp
> Your Ldpps Most Humble and Obedt Servt
> [symbol]

Augt 31.

MS.: Duke of Portland, Defoe Papers, 2 f. 145. *Pub.*: *H.M.C. Portland*, v. 491–2. *Address*: none.

231. [*To* ROBERT HARLEY, EARL OF OXFORD].
28 September 1714

My Lord

It is not want of Duty or of a Sence of Duty that I have Layn Still at a Time when Others take Such an Unbounded Liberty, but in Such a juncture who can direct his Own steps?

I presume The Artifice of the present Politicians[2] is Now to have it believed That all who acted under The late administration were Enemies to the Succession of the Present King,[3] and in Such a Stream as Now Runs Such Absurdityes may go down; how Evedent So Ever the Contrary May be; Honest Men then must Reserv themselves for better Fortunes, and For times when Truth May be more quietly heard.

In the Mean Time as I am and shall be Ever Watchfull for your Ldpps Intrest, I Could not but Send the Enclosed[4] to your Ldpp, which came to my hand Very Odly, But is the Originall and as Directed was Sent to the Writer of Dyers News to Publish;

[1] Arthur Annesley (1676–1737), fifth Earl of Anglesey, a leader of the Hanoverian Tories, was at this time one of the Lords Justices, having been named by George himself. But the letter that Defoe had edited implied that Anglesey was a Jacobite, a charge that a Regent could hardly ignore. He complained to his fellow Regents, and the arrests followed at their order. See Lee, *Life*, i. 233–5, where the offending letter is reprinted.

[2] The King had arrived in England on 18 Sept., and the new Whig Government was beginning to take shape.

[3] In the following June Harley, Bolingbroke, Ormonde, and Strafford were impeached, the first three for high treason (*J.H.C.* xviii. 166 and 182–3).

[4] Missing.

That it was written in Town is most probable, because There is
a Frank on the Outside and yet no Post Mark on the back, and
The Frank I Suppose is a Counterfeit also.

Your Ldpp will kno' what use to make of it, without shewing
the Superscription. Mean time I have Obtained that it shall
not be put into the News Letter, if they keep their Word with me.

I Can not but humbly Remind your Ldpp of the Case between my Ld Anglesey &c. I hope your Ldpp will prevail with
him to drop a prosecution which None but his Enemyes Prompt
him to, and Against a Man that did Nothing but with a Sincere
Design to Serv him, haveing done Nothing towards the Letter
published but Taken Out what was Most Injurious to his Ldpp.[1]

God Preserv your Ldpp From the Rage of those who haveing
Long had a will Now think they have power to hurt you.

> I am, May it Please your Ldpp
> Your Ldpps Ever faithfull and Obedt Servt

Septembr. 28. 1714   [symbol]

MS.: Duke of Portland, Defoe Papers, 2 f. 147. *Pub.*: *H.M.C. Portland*, v.
496. *Address*: none.

232. *To* SAMUEL KEIMER.[2] [*1717?*]

Mr. Keimer,

I Have your Letter: The Account you give of your Hardships
is indeed very moving; the Relief I have been able to give you,

[1] Harley was powerless to prevent the prosecution and on 15 July 1715 Defoe
was brought to trial and found guilty. Sentence, however, was never passed. See
Lee, *Life*, i. 251–8.

[2] Samuel Keimer (d. *c.* 1738), printer and religious eccentric, had formerly
been one of Defoe's publishers. Keimer learned his trade from Robert Tookey,
and his religious aberrations from the 'French Prophets'. As a member of their
sect, he grew a beard, wore yard-lengths of green ribbon, and wrote his name on
large apples. In 1713 he married and set up his own printing office. In 1715 he
published at least nine pamphlets for Defoe, and established a paper called the
London Post; but in the same year he went into bankruptcy and was committed to
the Fleet for debt. While he was still there, in 1717, some objectionable matter
appeared in the *Weekly Journal*, which was printed at his establishment. As a
result, he was now suffering the miseries of being confined in the Gatehouse, and,
having abandoned the Prophets, was abandoned by them. He was released after
17 weeks, but only to return to the Fleet. When he was finally set free, in 1721, he
deserted his wife and sailed to America. In 1723 he set up a press in Philadelphia
and gave employment to young Benjamin Franklin. Among his Philadelphia
enterprises was a periodical entitled *The Universal Instructor in All Arts and Sciences*,
in which he reprinted selections from Defoe's *Religious Courtship*. Keimer later went
to Barbados, where he founded the *Barbadoes Gazette* in 1731 and published it until
1738, near the time of his death. See Keimer's *Brand Pluck'd from the Burning*, 1718;
Dottin, *Defoe*, pp. 822–5; *Dictionary of American Biography*; and Stephen Bloore,
'Samuel Keimer', *Pennsylvania Magazine of History and Biography*, Philadelphia, liv
(1930), 255–87.

has been very small; however I have repeated it by the same kind Messenger.

Of all your Letter, nothing pleases me so much as to find you hint something of your being touch'd with a Sense of breaking in upon Principle and Conscience; God grant the Motion may be sincere. Afflictions do not rise out of the Dust: They seem to leave God himself no other room but that of Vengeance to deal with them, who are neither better'd by Mercies or Afflictions. The Time of Sorrow is a Time to reflect, and to look and see wherefore he that is righteous is contending with you. Only remember that he is not mocked. Nothing but a deep thorough unfeigned sincere Humiliation is accepted by him. God restore you to your Health, Liberty and Prosperity; and last of all to his Blessing and Favour.

Shall I recommend a sincere Prayer put up to Heaven, tho' in Verse, by one[1] I knew under deep and dreadful Afflictions? I'll write you but a few of them;

> Lord, whatsoever Troubles wrack my Breast,
> Till Sin removes too, let me take no Rest;
> How dark soe'er my Case, or sharp my Pain,
> O let no Sorrows cease, and Sin remain!
> For JESUS Sake, remove not my Distress
> Till thy Almighty Grace shall repossess
> The vacant Throne, from whence my Crimes depart,
> And makes a willing Captive of my Heart.

These are serious Lines, tho' Poetical. Its a Prayer, I doubt few can make: But the Moral is excellent; if Afflictions cease, and Cause of Afflictions remain, the Joy of your Deliverance will be short.

I have sent you the printed Paper you wrote for.— I should be glad to render you any Service within my Power, having been always perhaps more than you imagin'd,

Your sincere Friend and Servant,[2]

MS.: untraced. *Pub.*: Samuel Keimer, *A Brand Pluck'd from the Burning*, 1718, pp. 98–99. *Address*: none recorded.

[1] Probably Defoe himself.

[2] Although Keimer did not identify his correspondent by name, he prefaced the letter with a sentence that seems to point to Defoe: 'My outward Wants encreasing, I wrote to several of my former Acquaintance for Relief, but with little Success, except from one who had known the different Stations of Life, from the Closet Conversation of a KING and QUEEN, to the fatiguing Difficulties of a Dungeon, who with his welcome Kindness, sent me the following Lines' (*A Brand Pluck'd from the Burning*, 1718, p. 98). The letter was first attributed to Defoe by James Crossley (*Notes and Queries*, 1 S, iv [1869], 422).

233. [*To* CHARLES DE LA FAYE].[1] *12 April 1718*

Sir

I could Not Read without Pain to day in The Publick Prints Some thing of An Account of that Traiterous Pamphlet being Printed,[2] I Mean that which I Shewed you and which I Sent to my Lord Sunderland.[3]

I beg you will Please to Assure his Ldpp[4] From me, That the Originall which I Shewed you is still in my hand, and has Never been Out of my Keeping, Nor has any Eye Seen it, or any Coppy been taken of it, that One Excepted which I Sent to his Ldpp.

I here Enclose a Letter[5] which I have stopt, which I Think is Worth his Ldpps Notice. I dare not yet Come Abroad but hope to See you in three or four dayes if the Cold Weather abates.

I am, Sir, Your Most Humble Servt
DE FOE

Newington Aprll 12. 1718

MS.: P.R.O., S.P. 35/11/87. *Pub.*: *Notes and Queries*, 3 S, vi (1864), 527. *Address*: none.

234. [*To* CHARLES DE LA FAYE]. *26 April 1718*

Sir

Tho' I doubt Not but you have Accquainted My Ld Stanhope[6] with what Humble Sence of his Ldpps goodness I Recd The Account you were Pleased to Give me, That My Little Services are Accepted, and That his Ldpp is Satisfyed to go on

---

[1] Charles De la Faye was Under-secretary in the office of the Secretary of State for the Northern Department, to which post James, Viscount Stanhope, had been sworn two weeks earlier. Defoe was now once again in secret service, this time for a Whig Ministry. In 1715, on the recommendation of Lord Chief Justice Parker, he had entered the service of Lord Townshend, one of the new Whig Secretaries. Public knowledge of Defoe's allegiance to the old Tory Government, instead of precluding his enlistment under the banner of the triumphant Whigs, had been made the very basis for that enlistment. Defoe was to pretend to be still in the Tory interest and was to continue writing for Tory papers; but his real mission was to intercept and suppress the more virulent contributions to those papers, to water down whatever they did print, and to keep the Government fully informed concerning the opposition press. Cf. No. 234.

[2] Perhaps 'Sultan Galga', mentioned in the postscript of the following letter (p. 454).

[3] De la Faye had been Under-secretary to the Earl of Sunderland, who had preceded Stanhope as Northern Secretary. Sunderland had resigned on 2 Mar., and was now First Lord of the Treasury and Lord President.

[4] Probably Sunderland, to whom Defoe had sent the manuscript, rather than Stanhope, De la Faye's new superior.   [5] Missing.

[6] James Stanhope (1673–1721), first Earl Stanhope, Secretary of State for the Northern Department. For a letter from Defoe to Stanhope, see No. 132.

Upon the Foot of Former Capitulations &c., yet I Confess Sir I have been Anxious On Many Accounts, with Respect as Well to the Service it Self, as to my Own Safety, Least My Lord May Think himself ill Served by me, Even when I may have best Perform'd My Duty:

I Thought it therefore Not Onely a Debt to my Self, But a Duty to his Ldpp that I should give his Ldpp a Short Account as Clear as I can, How far my former Instructions Empowred me to Act, and in a Word what this Little Peice of Secret Service is for which I am So much a Subject of his Ldpps Present Favour and Bounty.

It was in the Ministry of My Lord Townshend,[1] When My Ld Chief Justice Parker to whom I stand Obliged for the favour, Was pleased So farr to state my Case, That Notwithstanding the Missrepresentations Under which I had Suffred,[2] and Notwithstanding Some Mistakes which I was the first to Acknowlege,[3] I Was So happy as to be believ'd in the Professions I made of a Sincere attachmt to The Intrest of the Present Governmt; and speaking with all Possible Humillity, I hope I Have not Dishonourd My Ld Parkers Recommendation.[4]

In Considring after this which Way I might be Rendred Most usefull to the Government, It was proposed By My Lord Townshend That I should still appear as if I were as before under the Displeasure of the Governmt; and Seperated From the Whiggs; and That I might be more Servicable in a kind of Disguise, Than If I appeard openly; and Upon this foot a Weekly Paper which I was at first Directed to Write, in Opposition to a Scandalous paper called the Shif shifted,[5] was Lay'd

---

[1] Charles Townshend (1674–1738), second Viscount Townshend, had been Northern Secretary from Sept. 1714 to Dec. 1716.

[2] In the case of the three pamphlets of 1713 (No. 204).

[3] His criticisms of the conduct of Lord Chief Justice Parker while Defoe was on trial for writing the three pamphlets (p. 409, n. 2).

[4] Defoe seems to have won Parker's favour when he wrote a letter to the Lord Chief Justice while awaiting sentence from his Court for libelling Anglesey (p. 447, n. 1). 'The letter was so strenuous in argument, so pathetic in its eloquence, and so moving and persuasive, that as soon as the judge read it he sent him word he should be easy, for he would endeavour to make that matter light to him; and in a word, never left until he obtained to stop prosecution, and restore him to his liberty and to his family' ('Vision of the Angelic World', *Serious Reflections during the Life and Surprising Adventures of Robinson Crusoe*, Aitken ed., p. 281). In this passage, Defoe pretends to be speaking of a friend's experience, but it was doubtless his own.

[5] The *Shift Shifted* was a Jacobite weekly edited by George Flint. It had first appeared, under the name *Robin's Last Shift*, on 18 Feb. 1715–16; the name was changed on 5 May 1716 (Laurence Hanson, *Government and the Press*, 1936, p. 102, and *C.B.E.L.* ii. 712).

aside; and The first thing I Engaged in was a Monthly Book called Mercurius Politicus[1] of which Presently.

In the Intervall of This, Dyer The News Letter Writer haveing been Dead,[2] and Dormer his Successor being Unable by his Troubles to Carry on that Work, I had an Offer of a share in The Property as Well as in the Mannagemt of that Work.[3]

I Imediately Accquainted my Ld Townshend of it, who by Mr Buckley[4] let me know, it Would be a Very Acceptable Peice of Service; for that Letter Was Really Very Prejudiciall to the Public, and the most Difficult to Come at in a judiciall way, in Case of Offence Given; My Ld was pleased to Add by Mr Buckley that he would Consider[5] my Service in that Case as he afterwards did.

Upon This I Engaged in it, and That So far, that Tho' the Property was not wholly my Own, yet the Conduct, and Governmt of the stile and News, was So Entirely in Me, that I Ventur'd to assure his Ldpp the sting of that Mischeivous Paper should be Entirely Taken out, Tho' it was Granted that the stile should Continue Tory, as it was, that the Party might be Amused, and Not Set up another, which Would have destroy'd the Design, and This Part I therefore Take Entirely on my Self still.

This Went on for a year, before My Ld Townshend Went Out of The Office;[6] and his Ldpp in Consideration of This Service, Made me the Appointment which Mr Buckley knows of, with Promise of a Further allowance as Service Presented.

My Ld Sunderland[7] to whose Goodness I had Many yeares

---

[1] *Mercurius Politicus: Being Monthly Observations on the Affairs of Great Britain* ran from May 1716 to Dec. 1720 (*C.B.E.L.* ii. 676).

[2] John Dyer, Defoe's old adversary (see No. 134), had died on 6 Sept. 1713 (John Nichols, *Literary Anecdotes of the Eighteenth Century*, 1812–16, i. 71–72).

[3] According to Lee, 'Defoe became part proprietor and manager in June, 1716, and Mr. Dormer died in March, 1718, but was succeeded by his brother. Defoe continued connected with the Paper until August following, but I cannot state whether it then terminated or not . . .' (*Life*, i. 266).

[4] Samuel Buckley had published the Whiggish *Daily Courant* since 1702 and had been Gazetteer since Sept. 1714 (Laurence Hanson, *Government and the Press*, 1936, p. 91). Buckley and Defoe now co-operated in a common cause, but in earlier days they had often denounced one another. See, for instances, the *Review* for 22 July 1704, and Dunton, *Life and Errors*, 1818, ii. 434–5.   [5] i.e. recompense.

[6] Early in Dec. 1716. He was succeeded by Stanhope, who held the office for four months.

[7] Charles Spencer (1674–1722), third Earl of Sunderland, had become Northern Secretary on 15 Apr. 1717. Defoe had corresponded with Sunderland in the days of the Godolphin Ministry (Nos. 129 and 130), and when Sunderland was dismissed from the Ministry in 1710, Defoe had celebrated him in three consecutive issues of the *Review* (17, 20, and 22 June).

agoe been Obliged when I was in a Secret Commission Sent to scotland,[1] was pleased to approve and Continue this Service, and the Appointmt Annexed; And with his Ldpps Approbation, I Introduced my Self in the Disguise of a Translator of the Forreign News to be So farr Concernd in This Weekly Paper of *Mists*,[2] as to be able to keep it within the Circle of a Secret Mannagement, also, prevent the Mischievous Part of it, and yet Neither Mist or any of those Concernd with him have the least Guess or Suspicion By whose Direction I do it.

But here it becomes Necessary to Accquaint My Lord (as I hinted to you Sir) That This paper called the journall is not in My Self in Property, as the Other;[3] Onely in Mannagemt; with this Express Difference, that if any thing happens to be put in without my knowlege, which may Give Offence; Or if any thing slips my Observation which may be ill Taken; His Ldpp shall be Sure allways to kno', whether he has a Servant to Reprove, or a stranger to Correct.

Upon the whole However, this is the Consequence, that by this Mannagemt The Weekly Journall and Dormers Letter as Also the Mercurius Politicus, which is in the Same Nature of Mannagemt as The journall, Will be allways kept (mistakes Excepted) To Pass as Tory Papers, and yet be Dissabled and Ennervated, So as to do no Mischief or give any Offence to the Governmt.

[1] In 1708 (Nos. 129 and 130).

[2] The *Weekly Journal, or Saturday's Post* first appeared on 15 Dec. 1716, and under the proprietorship of Nathaniel Mist (d. 1737) 'soon gained repute as the most popular weekly of the opposition' (Laurence Hanson, *Government and the Press*, 1936, pp. 102–3). Defoe probably joined the paper as a translator in Aug. 1717, and by December was contributing articles to it. He succeeded for a while in moderating the Toryism of the *Journal*—one reader complained that the paper was turning Whig—but by the autumn of 1718, Mist was out of Defoe's control and De la Faye complained that the *Journal* was doing 'more mischief than any other libel being wrote *ad captum* of the common people' (Hanson, op. cit., pp. 104–5). In Oct. 1718 Mist was seized and examined by De la Faye; in November he was summoned before both Secretaries of State; and in December the Middlesex grand jury found the *Journal* a 'false, seditious, scandalous, and profane libel'. At about this point Defoe withdrew from the paper, but he returned in Jan. 1719, perhaps upon Mist's promise to maintain a more moderate tone. By June 1720, however, Mist had again overstepped the bounds, and in December he was sentenced to be pilloried, fined, and imprisoned. Defoe again withdrew from the paper, but urged clemency for Mist, visited him in prison, and helped him, during his confinement, to prepare an edition of letters selected from the *Journal*. At about the end of 1724, the relationship between Defoe and Mist came to an end in a violent quarrel, during which, it is said, they drew swords and Defoe wounded his adversary. See Lee, *Life*, i. 273; Hanson, op. cit., pp. 102–5; and G. A. Aitken, 'Defoe and Mist's "Weekly Journal"', *The Athenaeum*, 26 Aug. 1893, pp. 287–8.

[3] Dormer's *News-letter*.

I Beg leav to Observ Sir one Thing More to his Ldpp in my Own behalf, And without which Indeed I May one Time Or other Run the hazard of fatall Missconstructions: I am Sir for This Service, Posted among Papists, Jacobites, and Enraged High Torys, a Generation who I Profess My Very Soul abhorrs; I am Oblig'd to hear Trayterous Expressions, and Outrageous Words against his Majties Person, and Governmt, and his Most faithfull Servants; and Smile at it all as if I Approv'd it; I am Oblig'd to take all the Scandalous and Indeed Villainous papers that Come, and keep them by Me as if I Would gather Materialls from Them to Put them into the News; Nay I often Venture to Let things pass which are a little shocking that I may not Render my Self Suspected.

Thus I bow in The House of *Rimmon*; and must Humbly Recommend my Self to his Lordpps Protection, or I may be Undone the Sooner, by how much the more faithfully I Execute The Commands I am Under.

I forbear to Enlarge. I beg you Sir to Represent these Circumstances to his Ldpp in Behalf of a faithfull Servant That Shall allways Endeavour to approve his fidellity by actions Rather Than Words.

I am, Sir, Your Most Humble Servt

DE FOE

Newington, Aprll 26. 1718

P.S. I Send you here One of the Letters stopt at the Press as I Mention'd to you. As to the Manuscript of Sultan Galga, another Villainous Paper, I Sent the Coppy to my Ld Sunderland; if the Originall be of any Service it is Ready at your first orders.[1]

MS.: P.R.O., S.P. 35/11/124. *Pub.*: *The London Review of Politics, Society, Literature, Art, and Science*, 4 June 1864, p. 591. *Address*: none.

235. [*To* CHARLES DE LA FAYE]. *10 May 1718*

Sir

I am Extreamly Concern'd That the Journall of this day has Coppyed from the Post boy That Ridiculous Paragraph of The Pretenders being in the List of The Queen Dowagers Legitimate Children, and I have spoken my Mind Very Freely to him of it.[2]

---

[1] Cf. No. 233.

[2] In reporting the death on 26 Apr. of Mary of Modena, widow of James II, Mist's *Journal* had named as her fifth child 'James Francis-Edward, born at St. James's the 10th of June, 1688, the Person who is now stiled the Pretender.' The

But Sir I think in Consequence of what I wrote last to you, it is my Duty to assure My Ld That I have no Part in this slip, but that Mr Mist did it after I had lookt Over what he had Gotten Together, which it Seems was not Sufficient; and Tho' I Would If I may Presume So far Intercede for him, yet My Ld May be assured I have no Concern in it Directly or Indirectly; This Sir I Say I thot my Self oblig'd to Notice to you, to make good what I Said in my Last (Viz) that if any mistake happend my Ld should allwayes kno' whether he had a Servant to Reprove, or a stranger to Punish.

I am, Sir, Your Most Humble Servt
D E F O E

May. 10. 1718

P S He has Renew'd his Promise to me that he will be more wary, and I do think Verily it was not done Malitiously, But that I leave as I find it.

MS.: P.R.O., S.P. 35/12/13. *Pub.*: *The London Review of Politics, Society, Literature, Art, and Science*, 4 June 1864, p. 591. *Address*: none.

236. [*To* CHARLES DE LA FAYE]. *23 May 1718*

Sir

When I had the Favour of Seeing you last, you were pleased to Mention to me My Perticular Concern, and That you would intrest your Self in That Part for me; The Exceeding kindness of that Offer Sir Encourages me to give you This Trouble and to Observe to you That the half year Expired The 17th Instt.[1]

I Need Say no More but to Ask you Pardon for this Freedome

inclusion of the Pretender's name was an implicit denial of the old story of his supposititious birth, a story which Defoe and many Whigs, however, had once considered to be unimportant because irrelevant. 'I have nothing to say here to his Legitimacy of Birth, I always thought that to be a Dispute we have no manner of Concern in, I take it to be no Damage to our Establishment, that he be taken for the true Son of King *James*, nor did I ever lay any stress upon the Thing call'd his Legitimacy; indeed, I think, we are no way Concern'd about it; and so I have said always, my Reason lies here. *It is the Undoubted Right of the Parliament of Great Britain, to Limit the Succession of the Crown*' (*Review*, 16 Sept. 1712). That the Pretender's legitimacy should now have become a question of high moment is perhaps evidence of the new fears and tensions generated by the Jacobite uprising of 1715.

[1] On the previous 13 Dec. Defoe had given Sunderland a receipt for £25 received from Samuel Buckley, 'being to 17 Nov. last' (*H.M.C. Eighth Report*, p. 27). From Mist, Defoe received at first 20 shillings per week. His salary was increased to 40 shillings, apparently in the autumn of 1718 (G. A. Aitken, 'Defoe and Mist's "Weekly Journal" ', *The Athenueum*, 26 Aug. 1893, p. 288).

and Leave the Rest to your Own Time and Methods, and shall attend at what Time you please to Appoint.

I hope I have kept the Difficult people I have to do with within the bounds of Duty, and am in hopes to Draw them Gradually into yet Narrower Limits of Respect; It is a hard Matter to please the Tory Party as their present Temper Operates, without abuseing not Onely The Government but the Persons of Our Governours in Every thing they Write, But to the best of my skill I Cause all letters and Paragraphs which look that Way to be intercepted and stop't at the press.

I am a Little Allarm'd at a prosecution against Morphew in the kings Bench Court for a passage in The Mercurius Politicus, which began in a Private Person Sueing Morphew on Pretence of Damages on a Paragraph printed from another printed paper of a Person Hang'd at York for Three half pence. But it Seems the Court Resenting a line or Two in it as a Reflection on the Judges have Made it a public Cause and have Committed Morphew till sentence, which it is Fear'd will be severe.[1]

But Sir I think my Self oblig'd to Lay before my Ld stanhope the following perticulars in Case they should Offer to Concern me in it; first That it is Two year or More Since this was done, and Consequently before the Capitulation made in My Ld Townshends time when all former Mistakes of Mine We[re][2] forgiven,[3] Secondly, That The Thing it Self was not Myne, neither can any One Pretend to Charge it o[n] me, otherwise than It might be Said I Saw or Overlookt the book, nor indeed can they prove So Much as tha[t,] So that I can in No Wise be Said to have faild in my Duty on account of this Latent affair, which indeed Seems to me to be but Triffling in it Self.

I have an Entire Dependence on my Lds Justice and Goodness That no Offence formerly Committed (were this Really So) Shall be Remembred to my Prejudice; However I thought it my Duty to give his Ldpp this Account, That my Enemyes

---

[1] *Mercurius Politicus* for Sept. 1716 reported the case of Thomas Barron and Edward Bourn, who had been hanged at York for 'demanding' three half-pence from 'one Mr. King and one Jackson a Printer, on the road to *Clifton* near *York*'. The article went on to say that 'they were greatly lamented by the Country, and especially upon the publishing their Case afterwards; the simplicity and downright way of expressing themselves, causing People universally to think they were not Guilty of the Fact', and concluded that 'Three Half-pence is a very small Sum to be hang'd for, and he must be a very hard-mouthed Fellow that swore it a Robbery.'

[2] MS. torn, affecting this and two words below.

[3] The 'capitulation' took place therefore between Sept. 1716 (when the offending article appeared) and Dec. 1716 (when Townshend left office).

may not Anticipate me by giveing Wrong and injurious Accounts of it before me.

I am, Sir, Your Most Humble Servt
D E F O E

May. 23. 1718

N.B. The words as I hear them which the Judges take offence at are in the Introduceing the story of the Fellow that was Excecuted Saying, *it was a peice of Justice Unmix'd with Mercy.*[1]

MS.: P.R.O., S.P. 35/12/29. *Pub.*: *The London Review of Politics, Society, Literature, Art, and Science*, 11 June 1864, p. 618. *Address*: none.

---

237. [*To* CHARLES DE LA FAYE]. *4 June 1718*

Sir

Since Our last Conference I have Entred into a New Treaty with Mr Mist. I need not Trouble you with the Perticulars But in a Word he Professes himself Convinc't that he has been Wrong, that the Governmt has Treated him with Lenety and Forbearance, and he Sollemnly Engages to me to give no more offence.[2]

The Libertys Mr Buckley[3] Mentioned (Viz) to Seem on the Same Side as before, *to Rally the Flying Post*,[4] the Whig writers, and even the Word Whig &c., and to admit foolish and Triffling things in Favour of the Tories, This as I Represented it to him he Agrees is liberty Enough and Resolves his Paper shall For the Future Amuse the Tories But not affront the Governmt.

I have Freely Told him That this is the Onely Way to preserv his paper, to keep himself from a Jail, and to Secure The Advantages which Now Rise to him From it, for that he might be assured the Complaint against him Was So Generall that the Governmt could bear it No longer.

I Said Sir all that Could be Said on that head, Onely

---

[1] The article opens: 'We begin with the Affairs at *York*, where an Example of Justice, unmix'd with Mercy was shewn, as the like has not happen'd in our Memory, or scarce in History . . . .'

[2] Mist had been in trouble with the Government on three different occasions in the previous year, in April, May, and December, but in each instance he had escaped without penalty.

[3] See p. 452, n. 4.

[4] Probably someone other than Defoe underscored this passage, opposite which appears the marginal comment, 'not true'.

Reserving the Secret of who I spoke from,[1] and Concluded that Unless he Would keep Measures with me and be Punctuall in these things, I Could not Serve him any farther Or be Concern'd any More.

Thus far Sir I have acted I hope in a Right Method, in Persuance of which, in his Next paper he is to make a kind of a Declaration in Answer to Two letters printed in his Last, wherein he shall Publish his Resolution Not to Meddle with or write any thing Offensiv to the Governmt.[2]

In Prosecution also of this Reformation he Brought me this Morning the Enclosed Letter,[3] which Indeed I was glad to See, because Tho' it Seems Couch'd in Terms which might have been made publick, yet has a Secret Gall in it, and a Manifest Tendency to Reproach the Governmt with Partiallity and Injustice, and (as it acknowleges Expressly) Was Written to Serv a Present Turn; As This is an Earnest of his just Intention, I hope he will Go on to your Satisfaction.

Give me Leave Sir to Mention here a Circumstance which Concerns my Self and which Indeed is a little hardship upon me (Viz) That I Seem to Merit less when I Intercept a peice of Barefac'd flagrant Treason at the Press than when I stop Such a letter as this Enclosed, Because One Seems to be of a kind which no Man Would Dare to Meddle with. But I Would Perswade my Self Sir that stopping Such Notorious things is not without its good Effect, perticularly because as it is True that Some people are generally found who do Venture to print anything that offers; So stopping them here is Some Discouragemt and Dissappointmt to them, and they often Dye in our hands.

I speak this Sir as Well on Occasion of what you Were pleas'd to Say upon that letter which I Sent you formerly about Killing No Murther[4] as upon Another with Verses in it which Mr Mist Gave me yesterday, which Upon my Word is So Villainous and scandalous that I scarce Dare to Send it without

---

[1] That Defoe was writing for Mist's and other Tory publications was well enough known at the time. But that he was engaged to do so by the Whig Ministry was a secret so well kept that it did not become public knowledge until five of his letters to De la Faye were published by the *London Review* in 1864.

[2] The issue for 7 June begins with an article in which the *Journal* declares its loyalty to the King and Government, its disavowal of Jacobitism, and its intention 'to be more watchful hereafter than perhaps we have been, of giving our Enemies any Advantage against us for Words capable of their ill natur'd Constructions'.

[3] Missing.

[4] Perhaps written by 'Paul Fogg'. See Lee, *Life*, ii. 28.

your Order and an assurance That my doeing So Shall be Taken Well. For I confess it has a Peculiar Insolence in it against his Majties Person which (as Blasphemous Words against God) are scarce fit to be repeated.

I am the More Concern'd you should know this also because if I Guess Right, and Mr Mist is of that Opinion too, it is the Same hand that the Manuscript which I shewed Mr Buckley of Sultan Galga[1] Was Writen in, and I Suppose Comes From the Same Quarter.

If you please to ordr my Sending it I shall Obey, and in the Mean time assure you No Eye Shall See it.

Here has been a Very Barbarous attempt made by Curl the Bookseller upon Mr Mist (Viz) to Trepann him into Words Against the Governmt with a Design to Inform against him;[2] I think Mist has Escaped him but if he brings it into your office I shall Lay a Clear state of the Matter before you. I kno' the Government is Sufficient to it self for punishing Offendors, and is Above Employing Trepanns to Draw men into offences On Purpose to Resent them.

I am, Sir, Your Most Humble and Obedt Servt
DE FOE

Newington June. 4th 1718

MS.: P.R.O., S.P. 35/12/38. *Pub.*: *The London Review of Politics, Society, Literature, Art, and Science*, 11 June 1864, p. 618. *Address*: none.

[1] See p. 454.
[2] Edmund Curll (1675?–1747), the 'unspeakable' bookseller, was notorious for the unscrupulousness of his methods and the pornography of some of his publications. Curll had been the subject of a merciless 'letter', printed in Mist's *Journal* for 5 Apr., which called upon the authorities to suppress 'Curlicism'. The attack was signed 'your Friend H', but was probably the work of Defoe. 'The Fellow', ran part of the account, 'is a contemptible Wretch a thousand Ways; he is odious in his Person, scandalous in his Fame, he is mark'd by Nature, for he has a bawdy Countenance, and a debauch'd Mein, his Tongue is an Ecchoe of all the beastly Language his Shop is fill'd with, and Filthiness drivels in the very Tone of his Voice'. Curll lashed back at Mist in a pamphlet entitled *Curlicism Display'd*, published on 31 May, in which he defended his own activities, sneered at Mist's 'super-annuated Letter-Writer', alluringly advertised the very kind of publication complained of, and intimated that Mist himself, in Curll's presence, had publicly revealed his disloyalty to the Government. Defoe here seeks to discredit Curll's grave charge, which had appeared in print only five days before, and which probably frightened Mist into his present good resolutions. Curll was publisher of at least two works attributed to Defoe's pen: *Memoirs of the Life and Eminent Conduct of That Learned and Reverend Divine, Daniel Williams* in Feb. 1718; and *The History of the Life and Adventures of Mr Duncan Campbell* in Apr. 1720. See Ralph Straus, *The Unspeakable Curll*, 1928, pp. 79–82, 250, and 261.

459

238. *[To* CHARLES DE LA FAYE]. *13 June 1718*

Sir

I gave you the Trouble of a Letter a few days agoe. The account I Gave you There of the Conditions I had Engag'd Mr M. . .t to Will I hope be Satisfactory and Perticularly in his Performance of those Conditions.

I Suppose you Will Remember I Hinted when I had last the favour of Waiting on you that there was a Book Printing at his house Scandalously Reflecting on My Ld Sund. . . and that M. . . . was willing as a Testimoney of his Sincerity to Consent to a method how to put it into his Ldpps hands.

I have gotten the sheets into my hands in Performance of this Promise, and Would Gladly Reciev your Commands about them.

I believ the Time is Come when the Journall instead of affronting and Offending the Governmt may many ways be made Serviceable to the Governmt, and I have Mr M. . . So absolutely Resign'd to proper Measures for it That I am perswaded I may answer for it.[1]

I am, Sir, Your Most Humble and Obedt Servant

DE FOE

June. 13. 1718

MS.: P.R.O., S.P. 35/12/47. *Pub.*: *The London Review of Politics, Society, Literature, Art, and Science*, 11 June 1864, p. 618. *Address*: none.

239. *To* CHARLES DE LA FAYE. *7 June 1720*

Sir

If I was not Very ill and in no Condition to Come abroad I should have waited on you imediately, and I acknowlege with all possible Thankfullness your Kindness in Sending in So Obligeing a Manner.

The Small share I had in Mr Mists journall[2] at That Time

[1] But Mist disappointed Defoe's expectations. See p. 453, n. 2.

[2] On 2 June the Bishop of Gloucester had complained in the House of Lords that several issues of Mist's *Journal* had reflected against the conduct of the Protestants of the Palatinate and had criticized the efforts of the Protestant powers to interpose in their favour. Upon hearing the paragraphs read, the Lords resolved to address the King 'that His Majesty will be pleased to direct a Prosecution of the Author, Printer, and publisher, of the said Papers' (*J.H.L.* xxi. 344). As a result, Mist was now under examination. He was prosecuted, convicted, and in the following February sentenced to stand twice in the pillory, pay a fine of £50, spend three months in prison, and give security for his good behaviour for seven years (William Lee, 'Daniel Defoe the Newswriter', *Notes and Queries*, 3 S, vii [1865], 343). Defoe seems to have escaped prosecution.

gives him no ground to Say I had the Direction of it, Nor indeed did I Some times See what was or was not Put in, There being Severall people Employ'd by him at The Same time who I had no knowlege of.

I am Very Well assur'd I had no Concern in the Paragraph in question,[1] and he can not Lay it justly to my Charge unless he has my Coppie to produce:[2] It is indeed hard to be Certain at This distance of Time, But I hope I shall be Treated with Clemency as Well as justice in a Case where my whole study was to keep things Out of the paper which might give Offence, and Especially after I had by Inadvertancy given Offence before,[3] as you kno' Sir, for which I am a Sincere Penitent and a Great Sufferer, and after which I Endeavod by all ways possible to be Servisable in The paper.

If my attendance be absolutely necessary, which I hope it may not, I Will not fail to Wait on you in a Few dayes if I am able to Come Abroad.

　　　　I am, Sir, Your Most Humble And Obedient Servt
　　　　　　　　　　　　　　　　　　　DE FOE
June. 7. 1720

MS.: Historical Society of Pennsylvania, Philadelphia. *Pub.*: George A. Aitken, 'Defoe and Mist's "Weekly Journal"', *The Athenaeum*, 26 Aug. 1893, p. 288. *Address*: 'To Cha: De la faye Esqr., Present.' *Endorsed*: 'De Foe.'

240. *To* HENRY BAKER.[4] *23 August 1728*

I cannot but say I am concerned on many Accounts, to see an Affair of this Nature hang thus in Suspence; and you will

[1] The particular paragraphs cannot be identified. The bishop had cited excerpts from the *Journal* for 2 Jan. and 2, 9, and 16 Apr. Boyer reprinted the latter three, and added similar matter from five more issues that the bishop apparently overlooked (*Political State*, June 1720, xix. 632–40).

[2] But according to Mist's statement to the Secretaries of State, given in Nov. 1718, Defoe habitually destroyed his copy, so that 'it should not be known who was the author' (G. A. Aitken, 'Defoe and Mist's "Weekly Journal" ', *The Athenaeum*, 26 Aug. 1893, p. 287).

[3] On 25 Oct. 1718 a letter opposing the war with Spain had appeared in the *Journal* over the signature of 'Sir Andrew Politick'. The Government took offence, and on 1 Nov. Mist was examined by Stanhope and Craggs, and Thomas Warner, bookseller, was examined by Stanhope and De la Faye. Both Mist and Warner testified that the offending letter was written by Defoe. In any case, whether he wrote it or merely allowed it to pass, he had embarrassed the Ministry. That lapse is possibly the 'inadvertancy' here mentioned. See G. A. Aitken, op. cit., p. 289.

[4] In the previous year, Defoe had given his consent to the betrothal of Sophia, his youngest daughter, to Henry Baker of Enfield. But almost immediately thereafter the two men began what became a tedious and unprofitable debate over the marriage settlement. Defoe maintained that he was at this time unable to furnish a dowry, but that he would provide for one in his will. Baker declined to accept

not take it ill that I add, It is more than I expected, and that it is highly reasonable it should be brought to an Issue.

As I said to you at first, that if you design'd to ask my Daughter, you must take her as I could give her, so I think it is far from being out of the Way to repeat it: adding with it that I also think I have endeavoured to shew the Respect I profess'd for you, by making as good proposals as my affairs will admit.

The first Proposal you have rejected, and also a second;[1] You and I will no more debate the Reasons of it, because whether I think it fair or kind or otherwise, Yet as I resolve to take nothing ill from You, so I choose to say no more of it, I think my Offer was fully consistent with my first proposal as it is with my Ability.

You have since plac'd the Affair in another Situation demand-

this proposal, and refused to go through with the marriage until the dowry should be better assured. At the end of almost two years of haggling, during which Defoe and Baker increasingly exasperated each other, the distracted Sophia suffered a breakdown. Thereupon the two men quickly reached a compromise, and the marriage was celebrated on 30 Apr. 1729. See Wright, *Life* (1894), 355–63 and 369–70; and G. R. Potter, 'Henry Baker, F.R.S. (1698–1774)', *Modern Philology*, xxix (1932), 308–17. Baker, who had served an apprenticeship to a bookseller and had published three volumes of verse, was now living at Enfield with the family of a relative, John Forster, three of whose deaf-and-dumb children Baker taught to overcome their handicap. He never divulged his method, but he developed it so successfully and practised it so widely that by the end of his life he was comfortably well off. In Oct. 1728 he founded the *Universal Spectator and Weekly Journal*, for which Defoe, in spite of their dispute over the dowry, wrote the first number. Of Baker's writings, which cover a variety of interests, the best known is *The Microscope Made Easy*, 1743. In 1740 he became a Fellow of both the Society of Antiquaries and the Royal Society, and in 1754 he helped to found the Society of Arts. See John Nichols, *Literary Anecdotes of the Eighteenth Century*, 1812–16, v. 272–8. The story of Baker's courtship of Sophia Defoe is told in his 'Autobiographical Memoranda', a brief manuscript preserved in the Forster Collection of the Victoria and Albert Museum and published by G. R. Potter in the article cited above.

[1] Defoe had once hoped to give Sophia a cash dowry. According to Baker's account, Defoe had said: 'I cannot pretend to give her a Portion equal to Mr. B——'s Merit, but he shall not take her like a Charity Girl with Nothing, I hope she will bring him at least [eradicated in MS.] Pounds, which added to as much of his, if properly secured will be some Provision for her and her Children (if God sends them) in Case of Accident. I wish I could promise more, but what she wants in Money I hope she will make up in Goodness' (Potter, op. cit., pp. 313–14). In that expectation, Baker had pressed his courtship, and having won Sophia's consent to the marriage 'he took the first occasion to inform Mr. D—— how happy he thought himself in the Affection of his fair Daughter, and requested him to order proper Settlements to be drawn up in the Manner he had proposed. His Answer was, that formal Articles he thought unnecessary: that he could confide in the Honour of Mr. B——: that when they talked before he did not know the true State of his own Affairs: that on due Consideration he found he could not part with any Money in present, but at his Death his Daughter Sophy's Share would be more than he had promised.—This was a cutting Disappointment' (Potter, op. cit., p. 315). This is perhaps what Defoe here refers to as his 'first Proposal'. What his second one was cannot now be reconstructed.

ing [   ]¹ down, which I said I would consider of. Many intervening Accidents have made the Time much longer than I intended to take in giving my Answer. I have now drawn it up and sent it herewith to my Daughter, to show you: I have only to add, that as this is my *Ultimatum,* not that I shall but that I can make an Offer of, I intreat, that you will consider of it so effectually, that your answer may put an end to the whole affair, one way or other; which I think highly necessary, as well for yourself, who have much trouble in it, as for my child, who I am too heartily concerned for to think it proper to leave it longer in Suspence.

I am (and shall be which way soever this matter may issue) always

Your sincere Friend and Servant

London, August 23rd, 1728

[Enclosure]

Mr. B—r's last Demand as of [   ]² down, and my Return is thus—

My Affairs do not permit me to advance the money presently, but I offer this as Equivalent.

1. That I will pay [   ]² at a certain Term, or sooner if it may be.

2. That till it be paid I will pay the Interest annually at £4 per cent., which is the ordinary Interest of Money.

3. That in Case of Mortality, Hannah will oblige herself to pay the [   ]² out of the Essex Estate,³ which shall be legally vested in her to enable her to perform it, and to come immediately upon my Decease into her Hands.

This I take to be paying the Money down, seeing Mr. B—r does not pretend to want the Money otherwise than to put it out to Interest.

August 23rd, 1728

MS.: untraced. *Pub.*: Wright, *Life* (1894), pp. 399–400. *Address*: none recorded.

¹ 'Word or sum scratched out' (Wright's note).
² 'Scratched out' (Wright's note).
³ Defoe held a 99-year lease on Kingswood Heath, an estate worth about £300 per annum, in the parish of St. Michael, Mile End, Colchester. He had acquired the lease for the benefit of his daughter Hannah. See J. R. Sutherland, 'A Note on the Last Years of Defoe', *Modern Language Review*, xxix (1934), 140; and Wright, *Life* (1894), pp. 297–8.

241. *To* HENRY BAKER. *27 August 1728*

Sir

I am Sorry there Should be any Manner of Room for an Objection when We are So Near a Conclusion of an Affair like This. I should be Very Uneasie when I give you a Gift I So much Value (and I hope I do not Over Rate her Neither) There Should be any Reserv among us, that Should leav the least Room for Unkindness, or So much as thinking of Unkindness, no not so Much as of the Word.

But there is a Family Reason why I am Tyed down to the Words of Four per Cent, and I can not Think Mr Baker Should Dispute So small a Matter with me, after I Tell him So (Viz) that I am So Tyed Down; I can I believ many Wayes make him up the Little Summ of Five pound a year,[1] and when I Tell you Thus under my hand, that I shall Think my Self Obligd to do it *Durante Vita*, I shall add that, I shall Think my Self more Obligd to do So, than if you had it Under Hand and Seal.

But if you are not Willing to Trust me on my Parole, for So Small a [summ],[2] and that According To the Great Treatys abroad, there must be a [secr]et Article in Our Negotiation; I Say if it must be So, I Would fain put my Self in a Condition to Deny you Nothing, which you can ask, believing you Will ask nothing of me which I ought to Denye.

When you Speak of a childs Fortune, which I Own you do Very Modestly, you Must give me leave to Say Onely this, you must accept of this in Bar of any Claim from the City Customes;[3] and I doubt you will have but Too much Reason, Seeing I can hardly hope to do Equally for all the Rest, as I shall for my Dear *Sophie*: But after that, you shall Onely allow me to Say, and that you shall Depend upon, what Ever it shall please God to bless me with, None Shall have a Deeper share in it, and you Need do no more Than Remember, That she is, Ever was, and Ever Will be My Dearest and Best Beloved: and let me add again I hope you will Take it for a Mark of my Singular and affectionate Concern for you, That I Thus giv her you, and

---

[1] The dowry, upon which Defoe offered 4 per cent. interest until paid, was probably to be £500. If so, this difference of £5 per year indicates that Baker was asking 5 per cent. interest. Wright omitted the words 'Five pound' from his transcript and explained that the sum was 'scratched out', a procedure for which the MS. offers no justification.

[2] A bleached spot affects the beginning of two lines of the MS.

[3] I cannot explain this passage.

That I Say too If I could giv her much More it should be to you, with the Same affection.

Yours Without Flattery

D F

Augt 27th 1728

MS.: Victoria and Albert Museum, Forster Collection, No. 142. *Pub.*: John Forster, *Oliver Cromwell, Daniel De Foe, Sir Richard Steele, Charles Churchill, Samuel Foote: Biographical Essays*, 3rd ed., 1860, pp. 153-4. *Address*: 'To Mr Baker, Present.'

242. *To* HENRY BAKER. *9 September 1728*

Sir

I am Very Sorry to Hear that Mr Forster[1] should Say I have not acted with Honour in this affair. I must ask your leav to think quite otherwise, and that I am not Well used atall.

From the begining I Said both to you and to Mr Forster that I Would not Mortgage the Triffle I have in Essex for the Security of this affair.[2] I did not speak ambiguously in it atall, but in Words at length and Explicit Such as Were Capable of no other Meaning, So as an Honest Man Ought allways to speak.

Mr Forster Concludes from Hence that It is allready Mortgagd, which is Something hard. I told him it was indeed at first Engagd for 200*l*, which is since paid off.[3]

But that I may more fully Explain it, If it must be So, the Case [is][4] this and nothing Elce Viz/that being arrivd to an age when if Ever it is Needfull to Settle what little I have among my Children, This is So Settled and So Engagd and no otherwise, and I can not think it a Breach of Honour that I do not think it proper to Expose, no not to my Own Children, all the Perticulars of my Family Settlement while I am still living, and as this is the Onely Reason, and that no Mortgage or other Engagemt is made on the Estate but this, and yet that this binds me not to make any other Disposition of it, I can not see how I act Dishonourably and I think ought not to be told so.

I am Sorry I am Obligd to Say this, but Since this is Truth,

---

[1] John Forster, attorney, of Enfield, with whom Baker made his home (p. 461, n. 4).
[2] See p. 463, n. 3.
[3] In order to buy the lease, Defoe in 1723 had mortgaged the Essex estate to Mary Newton for £200. He cleared the incumbrance on 13 Nov. 1727. See Wright, *Life* (1894), p. 298.
[4] MS. stained.

and that the Circumstances Oblige me to speak it, I hope you will Excuse my freedom. I shall still be with respect as before,

Your Humble Servt
DE FOE

Newington, Monday Sept. 9th 1728

MS.: Mrs. Margaret E. De Foe Latham, Woodhall Spa, Lincs. *Pub.*: Wright, *Life* (1894), pp. 400–1. *Address*: 'To Mr Henry Baker at Mr Forsters in Baker Street, Enfield.'

243. HENRY BAKER *to* DEFOE. *7 January* [*1728/29?*][1]

I can't help objecting to that part of your paper which provides that in case your daughter dies without issue her portion shall revert to your executors. Will you consent if I die childless that what I leave shall go among my relations. I know you won't. And is not your negative a good argument for my objection?

MS.: untraced. *Pub.*: Wright, *Life* (1894), p. 359. *Address*: none recorded.

244. *To* HENRY BAKER. *9 January* [*1728/9?*]

Sir,

I must acknowledge I am very Sorry we should break at last upon a Point so very nice and yet so important as This, and I am the more concerned because I think we have been both wrong in omitting a more early Debate about it.

After the Frankness with which I at first treated your proposal, and the Kindness with which I always treated you personally, I should be very sorry to offer anything now that should seem less kind than at first. Nor can I see the least room to have it thought so; but at the same time that I desire to be thought kind, you will not, I hope, offer anything that shall look like unkind.

The Thing proposed,[2] I confess, is in my Opinion consistent not with kindness only, but with Justice. And, indeed, Justice to the rest of my little Family commands it from Me: It is a little hard to put a Father to express himself upon it, but at the same time that You argue your Case as an Husband, with what Horror (excuse the Word) must I suppose the case before I can

---

[1] In transcribing this letter, Wright, who presumably saw the MS., says 'This was on Jan. 7th, 1728.' But since Wright seems to have recorded his dates just as he found them, without adjusting them to modern reckoning, I take the letter to belong to 1728–9.

[2] i.e. that if Sophia should die childless, her portion should revert to Defoe's estate.

argue upon it as a Father. I must suppose My Child lost, dead, childless. Mr. Baker, who now I value and shall (before that) say I value and love, lost to me; the Relation sunk out of Nature and embarked perhaps in another Family, how can I look on the rest of my Children disinherited and impoverisht by the double Loss of their Sister and their Fortune! Make the Case your own if that be possible.

I can say no more! 'tis my Weakness: I would hope for long Life and a Family between you. God in his mercy grant it if you come together: but how can You (and I much less) enter upon the melancholy and mornful Negative and suppose me deprived doubly and made miserable, and yourself supported at the expence of the Family.

Besides what Necessity as well as what Justice to lay such a dead weight always on a Father's Thoughts ready to sink with but the mention of it.

If you live and encrease, the Thing is at an end; if not, the Occasion is at least lessened. I hope the odds is in your Favour: may it be to you and yours for ever; and if there is so apparent Hopes, why should you lay so much more weight on the melancholy part: I run the Risque Equally and indeed much more than you, for upon the whole you run no Risque at all. If you lose your Wife you have all your own with its encrease, and I can not call it a maintaining her in the mean time; if she will not more than merit her maintenance, She will be a worse Wife than I would wish Mr. Baker to have, and much worse than I hope she will make.

I am very sorry my Family circumstances make it needful to me to say this, but as it is nothing but what is consistent with my first offer, and with the Nature of the Thing customary in like Cases, and which I yielded to myself on the like occasion, I can not be chargeable with taking the least step aside, from what I proposed and what you had accepted.

I am, with the same kindness and sincerity as before,

Your Friend affectionately,

D. F.

Newington, January 9th, 1728[1]

P. S. Pray reflect on the risque on my Side if my Child should drop off in a year or two or less, as often happens. The very Thought afflicts me so I cannot go on writing upon it.

[1] Wright gives this date in the caption of his transcript. See p. 466, n. 1.

Suppose again you should be taken from her in a few Years before you had encreased sufficiently for the support of a Family which may be left: Where would that dead weight lye?

God avert these melancholy Things! but they are all possible.

MS.: untraced. *Pub.*: Wright, *Life* (1894), pp. 397–8. *Address*: none recorded.

245. *To* HENRY BAKER. *21 January* [*1728/9*?]

Sir

I believ you Will now be Convinc'd that What I Suggested in this affair Was Right Judg'd, Tho' as I Was not Sure, you might then think me Mistaken.

The Sending me to Sutton[1] to Mend a Title which I have not t[he least[2] re]ason to think Precarious has had the Effect I Expected [and has] put Vain Conciets in his head of his power, which however I Se no Weight in, yet puffs him up to Refuse, what I have Really no Occasion to ask, and you will See if you please to judge Impartially that I Was not Wrong when I Said it Was Harassing me and without Cause too.

However Nothing shall Move me to have any Disputes with Mr Baker, or to lessen my Respect for him, and for that reason, if my Circumstances allow me not to offer any thing that He thinks fit to accept, (I can Onely Say I am Sorry for it) and I shall make no Remarks upon it here.

If you please to let my Lease be Returnd Either to my

[1] Timothy Sutton was owner of the house occupied by Defoe and his family in Stoke Newington. Baker and Defoe were now nearing a settlement of their differences. 'At length however,' wrote Baker, 'after almost two years, Mr. D—— consented to engage his House at Newington as a Security, and Articles being accordingly executed, the Marriage was celebrated April 30th, 1729' (G. R. Potter, 'Henry Baker, F.R.S.', *Modern Philology*, xxix [1932], 316). But Defoe did not at this time own the basic lease on the property. He had bought the lease in 1727, but had immediately assigned it to George Virgoe, a London merchant, perhaps to protect himself from creditors (p. 474, n. 1). Baker had apparently questioned Defoe's rights in the property upon which the dowry was to be secured. At any rate Defoe repurchased the lease on 3 Apr. 1729, and two days later gave Baker a bond for £500 and engaged the lease as security. On 25 Apr., five days before the marriage, he gave Baker a 34½-year mortgage on the lease at a peppercorn rent, with the understanding that the mortgage was to be cancelled if he paid Baker £500 with interest at 5 per cent. Ten years after Defoe's death, Baker bought the house from Sutton. See A. W. Secord, 'Defoe in Stoke Newington', *PMLA*, lxvi (1951), 215–20.

[2] Defects in the MS. obscure the text at two points.

Daughter or to my Son in Finch Lane,¹ I shall leav your
Receipt with Either of them as you Shall Direct.

I am, Sir, Your Very Humble Servt
DE FOE
Jan. 21th 1728

MS.: Mrs. Margaret E. De Foe Latham, Woodhall Spa, Lincs. *Pub.*:
Wright, *Life* (1894), pp. 398–9. *Address*: 'To Mr Baker, Present.'

246. HENRY BAKER *to* DEFOE. [*21–25 January 1728/9?*]

I never suppos'd You could force Sutton, but presumed I
might without Offence desire your Endeavours towards another
Lease.

You have try'd it seems in vain: if then it can't be done, we
must make the best of Things without it. I never shall exact
Impossibilities; but indeed wonder'd at your unwillingness to
attempt it. But I [never?] intended it as the sine qua non.

To have the House is not my Wish, & if You please as yourself propos'd to secure the Yearly payments, I shall not only be
well contented, but be in the Sincerest Manner

Your most Obliged humble Servt

MS.: untraced; the text is taken from a draft scribbled upon the back of
the preceding letter, owned by Mrs. Margaret E. De Foe Latham, Woodhall
Spa, Lincs. *Pub.*: Wright, *Life* (1894), p. 399. *Address*: none.

247. *To* HENRY BAKER. [*25 January 1728/9?*]
Sir

I am Very much Surpris'd that Now you plainly see the
Difficultys which I foresaw Would Occur in this Affair have
happend accordingly, you Now Drop them as things which may
be let alone, after they had been Insisted upon before as Absolutely Necessary, and after [you]² have by this brought me into
a Labirinth, which I do not see [any] Way out of, and like Some
other people, Ventur'd to Raise a [Work] they can not help to
finish. Had you done it before, the thing had been [   ].

What you Expect [   ]³ I kno' not, or what after having
been so Handled you can desire me to do next, and Therefore

¹ The address is that of Daniel Defoe, junior (Bernard Drew, *The London
Assurance: a Second Chronicle*, 1949, p. 136).
² A large lacuna in the copy from which this text is derived accounts for the
several omissions, and suggests that a piece had been torn out of the original MS.
³ Illegible word.

must Desire you Will please to let the Lease be left with my [Son]¹ in Finch Lane, where I will also leav your Reciept for it: I am Sorry my poor Child has the Missfortune to have no better Treatment after So long being Exposed, But I hope God will Provide for her his Own Way.

I am, Sir, Your Frd and Humble Servt
DE FOE

Fryday Jan. 25th² 1728

MS.: untraced; the text is taken from a copy, apparently a tracing, owned by Mrs. Margaret E. De Foe Latham, Woodhall Spa, Lincs. *Pub.*: Wright, *Life* (1894), p. 361. *Address*: 'To Mr Baker.'

248. *To* HENRY BAKER. [*April 1729?*]

Sir

I have Perused the Writing and See nothing amiss in it, if you Think the Security against the Lost Writings is Sufficient: but I Thot Mr Curryer³ in whose Posession they were left, and by whom they are lost (or by persons Entrusted by him) should have given Something under his hand, Obliging him to Deliver up the Old Deed and Assignmt to be Cancelld, if it should Come to his hand; and should have Indemnifyed D F from all Claims or Pretensions which might hereafter be made by any person on the foot of those writings: nothing of which is Mentiond in this Deed.⁴

There is a Small Objection which Occurrs to me against a Clause in the Draught of the Marriage Contract which I perusd but Hastily and in Disorder that night on Account of our family being So Disscomposd.⁴ I Suppose 'tis not too late.

The paymt of the 200*l* is made to take place within a Month after my Decease, which is Sooner than it can be Supposed Excecutors can be in Readyness after such a Revolution in the family. Such things have usually Twelv months time allowed, and as my Effects will lye much abroad, I think it can not be

¹ In the MS. copy, this word is followed by a kind of superscripture, which casts doubt on the reading. But see p. 469, n. 1.
² An error in either the day of the week or the day of the month. In 1728–9, Jan. 25th fell on Saturday; in 1727–8, on Thursday.
³ Unidentified.
⁴ On 5 Apr. 1729 Defoe repurchased the basic lease on the house in Stoke Newington. The missing papers probably covered the transaction of 1727, at which time he had purchased the lease and assigned it to George Virgoe. See A. W. Secord, 'Defoe in Stoke Newington', *PMLA*, lxvi (1951), 216.
⁵ The discomposure was probably due to Sophia's illness. See Wright, *Life* (1894), p. 370.

Expected in less. This is a matter So Reasonble that I hope you can not Scruple the alterations.

I am, your Friend & Servt
D E F O E

Fryday night

MS.: Mrs. Margaret E. De Foe Latham, Woodhall Spa, Lincs. *Pub.*: Wright, *Life* (1894), p. 401. *Address*: 'To Mr Baker, Present.'

249. *To* Mrs. Sophia Defoe Baker. *9 June* [*1729*]

My Dearest Sophia

Allow me to begin with a Little Phylosophy. Where Affections are strongest they are allways most Sencible of a shock, and Unkindnesses (Nay tho' but Seeming Such) make the Deepest Impressions: Hence Cæsar Tho' of a Spirit Invincible Gave up to Death, when he felt a stroke From his Adopted Brutus, and Said no More But (et tuo quoque mi fili! Tue Brute!) What! and Thou too Brutus! My Son! Nay, Hence the Wise man Says, a Brother Offended is harder to be Won, than the Barrs of a Castle. Love is of So Nice a Nature, That like the heart, it faints with the least Touch. Where it is not So, it must be because Such kno' not how to Love.

If I have been more Sencibly Grievd at what I thot Unkind in my Sophi (Say it was Onely that I thot So), if I Took Fire more Than another Would have done, it Was because I Lov'd you More Than Ever any lovd, or will or can love you (he that has you Excepted). Had Deb,[1] The *Hasty*, the *Rash*, and So far *Weak*, Said Ten Times as much to me, it had Made no Impression atall: But From Sophi, Thee Sophi! whose Image Sits close to my affections, and who I Lov beyond the Power of Expressing: I acknowlege it Wounded my Very Soul; and my Weakness is So much the more, as that Affection is strong; So that I can as ill Express The Satisfaction I have from your Letter, as I could the grief of what I thot an Unkindness.[2]

Perhaps I do not write like a Father. But perhaps I do too, if it be Considred That Love is the Same, let the Relation be what it will; besides, as a father, I hope I may be allowed not to Love in a less Exalted and Sublime Manner, but a greater; and From thence I still Inferr, as my affection made my Grief the greater, So the Same Affection Doubles the Satisfaction I

[1] Unidentified. No member of Defoe's family was named Deborah, but 'Deb' may have been a nickname for one of the other daughters.
[2] What had caused the difference between Sophia and her father remains unknown.

have at my Dear Sophys Return: I Reciev your Letter my Dear, with a joy not to be Describ'd, but in the Deepest Silence, or Expressd but in Teares.

From Hence I Forbear to Enter upon the Subject of this Irruption, & shall Onely hint, That you mistake it; and be it That you mistake it, yet as on that Mistake you Are So Generous as to make this Reparation, I will believ you Would with the Same filial goodness have made The like *and* more, if you had been Sencible in what Tender part you gave the Wound.

But you have heald it. One Word can Wound where Love is Nice, and One Word can Heal where Sincerity Joyns the Affection; you have heald it at Once; and Since you do not yet See where the hurt Was, I choose to leav it Conceald, because what ever I had, I Would have you feel no grief.

I Would Say more, but hope I need not. Let this Tell you, I am Satisfyed, and Rejoyce That you Think your fathers Affection worth preserving; I am perswaded I shall Never giv you Room to Lessen your Value for it, humane Frailty Excepted: I shall Conclude Onely with letting you See, with what a Sincere heart I was acting when this happened, and how little I thought of Dissobliging you or Mr Forster:[1] and This I can not do better, than in Sending you the Letter (Unopend) which I had written to Mr Baker and had in my hand to giv you. Let this speak for me, and believ it to be the Very Meaning and Intent of my heart, and I am Sure you Will Continue your affection to your Father upon the Very Conviction of it.

All the Pennance I shall Enjoyn you on this whole affair, is that you Will give Mr Baker the Letter, let him kno' when I wrote it, and Desire him to Lend me a Kiss of Peace to his Sophi, and I'll pay it him in Kind.

My Dearest Sophi I am and Ever shall be
Your Most Affectionate Father

D F

(But Very much Tormented
With Pain Ever Since)

Newington Monday June 9th

Thank Mr Baker for his Enclosed paper about the Customs.[2]

MS.: Mrs. Margaret E. De Foe Latham, Woodhall Spa, Lincs. *Pub.*: Wright, *Life* (1894), pp. 371–2. *Address*: 'To my Daughter.'

[1] Probably John Forster of Enfield, with whom Henry Baker had made his home, and who had taken an interest in the negotiations concerning Sophia's dowry. [2] Cf. p. 464.

250. *To* JOHN WATTS.[1] *10 September 1729*

Sir

I am to ask your Pardon for keeping the Enclosed[2] so long, Mr Baker having told me your Resolution of taking it in hand and Working it off, But I have been Exceeding ill.

I have Revisd it again and Contracted it Very Much, and hope to bring it within the Bulk you Desire or as Near it as Possible.

But this and Some Needfull alterations will Oblige you to much Trouble in the first sheet, perhaps allmost as bad as Setting it over again, which Can not be avoided.

I will Endeavour to send the Rest of the Coppy So Well Corrected as to give you Very little Trouble.

I here Return the first sheet[3] and as much Coppy as Will make near 3 sheets more. You shall have all the remainder So as not to let you stand still atall.

> I am, Sir, Your Most Humble Servt
>
> DE FOE

Sept. 10. 1729

MS.: Bodleian, Montagu MS. d. 17, f. 76. *Pub.*: Wilson, *Life*, iii. 599. *Address*: 'To Mr J Watts, in Wild Court, Present.'

251. *To* HENRY BAKER. *12 August 1730*

Dear Mr Baker,

I have your very kind and affectionate Letter of the 1st: But not come to my hand till the 10th; where it had been delay'd I kno' not. As your kind Manner, and Kinder Thought, from which it flows, (for I take all you say to be as I always believed you to be, sincere and Nathaniel like, without Guile,) was a particular Satisfaction to me; so the stop of a Letter, however it happened, depriv'd me of that Cordial too many Days, considering how much I stood in need of it, to support a Mind

---

[1] John Watts (d. 1763), patron of the elder William Caslon and one-time employer of Benjamin Franklin, was proprietor of one of the largest printing houses in London (W. M. Sale, *Samuel Richardson: Master Printer*, Ithaca, New York, 1950, pp. 18–19 and 21).

[2] Missing, but it was the first proof-sheet of Defoe's *Compleat English Gentleman*. Watts seems to have printed no more than the one sheet, but why the project was abandoned is not now known. The unfinished manuscript remained in Defoe's family for a century and was eventually acquired by the British Museum (Add. MS. 32555). See K. D. Bülbring, ed. *The Compleat English Gentleman*, 1890, pp. ix–xxxii.

[3] A copy of this sheet, with corrections in a hand other than Defoe's, has been preserved with the manuscript of the book in the British Museum.

sinking under the Weight of Affliction too heavy for my Strength, and looking on myself as Abandon'd of every Comfort, every Friend, and every Relative, except such only as are able to give me no Assistance.[1]

I was sorry you should say at the Beginning of your Letter, you were debarred seeing me. Depend upon my Sincerity for this, I am far from debarring you. On the contrary, it would be a greater Comfort to me than any I now enjoy, that I could have your agreeable Visits with Safety, and could see both you and my dear Sophia, could it be without giving her the Grief of seeing her Father *in tenebris,* and under the Load of insupportable Sorrows. I am sorry I must open my Griefs so far as to tell her, it is not the Blow I recd from a wicked, perjur'd, and contemptible Enemy, that has broken in upon my Spirit; which as she well knows, has carryed me on thro' greater Disasters than these. But it has been the injustice, unkindness, and, I must say, inhuman dealings of my own Son,[2] which has both ruin'd my Family, and, in a Word, has broken my Heart; and as I am at this Time under a weight of very heavy Illness, which I think will be a Fever, I take this Occasion to vent my

[1] The aged Defoe was once more a fugitive, separated from family and friends, and writing from an undisclosed hiding place. Once more, the cause of his distress was a creditor. Although Defoe does not identify the 'wicked, perjur'd, and contemptible Enemy' who had caused his flight, his adversary was almost certainly Mary Brooke. Her claims, which Defoe maintained had long since been discharged, arose out of financial disasters that had struck Defoe 35 or 40 years earlier. About the year 1695, Defoe was obliged to make a composition with his creditors, among them Samuel Stancliffe. After Samuel's death, administration of his estate passed to his brother James (to whom No. 4 is addressed). In 1704 or thereabouts, Defoe was again compelled to compound with his creditors. This time he surrendered all his possessions to James Stancliffe, who was himself a creditor (both in his own right and as administrator of his brother's estate), but who as Defoe's trustee was to satisfy all creditors, including himself, out of Defoe's assets. Defoe maintained that these assets were sufficient, and that Stancliffe paid, or should have paid, all of Defoe's creditors who entered into the agreement. But Stancliffe died (date unrecorded) without rendering an account of his trusteeship, and though he may have satisfied the claims of himself and his brother's estate, he left no evidence to clear Defoe of these obligations. Samuel Brooke, weaver, took out administration to Stancliffe's estate, noted that Defoe appeared to be indebted to the estate for large sums, but according to Defoe accepted his explanation and agreed to discharge him. Then Brooke died, but his wife Mary, who took out administration of his estate, refused to believe that the old Stancliffe debts had ever been discharged, and she set out to recover them from Defoe.

In 1727 or thereabouts Mary Brooke opened proceedings against Defoe in the Courts of King's Bench and Exchequer. Defoe countered in 1728 and again in 1730 by filing Bills in Chancery. But his suit failed, and he apparently felt that his only protection from disaster lay in flight. See J. R. Sutherland, 'A Note on the Last Years of Defoe', *Modern Language Review,* xxix (1934), 137–40.

[2] Presumably Daniel Defoe, junior, to whom he had perhaps transferred his property to protect it from Mary Brooke (Sutherland, *Defoe,* p. 273).

Grief in the Breasts who I know will make a prudent use of it, and tell you, that nothing but this has conquered or could conquer me. *Et tu! Brute.* I depended upon him, I trusted him, I gave up my two dear unprovided Children[1] into his Hands; but he has no Compassion, but suffers them and their poor, dying Mother[2] to beg their Bread at his Door, and to crave, as if it were an Alms, what he is bound under Hand and Seal, besides the most sacred promises, to supply them with; himself, at the same Time, living in a profusion of Plenty. It is too much for me. Excuse my Infirmity, I can say no more; my Heart is too full. I only ask one Thing of you as a dying request. Stand by them when I am gone, and let them not be wrong'd, while he is able to do them right. Stand by them as a Brother; and if you have anything within you owing to my Memory, who have bestow'd on you the best Gift I had to give, let them not be injured and trampled on by false Pretences, and unnatural Reflections. I hope they will want no help but that of Comfort and Council; but that they will indeed want, being too easie to be manag'd by Words and Promises.

It adds to my Grief that it is so difficult to me to see you. I am at a distance from London in Kent; nor have I Lodging in London, nor have I been at that Place in the Old Bailey, since I wrote you I was removed from it. At present I am weak, having had some fits of a Fever that have left me low. But those Things much more.

I have not seen Son or Daughter, Wife or Child, many Weeks, and kno' not which Way to see them. They dare not come by Water, and by Land there is no Coach, and I kno' not what to do.

It is not possible for me to come to Enfield,[3] unless you could find a retired Lodging for me, where I might not be known, and might have the Comfort of seeing you both now and then; Upon such a circumstance, I could gladly give the days to Solitude, to have the Comfort of half an Hour now and then, with you both, for two or three Weeks. But just to come and look at you, and retire immediately, 'tis a Burden too heavy. The Parting will be a Price beyond the Enjoyment.

I would Say, (I hope) with Comfort, that 'tis yet well. I am so near my Journey's end, and am hastening to the Place

[1] Hannah and Henrietta, his unmarried daughters.
[2] Mrs. Defoe died in 1732.
[3] Where Baker resided.

where the Weary are at Rest, and where the Wicked cease to trouble; be it that the Passage is rough, and the Day stormy, by what Way soever He please to bring me to the End of it, I desire to finish Life with this temper of Soul in all Cases: *Te Deum Laudamus.*[1]

I congratulate you on the Occasion of your happy advance in your Employment. May all you do be prosperous, and all you meet with pleasant; and may you both escape the torments and troubles of uneasie Life. May you Sail the dangerous Voyage of Life with *a forcing Wind*, and make the Port of Heaven *without a Storm*.

It adds to my Grief that I must never see the pledge of your mutual Love, my little Grandson.[2] Give him my Blessing, and may he be to you both your Joy in Youth, and Your Comfort in Age, and never add a Sigh to your Sorrow. But, alas! that is not to be expected. Kiss my dear Sophy once more for me; and if I must see her no more, tell her this is from a Father that loved her above all his Comforts, to his last Breath.

Your unhappy,
D. F.

About two Miles from Greenwich, Kent,
Tuesday, Augst 12, 1730

P.S.   I wrote you a Letter some Months ago, in answer to one from you, about selling the House; but you never signified to me whether you received it. I have not the Policy of Assurance; I suppose my Wife, or Hannah, may have it.[3]

Idem.
D. F.

MS.: untraced. *Pub.*: Wilson, *Life*, iii. 605–8. *Address*: none recorded.

[1] Defoe died on 26 Apr. 1731.
[2] David Erskine Baker, born 30 Jan. 1730.
[3] An insurance policy of Defoe's is reported in Bernard Drew, *The London Assurance: a Second Chronicle*, 1949, p. 136.

INDEX

Italic numerals refer to the notes, both at the foot of the page and at the end of each letter.

to depart from facts, 41; and lying, 42; and management of Dissenters, 53–56; said to be in custody, 59; seeks Harley's protection, 59; denies offending Rooke, 60; stands for moderation and peace, 60, 102, 207, 271–2, *275*, 289, 291, 303, 444–5; at Cambridge, 58; at Bury St. Edmunds, 59; returns from journey, 63; his 'letters about the battail', 63; his conversation, 65; defends Harley, 67; advice to King William, 68; recommends Lord Somers, 69; and Occasional Conformity Bill (1704), *69*, 72; sends pamphlets all over England, 72; advises Lords on manning the Fleet, 73–77; and wages of seamen, 74–77; like the cripple at the pool, 81; willing to serve Lord Halifax, 81–83, 86; refused to betray King William, 82; agrees to write for Halifax, 82; receives money for his services, 86, 103, 127, 130, 141, 147 & n., 159, 170 & n., 247, 289 & n., 296, *312*, 334, 362, 373 & n., 442; a plain, unpolished man, 86; soured by afflictions, 86; honest, 87; to begin journey to the west, 88; his seven children, 89; answers *Memorial of the Church of England*, 90–91; sends pamphlets to Godolphin, 92; bribed Stephens, the Messenger, 92; begins western journey, 93; sends pamphlets to Halifax, 93; at Crediton, 94; and Capt. Turner of Guernsey, 97 & n.; shows Harley's pass, 99; Harley worried about, 99; conceals nature of work, 100; and Hugh Stafford, 101–2; said to owe £3,000, 106; lost £3,000 in 1703, 106; an expert guesser, 107; abstract of his 1705 journey, 108–13; honesty of, questioned by creditors, 114; reduces indebtedness from £17,000 to £5,000, 115; and Yarmouth creditors, 115; asks to be sent abroad, 120; persecuted for serving the Queen, 120, 274; asks for apartment in Whitehall, 121; his verses on Ramillies, 122 & n.; defends his honesty, 123; could not have prevented business failure, 123; had not 5 shillings, 123; creditors cost him £5,000, 123; may quit kingdom, 123; portrait of, published, 124 & n.; in bankruptcy, 124–5; prevents publication of anti-Union tract, 125 & n.; quotes Juvenal, 127 & n.; surrenders every-

thing to creditors, 127; buys equipment for journey, 127; leaves 'widow' and 7 children to Harley, 128; sets out for Scotland, 128; 9 days in the rain, 128–9; John Bell's estimate of, *130–2*; buys a horse, 131; threatened by Edinburgh mob, 134; in ill health, 134, 200, 371, *378*, 381, 408–9, 412, 422, 427, *441*, 460, 473–6; and the stage, 138–9; pretends he will settle in Scotland, 141 & n., 159; 'that vile monster and wretch', *142*; his mission in Scotland unsuspected, *142*, 143, 158 & n., 196–7; serves on Committee of Equivalents, 144; suggests rate of excise on ale, 145; requests troops on Border, 147, 150; solicited by Lord Halifax, 147; dares not visit Glasgow, 151–2; advises on customs duties, 154; sends Pierce to west, 163–4; conceals mission from Halifax, 167; asks draft of Harley's arms, 167–8; and the coronation oath, 173–5; sympathetic with Scottish clergy, 173–5, 176; and the abjuration oath, 174; dines with Cessnock, 176; death of his father, James Foe, 180; reports Pierce's visit to the west, 181 & n.; servant of, 183, 206; again sends Pierce to west, 183; changes lodgings for safety, 184; wishes to settle in Scotland, 188; ready to leave Scotland, 190–1; and Kirk Test for Englishmen, 192; pleads for Scottish clergy, 193–4; and James Webster, 195 & n., 196; defends Dissenters, 196; his methods of concealment, 196–7; his bankruptcy of 1706, 197 & n.; distressed for his family, 197; hopes to return home, 199; disturbed at Harley's illness, 199–200; has despised sleep, hours, and rules, 200; attacked by Webster, 201; will buy claret for Harley, 206–7, 211; again asks draft of Harley's arms, 208; his controversy with Webster, 209–10; called drunkard, swearer, and blasphemer, 210; and the Copyright Bill (1707), 212 & n.; his reputation hurt, 217; his letters tampered with, 219; family of, makes demands, 221; asked for government post, 224, 225 & n., 227; travelling and disputing, 226; mistakes date, *227*; Harley no longer to pay, 229; willing to go to north, 230; and threat to steal the Equivalent, 231; neglected by Harley, 231, 241–5; to confer with Sir John Cope, 235; declines government post, 236 & n.; counsels leniency for Scottish smugglers, 240; bred like a man, 241; enemies of, 241, 249, 253 & n.; risked life, 242; grown shabby, 242; reproaches Harley, 242; asks Godolphin for money, 243, 264; friends of, would help, 244–5; can hold out no longer, 245; to sit with Synod, 246; without subsistence for half a year, 246; at Gainsborough, 249; returns to London (1708), 249; and resignation of Harley, 250; employed by Godolphin, 254 & n.; presented to Queen, *254*; introduction to Lord Leven, *255*; visits Belhaven in prison, 255 & n., 256; at Edinburgh, 256; abhors anything clandestine, 260; and the *Paris Gazette*, 263; denounces Sacheverell to Stanhope, 256 & n., 257; denounces Cooper, 267–8; resumes correspondence with Harley, 270; regrets serving Harley's enemies, 273; cast upon Harley by Providence, 273; entirely void of ceremony, 274; maintains a correspondence network, 276; opposes Calamy, 285–6; grateful to the Queen, 287; suggests journey to the north, 287; 1705 journey a success, 288; to go to Scotland (1710), 289–90; arrives at Edinburgh, 291 & n.; separates from John Bell, 292; employs cipher in his letters, 293–5, 298, 301–2; his spectacles mended, 305; deludes Harley concerning *Atalantis Major*, 307 & n.; opposes toleration in Scotland, 308; recommends Commissioners to Church of Scotland, 313–15; willing to return to Scotland, 319–20; corresponds with Scottish clergy, 320; disturbed by Greenshields case, 317–20; and Guiscard's assault on Harley, 326–7; recommends Buchan, 314–15, 328; and printing the Bible in Scotland, 330 & n., 342 & n., 357–8; regrets loss of Harley's favour, 331; declines commissionership of customs, 331; chooses secret service instead of government office, 331; and the South Sea Company, 338–41, 343–9; proposes English colonies in South America, 343–9; confided South Seas plan to King William, 345; burned papers to thwart Nottingham, 345; proposes journey to north, 351, 354; prefers to see Harley secretly, 358; recommends Commander-in-Chief for Scotland, 359–60; signs receipt, 362; attacked by Ridpath, 362 & n.; and Occasional Conformity Act (1711), 363–5; and the Newcastle keelmen, 369; ready to lay down his pen, 370; may stop printing, 370; used badly by Whigs and Dissenters, 370; quotes Aesop, 374; and the 'restraining orders', 375 & n.; sends books to Harley, 376; and the Dutch, 376 & n., 377; criticizes Argyll, 378 & n.; declares Harley never influenced his writings, 379, 380 & n.; wishes to go to north, 380, 384; correspondent of, reports from Scotland, 382–3; enemy of religious coercion and enthusiasm, 384; visits Scotland (1712), 389; has lost Harley's favour, 392 & n., 393; suffers for Harley's sake, 393; accuses Ridpath, 395; seized for debt, 401, *402*; prosecuted for three pamphlets (1713), 405 & n., 406 & n., 407 & n., 409 & n., 410 & n., 411 & n., 412, 415, 418; thrice rescued from jail by Harley, 408 & n.; bail given for, 408 & n.; scheme to escape prosecution, 411 & n.; petitions for pardon, 415 & n.; and the Treaty of Commerce with France, 416–21, 423; ordered to plead, 422; writes *Letter to the Dissenters*, 424; and the Queen's pardon, 425 & n.; and death of Harley's daughter, 425 & n.; urges expulsion of Steele, 430 & n.; compiles 'Collection of Scandal' from Steele's writings, 433–8; and Dunton's *Neck or Nothing*, 438; protests against *Flying Post*, 438–9; and the Schism Bill, 440–1; at the end of Harley's political career, 443–5; and vindication of Harley, 444 & n.; and the second *Flying Post*, 446 & n.; in trouble for offending Anglesey, 446, 447 & n., 448 & n.; verses by, 449; in service of Stanhope, 450–1; sincerely attached to Whigs, 451; favoured by Sunderland, 452–3; and Mist's *Weekly Journal*, 453 & n.; bows in the house of Rimmon, 454; asks De la Faye for money, 455; to attend De la Faye, 456; admonishes Mist, 457–8, 460; denies writing offensive material, 460 & n., 461; his love for his daughter Sophia, 471–2, 476; sends corrected proofs to Watts, 473; dis-

494

PRINTED IN
GREAT BRITAIN
AT THE
UNIVERSITY PRESS
OXFORD
BY
CHARLES BATEY
PRINTER
TO THE
UNIVERSITY

SELECTED POEMS

OF

WILLIAM VAUGHN MOODY

Edited, with Introduction, by
ROBERT MORSS LOVETT

BOSTON AND NEW YORK
HOUGHTON MIFFLIN COMPANY
The Riverside Press
1931

𝕿𝖍𝖊 𝕽𝖎𝖛𝖊𝖗𝖘𝖎𝖉𝖊 𝕻𝖗𝖊𝖘𝖘
CAMBRIDGE · MASSACHUSETTS
PRINTED IN THE U.S.A.

PREFACE

THE present volume is a selection of the poems of William Vaughn Moody, as published in the two-volume edition of his work in 1912. In compiling it I have had the assistance of Mrs. Moody, and of his friends, Ferdinand Schevill, Ridgely Torrence, and Daniel Gregory Mason. My first intention was to exclude the poetic dramas, but these are so characteristic of Moody's mature style that a full comprehension of his career as poet is scarcely possible without them. I have therefore included the songs and lyric passages in the hope that some readers will be moved to turn to the works in their completeness.

In the Introduction I found it impossible to write of Moody except from my personal recollection of him. This I have supplemented by the memories of others, especially those mentioned above. I have drawn freely upon Professor John Matthews Manly's Introduction to the

two-volume edition, and upon that of
Daniel Gregory Mason's volume, *Some
Letters of William Vaughn Moody*. I have
also included in the Introduction, or in
the Notes, critical comments on Moody's
poetry from Professor Paul Shorey, William Morton Payne, and others, to show
the place accorded him by contemporary
critics. To all these my thanks are due;
and to Miss Elizabeth Greenebaum for
assistance on the text and notes. I am
especially indebted to Mrs. Julia Moody
Schmalz, of Mountain Lakes, New Jersey,
for facts in regard to Moody's family and
early life.

R. M. L.

TABLE OF CONTENTS

From *Second Coming and Later Poems*

SONGS AND LYRIC PASSAGES

From *The Fire-Bringer*

SONGS AND LYRIC PASSAGES

From *The Masque of Judgment*

From *The Death of Eve*

INTRODUCTION

I

WILLIAM VAUGHN MOODY was born at Spencer, Indiana, July 8, 1869. His father, Francis Burdette Moody, with two brothers, Norman and Gideon, had moved from Central New York about 1852. Norman, a lawyer, settled in Illinois. Gideon, also trained for the law, went to South Dakota, whence he was sent to the United States Senate. Francis Burdette settled in New Albany, Indiana, where he married Henrietta Emily Stoy, of mingled English, French, and Scotch descent, a daughter of one of the earliest pioneer families of southern Indiana. For years Francis Moody commanded a steamer, in which he owned a half-interest, one of the floating palaces of that picturesque era, plying between Pittsburgh and New Orleans. At the outbreak of the Civil War, his vessel was seized and held by Southern troops. After this financial loss he did not return to the river, but went into business in Spencer, Indiana. Returning to New Albany in 1871, he was, until his death, secretary of the Ohio Falls Iron Works in which he held a small interest. Thus it was at New Albany that the family chiefly lived — William Vaughn from about his second to his eighteenth year.

To Francis and Henrietta Moody were born three sons and four daughters, of whom William was next to the youngest. They lived in a pleasant, comfortable house of red brick with white porches, near the center of the town. Francis Moody was a handsome man, six feet two in height. He was not what the townsfolk called religious, but a great nature-lover, and a lover of books. His library was well supplied with the English classics, Scott, Dickens, Thackeray, and the English poets. The memory of Mrs. Moody's beauty and spiritual grace survives in the tenderly beautiful lines of "The Daguerreotype." It was perhaps due to her influence that the children were brought up to go to church and Sunday-School, though Francis Moody was a strict disciplinarian on this point. In every way he upheld the mother's wishes regarding the children. There were also in the family a number of old retainers, especially Jane, a quaint character who served the family for three generations. Next to her, in leaving an impression upon the imagination of the children, was an old Negro, Uncle Billy, who abounded in stories of the Civil War, in which the family had suffered. Religion and patriotism were thus two elements in Moody's early life.

In course of time the children went to grammar and high school, where William early showed ambition and promise. It was no effort for him to keep well ahead of his class. He had a remarkably strong and symmetrical body, and outdoor sports held decidedly more interest for him at times than his books. He was fond of music and played the guitar, an instrument in which he always took a shy pleasure. Drawing and painting interested him so deeply that after leaving high school he studied for a year at the local art academy, the Pritchett Institute of Design, at Louisville, Kentucky. To this pursuit he returned in after life, surprising his friends by his assured technique and sense of values. He was editor of two high-school papers and wrote poems which, with a self-criticism always characteristic of him, he usually tore up as soon as they were written. Among questions of the day he was particularly alive to those of faith and morals. Very early he showed a zest for experience of all kinds, religious, æsthetic, moral, and physical. It would seem that the only interest which Moody as boy and man failed to share was the acquisition and possession of material things.

In 1884, the happy, prosperous home was shattered by the death of Mrs. Moody. It throws a revealing light on the nature of Moody's father that he never recovered from the blow. He died two years later. After this the family was scattered. Two of Moody's sisters, Charlotte and Julia, went East to school under the guardianship of a cousin, Charles Rowley, of Poughkeepsie, New York. Henrietta, the youngest of the family, went to live with the eldest brother, Francis Burdette, who was married and living at Lafayette, Indiana. William Vaughn, his delightful studies at the Pritchett Institute ended, found a place as teacher of a district school near New Albany, living with his cousin, Elizabeth Stoy. Charles Rowley, however, became interested in the lad, of whom his sisters spoke so often, and the next year brought him to the Riverview Academy, where he spent two years in preparation for college, at the same time tutoring Rowley's son for Yale.

Riverview was a military school, and the discipline was severe. The only reminiscence of his life there that I ever heard fall from Moody's lips was of marching around the drill field (with many others) a stated number of times as a penalty for smoking. He had other memories which he did not divulge. The head master was Harlan Page Amen, afterwards head master of Phillips Academy, Exeter, whom Moody loved and admired always. To Amen's fine ideals of scholarship and discipline Moody owed the rare intellectual training, especially in the classics, which fitted him for a distinguished university career. This, however, he renounced in favor of poetry.

In 1889, Moody entered Harvard, with the class of 1893. He had some money saved from school teaching, and his uncle Gideon Moody advanced a thousand dollars which his nephew repaid from his earnings by writing and tutoring during the summers. Although he worked his way through college in this manner, he suffered no real handicap. No student ever took fuller advantage of the opportunities of Harvard, which were then becoming magnificent. It was for such as he that Eliot carried through the elective system, and the use which Moody made of it must have delighted the President, who followed the careers of individual students more closely than most of them imagined. Moody chose his courses with fine economy, selecting subjects in which guidance counted most and avoiding those which he could master by himself. He took the classics and modern languages, and later, in a year of graduate study, modern philology. I do not remember him in any English literature or composition courses, and natural and social science I believe he ignored. He acted wisely in avoiding any academic influence upon his own reading and writing. To history and social theory he came later with a freshness and naïveté of mind that submitted the matter to the uses of the imagination, free from dulling memories of the classroom. He was, next to David S. Muzzey, now Professor of History at Columbia, the first student in his class, and held the largest scholarship, the Richard Augustin Gambrill, which yielded four hundred dollars.

My own recollection of Moody goes back to his freshman year. In Latin D, which was an advanced class for freshmen, we were reading the *Phormio*, when Professor C. L. Smith called, "Mr. Moody next," and for the first time I heard the clear, vibrant, musical voice which always expressed so perfectly the man and the poet. He sat directly behind me, and for many weeks he re-

mained for me only a voice. Later in
that year I read his first poem in the
Harvard Monthly, "A Chorus of Wagner,"
and as I was a candidate for the *Monthly*
myself, the thought of having Moody for
a colleague lent energy to my striving.
I came to know him by sight, and I suppose he knew me likewise, but it was
perhaps characteristic of Harvard in the
nineties that we never spoke. The *Harvard Monthly* represented a high ambition in those days. The brilliancy of the
first board of editors, Alanson Bigelow
Houghton, George Santayana, George
Rice Carpenter, and others, and of their
immediate successors, George Pierce
Baker and Bernhard Berenson, was a recent memory. It was the only undergraduate publication admitted to *Poole's Index*.
Robert Herrick and Norman Hapgood
divided the editorship-in-chief that year,
and under their somewhat skeptical guidance Moody and I were admitted to the
board.

During the next two years we were
thrown much together by the *Monthly*
and other interests. Moody was not

an organization man. A figure of speech or a single flawless line of verse meant more to him than any institution. But as if he recognized this bias as a danger, he showed a heroic patience in performing any task that was laid upon him. You had only to say, "You ought to do that," and with dogged obedience he went about it.

It was always a keen pleasure to walk and talk with Moody. His joy in the purple shadows of the pines on the snow, in the smell of violets in fresh earth, was an experience which he gladly shared. Years later, walking around the Marmolada in the early morning, we came to a spot where the retreating snow-field met the green grass in a sharp edge, and Moody at once proposed that we should strip and take our morning bath by rolling down the slope to feel the stinging cold of the snow on our bodies, and the sudden release of the sun-warmed earth. Equal to his joy in nature was his joy in mind, in intellectual play. Norman Hapgood, who sometimes joined us, used to remark on Moody's faculty for setting a figure of speech in motion and following its implications in a sort of mock argument.

All this time Moody's verse was growing. Even in youth Moody felt himself dedicated to poetry, as Milton and Wordsworth had before him. He was not ashamed to learn from the masters. He was, perhaps unconsciously, preparing himself for a long career, and was content to begin at the beginning, with a thorough mastery of the great tradition in which he was to work. I remember once speaking in discouraged mood of the difficulty of achieving anything distinctive in a crowded world, to which he replied, with boyish solemnity, "No man can refuse to run at Olympia."

Most of Moody's verse of this time was destroyed, or is to be found only in the files of the *Harvard Monthly*. He was too critical of himself to preserve his juvenilia. One sonnet, however, is so characteristic in its inspiration, so perfect in its expression of what was in his soul at this time, that I hope to be forgiven any impiety in quoting it. A remark by Professor Tar-

bell in a Greek course, a journey to the
Boston Art Museum, and the next evening he read to the *Monthly* Board, "To
the Niké of Paionios."

I wonder did he dream of battle spears
Ahurtle on Greek hillsides in the sun;
Or of the moment when, the wild race won,
Some hyacinthine boy stands panting, hears
Like surf beat on the sands, the shouts and cheers;
Or of such ecstasy the poet knows
When dazed and dumb he feeleth round his brows
The dusk-leaved ivy Dionysus wears;

Or haply did he look beyond the dawn
That paled above the purple eastern sea,
Beyond the things that seem to things that be,
And listen to the lips that trumpet on
From star-depth unto star-depth "Victory"!
Paionios — What time he fashioned thee?

If Moody ever thought of his vocation
to poetry in such terms as Milton and
Wordsworth, he must have recognized
that in one respect his apprenticeship
was happier than theirs. They found
their English Cambridge a harsh and cold
nurse; Moody found his altogether sympathetic and stimulating. Indeed, in
these middle years of Eliot's presidency,

Harvard offered to the undergraduate a life of extraordinary variety and freedom. The spirit of free election permeated all relations. The stiff aloofness between Harvard and what was then the Annex had broken down. There was the Comedy Club, a mixed group for acting plays, and the Browning Club which used to meet alternately in college rooms and Cambridge homes. The austere corridors of Hollis and Thayer without protest beheld ladies coming for an evening to read *Bishop Blougram's Apology*. There was no rule against it, and the absence of all bathing facilities in the dormitories obviated disconcerting encounters. Moody belonged to these groups, as well as to the regular college clubs — the Signet, the Delta Upsilon, and the O.K. In those days also, as a result of the elective system, there was free exchange between faculty and undergraduates, or such of the latter as cared to trade. The Hapgoods were great friends of William James, Charles Carroll Everett, and Crawford Howell Toy. I think it was Norman Hapgood who introduced Moody to the Toys, in whose home the boy, whose own home had long been only a sacred memory, found not only intellectual stimulation, but quiet happiness.   There were a number of younger men, lately returned from Europe, bringing a new learning: George Santayana in philosophy, Edward Cummings in sociology, Arthur R. Marsh in comparative literature, and a little later, in English, Lewis E. Gates, who became Moody's close friend and critic.

Moody finished the courses required for his degree in three years, and spent his fourth abroad, in company with Ingersoll Bowditch, whom he prepared for college. That summer Norman Hapgood, Louis Henry Dow, and I were getting our first glimpse of Europe, and were met on the Rhine by Moody and his pupil.   The five of us walked through the Black Forest and Switzerland.   I remember particularly Moody's enthusiasm when after a night spent in a hut above Zermatt, and an early morning climb through mist and sleet on the Cima di Jazzi, we came out on the sunny slope above Domodossola, and gained our first view of Italy, a land which he was to love so much. At Milan, Moody left us to go to England, but later in the year he came south again and made a long stay in Athens. Italy and Greece were two countries which, through landscape, history, literature, and contemporary peasant life, entered most deeply into Moody's consciousness. Both were associated in his mind with a solemn sense of humanity and the unseen powers which rule its fate: Italy with the medieval mysticism of Dante's theology, Greece with the classic feeling of joy in life restrained by measure and the decrees of the gods. One is the inspiration of *The Masque of Judgment*, the other of *The Fire-Bringer*.

During his absence Moody was elected Class Poet, and returned to deliver his poem on Class Day, 1893. In the summer he and I undertook a revision of Bulfinch's *Age of Fable*, and sought relaxation in cruising about Buzzard's Bay. For the next year he was a graduate student at Harvard, chiefly in medieval philology, and in the year following, he assisted Lewis E. Gates in reading manuscript for a sophomore course in composition, English 22. During these years he found new companions in Trumbull Stickney, who in the *Monthly* was giving promise of the career in poetry which was to be so untimely ended; in Josephine Preston Peabody, who made an enduring contribution to American poetry before her death; and in Daniel Gregory Mason, composer and writer on music. A special chapter should be written on Moody's friendships, and it should be written by a poet: His companionship was a precious thing, and though he had sometimes the reputation of being aloof and indifferent, he gave it generously to many. He could discern and delight in genuine human quality in very simple, humble forms. But he was at his best in association with the makers — those who like himself had seen the vision and not been disobedient to it.

Moody enjoyed the pleasant, civilized life of Cambridge, and renounced it with regret. Obligations to his family, however, made it necessary for him to add at once to his resources. Two positions were open: Mr. Amen asked him to teach at Exeter, and Robert Herrick and I urged him to join us in the Department of English at the University of Chicago. He chose the latter, fortunately, I think.

Before beginning as an instructor at Chicago, however, he spent three months in France with Daniel Gregory Mason. Professor Gates joined them for a short trip through Brussels, Ghent, Bruges, Lille, Amiens, and Beauvais. Of this trip Mr. Mason says, in *Some Letters of William Vaughn Moody*:

Moody's delight in the beauty of the cathedrals, the picturesqueness of the landscapes, and the bits of talk with peasants, servants, and railway acquaintances which he never failed to snatch, was a constant pleasure. The easy transitions his mind made from poetic feeling and imagery to the broadest colloquial humor made him an incomparable companion. At Amiens, for example, he calls the delicate rose-window of the cathedral "God's spider-web"; at Comines, on the border of France, charmed with the pure French of the waitress, he asks the names of all the viands, and in return communicates that the English name of raspberry jam is "Red-goo," and with a

solemnity that convulses us watches her efforts
to reproduce it, with much rolling of the R.

Of the short walking tour that followed
Gates's departure, Mr. Mason says:

At Caen, on a rainy afternoon, Moody made
the first sketch of a poem which eventually,
after much revision, became "Jetsam." At
Tessy-sur-Vire we were awakened before
dawn one morning by the bugles of a regiment
passing up one of the narrow streets — a
valorous music strangely impressive in that
darkness and silence. Moody has commem-
orated it in the speech of the Third Youth in
Act IV of *The Masque of Judgment*:

But always ere the dayspring took the sky,
Somewhere the silver trumpets were acry —
Sweet, high, oh, high and sweet!
What voice could summon so but the Soul's
    Paraclete?
Whom should such voices call but me, to dare and
    die?
O ye asleep here in the eyrie town,
Ye mothers, babes, and maids, and aged men,
The plain is full of foe-men! Turn again —
Sleep sound, or waken half
Only to hear our happy bugles laugh
Lovely defiance down,
As through the steep
Grey streets we sweep,
Each horse and man a ribbéd fan to scatter all
    that chaff!

The fundamental question concerning his decision to leave Cambridge for Chicago has to do with the effect of this translation on his own development as a poet. Moody had gone to Cambridge a youth from the Middle West, and had seized with genuine hunger upon the rich intellectual and civilizing influences which he found there. He was spiritually homesick at leaving them. The crudeness of the western scene as found in Chicago oppressed him sorely, and he resented still more at first the somewhat forced and pretentious quality of its nascent culture. In the end, however, it is impossible to doubt that the result was good, for it passed his own close criticism of himself as good. The experience brought him into contact with the stern necessities of living in a world which could only be described as realistic. The very bleakness of the environment forced him to take strong measures for defending his own inner life, of whose needs and responsibilities he became increasingly conscious. Even in the striving toward higher things by those whose efforts he was tempted to dismiss as vague and futile, he came to recognize a genuine and honest effort with which in the end he could not fail to sympathize.   In the midst of much that was shallow and spurious, he had an unerring instinct for what was sound and true.   He found others, like himself, conscious of a feeling of exile, and was closely drawn to them. His years in Chicago were years of growth as a human being, and humanity was the essence of his poetry.

This conclusion is borne out by his letters written at this time to friends of the Cambridge circle, collected by Mr. Mason in *Some Letters of William Vaughn Moody*.   Here the theme of East and West is treated with all the gusto of personal experience.   That Moody appreciated the momentous nature of his choice is shown in a letter to Josephine Preston Peabody, dated September 22, 1895 — a few days after his arrival in the western city.

I do not know what this place is going to do for me, but am sure of its potency — its alchemical power to change and transmute.

It is appallingly ugly for one thing — so ugly
that the double curtain of night and sleep does
not screen the aching sense. For another
thing it is absorbing — crude juice of life —
intellectual and social protoplasm. Far aloft
hovers phantom Poetry, no longer my delicate
familiar. But I dream of another coming of
hers, a new companionship more valorous and
simple hearted....

A later letter to the same correspondent
reveals clearly his nostalgia for Cambridge, his sense of the abundant life
about him, and a certain despair of
breaking through the academic trammels
and reaching down into it.

The truth of the matter is, I suppose, that
I am dissatisfied to the point of desperation
with the kind of life that is possible out here.
I used to have days in the east when a hedge of
lilac over a Brattle Street fence or a strenuous
young head caught against a windy sweep of
sunset on Harvard Bridge, filled me with
poignant perceptions of a freer life of sense and
spirit — and I was frequently vaguely unhappy
over it. But after all one hadn't far to go before finding some refinement of feeling, some
delicate arabesque of convention, to help
make up for the lack of liberty. Out here
there is even less liberty (because less thought)
and there is nothing — or next to nothing —

to compensate. If my lines were cast in other places — even other places in this gigantic ink-blot of a town — I could make shift to enjoy my breath. I should make a very happy and efficient peanut-vender on Clark or Randolph Street, because the rush and noise of the blood in the city's pulse would continually solicit and engage me. The life of a motorman is not without exhilarating and even romantic features, and an imaginative boot-black is lord of unskirted realms. But out here, where there is no city life to gaze at, nothing to relieve the gaseous tedium of a mushroom intellectuality, no straining wickedness or valiant wrestling with hunger to break the spectacle of Gospel-peddling comfort — the imagination doth boggle at it!...

A very just perception of a weakness arising from the middle-western spirit of tolerance with which even the better part of Chicago regarded what it sadly termed its lack of standards, appears in a letter to Mrs. Mary L. Mason, dated January 11, 1896.

The enervating thing about the place is its shallow kindness. People are so eager to give you credit for virtues that you do not possess that you feel ashamed to put forth those that are yours. Then when you do take heart of grace, and do or say or think a really good thing, and win the facile applause, you have a bad taste in the mouth to think that any jigster's trick would have won you the same magnificent triumph....

That he was, nevertheless, from the outset fitting his environment to his own needs, appears from letters written to Daniel Gregory Mason. In October, 1895, he says:

I experience aching diastoles [a term, his editor explains, borrowed from physiology to denote moods of spiritual elation], however, and that is the great thing to my thinking. To be a poet is a much better thing than to write poetry — out here, at least, watched by these wide horizons, beckoned to by these swift streamers of victorious sunset.

That he, like Wordsworth, was coming to feel the value to the poet of a "wise passiveness," though in his case touched by stoicism, is clear from another letter to Mason:

The hard bright sun of a western morning, with theme classes superimposed, reduces the golden tongue to phantom thinness of song and banishes the lute into the limbo of the ridiculous, but I plod on evening-wards with

mole-like assiduity.   I have come to realize
the wonderful resources of passive enjoyment
better than I ever did before — perhaps
perversely, perhaps according to a mere instinct of self-preservation against the hurry
and remorseless effectiveness of life out here....

In another letter written to Mason the
following year, he voices the conviction,
which he shared with Browning, that it is
better to live poetry than to write it:

If you can only throttle your Dæmon, or
make him forego his leonine admonition
"Accomplish," and roar you as any sucking
dove the sweet vocable, "Be," — you ought to
live.   I have got mine trained to that pardee!
and his voice grows not untunable.   I pick
up shreds of comfort out of this or that one of
God's ashbarrels.   Yesterday I was skating on
a patch of ice in the park, under a poverty-
stricken sky flying a pitiful rag of sunset.
Some little muckers were guying a slim raw-
boned Irish girl of fifteen, who circled and
darted under their banter with complete unconcern.   She was in the fledgling stage, all
legs and arms, tall and adorably awkward,
with a huge hat full of rusty feathers, thin
skirts tucked up above spindling ankles, and
a gay aplomb and swing in the body that was
ravishing.   We caught hands in midflight,
and skated for an hour, almost alone and quite

silent, while the rag of sunset rotted to pieces. ... I came away mystically shaken and elate. ... It is thus the angels converse. She was something absolutely authentic, new, and inexpressible, something which only nature could mix for the heart's intoxication, a compound of ragamuffin, pal, mistress, nun, sister, harlequin, outcast, and bird of God — with something else bafflingly suffused, something ridiculous and frail and savage and tender. With a world offering such rencontres, such aery strifes and adventures, who would not live a thousand years stone dumb?

A serious appraisal of his life at Chicago after a year appears in a letter to Mrs. Toy:

As for Chicago, I find that it gives me days or at least hours of broad-gauge Whitmanesque enthusiasm, meagrely sprinkled over weeks of tedium. The tedium is not of the acid-bath sort, however. Genuinely, I feel mellower, deeper-lunged, more of a lover of life, than I have ever felt before, and the reason is that I have had long somnolent spaces in which to feel the alchemy of rest.

One thing which Moody found from the beginning at the University of Chicago was an intellectual companionship and stimulus fully as valuable as that which Harvard had to offer. He possessed the instinct of humane scholarship, and went to the past not only with his mind but with his heart. It was the beauty perceived and uttered by poets that moved him, and as his vision of poetry widened, this tradition meant more and more to him. His colleagues at Chicago whose knowledge he laid most fruitfully under contribution were Paul Shorey in Greek, Ferdinand Schevill in the Italian Middle Age and Renaissance, and John Matthews Manly in English literature, all scholars of imagination and sympathetic understanding. At Harvard, Moody found plenty of critics who were abundantly useful to him, but I think, except perhaps for Professor Toy, he found no scholastic influence so directly contributing to his own creative life as at the University of Chicago.

Among other influences of his new environment must be set down his own teaching. Instead of acting as reader and consultant to a large course of sophomores, he had his own classes, limited to thirty, which involved close contact with a variety of human types. Close, but seldom intimate. One of his pupils writing in later years speaks of "the dreamy aloofness, the habit of slow, impersonal, vivid epigram which we associated with Mr. Moody." Moody never achieved such a degree of self-conquest as to suffer fools gladly, but he did suffer them patiently and courteously. Of the pupils in whom he took most genuine interest I recall two, Katharine Bates, who was afterwards instructor at Wellesley College, and Mrs. Katherine Gibbs, a woman who had come to college late in life, but fresh in mind and as ambitious as youth. I have always thought that his understanding of old age came to him largely through the woman whom he called, with real affection, Grandma Gibbs.

In all ways, Moody was an admirable teacher. Whether tutoring individual pupils or conducting classes, he gave his full mind to every exercise. His lectures were carefully thought out and delivered in perfect form. I have seen hundreds of students' themes, painfully corrected in red ink, with elaborate comment on the outside page written in his clear, beautiful hand. He was obliged to augment his salary by preparing texts for school use, among them an edition of Bunyan's *Pilgrim's Progress* for Houghton Mifflin Company's Riverside Literature Series, to which his introduction is a little masterpiece. His workmanlike instinct appeared in every task, and it may be said that, by virtue of an economy which consisted in putting his full strength into every undertaking, nothing that he did was without value to him.

In that first year in Chicago we had a coöperative household at 5488 East End Avenue, managed by my wife, with Moody and Ferdinand Schevill as members. We were all poor, but living was cheap in the days after the World's Fair. When the weekly budget was $8.38 for rent, service, and food, we felt entitled to a celebration in a private room at the Bismarck, where real Pschorrbräu made up for our exile from Jakey Wirth's ale in Boston. The youngest of the Hapgood brothers, William Powers, and his room-

mate Edward Kennard Rand, who had
come to the University as tutor in Latin,
regularly dined at our apartment, and
joined in these parties. For some reason
we used now and then to dress for these
occasions, and I remember Moody in
his tail coat, doing a dance to the tune
of "Twinkle, Twinkle, Little Star," with
a humorous solemnity that was most engaging. The guitar was often in play
as accompaniment to his varied store
of songs. Chicago's freer atmosphere
brought to Moody, as to all of us, a certain expansion of mood after the decorum
of Cambridge. I had never known him
so natural, so easy, so blithe.

During his second year in Chicago,
Moody lived in the family of Robert
Herrick. These months are chiefly
memorable for his work in editing
Milton's poems, English and Latin,
for Houghton Mifflin Company's Cambridge Poets Series. This he did with
a thoroughness which lifted the task far
above hack-work. The contract called
for the conventional text, with introduction and notes, but Moody could not

let it go at that.   He scrutinized the text in the light of all the readings, and with a sure feeling for the atmosphere of the poems he returned to Milton's original spelling.   He made a new translation of the Latin poems.   Later, the accuracy of his rendering was in some cases challenged, but Professor Rand, who revised the work, informs me that in most cases of departure from the literal, he recognized Moody's sense of values in his adherence to poetic rather than grammatical accuracy.   His essays introducing the several divisions of Milton's work are fine examples of exposition and appreciation, beautifully and eloquently written.   All this was done for the fee originally agreed upon, which the publishers, however, voluntarily increased.   But Moody's real compensation was far greater.   Milton was not one of the poets for whom in his youth he greatly cared.   He preferred the more lavish art of Shakespeare or Shelley.   Moreover, Milton's theology was repulsive to him.   But by dint of a conscientious effort to enter into the spirit of the Puritan poet, he learned to know his greatness. When Moody himself came to deal with the highest things, he had the example of Milton clearly before him, and his latest poetry shows this influence more than any other.

The result of Moody's emigration to Chicago is to be seen in his own poetry. Hitherto his inspiration had been literary and the result largely imitative. Now for the first time he drew on his own experience for subject-matter, and achieved a freer and more personal manner. A letter to Daniel Gregory Mason dated May 16, 1896, accompanied by the poem "Wilding Flower," rewritten as "Heart's Wild-Flower," contains the significant sentence, "I hope you will like it because it is almost the first thing I have done which has been a direct impulse from 'real life,' and you know I have theories about that."

This first continuous year and a half in Chicago was rewarded by the six months of freedom which followed, and which saw the beginning, not indeed of his life in poetry, but of his career as a poet.   The force which had been expanding against the resistance of circumstances found sudden release.   He sailed for Naples, and at Sorrento the experience befell him which he has recorded in "Good Friday Night."   Joining Ferdinand Schevill on a bicycle trip northward, he found such joy and hope on a morning ride out of Orvieto as inspired the "Road-Hymn for the Start."   In June he joined my family at Venice, at the Casa Frollo on the Giudecca.   The Casa ran completely across the island, in two wings enclosing a garden.   Moody's room was somewhere near the extremity of one of the wings, and though the insect life tormented him at night, still the nightingales sang in the garden.   In our gondola, manned by one Luigi, we used to proceed to the Lido every morning, or took longer trips to Torcello and Murano, where Moody was endlessly enthralled by the skill of the glass-blowers.   Craftsmanship in every form delighted him. One of our happiest memories is of his affection for my little son, about a year old, with whom he used to play for hours on the floor. In the evenings the singing on the Grand Canal charmed him, and I remember his full, clear baritone trolling out the chorus:

> Vieni sul mar;
> Vieni a vogar;
> Sentirai l'ebbrezza
> Del tu' marinar.

At Venice we went occasionally to an exhibition of modern art which included a triptych representing the Last Judgment: in the center, the Deity in his wrath, and on the sides the contorted bodies of the damned. I wondered at the fascination which that picture held for Moody. Later I realized that it was one of the sources of *The Masque of Judgment*.

From Venice, Moody and I bicycled to Asolo, where we found decent lodging, and foraged for food among the three little inns of the town. We had some thought of settling there for the summer, and engaged in long negotiations with Robert Barrett Browning who owned the only practicable villas, but Mr. Browning could not quite make up his mind which of them to rent.   Miss Browning, the poet's sister, the *sindaco* of Asolo, and the postmaster, assisted at these conversations, and Moody often recalled the argument of the *sindaco* that it would be dangerous for a *bambino* to pass *subito* from Venice to the Dolomites, without breaking the journey in the hills.   It grew hot in Asolo.   At night we took our blankets to the hillside beneath the Rocca, and slept, to be wakened before dawn by the noise of men and women on their way to work, a confusion of forms vaguely moving in the twilight, with voices strangely subdued.   My range of activity was limited by the fever I had brought from Rome, but Moody made bicycle trips to Bergamo and other places.   It was difficult to induce him to take the road again, but at length our departure was fixed for an evening, when we were to ride to Feltre to take the diligence for San Martino di Castrozza next morning. At sunset, Moody had not appeared, and I finally set out alone.   In the early morning at Feltre, I mounted the diligence ready to start, when far down the

,road I saw a little cloud of dust, out of which slowly emerged a man, pedaling for all he was worth. I assured the driver that it was another passenger. Five minutes later, Moody, covered with .dust, came alongside, swung himself up ,and collapsed beside me, while his wheel was loaded on behind. For a long time he did not speak a word. Then he showed me two or three little notes in Italian — *sempre, sempre, ricordati di me* — signed Annunziata.

At San Martino we sent our bicycles ahead to Innsbruck and footed it across to Belluno. There we met my family and took carriage to Cortina, where we found rooms at the Bella Vista, with Cristallo and Tofana and Sorapis rising menacingly above the smiling valley. There was a *Schwimbad*, fed by icy streams from the glacier, in which we plunged daily. One evening we went to a Passion Play given in Italian by boys of the neighborhood.

Here Moody began to write *The Masque of Judgment*, the origins of which are clear. The picture at Venice gave the emotional shock, indignation that God could so treat his creation. The Dolomites furnished the setting. Milton supplied the intellectual background; in his capacity as attorney for the defense, justifying the ways of God to men, he challenged Moody to vigorous argument on the side of humanity, the plaintiff.

Moody wrote industriously through the mornings, complaining with some humor of the loquacity of Raphael, and wishing he would have done talking in order that we might start on our further tour of the Dolomites. At length the Archangel stayed his speech, and we set out afoot, going by way of Tre Croci, Lake Misurina and the Drei Zinnen. One morning we lay for an hour confronting a mass of tawny rock with huge red stains like congealed blood on its face, as if it had been gashed by a giant axe. Another glorious morning we walked around the Marmolada taking our bath in the snow. It was on this morning that I found in my mail the *Boston Transcript* with William James's oration on the dedication of the monument to Robert Gould Shaw, which gave the keynote to the "Ode in Time of Hesitation."

Our last exploit on this trip was an ascent of the Gross Venediger, from which we hoped to see Venice once more, but the mountain belied its name. We were shockingly unprepared for high altitudes. After we reached Innsbruck and I had started back to Cortina, leaving Moody alone, he was ill from exposure for some days. It was the first breach in his magnificent bodily health.

Moody rode back to Italy over the Brenner to Verona, and thence to Ravenna to see the mosaics, which perhaps also played their part in the imagery of *The Masque of Judgment*. From Ravenna he crossed Italy, riding by night on account of the heat, to Viareggio. He made his way to Genoa, where he was again ill, lying half-conscious for days at an Italian inn, until one morning he realized that his steamer was due to sail on that day. Thereupon he got up, packed his bags, and made his way to the quay, to fall again unconscious in his berth.

In the succeeding years, Moody found conditions at Chicago more favorable to poetry. In 1898, John Matthews Manly became head of the Department of English, and Moody's close friend. Under his leadership the work of the department was reorganized, and Moody was relieved of much of the drudgery of composition courses. His special field was the early seventeenth century, whose poets and dramatists he came to know with the thoroughness which his conscientious preparation for teaching made necessary. He found also a group of writers in Chicago, Harriet Monroe, Hamlin Garland, Henry B. Fuller, William Morton Payne. With these he consorted at "The Little Room." He also found a welcome at 2970 Groveland Avenue, where Mrs. Harriet Brainerd was hostess to many young people of promise, such as William Penhallow Henderson, the painter; Alice Corbin (now Mrs. Henderson) the poet; Swinburne Hale and Milton Sills. For out-of-town excursions we discovered Saint Joseph, across the lake; and Lake Zurich, where there was a primitive country club.

Of his longer vacations one was spent on Cape Ann with Mason, another at Mackinac Island, where Mrs. Brainerd had a cottage, and a third on a horseback trip with Hamlin Garland, camping among the mountains of Colorado. His first extended stay in New York was from April to July of 1898. Here he worked on his edition of Milton, and finished the first draft of *The Masque of Judgment*. Here also he fell in with a group of rising young dramatists, as he wrote to Daniel Gregory Mason, "full of enthusiasm and practical expedient. The great thing about them is that they get their things played, and that sort of thing, begad, begins to appeal to me. Do not believe me quite recreant to ideals; Cambridge and her elegiac air seems still lovely and of good report. But these chaps here, though very moderately elegiac and of a dubious report, are splendidly American and contemporary; and I feel convinced that this is the place for young Americans who want to do something.

(N.B. *I have not enlisted in the marines.*)"
A different attitude toward his New York
associates is suggested in a later letter to
the same correspondent: "I am going in
for people now, having made the discovery that the average man is among the
most unexpected and absorbing of be-
ings." For the rest of his teaching career,
residence in Chicago was alternated with
periods spent in Boston or New York.

The various influences of persons and
places show clearly in his poetry. The
Spanish War, fought in the summer of
1898, blended with memories of the Civil
War in the "Ode in Time of Hesitation,"
written in Boston, early in 1900. There
was strong feeling in Chicago against the
subjugation by arms of the Philippines,
which Moody expressed in his lines "On
a Soldier Fallen in the Philippines,"
published in the *Atlantic Monthly* for
February, 1901 — a very bold utterance
which, in a university less tolerant than
that of Chicago under President Harper,
might have cost an instructor his position. Henry B. Fuller was an ardent
anti-imperialist, and Hamlin Garland

was a disciple of Henry George. The latter certainly was of influence in turning Moody's thought to social matters, of which "Gloucester Moors," published in *Scribner's Magazine* for December, 1900, is unmistakable evidence. At the same time, Moody's power of rendering actual experience was growing. Even a trivial event was for him hung about with mysterious intimations of high meaning. An example of this is found in "Old Pourquoi," of which the germ incident had occurred on the walking trip in Northern France in 1895.

In July, 1900, Moody read the "Anniversary Ode," at Cambridge, on the one hundred and twenty-fifth anniversary of Washington taking command of the American Army, published in the *Harvard Monthly* for October of that year. In the course of the same year appeared *The Masque of Judgment*, published by Small, Maynard and Company, and in 1901 his first collected *Poems*. In the fall of that year I joined him in Boston, where we worked through the winter on *A History of English Literature*. The *History* was a fortunate venture, for by it Moody became independent of teaching, which he forthwith renounced. President Harper made him a standing offer of a single quarter's service at the rate of a professor's salary, and Manly patiently arranged and announced courses for him, but they were always withdrawn. Aside from the necessity of saving himself for his true work, he felt that the formal teaching of literature involved a kind of sacrilege. He said to Manly, "I cannot do it. At every lecture I slay a poet."

In the spring of 1902, while Moody was visiting Mrs. Brainerd at Cape Henry, he spoke one evening of the Prometheus legend, as affording another expression of the problem of man's separation from God. This was the origin of *The Fire-Bringer*. The next morning he started for Greece. Here his most notable experience was traveling with a donkey through the Peloponnesus. Here also he felt, at Corinth, that sense of the power of human love to annihilate distance which is the subject of "The

Moon-Moth," and while in Crete he had for a second time a vision of the actual presence of Christ, recorded in "Second Coming." No one who knew Moody can doubt that these were real experiences —

Closer to him than breathing, and nearer than hands and feet.

In July of that year, I found him in Paris in Trumbull Stickney's rooms on the rue d'Assas, where he was reading the entire body of Greek tragedy. Stickney, who was writing his thesis for his doctorate at the Sorbonne, in Greek literature, was an incomparable guide and stimulus. He had himself written a lyric drama, *Prometheus Pyrfuros*, the influence of which is discernible in Moody's larger, full-bodied work.

In the autumn of 1902, Moody was in the Tyrol. After his return to America he made his headquarters in New York, at 50 West Tenth Street, later, at 107 Waverly Place, but he was a frequent visitor at Mrs. Brainerd's home in Chicago. In New York he had his intimate friend, Daniel Gregory Mason, and he was the center of a group of younger poets, especially Ridgely Torrence, Edwin Arlington Robinson, and Percy MacKaye. Mrs. C. P. Davidge was the hospitable friend of all this circle, and their intimate ways and sayings were constantly recalled in her vivid conversation. At this time Moody returned to his old love of painting, and found expression for his seeing eye and firm, sensitive fingers in pastel and oil.

Most of this time Moody was receiving a small income from the *History of English Literature*, but his livelihood, until the success of *The Great Divide*, was far from assured. There was a steady market for his verse in the *Atlantic Monthly*, the *Century*, and *Scribner's*, but he refused to exploit it. He was exceedingly scrupulous about giving his poetry to the world. He would rather go hungry than publish a poem which he thought unfinished, or beneath the best that he could do. He never starved, but he did meet hardship and denial like a good soldier in a cause which he would not betray, even by compromise.

The Fire-Bringer was published in 1904, and it is not too much to say that it was accepted by critics as placing Moody at the head of American poetry. Already William Morton Payne had written in *The Dial* (January 1, 1901): "No other new poet in the past score of years, either in America or in England, has displayed a finer promise upon the occasion of his first appearance, or has been deserving of more respectful consideration." Now Richard Watson Gilder welcomed him as a new poet in his stanzas published in the *Atlantic Monthly* of June, 1905:

Friends, beware!
A sound of singing in the air!
The love-song of a man who loves his fellow men:
Mother-love and country-love and the love of
    sea and fen;
Lovely thoughts and mighty thoughts that linger
    long;
There has come to the old world's singing the
    thrill of a brave new song.

They said there were no more singers,
But listen! — a master's voice!
A voice of the true joy-bringers!
Now will ye heed and rejoice
Or pass on the other side,

And wait till the singer has died —
Then weep o'er his voiceless clay?
Friends, beware!
A keen new sound is in the air —
Know ye a poet's coming is the old world's
       Judgment Day!

His work had been noted in England, where William Archer included the "Ode in Time of Hesitation" in an anthology of modern verse, and whence May Sinclair wrote for the *Atlantic Monthly* (September, 1906), an enthusiastic criticism hailing him as the first of a trio of American poets, the others being his friends, Edwin Arlington Robinson and Ridgely Torrence. It was, however, at this time that he chose to turn to prose drama, although from no temptation of "thieving ambition or paltering gain."

Moody was always fascinated by the dramatic form. It appealed to him as a vehicle for representing human experience, and it challenged his instinct of craftsmanship. As far back as 1896, he was taking a keen interest in the newspaper accounts of the work of a western faith healer named Schlatter, and speaking of him as a subject for a play. After *The Fire-Bringer* had appeared in 1904, and *A First View of English Literature* was finished, he went seriously to work on a prose play, which he at first called *The Sabine Woman*, subsequently *The Great Divide*.

It was generally thought that this play owed its inception to a trip to Arizona which he took in the spring of 1905 with Ferdinand Schevill, in the course of which they spent a week at Oraibi among the Hopi and saw the spring dance at Walpis. But this excursion gave confirmation rather than color to his background, for the play was already practically finished. It was based on a story from real life, related to him by Mrs. Brainerd. The first act keeps closely to the facts as they were told to him, but the rest of the play is Moody's development, through this situation, of a contrast which had always presented itself to him most forcibly: Puritan New England, as opposed to the pioneering West. It is obvious that he understood the latter far better, and was more fully in sympathy with it. It is noteworthy also that the difference in quality between the first, almost re-portorial act, and those following, is perceptible even without a clue to its cause. The success of his first play does not cloud the fact that Moody was a poet rather than a dramatist; rather, it testifies to his superb endowment with those qualities which are common to both.

The Great Divide centers about the attack on a New England girl, alone in a cabin in Arizona, by a band of outlaws, one of whom, an American, buys her with gold from the others. She goes through with the bargain of marriage, but, though she comes to love her captor, she is possessed by a desperate necessity of earning and repaying the price for which she was bought. This accomplished, she parts from her husband, with pain on both sides, and returns to her New England home, where the reconciliation takes place. The play was shown to Miss Margaret Anglin, who was playing in Chicago in the spring of 1906, and she resolved to give it a trial at the close of her engagement. No one who was present on the opening night will forget the circumstances, almost as dramatic as the play itself. The curtain went down on the first act amid a whirlwind of applause. Then Miss Anglin's management summoned Moody from the audience and presented him with a contract to sign, threatening that otherwise they would not permit the play to continue. Moody hesitated. He had been warned by his friend Percy MacKaye of the danger of hasty engagements, illustrated so tragically in the case of the latter's father, Steele MacKaye. A lawyer was called from the body of the house, and while he scanned the document the audience waited in tension for the outcome of the drama which was being enacted during the intermission. At last an agreement was effected, and the curtain went up. The second act, which was mainly carried by the principals, went off fairly well. But the supporting company, inadequately rehearsed, had gone cold during the long wait. In the third act they forgot their lines and wandered vaguely about the stage, opening and shutting windows or reading newspapers. Toward midnight the play staggered to a lamentable conclusion. It was a harrowing experience for a man of Moody's sensitive temperament, but he was not blind to its humorous aspect.

In the summer he was resolutely at work revising the play, living at Cornish, New Hampshire, where I had an opportunity to see it grow anew under his hand. I had known Moody as a most conscientious and meticulous craftsman, but I had not known, nor ever have seen since, anything like his fierce power of concentration. There were many friends near by: the Herricks, the Hapgoods, the Churchills, Miss Ethel Barrymore. But Moody was not to be diverted for more than an occasional set at tennis, or a plunge in the swimming-pool. In the autumn the play was triumphantly produced in New York as *The Great Divide*, by Miss Anglin and Henry Miller, and has remained a landmark in the history of the American drama.

Moody had intended to complete his

trilogy of poetic dramas by a third member. He had dealt with the Greek conception of the power behind the human scene in *The Fire-Bringer* and with the medieval in *The Masque of Judgment.* These have to do with the separation of Man from God. For the third member, dealing with reconciliation, he went directly to the Hebrew theme. *The Death of Eve* was the subject, not only of his poetic drama, but of an epic fragment published in the *Century Magazine* for December, 1906. That he never finished this drama was clearly a misfortune, and was felt by Moody as a kind of betrayal of his vocation.

The theme of *The Faith Healer* which had so long haunted him came to fruition in the play of that name, produced in St. Louis in the autumn of 1909, and in New York in December of that year, by Henry Miller, to whom Moody was indebted for genuine friendship and stimulating advice. This play cost Moody dearly in time and effort. It is, to a greater extent than is commonly supposed, a personal document. It embodies the question, always insistent in Moody's mind, to what extent a man who is dedicated to a great purpose may share the common lot. The fact that he threw the discussion into the life of a mystic, an itinerant healer, was owing to his early interest in the case of Schlatter, which seemed to Moody's imagination to offer precisely the example he needed of the opposition between the sense of a high calling and the joy of a human love. That the play was a discussion with himself is shown by the three versions extant, written at considerable intervals of time. In the first, the healer gives up his love for the sake of his healing; in the second, he surrenders his healing for love; in the final version he realizes that his dedication to his work must also include the reaction of love upon that work.

Moody's health in early years was perfect. My first knowledge of any illness of his was after the ascent of the Gross Venediger, when he suffered from exposure, as later from continued exercise in the tropic heat of an Italian summer.

The effects seemed to have passed away completely. He had, however, a severe fall while climbing Mount Parnassus on his trip to the Peloponnesus in 1902; some four years later, I met him in New York, walking quite unconcernedly to Dr. Bull's hospital to have a growth removed from his injured thigh. The operation proved more serious than was anticipated, but the surgeon assured him that, if there was no recurrence of the symptoms within a year, he might be pronounced cured. In the spring of 1907, he made an expedition to Spain, Italy, and France with Ridgely Torrence. While they were walking up the hill of Posilippo near Naples, Moody suddenly stopped and lay down. The pain in his thigh had come back. From that time on, Torrence saw a change in him — his usual even spirits yielded to deep depression. It must be remembered by those who noted a falling-off in Moody's work and an increasing withdrawal from human relations that from then on he walked in the shadow of doom. In 1908, he had a severe attack of typhoid fever. A

cheering mark of recognition came to him
that year in the degree of Doctor of Letters
awarded him by Yale University. The
summer was spent largely on the island
of Monhegan off the Maine coast with
Ridgely Torrence, whence he returned
in better health and spirits. But the
recurring growth proved to be malignant,
and at last symptoms appeared in the
brain. It was the same terrible malady
from which Trumbull Stickney had died,
and Moody must have had its horror
clearly before him, but he bore himself
always with stoical courage. My last
meeting with him was in the winter of
1909, when he came out to Jackson Park
for an afternoon of skating, a pastime he
always greatly enjoyed. After twenty
minutes he drew up at the bank, took off
his skates, and we walked slowly away
under the trees, which suddenly reminded
him of the snowy woods on Arlington
Heights above Cambridge, where we
had spent many winter afternoons in his
student days.

Later that winter, he went to Cali-
fornia, where he painted with William

Wendt, and seemed to regain strength and hope. He was married to Mrs. Harriet C. Brainerd in Quebec, May 7, 1909, and spent the summer in England. The devoted care of his wife and his sister Charlotte and the frequent companionship of Ferdinand Schevill were his last happiness. To the latter he confided his constant regret that he had given so much of his last precious time to prose, which he, like Milton, reckoned to be but "the work of his left hand." Once he said, "It is perhaps a judgment that this confusion has come upon me." He died at Colorado Springs on the seventeenth of October, 1910. The night before his death there came to him one of those visions which he had always held as the source of his highest poetry — as commands not to be disobeyed. This vision is touched upon in a stanza of the heartfelt threnody which Percy MacKaye wrote on his dead friend. (*North American Review*, October, 1911.)

Darkling those constellations of his soul
Glimmered, while racks of stellar lightnings shot
The white, creative meteors of thought

Through that last night, where — clad in cloudy
    stole —
Beside his ebbing shoal
Of life-blood, stood Saint Paul, blazing a theme
Of living drama from a fiery scroll
Across his stretchéd vision as in dream —
When death, with blind dark, blotted out the
    whole.

II

It is difficult to think of a human being
more perfectly endowed with strength and
beauty of body and mind than William
Vaughn Moody. Physically he was
slightly above medium height, graceful
and well proportioned, in young man-
hood with a strength beyond his stature,
and with great endurance. In college he
wore a mustache; later in life, a Van
Dyke beard. His hands were unusually
deft and sensitive. His voice was clear
and resonant. Professor Manly speaks of
his "wonderful eyes, light, clear blue, and
shining like large gems because of the
sailor-like ruddiness that wind and sun
had laid upon his cheek and brow."

He was fond of all the grander phases of
the physical world, the forest, the sea, the

mountains, the desert.   Whether his delight in nature or in the arts were the greater, there is no doubt that his senses, naturally keen, were schooled to a closer perception of values and a richer enjoyment by his æsthetic training in music, painting, and poetry.   Moody respected his sensuous equipment as part of his endowment for his vocation.   He was very fond of tobacco, but he declared once that if he thought smoking tended to dull the senses, he would never light his pipe again.   In physical as in intellectual quality, he was a young Euphues, and he bore himself as if conscious of his distinction.   When in college I first came on the portrait of Flavian in *Marius the Epicurean*, I instantly thought of Moody.   In youth his habitual expression was one of calm self-possession, in the literal sense of the word.   Certainly he did not wear his heart upon his sleeve and he abhorred sentimentality.   Yet a guarded joy looked out from his eyes, with gleams of ironical amusement, and now and again his whole being would flame up in laughter.   There was something of the faun in him, and oc-

casionally his mood would verge toward
the satyric when the flesh would threaten
the control of the spirit.   Later in life, his
face took on the more somber, deeply
inward expression shown in his portrait
of himself.

He was always a good companion,
walking, swimming, riding, at a concert
or art gallery, spending the night smoking
before the fire or under the stars.   I think
he was at his best with one other person,
or at least a small group, for his rare
personal quality came out mostly in the
warmth of intimacy.   Daniel Gregory
Mason gives a delightful picture of him in
conversation, "slightly knitting his brows,
as if taking, from under half-closed lids, a
bird's-eye view of the broadest possible
stretch of his subject, while he communed
with his pipe, frequently pressing down
the tobacco with a forefinger long enured
to that service, and finally producing a
brief comment, usually metaphorical and
often madly exaggerative, that liberated
the mind more than floods of ordinary
talk."   In this personal intercourse, his
faculty for making all communication a

sort of fine art had full scope. Of such
intimacy his play with words was a distinct promotion. About him there always grew up a special vocabulary which
constituted a kind of secret language.
Mason gives some examples: " 'It' is everything, taken together, that may be the
object of a youthful idealist's devotion; it
is the sum total of all that is beautiful and
worthy of loyalty in the world."   "A
'diastole' is a mood in which, so to speak,
the spiritual circulation is good:... it is a
mood of vitality, of realization, of fulfill-
ment."   In large groups, or with people
whom he did not know well, Moody was
inclined to be self-conscious. Sometimes
he played up with an effort; sometimes,
especially when the company bored him,
he fell utterly silent. His social sense,
however, grew along with his capacity for
life in other directions.   I can quite believe that he found the group of literary
men in New York, poets and playwrights,
a most congenial company, and brought
to them the larger conviviality which
Percy MacKaye has noted in his poem
"Uriel."

Places and human associations had a special significance for Moody, and as a true artist he did not mix his *genres*. His reticence in personal matters was extraordinary. At college I never heard him speak of his family or home, almost never of his school life. In Chicago he seldom talked of Cambridge, and the depth of his feeling for it revealed in his letters came to me as a surprise. Even with his intimate friends he was more given to impersonal talk than to that form of amusement which Mr. Howells says is described in Cambridge, not as gossip, but as "gathering material for formulating character." With his joy in life, with the extraordinary gusto which he brought to experience, with a sense of humor which did not fail to include himself, he had a personal reserve, an exact sense of values, and a fundamental seriousness, which set him apart from others, and which constituted an essential part of his character as poet.

Of Trumbull Stickney, Moody wrote in an article in the *North American Review* (November, 1906): "Though he had a richly varied and most human existence, with senses, affections, curiosities, all in vivid action, the truth indeed was that poetry was both the root and flower of his life, the point of repair for all his vital powers." So it was with Moody himself. His very being was poetry. He lived in the highest sense in his own, and he took the fullest pleasure in the poetry of others. When he read aloud, his voice was full of unforgettable emotion and reverence.

He grew up in the tradition of English poetry. It was natural that his first efforts should be imitative, and the fact that the imitation was so perfect has done some wrong to his later fame. In college he passed from one master to another, and the poets whom he was reading at the time found echoes in his verse — Wordsworth, Keats, Shelley, Tennyson, Browning, Rossetti, Swinburne. Later the robust manner of Kipling appealed to him, and his medieval fancy turned from Tennyson to William Morris. Professor Gates brought Francis Thompson to his attention, and during his first year in Chicago he read us "The Hound of

Heaven," "Dream Tryst," and especially, "The Poppy" and "To Monica Thought Dying." Professor Sophie C. Hart, of Wellesley, who met Thompson a little later, remembers his asking her about Moody, "the man in America who writes like me." A fine passage would haunt his mind for years. I remember on our walk through the Black Forest his quoting quite suddenly the lines from Dante which stand as the text of "A Dialogue in Purgatory," written much later. The great masters of poetry, those who exercised an enduring influence upon him, came to him sometimes as the result of circumstances. Dante he had never read until he reviewed, for the *Harvard Monthly*, Professor Charles Eliot Norton's translation of the *Inferno*. The occasion of his deep interest in Milton I have already indicated. Of Greek poetry, however, he was a student in his undergraduate time, and later the whole glorious body of Greek tragedy was vivified for 'him 'by his reading of it with Trumbull Stickney.

Such of Moody's early imitative verse as survived at all is to be found in the pages of the *Harvard Monthly* between 1889 and 1894. Throughout the poems published in the volume of collected verse will be found echoes of the Victorian poets, echoes which his friendly critic, Professor Gates, pointed out unsparingly in his review in *The Nation*, August 22, 1901. It was fortunate, however, that Moody did not suppress such poems as "Harmonics," "Heart's Wild-Flower," "The Bracelet of Grass," "A Grey Day," "The Brute," or "The Menagerie," because of similarities in manner to older poets. These poems all deal with experiences and thoughts which were his own, and through them we can see coming into full authority a form and mode of utterance in which imitation has given way to genuine assimilation. Of this aspect of Moody's work, Professor Paul Shorey has given an illuminating discussion in a lecture at the University of Chicago, republished in the *University of Chicago Record*, July, 1927:

At the most, we are haunted by a faintly familiar aroma, and say not, That is from Marlowe's *Faustus*, Shelley's *Prometheus*, or Keats's *Hyperion*, but, That is Moody writing as Marlowe, Shelley, or Keats might have written.... We cannot say what, if any, passage of Shakespeare or Æschylus suggested the line:

> But yet conjecture clamors at thy heart.

We can only say that it is an Æschylean or Shakespearean line.... We need not quote Marlowe in a footnote, but we think of Marlowe when we read:

Look where the giant wings rock down the slope,

or

> Lo! where God's body hangs upon the cross,
> Drooping from out yon skyey Golgotha.

Still more distinct perhaps is the note of Shelley in:

> All palpitant and doubtful on her head
> A soft-winged splendour lit.

And faint echoes of Milton, whom Moody edited, are everywhere.

>   past the walls
> Rhipean and the Arimaspian caves
> I sought the far hyperborean day.

More explicit borrowings are rare.

As a fawn from the green windows of a wood,
Slave of the panic woodland fear,

recalls the fawn in Murray's translation of the *Bacchæ*, Moody's favorite Greek play.... It

pleases me to believe that the explicit quotation
of Pindar in "The Moon-Moth,"

> as if Pindar heard
> And loved again the sweet fruit of his breast,

preserves the memory of the afternoon when
I called his attention to that phrase of Pindar.

It is Moody's strength and glory that
he worked in the great tradition of the
poetry of the world.   He was a scholar.
He made scholarship a high and living
thing in its preservation of the noble and
beautiful things of the past and its contribution to the wealth of those who would
live nobly and beautifully in the present.

Possibly the most immediate and ele-
mentary quality to be noted in Moody's
poetry is his sense of values in his medium,
his craftsmanship in the use of his tools.
He was always enamoured of words, both
the noble and the base-born. An incident
which occurred just after his arrival in
Chicago affords a homely illustration of
this trait.   We had stepped into a bar,
where an habitué accosted him with a
familiarity from which Moody withdrew
with some accentuation of the Cambridge
manner, whereupon the stranger in-

quired, with resentment, why he was so "abrupt." Moody always enjoyed recalling the adjective in its new sense. Indeed, a great deal of the spice of our conversation in those days was his play with words. In his copies of Hardy's novels I find the fly-leaves containing lists of folk-words from that writer's vocabulary. Undoubtedly Moody's delight in Francis Thompson was in part due to that poet's power of fusing recalcitrant verbal material into poetic harmony. Miss Sinclair, in her appreciative criticism of Moody's poetry in the *Atlantic Monthly* (September, 1906), comments on his use of archaic or unfamiliar terms: *bataillous*, *vesperine*, *energic*, *margent*, *blooth*, and *windelstræ*. Undoubtedly Moody laid himself open to criticism in this matter, but he had the spirit of the pioneer, he was willing to take chances. "I think," he wrote to Mason, "you are not tolerant enough of the instinct of conquest in language, the attempt to push out its boundaries, to win for it continually some new swiftness, some rare compression, to distil from it a more opaline drop. Isn't it possible, too, to be pedantic in the demand for simplicity? It's a cry which, if I notice aright, Nature has a jaunty way of disregarding."

Moody always dissented from Wordsworth's theory that there should be no difference between the diction of poetry and that of prose. For him the word with all its associations and imaginative suggestions was in itself an element of poetry and history, and he employed it with a reverent sense of its use by poets of the past and also by the mass of men and women to whom it had been part of life. At the same time he had a genuine feeling for present-day colloquial values. To those who knew him "The Menagerie" has a unique worth in preserving one phase of his personality. Even in his use of slang, Moody kept a certain fastidiousness. If he sacrificed something of what is called purity of diction to the demands of his theme, it was because he felt those demands truly. He strove for precision, *le mot juste*, and if the word he needed was unfamiliar or had to be reminted, he yielded to the necessity. This necessity was not merely one of thought, but also of mood and feeling. "A word was to him," wrote William Morton Payne in *The Dial* (December 16, 1912), "like a jewel reflecting manifold hues from its facets, or like the note of a violin with its gamut of attendant overtones which he made us overhear."

Akin to Moody's instinct for words was his pursuit of figures of speech to which they invited him. I have spoken of this also as characterizing his daily use and wont. Once coming back from a walk with Norman Hapgood, he said with satisfaction, "We chased a metaphor all the way across the Harvard Bridge and back again." This opulence of imagery was again a ground of criticism, particularly of his early work. Mr. Santayana once remarked that Moody's early verse reminded him of stained-glass windows. The critic in *The Nation* (February 6, 1913) declares that "The image has come in many cases to override the idea, until it is no longer a figure but a symbol. In this way there is something almost allegorical and even enigmatical about much of his verse, like 'The Quarry,' 'The Brute,' or even 'The Moon-Moth.'" This is an extreme statement of Moody's romantic tendency. On the other hand, we have Miss Sinclair praising him for the submission of this romantic strain to order: "His quality is opulence, a certain gorgeousness that is never barbaric, owing to his power of classic restraint. His sweetness is crystal, never luscious or impure."

In his use of meter, rhythm, and stanza-form, Moody was again an artist with a background of scholarship. He learned the practice of the English poets in these matters even before he knew the technical terms. Later, his study of primitive poetry, Old French and Old Norse, enriched his store of memories, and finally he found in Professor Shorey a guide to the more intricate effects of Greek tragic poetry and the ode. His genius was essentially lyrical; his greatest originality shows itself in his use of the simplest forms, to which he gave an accent peculiarly his own. For the dramas he drew on the great tradition of English blank verse, from Marlowe and Shakespeare to Milton, and thence to Keats and Swinburne. In movement, even more than in diction, we have echoes of these masters, giving a constant enrichment of tone. The ode, however, was his favorite form, with its effect of lyric freedom secured within the limits of precise measure and controlled variation. The "Ode in Time of Hesitation" marks the height of public poetry in America; it has an eloquence of form which is as native as its subject-matter. And it is impossible to close this brief technical consideration of Moody's poetry without calling attention to certain minor effects of phrasing and movement in which resides the poetic dispensation that Matthew Arnold called Natural Magic. There is the sense of sullen resistance in the consonants of the lines:

As now, blind bulks of sheep, or hunger bitten
To creep the stagnant bottom of the world;

and the fleetness of anapestic flight in

Must she seek her lover, her king of kings
Naked, stripped of her costly things?
Must she have no garment but love?

Professor Shorey, with his sure sense of poetic values, recalls the lines from "Old Pourquoi":

> Couched in the sweet, satirical,
> Impudent tongue of France,

"for sheer delight in the calculated effect of the division of the second epithet from the third by the verse-ending."

Alike in diction and in movement, Moody's poetry gives the impression of abundance and extraordinary variety, of a technical mastery quite complete. Among his lyrics the best known through anthologies and frequent quotation is Pandora's Song, "Of wounds and sore defeat." It may be noticed that the theme, victory in defeat, is one which has attracted many poets. Matthew Arnold has given utterance to it in a short lyric, "The Last Word," which may be quoted here for the sake of comparison.

> Creep into thy narrow bed,
> Creep, and let no more be said!
> Vain thy onset! all stands fast.
> Thou thyself must break at last.
>
> Let the long contention cease!
> Geese are swans, and swans are geese.

Let them have it how they will!
Thou art tired, best be still.

They out-talk'd thee, hissed thee, tore thee?
Better men fared thus before thee;
Fired their ringing shot and pass'd,
Hotly charged — and sank at last.

Charge once more, then, and be dumb!
Let the victors, when they come,
When the forts of folly fall,
Find thy body by the wall!

It is clear that Arnold's poem depends on the vividness of its picture, and the suggestion of its story. It is a direct statement of experience, and is full of the quality on which he based his famous definition of poetry as "criticism of life." Moody's lyric contains no story and no single picture, though it is full of appeal to the eye as to the ear. The theme is carried by the opposition of terms, those denoting defeat and others renewed combat: "wounds" and "sore defeat" surmounted by "battlestay"; "wingéd sandals" against "delay"; "weariness and fear" issuing in "shouting spear"; and "loss and doubt and dread," in "helmet and plume"; "the shutting mist of death," "the failure of the breath," becoming the

> battle horn to blow
> Across the vales of overthrow,

to which Pandora bids hearken

> Where its echoes bring,
> Down the gray disastrous morn,
> Laughter and rallying.

It was altogether like Moody to associate triumph with "silver scorn," and "laughter" with "rallying." His poem cannot be termed deficient in criticism of life; its popularity shows that it reaches many readers who enjoy poetry primarily for its meaning. But even to them the subtlety of suggestion by which that meaning is conveyed, through the connotation of words and the variation of movement, now retarded, then springing forward with triumphant acceleration, brings, perhaps unconsciously, an emotional reenforcement of the theme. Arnold encourages to life by exhortation; Moody, by exhilaration. In such poems as Pandora's Song we find an illustration of what Walter Pater declared that all fine art, and poetry most of all, was seeking: the approximation to pure feeling which is characteristic of music.

If the dominant effect of Moody's poetry is richness and abundance, it must be recognized that he escaped or conquered the temptation which comes to poets of lavish and facile art. He never allowed himself to be betrayed into excesses of publication. The great bulk of his writing up to the time of his death was experimental, and as such was destroyed. "It is certain," says Professor Shorey, "that unlike some other great poets — Shelley, Byron, Wordsworth, and even Keats, for instance — he gave to posterity no absolutely bad and silly verse, and very little if any that is plainly weak and commonplace."

As Moody progressed, his poetry took on a more austere and somber cast. In that written after *The Fire-Bringer* he achieved a freedom of utterance and a manner entirely his own, largely by a process of limitation and exclusion, setting the force within him to expand against the pressure of constant and severe restraint. This gives to such poems as "I am the Woman" and "The Death of Eve" a strain of sheer, concentrated energy· which we find only in the greatest poets. The dialogue between Eve and Cain in the latter poem furnishes an excellent example, the force of which may be fully realized if we place beside it an older and more famous rendering of the same characters in Byron's "Cain." "For all the dramatic compression of Moody's lines," says Professor Manly, "they never cease to sing. Only a master of English verse could make lines of such length move at all, while to make them run and dance and sparkle with light is a triumphant achievement."

It is perhaps superfluous to point out that the two elements in Moody's poetic style, abundance and austerity, reflect two elements in his character and experience. He had, on the one hand, a great joy in nature and life, a natural paganism to which the visible and tangible world made instant and constant appeal; and on the other, a solemn sense of the mystery behind the external frame, which filled him with reverence and awe. At times he felt himself in immediate contact or communication with the spirits who on earth have freely and confidently touched the things beyond and unseen, especially with Him who said "The kingdom of Heaven is within you." It was Moody's task, as it was Keats's, to subdue the clamorous world of sense, to refine by meditation and discipline his mind and his art to the imperative demands of a vision and a music that came to him with an authority which he recognized as divine. But it was a transfiguration, not a renunciation. Moody was no ascetic. He would not have subscribed to Tennyson's "Higher Pantheism":

The earth, these solid stars, this weight of body
    and limb,
Are they not sign and symbol of thy division from
    Him?

Rather, he felt them the revelation of God; they wove "the garment thou seest Him by."

To Moody the separation of man from God was not of the senses, but of the in-

tellect; to show the unity of the world
with God was therefore the philosophical
task to which he set himself in his trilogy
of poetic dramas.   The first, in his final
order, deals with the striving of man in
his great prototype, Prometheus, to rise in
his own right from the elemental matter,
to take part in the creative struggle.   The
second reveals the tragedy of a God who
denies this element in his creation, and
who through his annihilation of his world
is himself involved in ruin.   The third
was to have set forth the search of mankind for reconciliation with God, through
Eve who was the original means of the
separation.   It must not be forgotten
that, though Moody in this trilogy is presenting a theme which was the center of
his own thought, he is working through
conceptions which, as myths or theologies,
have expressed throughout history mankind's sense of its relation to God.   This
is explained admirably in the letters on
The Masque of Judgment, quoted in the
Notes, which remove a misconception
too common among readers of the poetic
dramas.

It would, therefore, be a mistake to judge Moody's poetic dramas as a cosmology. Far deeper than the definition of the philosophical inseparableness of man from God is the sense of a moral unity. And this is a pervading conception through all Moody's poetry. It was so recognized by his critics in the period between the appearance of *The Masque of Judgment* and that of the two-volume collection of his works in 1912. Professor Gates wrote on the first (*The Nation*, March 28, 1901):

Doubtless *The Masque* is, on the whole, a plea for the rights of the "sanguine stain" and the "senses five." And yet, quite as surely, passion and richness of experience, as Mr. Moody conceives of them, have a spiritual cast and color, and the impression that the entire *Masque* leaves is that of a noble and lofty idealism.

Miss May Sinclair wrote in the *Atlantic Monthly* for September, 1906:

He knows that the spirit does not maintain its purity by mere divorce from Nature.... It is the same divine thing which is housed in the flesh and shrined in the spirit of man, and the process of the world is the process of its unfolding.

Professor Charleton M. Lewis (*Yale Review*, July, 1913) puts the matter very justly:

Moody saw in evil not exactly the implacable foe of good, but rather its twin brother, bone of its bone and flesh of its flesh, since both good and evil are children of passion and will.... Life is rich and wonderful because our spirits are charged with aspiration and liberty and love. If we are swayed also by jealousy and wrath, license and lust, these are but other manifestations of the same primal forces. The concords and discords are sounded on the same strings, and are essential parts of one divine harmony.

A final and exhaustive criticism on Moody's collected works by William Morton Payne may be quoted as summing up the impressions made by Moody upon one of the most catholic and fastidious of contemporary critics. (*The Dial*, December 16, 1912.)

The main thing to be emphasized concerning Moody is that he was a poet by the grace of God, and such a poet as had not been raised up before him in America — or even in the English-speaking world — since the eclipse of the great line of the older singers.... He seems to be the one authentic "maker" that our young century has given to the world, achieving a height that none of his contemporary fellow craftsmen in the poetic art, either in England or America, could attain....

The stupendous task which Moody set himself in the trilogy is the highest which poetry has ever attempted. It is the task of Æschylus and Dante and Milton, the task of Goethe in his *Faust* and of Shelley in his *Prometheus Unbound*. It is Milton's attempt to "justify the ways of God to man" coupled with the attempt of the later poets to justify the ways of man to God.

In the light of such sincere appreciation by the critics of his own decade, it is necessary to inquire why it is that during the twenty years succeeding, Moody's popularity has not been in any way commensurate with his achievement. It must be remembered that during the years after his death, poetry in England and America made a sudden turn into new fields and took on new forms of expression. In 1911, the group of poets who called themselves the Imagists was formed in London including Amy Lowell, Ezra Pound, Richard Aldington, and H. D.

They felt, perhaps rightly, that the chief obstacle they had to encounter in conquering their public was its adherence to conventions of poetic form, traditional rhythms, limited meters, and rhyme. It was natural that they should adopt a certain militancy in their enterprise. I remember an occasion when Miss Lowell, inquiring about Moody, whom she had never met, murmured, as if to herself: "I wonder if he could have kept us back."

It is not to be inferred that the Imagists and poets of free verse made any organized attack upon their predecessors who worked within traditions which they considered hampering; but their success brought up a new generation of poets, critics, and readers, who were indifferent to older poetry and its masters. If Moody had lived, he would have held his own in the renaissance of poetry. It must be remembered that when he appeared, the public interest in poetry was at its ebb. In contrast to 1928, when fifty volumes were presented for the Pulitzer Prize, in 1900, publishers were reluctant to engage in what they assumed would be a losing venture, and Moody had his first volume of collected verse rejected by a leading house before Houghton Mifflin Company accepted it.   In the decade which followed, the interest in contemporary poetry increased, partly in consequence of Moody's own powerful example; but a poetic reputation was still of slow growth, as in the past.   Ten years did not afford time for Moody's poetry to secure a large number of readers, or for his reputation to become deeply rooted in the literature that comes to be historical.   And close upon his death there came a revolution. To the tragedies of poets who died untimely, Chatterton, Shelley, Keats, Thomson, Brooke, Moody adds one of special poignancy.

Part of that poignancy lies in the fact that Moody had already shown himself in sympathy with much in the new program. The Imagists defined their æsthetic of poetry as: the presentation of a visual situation in the fewest possible concrete words, free from adjectives and conventional phrasing, unhampered by moralizing or speculation upon the philosophical significance of the visual idea — the form and rhythm developing out of the subject, not imposed upon it; the rhyme and meter determined by the judgment of the author. Some of these objectives Moody had already achieved; toward others he was clearly progressing. It is true that he would never have been satisfied with the visible world as a spectacle merely, with no curiosity as to its meaning; but the æsthetic principle that the form of poetry should grow out of the subject, rather than that the subject should be fitted to a given form, was entirely his own. His own practice tended constantly toward precision in diction and freedom in meter. For the latter reason he preferred the ode, and we find him, as early as 1898, writing of Milton's *Samson Agonistes*, "The idea might naturally have occurred to him of casting away the fixed line altogether as a useless fiction."

There are many other aspects of Moody's poetry in which he anticipates the most modern of his successors. The critic of *The Nation* (February 6, 1913) notes one which is akin to Expressionism:

His significance lies rather in his manner of reproducing a complicated state of consciousness, even in the presence of plain and familiar objects.

And again,

The clash of incongruous moods produces an effective sort of irony — a kind of grim cosmical humor — which is, after all, Moody's most original and powerful note.

With all his forward-looking qualities, Moody was, after all, distinctly a poet of his age. In looking back over his work, it is interesting to note how the forces of the time wrought themselves out in the form and substance of his verse. There is the eclecticism of the dying Victorian period, and its self-consciousness, its moral striving. There is something of the realism which reflected the influence of science, and the tendency of realism to extend itself into symbolism by the intimations which it carries of the world beyond that which we see and touch. Moody passed from the realm ruled by Tennyson and Browning, Rossetti and Swinburne, to that in which he was akin to Maeterlinck, Francis Thompson, Arthur Symons, and

Ernest Dowson. Like the last, he confronted the eternal problem of the dualism of flesh and spirit and their inevitable union, although his solution was not the same. I feel sure that he wrote "Good Friday Night" and "Second Coming" before he knew Dowson's poetry, and in any case the impulse of these poems was entirely personal, but the kinship of the two poets is unmistakable. Like Dowson and Symons he was a lover of Verlaine and the early symbolists. In *The Masque* and *The Fire-Bringer* he shared in the revival of the poetic drama as a literary form, and his prose plays were the most distinctive contribution in the United States to the movement initiated by Ibsen to make the stage once more a vehicle for serious and significant criticism of life. Thus, historically, Moody has an important place in American literature — and, like Milton, he "has left something so written to after times as they should not willingly let it die."

ROBERT MORSS LOVETT

YORK VILLAGE

From *Gloucester Moors and Other Poems*

GLOUCESTER MOORS

A MILE behind is Gloucester town
Where the fishing fleets put in,
A mile ahead the land dips down
And the woods and farms begin.
Here, where the moors stretch free
In the high blue afternoon,
Are the marching sun and talking sea,
And the racing winds that wheel and flee
On the flying heels of June.

Jill-o'er-the-ground is purple blue,
Blue is the quaker-maid,
The wild geranium holds its dew
Long in the boulder's shade.
Wax-red hangs the cup
From the huckleberry boughs,
In barberry bells the grey moths sup,
Or where the choke-cherry lifts high up
Sweet bowls for their carouse.

Over the shelf of the sandy cove
Beach-peas blossom late.
By copse and cliff the swallows rove
Each calling to his mate.

Seaward the sea-gulls go,
And the land-birds all are here;
That green-gold flash was a vireo,
And yonder flame where the marsh-flags
      grow
Was a scarlet tanager.

This earth is not the steadfast place
We landsmen build upon;
From deep to deep she varies pace,
And while she comes is gone.
Beneath my feet I feel
Her smooth bulk heave and dip;
With velvet plunge and soft upreel
She swings and steadies to her keel
Like a gallant, gallant ship.

These summer clouds she sets for sail,
The sun is her masthead light,
She tows the moon like a pinnace frail
Where her phosphor wake churns bright.
Now hid, now looming clear,
On the face of the dangerous blue
The star fleets tack and wheel and veer,
But on, but on does the old earth steer
As if her port she knew.

God, dear God! Does she know her port,
Though she goes so far about?
Or blind astray, does she make her sport
To brazen and chance it out?
I watched when her captains passed:
She were better captainless.
Men in the cabin, before the mast,
But some were reckless and some aghast,
And some sat gorged at mess.

By her battened hatch I leaned and caught
Sounds from the noisome hold, —
Cursing and sighing of souls distraught
And cries too sad to be told.
Then I strove to go down and see;
But they said, "Thou art not of us!"
I turned to those on the deck with me
And cried, "Give help!"   But they said,
        "Let be:
Our ship sails faster thus."

Jill-o'er-the-ground is purple blue,
Blue is the quaker-maid,
The alder-clump where the brook comes
        through
Breeds cresses in its shade.
To be out of the moiling street

With its swelter and its sin!
Who has given to me this sweet,
And given my brother dust to eat?
And when will his wage come in?

Scattering wide or blown in ranks,
Yellow and white and brown,
Boats and boats from the fishing banks
Come home to Gloucester town.
There is cash to purse and spend,
There are wives to be embraced,
Hearts to borrow and hearts to lend,
And hearts to take and keep to the end, —
O littie sails, make haste!

But thou, vast outbound ship of souls,
What harbor town for thee?
What shapes, when thy arriving tolls,
Shall crowd the banks to see?
Shall all the happy shipmates then
Stand singing brotherly?
Or shall a haggard ruthless few
Warp her over and bring her to,
While the many broken souls of men
Fester down in the slaver's pen,
And nothing to say or do?

GOOD FRIDAY NIGHT

At last the bird that sang so long
In twilight circles, hushed his song:
Above the ancient square
The stars came here and there.

Good Friday night! Some hearts were
        bowed,
But some amid the waiting crowd
Because of too much youth
Felt not that mystic ruth;

And of these hearts my heart was one:
Nor when beneath the arch of stone
With dirge and candle flame
The cross of passion came,

Did my glad spirit feel reproof,
Though on the awful tree aloof,
Unspiritual, dead,
Drooped the ensanguined Head.

To one who stood where myrtles made
A little space of deeper shade

(As I could half descry,
A stranger, even as I),

I said, "These youths who bear along
The symbols of their Saviour's wrong,
The spear, the garment torn,
The flaggel, and the thorn, —

"Why do they make this mummery?
Would not a brave man gladly die
For a much smaller thing
Than to be Christ and king?"

He answered nothing, and I turned.
Throned in its hundred candles burned
The jeweled eidolon
Of her who bore the Son.

The crowd was prostrate; still, I felt
No shame until the stranger knelt;
Then not to kneel, almost
Seemed like a vulgar boast.

I knelt.   The doll-face, waxen white,
Flowered out a living dimness; bright
Dawned the dear mortal grace
Of my own mother's face.

When we were risen up, the street
Was vacant; all the air hung sweet
With lemon-flowers; and soon
The sky would hold the moon.

More silently than new-found friends
To whom much silence makes amends
For the much babble vain
While yet their lives were twain,

We walked along the odorous hill.
The light was little yet; his will
I could not see to trace
Upon his form or face.

So when aloft the gold moon broke,
I cried, heart-stung.   As one who woke
He turned unto my cries
The anguish of his eyes.

"Friend! Master!"   I cried falteringly,
"Thou seest the thing they make of thee.
Oh, by the light divine
My mother shares with thine,

"I beg that I may lay my head
Upon thy shoulder and be fed

With thoughts of brotherhood!"
So through the odorous wood,

More silently than friends new-found
We walked.   At the first meadow bound
His figure ashen-stoled
Sank in the moon's broad gold.

ROAD–HYMN FOR THE START

Leave the early bells at chime,
    Leave the kindled hearth to blaze,
Leave the trellised panes where children
        linger out the waking-time,
Leave the forms of sons and fathers
        trudging through the misty ways,
Leave the sounds of mothers taking up
        their sweet laborious days.

Pass them by! even while our soul
    Yearns to them with keen distress.
Unto them a part is given; we will strive
        to see the whole.
Dear shall be the banquet table where
        their singing spirits press;
Dearer be our sacred hunger, and our
        pilgrim loneliness.

We have felt the ancient swaying
    Of the earth before the sun,
On the darkened marge of midnight heard
        sidereal rivers playing;

Rash it was to bathe our souls there, but
    we plunged and all was done.
That is lives and lives behind us — lo, our
    journey is begun!

Careless where our face is set,
    Let us take the open way.
What we are no tongue has told us:
    Errand-goers who forget?
Soldiers heedless of their harry?   Pilgrim
    people gone astray?
We have heard a voice cry "Wander!"
    That was all we heard it say.

Ask no more: 'tis much, 'tis much!
    Down the road the day-star calls;
Touched with change in the wide heavens,
    like a leaf the frost winds touch,
Flames the failing moon a moment, ere it
    shrivels white and falls;
Hid aloft, a wild throat holdeth sweet
    and sweeter intervals.

Leave him still to ease in song
    Half his little heart's unrest:
Speech is his, but we may journey to-
    ward the life for which we long.

God, who gives the bird its anguish, mak-
    eth nothing manifest,
But upon our lifted foreheads pours the
    boon of endless quest.

AN ODE IN TIME OF HESITATION

(After seeing at Boston the statue of Robert Gould Shaw, killed while storming Fort Wagner, July 18, 1863, at the head of the first enlisted Negro regiment, the Fifty-fourth Massachusetts.)

I

BEFORE the solemn bronze Saint Gaudens made
    To thrill the heedless passer's heart with awe,
And set here in the city's talk and trade
To the good memory of Robert Shaw,
This bright March morn I stand,
And hear the distant spring come up the land;
Knowing that what I hear is not unheard
Of this boy soldier and his negro band,
For all their gaze is fixed so stern ahead,
For all the fatal rhythm of their tread.
The land they died to save from death and shame
    Trembles and waits, hearing the spring's great name,
And by her pangs these resolute ghosts are stirred.

II

Through street and mall the tides of peo-
    ple go
Heedless; the trees upon the Common show
No hint of green; but to my listening heart
The still earth doth impart
Assurance of her jubilant emprise,
And it is clear to my long-searching eyes
That love at last has might upon the skies.
The ice is runneled on the little pond;
A telltale patter drips from off the trees;
The air is touched with southland spicer-
    ies,
As if but yesterday it tossed the frond
Of pendant mosses where the live-oaks
    grow
Beyond Virginia and the Carolines,
Or had its will among the fruits and vines
Of aromatic isles asleep beyond
Florida and the Gulf of Mexico.

III

Soon shall the Cape Ann children shout
    in glee,
Spying the arbutus, spring's dear recluse;
Hill lads at dawn shall hearken the wild
    goose

Go honking northward over Tennessee;
West from Oswego to Sault Sainte-Marie,
And on to where the Pictured Rocks are
      hung,
And yonder where, gigantic, wilful,
      young,
Chicago sitteth at the northwest gates,
With restless violent hands and casual
      tongue
Moulding her mighty fates,
The Lakes shall robe them in ethereal
      sheen;
And like a larger sea, the vital green
Of springing wheat shall vastly be out-
      flung
Over Dakota and the prairie states.
By desert people immemorial
On Arizonan mesas shall be done
Dim rites unto the thunder and the sun;
Nor shall the primal gods lack sacrifice
More splendid, when the white Sierras
      call
Unto the Rockies straightway to arise
And dance before the unveiled ark of the
      year,
Sounding their windy cedars as for
      shawms,

Unrolling rivers clear
For flutter of broad phylacteries;
While Shasta signals to Alaskan seas
That watch old sluggish glaciers down-
      ward creep
To fling their icebergs thundering from
      the steep,
And Mariposa through the purple calms
Gazes at far Hawaii crowned with palms
Where East and West are met, —
A rich seal on the ocean's bosom set
To say that East and West are twain,
With different loss and gain:
The Lord hath sundered them; let them
      be sundered yet.

IV

Alas! what sounds are these that come
Sullenly over the Pacific seas, —
Sounds of ignoble battle, striking dumb
The season's half-awakened ecstasies?
Must I be humble, then,
Now when my heart hath need of pride?
Wild love falls on me from these sculp-
      tured men;
By loving much the land for which they
      died

I would be justified.
My spirit was away on pinions wide
To soothe in praise of her its passionate
    mood
And ease it of its ache of gratitude.
Too sorely heavy is the debt they lay
On me and the companions of my day.
I would remember now
My country's goodliness, make sweet her
    name.
Alas! what shade art thou
Of sorrow or of blame
Liftest the lyric leafage from her brow,
And pointest a slow finger at her shame?

V

Lies! lies! It cannot be! The wars we
    wage
Are noble, and our battles still are won
By justice for us, ere we lift the gage.
We have not sold our loftiest heritage.
The proud republic hath not stooped to
    cheat
And scramble in the market-place of war;
Her forehead weareth yet its solemn star.
Here is her witness: this, her perfect son,
This delicate and proud New England soul

Who leads despisèd men, with just-un-
    shackled feet,
Up the large ways where death and glory
    meet,
To show all peoples that our shame is done,
That once more we are clean and spirit-
    whole.

VI

Crouched in the sea fog on the moaning
    sand
All night he lay, speaking some simple
    word
From hour to hour to the slow minds
    that heard,
Holding each poor life gently in his hand
And breathing on the base rejected clay
Till each dark face shone mystical and
    grand
Against the breaking day;
And lo, the shard the potter cast away
Was grown a fiery chalice crystal-fine
Fulfilled of the divine
Great wine of battle wrath by God's ring-
    finger stirred.
Then upward, where the shadowy bastion
    loomed

Huge on the mountain in the wet sea
      light,
Whence now, and now, infernal flowerage
      bloomed,
Bloomed, burst, and scattered down its
      deadly seed, —
They swept, and died like freemen on the
      height,
Like freemen, and like men of noble
      breed;
And when the battle fell away at night
By hasty and contemptuous hands were
      thrust
Obscurely in a common grave with him
The fair-haired keeper of their love and
      trust.
Now limb doth mingle with dissolvèd
      limb
In nature's busy old democracy
To flush the mountain laurel when she
      blows
Sweet by the southern sea,
And heart with crumbled heart climbs in
      the rose: —
The untaught hearts with the high heart
      that knew
This mountain fortress for no earthly hold

Of temporal quarrel, but the bastion old
Of spiritual wrong,
Built by an unjust nation sheer and strong,
Expugnable but by a nation's rue
And bowing down before that equal
        shrine
By all men held divine,
Whereof his band and he were the most
        holy sign.

VII

O bitter, bitter shade!
Wilt thou not put the scorn
And instant tragic question from thine
        eye?
Do thy dark brows yet crave
That swift and angry stave —
Unmeet for this desirous morn —
That I have striven, striven to evade?
Gazing on him, must I not deem they
        err
Whose careless lips in street and shop aver
As common tidings, deeds to make his
        cheek
Flush from the bronze, and his dead
        throat to speak?
Surely some elder singer would arise,

Whose harp hath leave to threaten and to
    mourn
Above this people when they go astray.
Is Whitman, the strong spirit, overworn?
Has Whittier put his yearning wrath
    away?
I will not and I dare not yet believe!
Though furtively the sunlight seems to
    grieve,
And the spring-laden breeze
Out of the gladdening west is sinister
With sounds of nameless battle overseas;
Though when we turn and question in
    suspense
If these things be indeed after these ways,
And what things are to follow after these,
Our fluent men of place and consequence
Fumble and fill their mouths with hollow
    phrase,
Or for the end-all of deep arguments
Intone their dull commercial liturgies —
I dare not yet believe! My ears are
    shut!
I will not hear the thin satiric praise
And muffled laughter of our enemies,
Bidding us never sheathe our valiant
    sword

Till we have changed our birthright for a
     gourd
Of wild pulse stolen from a barbarian's
     hut;
Showing how wise it is to cast away
The symbols of our spiritual sway,
That so our hands with better ease
May wield the driver's whip and grasp
     the jailer's keys.

VIII

Was it for this our fathers kept the law?
This crown shall crown their struggle and
     their ruth?
Are we the eagle nation Milton saw
Mewing its mighty youth,
Soon to possess the mountain winds of
     truth,
And be a swift familiar of the sun
Where aye before God's face his trumpets
     run?
Or have we but the talons and the maw,
And for the abject likeness of our heart
Shall some less lordly bird be set apart? —
Some gross-billed wader where the
     swamps are fat?
Some gorger in the sun?   Some prowler
     with the bat?

IX

Ah no!
We have not fallen so.
We are our fathers' sons: let those who
     lead us know!
'Twas only yesterday sick Cuba's cry
Came up the tropic wind, "Now help us,
     for we die!"
Then Alabama heard,
And rising, pale, to Maine and Idaho
Shouted a burning word.
Proud state with proud impassioned state
     conferred,
And at the lifting of a hand sprang forth,
East, west, and south, and north,
Beautiful armies. Oh, by the sweet
     blood and young
Shed on the awful hill slope at San Juan,
By the unforgotten names of eager boys
Who might have tasted girls' love and
     been stung
With the old mystic joys
And starry griefs, now the spring nights
     come on,
But that the heart of youth is generous, —
We charge you, ye who lead us,
Breathe on their chivalry no hint of stain!

Turn not their new-world victories to
   gain!
One least leaf plucked for chaffer from the
   bays
Of their dear praise,
One jot of their pure conquest put to hire,
The implacable republic will require;
With clamor, in the glare and gaze of
   noon,
Or subtly, coming as a thief at night,
But surely, very surely, slow or soon
That insult deep we deeply will requite.
Tempt not our weakness, our cupidity!
For save we let the island men go free,
Those baffled and dislaureled ghosts
Will curse us from the lamentable coasts
Where walk the frustrate dead.
The cup of trembling shall be drainèd
   quite,
Eaten the sour bread of astonishment,
With ashes of the hearth shall be made
   white
Our hair, and wailing shall be in the tent;
Then on your guiltier head
Shall our intolerable self-disdain
Wreak suddenly its anger and its pain;
For manifest in that disastrous light

We shall discern the right
And do it, tardily. — O ye who lead,
Take heed!
Blindness we may forgive, but baseness
      we will smite.

THE QUARRY

BETWEEN the rice swamps and the fields
     of tea
I met a sacred elephant, snow-white.
Upon his back a huge pagoda towered
Full of brass gods and food of sacrifice.
Upon his forehead sat a golden throne,
The massy metal twisted into shapes
Grotesque, antediluvian, such as move
In myth or have their broken images
Sealed in the stony middle of the hills.
A peacock spread his thousand dyes to
     screen
The yellow sunlight from the head of one
Who sat upon the throne, clad stiff with
     gems,
Heirlooms of dynasties of buried kings, —
Himself the likeness of a buried king,
With frozen gesture and unfocused eyes.
The trappings of the beast were over-
     scrawled
With broideries — sea-shapes and flying
     things,
Fan-trees and dwarfed nodosities of pine,

Mixed with old alphabets, and faded lore
Fallen from ecstatic mouths before the
    Flood,
Or gathered by the daughters when they
    walked
Eastward in Eden with the Sons of God
Whom love and the deep moon made
    garrulous.
Between the carven tusks his trunk hung
    dead;
Blind as the eyes of pearl in Buddha's
    brow
His beaded eyes stared thwart upon the
    road;
And feebler than the doting knees of eld,
His joints, of size to swing the builder's
    crane
Across the war-walls of the Anakim,
Made vain and shaken haste.   Good need
    was his
To hasten: panting, foaming, on the slot
Came many brutes of prey, their several
    hates
Laid by until the sharing of the spoil.
Just as they gathered stomach for the leap,
The sun was darkened, and wide-bal-
    anced wings

Beat downward on the trade-wind from
      the sea.
A wheel of shadow sped along the fields
And o'er the dreaming cities. Suddenly
My heart misgave me, and I cried aloud,
"Alas! What dost thou here? What dost
      thou here?"
The great beasts and the little halted
      sharp,
Eyed the grand circler, doubting his in-
      tent.
Straightway the wind flawed and he came
      about,
Stooping to take the vanward of the pack;
Then turned, between the chasers and
      the chased,
Crying a word I could not understand, —
But stiller-tongued, with eyes somewhat
      askance,
They settled to the slot and disappeared.

ON A SOLDIER FALLEN IN
THE PHILIPPINES

STREETS of the roaring town,
Hush for him, hush, be still!
He comes, who was stricken down
Doing the word of our will.
Hush! Let him have his state,
Give him his soldier's crown.
The grists of trade can wait
Their grinding at the mill,
But he cannot wait for his honor, now the
      trumpet has been blown;
Wreathe pride now for his granite brow,
      lay love on his breast of stone.

Toll! Let the great bells toll
Till the clashing air is dim.
Did we wrong this parted soul?
We will make up it to him.
Toll! Let him never guess
What work we set him to.
Laurel, laurel, yes;
He did what we bade him do.
Praise, and never a whispered hint but the
      fight he fought was good;

Never a word that the blood on his sword
     was his country's own heart's-
     blood.

A flag for the soldier's bier
Who dies that his land may live;
O, banners, banners here,
That he doubt not nor misgive!
That he heed not from the tomb
The evil days draw near
When the nation, robed in gloom,
With its faithless past shall strive.
Let him never dream that his bullet's
     scream went wide of its island
     mark,
Home to the heart of his darling land
     where she stumbled and sinned in
     the dark.

THE BRUTE

THROUGH his might men work their wills.
They have boweled out the hills
For food to keep him toiling in the cages
    they have wrought;
And they fling him, hour by hour,
Limbs of men to give him power;
Brains of men to give him cunning; and
    for dainties to devour
Children's souls, the little worth; hearts of
    women, cheaply bought:
He takes them and he breaks them, but
    he gives them scanty thought.

For about the noisy land,
Roaring, quivering 'neath his hand,
His thoughts brood fierce and sullen or
    laugh in lust of pride
O'er the stubborn things that he
Breaks to dust and brings to be.
Some he mightily establishes, some flings
    down utterly.
There is thunder in his stride, nothing
    ancient can abide,

When he hales the hills together and
   bridles up the tide.

Quietude and loveliness,
Holy sights that heal and bless,
They are scattered and abolished where
   his iron hoof is set;
When he splashes through the brae
Silver streams are choked with clay,
When he snorts the bright cliffs crumble
   and the woods go down like hay;
He lairs in pleasant cities, and the hag-
   gard people fret
Squalid 'mid their new-got riches, soot-
   begrimed and desolate.

They who caught and bound him tight
Laughed exultant at his might,
Saying, "Now behold, the good time
   comes for the weariest and the
   least!
We will use this lusty knave:
No more need for men to slave;
We may rise and look about us and have
   knowledge ere the grave."
But the Brute said in his breast, "Till the
   mills I grind have ceased,

The riches shall be dust of dust, dry ashes
      be the feast!

"On the strong and cunning few
Cynic favors I will strew;
I will stuff their maw with overplus until
      their spirit dies;
From the patient and the low
I will take the joys they know;
They shall hunger after vanities and still
      an-hungered go.
Madness shall be on the people, ghastly
      jealousies arise;
Brother's blood shall cry on brother up the
      dead and empty skies.

"I will burn and dig and hack
Till the heavens suffer lack;
God shall feel a pleasure fail Him, crying
      to his cherubim,
'Who hath flung yon mud-ball there
Where my world went green and fair?'
I shall laugh and hug me, hearing how
      his sentinels declare,
"'Tis the Brute they chained to labor!
      He has made the bright earth
      dim.

Stores of wares and pelf a plenty, but they
     got no good of him.'"

So he plotted in his rage:
So he deals it, age by age.
But even as he roared his curse a still small
     Voice befell;
Lo, a still and pleasant voice bade them
     none the less rejoice,
For the Brute must bring the good time
     on; he has no other choice.
He may struggle, sweat, and yell, but he
     knows exceeding well
He must work them out salvation ere they
     send him back to hell.

All the desert that he made
He must treble bless with shade,
In primal wastes set precious seed of rap-
     ture and of pain;
All the strongholds that he built
For the powers of greed and guilt —
He must strew their bastions down the sea
     and choke their towers with silt;
He must make the temples clean for the
     gods to come again,

And lift the lordly cities under skies with-
    out a stain.

In a very cunning tether
He must lead the tyrant weather;
He must loose the curse of Adam from the
    worn neck of the race;
He must cast out hate and fear,
Dry away each fruitless tear,
And make the fruitful tears to gush from
    the deep heart and clear.
He must give each man his portion, each
    his pride and worthy place;
He must batter down the arrogant and
    lift the weary face,
On each vile mouth set purity, on each
    low forehead grace.

Then, perhaps, at the last day,
They will whistle him away,
Lay a hand upon his muzzle in the face of
    God, and say,
"Honor, Lord, the Thing we tamed!
Let him not be scourged or blamed,
Even through his wrath and fierceness
    was thy fierce wroth world re-
    claimed!

Honor Thou thy servants' servant; let thy
    justice now be shown."
Then the Lord will heed their saying, and
    the Brute come to his own,
'Twixt the Lion and the Eagle, by the
    armpost of the Throne.

THE MENAGERIE

Thank God my brain is not inclined to
    cut
Such capers every day!   I'm just about
Mellow, but then — There goes the tent-
    flap shut.
Rain's in the wind.   I thought so: every
    snout
Was twitching when the keeper turned
    me out.

That screaming parrot makes my blood
    run cold.
Gabriel's trump! the big bull elephant
Squeals "Rain!" to the parched herd.
    The monkeys scold,
And jabber that it's rain water they want.
(It makes me sick to see a monkey pant.)

I'll foot it home, to try and make be-
    lieve
I'm sober.   After this I stick to beer,
And drop the circus when the sane folks
    leave.

A man's a fool to look at things too near:
They look back, and begin to cut up
    queer.

Beasts do, at any rate; especially
Wild devils caged.   They have the cool-
    est way
Of being something else than what you
    see:
You pass a sleek young zebra nosing hay,
A nylghau looking bored and distingué, —

And think you've seen a donkey and a
    bird.
Not on your life!   Just glance back, if you
    dare.
The zebra chews, the nylghau hasn't
    stirred;
But something's happened, Heaven knows
    what or where
To freeze your scalp and pompadour
    your hair.

I'm not precisely an æolian lute
Hung in the wandering winds of senti-
    ment,
But drown me if the ugliest, meanest brute

Grunting and fretting in that sultry tent
Didn't just floor me with embarrassment!

'Twas like a thunder-clap from out the
    clear, —
One minute they were circus beasts, some
    grand,
Some ugly, some amusing, and some
    queer:
Rival attractions to the hobo band,
The flying jenny, and the peanut stand.

Next minute they were old hearth-mates
    of mine!
Lost people, eyeing me with such a stare!
Patient, satiric, devilish, divine;
A gaze of hopeless envy, squalid care,
Hatred, and thwarted love, and dim de-
    spair.

Within my blood my ancient kindred
    spoke, —
Grotesque and monstrous voices, heard
    afar
Down ocean caves when behemoth awoke,
Or through fern forests roared the plesio-
    saur
Locked with the giant-bat in ghastly war.

And suddenly, as in a flash of light,
I saw great Nature working out her plan;
Through all her shapes from mastodon to
          mite
Forever groping, testing, passing on
To find at last the shape and soul of Man.

Till in the fullness of accomplished time,
Comes brother Forepaugh, upon business
          bent,
Tracks her through frozen and through
          torrid clime,
And shows us, neatly labeled in a tent,
The stages of her huge experiment;

Blabbing aloud her shy and reticent hours;
Dragging to light her blinking, slothful
          moods;
Publishing fretful seasons when her powers
Worked wild and sullen in her solitudes,
Or when her mordant laughter shook the
          woods.

Here, round about me, were her vagrant
          births;
Sick dreams she had, fierce projects she
          essayed;

Her qualms, her fiery prides, her crazy
　　　mirths;
The troublings of her spirit as she strayed,
Cringed, gloated, mocked, was lordly,
　　　was afraid,

On that long road she went to seek man-
　　　kind;
Here were the darkling coverts that she
　　　beat
To find the Hider she was sent to find;
Here the distracted footprints of her feet
Whereby her soul's Desire she came to
　　　greet.

But why should they, her botch-work,
　　　turn about
And stare disdain at me, her finished job?
Why was the place one vast suspended
　　　shout
Of laughter?　Why did all the daylight
　　　throb
With soundless guffaw and dumb-stricken
　　　sob?

Helpless I stood among those awful cages;
The beasts were walking loose, and I was
　　　bagged!

I, I, last product of the toiling ages,
Goal of heroic feet that never lagged, —
A little man in trousers, slightly jagged.

Deliver me from such another jury!
The Judgment Day will be a picnic to 't.
Their satire was more dreadful than their
        fury,
And worst of all was just a kind of brute
Disgust, and giving up, and sinking mute.

Survival of the fittest, adaptation,
And all their other evolution terms,
Seem to omit one small consideration,
To wit, that tumblebugs and angleworms
Have souls: there's soul in everything that
        squirms.

And souls are restless, plagued, impatient
        things,
All dream and unaccountable desire;
Crawling, but pestered with the thought
        of wings;
Spreading through every inch of earth's
        old mire
Mystical hanker after something higher.

Wishes *are* horses, as I understand.
I guess a wistful polyp that has strokes
Of feeling faint to gallivant on land
Will come to be a scandal to his folks;
Legs he will sprout, in spite of threats and
      jokes.

And at the core of every life that crawls
Or runs or flies or swims or vegetates —
Churning the mammoth's heart-blood, in
      the galls
Of shark and tiger planting gorgeous
      hates,
Lighting the love of eagles for their mates;

Yes, in the dim brain of the jellied fish
That is and is not living — moved and
      stirred
From the beginning a mysterious wish,
A vision, a command, a fatal Word:
The name of Man was uttered, and they
      heard.

Upward along the æons of old war
They sought him: wing and shank-bone,
      claw and bill
Were fashioned and rejected; wide and far

They roamed the twilight jungles of their
      will;
But still they sought him, and desired him
      still.

Man they desired, but mind you, Perfect
      Man,
The radiant and the loving, yet to be!
I hardly wonder, when they came to scan
The upshot of their strenuosity,
They gazed with mixed emotions upon
      me.

Well, my advice to you is, Face the
      creatures,
Or spot them sideways with your weather
      eye,
Just to keep tab on their expansive fea-
      tures;
It isn't pleasant when you're stepping
      high
To catch a giraffe smiling on the sly.

If nature made you graceful, don't get
      gay
Back-to before the hippopotamus;
If meek and godly, find some place to play

Besides right where three mad hyenas fuss:
You may hear language that we won't
      discuss.

If you're a sweet thing in a flower-bed hat,
Or her best fellow with your tie tucked in,
Don't squander love's bright springtime
      girding at
An old chimpanzee with an Irish chin:
There may be hidden meaning in his grin.

HEART'S WILD–FLOWER

TO-NIGHT her lids shall lift again, slow,
    soft, with vague desire,
And lay about my breast and brain their
    hush of spirit fire,
And I shall take the sweet of pain as the
    laborer his hire.

And though no word shall e'er be said to
    ease the ghostly sting,
And though our hearts, unhoused, unfed,
    must still go wandering,
My sign is set upon her head while stars
    do meet and sing.

Not such a sign as women wear who make
    their foreheads tame
With life's long tolerance, and bear love's
    sweetest, humblest name,
Nor such as passion eateth bare with its
    crown of tears and flame.

Nor such a sign as happy friend sets on his
    friend's dear brow

When meadow-pipings break and blend
    to a key of autumn woe,
And the woodland says playtime's at end,
    best unclasp hands and go.

But where she strays, through blight or
    blooth, one fadeless flower she
    wears,
A little gift God gave my youth, — whose
    petals dim were fears,
Awes, adorations, songs of ruth, hesitan-
    cies, and tears.

O heart of mine, with all thy powers of
    white beatitude,
What are the dearest of God's dowers to
    the children of his blood?
How blow the shy, shy wilding flowers in
    the hollows of his wood!

HARMONICS

THIS string upon my harp was best be-
    loved:
I thought I knew its secrets through and
    through;
Till an old man, whose young eyes light-
    ened blue
'Neath his white hair, bent over me and
    moved
His fingers up and down, and broke the
    wire
To such a laddered music, rung on rung,
As from the patriarch's pillow skyward
    sprung
Crowded with wide-flung wings and feet
    of fire.

O vibrant heart! so metely tuned and
    strung
That any untaught hand can draw from
    thee
One clear gold note that makes the tired
    years young —
What of the time when Love had whis-
    pered me

Where slept thy nodes, and my hand
      pausefully
Gave to the dim harmonics voice and
      tongue?

ON THE RIVER

THE faint stars wake and wonder,
Fade and find heart anew;
Above us and far under
Sphereth the watchful blue.

Silent she sits, outbending,
A wild pathetic grace,
A beauty strange, heart-rending,
Upon her hair and face.

O spirit cries that sever
The cricket's level drone!
O to give o'er endeavor
And let love have its own!

Within the mirrored bushes
There wakes a little stir;
The white-throat moves, and hushes
Her nestlings under her.

Beneath, the lustrous river,
The watchful sky o'erhead.
God, God, that Thou should'st ever
Poison thy children's bread!

THE BRACELET OF GRASS

THE opal heart of afternoon
Was clouding on to throbs of storm,
Ashen within the ardent west
The lips of thunder muttered harm,
And as a bubble like to break
Hung heaven's trembling amethyst,
When with the sedge-grass by the lake
I braceleted her wrist.

And when the ribbon grass was tied,
Sad with the happiness we planned,
Palm linked in palm we stood awhile
And watched the raindrops dot the sand;
Until the anger of the breeze
Chid all the lake's bright breathing down,
And ravished all the radiancies
From her deep eyes of brown.

We gazed from shelter on the storm,
And through our hearts swept ghostly pain
To see the shards of day sweep past,
Broken, and none might mend again
Broken, that none shall ever mend;

Loosened, that none shall ever tie.
O the wind and the wind, will it never
      end?
O the sweeping past of the ruined sky!

A GREY DAY

GREY drizzling mists the moorlands drape,
Rain whitens the dead sea,
From headland dim to sullen cape
Grey sails creep wearily.
I know not how that merchantman
Has found the heart; but 'tis her plan
Seaward her endless course to shape.

Unreal as insects that appall
A drunkard's peevish brain,
O'er the grey deep the dories crawl,
Four-legged, with rowers twain:
Midgets and minims of the earth,
Across old ocean's vasty girth
Toiling — heroic, comical!

I wonder how that merchant's crew
Have ever found the will!
I wonder what the fishers do
To keep them toiling still!
I wonder how the heart of man
Has patience to live out its span,
Or wait until its dreams come true.

THE RIDE BACK

Before the coming of the dark, he dreamed
An old-world faded story: of a knight,
Much like in need to him, who was no knight!
And of a road, much like the road his soul
Groped over, desperate to meet Her soul.
Beside the bed Death waited.   And he dreamed.

His limbs were heavy from the fight,
His mail was dark with dust and blood;
On his good horse they bound him tight,
And on his breast they bound the rood
To help him in the ride that night.

When he crashed through the wood's wet
      rim,
About the dabbled reeds a breeze
Went moaning broken words and dim;
The haggard shapes of twilight trees
Caught with their scrawny hands at him.

Between the doubtful aisles of day
Strange folk and lamentable stood
To maze and beckon him astray,
But through the grey wrath of the wood
He held right on his bitter way.

When he came where the trees were thin,
The moon sat waiting there to see;
On her worn palm she laid her chin,
And laughed awhile in sober glee
To think how strong this knight had
      been.

When he rode past the pallid lake
The withered yellow stems of flags
Stood breast-high for his horse to break;
Lewd as the palsied lips of hags
The petals in the moon did shake.

When he came by the mountain wall,
The snow upon the heights looked down
And said, "The sight is pitiful.
The nostrils of his steed are brown
With frozen blood; and he will fall."

The iron passes of the hills
With question were importunate;
And, but the sharp-tongued icy rills
Had grown for once compassionate,
The spiteful shades had had their wills.

Just when the ache in breast and brain
And the frost smiting at his face

Had sealed his spirit up with pain,
He came out in a better place,
And morning lay across the plain.

He saw the wet snails crawl and cling
On fern-stalks where the rime had run,
The careless birds went wing and wing,
And in the low smile of the sun
Life seemed almost a pleasant thing.

Right on the panting charger swung
Through the bright depths of quiet grass;
The knight's lips moved as if they sung,
And through the peace there came to pass
The flattery of lute and tongue.

From the mid-flowering of the mead
There swelled a sob of minstrelsy,
Faint sackbuts and the dreamy reed,
And plaintive lips of maids thereby,
And songs blown out like thistle seed.

Forth from her maidens came the bride,
And as his loosened rein fell slack
He muttered, "In their throats they lied
Who said that I should ne'er win back
To kiss her lips before I died!"

SONG–FLOWER AND POPPY

I

IN NEW YORK

HE plays the deuce with my writing time,
For the penny my sixth-floor neighbor
      throws;
He finds me proud of my pondered
      rhyme,
And he leaves me — well, God knows
It takes the shine from a tunester's line
When a little mate of the deathless Nine
Pipes up under your nose!

For listen, there is his voice again,
Wistful and clear and piercing sweet.
Where did the boy find such a strain
To make a dead heart beat?
And how in the name of care can he bear
To jet such a fountain into the air
In this grey gulch of a street?

Tuscan slopes or the Piedmontese?
Umbria under the Apennine?

South, where the terraced lemon-trees
Round rich Sorrento shine?
Venice moon on the smooth lagoon? —
Where have I heard that aching tune,
That boyish throat divine?

Beyond my roofs and chimney pots
A rag of sunset crumbles grey;
Below, fierce radiance hangs in clots
O'er the streams that never stay.
Shrill and high, newsboys cry
The worst of the city's infamy
For one more sordid day.

But my desire has taken sail
For lands beyond, soft-horizoned:
Down languorous leagues I hold the trail,
From Marmolada, steeply throned
Above high pastures washed with light,
Where dolomite by dolomite
Looms sheer and spectral-coned,

To purple vineyards looking south
On reaches of the still Tyrrhene;
Virgilian headlands, and the mouth
Of Tiber, where that ship put in
To take the dead men home to God,

Whereof Casella told the mode
To the great Florentine.

Up stairways blue with flowering weed
I climb to hill-hung Bergamo;
All day I watch the thunder breed
Golden above the springs of Po,
Till the voice makes sure its wavering lure,
And by Assisi's portals pure
I stand, with heart bent low.

O hear, how it blooms in the blear day-
        fall,
That flower of passionate wistful song!
How it blows like a rose by the iron wall
Of the city loud and strong.
How it cries "Nay, nay" to the world-
        ling's way,
To the heart's clear dream how it whis-
        pers, "Yea,
Time comes, though the time is long."

Beyond my roofs and chimney piles
Sunset crumbles, ragged, dire;
The roaring street is hung for miles
With fierce electric fire.
Shrill and high, newsboys cry

The gross of the planet's destiny
Through one more sullen gyre.

Stolidly the town flings down
Its lust by day for its nightly lust;
Who does his given stint, 'tis known,
Shall have his mug and crust. —
Too base of mood, too harsh of blood,
Too stout to seize the grosser good,
Too hungry after dust!

O hark! how it blooms in the falling dark,
That flower of mystical yearning song:
Sad as a hermit thrush, as a lark
Uplifted, glad, and strong.
Heart, we have chosen the better part!
Save sacred love and sacred art
Nothing is good for long.

II

AT ASSISI

Before Saint Francis' burg I wait,
Frozen in spirit, faint with dread;
His presence stands within the gate,
Mild splendor rings his head.
Gently he seems to welcome me:

Knows he not I am quick, and he
Is dead, and priest of the dead?

I turn away from the grey church pile;
I dare not enter, thus undone:
Here in the roadside grass awhile
I will lie and watch for the sun.
Too purged of earth's good glee and strife,
Too drained of the honied lusts of life,
Was the peace these old saints won!

And lo! how the laughing earth says no
To the fear that mastered me;
To the blood that aches and clamors so
How it whispers "Verily."
Here by my side, marvelous-dyed,
Bold stray-away from the courts of pride,
A poppy-bell flaunts free.

Saint Francis sleeps upon his hill,
And a poppy flower laughs down his
        creed;
Triumphant light her petals spill,
His shrines are dim indeed.
Men build and plan, but the soul of man,
Coming with haughty eyes to scan,
Feels richer, wilder need.

How long, old builder Time, wilt bide
Till at thy thrilling word
Life's crimson pride shall have to bride
The spirit's white accord,
Within that gate of good estate
Which thou must build us soon or late,
Hoar workman of the Lord?

A DIALOGUE IN PURGATORY

Poi disse un altro.... "*Io son Buonconte:*
Giovanna o altri non ha di me cura;
Per ch' io vo tra costor con bassa fronte."

Seguito il terzo spirito al secondo,
"*Ricorditi di me, che son la Pia;*
Siena mi fe, disfecemi Maremma.
Salsi colui che inannellata pria
Disposata m' avea colla sua gemma."

PURGATORIO, CANTO V.

I

BUONCONTE

SISTER, the sun has ceased to shine;
By companies of twain and trine
Stars gather; from the sea
The moon comes momently.

On all the roads that ring our hill
The sighing and the hymns are still;
It is our time to gain
Strength for to-morrow's pain.

Yet still your eyes are wholly bent
Upon the way that Virgil went,

Following Sordello's sign,
With the dark Florentine.

Night now has barred their upward track:
There where the mountain-side folds back
And in the Vale of Flowers
The Princes count their hours

Those three friends sit in the clear star-
      light
With the green-clad angels left and
      right, —
Soul made by wakeful soul
More earnest for the goal.

So let us, sister, though our place
Is barren of that Valley's grace,
Sit hand in hand, till we
Seem rich as those friends be.

II

LA PIA

Brother, 'twere sweet your hand to feel
In mine; it would a little heal
The shame that makes me poor,
And dumb at the heart's core.

But where our spirits felt Love's dearth,
Down on the green and pleasant earth,
Remains the fleshly shell,
Love's garment tangible.

So now our hands have naught to say:
Heart unto heart some other way
Must utter forth its pain,
Must glee or comfort gain.

Ah, no!   For souls like you and me
Some comfort waits, but never glee:
Not yours the young men's singing
In Heaven, at the bride-bringing;

Not mine, beside God's living waters,
Dance of the marriageable daughters,
The laughter and the ease
Beneath His summer trees.

III

BUONCONTE

In fair Arezzo's halls and bowers
My Giovanna speeds her hours
Delicately, nor cares
To shorten by her prayers

My days upon this mount of ruth:
If those who come from earth speak
      sooth,
Though still I call and call,
She does not heed at all.

And if aright your words I read
At Dante's passing, he you wed
Dipped from the drains of Hell
The marriage hydromel.

O therefore, while the moon intense
Holds yonder dreaming sea suspense,
And round the shadowy coasts
Gather the wistful ghosts,

Let us sit quiet all the night,
And wonder, wonder on the light
Worn by those spirits fair
Whom Love has not left bare.

IV

LA PIA

Even as theirs, the chance was mine
To meet and mate beneath Love's sign,

To feel in soul and sense
The solemn influence

Which, breathed upon a man or maid,
Maketh forever unafraid,
Though life with death unite
That spirit to affright, —

Which lifts the changèd heart high up,
As the priest lifts the changèd cup,
Boldens the feet to pace
Before God's proving face.

O just a thought beyond the blue
The wings of the dove yearned down and
   through!
Even now I hear and hear
How near they were, how near!

I murmur not.   Rightly disgraced,
The weak hand stretched abroad in haste
For gifts barely allowed
The tacit, strong, and proud.

But therefore was I so intent
To watch where Dante onward went

With the Roman spirit pure
And the grave troubadour,

Because my mind was busy then
With the loves that wait those gentle
     men:
Cunizza one; and one
Bice, above the sun;

And for the other, more and less
Than woman's near-felt tenderness,
A million voices dim
Praising him, praising him.

V

BUONCONTE

The waves that wash this mountain's
     base
Were crimson in the sun's low rays,
When, singing high and fast,
An angel downward passed,

To bid some patient soul arise
And make it fair for Paradise;
And upward, so attended,
That soul its journey wended;

Yet you, who in these lower rings
Wait for the coming of such wings,
Turned not your eyes to view
Whether they came for you,

But watched, but watched great Virgil
     stayed
Greeting Sordello's couchant shade,
Which to salute him rose
Like lion from its pose;

While humbly by those lords of song
Stood he whose living limbs are strong
To mount where Mary's bliss
Is shed on Beatrice.

On him your gaze was fastened, more
Than on those great names Mantua bore:
Your eyes hold the distress
Still, of that wistfulness.

Yea, fit he seemed much love to rouse
His pilgrim lips and iron brows
Grew like a woman's, dim,
While you held speech with him;

And troubled came his mortal breath
The while I told him of my death;

His looks were changed and wan
When Virgil led him on.

VI

LA PIA

E'er since Casella came this morn,
Newly o'er yonder ocean borne,
Bound upward for the choir
Who purge themselves in fire,

And from that meinie he was of
Stayed backward at my cry of love,
To speak awhile with me
Of life and Tuscany,

And, parting, told us how e'er day
Was done, Dante would come this way,
With mortal feet, to find
His sweetheart, sky-enshrined, —

E'er since Casella spoke such news
My heart has lain in a golden muse,
Picturing him and her,
What starry ones they were.

And now the moon sheds its compassion
O'er the hushed mount, I try to fashion

The manner of their meeting,
Their few first words of greeting.

O well for them, with claspèd hands,
Unshamed amid the heavenly bands!
They hear no pitying pair
Of old-time lovers there

Look down and say in an undertone,
"This latest-come, who comes alone,
Was still alone on earth,
And lonely from his birth."

Nor feel a sudden whisper mar
God's weather, "Dost thou see the scar
That spirit hideth so?
Who dealt her such a blow

"That God can hardly wipe it out?"
And answer, "She gave love, no doubt,
To one who saw not fit
To set much store by it."

THE DAGUERREOTYPE

THIS, then, is she,
My mother as she looked at seventeen,
When she first met my father.   Young
      incredibly,
Younger than spring, without the faintest
      trace
Of disappointment, weariness, or teen
Upon the childlike earnestness and grace
Of the waiting face.
These close-wound ropes of pearl
(Or common beads made precious by
      their use)
Seem heavy for so slight a throat to wear;
But the low bodice leaves the shoulders
      bare
And half the glad swell of the breast, for
      news
That now the woman stirs within the girl.
And yet,
Even so, the loops and globes
Of beaten gold
And jet
Hung, in the stately way of old,

From the ears' drooping lobes
On festivals and Lord's-day of the week,
Show all too matron-sober for the
    cheek, —
Which, now I look again, is perfect child,
Or no — or no — 'tis girlhood's very self,
Moulded by some deep, mischief-ridden
    elf
So meek, so maiden mild,
But startling the close gazer with the
    sense
Of passions forest-shy and forest-wild,
And delicate delirious merriments.

As a moth beats sidewise
And up and over, and tries
To skirt the irresistible lure
Of the flame that has him sure,
My spirit, that is none too strong to-day,
Flutters and makes delay, —
Pausing to wonder on the perfect lips,
Lifting to muse upon the low-drawn hair
And each hid radiance there,
But powerless to stem the tide-race bright,
The vehement peace which drifts it to-
    ward the light
Where soon — ah, now, with cries

Of grief and giving-up unto its gain
It shrinks no longer nor denies,
But dips
Hurriedly home to the exquisite heart of
      pain, —
And all is well, for I have seen them plain,
The unforgettable, the unforgotten eyes!
Across the blinding gush of these good
      tears
They shine as in the sweet and heavy years
When by her bed and chair
We children gathered jealously to share
The sunlit aura breathing myrrh and
      thyme,
Where the sore-stricken body made a
      clime
Gentler than May and pleasanter than
      rhyme,
Holier and more mystical than prayer.

God, how thy ways are strange!
That this should be, even this,
The patient head
Which suffered years ago the dreary
      change!
That these so dewy lips should be the
      same

As those I stooped to kiss
And heard my harrowing half-spoken
name,
A little ere the one who bowed above her,
Our father and her very constant lover,
Rose stoical, and we knew that she was
dead.
Then I, who could not understand or
share
His antique nobleness,
Being unapt to bear
The insults which time flings us for our
proof,
Fled from the horrible roof
Into the alien sunshine merciless,
The shrill satiric fields ghastly with day,
Raging to front God in his pride of sway
And hurl across the lifted swords of fate
That ringed Him where He sat
My puny gage of scorn and desolate hate
Which somehow should undo Him, after
all!
That this girl face, expectant, virginal,
Which gazes out at me
Boon as a sweetheart, as if nothing loth
(Save for the eyes, with other presage
stored)

To pledge me troth,
And in the kingdom where the heart is
    lord
Take sail on the terrible gladness of the
    deep
Whose winds the grey Norns keep, —
That this should be indeed
The flesh which caught my soul, a flying
    seed,
Out of the to and fro
Of scattering hands where the seedsman
    Mage,
Stooping from star to star and age to age
Sings as he sows!
That underneath this breast
Nine moons I fed
Deep of divine unrest,
While over and over in the dark she said,
"Blessèd! but not as happier children
    blessed" —
That this should be
Even she....
God, how with time and change
Thou makest thy footsteps strange!
Ah, now I know
They play upon me, and it is not so.
Why, 'tis a girl I never saw before,

A little thing to flatter and make weep,
To tease until her heart is sore,
Then kiss and clear the score;
A gypsy run-the-fields,
A little liberal daughter of the earth,
Good for what hour of truancy and mirth
The careless season yields
Hither-side the flood of the year and
      yonder of the neap;
Then thank you, thanks again, and twenty
      light good-byes. —
O shrined above the skies,
Frown not, clear brow,
Darken not, holy eyes!
Thou knowest well I know that it is thou!
Only to save me from such memories
As would unman me quite,
Here in this web of strangeness caught
And prey to troubled thought
Do I devise
These foolish shifts and slight;
Only to shield me from the afflicting sense
Of some waste influence
Which from this morning face and lus-
      trous hair
Breathes on me sudden ruin and despair.
In any other guise,

With any but this girlish depth of gaze,
Your coming had not so unsealed and
    poured
The dusty amphoras where I had stored
The drippings of the winepress of my
    days.
I think these eyes foresee,
Now in their unawakened virgin time,
Their mother's pride in me,
And dream even now, unconsciously,
Upon each soaring peak and sky-hung
    lea
You pictured I should climb.
Broken premonitions come,
Shapes, gestures visionary,
Not as once to maiden Mary
The manifest angel with fresh lilies came
Intelligibly calling her by name;
But vanishingly, dumb,
Thwarted and bright and wild,
As heralding a sin-defiled,
Earth-encumbered, blood-begotten, pas-
    sionate man-child,
Who yet should be a trump of mighty call
Blown in the gates of evil kings
To make them fall;
Who yet should be a sword of flame before

The soul's inviolate door
To beat away the clang of hellish wings;
Who yet should be a lyre
Of high unquenchable desire
In the day of little things. —
Look, where the amphoras,
The yield of many days,
Trod by my hot soul from the pulp of
    self
And set upon the shelf
In sullen pride
The Vineyard-master's tasting to abide —
O mother mine!
Are these the bringings-in, the doings fine,
Of him you used to praise?
Emptied and overthrown
The jars lie strown.
These, for their flavor duly nursed,
Drip from the stopples vinegar accursed;
These, I thought honied to the very seal,
Dry, dry, — a little acid meal,
A pinch of mouldy dust,
Sole leavings of the amber-mantling
    must;
These, rude to look upon,
But flasking up the liquor dearest won,
Through sacred hours and hard,

With watching and with wrestlings and
     with grief,
Even of these, of these in chief,
The stale breath sickens, reeking from the
     shard.
Nothing is left.   Ay, how much less than
     naught!
What shall be said or thought
Of the slack hours and waste imaginings,
The cynic rending of the wings,
Known to that froward, that unreckoning
     heart
Whereof this brewage was the precious
     part,
Treasured and set away with furtive
     boast?
O dear and cruel ghost,
Be merciful, be just!
See, I was yours and I am in the dust.
Then look not so, as if all things were well!
Take your eyes from me, leave me to my
     shame,
Or else, if gaze they must,
Steel them with judgment, darken them
     with blame;
But by the ways of light ineffable
You bade me go and I have faltered from,

By the low waters moaning out of hell
Whereto my feet have come,
Lay not on me these intolerable
Looks of rejoicing love, of pride, of happy
   trust!

Nothing dismayed?
By all I say and all I hint not made
Afraid?
O then, stay by me!   Let
These eyes afflict me, cleanse me, keep
   me yet
Brave eyes and true!
See how the shriveled heart, that long has
   lain
Dead to delight and pain,
Stirs, and begins again
To utter pleasant life, as if it knew
The wintry days were through;
As if in its awakening boughs it heard
The quick, sweet-spoken bird.
Strong eyes and brave,
Inexorable to save!

JETSAM

I WONDER can this be the world it was
At sunset?   I remember the sky fell
Green as pale meadows, at the long street-
ends,
But overhead the smoke-wrack hugged
the roofs
As if to shut the city from God's eyes
Till dawn should quench the laughter and
the lights.
Beneath the gas flare stolid faces passed,
Too dull for sin; old loosened lips set
hard
To drain the stale lees from the cup of
sense;
Or if a young face yearned from out the
mist
Made by its own bright hair, the eyes
were wan
With desolate fore-knowledge of the end.
My life lay waste about me: as I walked,
From the gross dark of unfrequented
streets

The face of my own youth peered forth at
　　me,
Struck white with pity at the thing I was;
And globed in ghostly fire, thrice-virginal,
With lifted face star-strong, went one who
　　sang
Lost verses from my youth's gold canticle.
Out of the void dark came my face and
　　hers
One vivid moment — then the street was
　　there;
Bloat shapes and mean eyes blotted the
　　sear dusk;
And in the curtained window of a house
Whence sin reeked on the night, a shame-
　　ful head
Was silhouetted black as Satan's face
Against eternal fires.　I stumbled on
Down the dark slope that reaches river·
　　ward,
Stretching blind hands to find the throat
　　of God
And crush Him in his lies.　The river lay
Coiled in its factory filth and few lean
　　trees.
All was too hateful — I could not die
　　there!

I whom the Spring had strained unto her
      breast,
Whose lips had felt the wet vague lips of
      dawn.
So under the thin willows' leprous shade
And through the tangled ranks of river-
      weed
I pushed — till lo, God heard me! I
      came forth
Where, 'neath the shoreless hush of region
      light,
Through a new world, undreamed of,
      undesired,
Beyond imagining of man's weary heart,
Far to the white marge of the wondering
      sea
This still plain widens, and this moon
      rains down
Insufferable ecstasy of peace.

My heart is man's heart, strong to bear
      this night's
Unspeakable affliction of mute love
That crazes lesser things.   The rocks and
      clods
Dissemble, feign a busy intercourse;
The bushes deal in shadowy subterfuge,

Lurk dull, dart spiteful out, make heart-
 less signs,
Utter awestricken purpose of no sense, —
But I walk quiet, crush aside the hands
Stretched furtively to drag me madmen's
 ways.
I know the thing they suffer, and the
 tricks
They must be at to help themselves en-
 dure.
I would not be too boastful; I am weak,
Too weak to put aside the utter ache
Of this lone splendor long enough to see
Whether the moon is still her white
 strange self
Or something whiter, stranger, even the
 face
Which by the changed face of my risen
 youth
Sang, globed in fire, her golden canticle.
I dare not look again; another gaze
Might drive me to the wavering coppice
 there,
Where bat-winged madness brushed me,
 the wild laugh
Of naked nature crashed across my blood.
So rank it was with earthy presences,

Faun-shapes in goatish dance, young
      witches' eyes
Slanting deep invitation, whinnying calls
Ambiguous, shocks and whirlwinds of
      wild mirth, —
They had undone me in the darkness
      there,
But that within me, smiting through my
      lids
Lowered to shut in the thick whirl of
      sense,
The dumb light ached and rummaged,
      and without,
The soaring splendor summoned me
      aloud
To leave the low dank thickets of the
      flesh
Where man meets beast and makes his lair
      with him,
For spirit reaches of the strenuous vast,
Where stalwart stars reap grain to make
      the bread
God breaketh at his tables and is glad.
I came out in the moonlight cleansed and
      strong,
And gazed up at the lyric face to see
All sweetness tasted of in earthen cups

Ere it be dashed and spilled, all radiance
    flung
Beyond experience, every benison dream,
Treasured and mystically crescent there.

O, who will shield me from her?   Who
    will place
A veil between me and the fierce in-
    throng
Of her inexorable benedicite?
See, I have loved her well and been with
    her!
Through tragic twilights when the
    stricken sea
Groveled with fear; or when she made her
    throne
In imminent cities built of gorgeous winds
And paved with lightnings; or when the
    sobering stars
Would lead her home 'mid wealth of
    plundered May
Along the violet slopes of evensong.
Of all the sights that starred the dreamy
    year,
For me one sight stood peerless and apart:
Bright rivers tacit; low hills prone and
    dumb;

Forests that hushed their tiniest voice to
    hear;
Skies for the unutterable advent robed
In purple like the opening iris buds;
And by some lone expectant pool, one
    tree
Whose grey boughs shivered with excess
    of awe, —
As with preluding gush of amber light,
And herald trumpets softly lifted through,
Across the palpitant horizon marge
Crocus-filleted came the singing moon.
Out of her changing lights I wove my
    youth
A place to dwell in, sweet and spiritual,
And all the bitter years of my exile
My heart has called afar off unto her.
Lo, after many days love finds its own!
The futile adorations, the waste tears,
The hymns that fluttered low in the false
    dawn,
She has uptreasured as a lover's gifts;
They are the mystic garment that she
    wears
Against the bridal, and the crocus flowers
She twined her brow with at the going
    forth;

They are the burden of the song she made
In coming through the quiet fields of
    space,
And breathe between her passion-parted
    lips
Calling me out along the flowering road
Which summers through the dimness of
    the sea.

Hark, where the deep feels round its
    thousand shores
To find remembered respite, and far
    drawn
Through weed-strewn shelves and cran-
    nies of the coast
The myriad silence yearns to myriad
    speech.
O sea that yearns a day, shall thy tongues
    be
So eloquent, and heart, shall all thy
    tongues
Be dumb to speak thy longing? Say I
    hold
Life as a broken jewel in my hand,
And fain would buy a little love with it
For comfort, say I fain would make it
    shine

Once in remembering eyes ere it be
  dust, —
Were life not worthy spent?   Then what
  of this,
When all my spirit hungers to repay
The beauty that has drenched my soul
  with peace?
Once at a simple turning of the way
I met God walking; and although the
  dawn
Was large behind Him, and the morning
  stars
Circled and sang about his face as
  birds
About the fieldward morning cottager,
My coward heart said faintly, "Let us
  haste!
Day grows and it is far to market-town."
Once where I lay in darkness after fight,
Sore smitten, thrilled a little thread of
  song
Searching and searching at my muffled
  sense
Until it shook sweet pangs through all
  my blood,
And I beheld one globed in ghostly fire
Singing, star-strong, her golden canticle;

And her mouth sang, "The hosts of Hate
    roll past,
A dance of dust motes in the sliding sun;
Love's battle comes on the wide wings
    of storm,
From east to west one legion! Wilt thou
    strive?"
Then, since the splendor of her sword-
    bright gaze
Was heavy on me with yearning and with
    scorn
My sick heart muttered, "Yea, the little
    strife,
Yet see, the grievous wounds! I fain
    would sleep."
O heart, shalt thou not once be strong to
    go
Where all sweet throats are calling, once
    be brave
To slake with deed thy dumbness?   Let
    us go
The path her singing face looms low to
    point,
Pendulous, blanched with longing, shed-
    ding flame
Of silver on the brown grope of the flood;
For all my spirit's soilure is put by

And all my body's soilure, lacking now
But the last lustral sacrament of death
To make me clean for those near-search-
      ing eyes
That question yonder whether all be well,
And pause a little ere they dare rejoice.

Question and be thou answered, passion-
      ate face!
For I am worthy, worthy now at last
After so long unworth; strong now at last
To give myself to beauty and be saved;
Now, being man, to give myself to thee,
As once the tumult of my boyish heart
Companioned thee with rapture through
      the world,
Forth from a land whereof no poet's lip
Made mention how the leas were lily-
      sprent,
Into a land God's eyes had looked not on
To love the tender bloom upon the hills.
To-morrow, when the fishers come at
      dawn
Upon that shell of me the sea has tossed
To land, as fit for earth to use again,
Men, meeting at the shops and corner
      streets,

Will speak a word of pity, glossing o'er
With altered accent, dubious sweep of
    hand,
Their virile, just contempt for one who
    failed.
But they can never cast my earnings up,
Who know so well my losses.   Even you
Who in the mild light of the spirit walk
And hold yourselves acquainted with the
    truth,
Be not too swift to judge and cast me out!
You shall find other, nobler ways than
    mine
To work your soul's redemption, — glori-
    ous noons
Of battle 'neath the heaven-suspended
    sign,
And nightly refuge 'neath God's ægis-rim;
Increase of wisdom, and acquaintance
    held
With the heart's austerities; still govern-
    ance,
And ripening of the blood in the weekday
    sun
To make the full-orbed consecrated fruit
At life's end for the Sabbath supper meet.
I shall not sit beside you at that feast,

For ere a seedling of my golden tree
Pushed off its petals to get room to grow,
I stripped the boughs to make an April
    gaud
And wreathe a spendthrift garland for my
    hair.
But mine is not the failure God deplores;
For I of old am beauty's votarist,
Long recreant, often foiled and led astray,
But resolute at last to seek her there
Where most she does abide, and crave
    with tears
That she assoil me of my blemishment.
Low looms her singing face to point the
    way,
Pendulous, blanched with longing, shed-
    ding flame
Of silver on the brown grope of the flood.
The stars are for me; the horizon wakes
Its pilgrim chanting; and the little sand
Grows musical of hope beneath my feet.
The waves that leap to meet my swim-
    ming breast
Gossip sweet secrets of the light-drenched
    way,
And when the deep throbs of the rising
    surge

Pulse upward with me, and a rain of
     wings
Blurs round the moon's pale place, she
     stoops to reach
Still welcome of bright hands across the
     wave
And sings low, low, globed all in ghostly
     fire,
Lost verses from my youth's gold canticle.

From *Second Coming and Later Poems*

SECOND COMING

Once, by an arch of ancient stone,
  Beneath Italian olive-trees
(In pentecostal youth, too prone
  To visions such as these),

And now a second time, to-day,
  Yonder, an hour ago! 'Tis strange.
— The hot beach shelving to the bay,
  That far white mountain range,

The motley town where Turk and Greek
  Spit scorn and hatred as I pass;
Seraglio windows, doors that reek
  Sick perfume of the mass;

The muezzin cry from Allah's tower,
  French sailors singing in the street;
The Western meets the Eastern power,
  And mingles — this is Crete.

Yonder on snowy Ida, Zeus
  Was cradled; through those mountain
    haunts

The new moon hurried, letting loose
  The raving Corybants,

Who after thrid the Cyclades
  To Thebes of Cadmos, with the slim
Wild god for whom Euripides
  Fashioned the deathless hymn.

And yonder, ere in Ajalon
  Young Judah's lion ramped for war,
Dædalus built the Knossian
  House of the Minotaur.

— 'Tis strange! No wonder and no dread
  Was on me; hardly even surprise.
I knew before he raised his head
  Or fixed me with his eyes

That it was he; far off I knew
  The leaning figure by the boat,
The long straight gown of faded hue;
  The hair that round his throat

Fell forward as he bent in speech
  Above the naked sailor there,
Calking his vessel on the beach,
  Full in the noonday glare.

Sharp rang the sailor's mallet-stroke
   Pounding the tow into the seam;
He paused and mused, and would have
      spoke,
   Lifting great eyes of dream

Unto those eyes which slowly turned —
   As once before, even so now —
Till full on mine their passion burned
   With, "Yes, and is it thou?"

Then o'er the face about to speak
   Again he leaned; the sunburnt hair,
Fallen forward, hid the tawny cheek;
   And I who, for my share,

Had but the instant's gaze, no more,
   And sweat and shuddering of the mind,
Stumbled along the dazzling shore,
   Until a cool sweet wind

From far-off Ida's silver caves
   Said, "Stay"; and here I sit the while.
— Silken Mediterranean waves,
   From isle to fabled isle,

Flame softly north to Sunium,
   And west by England's war-cliff strong

To where Ulysses' men saw loom
  The mount of Dante's song.

As far as where the coast-line dies
  In sharp sun-dazzle, goes the light
Dance-dance of amber butterflies
  Above the beach-flowers, bright

And jealous as the sudden blood
  The lovers of these island girls
Spill in their frays; o'er flower and bud
  The light dance dips and whirls.

And all my being, for an hour,
  Has sat in stupor, without thought,
Empty of memory, love, or power,
  A dumb wild creature caught

In toils of purpose not its own!
  But now at last the ebbed will turns;
Feeding on spirit, blood, and bone,
  The ghostly protest burns.

"Yea, it is I, 'tis I indeed!
  But who art thou, and plannest what?
Beyond all use, beyond all need!
  Importunate, unbesought,

"Unwelcome, unendurable!
  To the vague boy I was before —
O unto him thou camest well;
  But now, a boy no more,

"Firm-seated in my proper good,
  Clear-operant in my functions due,
Potent and plenteous of my mood, —
  What hast thou here to do?

"Yes, I have loved thee — love thee,
      yes;
  But also — hear'st thou? — also him
Who out of Ida's wilderness
  Over the bright sea-rim,

"With shaken cones and mystic dance,
  To Dirce and her seven waters
Led on the raving Corybants,
  And lured the Theban daughters

"To play on the delirious hills
  Three summer days, three summer
      nights,
Where wert thou when these had their
      wills?
  How liked thee their delights?

"Past Melos, Delos, to the straits,
   The waters roll their spangled mirth,
And westward, through Gibraltar gates,
   To my own under-earth,

"My glad, great land, which at the most
   Knows that its fathers knew thee; so
Will spend for thee nor count the cost;
   But follow thee?   Ah, no!

"Thine image gently fades from earth!
   Thy churches are as empty shells,
Dim-plaining of thy words and worth,
   And of thy funerals!

"But oh, upon what errand, then,
   Leanest thou at the sailor's ear?
Hast thou yet more to say, that men
   Have heard not, and must hear?"

OLD POURQUOI

'Twas not yet night, but night was due;
The earth had fallen chalky-dun;
Our road dipped straight as eye could
      run,
Between the poles, set two and two,
And poplars, one and one,

Then rose to where far roofs and spires
Etched a vague strip of Norman sky:
The sea-wind had begun to sigh
From tree to tree, and up the wires
Slid its frail, mounting cry.

All afternoon our minds had reveled
In steep, skylarking enterprise;
Our hearts had climbed a dozen skies,
And fifty frowning strongholds leveled
Of Life's old enemies.

A trifle, here and there, was spared
Till morning found us more adept;
But, broadly speaking, we had swept
Earth of her wrongs; light had been flared
Where the last Error slept!

Then, nothing said and nothing seen,
Misgiving gripped us.   Treeless, bare,
The moorland country everywhere
Lay blackened; but a powdery sheen
Hung tangled in the air.

And Heaven knows what suspense and
          doubt
Prowled in the dusk!   A peasant's door,
Where naught was visible before,
Opened, and let the lamp shine out
Across the crumpled moor.

A stone's-throw off some drowsy sheep
Took fright; across a rise of land
In shadowy scamper went the band;
Three bleating ewes held back to keep
Their coward young in hand.

And borne across the shallow vale,
Along the highway from the town,
A voice the distance could not drown
Chanted an eerie, endless tale,
Now shrill, now dropping down

To querulous, questioning minor song;
Now sweeping in a solemn gust,

As if some great dishonoured dust
Came crying its ancestral wrong,
And found no listener just.

And as the voice drew nearer toward,
It dropped through vague disastrous bars,
Heart-broken roulades, sudden jars
Of discord; then superbly soared
Into a heaven whose stars

Twinkled to some immortal jest,
And satire was the cosmic mood; —
Upon which, down the twilight road,
With stolid haste, monotonous zest,
Shuffled or limped or strode, —

Who? What? King David, crazed and
       free!
Hamlet, grown old, and wandering!
The ghost of Tiryns' murdered king
Clamorous by its native sea;
Or his who made to sing

The Frogs, and set the Wasps to buzz
Round plague-struck Athens; the mid-
       pain
Of old Laocoön; Paul Verlaine,

In high talk with the Man of Uz
Outside his prison-pane!

One moment by the darkening West
We saw the grand old grizzled head,
The stricken face, the rolling, red,
Quizzical eyeballs, the bared chest,
Hairy, Homeric, spread

And laboring with the grievous chant,
The knotted hands raised high and wrung,
As, craning through the gloom, he flung
Into our teeth that iterant
Enormous word he sung.

Then he was gone.   Slow up the hill,
And faster down the other side,
The wild monotonous question died;
Again the sea-wind whispered shrill,
As if the sea replied.

I muttered, "Did you hear?" and you
Nodded.   In silence half a mile
We stumbled onward: you meanwhile
Had paper out, your pencil flew
In quirk and quiddet vile.

Till in disgust I seized your hand,
And thundered, "Scratching music, clod?
Getting his tune down?   Suffering God!
Have you no heart to understand?"
One more New-England nod,

And "Yes, I heard, my son, I heard.
A tune fit for the mutinous dead
To march to when, Prometheus-led,
They storm high Heaven! As for his word,
Pourquoi? was all he said!"

Pourquoi? Pourquoi? Yes, that was all!
Only the darkest cry that haunts
The corridors of tragic chance,
Couched in the sweet, satirical,
Impudent tongue of France.

Only the bitterest wail flung out
From worlds that traffic to their mart
Without a pilot or a chart;
With "What?" the body of their doubt,
And "Why?" the quaking heart.

Old bard and brother to the Sphinx!
I wonder what abysmal luck
Had left your face so planet-struck,

And driven you on such horrid brinks
To play the run-amuck.

I wonder down what road to-night
You shuffle; from what plunging star
Your gnarled old hands uplifted are,
Between moth-light and cockshut-light,
Calling young hearts to war!

I AM THE WOMAN

I AM the Woman, ark of the law and its
      breaker,
Who chastened her step and taught her
      knees to be meek,
Bridled and bitted her heart and humbled
      her cheek,
Parceled her will, and cried, "Take
      more!" to the taker,
Shunned what they told her to shun,
      sought what they bade her seek,
Locked up her mouth from scornful
      speaking: now it is open to speak.

I am she that is terribly fashioned, the
      creature
Wrought in God's perilous mood, in His
      unsafe hour.
The morning star was mute, beholding
      my feature,
Seeing the rapture I was, the shame, and
      the power,
Scared at my manifold meaning; he heard
      me call,

"O fairest among ten thousand, accept-
    able brother!"
And he answered not, for doubt; till he
    saw me crawl
And whisper down to the secret worm,
    "O mother,
Be not wroth in the ancient house; thy
    daughter forgets not at all!"

I am the Woman, fleer away,
Soft withdrawer back from the maddened
    mate,
Lurer inward and down to the gates of day
And crier there in the gate,
"What shall I give for thee, wild one,
    say!
The long, slow rapture and patient an-
    guish of life,
Or art thou minded a swifter way?
Ask if thou canst, the gold, but O, if thou
    must,
Good is the shining dross, lovely the
    dust!
Look at me, I am the Woman, harlot and
    heavenly wife;
Tell me thy price, be unashamed; I will
    assuredly pay!"

I am also the Mother: of two that I bore
I comfort and feed the slayer, feed and
    comfort the slain.
Did they number my daughters and sons?
    I am mother of more!
Many a head they marked not, here in
    my bosom has lain,
Babbling with unborn lips in a tongue
    to be,
Far, incredible matters, all familiar to me.
Still would the man come whispering,
    "Wife!" but many a time my
    breast
Took him not as a husband: I soothed him
    and laid him to rest
Even as the babe of my body, and knew
    him for such.
My mouth is open to speak, that was
    dumb too much!
I say to you I am the Mother; and under
    the sword
Which flamed each way to harry us forth
    from the Lord,
I saw Him young at the portal, weeping
    and staying the rod,
And I, even I was His mother, and I
    yearned as the mother of God.

I am also the Spirit.   The Sisters laughed
When I sat with them dumb in the por-
　　　tals, over my lamp, —
Half asleep in the doors: for my gown
　　　was raught
Off at the shoulder to shield from the
　　　wind and the rain
The wick I tended against the mysterious
　　　hour
When the silent City of Being should ring
　　　with song,
As the Lord came in with Life to the
　　　marriage bower.
"Look!" laughed the elder Sisters; and
　　　crimson with shame
I hid my breast away from the rosy
　　　flame.
"Ah!" cried the leaning Sisters, pointing,
　　　doing me wrong;
"Do you see?" laughed the wanton Sis-
　　　ters.   "She will get her a lover
　　　erelong!"
And it was but a little while till unto my
　　　need
He was given, indeed,
And we walked where waxing world after
　　　world went by;

And I said to my lover, "Let us begone,
O, let us begone, and try
Which of them all the fairest to dwell
in is,
Which is the place for us, our desirable
clime!"
But he said, "They are only the huts and
the little villages,
Pleasant to go and lodge in rudely over
the vintage-time!"
Scornfully spake he, being unwise,
Being flushed at heart because of our
walking together.
But I was mute with passionate prophe-
cies;
My heart went veiled and faint in the
golden weather,
While universe drifted by after still uni-
verse.
Then I cried, "Alas, we must hasten and
lodge therein,
One after one, and in every star that they
shed!
A dark and a weary thing is come on our
head —
To search obedience out in the bosom of
sin,

To listen deep for love when thunders the
    curse;
For O my love, behold where the Lord
    hath planted
In every star in the midst his dangerous
    Tree!
Still I must pluck thereof and bring unto
    thee,
Saying, "The coolness for which all night
    we have panted;
Taste of the goodly thing, I have tasted
    first!"
Bringing us noway coolness, but burning
    thirst,
Giving us noway peace, but implacable
    strife,
Loosing upon us the wounding joy and
    the wasting sorrow of life!

I am the Woman, ark of the Law and
    sacred arm to upbear it,
Heathen trumpet to overthrow and idola-
    trous sword to shear it:
Yea, she whose arm was round the neck
    of the morning star at song,
Is she who kneeleth now in the dust and
    cries at the secret door,

"Open to me, O sleeping mother! The
    gate is heavy and strong.
Open to me, I am come at last; be wroth
    with thy child no more.
Let me lie down with thee there in the
    dark, and be slothful with thee as
    before!"

THE DEATH OF EVE

I

At dawn they came to the stream Hiddekel,
Old Eve and her red first-born, who was now
Greyer than she, and bowed with more than years.
Then Cain beneath his level palm looked hard
Across the desert, and turned with outspread hand
As one who says, "Thou seest; we are fooled."
But Eve, with clutching fingers on his arm,
And pointing eastward where the risen sun
Made a low mist of light, said, "It is there!"

II

For, many, many months, in the great tent
Of Enoch, Eve had pined, and dared not tell

Her longing: not to Irad, Enoch's son,
Masterful like his father, who had held
Harsh rule, and named the tent-place
    with his name;
Not to mild Seth, given her in Abel's
    stead;
Not unto angry Lamech, nor his wives,
Usurpers of her honor in the house;
Not to young Jubal, songs-man of the
    tribe,
Who touched his harp at twilight by her
    door;
And not to bed-rid Adam, most of all
Not unto Adam.   Yet at last, the spring
Being at end, and evening with warm
    stars
Falling upon them by the camel kraal,
Weary with long desire she spoke to Seth,
Touching her meaning faintly and far off
To try him.   With still scrutiny awhile
He looked at her; then, lifting doubtful
    hands
Of prayer, he led her homeward to the
    tent,
With tremulous speech of small and week-
    day things.
Next, as she lay by Adam before dawn,

His big and wasted hand groping for
    hers
Suddenly made her half-awakened heart
Break back and back across the shadowy
    years
To Eden, and God calling in the dew,
And all that song of Paradise foredone
Which Jubal made in secret, fearing her
The storied mother; but in secret, too,
Herself had listened, while the maids at
    toil
Or by the well at evening sang of her
Untruthful things, which, when she once
    had heard,
Seemed truthful. Now, bowed upon
    Adam's breast,
In the deep hush that comes before the
    dawn,
She whispered hints and fragments of her
    will;
And when the shaggy forehead made no
    sign,
And the blind face searched still as quietly
In the tent-roof for what, these many
    months,
It seemed to seek for there, she held him
    close

And poured her whole wild meaning in
    his ear.
But as a man upon his death-bed dreams
That he should know a matter, and knows
    it not,
Nor who they are who fain would have
    him know,
He turned to hers his dim, disastrous
    eyes,
Wherein the knowledge of her and the
    long love
Glimmered through veil on veil of va-
    cancy.
That evening little Jubal, coming home
Singing behind his flock, saw ancient
    Eve
Crouched by the ruined altar in the glade,
The accursèd place, sown deep each early
    spring
With stones and salt — the Valley of the
    Blood;
And that same night Eve fled under the
    stars
Eastward to Nod, the land of violence,
To Cain, and the strong city he had
    built
Against all men who hunted for his soul.

III

She gave her message darkly in the gates,
And waited trembling.   At day-fall he
    came.
She knew him not beneath his whitened
    hair;
But when at length she knew him, and
    was known,
The whitened hair, the bent and listening
    frame,
The savage misery of the sidelong eyes,
Fell on her heart with strangling.   So it
    was
That now for many days she held her
    peace,
Abiding with him till he seemed again
The babe she bare first in the wilderness,
Her maiden fruits to Adam, the new joy
The desert bloomed with, which the
    desert stars
Whispered concerning.   Yet she held her
    peace,
Until he seemed a young man in the
    house,
A gold frontlet of pride and a green cedar;
Then, leading him apart, Eve told her
    wish,

Not faltering now nor uttering it far off,
But as a sovereign mother to her son
Speaks simple destiny.   He looked at
    her
Dimly, as if he saw her not; then stooped,
Sharpening his brows upon her.   With a
    cry
She laid fierce, shaken hands about his
    breast,
Drew down his neck, and harshly from his
    brow
Pushing the head-band and the matted
    locks,
Baring the livid flesh with violence,
She kissed him on the Sign.   Cain bowed
    his head
Upon her shoulder, saying, "I will go!"

IV

Now they had come to the stream Hid-
    dekel,
And passed beyond the stream.   There,
    full in face,
Where the low morning made a mist of
    light,
The Garden and its gates lay like a flower
Afloat on the still waters of the dawn.

The clicking leap of bright-mailed grass-
     hoppers,
The dropping of sage-beetles from their
     perch
On the gnawed cactus, even the pulsing
     drum
Of blood-beats in their ears, merged sud-
     denly
Into ethereal hush.   Then Cain made
     halt,
Held her, and muttered, "'Tis enough.
     Thou sawest!
His Angel stood and threatened in the
     sun!"
And Eve said, "Yea, and though the day
     were set
With sworded angels, thou would'st wait
     for me
Yonder, before the gates; which, look you,
     child,
Lie open to me as the gates to him,
Thy father, when he entered in his rage,
Calling thee from the dark, where of old
     days
I kept thee folded, hidden, till he called."
So grey Cain by the unguarded portal
     sat,

His arms crossed o'er his forehead, and
    his face
Hid in his meagre knees; but ancient Eve
Passed on into the vales of Paradise.

V

Trancèd in lonely radiance stood the
    Tree,
As Eve put back the glimmering ferns and
    vines
And crept into the place.   Awhile she
    stooped,
And as a wild thing by the drinking-pool
Peers ere it drinks, she peered.   Then,
    laughing low,
Her frame of grief and body of her years
She lifted proudly to its virgin height,
Flung her lean arms into the pouring
    day,
And circling with slow paces round the
    Tree,
She sang her stifled meaning out to God.

EVE'S SONG

Behold, against thy will, against thy word,
Against the wrath and warning of thy sword,
Eve has been Eve, O Lord!

A pitcher filled, she comes back from the brook,
A wain she comes, laden with mellow ears;
She is a roll inscribed, a prophet's book
Writ strong with characters.
Behold, Eve willed it so; look, if it be so,
   look!

Early at dawn, while yet thy watchers slept,
Lightly her untamed spirit over-leapt
The walls where she was kept.
As a young comely leopardess she stood:
Her lustrous fell, her sullen grace, her fleetness,
They gave her foretaste, in thy tangled wood,
Of many a savage sweetness,
Good to fore-gloat upon; being tasted, sweet and
   good.

O swayer in the sunlit tops of trees,
O comer up with cloud out of the seas,
O laugher at thine ease
Over thine everlasting dream of mirth,
O lord of savage pleasures, savage pains,
Knew'st Thou not Eve, who broughtest her to
   birth?
Searcher of breast and reins,
Thou should'st have searched thy Woman, the
   seed-pod of thine earth!

Herself hath searched her softly through and
    through;
Singing she lifts her full soul up to view;
Lord, do Thou praise it, too!
Look, as she turns it, how it dartles free
Its gathered meanings: woman, mother, wife,
Spirit that was and is and waits to be,
Worm of the dust of life,
Child, sister — ghostly rays!   What lights are
    these, Lord, see!

Look where Eve lifts her storied soul on high,
And turns it as a ball, she knows not why,
Save that she could not die
Till she had shown Thee all the secret sphere —
The bright rays and the dim, and these that
    run
Bright-darkling, making Thee to doubt and
    fear, —
Oh, love them every one!
Eve pardons Thee not one, not one, Lord; dost
    Thou hear?

Lovely to Eve was Adam's praising breath;
His face averted bitter was as death;
Abel, her son, and Seth
Lifted her heart to heaven, praising her;

Cain with a little frown darkened the stars;
And when the strings of Jubal's harp would
*   stir,*
Like honey in cool jars
The words he praised her with, like rain his
*   praises were.*

Still, still with prayer and ecstasy she strove
To be the woman they did well approve,
That, narrowed to their love,
She might have done with bitterness and blame;
But still along the yonder edge of prayer
A spirit in a fiery whirlwind came —
Eve's spirit, wild and fair —
Crying with Eve's own voice the number of her
*   name.*

Yea, turning in the whirlwind and the fire,
Eve saw her own proud being all entire
Made perfect by desire;
And from the rounded gladness of that sphere
Came bridal songs and harpings and fresh
*   laughter;*
"Glory unto the faithful!" sounded clear,
And then, a little after,
"Whoso denyeth aught, let him depart from
*   here!"*

Now, therefore, Eve, with mystic years o'er-
scored,
Danceth and doeth pleasure to Thee, Lord,
According to the word
That Thou hast spoken to her by her dream.
Singing a song she dimly understands,
She lifts her soul to let the splendor stream.
Lord, take away thy hands!
Let this beam pierce thy heart, and this most
piercing beam!

Far off, rebelliously, yet for thy sake,
She gathered them, O Thou who lovest to break
A thousand souls, and shake
Their dust along the wind, but sleeplessly
Searchest the Bride fulfilled in limb and feature,
Ready and boon to be fulfilled of Thee,
Thine ample, tameless creature, —
Against thy will and word, behold, Lord, this is
She!

VI

From carven plinth and thousand-gal-
leried green
Cedars, and all close boughs that over-
tower,
The shadows lengthened eastward from
the gates,

And still Cain hid his forehead in his
    knees,
Nor dared to look abroad lest he might
    find
More watchers in the portals: for he heard
What seemed the rush of wings; from
    while to while
A pallor grew and faded in his brain,
As if a great light passed him near at
    hand.
But when above the darkening desert
    swales
The moon came, shedding white, unlikely
    day,
Cain rose, and with his back against the
    stones,
As a keen fighter at the desperate odds,
Glared round him.   Cool and silent lay
    the night,
Empty of any foe.   Then, as a man
Who has a thing to do, and makes his fear
An icy wind to freeze his purpose firm,
He stole in through the pillars of the gate,
Down aisles of shadow windowed with the
    moon,
By meads with the still stars communi-
    cant,

Past heaven-bosoming pool and poolèd
    stream,
Until he saw, through tangled fern and
    vine,
The Tree, where God had made its
    habitation:
And crouched above the shape that had
    been Eve,
With savage, listening frame and sidelong
    eyes,
Cain waited for the coming of the dawn.

A PRAIRIE RIDE

I

WHEN I look back and say, of all our hours
This one or that was best,
Straightway, from north and south, from
    east and west,
With banners strange and tributary pow-
    ers
The others camp against me.   Thus,
Now for many nights and days,
The hills of memory are mutinous,
Hearing me raise
Above all other praise
That autumn morn
When league on league between ripe
    fields of corn,
Galloping neck and neck or loitering
    hand in hand,
We rode across the prairie land
Where I was born.

II

I never knew how good
Were those fields and happy farms,

Till, leaning from her horse, she stretched
     her arms
To greet and to receive them; nor for all
My knowing, did I know her woman-
     hood
Until I saw the gesture understood,
And answer made, and amity begun.
On the proud fields and on her proud
     bent head
The sunlight like a covenant did fall;
Then with a gesture rich and liberal
She raised her hands with laughter to the
     sun, —
And it was done,
Never in life or death to be gainsaid!
And I, till then,
Home-come yet alien,
Held by some thwart and skeptic mind
     aloof
From nature's dear behoof,
Knelt down in heart and kissed the kindly
     earth,
And, having swept on wings of mirth
The big horizon round, I swiftly clomb,
And from the utter dome
Of most high morning laughed, and sang
     my loved one home!

Meanwhile, within the rings our laughter
    made,
Bending like a water-arum
Where impetuous waters meet,
Rhythmic to the strong alarum,
Of her horse's rushing feet,
Before me and beside me and on before
    me swayed
Her body like a water-arum blade,
Like a slanted gull for motion,
And the blown corn like an ocean
For its billows and their rumor, and the
    tassels snapping free
As whittled foam and brine-scud of the
    sea.
Thanks to God,
No ocean, but the rife and homely sod,
And golden corn to feed
A universe at need!
Land of mine, my mother's country!
My heritage! — But through her loosen-
    ing hair
She has tossed me back the dare.
Drunken-hearted! shall it be a race in-
    deed?
Then drink again, and drink again, to
    reeling drink the winy speed!

III

Ye on the jealous hills,
Ye shall not have your wills
For many a dreaming day
And haunted night.
To that high morning, walled and domed
      with light,
I am given away;
And often here, above the weary feet
That pour along this fierce and jaded
      street,
As from a taintless source
Of power and grace,
Anxious and shrill and sweet
I hear her strong unblemished horse
Neigh to the pastured mothers of the race.

SONG

My love is gone into the East
Across the wide dawn-kindled sea;
My love remembreth naught of me
Nor of my lips nor of my breast,
For he has gone where morning dwells
Into the land of dreams and spells.

But yet sometimes deep in the night
A foolish little cricket thing,
A kind of voice, will wake and sing
And drone and sing till it is light;
I am not sure, but every day
I grow to think he sings this way: —

"Into the West, or late or soon,
Across dim seas into the West,
Thy lover will sail back in quest
Of Earth's one gift and life's one boon,
Of simple love that comes to pass
As dew falls or as springs the grass."

MUSA MERETRIX

I TURN the last leaf down, and lay
The flaunting rubbish in the grass;
With folded arms across my face
I shut the summer light away.
On him too the old trick to play!
    Too dull, too base!

I see again his dream-worn hand
Shaken by my poor praise, his brow
Flushed by the words I scarce knew how
To speak at all, so shadowy grand
He stalked there in Song's lonely land,
    Under the vow.

So rare a spirit, and if frail —
Curse thee! what should a spirit be
That ate not, drank not, save for thee?
Flat brothel-jestress, thing of sale,
On his head too to pour the stale
    Indignity!

THE COUNTING MAN

I

Eeny, meeny, miney, mo,
Cracka feeny, finey, fo;
Omma nooja, oppa tooja,
Rick, bick, ban, do!

II

Eeny, meeny, miney, mo, —
All the children in a row.
Cracka feeny, who is he,
Counting out so solemnly?

III

Eeny, meeny, look how tall,
Like a shadow on the wall!
When did he come down the street,
Muffled up from head to feet?

IV

Listen!   Don't you hear the shiny
Shadow-man count meeny-miney?
Hush! when all the counting's done
Maybe I might be The One!

V

Cracka feeny, finey, fo,
Watch his shining fingers go!
He can see enough to play,
Though he hides his face away.

VI

Oppa tooja, rick, bick, ban,
O the solemn Counting Man!
Forty-'leven from the top —
Now where *will* his fingers stop?

VII

Eeny, meeny, miney, mo,
Cracka feeny, finey, fo;
Omma nooja, oppa tooja,
Rick, bick, ban, do!

THE MOON–MOTH

ᴀɢᴀɪɴ the steep path turns, and pained at
 heart
With prescience of the beauty soon to
 be,
Climbing I break the flowering weeds
 apart
And the low vines that mat about my
 knee,
Till airy-strong against the sky and sea
Juts out the fragment of a temple's base
And one great corner-stone.
Deep, deep, within me, in some deepest
 place
Of unknown being, laughter wakes, and
 moans,
As on the marble ledge I lay my face,
Bowed down with thoughts of Her who
 had this house and throne.

Above the market and the popular well
Within whose carven niche the old men
 sat
To murmur at Medea, and to tell

How her witch-love for Jason turned to
      hate,
High o'er the struggles old men wonder at,
High in the delicate heavens, beheld of
      none
Save who should climb above
Yonder hill-fountain where Bellerophon
Snared the winged horse and backed him
      in the moon, —
Corinth the city raised up unto Love
This specular temple pure and its far-
      gazing grove;

That in the intense zenith laughing free,
Making inviolable light its screen,
Passion might know a wilder secrecy,
To an abandonment more wounding
      lean,
More richly healing of a hurt more keen;
That, high in prospect of all Hellene
      story,
Love, which will gather power
From all it sees of beauty and of glory,
And on the top of every lifted hour
Stand singing of itself as from a tower,
Might stand and sing at ease from this
      bright promontory.

Temple and grove are gone; the summit
    lies
Bare to the feet of the fantastic year.
Weeds of strange flower, and moths of
    many dyes,
Creepers and flyers small, that, watched
    anear,
Are as outlandish gods and things of
    fear
Seen at their amorous revels and their
    wars —
These only keep the height,
These and the jeweled air that laps and
    jars
In tide and gulf-stream of ecstatic light,
Through pale gold deeps, whereof no
    ripple mars
Outspreaded Greece flame-pale and more
    than earthly bright.

Those faint vermilion hills that southward
    peer
Look over into Clytemnestra's land,
As if each crouching summit leaned to
    hear
White-lipped   Cassandra,   by   Apollo
    banned

To drink with cries of loathing from his
        hand
Her horrid vision of the house of sin;
Those heights of flame and dew,
Gleaming far westward, lock Arcadia in;
And where the olive-mottled gulf burns
        blue,
The Muses' mount, with silver summits
        twin,
Shines o'er the violet steep that Delphi
        clings unto.

Yonder a name, yonder a name, and
        yonder
A name to make the troubled blood beat
        fast
And the o'ertaken spirit ache with won-
        der:
Daphne, whose slope the spring-time
        revelers passed,
With Eleusinian Demeter to taste
The bread of resurrection; Sunion,
Glad shrine and pharos glad;
Hymettos and grape-dark Pentelicon;
And bright, O bright against their bronzen
        shade,
Athens, by time and ruin undismayed,

Lifting her solemn crown of temples to the
    sun.

Mountains and seas, cities and isles and
    capes, .
All frail as dream and painted like a
    dream,
All swimming with the fairy light that
    drapes
A bubble, when the colors curl and
    stream
And meet and flee asunder.   I could
    deem
This earth, this air, my dizzy soul, the sky,
Time, knowledge, and the gods
Were lapsing, curling, streaming lazily
Down a great bubble's rondure, dye on
    dye,
To swell the perilous clinging drop that
    nods,
Gathers, and nods, and clings, through all
    eternity.

We cry with drowsy lips how life is
    strange,
And shadowy hands pour for us while we
    speak

Old bowls of slumber, that the stars may
    range
And the gods walk unhowled-at.... To
    my cheek
This stone feels blessèd cool. My heart
    could break
Of its long searching and its finding not,
But that it has forgot
What 'twas it searched, and how it failed
    thereof.
— O soft, ye flute-players! No temple
    dove
Be fluttered! Soft, sing soft, ye lyric girls,
Till the shrine portals ope and the blue
    smoke outcurls!

Dance slowly, singing as if Pindar heard
And loved again this sweet fruit of his
    breast.
O let the strophe, like a smooth sea-bird,
Drift down the wave, and wheel again to
    rest
One long, long instant on the glittering
    crest.
Scare not the sacred peacock where he
    spreads
His fan upon the wall;

Let not a flower, let not a petal fall
From those fresh-woven garlands on your
    heads;
Dance delicately slow as yon light treads
From isle to isle: though late, love comes
    at last to all!

And might it not be sweeter late than
    soon?
What though the western radiance flame
    and fail?
What though the ivory circle of the
    moon
Deepen to gold?   What though the keen
    stars tell
Through Heaven's abysm their midnight
    and all's-well,
And still not yet the jealous doors unclose?
Despair not; these delays
We know are Paphian, and the waked
    thrush knows
Who from the grove chants love's heart-
    broken praise.
"Too late, too soon! Too soon, too late!"
    he says,
"O goddess, hear them now, before the
    sweet night goes!"

Aye, deeply heard!   In Aphrodite's
    porch
Perfect of her the slumbering lovers lie,
And on the shrine steps where her saffron
    torch
Lights their young bosoms when they
    turn and sigh,
And in the moonlit grove, and round the
    high
Plinth, where her fiery urns purpureal
Signal her native deep;
To these she giveth all things, even sleep.
But, rich, rich giver, hast thou given
    all?
Dost thou not some diviner secret keep
For me, though outland, though half-
    atheist in thy hall?

— Shattered!   And I awake.   The prayer
    was rash.
Daylight is hardly touched with failure
    yet,
Though there a glowing headland drops
    to ash
And there a chanting island will forget
Its glory soon.   The stones with dew are
    wet.

The moon sings up the world — or in my
    blood
Climbs it, the choiring peace?
What have I done, what suffered or with-
    stood,
That all within me is so bright and good?
— Look, lo, the rainbow-colored pinions
    please
To settle!   A moon-moth, by all my
    dreams it is!

Rich as a pulse a worshiped head rests
    on,
The glimmering vans that time the trem-
    bling life
Open and close above the moon-washed
    stone,
As if the fairy heart were fugitive,
As if it halted panting from a strife
Too large for its frail day.   O missionary
Winds of the far and dear!
O elfin ship, why flap your gallants there?
My heart has many a brimming estuary
Where you can ease you from the endless
    air,
The ocean light you sailed to bring me
    news of her!

Our souls had risen from their second
　　birth,
And were at peace within the land
　　thereof;
With tears we trod there, and with care-
　　less mirth:
And sometimes on the bosom of my love,
Or on her lips or brow, or poised above
All palpitant and doubtful on her head,
A soft-winged splendor lit;
And I would say, "The Butterfly!" and
　　sit
Loving it till it went.　And once I said
"Hush, the Moon-Moth!"　That evening
　　we were wed
Anew, and we were glad as the uprisen
　　dead.

And now, what gladness ails thee now, my
　　soul?
For all the desolate, all the wasted days
Nothing but strong delight?　The lifted
　　bowl,
The cones of ecstasy, the wands of praise,
Tossing delirious down the mountain ways
Of all that's forfeit, all that is foregone?
Triumphing through the seas,

And past the ghostly power that, leagued
    with these,
Did make as if the bolts of God were
    drawn
Between her life and me? And like a
    fawn
Thou'lt dance there in the moon, where
    now the moon-moth flees?

But whither, flame of pearl, vapor of
    pearl,
Breath and decantment of sea-buried
    gems
That with the foam-born Woman did
    upswirl
To wreathe their brightness round her
    breast and limbs
And give their color to the cup that dims
Earth's piercing cry to music, — whither
    now
Do the weighed wings intend?
Fawn heart of me, that with the upflung
    brow
Followest on, where will thy dances end?
O after many days! O let me bow,
Let me be risen lordly up! My love, my
    friend,

My wild one, my soul's need, my song of
    life!
Through the strange seas and past the
    ghostly powers
Safe come and sure, and like a festal wife,
Admonished of the seasons and the hours,
The time of times and the preparèd
    bowers!
Above thy brow floats like an influence
The moon-moth, our dear sign,
No plainer now than when these eyes of
    mine
In faith imagined and beheld it once,
As these thy hands to all my thirsting
    sense,
To lips and breast and brow, are palpable
    as then.

More palpable, by that dark curtain wove
And hung between us for Earth's lie of
    lies!
Which these our meeting hands make
    nothing of
And this thy happy bending-down denies,
And these our clinging lips and closèd eyes
And mating breasts have never, never
    known

But for the cheat it was.
— Sigh not, love; tremble not!   Be all at
    peace!
You will not go because the moth is
    flown?
— Gone, beyond passion's cry! — The
    moon-washed stone,
The sleeping weeds, the stars few over
    dreaming Greece.

And my far country swims into the light.
The seaboard states are up, the prairies
    stay
But little longer now to make them bright.
Westward the burning bugles of the
    day
Are blowing strong across America.
New laws, new arts, new gods, new souls
    of men,
New hopes and charities!
Why do I traffic where no profit is,
Taking but one or two where they take
    ten
Who trade to their own shores, and back
    again
To their own shores?   O my beloved!
    Who replies

But thou, fled heart, who cling'st here
    close and true!
For us the future was, the past will be,
And all the holy human years are new,
And all are tasted of eternally,
And still the eaten fruit shines on the
    tree.
— Let us go down.   There, in that naked
    glen,
Bellerophon played the thief.
Much lower lies the well where the old
    men
Sat murmuring at Medea, and at their
    chief
Spoused to the witch.   Love, we'll not
    grieve again,
We ne'er shall grieve again, not what we
    could call grief!

THAMMUZ

DAUGHTERS, daughters, do ye grieve?
Crimson dark the freshes flow!
Were ye violent at eve?
Crimson stains where the rushes grow!
What is this that I must know?

Mourners by the dark red waters,
Met ye Thammuz at his play?
Was your mood upon you, daughters?
Had ye drunken?   O how grey
Looks your hair in the rising day!

Mourners, mourn not overmuch
That ye slew your lovely one.
Such ye are; and be ye such!
Lift your heads; the waters run
Ruby bright in the climbing sun.

Raven hair and hair of gold,
Look who bendeth over you!
This is not the shepherd old;
This is Thammuz, whom ye slew,
Radiant Thammuz, risen anew!

Songs and Lyric Passages from
The Fire-Bringer

PANDORA'S SONGS

I

Along the earth and up the sky
*   The Fowler spreads his net:*
O soul, what pinions wild and shy
*   Are on thy shoulders set?*
What wings of longing undeterred
Are native to thee, spirit bird?

What sky is thine behind the sky,
For refuge and for ecstasy?
Of all thy heavens of clear delight
Why is each heaven twain,
O soul! that when the lure is cast
Before thy heedless flight,
And thou art snared and taken fast
Within one sky of light,
Behold, the net is empty, the cast is vain,
And from thy circling in the other sky the lyric
*   laughters rain!*

II

Of wounds and sore defeat
I made my battle stay;

Wingèd sandals for my feet
I wove of my delay;
Of weariness and fear,
I made my shouting spear;
Of loss, and doubt, and dread,
And swift oncoming doom
I made a helmet for my head
And a floating plume.
From the shutting mist of death,
From the failure of the breath,
I made a battle-horn to blow
Across the vales of overthrow.
O hearken, love, the battle-horn!
The triumph clear, the silver scorn!
O hearken where the echoes bring,
Down the grey disastrous morn,
Laughter and rallying!

III

Because one creature of his breath
Sang loud into the face of death,
Because one child of his despair
Could strangely hope and wildly dare,
The Spirit comes to the Bride again,
And breathes at her door the name of the child;
"This is the son that ye bore me!   When
Shall we kiss, and be reconciled?"

Furtive, dumb, in the tardy stone,
With gropings sweet in the patient sod,
In the roots of the pine, in the crumbled cone,
With cries of haste in the willow-rod, —
By pools where the hyla swells his throat
And the partridge drums to his crouching mate,
Where the moorland stag and the mountain
   goat
Strictly seek to the ones that wait, —
In seas aswing on the coral bar,
In feasting depths of the evening star,
In the dust where the mourner bows his head,
In the blood of the living, the bones of the
   dead, —
Wounded with love in breast and side,
The Spirit goes in to the Bride!

IV

Too far, too far, though hidden in thine arms;
Too darkly far, though lips on lips are laid!
Love, love, I am afraid;
I know not where to find thee in these storms
That dashed thy changèd breast my breast upon,
Here in the estranging dawn.
Unsteadfast! who didst call and hast not
   stayed.

Tryst-breaker!　I have heard
Thy voice in the green wood, and not deferred:—
O fold me closer, fugitive one, and say where
　　　thou art gone!

Nay, speak not, strive not, sorrow not at all!
O, dim and gradual! —
Belovèd, my belovèd, shall it be?
Keep me, keep me with thy kiss,
Save me with thy deep embrace;
For down the gulfs of spirit space,
The slow, the implacable winds, now un-
　　　escapably
Wheel us downward to our bliss,
Whelm us, darken us — O lethal winds! —
　　　down to our destined place.
Swimming faint, beneath, afar —
O lover, let there be
No haste, nor clamor of thy heart to see!
But I have seen, and I whisper thee
How the rivers of peace apparent are,
And the city of bridal peace
Waits, and wavers, and hardly is,
Fades, and is folded away from sight;
And now like a lily it openeth wistfully,
Whispering through its courts of light
"How long shall we be denied?

How long must the eastern gate stand wide,
Ere these who are called shall enter in, and the
bridegroom be with the bride?"

V

A thousand æons, nailed in pain
On the blown world's plunging prow,
That seeks across the eternal main, —
Down whatever storms we drift,
What disastrous headlands lift,
Festal lips, triumphant brow,
Light us with thy joy, as now!

VI

I stood within the heart of God;
It seemed a place that I had known:
(I was blood-sister to the clod,
Blood-brother to the stone.)

I found my love and labor there,
My house, my raiment, meat and wine,
My ancient rage, my old despair, —
Yea, all things that were mine.

I saw the spring and summer pass,
The trees grow bare, and winter come;

All was the same as once it was
Upon my hills at home.

Then suddenly in my own heart
I felt God walk and gaze about;
He spoke; his words seemed held apart
With gladness and with doubt.

"Here is my meat and wine," He said,
"My love, my toil, my ancient care;
Here is my cloak, my book, my bed,
And here my old despair.

"Here are my seasons: winter, spring,
Summer the same, and autumn spills
The fruits I look for; everything
As on my heavenly hills."

From Act II
A Girl's Voice

Once more, once more, O sisters, ere we
　　die
I will lift up my cry
To Him who loved us though He puts us
　　by.
For yonder singer with the golden mouth

Hath fallen upon us privily as falls
The still spring out of the south
On the shut passes and locked mountain
    walls,
And suddenly from out my frozen heart
Dark buds of sorrow start,
Freshets of thought through my faint
    being roll,
And dim remembrance gropes and trav-
    ails in my soul.

I will cry on Him piercingly
By reason of my girlhood how it ailed,
Then when I seemed
Unto myself a thing myself had dreamed,
And for whose sake the visionary Spring
High in the chilly meadows where she
    stood
With lips of passionate listening
In the sea-wind above the moaning wood,
Scattered her discrowned hair, and bowed
    herself, and wailed.
And then, a little after, came a day
That loosed my bands of ailing all away;
For somewhere in the wilds a spirit spoke,
The ghostly earth went past me like a
    stream,

And swooning suddenly aloft I woke
To an intenser dream.
Would mine were that same spirit's
    tongue to tell
The joy that then befell, —
Rather befell not, but refrained,
Lurked and withdrew,
And was an inner freshness in the dew,
A look inscrutable the stars put on,
A fount of secret color in the dawn,
After day-fall a daylight that remained
Brighter than what was gone.
O sisters, kiss the numbing death away
From off my heavy lips, and let me say
How fair my summoned spirit blossomed
    in its clay,
When the girls sang of me that I was
    his
Whose voice I heard treading the wilder-
    ness;
And I had followed him as the homing
    dove
That furtive way he went,
Till now he had brought me up into his
    tent,
Where flutes made mention of love, and
    wild throats said

With wine and honey of love were his
    tables spread,
Also the banner over us was love!

From Act III

PROMETHEUS

Be comforted; it is established sure.
Light shall arise from light, day follow
    day,
Season meet season, with all lovely signs
And portents of the year. These shall not
    fail;
From their appointed dance no star shall
    swerve,
Nor mar one accent of one whirling
    strophe
Of that unfathomed chorus that they
    sing
Within the porch and laughing house of
    Life,
Which Time and Space and Change,
    bright caryatids,
Do meanwhile pillar up. These shall not
    fail;
But O, these were the least I brought you
    home!

The sun whose rising and whose going
    down
Are joy and grief and wonder in the
    heart;
The moon whose tides are passion,
    thought, and will;
The signs and portents of the spirit year,—
For these, if you would keep them, you
    must strive
Morning and night against the jealous gods
With anger, and with laughter, and with
    love;
And no man hath them till he brings them
    down
With love, and rage, and laughter from
    the heavens, —
Himself the heavens, himself the scornful
    gods,
The sun, the sun-thief, and the flaming
    reed
That kindles new the beauty of the world.

He draws Æolus and Rhodope to him.

For you the moon stilly imagineth
Her loiterings and her soft vicissitudes;
For you the Pleiades are seven, and one
Wanders invisible because of you;

For you the snake is burnished in the
    spring,
The flower has plots touching its mar-
    riage time,
The queen-bee from her wassailed lords
    soars high
And high and high into the nuptial blue,
Till only one heroic lover now
Flies with her, and her royal wish is prone
To the elected one, whose dizzy heart
Presageth him of ecstasy and death.
For you the sea has rivers in the midst,
And fathomless abysses where it breeds
Fantastic life; and each its tiniest drop
Flung from the fisher's oar-blade in the
    sun
Has rivers, abysses, and fantastic life.
For your sakes it was spoken of the soul
That it shall be a sea whereon the moon
Has might, and the four winds shall walk
    upon it, —
Also it has great rivers in the midst,
Uncharted islands that no sailor sees,
And fathomless abysses where it breeds
Mysterious life; yea, each its tiniest drop
Flung from the fisher's oar-blade in the
    sun

Has rivers, tempests, and eternal tides,
Untouched-at isles, horizons never hailed,
And fathomless abysses where it breeds
Incredible life, without astonishment.

He bends over Deukalion.

O death, majestic mood!   Transfigured
    brow
And eyes heavy with vision, since the
    time
They saw creation sitting like a sphinx,
Woman and lion, riddling of herself
At twilight, in the place of parted souls —

He pauses, looks at the lighted cloud, and below at the
* darkening earth, where a mist is beginning to rise.*

As far as being goes out past the stars
Into unthinkable distance, and as far
As being inward goes unthinkably,
Traveling the atom to its fleeing core,
Through world in world, heaven beneath
    wheeling heaven,
Firmament under firmament, without
    end, —
To-day there is rejoicing, and the folk,
Though ignorant, call us blessèd in their
    hearts.
Yea, He who is the Life of all this life,

Death of this death and Riser from this
      death,
Calleth us blessèd in his heart of hearts;
And once again, in the dim end of things,
When the sun sickens, and the heaven of
      heavens
Flames as a frosty leaf unto the fall,
In swoon and anguish shall his stormèd
      heart
Cry unto us; his cry is ringing there
In the sun's core! I heard it when I stood
Where all things past and present and to
      come
Ray out in fiery patterns, fading, chang-
      ing,
Forevermore unfaded and unchanged.

CHORUS OF YOUNG MEN

One large last star, not yet persuaded
      well,
Expected till the mountains should de-
      clare;
But from his hesitant attitude,
From his wild and waiting mood,
Wildly, waitingly there came
Over sea and earth and air

And on our bended hearts there fell
Trembling and expectation of thy name,
Apollo!
Now the East to the West has flung
Sudden hands aloft, and sung
Thy titles, and thy certain coming-on;
Wheeling ever to the right hand, wheeling
    ever to the dawn,
The South has danced before the North,
And the text of her talking feet is the news
    of thy going forth,
Apollo!   Apollo!   Apollo!
When radiance hid the Titan's face
And all was blind in the altar place,
Then we knew thee, O we cried upon thee
    then,
Apollo!   Apollo!
Past thee Dionysus swept,
The wings of Eros stirred and slept,
And we knew not the mist of thy song
    from the mist of the fire,
As out of the core of the light thy lyre
    laughed and thundered again!

Eros, how sweet
Is the cup of thy drunkenness!
Dionysus, how our feet

Hasten to the burning cup
Thou liftest up!
But O how sweetest and how most burn-
    ing it is
To drink of the wine of thy lightsome
    chalices,
Apollo! Apollo! To-day
We say we will follow thee and put all
    others away.
For thou alone, O thou alone art he
Who settest the prisoned spirit free,
And sometimes leadest the rapt soul on
Where never mortal thought has gone;
Till by the ultimate stream
Of vision and of dream
She stands
With startled eyes and outstretched
    hands,
Looking where other suns rise over other
    lands,
And rends the lonely skies with her
    prophetic scream.

Songs and Lyric Passages from
The Masque of Judgment

From The Prelude, Scene I

Raphael

The late moon would not stay,
The stars grow far and few;
Into her house of day
Hung with Sidonian blue
Stealeth the earth, as a mænad girl
Steals to her home when the orgies are o'er
That startled the glens and the sleeping shore,
And up from the passionate deeps of night
Into the shallows and straits of light
Softly the forests whirl.
Laugh, earth!   For thy feigning-face is wise;
There is naught so clear as thy morning eyes;
And the sun thy lord is an easy lord!
What should they be to him, —
Thine hours of dance in the woodland dim,
The brandished torch and the shouted word,
The flight, the struggle, the honeyed swoon
'Neath the wild, wild lips of the moon?

A Girl's Voice

O daughters of Jerusalem!
What said ye unto her

Who took her love by the garment's hem,
Where the tanned grape-gatherers were?
Did any go down and see
If she led him into her house?
Or was it aloft where the wild harts flee,
Was it high in the hills, 'neath the cedar-tree,
That she kissed him and called him spouse?

O keepers of the city walls!
Have ye taken her veil away,
Whose hasting feet and low love-calls
Ye heard at the drop of day?
Have ye taken her ankle-rings,
Who is fair, who hath eyes like a dove?
Must she seek her lover, her king of kings,
Naked, stripped of her costly things?
Must she have no garment but love?

THE ANGEL OF THE PALE HORSE

The scourge of the wrath of God
We swing and we stay:
(Rest, my steed, rest!)
On the green of the hill we have trod,
And the green is grey.
Ours is his scourging rod.

Yea, thy hoofs long to be fleet
On the armied hills;
(Yet rest, my steed, rest!)
Scent of the arrowy sleet
Broadens thy nostrils;
The mown field smelleth sweet.

God giveth his loins' increase
Into our hand;
(Rest, my steed, rest!)
We shall establish his peace
By sea and by land.
Soon shall their troubling cease!

From Act I, Scene I

A high mountain pass, down which flows a brook, with pools and waterfalls. Early morning.

RAPHAEL

Climbing, sings:
On earth all is well, all is well on the sea;
Though the day breaks dull
All is well.
Ere the thunder had ceased to yell
I flew through the wash of the sea
Wing and wing with my brother the gull.

On the crumbling comb of the swell,
With the spindrift slashing to lee,
Poised we;
The petrel thought us asleep
Till sidewise round on stiffened wing,
Keen and taut to take the swing
With the glass-green avalanches in their swerv-
        ing plunge and sweep,
Down the glassy, down the prone,
Swift as swerving thunder-stone,
We shot the green crevasses
And we hallooed down the passes
Of the deep.

On earth all is well, all is well.
In the weeds of the beach lay the shell
With the sleeper within,
And the pulse of the sleeper showed through
The walls of his delicate house
That will wake with the sun into silver and
        purple and blue.
Where the creek makes out and the sea makes in
Between the low cliff-brows
Was borne the talk of the aldered linn
Matching the meadow's subtile din;
And hark, from the grey high overhead
The lark's keen joy was shed!

For what though the morning sulky was
And the punctual sun belated,
His nest was snug in the tufted grass,
Soft-lined and stoutly plaited,
And shine sun may or stay away
Nests must be celebrated!

Drowsy with dawn, barely asail,
Buzzes the blue-bottle over the shale,
Scared from the pool by the leaping trout;
And the brood of turtlings clamber out
On the log by their oozy house.
Round the roots of the cresses and stems of the ferns
The muskrat goes by dodges and turns;
Till she has seized her prey she heeds not the
        whine of her mouse.
Lovingly, spitefully, each
Kind unto kind makes speech;
Marriage and birth and war, passion and hun-
        ger and thirst,
Song and plotting and dream, as it was meant
        from the first!

He climbs higher, and sings:
        Peering in the dust I thought
        "How all creatures, small and great,
        For His pleasure God hath wrought!"

When I saw the robins mate
Low I sang unto my harp,
"Happy, happy, His estate!

"Down curved spaces He may warp
With old planets; long and long,
Where the snail doth tease and carp,

"Asking with its jellied prong,
A whole summer He may bide,
Wondrous tiny lives among,
Curious, unsatisfied."

From ACT I, SCENE II

VOICES

Through the vines of tangled light
In the jungles of the sun
Swept the Hunter in his might
And his lion-beagle dun
Gaped for prey to left and right.

O'er the passes of the moon
Strode the Hunter in his wrath:
The eagle sniffed the icy noon,
"Master, knowest thou the path?
Shall we meet thy foe-man soon?

"On what interstellar plain,
'Mid what comet's blinding haze,
Storm of star dust, meteor rain,
Shall we spy his crouching gaze,
Leap at him, and end thy pain?"

Peace is on the heavenly meres,
Sabbath lies on Paradise;
But the little Throne-Lamp fears,
For she sees the Master's eyes,
And she tastes the Master's tears.

Where had his gadding spirit led?
Beside what peopled water-head
Stooped he, or on what sleeping face
Was he intent the dream to trace?
Had creature love upon him fawned
Or had he drunk of mortal mirth
That he knew not what a morning dawned
Over his darling earth?
Heard not the storm, heard not the cries,
Heard not the talk of the startled skies
Over the guilty earth?

From Act II

RAPHAEL

Shore-birds wet with deep-sea dew,
Fold your wings and stay your flight;
Stay, stay!
Long was the way,
Grieved with wind is your tender light,
Stay, till our love rekindle you

Wood-birds that through lunar glens
Flood the noon of night with singing,
Hearken, hearken!
Our minds undarken:
O'er your phosphor forests winging,
Say, what shadow scared you thence?

From Act III, Scene I

RAPHAEL

O heart of man, how I have loved thee!
Hidden in sunlight what sweet hours were
    mine
Of lover-like espial upon thine;
Thrilled with thy shadowy fears, half
    guessing
The hope that lit thy veins like wine,

Musing why this was bane and that thy
      blessing,
My angel-ichor moved by all that moved
      thee;
Though oft the meanings of thy joy and
      woe
Were hid, were hard to know;
For deep beneath the clear crystalline
      waters
That feed the hearts of Heaven's sons and
      daughters,
The roots of thy life go.
O dreamer! O desirer! Goer down
Unto untraveled seas in untried ships!
O crusher of the unimagined grape
On unconceivèd lips!
O player upon a lordly instrument
No man or god hath had in mind to in-
      vent;
O cunning how to shape
Effulgent Heaven and scoop out bitter
      Hell
From the little shine and saltness of a
      tear;
Sieger and harrier,
Beyond the moon, of thine own builded
      town,

Each morning won, each eve impregna-
    ble,
Each noon evanished sheer!

Thou fiery essence in a vase of fire!
What quarry gathered and packed down
    the clay
To make this delicate vessel of desire?
Who digged it?   In what mortar did he
    bray?
Whose wistful hand did lead
All round the lyric brede?
Who tinted it, and burned the dross away?
"He, He," (doth some one say?)
"Whose mallet-arm is lift and knitted hard
To break it into shard!"
Were that the Maker's way?
Who brings to being aught,
Love is his skill untaught,
Love is his ore, his furnace, and his tool;
Who makes, destroyeth not,
But much is dashed in pieces by the fool.

O struggler in the mesh
Of spirit and of flesh
Some subtle hand hath tied to make thee
    Man,

That now is unto thee a wide domain
To laugh and love and dare in for a
    span,
And straightway is a prison-house of
    pain,
A den of loathing, and a violent place,
A hold for unclean wing and cruel face
That mock the searèd heart and darkened
    brain, —
My bosom yearns above thee at the end,
Thinking of all thy gladness, all thy
    woe;
Whoever is thy foe,
I am thy friend, thy friend!
As thou hast striven, I strove to compre-
    hend
The piteous sundering set betwixt the
    zenith
And nadir of thy fates,
Whose life doth serious message send
To moon and stars, anon itself demeaneth
Below the brute estates.
Wild heart, that through the steepening
    arcs art whirled
To a bright master-world,
And in a trice must blindly backward
    hark

To the subtèrrene dark,
Deem not that mighty gamut-frame was
     set
For wanton finger-fret!
No empty-hearted gymnast of the strings
Gave the wild treble wings,
Or flung the shuddering bass from Hell's
     last parapet.
Though now the Master sad
With vehemence shall break thee,
Not lightly did He make thee,
That morning when his heart was music-
     mad:
Lovely importings then his looks and
     gestures had.

Whatever cometh with to-morrow's light,
Oh, deem not that in idlesse or in spite
The strong knot of thy fate
Was woven so implicate,
Or that a jester put thee in that plight.
Darkly, but oh, for good, for good,
The spirit infinite
Was throned upon the perishable blood;
To moan and to be abject at the neap,
To ride portentous on the shrieking scud
Of the arousèd flood,

And halcyon hours to preen and prate in
     the boon
Tropical afternoon.

Not in vain, not in vain,
The spirit hath its sanguine stain,
And from its senses five doth peer
As a fawn from the green windows of a
     wood;
Slave of the panic woodland fear,
Boon-fellow in the game of blood and lust
That fills with tragic mirth the woodland
     year,
Searched with starry agonies
Through the breast and through the reins,
Maddened and led by lone moon-wan-
     dering cries.
Dust unto dust complains,
Dust laugheth out to dust,
Sod unto sod moves fellowship,
And the soul utters, as she must,
Her meanings with a loose and carnal lip;
But deep in her ambiguous eyes
Forever shine and slip
Quenchless expectancies,
And in a far-off day she seems to put her
     trust.

From Act III, Scene II

REDEEMED SPIRITS

Sing, as they fly past below:

> *In the wilds of life astray,*
> *Held far from our delight,*
> *Following the cloud by day*
> *And the fire by night,*
> *Came we a desert way.*
> *O Lord, with apples feed us,*
> *With flagons stay!*
> *By Thy still waters lead us!*
>
> *As bird torn from the breast*
> *Of mother-cherishings,*
> *Far from the swaying nest*
> *Dies for the mother wings,*
> *So did the birth-hour wrest*
> *From Thy sweet will and word*
> *Our souls distressed.*
> *Open Thy breast, thou Bird!*

From Act IV

VOICES OF THE DAMNED

A YOUTH

Oh, for a voice
Here in the doors of death

To speak the praise of life, existence mere,
The simple come and go of natural
    breath,
And habitation of the body's house with
    its five windows clear!
O souls defeated, broken, and undone,
Rejoice with me, rejoice
That we have walked beneath the moon
    and sun
Not churlishly, nor slanderous of the bliss;
But rather leaving this
To the many prophets strict and sedulous
Of that sad-spoken god
Who now hath conquered and is surely
    king,
Have given our lips for life to closely kiss,
Have heard the sweet persuasion of the
    sod
And been heart-credulous
To trust the signs and whispers of the
    spring.

A GIRL'S VOICE

I waited patiently and thought to hear
The secret reason dark,
The secret reason dark and dear

Why none of us had heart to mark
The pale evangel whispering from the
        sphere.
For oft the moon between the garden
        boughs
Her looks of summer longing would ef-
        face,
And come to be a halo round the brows
Of Him who died to give the sinner grace,
Now saddening o'er His purchase from
        that place.
And oft at dawn I heard the Sons of
        Morning
Silvered with lovely menace fill the sky,
And heard their solemn lips deliver warn-
        ing
What time the central singer lifted high,
In the deep hush 'twixt ode and palinode,
The sangrael of the sun, brimmed with
        redeeming blood.
But how might I attend the minatory
Voices of many angels breathing doom,
When from the window of the little room
My love's face had not faded, and the
        story
His wakeful mouth had whispered in the
        gloom

Spake in my pulses yet? And how at
    evening turn
To feel those sad eyes down the moonlight
    yearn,
When mouth to mouth and breast to
    aching breast
I held my lover close, and by his nest
The nightingale, scarce master of his
    mood,
Now after faint essay
And amorous dim delay
Suddenly steeped his heart in song's mad
    plenitude?

A WOMAN'S VOICE

What unripe girl is this who maketh bold
To speak for lovers at the extreme hour,
Yet fancy-paints the flower?
Yet hides with image-gilt the naked gold?
O sisters, brothers, help me to arise!
Of God's two-hornèd throne I will lay
    hold
And let Him see my eyes;
That He may understand what love can
    be,
And raise his curse, and set his children free.

Passages from *The Death of Eve*

Chorus of Water-Bearers

Two groups, one of young, the other of old women, sing in alternation.

Old Women

Like a hunter in his mountain walks the purpose of the Lord!

Young Women

O, the prey alert and little, be its littleness its ward!

Old Women

Like a linnet on the lime-twig sings the bow-string on the bow.

Young Women

O, the serpent when he sitteth on his coils singeth so!

Chorus (in unison)

Even though, even though!
Be it ours to flee and double, be it His to bring us low.

*Blessed she who tastes His arrow and lies
        broken in the wood.*
She has fled, she has fallen: it is good.

They fill their jars at the well.

As they ascend the slope behind and pass through the
    gate.

Till the coming up of day,
Till the cool night flee away,
Till the Hunter rises up to pursue,
O my sisters, we will laugh, we will play!
Though He wake and walk anear us,
He is mused, He will not hear us;
Though He wanders lone and late,
*He will never hear how mate whispereth to
        darkling mate.*
Yea, and though He hear, and though!
Will He judge us, even so?
*He is mused, He walketh harmless.   In the
        shadowy mountain hid*
*We will lure our lovers to us, even as our
        mothers did!*
*When He cometh forth at dawn, and His anger
        burns anew,*
As our hunted mothers did, even so we will do:
*Flee and crouch and feint and double, leap the
        snare or gnaw it through!*

Cain and Eve

He draws her to him, and sinks on the bench, — she at his feet, her head buried in his knees.

Cain

The first that I remember of my life
Was such a place, such a still afternoon,
I sitting thus, thy bright head in my knees,
And such a bird above us as him yonder
Who dips and hushes, lifts and takes his
      note.
I know not what child's trespass I had
      done,
Nor why it drove the girl out of thy face,
Clutched at thy heart with panic, and in
      thine eyes
Set shuddering love.

Eve

      O my first-born, my child!
O herald star in the wilderness appearing,
After the nine-fold moon of dubious
      speech,
Proclaiming silence soon to fall in
      Heaven —
The everlasting silence that soon did fall,

When by me lay thy little frame of breath-
    ing,
And blind and weak thou foundest out
    the breast!

Cain

There was a day when winter held the hills
And all the lower places looking sunward
Knew that the spring was near.   Until
    that day
I had but walked in a boy's dream and
    dazzle,
And in soft darkness folded on herself
My soul had spun her blind and silken
    house.
It was my birthday, for at earliest dawn
You had crept to me in the outer tent,
Kissed me with tears and laughter,
    whispering low
That I was born, and that the world was
    there,
A gift you had imagined and made for me.
Now, as I climbed the morning hills, be-
    hold,
Those words were true: the world at last
    was there;
At last 'twas mine, and I was born at last.

I walked, and on my shoulders and my
    reins
Strength rang like armor; I sat, and in
    my belly
Strength gnawed like a new vinegar; I ran
And strength was on me like superfluous
    wings,
Even the six wings of the cherubim,
Twice twain to cover me and twain to fly.

Eve's Command to Cain

Thou wilt not hear me?   Yea, but thou
    wilt hear!
Thy ears be not thy ears.   I moulded
    them.
Thy life is not thy life.   I gave it thee,
And do require it back.   Thy beating
    heart
Beats not unto itself, but unto me,
Whose voice did tell it when to beat and
    how.
Thy deeds are not thy deeds.   Ye conned
    them here,
Under this breast, where lay great store
    of deeds
Undone, for thee to choose from.

She uncovers the Sign on his forehead.

'Tis not thy head
Weareth this Sign.   'Tis my most cruel head,
Whose cruel hand, whose swift and bloody hand
Smote in its rage my own fair man-child down.
Not thy hand, Cain, not thine; but my dark hand;
And my dark forehead wears the sign thereof,
As now I take it on me.

She kisses him on the Sign.